1,000,000 Books

are available to read at

orgotten ooks

www.ForgottenBooks.com

Read online
Download PDF
Purchase in print

ISBN 978-1-333-01709-5
PIBN 10451753

This book is a reproduction of an important historical work. Forgotten Books uses state-of-the-art technology to digitally reconstruct the work, preserving the original format whilst repairing imperfections present in the aged copy. In rare cases, an imperfection in the original, such as a blemish or missing page, may be replicated in our edition. We do, however, repair the vast majority of imperfections successfully; any imperfections that remain are intentionally left to preserve the state of such historical works.

Forgotten Books is a registered trademark of FB &c Ltd.
Copyright © 2018 FB &c Ltd.
FB &c Ltd, Dalton House, 60 Windsor Avenue, London, SW19 2RR.
Company number 08720141. Registered in England and Wales.

For support please visit www.forgottenbooks.com

1 MONTH OF FREE READING

at
www.ForgottenBooks.com

By purchasing this book you are eligible for one month membership to ForgottenBooks.com, giving you unlimited access to our entire collection of over 1,000,000 titles via our web site and mobile apps.

To claim your free month visit:
www.forgottenbooks.com/free451753

* Offer is valid for 45 days from date of purchase. Terms and conditions apply.

English
Français
Deutsche
Italiano
Español
Português

www.forgottenbooks.com

Mythology Photography **Fiction**
Fishing Christianity **Art** Cooking
Essays Buddhism Freemasonry
Medicine **Biology** Music **Ancient
Egypt** Evolution Carpentry Physics
Dance Geology **Mathematics** Fitness
Shakespeare **Folklore** Yoga Marketing
Confidence Immortality Biographies
Poetry **Psychology** Witchcraft
Electronics Chemistry History **Law**
Accounting **Philosophy** Anthropology
Alchemy Drama Quantum Mechanics
Atheism Sexual Health **Ancient History**
Entrepreneurship Languages Sport
Paleontology Needlework Islam
Metaphysics Investment Archaeology
Parenting Statistics Criminology
Motivational

CORRESPONDENCE

OF

MATTHEW PARKER, D.D.,
ARCHBISHOP OF CANTERBURY.

The Parker Society.

Instituted A.D. M.DCCC.XL.

For the Publication of the Works of the Fathers and Early Writers of the Reformed English Church.

CORRESPONDENCE

OF

MATTHEW PARKER, D.D.

ARCHBISHOP OF CANTERBURY.

COMPRISING

LETTERS WRITTEN BY AND TO HIM, FROM A.D. 1535,

TO HIS DEATH, A.D. 1575.

EDITED FOR

𝕿𝖍𝖊 𝕻𝖆𝖗𝖐𝖊𝖗 𝕾𝖔𝖈𝖎𝖊𝖙𝖞,

BY

JOHN BRUCE, ESQ.

AND THE

REV. THOMAS THOMASON PEROWNE, M.A.
FELLOW OF CORPUS CHRISTI COLLEGE, CAMBRIDGE.

CAMBRIDGE:
PRINTED AT
THE UNIVERSITY PRESS.

M.DCCC.LIII.

INTRODUCTORY NOTICE.

It is not deemed necessary to introduce the Correspondence of Archbishop Parker to the members of the society which bears his name, by any lengthened or express biography. To consider his career in detail, would be to write the ecclesiastical history, and indeed no small portion also of the literary history, of the most important part of the reign of Queen Elizabeth. Such a work, however valuable, would be foreign to the purpose of the Parker Society; the design of which is to furnish materials, rather than treatises; to publish authorities, rather than to draw conclusions.

But, in truth, although not in the form of an express biography, this volume contains within itself what is really and truly a Life of Archbishop Parker. In what esteem he was held by Archbishop Cranmer and others of the Reformers of the English church[1], by what steps he rose to the archbishoprick, how he exercised the authority of that exalted office, what difficulties he had to encounter, and by what spirit the whole tenour of his life was animated, these things—

[1] One interesting proof of this esteem, the MS. of which was searched for in vain when the early portion of the Correspondence went to press, may find a place here. It is a letter from Latimer to Parker, which, having escaped from its old place of deposit, has lately been added to the Library of the British Museum, where it stands, Additional MS. 19,400, No. 21. It was probably written in 1535, when Parker was chaplain to Anne Boleyn.

"Mine own good master Parcare, *salutem*. And as yet I have devised nothing, nor yet will, till I have spoken with the King's grace, and have passed through the next parliament. And then, what I shall alter and change, found and confound, you shall not be ignorant thereof. *Vale*, and do as master Latymer shall move you to do. *Ostende teipsum mundo; delitescere diutius nolito; operare bonum dum tempus habes, veniet nox quando nemo poterit operari. Notum est quid potes, fac non minus velis quam potes. Vale. Tuus*,

H. Latymer, of Worcester.

To his well-beloved, master Parcare, chaplain to the Queen's good grace."

254295

which are the essence of his biography—all appear clearly in the present volume, written unmistakeably by his own pen, and by the pens of his correspondents. No one who will take the trouble to peruse the following pages will need any biographer to instruct him farther as to the character, or as to the opinions, of Archbishop Parker.

Some few facts, principally relating to his early and his domestic history, were registered by the Archbishop himself in a small roll of parchment, which is preserved with peculiar care in Corpus Christi College, Cambridge. These autobiographical *memoranda*, not being of the character of Correspondence, could not find a place in the body of the present volume, but they are necessary to be read in connection with the Letters, and tend to complete the information which they contain. The *memoranda* are as follows[1]:—

"IN THE YEAR of our Lord 1504, on the 6th of August, letter G and F[2], MATTHEW PARKER was born at Norwich, in the parish of Saint Saviour; and was brought up in the parish of All Saints near Fye-bridge gates, and educated in the parish of Saint Clement near Fye-bridge, under WILLIAM, his father, who lived to A.D. 1516, and to the 48th year of his age; ALICE, his mother, who lived to A.D. 1553, and to the 83rd year of her age.

He was instructed
{ in reading 1.
  in writing 2.
  in singing 3.
  in grammar 4. }
by
1. { Thomas Benis, Bachelor of Theology, rector of St Clement's, and partly by Richard Pope, priest.
2. William Prior, clerk, of the church of St Benedict.
3. { W. Love, priest
     R. Manthorp, clerk } of St Stephen's, severe teachers.
4. William Neve, an easy and kind schoolmaster.

YEAR
1522. 8th of September, about the 17th year of my age[3], sent to

---

[1] The original Latin in which these entries are made, is printed in the Appendix, No. I. p. 481.

[2] The Dominical Letter.

[3] Strype, in the body of his work, (Bk. I. c. 1, p. 8), gives 1520 as the date of Parker's going to Cambridge. This is certainly wrong. Parker's own autobiographical roll gives "A°. 1522, 8°. Septembr. circa a^m. ætatis meæ 17;" but this must be a mistake for 1521, for he was born in August 1504, and would therefore have been in his 18th, not his 17th year, in September 1522. Moreover, at the foot of a document written by Stephen Gardiner (Parker MSS., C. C. Coll., Camb., CVI. art. 15, p. 63, Orig.), there is this note, apparently in Parker's handwriting: "Hoc anno in festo Nativitatis

YEAR	
	Cambridge (by the help of Mr Bunge, of the parish of St George, but at my mother's expense); and in Corpus Christi College, under a tutor, Robert Cowper, a Master of Arts, but of small learning, instructed in dialectics and philosophy; partly in Saint Mary's Hostel, and partly in [Corpus] Christi College.
1522.[4]	In the month of March elected a Bible-clerk of Corpus Christi College.
1525.	Admitted Bachelor of Arts.
1526.	22nd of December. Made Sub-deacon under the titles of Barnwell, and the Chapel in the fields, Norwich.
1527.	20th of April. Made Deacon.
1527.	15th of June. Made Priest.
1527.	6th of September. Elected a Fellow of Corpus Christi College.
1527.[5]	3rd. Created Master of Arts.
1533.	On the first Sunday in Advent entered on the office of preaching. {Granchester 1, Beach [Landbeach] 2, St Benet's Church [Cambridge] 3, Madingley, and Barton. 4, 5} Sunday in Advent[6].
1535.	30th of March. Called to the Court of Queen Anne[7].
1535.	14th of July. Made Bachelor of Divinity.
1535.	4th of November. Promoted to the deanery of Stoke Clare by Queen Anne, in the 27th year of Henry VIII.
1537.	1st of March. Called to the court of the King, and made chaplain of Henry VIII.
1538.	1st of July. Created Doctor of Divinity.
1542.	27th of May. Presented to the rectory of Ashen in Essex.
1541.[8]	28th of October. Installed into the second prebend in the church of Ely, by collation of Henry VIII.
1544.	4th of December. Elected Master of Corpus Christi College by commendatory letters of Henry VIII.
1544.	30th of April. Resigned the rectory of Ashen.
1544.	1st of May. Presented to the rectory of Burlingham, Norfolk.

beatæ Mariæ M. P. accessit Cantabrigiam." Now the festival in question falls on the 8th of September, but the date of Gardiner's document is, "Anno Domini millesimo quingentesimo vicesimo primo."

[4] *i. e.* 1522-3.

[5] Probably this should be 3rd of July, 1528.

[6] The figures 1, 2, 3, 4, 5, here seem to intimate the order of Parker's first five sermons, of which the first four were preached on the Sundays in Advent, the fifth on Christmas-day, which fell that year on a Sunday.

[7] Anne Boleyn.

[8] This date is printed in the chronological order in which it stands in the original MS.

YEAR
1544.[1] 25th of January. First elected to the office of Vice-Chancellor of Cambridge.
1545. 22nd of September. Presented to the rectory of Landbeach.
1547. 1st of April. Resigned the deanery of Stoke in obedience to an Act of Parliament.
1548.[2] 7th of February. Elected a second time to the office of Vice-Chancellor of Cambridge.
1550. 1st of October. Resigned the rectory of Burlingham St Andrew's.
1552. 1st of June. Presented to the prebend of Coringham } by the illustrious Prince Edward the Sixth.
1552 8th of June. Nominated to the deanery of Lincoln
1552. 9th of July. Installed into the prebend aforesaid.
1552. 30th of July. Elected dean of Lincoln.
1552. 7th of October. Installed into the deanery in person.

1553. —— of December. Resigned the office of Master of Corpus Christi College to Laurence Moptyd, whom, under constraint, I had myself chosen as my successor.
1554. 2nd of April. Deprived of my prebend in the Church of Ely, and deprived of my rectory of Landbeach, to which church I procured to be presented, William Whalley, canon of Lincoln, whom I chose as my successor, and he was instituted on the 30th of September.
1554. 21st of May. Despoiled of my deanery of Lincoln, as also on the same day of my prebend of Coringham in the same Church, to which Mr George Pierpoint was presented by virtue of an advowson of the same granted [to me] by the bishop of Lincoln, J. Taylor. The deanery was conferred upon Francis Malet, Doctor of Divinity, by Queen Mary.

After this I lived as a private individual, so happy before God in my conscience, and so far from being either ashamed or dejected, that the delightful literary leisure to which the good providence of God recalled me yielded me much greater and more solid enjoyments, than my former busy and dangerous kind of life had ever afforded me. What shall befal me hereafter I know not: but to God, who cares for all men, who will one day reveal the secrets of the hearts, I commit myself wholly, and my good and virtuous wife, with my two very dear children. And I beseech the same most merciful and almighty God that for the time to come we may so bear the reproach of Christ with unbroken courage as ever to remember that here we have no continuing city, but may seek one to come by the grace and mercy of our Lord Jesus Christ; to whom with

---

[1] *i.e.* 1544-5.   [2] *i.e.* 1548-9

the Father and the Holy Ghost be all honour and dominion. Amen.

26th of October, A.D. 1554.

And still on this 6th of August, A.D. 1557, I persevere in the same constancy, supported by the grace and goodness of my Lord and Saviour Jesus Christ; by whose inspiration I have completed a metrical version of the Psalter into the vulgar tongue. And I have written a defence of the marriage of priests against Thomas Martin.

3rd of February, A.D. 1552[5?].

Hitherto so happy before God and content with my own lot have I lived, as neither to envy my superiors, nor despise my inferiors, directing all my efforts to this end: to serve God in a pure conscience, and to be neither despised by those above me nor feared by those beneath me.

14th of October, A.D. 1556.

And I still live happy, contented with my lot, trusting in the testimony of my conscience in the Lord, relying on his word, waiting for the redemption of my body through Christ my Saviour.

SERMONS.

YEAR	
1534.	Before the bishop of Ely; at his visitation, at Balsham.
1535.	Before the lady Elizabeth[3], at Hundeston.
1535.	Before King Henry VIII., at the Court, on the third Sunday in Lent, from the Epistle.
1539.	Before prince Edward.
1540.	Before the lady Elizabeth, at Hatfield.
1548.	Before King Edward, at the Court at Westminster, on the third Sunday in Lent, from the Gospel[4].

[3] Afterwards Queen Elizabeth; she and her sister Mary at this time resided at Hunsdon palace, Hertfordshire, under the care of Lady Bryan.

[4] Archbishop Cranmer's summons to Parker to preach this sermon, is printed below, p. 40. Parker does not include in this list his sermons preached at St Paul's Cross. Besides the summons to preach there, printed in the Correspondence, p. 39, there is another addressed to him by Archbishop Cranmer in Additional MS. Brit. Mus. 19,400, No. 2. It is dated 8th January, 1550, and informs him that he had been appointed by the Council to preach "at Paul's Cross, on Sunday, the 16th day of March." Cranmer adds, "wherefore I pray you purely and sincerely to set forth God's word there, and to exhort your audience to their due obedience to his majesty's highness's laws and statutes, and to unity and charity among themselves, as appertaineth."

[PARK. COR.]

INTRODUCTORY NOTICE.

YEAR

1551. Before his Majesty King Edward, in Lent, that is to say on alternate Wednesdays, viz. on the 9th, 23rd, and 25th of March, my colleague being Mr Harlow[1], bishop of Hereford.

1559. Before our sovereign lady Queen Elizabeth twice in Lent.

[1547.] A.D. 1547, 24th June, I married Margaret, daughter of Robert Harlston, of Mattishall in the county of Norfolk, gentleman, who was born A.D. 1519, Sunday-letter B, on the 23rd June, in which year the festival of Corpus Christi fell on the Eve of St John Baptist.
In the 43rd year of my age.
In the 28th year of her age.

1570. This Margaret, my most dearly beloved and virtuous wife, lived with me some twenty-six years, and died right Christianly on the 17th of August, 1570, about eleven o'clock in the forenoon, and lies buried in the Duke of Norfolk's chapel at Lambeth.

[1548.] She bore me a son, John, A.D. 1548, on the 5th of May, Sunday letter G, at six in the morning.

1566. He married Joanna, daughter of the bishop of Ely[2], on the 28th of January.

[1550.] In the year 1550, on the 27th of August, Sunday letter E, at eleven o'clock at night, I had born to me another son, Matthew, who departed this life on the 8th of January, the same year.

[1551.] In the year 1551, on the first of September, between two and three in the afternoon, Sunday letter D, I had a third son, Matthew, born to me.

1569. He married Frances, daughter of the bishop of Chichester[3], on the 29th of December.

[1556.] In the year 1556, on the 12th of September, between seven and eight in the evening, I had a fourth son, Joseph, born to me, who died in the same year.

[1559.] On the 17th of December, in the year 1559, I was consecrated archbishop of Canterbury.

Alas! alas! O Lord God, for what times hast thou kept me. Now am I come into deep waters, and the flood hath overwhelmed me. O Lord, I am oppressed, answer for me, and strengthen me with thy free Spirit: for I am a man, and have but a short time to live, and am less, &c. Give me of thy sure mercies, &c.

John Parker, born on the 5th of May, 1548, married Joanna Cox, born on the 1st of April, 1551, of whom he had
Margaret, born at Lambeth, on the 21st of March, 1568.

---

[1] No doubt Harley, consecrated Bishop of Hereford, May 26, 1553; deprived, 1554.

[2] Bishop Cox.   [3] Bishop Barlow.

Matthew, his heir, at Canterbury, on the 19th of May, 1570.
Jane, born at Lambeth, on the 19th of March, 1571.
Richard, born at Canterbury (?) on the 20th of May, 1577.
James, born at Bekesborne, on the 30th of May, 1585 [?].
John, born in the Isle of Ely, on the 4th of May, 1589.
Elizabeth and John died children."

The last eight of these entries were made by some other person than the Archbishop, who died at Lambeth on the 17th May, 1575, exactly one month after the last letter we have printed. That letter, according to his wish, was probably the last he was called upon to write (p. 477). His body was interred in the private chapel of Lambeth palace, on the south side of the communion-table, under a monument erected by himself, close to the place where he used to kneel in prayer. During the Great Rebellion not only the original monument was removed, but even the body of the archbishop was taken from its resting place and treated with shameful indignity. Archbishop Sancroft, on the suggestion of Sir William Dugdale, and under the authority of an order of the House of Lords, brought back into the archiepiscopal chapel the bones of his venerable predecessor, from the place whither they had been ignominiously thrown, and set up again the original monument erected to his memory. Archbishop Sancroft also commemorated the removal and restoration in an inscription which still remains[4].

One other document which it seems desirable to include in the present volume, although not ranging under the title of Correspondence, relates to the archbishop's application of the revenues of his see. When Parker succeeded to the archiepiscopate, arrangements were made with reference to the temporalities of the see which considerably reduced the income of its possessor. Although of his own nature a lover of hospitality, and far from disinclined to maintain the dignity of his position, he was consequently unable to make the

---

[4] See the inscription and many particulars of Parker's interment and the disturbance of his remains, in Strype's Parker, Book IV. chap. xliv. Strype also published the archbishop's Will, Appendix, Book IV., No. c. An inventory and appraisement of his effects, communicated by William Sandys, Esq., F.S A., was printed in the Archæologia, Vol. XXX. p. 1.

splendid display, especially upon public occasions, for which Cardinal Pole (who received a large pension in addition to the ordinary income of the see) and others of his predecessors had been remarkable. This occasioned rumours of Parker's penuriousness. During his lifetime he satisfactorily vindicated himself; and, in a MS. which is now in Lambeth Library, his son John has left on record what appears to be an ample refutation. The falsehood of the accusation is indeed too obvious for any one now to dwell upon it, but the answer of the archbishop's son, although not needed for the purpose for which it was designed, contains in a brief space information of such value respecting the revenues of the see, and the means with which the archbishop was able to perform his many acts of liberality, that we think it right to print the paper as it stands:—

The true Estate of the Archbishoprick of Canterbury, tempore Matthæi Parker Archiepiscopi.

The yearly revenue about 3128 *l*. By fines for leases, wardships, *et quo quomodo, communibus annis*, 300 *l*., *in toto* 3428 *l*.

The certain yearly disbursements in fees to certain officers, pensions to curates, to two hospitals, &c , 800 *l*.; household achates [1] *communibus annis*, 1300 *l*.; wages and liveries to household servants and retainers, 300 *l*.;—2400 *l*.

So is there a remainder towards these particular disbursements, 1028 *l*.

He christened with the Queen and duke of Norfolk, Edwardus Fortunatus, the lady Cecilia her son, and gáve above 100 *l*. [2]

His entertainment of the Queen at Canterbury and other houses, with his gifts to her and the lords and ladies, above 2000 *l*.

At Canterbury he gave besides, in rewards to the Queen's officers of household, 500 crowns, 170 *l*.

His foundations of fellowships and scholarships at Cambridge, yearly sermons, and to the poor at Mattishall for ever, increase of perpetual fees and commons at Benet College, had stood him in 2000 *l*.

The purchase of the soil of the University street and buildings on either sides, cost him 500 *l*.

---

[1] Provisions.

[2] The Lady Cecilia was a sister of the king of Sweden, and wife of Christopher, Margrave of Baden. The christening alluded to took place in 1565.

He gave to Glover, alias Somerset, a herald, for a pedigree of the ancient nobility, 100*l*.

He gave to Alexander Nevile for writing the story of Kett's rebellion, entitled Norwicus, 100*l*.[3]

Also silver and gilt plate to Benet College, to Caius College, to Trinity Hall, about 400*l*.

He gave to Thomas Doyly, Esq., that married one of his nieces, in money and money's worth, 300*l*.

To another niece, married to Jo. Heth, gent., that was worth to their purse [by an advowson] 500*l*.

To his niece Clerk, &c., 300*l*.

To Sir Thomas Josseline's brother, an antiquary in his house, who wrote this history, De Antiquitate Britannicæ ecclesiæ, a prebend worth 30*l*. per annum, and procured for him 300*l*.

He expended upon repairing of his palace at Canterbury, his chief lodging, being burnt in Archbishop Cranmer's time, and upon his other houses, chancels, &c., to about 2600*l*.[4]

This paper gives but little idea of the eminent value of the archbishop's patronage of literature, and none of his own personal labours as an author. These are points to which there are frequent allusions in the volume now published; and it was our intention to enter freely upon both of them in the present Introduction; but the Correspondence has extended to a length very far beyond what was anticipated, and has thus deprived us of the opportunity of doing so. The former point is one which would especially repay inquiry, and it is also one as to which there can fortunately be no difference of opinion. The archbishop's labours as the first publisher of the materials for English History, acquired for him the respect even of the historian Gibbon.

The same necessity for compressing this Introduction within the briefest limits has led to the exclusion of an intended Catalogue of all the Letters to or from the Archbishop, notices of which have come to light during the compilation of the present volume, without our being able to recover the letters themselves. We have printed all the letters of the archbishop with which we are acquainted, but there are probably many others scattered abroad which have escaped our inquiries. Letters have turned up from time to time in

---

[3] De furoribus Norfolciensium Ketto duce. 4to. Bynneman, 1575.

[4] Lambeth MS. 959, art. 46. The paper is inserted in a copy of Parker's Antiquitates.

quarters where their existence was never suspected, and the publication of the present volume will doubtless lead to the production of others.

In a few instances letters alluded to by Strype will not be found in the present volume. There are two causes of their omission. In some cases, Strype has been found to have been mistaken in the authorship or in the address, as where a letter written by Bishop Bonner was by him supposed to have been addressed to Parker instead of to Dr Edmunds; in other cases, letters, alluded to by Strype as being in certain repositories, are not now to be found either there or in any other place to which we have had access.

It is perhaps scarcely necessary after recent investigations respecting Strype's mode of publication, to remark that, in cases where our text of a letter published by Strype differs from his, even where words and sentences appear in the present volume which do not occur in Strype, it should not be taken for granted that the present publication is in error. Our desire has been to print the letters correctly, without encumbering the page with references to the mistakes of others.

It would be unjust, as well as uncourteous, were we to conclude without pointing out to the Members of the Parker Society, how much they are indebted to the Master and Fellows of Corpus Christi College, Cambridge, for the very great facility of access they have given us to the Parker MSS. The same kindness has been shewn us by the Benchers of the Inner Temple, with reference to the Petyt MSS., and indeed by all the other possessors of MSS., to whom we have found it necessary to apply.

CONTENTS.

LETTER			PAGE
I.	1534-5,	23rd March....John Skypp to Matthew Parker............	1
II.	—	23rd March....The same to the same	2
III.	1535,	23rd March....Sir John Cheke to the same..................	2
IV.	—	11th Oct........Henry VIII. to the same	4
V.	—	4th Nov........Queen Anne Boleyn to the Bishop of Norwich	4
VI.	1537,	4th Nov........Thomas Lord Cromwell to Matthew Parker	5
VII.	1537-8,	13th Feb.......John Skypp to the same	5
VIII.	1539,	—— ......Answer to Articles of Accusation sent to the Lord Audley against M. Parker by Mr G. Colt and other of Clare Town..	7
IX.	—	11th May ......John Skypp to Matthew Parker	9
X.	—	23rd Nov.......Matthew Parker to Dr Stokes	10
XI.	1544,	25th May ......Henry VIII. to the Dean and Prebendaries of Stoke....................................	15
XII.	—	14th Nov.......Queen Katherine Parr to Dr Matthew Parker	16
XIII.	—	30th Nov.......Henry VIII. to the Fellows of Corpus Christi College, Cambridge	16
XIV.	1544-5,	26th Jan........John Mere to Matthew Parker	17
XV.	—	24th March ...Queen Katherine Parr to the Dean and Fellows of Stoke............................	19
XVI.	1545,	27th March ...Bishop Gardiner to Dr Matthew Parker and Dr Thomas Smith	20
XVII.	—	3rd April ......Dr Parker to Bishop Gardiner...............	21
XVIII.	—	23rd April ...Bishop Gardiner to Dr Matthew Parker...	22
XIX.	—	8th May ......Dr Matthew Parker to Bishop Gardiner	24
XX.	—	12th May ......Bishop Gardiner to Dr Matthew Parker...	27
XXI.	—	16th May ......The Lords of the Council to the same ...	29
XXII.	—	21st August...Thomas Smith to the same	30
XXIII.	—	—— ...Dr Matthew Parker to the Council of Queen Katherine Parr	31
———	1545-6,	16th Jan........King Henry VIII. to Dr Matthew Parker	34n.
———	—	26th Feb.......Queen Katherine Parr to the Chancellor and Vice-Chancellor of Cambridge ...	36n.
XXIV.	1546,	—— ......Dr Matthew Parker's Minute of an interview with King Henry VIII.	34
XXV.	1547-8,	— Feb.......John Mere to Dr Matthew Parker	37
———	—	29th Feb.......Sir Anthony Denny to the Commissioners for the suppression of Colleges	33n.
XXVI.	—	13th March....William May to Dr Matthew Parker.....	38
XXVII.	1548,	5th May........Archbishop Cranmer to the same	39
XXVIII.	—	7th June ....Sir John Cheke to the same..................	39

CONTENTS

LETTER				PAGE
XXIX.	1548-9,	17th Feb.	Archbishop Cranmer to Dr Matthew Parker	40
XXX.	—	4th March.	Bishop Thirleby to the same.	41
XXXI.	1550,	—	Martin Bucer to the same	41
XXXII.	—	—	The same to the same	42
XXXIII.	1550-1,	— Feb.	The same to the same	42
XXXIV.	—	12th Feb.	Archbishop Cranmer to the same	43
XXXV.	—	9th March.	Sir John Cheke to the same	43
XXXVI.	1551,	25th July	Bishop Ridley to the same	45
XXXVII.	—	13th Dec.	The Lords of the Council to the same	46
XXXVIII.	—	—	Matthew Parker and Walter Haddon to the Guardians of the children of Martin Bucer	46
XXXIX.	1552-3,	6th Feb.	Sir John Cheke to Dr Matthew Parker	48
—	1553,	20th August	Queen Mary to Bishop Gardiner	54n.
—	—	25th August.	Bishop Gardiner to the University of Cambridge	56n.
XL.	1558,	9th Dec.	Sir Nicholas Bacon to Dr Matthew Parker	49
XLI.	—	Between 9th & 20th Dec.	Dr Matthew Parker to Sir Nicholas Bacon	50
XLII.	—	20th Dec.	The same to the same	52
XLIII.	—	30th Dec.	Sir William Cecil to Dr Matthew Parker	53
XLIV.	1558-9,	4th Jan.	Sir Nicholas Bacon to the same	53
XLV.	—	1st March	Dr Matthew Parker to Sir William Cecil	54
XLVI.	—	1st March	The same to Sir Nicholas Bacon	57
XLVII.	—	21st March.	Sir William Cecil to Dr Porie, Dr Matthew Parker, and Mr Edward Leeds	63
XLVIII.	—	21st March.	Sir T. Smith to Dr Porie, Dr Matthew Parker, and Mr Leeds	64
XLIX.	1559,	30th April	Dr Edmund Sandys to Dr Matthew Parker	65
L.	—	5th May	Sir William Cecil to the same	67
LI.	—	17th May	Sir Nicholas Bacon to the same	68
LII.	—	19th May	Sir Nicholas Bacon and Sir William Cecil to the same	68
LIII.	—	28th May	Lord Keeper Bacon and Sir William Cecil to the same	69
LIV.	—	28th June	Dr Matthew Parker to Queen Elizabeth	69
LV.	—	— June	Lord Keeper Bacon to Dr Matthew Parker	71
LVI.	—	8th August	Archbishop Parker and others to the University of Cambridge	71
LVII.	—	24th August	The Lords of the Council to Archbishop Parker and Bishop Grindal	72
LVIII.	—	27th August	Archbishop Parker to the Lords of the Council	73
LIX.	—	28th August	The Lords of the Council to Archbishop Parker	74
LX.	—	7th Sept.	The same to the same	75
LXI.	—	9th Sept.	Sir Nicholas Bacon to the same	76
LXII.	—	23rd Sept	The Lords of the Council to the same	76
LXIII.	—	27th Sept	The same to the same	77
LXIV.	—	2nd Oct.	Sir W. Cecil to the same	77
LXV.	—	5th Oct.	The same to the same	78
LXVI.	—	—	Archbishop Parker and others to Queen Elizabeth	79

CONTENTS. xvii

LETTER			PAGE
LXVII.	1559, 13th Oct.......	Sir Francis Knollys to Archbishop Parker	96
LXVIII.	—	15th Oct.......Archbishop Parker and four other bishops to Queen Elizabeth	97
LXIX.	—	26th Oct.......Queen Elizabeth to the Lord Treasurer and the Barons of the Exchequer	101
LXX.	—	2nd Nov. ......The Lords of the Council to Archbishop Parker	103
LXXI.	—	2nd Nov. ......Sir Thomas Parry and Sir William Cecil to the same.....................	104
LXXII.	—	6th Nov. ......Archbishop Parker to Sir William Cecil...	105
LXXIII.	—	9th Nov. ......The Lords of the Council to Archbishop Parker and the rest of the Ecclesiastical Commissioners............................	105
LXXIV.	—	18th Nov.......Archbishop Parker to Sir William Cecil	106
LXXV.	—	23rd Dec.......Archbishop Parker and others to the President and Chapter of Exeter.........	107
LXXVI.	1559-60, 27th Feb.......	Sir William Cecil to Archbishop Parker	108
LXXVII.	1560, 26th March ...	Archbishop Parker to Dr Nicholas Heath, deprived archbishop of York, and other deprived bishops............................	109
LXXVIII.	—	— April......Archbishop Parker to Warham St Leger	113
LXXIX.	—	3rd May ......Bishop Young to Archbishop Parker..... .	114
LXXX.	—	27th May ......Archbishop Parker to Bishop Grindal ...	115
LXXXI.	—	30th May ......The Lords of the Council to Archbishop Parker	117
LXXXII.	—	6th June ....Sir William Petre to the same...............	118
LXXXIII.	—	14th July ......The same to the same...........................	118
LXXXIV.	—	17th July ......Marquis Winchester to the same............	119
LXXXV.	—	24th July ......Lord Keeper Bacon to the same	120
LXXXVI.	—	15th August...Archbishop Parker to Bishop Grindal ...	120
LXXXVII.	—	4th Sept. ......The Lords of the Council to Archbishop Parker	121
LXXXVIII.	—	6th Sept. ......Archbishop Parker to Sir Edward Warner	122
LXXXIX.	—	16th Oct. ......The same to Sir William Cecil...............	123
XC.	—	24th Oct. ......Bishop Sandys to Archbishop Parker	124
XCI.	—	18th Nov.......Archbishop Parker to Bishop Grindal	127
XCII.	—	20th Nov......The same to Dr Yale	128
XCIII.	—	— ......Archbishop Parker and other Bishops to Queen Elizabeth	129
XCIV.	1560-1, 22nd Jan.......	Queen Elizabeth to Archbishop Parker and others	132
XCV.	—	15th Feb. ......Archbishop Parker to Bishop Grindal	134
XCVI.	1561, 13th April ...	The same to Lord Thomas Howard.........	136
——	—	16th April .....Richard Cheney to Sir William Cecil......	138n.
XCVII.	—	18th April ....Bishop Richard Davies to Archbishop Parker	137
XCVIII.	—	after 16th April, Sir William Cecil to the same...............	138
XCIX.	—	22nd May ....Flacius Illyricus to the same..................	139
C.	—	21st June ....Thomas Seckford to the same	142
CI.	—	24th June ......Queen Elizabeth to the same..................	142
CII.	—	1st July ....Archbishop Parker to Bishop Grindal.....	143
CIII.	—	{shortly after 30th June ...} The same to Dr Nicholas Wotton	144

CONTENTS.

LETTER			PAGE
CIV.	1561, 2nd July	Archbishop Parker to the Sheriff of Oxford and Berks	145
CV.	—	9th August ...Order of Queen Elizabeth prohibiting the residence of women in Colleges	146
CVI.	—	11th August...Archbishop Parker to Sir William Cecil	147
CVII.	—	12th August .. Sir William Cecil to Archbishop Parker...	148
CVIII.	—	22nd August...Queen Elizabeth to the same	149
CIX.	—	— August...Bishop Cox to the same	151
CX.	—	1st Sept.........Archbishop Parker to Bishop Grindal ...	152
CXI.	—	1st Oct..........The same to Archdeacons and other Ecclesiastical officers	153
CXII.	—	24th Oct. ......The Lords of the Council to Archbishop Parker	154
CXIII.	—	14th Dec.......The same to the same	155
CXIV.	—	——— ......Archbishop Parker to Sir William Cecil.	156
CXV.	—	——— ..... John Fox to Archbishop Parker and Bishop Grindal	160
CXVI.	1561 2, 1st Jan.	Sir William Cecil to Archbishop Parker.	161
CXVII.	—	25th Jan. ......Archbishop Parker to the Provost and Fellows of Eton College	162
CXVIII.	—	— Jan. ......Sir William Cecil to Archbishop Parker.	163
CXIX.	—	12th Feb. ......Queen Elizabeth to the same	163
CXX.	—	13th March ...Archbishop Parker and Bishop Grindal to Sir William Cecil	165
CXXI.	—	21st March ...Archbishop Parker to Mr Nevenson	165
CXXII.	1562,	2nd May ......The same to the Barons of the Exchequer	166
CXXIII.	—	28th Oct.......The same to Sir William Cecil	170
CXXIV.	—	about Nov. ...The same to Lord Keeper Bacon	171
CXXV.	1562-3, 23rd Feb.	Sir William Cecil to Archbishop Parker.	172
CXXVI.	—	27th Feb. ......The same to the same.	172
CXXVII.	1563,	shortly after 14th April } Archbishop Parker to Sir William Cecil.	173
CXXVIII.	—	shortly after 14th April } The same to each of his Suffragan Bishops	174
CXXIX.	—	16th May ......Queen Elizabeth to Archbishop Parker..	175
CXXX.	—	16th June ...Bishop Jewel to the same	176
CXXXI.	—	before Midsummer } Archbishop Parker to Sir William Cecil.	177
CXXXII.	—	26th June ...The Lords of the Council to Archbishop Parker	178
CXXXIII.	—	28th June ...The same to the same	179
CXXXIV.	—	9th July ......The same to the same	180
CXXXV.	—	23rd July ......Archbishop Parker to Sir William Cecil.	182
CXXXVI.	—	1st August ... Sir William Cecil to Archbishop Parker.	183
CXXXVII.	—	1st August ...Queen Elizabeth to the same	184
CXXXVIII.	—	6th August ...Archbishop Parker to Sir William Cecil.	185
CXXXIX.	—	22nd August. The same to the same	186
CXL.	—	25th August . Sir William Cecil to Archbishop Parker.	187
CXLI.	—	27th August . Archbishop Parker to Sir William Cecil.	187
CXLII.	—	4th Sept. ......Lord Robert Dudley to Archbishop Parker	190
CXLIII.	—	6th Sept. ...., .Archbishop Parker to Lord Robert Dudley	190

CONTENTS.

LETTER			PAGE
CXLIV.	1563,	7th Sept. ......Archbishop Parker to Sir William Cecil.	191
CXLV.	—	15th Sept......The Lords of the Council to Archbishop Parker	192
CXLVI.	—	16th Sept......Dr Thirleby to the same	193
CXLVII.	—	20th Sept......Archbishop Parker to Dr Thirleby	193
CXLVIII.	—	20th Sept......The same to Sir William Cecil	194
CXLIX.	—	23rd Sept......The Lords of the Council to Archbishop Parker	195
CL.	—	3rd Oct. ......Bishop Grindal to the same	196
CLI.	—	— Oct. ......Archbishop Parker to Sir George Howard	197
CLII.	—	20th Nov.......The same to Sir William Cecil	197
	—	29th Dec......Act of General Assembly of the Church of Scotland	205
CLIII.	—	......Archbishop Parker to Sir William Cecil.	199
CLIV.	1563-4,	2nd Jan. ... ..Bishop Grindal to Archbishop Parker ...	201
CLV.	—	6th Feb. ......Archbishop Parker to Sir William Cecil.	202
CLVI.	—	20th Jan. ......The same to the same	203
CLVII.	—	10th Feb.......Scottish Ministers to Archbishops Parker and Young	205
CLVIII.	—	18th March ...Archbishop Parker to Sir William Cecil.	207
CLIX.	1564,	14th April ...The same to the same	209
CLX.	—	7th May ......Master and Wardens of the Skinners' Company to Archbishop Parker.........	210
CLXI.	—	14th May......Queen Elizabeth to the same	212
CLXII.	—	About end of April ....} Archbishop Parker to Bishop Cheney....	213
CLXIII.	—	About end of April ....} The same to Mr Drury......................	213
CLXIV.	—	3rd June ......The same to Sir William Cecil	214
CLXV.	—	23rd June......The Lords of the Council to Archbishop Parker	217
CLXVI.	—	6th July ......Walter Haddon to the same..................	218
CLXVII.	—	......Archbishop Parker to Lady Bacon.........	219
CLXVIII.	—	......Bishop Pilkington to Archbishop Parker	221
CLXIX.	1564-5,	15th Jan. ......Sir William Cecil to the same...............	223
CLXX.	—	25th Jan........Queen Elizabeth to the same	223
CLXXI.	—	30th Jan. ......Archbishop Parker to Bishop Grindal ...	227
CLXXII.	—	7th Feb. ......John Fox to Archbishop Parker............	230
CLXXIII.	—	20th Feb.......Archbishop Parker to Sir John Holt and others, inhabitants of Rochdale	231
CLXXIV.	—	— Feb........The same to Mr Byron.......................	232
CLXXV.	—	3rd March ...The same to Sir William Cecil	233
CLXXVI.	—	8th March......The same to the same	234
CLXXVII.	—	14th March....Sir William Cecil to Archbishop Parker.	235
CLXXVIII.	—	24th March....Archbishop Parker to Sir William Cecil.	236
CLXXIX.	1565,	7th April.......The same to the same	237
CLXXX.	—	9th April.......The same to the same	238
CLXXXI.	—	About Easter.The same to the same	239
CLXXXII.	—	30th April......The same to the same	240
CLXXXIII.	—	12th May ...... The same to Bishop Grindal	242
CLXXXIV.	—	3rd June........Dr Sampson to Archbishop Parker	243
CLXXXV.	—	4th June ...... Archbishop Parker to Sir William Cecil.	244

CONTENTS.

LETTER				PAGE
CLXXXVI.	1565,	4th June	Archbishop Parker to Dr Sampson	244
CLXXXVII.	—	4th June	The same to Earl of Huntingdon	245
CLXXXVIII.	—	8th Dec.	The same to Sir William Cecil	245
—	—	13th Dec.	The same to the same	246n.
CLXXXIX.	—	19th Dec.	Bishop Parkhurst to Archbishop Parker.	247
CXC.	—	29th Dec.	Archbishop Parker to Sir William Cecil.	248
CXCI.	—	—	Bishop Geste to Archbishop Parker.	250
CXCII.	—	—	Dean Nowell to Archbishop Parker	251
CXCIII.	1565-6,	4th Jan.	Archbishop Parker to Sir William Cecil.	251
CXCIV.	—	24th Jan.	The same to the same	253
CXCV.	—	29th Jan.	The same to Sir William Cecil	254
CXCVI.	—	—	The same to the Duke of Norfolk.	255
CXCVII.	—	6th Feb	Bishop Sandys to Archbishop Parker	256
CXCVIII.	—	7th Feb.	Archbishop Parker to Sir William Cecil.	257
CXCIX.	—	12th Feb.	The same to the same	258
CC.	—	12th Feb.	The same to the same	259
CCI.	—	26th Feb.	The same to the same	260
CCII.	—	9th March	Archbishop Parker and Bishop Grindal to the same	261
CCIII.	—	12th March	Archbishop Parker to the same	262
CCIV.	—	19th March	Bishop Davies to Archbishop Parker	265
CCV.	—	20th March	Archbishop Parker and Bishop Grindal to Sir William Cecil	267
CCVI.	1566,	25th March	Archbishop Parker to the same	269
CCVII.	—	26th March	The same to the same	269
CCVIII.	—	28th March	The same to Bishop Davies	270
CCIX.	—	28th March	The same to Sir William Cecil	271
CCX.	—	28th March	The same to Bishop Grindal	272
CCXI.	—	3rd April	The same to Sir William Cecil	275
CCXII.	—	4th April	The same to the same	276
CCXIII.	—	12th April	The same to the same	277
CCXIV.	—	24th April	Bishop Davies to Archbishop Parker	279
CCXV.	—	28th April	Archbishop Parker to Sir William Cecil.	280
CCXVI.	—	3rd May	Bishop Cox to Archbishop Parker	281
CCXVII.	—	27th May	Dr Walter Haddon to the same	282
CCXVIII.	—	5th June	Archbishop Parker to Sir William Cecil.	283
CCXIX.	—	6th June	The same to Dr Walter Haddon	284
CCXX.	—	27th June	The same to Lord Abergavenny	285
CCXXI.	—	18th July	The same to Matthias Flacius Illyricus, John Wigand, and Matthias Judex.	286
CCXXII.	—	22nd July	The same to Sir William Cecil	289
CCXXIII.	—	26th Nov.	The same to the same	290
CCXXIV.	—	21st Dec.	The same to the same	290
CCXXV.	—	24th Dec.	Archbishop Parker and other Bishops to Queen Elizabeth	292
—	—	26th Dec.	Archbishop Young to Archbishop Parker	294n.
CCXXVI.	—	—	Richard Grafton to the same	295
CCXXVII.	1566-7,	5th March	Archbishop Parker to the Warden of All Souls' College, Oxford	296
CCXXVIII.	1567,	26th March	Archbishop Parker and others to the Warden and Fellows of All Souls' College, Oxford	297
CCXXIX.	—	8th April	Dr John Caius to Archbishop Parker	298

CONTENTS. xxi

LETTER			PAGE
CCXXX.	1567,	19th April ...Archbishop Parker and others to the Warden of All Souls' College, Oxford	300
CCXXXI.	—	middle of year ...Lord Leicester and Sir William Cecil to Archbishop Parker	301
	—	—— ......Lords of the Council to the same	302n.
CCXXXII.	—	3rd July ......Archbishop Parker to * * * *	303
CCXXXIII.	—	12th Aug......The same to Sir William Cecil	303
CCXXXIV.	—	12th Sept.......Sir William Cecil to Archbishop Parker.	305
CCXXXV.	—	5th Oct. ......Archbishop Parker to Sir William Cecil.	305
CCXXXVI.	—	27th Oct. ......Sir Robert Wingfield and others to Archbishop Parker	306
CCXXXVII.	—	before Nov. ...Archbishop Parker to Bishop Grindal ...	308
CCXXXVIII.	—	31st Dec. ......The same to Sir Gilbert Gerrard	308
CCXXXIX.	1567-8,	6th Feb. ......The same to Lady Bacon	309
CCXL.	—	3rd March ...Sir Henry Sydney to Archbishop Parker.	316
CCXLI.	1568,	25th March....Archbishop Parker to Frederic III., Elector Palatine	317
CCXLII.	—	29th March....The same to Sir William Cecil	318
CCXLIII.	—	3rd May ....Earl of Warwick to Archbishop Parker ..	319
CCXLIV.	—	12th May ......Archbishop Parker to the Warden of All Souls' College, Oxford	320
CCXLV.	—	13th May ......Queen Elizabeth to Archbishop Parker..	321
CCXLVI.	—	21st May ......Archbishop Parker to Sir William Cecil...	322
CCXLVII.	—	24th May ......The same to Bishop Grindal	323
CCXLVIII.	—	1st June ....The same to the Warden of All Souls' College, Oxford	324
CCXLIX.	—	11th June......The same to Sir William Cecil	324
CCL.	—	21st June..... The same to Sir Gilbert Gerrard	325
CCLI.	—	4th July......The same to Sir William Cecil	327
CCLII.	—	5th July........The Lords of the Council to Archbishop Parker	328
——	—	7th July ....Order of the Privy Council	327n.
CCLIII.	—	14th July......Archbishop Parker to the Lords of the Council	330
CCLIV.	—	19th August...The same to Sir William Cecil	331
CCLV.	—	16th Sept......Immanuel Tremellius to Archbp. Parker	332
CCLVI.	—	22nd Sept......Archbishop Parker to Sir William Cecil	333
CCLVII.	—	5th Oct. ......The same to the same .	334
CCLVIII.	—	5th Oct. ......The same to Queen Elizabeth	337
CCLIX.	—	—— ....The same to Mr Serjeant Manwood	338
——	1568-9,	4th Jan. ....Archbishop Parker and others to Sir William Cecil	343n.
CCLX.	—	16th Jan.......Antonius Corranus to Archbishop Parker	339
CCLXI.	—	17th Jan. ......Queen Elizabeth to the same	340
CCLXII.	—	22nd Feb.......Archbishop Parker to Sir William Cecil .	341
CCLXIII.	1569,	25th March....The same to the Bailiffs of Lydd	342
CCLXIV.	—	13th April. ...Archbishop Parker and other Ecclesiastical Commissioners to Sir William Cecil	343
CCLXV.	—	6th May........Archbishop Parker to Bishop Grindal ...	345
CCLXVI.	—	16th May......The same to the Dean and Chapter of York	347
CCLXVII.	—	18th May......The same to Sir William Cecil	348
CCLXVIII.	—	20th May ......Archbishop Parker and Bishop Grindal to the Vice-Chancellor and Heads of Houses at Cambridge	348

CONTENTS.

LETTER				PAGE
CCLXIX.	1569,	3rd June......	Archbishop Parker to Sir William Cecil .	350
CCLXX.	—	1st July . .	The same to the same	351
CCLXXI.	—	9th August ..	The same to the same	352
CCLXXII.	—	24th Sept.....	Sir William Cecil to Archbishop Parker.	354
CCLXXIII.	—	6th Nov.	The Lords of the Council to the same ...	355
CCLXXIV.	1569-70,	8th March.......	Archbishop Parker to Sir William Cecil.	358
CCLXXV.	1570,	30th March . .	The same to the same	359
CCLXXVI.	—	1st April	The same to the same	361
CCLXXVII.	—	3rd April	The same to the same	363
CCLXXVIII.	—	4th May	The same to the same	365
———	—	7th May	Thomas Keyes to Archbishop Parker.....	366n.
CCLXXIX.	—	26th May	Archbishop Parker to Sir William Cecil.	366
CCLXXX.	—	25th August...	The same to the same	368
CCLXXXI.	—	2nd Nov.	The same to the same	370
CCLXXXII.	—	27th Dec.......	The same to Queen Elizabeth...............	371
CCLXXXIII.	1570-1,	8th Jan.	The same to Sir William Cecil	375
CCLXXXIV.	—	21st Jan.	The same to the same	377
CCLXXXV.	—	2nd Feb.	The same to the same	378
CCLXXXVI.	—	6th Feb.	The same to the same	378
CCLXXXVII.	—	17th Feb.......	The Lords of the Council to Archbishop Parker and Lord Cobham.	379
CCLXXXVIII.	1571,	4th June	Archbishop Parker to Lord Burghley ...	381
CCLXXXIX.	—	7th June	Archbishop Parker and other Ecclesiastical Commissioners to Churchwardens and others	382
CCXC.	—	17th June.....	Archbishop Parker to Lord Burghley ...	384
CCXCI.	—	17th June......	The Lords of the Council to Archbishop Parker and Bishop Sandys	384
CCXCII.	—	20th August...	Queen Elizabeth to Archbishop Parker.	386
CCXCIII.	—	22nd August..	Order of the Earl of Arundel for supply of Deer to Archbishop Parker............	387
CCXCIV.	—	16th Dec.......	Archbishop Parker to * * * ...	388
CCXCV.	1571-2,	2nd Jan.	The same to Bishop Parkhurst	389
CCXCVI.	—	13th Jan.	Archbishop Parker and other Ecclesiastical Commissioners to the Duchess of Suffolk	390
CCXCVII.	1572,	19th May	Archbishop Parker to Lord Burghley ...	391
CCXCVIII.	—	22nd May......	The same to Bishop Barnes...................	392
CCXCIX.	—	31st May	Archbishop Parker and others to Lord Burghley	393
CCC.	—	2nd July	Archbishop Parker to the same	394
CCCI.	—	8th July	The same to the same	395
CCCII.	—	17th August..	The same to the same	396
CCCIII.	—	25th August...	The same to the same	397
CCCIV.	—	16th Sept.	The same to the same	398
CCCV.	—	6th Oct...........	The same to the same	400
CCCVI.	—	9th Oct..........	Archbishop Parker and other Ecclesiastical Commissioners to Bishop Parkhurst............	401
CCCVII.	—	29th Oct.	Archbishop Parker to Bishop Sandys ...	402
CCCVIII.	—	2nd Nov.	The same to Bishop Parkhurst	403
CCCIX.	—	5th Nov.	The same to Lord Burghley................. ..	404
CCCX.	—	7th Nov.	The same to Lord Burghley and the Earl of Leicester	405

CONTENTS. xxiii

LETTER			PAGE
CCCXI.	1572,	8th Nov. ......The same to Lord Burghley..................	406
CCCXII.	—	13th Nov. ......The same to the same......................	407
CCCXIII.	—	22nd Nov.......The same to the same	409
CCCXIV.	—	13th Dec.......The same to the same	411
CCCXV.	—	21st Dec.......The same to the same	412
CCCXVI.	—	25th Dec. ......The same to the same	413
CCCXVII.	1572-3,	2nd Jan. ......The same to Bishop Parkhurst..............	415
CCCXVIII.	—	9th Jan. ......The same to the Earl of Sussex	416
CCCXIX.	—	24th Feb.. ....The same to Bishop Parkhurst..............	416
CCCXX.	—	3rd March ...The same to the same........................	417
CCCXXI.	—	12th March .. The same to Lord Burghley	418
CCCXXII.	1573,	9th April......The same to the same........................	420
CCCXXIII.	—	25th April ...The same to the same	422
CCCXXIV.	—	27th April ...The same to the same.........................	423
CCCXXV.	—	9th May ......The same to the same.........................	424
CCCXXVI.	—	5th June .... .The same to the same.........................	427
CCCXXVII.	—	15th June......The same to the same.........................	427
CCCXXVIII.	—	15th June......The same to Queen Elizabeth	428
CCCXXIX.	—	19th June......The same to the same.........................	429
CCCXXX.	—	5th July ......Archbishop Parker and other Ecclesiastical Commissioners to the Vice-Chancellor of Cambridge	433
CCCXXXI.	—	6th July ......Archbishop Parker and Bishop Sandys to some other Bishop	434
CCCXXXII.	—	15th July ......Archbishop Parker to Lord Burghley ...	436
CCCXXXIII.	—	18th July ......The same to the same	437
CCCXXXIV.	—	23rd July ......The same to the same	440
CCCXXXV.	—	27th July ... . The same to the same	441
CCCXXXVI.	—	17th August...The same to the same	441
CCCXXXVII.	—	11th Sept. ....Lord Burghley to Archbishop Parker ...	444
CCCXXXVIII.	—	11th Sept .. .Archbishop Parker to Lord Burghley ..	444
CCCXXXIX.	—	3rd Nov. ......The same to the same	445
CCCXL.	—	7th Nov. ......The same to the same	447
CCCXLI.	—	9th Nov. ......The same to the same	447
CCCXLII.	—	11th Nov.......The same to the same	448
CCCXLIII.	—	13th Nov.. ..The same to the same	449
CCCXLIV.	—	15th Nov..... .The same to the same	449
CCCXLV.	—	24th Nov.......The same to Bishop Sandys.	451
CCCXLVI.	—	5th Dec. ......The same to Mr John Boys	452
CCCXLVII.	—	30th Dec.... .The same to Lord Burghley	453
CCCXLVIII.	—	——— ..... The same to the same	453
CCCXLIX.	1573-4,	13th Jan. ..... .The same to the Vidame of Chartres	455
CCCL.	1574,	25th March....The same to Mr Matchett	456
CCCLI.	—	17th May . ....The same to Bishop Parkhurst	457
CCCLII.	—	12th June......The same to the Earl of Sussex	458
CCCLIII.	—	14th June......The same to Bishop Parkhurst	459
CCCLIV.	—	19th June ....The same to Lord Burghley	460
CCCLV.	—	19th June......The same to the same	461
CCCLVI.	—	23rd June......The same to the same	462
CCCLVII.	—	26th June......The same to the same	462
CCCLVIII.	—	26th June......The same to the same	463
CCCLIX.	—	30th June......The same to the same	464
CCCLX.	—	13th August...The same to the same	465

CONTENTS.

LETTER				PAGE
CCCLXI.	1574,	2nd Oct.	......Archbishop Parker to the Earl of Sussex	466
CCCLXII.	—	7th Oct.	......The same to the same	467
CCCLXIII.	—	23rd Nov.	.......The same to Lord Burghley	467
CCCLXIV.	—	25th Nov.	.......The same to Dr Robert Norgate	469
CCCLXV.	1574-5,	9th Jan.	......The same to Lord Burghley.................	469
CCCLXVI.	—	24th Jan.	......The same to Peter Dathenus	471
CCCLXVII.	—	18th Feb.	......The same to Lord Burghley	472
CCCLXVIII.	—	17th March.	....The same to Archbishop Grindal	474
CCCLXIX.	1575,	11th April.	....The same to Lord Burghley	477

APPENDIX.

I.	1504-59,	———	Archbishop Parker's Autobiography	481
II.	1559,	30th March.	...Dr Matthew Parker to Sir William Cecil	485
		INDEX	....	487

CORRESPONDENCE

OF

ARCHBISHOP PARKER.

I.

JOHN SKYPP TO MATTHEW PARKER.

23rd March, 1534—5. Parker MSS. C. C. Coll. Camb. CVIII. art. 5. p. 73. Orig.

MR PARKER, I commend me heartily unto you. Our friend Master Betts[1] is departed out of this world. And the Queen's grace commanded me to write unto you to the intent that ye should come up and speak with her with all the speed that ye can. I would ye might come before Easter; but if ye cannot, I pray you in any wise to be here in the week after, and then shall ye know further of her pleasure. Thus fare ye well. From Hampton Court, the Tuesday after Palm Sunday[2].

Your,

JOHN SKIPPE.

Master Betts dead. Queen Ann's Boleyn desires to speak with Parker.

To my friend Mr Parker of Benet College this be delivered with speed.

[[1] He was a Fellow of Corpus Christi College, and chaplain to Queen Anne Boleyn, in which office Parker succeeded him.]

[[2] The following note is appended to this letter, apparently by the archbishop: "Hic J. Skyp erat ab eleemosinis Reginæ Annæ, postea episcopus Herefordensis, et tandem moritur in ædibus suis Londini." There is also added to this and the next letter by a subsequent hand the date "1533." We have assigned them to the year 1535, as a period more consistent with other facts in the biography of Parker. It appears from his autobiographical memoranda, that he did not take upon him the office of a preacher until the first Sunday in Advent in 1533, and that on the 30th March, 1535, probably the day on which he received these letters, he was "summoned to the court of queen Anne." See Appendix, No. I.]

II.

JOHN SKYPP TO MATTHEW PARKER.

23rd March, 1534—5. Parker MSS. C. C. Coll. Camb. cviii. art. 5. p. 73. Orig.

Being uncertain as to the delivery of his former letter, Skypp writes again to summon Parker to court.

MASTER Parker, I commend me heartily unto you. I sent you a letter by a carrier, but whether it shall be delivered or not I cannot tell. Therefore I write again praying you that ye will be at the court as shortly after Easter as ye can, for the Queen will see you; and for as much as Mr Betts is departed, I think her mind is to have you to her chaplain. I pray you resist not your calling, but come

Bring a long gown; that shall be enough.

in any wise to know further of her pleasure. Bring with you a long gown, and that shall be enough until ye shall return to Cambridge. We shall be this Easter at Richmond; we remove thither this same day. Thus fare ye well. From Hampton Court, the Tuesday after Palm Sunday.

Your,

JOHN SKYPPE.

III.

SIR JOHN CHEKE TO MATTHEW PARKER.

A.D. 1535.[1] Parker MSS. C. C. Coll. Camb. cxiv. art. 134. p. 405. Orig.

Old favour shewn by Parker to Cheke.

AUDEO equidem pro veteri tuo erga me favore familiariter impetrare, vir honestissime, ut tantum petitioni meæ honestæ tribuas quantum commodo tuo facere potes. Hoc in causa est. Accepimus et constans apud nos fama est de nobilis-

Queen Anne Boleyn's reputation for liberality towards students.

simæ Reginæ magnificentia, quæ, cum immensum quendam modum erga studiosos late patuit, nunc sit adaucta multum et amplificata quod ad compendii nostri primo quoque anno reditum dissolvendum spectat. Intelleximus autem nuper in

[[1] It seems probable that this letter was addressed to Parker at court. He was summoned thither as we have seen to become chaplain to queen Anne on the 30th of March, 1535, and he took possession of the deanery of Stoke in November of the same year. See Appendix, No. I. Strype, in his life of Cheke, places this letter under "ann. 1540, et seq.," but in his life of Parker he assigns it to 1534.]

se recepisse Reginam hoc ut faceret, et promisisse ut, si qui tenui in re et in egestate positi, quorum præterea morum ingenuitas et candor aliquis ingenii præluceret ad virtutis et literarum studia, libenter se illorum nomine dissoluturam atque illorum nomine perscripturam, modo illi significatio detur aliqua vel per D. Skippum vel aliquem ex vobis qui clarissimæ Reginæ a sacris estis, qualem se gerat et qualem se ostendat moribus ac eruditione. Jam vero cum nos habeamus apud nos adolescentulum literatum et honestum, qui et rerum cognitione abundat et integritate morum, qui venisset in sociorum numerum ad tempus Paschatis nisi quod ex hoc ære exire non potuit et pecuniam istam nequibat habere expeditam, D. Billum[2], multum a te desidero et requiro ut aliqua via ad Reginam perferatur esse adolescentulum gravi paupertate oppressum, cui iter ad victum suum interclusum est, quod colligere certam pecuniam nequeat, quam numerare ante debeat quam societatem inire posset. Quod si cures pro tua humanitate faciundum, facies rem valde piam et sanctam quod promoves ad studia et bonas literas eos quibus paupertatis malum ingravescit. Id si ante Omnium Sanctorum feceris, dupliciter demereberis nos tibi, et quod illum in locum suum curabis restitui, et quod alii dabis ansam in ejus locum quem nunc habet veniendi. Est enim solenne nobis ad festum Sanctorum Omnium creare novos discipulos qui in vacua eorum loca veniant quos ante hoc tempus abiisse hoc munere cognoverimus. Ergo hoc facto nos duplicem reportabimus commoditatem, et tu una ex re duplicem rapies laboris tui fructum. Me autem in infinitum tibi devinctum habes. Vale. Cantabrigiæ. Pridie Michaelm.

Tuus si quid potest,
JOANNES CHEEKUS.

Generoso viro Mattheo Parkaro,
  Reginæ a sacris.

[2 William Bill, afterwards Dean of Westminster, &c.]

IV.

HENRY VIII'S WARRANT FOR A DOE FOR MATTHEW PARKER.

11th October, 1535.   Parker MSS. C. C. Coll. Camb. cxiv. art. 4. p. 8. Orig.

HENRY R.[1]

BY THE KING.

We will and command you forthwith, upon the sight of these our letters and by warrant of the same, that ye deliver, or cause to be delivered unto our trusty and well-beloved Matthew Parker, chaplain to our dearest wife the Queen[2], or to the bringer hereof in his name, one doe of season, to be taken of our gift within our forest of Wayebridge, any restraint or other commandment heretofore had or made to the contrary hereof in anywise notwithstanding. Given under our signet at our city of Salisbury, the 11th day of October, in the 27th year of our reign.

One doe of season to be delivered to Matthew Parker, chaplain to the Queen.

To the Master Forester of our forest of Weybridge, and in his absence to his deputy or deputies there and to any of them.

V.

QUEEN ANNE BOLEYN TO THE BISHOP OF NORWICH.

4th November, 1535.   Parker MSS. C. C. Coll. Camb. cviii. art. 6. p. 74. Copy.

Anna, Dei gratia Regina Angliæ et Franciæ ac domina Hiberniæ, reverendo in Christo patri Richardo permissione divina Norwicen. episcopo, ejus ve in absentia vicario suo in spiritualibus generali, seu alio [sic] cuicunque jurisdictionem episcopalem ejusdem pro tempore habenti, salutem. Ad decanatum ecclesiæ nostræ collegiatæ sancti Johannis Baptistæ de Stoke[3] juxta Clare vestræ Norwicensis dioceseos modo per mortem naturalem magistri Roberti Shorten ultimi decani ibidem vacantem, et ad nostram collationem sive presentationem pleno jure spectantem, dilectum nobis in Christo magistrum Matheum Parker, sacræ theologiæ baccalarium, capel-

The deanery of the collegiate church of Stoke vacant by the death of Robert Shorton.

[1 The king's stamp.]   [2 Anne Boleyn.]
[3 This had been formerly a Benedictine priory, but was now a college of secular priests. See Strype's Parker, Book I. c. 2. pp. 15, 16. Oxf. 1821.]

1535.] QUEEN ANNE BOLEYN TO THE BISHOP OF NORWICH. 5

lanum nostrum vobis presentamus intuitu charitatis, rogantes ut eundem magistrum Matheum ad decanatum predictum admittere, ipsumque decanum in eodem canonice instituere cum suis juribus et pertinentibus universis, ceteraque peragere quæ vestro in hac parte incumbunt officio pastorali velitis cum favore. In cujus rei testimonium magnum sigillum nostrum presentibus apponi fecimus[4]. Datum apud castellum domini mei de Windesore, quarto die Novembris anno regni dicti domini mei Regis Henrici octavi vicesimo septimo. Anno Domini 1534[5].

Matthew Parker to be instituted thereto.

Per warrantum sub Signeto.

VI.
THOMAS LORD CROMWELL TO MATTHEW PARKER.
A.D. 1537. Parker MSS. C. C. Coll. Camb. CXIV. art. 129. p. 393. Orig.

IN my right hearty manner, I commend me unto you. And whereas, for the honest report of your learning in holy letters and uncorrupt judgment in the same, I have appointed you, among others, to occupy the room of a preacher one day at Paul's Cross; these be as well to signify unto you that the said day limited for you is the seventeenth Sunday after Trinity Sunday, being the 23rd day of September next coming, as also to require you that ye fail not to be there the same day, preparing in the mean time with such pure

Parker appointed by Cromwell to "occupy the room" of a preacher at Paul's cross on the 17th Sunday after Trinity, being 23rd September.

[4 At the foot of this letter is the following copy of the certificate of composition for firstfruits :

Decanatus Collegii divi Johannis Baptistæ de Stoke juxta Clare in com. Suff.	Diocesis Norvicensis. Memorandum : quinto die Novembris anno Regis Henrici VIII. xxvii°, Matheus Parker Clericus composuit coram Thoma Crumwell Armigero, primario Secretario Domini regis ac magistro Rotulorum Curiæ Cancellariæ Domini Regis pro primitiis dicti decanatus secundum formam statuti de concessione primitiarum editi et provisi.

Per JOHANNEM HALES.]

[5 This date is by the same hand as the rest of the letter. It should, however, be 1535, (see App. No. I.) which agrees with the 27th of King Henry VIII.]

sincereness truly to open the word of God at the said day as I may thereby take occasion to think the report made of you to be true; whereby ye shall not only do a right good deed, but also to minister unto me thankful pleasure, which I shall not fail to requite as occasion may thereunto serve[1]. And thus fare ye well.

Your friend,
THOMAS CRUMWELL.

To my loving friend Master Parker,
Dean of Stoke college in Suffolk.

VII.

JOHN SKYPP TO MATTHEW PARKER.

13th February, 1537_8. Parker MSS. C. C. Coll. Camb. CXIV. art. 17. p. 62. Orig.

Parker summoned to court to be appointed chaplain to Henry VIII.

RIGHT worshipful Mr Dean, I commend me heartily unto you. These my letters shall be to certify you that the King's grace hath not forgotten you, but hath you perfectly in his remembrance, and also willeth, that you at your convenient leisure repair unto the court, not only to be admitted chaplain unto his grace[2], but also at your coming thither to know further of his pleasure. This he willed me to signify unto you. He appointed you no certain day, wherefore sith you were minded before to be here about Mid-Lent, I think it best that you persevere in your purpose. Thus fare ye well. From Westminster, the 13th day of February.

Your,
JOHN SKYPPE[3].

To the right worshipful Mr Parker,
Dean of Stoke college.

[[1] Strype under the date 1537 says: "About this time, if not before, our Parker was sent for up by the lord Crumwell to take a turn at Paul's Cross." The date assigned to the 17th Sunday after Trinity, proves that this letter was written in 1537.]

[[2] "1537· 1° Martii. Vocatus ad aulam regis, et factus capellanus Henrici VIII." Autobiog. Mem. App. No. I.]

[[3] The words "quondam episcopus Hereforden.", are added by another hand. Dr Skypp was elected bishop of Hereford 24th October, 1539. He died 30th March, 1552.]

VIII.

ANSWER TO ARTICLES OF ACCUSATION SENT TO THE LORD AUDLEY, LORD CHANCELLOR, AGAINST M. PARKER BY MR G. COLT AND OTHER OF CLARE TOWN.

Probably A.D. 1539[4]. Parker MSS. C. C. Coll. Camb. CVIII. art. 38. p. 169. Orig. draft of the Answer.

The manner as they used the resurrection, with the ceremonies appertaining to the same, was but a pageant or an interlude. _{1st ART. That he ridiculed the ceremonies of Easter.}

Upon Easter Monday I had this text of St Paul to my theme, *Si consurrexistis cum Christo quæ sursum sunt sapite, &c.*; at what time I moved them to consider spiritually what was meant by their procession on Easter morning, when they followed the quire about the church with *Christus resurgens.* I said that it was an open protestation of their faith to believe that Christ died for their sins, and rose again for their justification, and that the ceremony of such following in their procession was to declare and testify openly to the world that they would henceforth follow Christ in their conversation; that as Christ once died, and died no more, that so would they cease and die to sin, no more to live therein, and as he rose from death to life, that so would they rise to a new life; and without this meditation and purpose their procession, with the solemnities thereof, was to them but a vain pageant whereof they had no profit. _{RESPONSIO. True meaning of Easter processions}

The cross that Christ died on was no holier than the crosses which the thieves died on. _{2nd ART. That he denied the holiness of the Cross.}

Upon Relic-Sunday I declared to them what were the true relics which we should worship, and moved them not to put their trust and affiance in the holiness and virtue of men's bones and coats, whereof we have no certainty whether they were the relics of saints or no; and I said, that be it in case that they were so as we have been made believe, as if we had indeed some pieces of Christ's cross, yet to forget the mystery of Christ's cross, and fall to the wor- _{RESPONSIO. We should not worship the wood of the Cross, and forget the mystery of the cross.}

[4 Lord Audley, who is here mentioned, was so created on the 29th November, 1538.]

shipping of the tree of his cross, was a superstitious worship, and reproved of St Ambrose *de obitu Theodosii*[1], which saith thus: *Invenit Helena titulum, regem adoravit, non lignum utique, nam hic Gentilis est error et vanitas impiorum. Sed adoravit illum qui pependit in ligno scriptus in titulo.*

"*Alii qui sanctiores se ostendere (?) volunt partem fimbriæ aut capillorum alligant et suspendunt. O impietas! majorem sanctitatem in suis vestimentis ostendere volentes quam in carne Christi; ut qui corpus ejus manducans sanatus non fuerit fimbriæ ejus sanctitate salvetur, ut desperans de misericordia (?) Dei confidat in vestimentis*.........[2].

_{3rd ART. That he said the King levied money of the commons to buy peace of other realms}

The King, with the money that he gathered of his commons, bought peace with other realms.

_{RESPONSIO.}

In the insurrection time[3], I considered the resort of soldiers and of divers other to the town of Clare, being one of the most people in that quarter of Suffolk, and thereupon I thought it then most expedient to go thither to courage their hearts with God's word to serve their prince in withstanding such traitors as was then risen, and in my sermon I inveighed against sedition, and declared the authority of a prince, and what commodities every realm enjoyed by such authority instituted by God. And, among other, I entreated of peace, what a benefit it was, by the means whereof we had the quiet fruition of our lives, goods, and lands, and thereby moved them, with good and ready wills to pay their taxes which was to be levied to some supportation of such charges as our peace was bought with, and _{That the King cannot defend his people without incurring charges, which should be cheerfully paid.} said thus, "Think you that our prince can maintain and defend us in so long continual peace against foreign realms without charges and expenses? and what is this little which

[1 Originally written "Chrysostom." See Opera. Ambros. II. 1210. ed. 1690.]

[2 These words "Alii qui sanctiores," &c., are not a continuation of the quotation from St Ambrose, nor has it been discovered whence they are taken. The sentence is left incomplete by the wearing away of the bottom of the leaf in the MS.]

[3 The allusion is to the Pilgrimage of Grace, and the rising in Lincolnshire under the prior of Barlings.]

is required of you compared to the rest of your goods which ye do peaceably enjoy, or compared to the charges that your prince is at for your protection and defence, &c."[4].

IX.

JOHN SKYPP TO MATTHEW PARKER.

11th May, probably 1539[5]. Parker MSS. C. C. Coll. Camb. cxix. art. 13. p. 36. Orig.

I COMMEND me heartily unto you, thanking you, beside other your kindness, for your last letters, wherein I perceive that the old and busy diligence in your new busy matters continueth still amongst you. We of the Convocation, by the reason of long absence from you, are decayed in quickness of wit, and so are become more dull and slow in our proceedings. Ye be hot and hasty: we be cold and tardy. We think that a great quantity of our qualities would do much good amongst you, and a little portion of your qualities were enough for us. Ye are so prudent and expert in all things that ye need never to use deliberation though your matters were greater than they be, but we, for lack of your properties, are fain to respect and consult in all matters that we entreat of. Therefore, seeing this diversity between us and you, ye cannot blame us though we proceed diversely. Fare ye well. I shall make an end of my letter another time. From Westminster, the 11th day of May.

Parker's old and busy diligence continueth still. Those of the Convocation slower in their proceedings.

They are fain to respect and consult in all matters that they deal wth.

J. SK.

*To the Right Worshipful Mr Doctor
Parker, Dean of Stoke.*

[[4] In Parker's handwriting is added: "These articles objected were thus answered by M. P., and sent to the lord chancellor, which heard, he blamed the promoters, and sent word that I should go on and fear not such enemies."]

[[5] Wilkins, Concilia, III. 845.]

X.

MATTHEW PARKER TO DR STOKES, FRIAR AUSTIN.

23rd November, probably 1539 or 1540. Parker MSS. C. C. Coll. Camb. CVIII.
art. 36. p. 161. Orig. draft.

Dr Stokes come from Norwich to reside at Clare.

IN my hearty manner, Mr Doctor, I commend me unto you. And this shall be to signify unto you, that forasmuch as ye informed me that ye be come from Norwich to be here resiant at Clare, I thought it convenient to write thus much following unto you: which I do of no other mind but of charity and of zeal toward the glory of God in his word; secondly, of my duty toward my prince, and of love towards his subjects in this quarter for their quietness and contentation, so far as God's truth may bear it; and finally, of a mind considering your own behoof and cause.

Parker presumes that at his leisure he will go abroad and preach, than which there can be no better service to God and the commonwealth.

Sir, I presuppose that at your leisure otherwhiles ye shall hereafter be occasioned to go abroad to preach and to speak your judgment as time and place shall serve you: which endeavour of your party, as of all other in this behalf, I cannot only favour and commend, but as my little power shall serve me, so shall I do my best to set it forward at all times and occasions, knowing that there can be no better service to God than sincerely to declare his will and pleasure, no sacrifice more acceptable than to convert the hearts of his reasonable creatures in true faith and knowledge unto him, and no ways better can we deserve of the commonwealth, than by our diligence to continue the commons in a quiet subjection and obedience toward their governors, and to further love and peace among themselves; which duty belonging to the minister of God's word I have done my best to perform, since my first coming into this country, and have bestowed some labour about it, and do yet, according to my vocation, intend to continue by the help of God, &c.

Parker has done his best to perform the same office since his first coming into that country. He now urges Dr Stokes to support him therein.

Now, Sir, my only purpose to you at this time is to require you, if that my foresaid endeavour hitherto seem allowable unto you, of your party, with that gift and talent of doctrine committed to your dispensation, to further it and to set it forward, and to attemper your speech in such wise that ye may be thought to consider rather the truth than private affection and custom. If ye should go about to sugill[1] and to decay the truth which I have (I trust and am assured) spoken, and I again should labour to use invections against you, we should learn our audiences but envy, discord, and dissension; we should offend God to abuse our office of peace to the slander of other, and consume our time in matters of controversy of our own, when otherwise it should be spent in edification of those to whom we speak; we should by our disagreement cause a roar and a schism in the people, and cause a murmur and parts-taking among themself; which inconveniences to foresee aforehand, and to provide for the avoiding of them, it were meet we should. For many times of such small sparks rise great commotions in the people, which once risen is not so easily ceased and stayed again.

Ye know what diligence our sovereign lord the King's grace bestoweth daily to reduce his people committed to his charge from their manifold blindness and superstitions they were in to the truth and right worship of God; it were meet for us that be speakers to the people to further his most godly purpose, not with covert inventions to labefact the credence of the people, and so to hatch privy rebellion and ill-will to his proceedings, not with ambiguous sophistication to fortify their misframed judgments. Ye know of late what dangers hung over the whole realm by wilful opinions and sturdy disobedience blown into them by secret dissimulation of some certain incomers, who hath now their deserved reward according to their privy malice. Peradventure some there be that will be glad and desire to hear you allow their old trade, and superstition, and papistical dregs, whereby in very deed ye should do some great pleasure; but then again ye should dishonour God in abusing that office which without all outward respects should denounce the truth, ye should work against your prince's purpose, ye should, in conclusion, work utter destruction of that mad and wilful people both in their souls and bodies, which should take courage by your words to utter the more boldly their ill-willing [?] hearts, and so to speak their own confusion to be taken in their words and have their deserving judged upon them. I think it were meet, seeing we

Also, to further the King's purpose of reclaiming the people from their manifold blindness and superstition.

[1 " To sugill," *sugillare*, to bruise; to defame or slander. The word is again used by Parker in this letter and also in a subsequent letter to Sir William Cecil: "If it be openly impugned or secretly *sugilled*."]

see the people so much bent to their customed inventions, to give them no maintenance by our qualifications to continue them still therein. I would desire, Mr Doctor, that we should proceed *eadem regula ut simus concordes, ut eodem spiritu ambulemus, ut uno ore glorificemus Deum et Patrem Domini nostri Jesu Christi.* In so doing our diligence and spending our time we should do good service to God, and to our prince, and to our country. I know that certain hath had some grudge toward me. The ground thereof and the cause I know very well. Notwithstanding, I stand not in such despair of the obedience of the people in this quarter, but that, with good and discreet calling on, they might be soon appeased and more indifferently hear that which some time was intolerable unto them. I would be loth now that any man should enter to imbecile the thing which they be toward, concerning the obedience of God's word, and the causes which the King's highness hath most like a christian prince taken in hand to set forth. Now before your beginning ye may take deliberation with yourself to ponder the weight of my considerations. "Had I wist" is too late. And as concerning that whatsoever I have at any time said and divulged, I will by God's grace justify at all times and before any indifferent judge defend it to my uttermost power, which I doubt not to do both by scripture, by the testimonies of the most approved authors in Christ's church, and by the Articles and Injunctions of the King's setting forth. As for the bishops' determinations, I know that there remaineth the agletts[1] setting on, and therefore I purpose not to stay certainly upon that, although yet whatsoever I have spoken I could justify it sufficiently by that which I read there. Howbeit I will neither use that book to prove or disprove as by the authority of that, until I see it have his full perfection; which yet I know it lacketh. But if in case report should be made unto you that I should teach that thing whereunto your judgment should not agree (for, as for so much as I spake this other day at Clare you allowed it and justified it to myself of your own accord undesired of my part,) I will then require thus much of you, to suspend your determination until ye know the truth by myself, that we may so dispute the cause pri-

[1 "Aglettes:" carved tags or ornaments. Fr. Aiguilettes. Here it is equivalent to finishing touches, the last revise.]

vately betwixt us to search out the truth, that thereupon either I may see sufficient learning of your part to agree unto your judgment, or else if I bring the same of my party, you to consent to the truth and you to agree to my judgment.

My request, Mr Doctor, I ensure you (as God knoweth my secret heart) riseth not of my fear either of your person or learning, that ye could or should hinder my poor estimation among my neighbours, which for the better credence of God's word in me I will endeavour myself to defend, otherwise not greatly careful therefore, but could refer all things to God's judgment;—it is not for my person's sake that I require you to this, but it is the cause's sake, God's sake, and the people's true and peaceable instruction that I regard. It is to cut away all occasion from seditious and tumultuous people; it is for the more quietness of both our parties that we should, without let or interruption of bye matters, effectuously go forward with the principal purpose of the office and vocation taken upon us, in converting and reversing the hearts of the fathers into [sic] their children, and the unbelievers to the wisdom of the just, to make the people ready for the Lord, to preach the gospel to the poor, to heal the broken in heart, to preach deliverance to the captive, and sight to the blind, to preach the acceptable year of the Lord[2]:—these ought to be our matters, not our own fame, lucre, and pre-eminence, and fancies. It were but foolishness to brawl for these before wise audience; and wisdom were it, not the one to desire to glory over the other, the one to labour to win sporis[3] of the other, and to allure the people's minds and fancies to ourself with depraving, sugilling, and noting the other. As for my part, I trust in God's grace I shall bear all personal injuries and slanders well in worth, as hitherto I have done; I could else have promoted some to their displeasure. But if the injury or slander redoundeth to the word of God, to the majesty of that, or to the decay of my prince's authority and lawful ordinances, or to the disturbance or commotion of the commons, I will never for friendship suffer that, but will do my uttermost to revenge it.

I would write many more things unto you, but my leisure will not suffer me. But thus shortly to conclude, If ye should go about, Mr Doctor, to get you a name, to hurt the

[2] Luc.   [[3] Spurs.]

If Dr Stokes calls in question the truth of scripture, or hinders the reformation intended by the King, Parker must oppose him.

truth of scripture, to deprave or hinder that reformation which the King's highness purposeth in matters of our religion, or to raise any schisure¹ or murmur in the people of this country, now metely in good stay and toward in the acceptation of the truth, under any open or colourable insinuation, verily ye cannot so secretly do it but it will brast out. It shall not so soon come to my knowledge, but I will, according to my duty, present it immediately². If, as I have better trust in your wisdom, circumspection, and conscience, ye intend truly and rightly to declare the verity, to the edification of the king's subjects, I will then promise to join hands with you the best I can; and to further you therein ye shall use me at all times at your commandment. Of this condition shall our friendship consist and stand betwixt us, and of no other intend I with no man, as I would no man should in no other respect bear his friendship to me. And thus the Holy Ghost be with you. At Stoke college, this 23rd day of November.

If he intends to declare the verity, Parker will join hands with him.

Your to his power,

MATTHUE PARKER.

Addressed,
To Doctor Stokes³.

[¹ i.e. schism.]

[² It seems that Dr Stokes neglected this warning, and took a course which ended in his imprisonment. There is extant (Parker MSS. C. C. Coll. Camb. cviii. art. 37. p. 167.) a letter of his to the Lord Privy Seal, in which he styles himself, "your simple prisoner, friar Stokes," and in which this passage occurs: "Also your lordship is formed that I should preach against the dean of Stoke. Truly, my lord, I commend him by name in my sermon for the declaring of certain verities the Sunday before me. And I did preach indifferently, as all the parish will testify, but and the word of God did touch him I cannot do thereto [?]."]

[³ There is added in Parker's hand: "He was an Austen friar, and prior in the Austens at Norwich, and doctor of divinity at Cambridge."]

XI.

HENRY VIII. TO THE DEAN AND PREBENDARIES OF STOKE.

25th May, 1544. Parker MSS. C. C. Coll. Camb. CXIV. art. 125. p. 387. Orig.

HENRY R.[4]   BY THE KING.

TRUSTY and well-beloved, we greet you well. And whereas between us and the Emperor, upon provocation of manifold injuries committed by the French king unto us both partienlarly, and for his confederation with the Turk against the whole commonwealth of Christendom, it is agreed that each of us apart, in person, with his puissant army, in several parts this summer, shall invade the realm of France; we let you wit that having not yet appointed so great a number for that purpose as is necessary, upon the good opinion we have of you with earnest good will to see us furnished as to our honour apperteineth, we have appointed you to send the number of four able footmen, whereof one to be an archer, furnished with a good bow in a case, with twenty-four arrows in a case, a good sword and a dagger; and the rest to be billmen, having, besides their bills, every of them a good sword and a dagger, to be levied of your own servants, tenants, and others: foreseeing that if any other man having tenants within your manors or lordships, be by our letters appointed to make us any men, he shall have the preferment of the making of the same his tenants to serve us in this army; not failing to have your said men in such a readiness, furnished with coats and hose of such colours as is appointed for our vanguard, as they fail not to be at our town of Sandwich, the 8th day of June, where order is taken for their transportation accordingly. Given under our signet, at our palace of Westminster, the 25th day of May, the 36th year of our reign. And our further pleasure is, that in any wise you send us the said number, being all picked and able men, as ye tender the advancement of our affairs, and for the contrary thereof will be put to the loss of their conduct and harness[5].

*To our trusty and well-beloved, the Dean
of our college of Stoke in Suffolk, and
the prebendaries of the same.*

[4 The King's stamp.]
[5 Henry VIII. invaded France in July 1554. He laid siege in

XII.

QUEEN KATHERINE PARR TO DR MATTHEW PARKER.

14th November 1544. Parker MSS. C. C. Coll. Camb. cxiv. art. 3. p. 7. Orig.

BY THE QUEEN.

Queen Katherine Parr recommends Dr Parker to appoint Randall Radclyff to the vacant office of bailiff of the college of Stoke.

KATERYN THE QUENE. K. P. Trusty and well-beloved, we greet you well. And whereas by credible report we are informed that the bailiwick of our college of Stoke is now void to dispose as you and certain other there shall think it meet and convenient: we therefore heartily desire you, at the contemplation of these our letters, to give the same office unto our well-beloved Randall Radclyff the bearer hereof, who hath already the goodwill of three of those that have interest in the granting of it. So that there rests no farther travail for him, your good will once obtained, the which at this our earnest request, we doubt not but that you will shew and declare effectuously, confirmable to our desire in this behalf, according to the expectation that we have hitherto conceived in you. Given under signet at my lord the King's majesty's palace of Westminster, the 14th of November, the 36th year of his majesty's most noble reign.

To our trusty and well-beloved doctor Parker, Dean of our College of Stoke.

XIII.

HENRY VIII. TO THE FELLOWS OF CORPUS CHRISTI COLLEGE, CAMBRIDGE.

30th November, 1544. Parker MSS. C. C. Coll. Camb. cxiv. art. 2. p. 5. Orig.

HENRY R.[1]   BY THE KING.

TRUSTY and well-beloved, we greet you well. And whereas it is come to our understanding that your master and governor[2] either lieth now at the extreme point of death, or

person to Boulogne, which surrendered on the 13th September following. State Papers of Henry VIII. x. 22. 68.]

[[1] The king's stamp.]

[[2] Dr William Sowode was master of the College from 1523 to his death on the 28th November, 1544. Masters' Hist. of Corpus Christi College, pp. 74—84. ed. Lamb.]

is already departed out of this transitory life, by occasion whereof ye be, or shortly are like to be, destitute of a good head and governor; we, therefore, for the zeal and love we bear to the advancement of good letters, desiring to see you furnished of such a governor as in all points may seem worthy of that room, have thought good by these our letters to commend unto you our well-beloved chaplain, doctor Parker, a man as well for his approved learning, wisdom, and honesty, as for his singular grace and industry in bringing up youth in virtue and learning, so apt for the exercise of the said room, as it is thought very hard to find the like for all respects and purposes. Wherefore, like as our trust is that at the contemplation of us ye will with one assent condescend to elect him for your head whom we have judged worthy for that office[3], so we doubt not that by the accomplishment of this our pleasure ye shall have cause to think yourselves furnished of such a master as appertaineth. Given under our signet, at our palace of Westminster, the last day of November, the 36th year of our reign.

King Henry VIII. recommends his chaplain, Dr Parker, as a man in all points fit for the mastership of Corpus Christi College.

To the fellows of Corpus Christi College within our University of Cambridge.

XIV.

JOHN MERE TO DR MATTHEW PARKER.

26th January, 1544—5[4]. Parker MSS. C. C. Coll. Camb. CVI. art. 150. p. 418*. Orig.

RIGHT worshipful, in most hearty wise I have me commended unto your worship, certifying the same that it hath pleased the University to choose you unto the office of the Vice-chancellor, and Mr proctors be very desirous to have you at home for to be admitted. Doctor Smith gave over his office on Saturday at iv. of the clock, and you were chosen on Sunday at iii. of the clock. Doctor Ridley and Doctor Standysh were named unto the office, and it was thought that there hath been labouring for them this

The University of Cambridge has elected Dr Parker Vice-chancellor.

Course of the election. The candidates.

[3 Parker was accordingly elected and admitted master on the 4th of December.]

[4 The voting paper appended to the letter bears date, 1544.]

[PARK. COR.]

se'nnight or fortnight; but very suddenly, even on the Sunday, all the labouring for them was turned unto very importune labour for Mr Atkinson vice-provost[1]; but he came nothing nigh you. Some suppose, and I think also, that it came not of himself; for on the Saturday after dinner he wished very heartily that ye might be, trusting that ye will be good master unto him this year; for on Friday last past he obtained his grace to go forth doctor. There was no doctor of Divinity present but D. Glyn; but in the law, doctors Poynt, Smith, Busby, and Harvey. In physic, both doctor Walkers, doctors Blyth and Hatcher. It was a very great house; the number of regents were four score and xviii.[2]

<small>Who were present at the election.</small>

<small>Parker's presence required at Cambridge.</small>

Ash-Wednesday draweth nigh[3], therefore it were very meet that there were an officer for admissions: and besides that, the keys of the common hutch and the seal of office be sealed up in a purse, that no man can come by them, whatsoever should need, until ye be admitted.

I delivered your letters and tokens unto my lords of Chichester[4] and Westminster[5], who received them very thankfully. Your letters directed unto my lord of Worcester[6] I brought home again, for he was gone in unto Worcestershire or I came there. I delivered also your letters and token at Mr Tanner's, but I have got none answer, but I look daily for to have. I cannot altogether excuse myself of negligence, though there were much slackness in Mr Canerner[?]. I would most heartily desire you to be so good as to know who receiveth the feofydye of West Walton in Marshlands, and to pay him xxx.*d.* for Mr parson Saunders, and I shall repay it at your return with hearty thanks.

I pray you have me commended [to] Mr Baker both young and old, to your brother Thomas, with all their wives[7].

[1 Of King's College.]

[2 From the voting paper it appears that the votes were, for Dr Parker 79, for Dr Ridley 5, for Dr Standysh 8, and for Mr Atkinson 6. In all, 98.]

[3 The 18th February 1544—5, was Ash-Wednesday.]

[4 Doctor Day. He was provost of King's College, Cambridge.]

[5 Doctor Thirleby.]

[6 Nicholas Heath.]

[7 Mr Baker the elder, here alluded to, married Dr Parker's mother after the death of her first husband. The younger Mr Ba-

Scribbled in haste, as appeareth, 26th January, by the hand of yours to command. *Deus te servet: per cujus filium, ut rebus ex sententia gestis corpore pariter ac animo cito nobis redeas incolumis percupide optarem, precaborque assidue.*

JOHN MERE[8].

To the right worshipful Mr doctor Parker, Vice-chancellor of Cambridge elect, this be delivered at Norwich.

XV.

QUEEN KATHERINE PARR TO THE DEAN AND FELLOWS OF STOKE.

24th March 1544—5. Parker MSS. C. C. Coll. Camb. cxiv. art. 126. p. 391. Orig.

BY THE QUEEN.

KATERYN THE QUENE. K. P. Trusty and well-beloved, we greet you well. And forasmuch as your manor or farm of Chipley in the county of Suffolk lieth in you to let and set at your will and pleasure, and that the same is very commodious for our well-beloved Edward Waldegrave, servant to our most dear and entirely beloved son the lord prince[9]; these therefore shall be heartily to desire and pray

The Queen recommends Edward Waldegrave, servant to the lord Prince, for a lease in reversion of the manor or farm of Chipley, in Suffolk.

ker, who was a son of that marriage, was afterwards the archbishop's treasurer. Parker's brother Thomas, here also alluded to, was a citizen of Norwich, and served the office of mayor of that city.]

[8 John Mere filled, successively, various offices in the University, of which he was "a hearty lover," and a considerable benefactor. He died in 1558. Parker was one of the overseers of his will, and received a legacy of books worth 20s. Mrs Parker was remembered with two gowns, valued at 20s., and their son John, probably Mere's godson, was left a silver cup, valued at 3l. 0s. 3d.—Masters's Hist. Corp. App. p. 46. ed. 1753.]

[9 Edward, afterwards sir Edward Waldegrave, and an officer in the household of princess Mary. He was one of the persons who were charged by the privy council of Edward VI. to see to the use of the communion service and discontinuance of the mass in Mary's establishment, and suffered imprisonment for not enforcing these orders. After the accession of Queen Mary he received considerable preferment, but on the accession of Queen Elizabeth, was again committed to the Tower, and died there on the 1st September, 1561.—Collins's Peerage, ed. Brydges, IV. 237.]

you to make a good and sufficient lease in reversion of the same unto the said Edward at this our earnest request: so that he may enjoy the effect of our desire (after the term expired of one Henry Hutton now farmer there) in as large and ample manner as the same Henry now holdeth it, and for so many years as you at the contemplation hereof can find in your heart to bestow on him for our sake. Wherein you shall not only acquire to yourself a farmer well reported of for his honesty and good behaviour, but also minister unto us grateful occasion to have your kind conformity thankfully in our remembrance, whensoever opportunity shall serve us to do you pleasure. Given under our signet at my lord the King's majesty's palace of Westminster, the 24th of March, the 36th year of his said majesty's most noble and prosperous reign.

XVI.

BISHOP GARDINER OF WINCHESTER[1] TO DR MATTHEW PARKER AND DR THOMAS SMITH.

27th March, 1545[2]. Parker MSS. C. C. Coll. Camb. CVI. art. 157. p. 437. Orig.

He has received Dr Smith's letters on the subject of provision for decayed cooks.

AFTER my right hearty commendations. I have received the letters of you, master Smith, and heard the request of this bearer concerning the order of such wilful persons as would frowardly break and dissolve the charitable purpose of those cooks, that have among themselves agreed by policy to provide for their own release, and the succour of other decayed.

He would have the present Vice-chancellor continue his predecessor's good order in the matter.

Wherein as ye, master Doctor Smith, have in the time of your office taken a good order in the matter, so I now desire you both to take the pains to travail together as the case shall require for the continuance of the same. There be small corrodies[3] in Cambridge for cooks decayed, and as great likelihood of their decay as in any other place. They may indeed endure longer with their small labour, but so

[[1] This letter is written by the bishop in his capacity of Chancellor of the university, to Dr Parker, the then vice-chancellor, and Dr Smith, his immediate predecessor in that office. See Lett. XIV.]

[[2] There is written on the letter in another hand: "procancellario D. Parker, A°. 1544. Mar. 27."]

[[3] "Corrody," a pension in money, or an allowance in meat or clothing, generally charged on the revenues of a religious house.]

much less do they gather for the smallness of the wages and gain; which if they perceive not presently, it shall be well done to bring them to conformity, and to interrupt the greediness of them that would abuse the occasion of such possessions as they have to their private advantage, with the detriment of other. Herein I pray you do what ye can, and the authority that wanteth shall be supplied hereafter.

Master Vice-chancellor, I have been informed that the youth in Christ's College, contrary to the mind of the master and president, hath of late played a tragedy called Pammachius, a part of which tragedy is so pestiferous as were intolerable. I will give no credit to the information but as I shall hear from you, wherein I pray you that I may shortly by you know the truth. If it be not so, I will be glad: and if it be so, I intend further to travail, as my duty is, for the reformation of it. I know mine office there, and mind to do in it as much as I may. Requiring you therefore that, in such matters of innovation and disorder, I may be diligently advertised from you from time to time. And so fare you well. At London, the xxviith of March.

He has been informed, that the youth of Christ's College had lately played a pestiferous tragedy called Pammachius. Inquiry to be made respecting the same.

Your loving friend,

STE. WINTON.

To my loving friend Mr Vice-chancellor of Cambridge, and to Mr Doctor Smith there, and to either of them.

XVII.

DR PARKER TO BISHOP GARDINER OF WINCHESTER.

3rd April, 1545. Parker MSS. C. C. Coll. Camb. CVI. art. 159. p. 443. Orig. draft.

AFTER my duty of lowly commendations to your honourable good lordship, pleaseth it you to be informed, that after I received your lordship's letters, I made the more exact inquiry of the tragedy late played in Christ's College: and thus I find that, where your lordship was informed that the youth of the house played this foresaid tragedy against the mind of the master there and president, the president himself, with whom I conferred in this cause, shewed me that it was not so; for he alleged that it cost the College well nigh twenty nobles,

After the receipt of Bp Gardiner's letter, Parker had made inquiry respecting the tragedy lately played in Christ's College. It was played with the concurrence of the master and the college, with the previous

omission of all objectionable passages.
No person who was present, had expressed himself dissatisfied.
Parker not present.

allowed by the master and the company. And where there is inspersed throughout the tragedy both slanderous cavillations and suspicious sentence, therefore, as I am credibly informed, they used this foresight, by the advertisement of the master and seniors, to omit all such matter whereby offence might justly have risen; and hitherto have I not seen any man that was present at it to shew himself grieved, albeit it was thought their time and labour might have been spent in a better handled matter. And forasmuch as I was not present myself at their playing, I have learned of others the cause to stand thus in these points aforesaid. And thus Almighty God long preserve your honourable estate in health and honour, to his pleasure and furtherance of our common wealth, with like good zeal as hitherto with thanks we be bound to acknowledge your lordship to have done. At Cambridge, this Good-Friday.

      Your bound orator,
        by duty to command,
          MATTHUE PARKER.

To the right honourable and my singular good lord, the lord of Winchester.

XVIII.

BISHOP GARDINER OF WINCHESTER TO DR MATTHEW PARKER.

23rd April, 1545. Parker MSS. C. C. Coll. Camb. cvi. art. 158. p. 439. Orig.

MASTER Vice-chancellor, after my hearty commendations, having commodity to send this bearer my chaplain to the University, I have thought good to signify further my mind unto you concerning the examination of the truth of the matter of the tragedy played in Christ's College, whereof I have heard more than I heard before, and have heard so much that I think it necessary for my discharge to travail with you to attain the knowledge of the very truth, and further to do therein as the case shall require. And to the intent it may appear that howsoever youth either of frailty, lightness, or malice would abuse their gifts, we that be heads

Gardiner has heard more respecting the tragedy played at Christ's College.

and rulers over them should not be seen either by sufferance
or negligence to be blameworthy of their fault, I will and require you that upon receipt of these my letters ye assemble the masters and presidents of the Colleges with the doctors of the University, and declaring unto them this matter, to require them to assist you in the trial of the truth concerning the said tragedy, and that by due examination of such as were there it may be truly known what was uttered, and so by their judgment approved for good, which by the order established by the King's majesty in this church is reproved, or by them reproved which by the King's majesty is allowed.
I have heard specialities, that they reproved Lent fastings, all ceremonies, and, albeit the words of sacrament and mass were not named, yet the rest of the matter written in that tragedy in the reproof of them was expressed. And if, as you wrote to me, they left out somewhat unspoken, it should appear that the rest being spoken was upon a judgment by consideration and deliberation allowed: which if it be true is a lamentable case, and such as hath not chanced, that such as by the King's majesty's privileges and supportation be there preserved in quiet to learn all virtue, should presumptuously mock and scorn the direction of their prince in matters of religion. I touch only herein the truth of obedience; for I esteem such offenders for unlearned and ignorant, unmeet to discern what is truth in the matter. But if the King's majesty's directions be not obeyed there, and by us dissembled, how shall we charge the rudeness abroad that may allege their example for pretence of their fault? This matter is greater than were expedient to be true, and is more certainly reported unto me than of likelihood can be totally false. It is not the fault of us that be heads to have in the number some naught, until we pass over their fault and suffer it unpunished. If I could have leisure to come myself, I would not spare to come thither for this purpose, being the special point of my charge. In mine absence, I require the aid of you to know by your examination the truth of the matter. Wherein I pray you use the assistance of the master, presidents, and doctors, as afore. And as wild wanton liberty sometime brasteth out in youth to their reproach, so let soberness and gravity appear in us requisite for the execution

He requireth Parker to assemble the masters and presidents with the doctors, and make trial of the truth of the matter.

What he has heard was specially condemned in the tragedy.

A presumptuous mock and scorn of the direction of the prince in matter of religion.

If he had leisure he would personally come thither to investigate the matter.

of our charge. Many hath of late repined at the King's majesty's munificence in our privileges and otherwise, and let not us give cause that they should justly so do. Our obedience should be example to all other in public directions, without occasion of all slander. If learning should now be an instrument to stir up dissension, and trouble the common quietness, their opinion should be confirmed which not many years past have laboured to prove in books printed in English that the Universities be the corruption of the realm.

<small>Oxford liveth quietly with fewer privileges than Cambridge.</small> Oxford liveth quietly with fewer privileges than we have; there be that would we had as few as they. I intreat this offence only worldly, because the capacity of the offenders seemeth to stretch no farther. And he that regardeth not his obedience to his prince, regardeth not much his obedience to God and his truth which he hath offended in the other. Wherefore, I pray you, let us by due examination find the fault where it is, and so purge ourself; and what ye shall find herein, I pray you advertise me with diligence. And so fare ye well. At London the 23. of April.

Your loving friend,

STE. WINTON.

*To Master Vice-chancellor of
the University of Cambridge.*

XIX.

DR MATTHEW PARKER TO BISHOP GARDINER OF WINCHESTER.

8th May, 1545. Parker MSS. C. C. Coll. Camb. CVI. art. 160. p. 445. Orig. draft.

<small>In compliance with the last letter from Bp Gardiner, Parker had made further inquiry as to the offence said to have been given by the performance of the tragedy at Christ's College.</small> PLEASETH it your honourable lordship, after my due commendations, to know that, according to your commandment in your last letters, I have used the wisdom of the doctors and presidents of all the Colleges of the University, for the trial of the truth concerning the tragedy, and thus was it agreed among us that every president should assemble their companies to know what they heard and wherewith they were offended, and so to declare so much as they found, whereupon I might make answer to your lordship, what was uttered

there. The answer of them all after their examination at our next meeting was, that none of all their companies declared unto them that they were offended with any thing, that now they remember was then spoken. Very many, whether of purpose or of chance, were absent: which can depose nothing. Moreover to a further trial what was uttered I thought good to send to your lordship a book of theirs, noted and cancelled all that was unspoken, the rest uttered. Which book was delivered me in presence of the master and all the fellows of Christ's College, whom I convented personally for the search of the truth. Among whom I found by inquisition not above two that were offended, of the which Mr Scot[1] being one declared that he was neither agreeable to the playing at the first, nor pleased with it when it was played, but offended in such points as he shewed me he hath already declared to your lordship.

With the deposition of the which Mr Scot to your lordship (known to them before I conferred with them) I perceived some of the company to be much grieved. Insomuch that there is now risen since our examination another matter betwixt them, whereof I had the hearing with the assistance of Mr doctors Wigan, Lockwood, and Wendy. Whereas, of words of displeasure spoken betwixt themselves at home, Mr Scot feared unquietness by certain of them, and came to me for his aid, I called them together to know their griefs, and purposed with the assistance aforesaid to have made a quietness betwixt them: and in their challenging one another there was uttered by Mr Crane and Mr Greenwall, players of the foresaid tragedy and fellows of the house, that the said Mr Scot should say at such time as the master and company consulted together for the playing of the said tragedy, that the said tragedy was throughout poison, and therefore liked not that it should be played. Whereto should the said Crane answer, that they intended not but to rebuke the pope's usurped power. Whereto should Scot answer, that under that pretence they would destroy all godliness. Which last words Mr Scot affirmed he said, but not the first, but said thus, that the book was throughout poisoned. With the ad-

[1] Strype supposes this to be the Scot who was made Bishop of Chester under Queen Mary.—Life of Parker, Book I. c. 5.]

vice of the foresaid assistance I caused their very words[1] to be written by their own hands; which I send to your lordship to be considered what weight is in them; and in the mean time we have them all bound with surety to be forthcoming, till such time as we shall hear again from your lordship and know your pleasure. Thus your lordship see the unquietness of some of that company among themselves, beside the outward vexation now of late risen of a townsman against our privileges, of which it may please your lordship to be informed by these letters of the University. And thus the Holy Ghost preserve your lordship in honourable estate to his pleasure. At Cambridge in Benet College this 8th of May.

Your orator at commandment there,
MATTHWE PARKER.

*To the right honourable and my singular
good lord, my lord of Winchester.*

[[1] The following copy of "the very words" is appended to the letter in the MS.

Anno 1545°. 8° Maii.

In the presence of Matthew Parker, Vice-chancellor, Dr Wigan, Dr Lockwood, Dr Wendy: these words spoken, underneath written, by the parties following.

I, John Crane, do say, that Mr Scot did affirm the tragedy of Pammachius to be throughout poison, about the xvith day of January.

JOHN CRANE.

Witnesseth that I, Nicholas Greenwall, heard him say that the tragedy was all throughout poison: xvith day of January.

NICHOLAS GRENEWALL.

And whereas we said that our intent was to pluck down the pope's usurped power, he answered, that under that pretence we would speak against all goodness.

JOHN CRANE.
MATHEW PARKER.
EDWARD WIGON.
HENRY LOCKEWOD.
THOMAS WENDEY.]

XX.

BISHOP GARDINER OF WINCHESTER TO DR MATTHEW PARKER.

12th May, 1545. Parker MSS. C. C. Coll. Camb. CVI. art. 161. p. 449. Orig.

MASTER Vice-chancellor, after my hearty commendations, I perceive by your letters which I have received with the book of the tragedy, that ye have assembled the sage of the University to know by their inquisition severally in their houses what was uttered that might and ought to offend godly ears in the playing of the same at Christ's College. Wherein, as appeareth by your letters, report was made unto you that no man is offended. And yet, perusing the book of the tragedy which ye sent me, I find much matter not stricken out, all which by the parties' own confession was uttered, very naught, and on the other part something not well omitted; where allowing and rejecting should proceed of judgment, and that to be taken for true which was uttered, and that for untrue which they note as untrue to be omitted and left unspoken. So as this book declareth the parties to have double offended, both in denying that is true and also approving that is false, as in some part by their notes doth appear. And indeed in the tragedy untruth is so maliciously weaved with truth, as making the bishop of Rome, with certain his abuses, the foundation of the matter, the author's reproach whereof is true, so many abominable and detestable lies be added and mingled with the other truth as no Christian ears should patiently hear, and cannot, in the process of the matter, be without a marvellous alteration, other than was now used, be[2] dissevered asunder. By mean whereof, where all other proof faileth there, the book maketh an undoubted proof of their lewdness to me here, and that which so many of the University being present heard and offended them not so deeply but it is now worn out and they be no longer offended, the same is by exhibition of the book so notified unto me, and so grieveth me, being absent, as, how soon soever I forget the offence upon their reconciliation, I shall hardly of a great while forget the matter. And if open and notorious faults which the

[[2] The word *be* is thus repeated in the MS. evidently by mistake.]

offenders in pomp and triumph so utter as they would have men know them and mark them, shall from henceforth without all reformation be neglected and forgotten, or so by silence hidden as they shall not appear to be corrected, there is small hope of conservation of good order, and a marvellous boldness given to offenders, the means of reformation thus taken away. Wise men have noted truly that it is *caput audaciæ impunitatis spes*, which must needs grow where open faults be thus neglected and pretermitted, wherein they be chiefly to be blamed that forbear to make report of that they have heard when they be required. I would not be over curious, unless the crime were notable, to bring to light his fault that himself hath used means to hide from the world. But, if the offender be so destitute of all fear and shame as these players were, why should any man forbear, when they walk in the street naked, to point them with his finger and say, There they go?

I hear many things to be very far out of order, both openly in the University and severally in the Colleges, whereof I am sorry, and amongst other in contempt of me the determination of the pronunciation of certain Greek letters agreed unto by the authority of the whole University, to be violate and broken without any correction therefor. The matter is low and the contempt so much the more. I was chosen Chancellor to be so honoured (although above my deserts) of them, and I have given no cause to be despised. I will do that I can for the maintenance of virtue and good order there, and challenge again, of duty, to be regarded after the proportion not of my qualities but mine office. Requiring you, Master Vice-chancellor, to communicate these my letters with the masters, presidents, and doctors, and on my behalf to desire them gravely to consider of what moment the good order of youth is, and to withstand the lewd li[cenc]e[1] of such as have neither shame, nor fear of punishment and correction. The lesson of obedience would be well taught and practised, and I will be more diligent to know how men profit in it than I have been. I have shewed the whole Council the words spoken by Master Scot, from whom ye shall shortly receive answer in that matter. And as touching those that were chief players in the tragedy I hear very evil matter, and I

[1 Part of this word has been torn away with the seal.]

pray you call them unto you and know whether they will acknowledge and confess their fault or no; and to signify the same unto me: and so fare ye well. At London the 12th of May.

The chief players to be summoned and required to confess their fault.

Your loving friend,
STE. WINTON.

To my loving friend Master Vice-chancellor of Cambridge.

XXI.

THE LORDS OF THE COUNCIL TO DR MATTHEW PARKER.

16th May, 1545. Parker MSS. C. C. Coll. Camb. CVI. art. 162. p. 453. Orig.

AFTER our hearty commendations, we have considered such words as you signified to your chancellor, our very good lord the bishop of Winchester, to have been spoken by one Mr Scot touching a certain tragedy played in Christ's College, and think it right expedient that, calling the parties before you, ye should admonish them to endeavour themselves so to employ their wits and studies in knowledge of that is good, true, and wholesome, as all that is indeed poison, either in learning or manners, be expelled and put out, and no such matter either in play or earnest to be moved or meddled with as should offend the laws and quiet of this realm, so as you, that there be assembled and under the King's majesty's special protection be maintained to live quietly for the increase of virtue and learning, do also in your manner and behaviour practise rest and quietness, and eschew all occasions that might impeach the same. Wherein ye that be heads and governors must have such special cure and care, as, if any misorder be among the youth, ye reform it from time to time, and do that may be for your discharge in that behalf. And thus, discharging the said master Scot, noted to have spoken the said words, to do, for reformation of those that have misused themselves in playing of the said tragedy, as to your wisdoms shall be thought requisite.

And thus we bid you right heartily well to fare. From St James, the 16th day of May, 1545.

Your loving friends,

T. WRIOTHESLEY.	J. RUSSELL.
STE. WINTON.	WILLM. PAGET.

To our very loving friends the Vice-chancellor, masters of Colleges, doctors and proctors of the University of Cambridge.

XXII.

THOMAS SMITH TO DR MATTHEW PARKER.

21st August, 1545.   Parker MSS. C. C. Coll. Camb. cvi. art. 183. p. 493.   Orig.

The King intendeth to assail his enemies.

He desires to be helped by prayers and processions in the University of Cambridge.

RIGHT worshipful, I have me commended unto you. You shall understand that letters is comen from the King's Council to my lord[1]. The tenor whereof is that the King's highness intendeth[2] with an army royal and a like and puissant navy, by the grace of God, with all speed to assail and repulse his enemies. To the which thing it is his grace's pleasure and desire to be helped with prayers and processions made throughout his realm, and warning thereof to be severally given in every diocese. Wherefore methinks you should do very well, if, as at such times in like cases you were wont, you did continue weekly your general processions in the University of Cambridge. There was at no time more need of common and hearty prayer than now.

Jesu keep you.   At Downham, the 21. day of August.

Your,

THOMAS SMYTH.

To the right worshipful Mr doctor Parker, Vice-chancellor of the University of Cambridge, or, in his absence, to his deputy there.

[1 Goodrich, Bishop of Ely, whose Chancellor Smith was when he wrote this letter. See Strype's Life of Sir Thomas Smith, p. 19. Oxf. 1820.]

[2 This intention was never carried out. In 1544, as we have before remarked, (p. 15, n. 5), Henry VIII. laid siege to Boulogne, with an "army royal," from July to September, and on the 14th of the latter month received its surrender in person. To aid in the re-

XXIII.

DR MATTHEW PARKER TO THE COUNCIL OF QUEEN KATHERINE PARR.

A.D. 1545. Parker MSS. C. C. Coll. Camb. CVIII. art. 23. p. 127. Orig. draft.

JESUS.

PLEASETH it your honourable estates, after my due recommendations to the same, to be advertised, that where, for the discharge of my governance of the Queen's grace' college of Stoke in Suffolk, committed to my trust, I have hitherto done my best diligence to employ that her grace['s] foundation not only agreeably thereto, but have also, of late, improved the state thereof somewhat above the first institution to no small cost and charge; and, moreover, have hitherto resisted such suit for surrender as might (by the occasion offered) have been both beneficial to me for the present commodity, as for a liberal pension with good assurance to have been obtained; and yet, weighing my duty to God and to the Queen's grace, in such respects as it may please your worshipful wisdom to peruse here following, I have not given place. But now, perceiving the continuance to be in danger, and not to be stayed by my ability[3], I thought it good in time to make my refuge to your worships, and to give your wisdoms occasion to consult (as ye do in other matters pertaining to the Queen's honour and commodity) what ye shall think meet to be done in this said case.

The suppression thereof cannot be great advancement to the King's majesty, the lands being but ccc*l*. and altogether covery of Boulogne, the French, in the year following, scoured the channel with their fleet, and did considerable damage on the shores of England. The intention here alluded to, was probably announced with the view of inspiriting the people of England in the unwonted naval circumstances in which the kingdom was then placed.]

[3 "In this same year [1545], being the 37th of the king, all colleges, chantries, hospitals, &c., were granted by parliament to him. This act struck full at Stoke College, which caused the dean to bestir himself, if it were possible, to prevent the dissolution of a place which he had laid out so much of his pains about to make it useful for the service of the king, the church, and commonwealth."— Strype's Parker, Bk. I. c. 6. The College was dissolved in the 1st year of Edward VI.]

The house in the midst of the Queen's tenants, who have the advantage of alms, hospitality, and education for their children.

(except a very little) standing in spiritual rents. The house standeth so that her grace's tenants be round about it, as well to be refreshed with alms and daily hospitality as is there kept, as to be instructed with God's word of certain of her grace's orators doing the same; beside the commodity that the childer of her grace's tenants and farmers fully enjoy by their teaching and bringing up, as well in grammar as in singing and playing, with other exercises and nurtures meet for their ages and capacities; being there sundry teachers attending upon their instructions in the same, the number of which scholars with other honourable and worshipful children amount[1] * * *.

Stoke the Queen's only college in that country, whence she draws part of her revenue.

Moreover, it may please your honourable wisdoms to call to remembrance, that her grace being lady and patroness but of that one in that country where her grace's honourable revenues in some part lieth, and the house being situate as it is, and so competently furnished with lodgings, for the entertaining of her grace's Council at their repair down, I trust ye will expend whether in this respect it were not convenient

It is therefore useful as a place of lodging for her Council, where they may meet her farmers and tenants.

some stay to be made therein, as heretofore have been received there at some survey the most part of her grace's Council viii. days together with the resort of the most part of her farmers and tenants to the same, and have been entertained there without cost or charge of the Queen's grace's coffers, in such wise as was to the contentation of them (worshipful as they were at that time): which expense, so by us gladly sustained, I report of, not for any other cause but to some little testification of our ready goodwill and service to the Queen's highness and her Council, and to declare no less readiness of service to remain in us hereafter to our abilities in the same.

These things stated by Parker for the information of the Queen, and that they may be suggested to the King.

Moreover, whatsoever your excellent wisdoms shall thus or otherwise more prudently consider in the premises, I thought it to be to the discharge of my duty and conscience, to signify unto you, as officers under God and the King, to provide for the preservation of the Queen's honour on this behalf, to the pleasure of God and relief of her poor orators and tenants, by suggesting such or like respects, and to the Queen's grace, for information of the King's majesty, who at

[1 A line is here unfortunately lost by the bottom of the leaf being cut off.]

the contemplation of her grace's suit, I doubt not will be good and gracious lord. As I have of late made supplication to the Queen's highness by myself, with declaration of these considerations aforesaid, it may please your worshipful goodness to pursue the same, as your opportunity shall serve you, whereby, beside the discharge of your conscience, I trust it shall redound to God's honour in especial, to whose merciful tuition I most humbly commit your honourable estate[2].

[[2] The result of Parker's interference on behalf of his college of Stoke, will be seen in the following letter from sir Anthony Denny to the commissioners for the suppression of such establishments, appointed in the succeeding reign. This letter occurs in Parker MSS. C. C. Coll. Camb. cviii. art. 16. p. 99.

"Besides most hearty commendations. For that heretofore I have been a suitor to the King, our late sovereign lord deceased, on the behalf of Mr Parker, dean of Stoke, whose honest and virtuous using of that college much also moved the same late King, in such wise as his majesty clearly resolved to permit the same to remain undissolved; I am much at this present stirred to require you to be favourable towards him. And albeit that I mean not to have the said college to endure in his former plight, knowing that of necessity it must now ensue the course of others, being in like state: yet that it might seem good unto you to consider the man's worthiness above the common sort: and that as he is in all points hath shewed himself not like to the rest, so likewise to be esteemed, and accordingly rewarded to his deserts; that is, in having an honest and convenient pension. Which although, peradventure, it shall seem the greater, yet may the King's majesty be soon thereof discharged by redemption of some other spiritual promotion, and the man nevertheless worthily advanced. Thus much I have thought good to write in his commendation and favour, whose worthiness I much esteem and tender. Trusting thereby, both for his desert's sake, and this my simple contemplation, ye will rather have respect towards him, as the cause and person require; and my thankfulness for the same may deservedly ensue. Fare ye right heartily well: from my house at Cheshunt, the last of February, 1547.

Sir Anthony Denny had been a suitor to Henry VIII. on behalf of Dr Parker, whose worthiness moved that King to allow Stoke to remain undissolved. Sir Anthony now appeals to the commissioners to consider Dr Parker's worthiness, which is "above the common sort," and to reward him with an honest and convenient pension until he is otherwise advanced.

29th February, 1547-8.

"Your own assured,

"A. DENNY."

To the right worshipful and my very assured friends, Mr Bacon, Mr Gosnold, and others of the King's commissioners in the county of Suffolk.

Beneath this letter Parker has written: "Sir Anthony Denny, knight, one of the privy chamber to King Henry, and after to King Edward."]

[PARK. COR.]

XXIV.

DR MATTHEW PARKER'S MINUTE OF AN INTERVIEW WITH KING HENRY VIII.

A.D. 1546.   Parker MSS. C. C. Coll. Camb. cviii. art. 84. p. 457. Orig.

THE repair up of M. Parker and W. May, after survey, to the King's Majesty.

King Henry VIII. persuaded to have the lands of the Universities surveyed.

Memorandum. That where certain officers in the court and others then in authority under the King, importunately suing to him to have the lands and possessions of both Universities surveyed, they meaning afterwards to enjoy the best of their lands and possessions by exchange of impropered benefices and such other improved lands, certain friends of the University, perceiving the sequel like to turn to a mischief, sued to the King for avoiding the great charges that should be sustained therein, not to send any of his costly officers to that purpose;

A commission sent thereupon to Parker and others,

and thereupon sent his commission to Matthew Parker, then Vice-chancellor, to John Redman, master of Trinity College, and to William May, master of the Queens' College, to survey them, and to make report to his highness what [was] the state of the revenues, and what number were sustained therewith[1].

[1 The following is the commission:
Parker MSS. C. C. Coll. Camb. cviii. art. 82. p. 448. Orig.

Dr M. Parker, Vice-chancellor, Dr Redman and Dr May, appointed commissioners,

BY THE KING. Trusty and well beloved, we greet you well, and let you wit that where as our most loving and obedient subjects, in this our last session of parliament, have freely given and granted unto us full power and authority to order, alter, change, and reform all the Colleges, Hospitals, Chantries, and Free Chapels, within this our realm of England, and other our dominions, or otherwise to use the same at our pleasure, as in the act made for that purpose more at length may appear: We minding to take such direction therein as shall be to the honour of God, the increase of good learning, and the common wealth of this our realm; and considering that the good establishment of the Colleges of our Universities of Oxford and Cambridge, wherein the great number of the youth of this our realm is nourished and educated in the exercise of all kinds of good literature, is specially to be provided for; have resolved to take such undelayed order with the same, as may both encourage the students to continue their studies, and also answer to the special trust and confidence committed unto us by our said subjects. And forasmuch as we know you to be men of notable virtue, learning, and knowledge, have therefore appointed you,

Which said commissioners, with the help of two clerks of the augmentation court, engrossed particularly the particular possessions of the University, Colleges and other spiritual lands there. In the end, the said commissioners resorted up to Hampton Court to present to the King a brief summary[?] written in a fair sheet of vellum (which very book is yet reserved in the college of Corpus Christi[2]) describing the revenues, the reprises, the allowances, and number and stipend of every College. Which book the King diligently perused; and in a certain admiration said to certain of his lords which stood by, that he thought he had not in his realm so many persons so honestly maintained in living, by so little land and rent: and where he asked of us what it meant that the most part of Colleges should seem to expend yearly more than their revenues amounted to; we answered that it rose partly of fines for leases and indentures of the farmers renewing their leases,

who executed the same with the assistance of two clerks of the augmentation court.

The commissioners presented a summary of the results to the King.

His remarks thereon:

and by these our letters give unto you full power and authority, not only to call before you the masters and heads of every of the Colleges and other houses endowed with any manner of possessions within that our University of Cambridge, and also such and as many other the officers and fellows of any of the said houses, as to you shall be thought meet and convenient; but also to peruse all and every their Foundations, Statutes, and Ordinances, and as well by examinations, as by all other ways and means that you shall think good, to learn the very truth, how the same Foundations, Statutes, and Ordinances be observed, of what values, kinds, and natures the whole possessions be which belong to every such College, Chantry, or other house of the sorts aforesaid, and in what shires the same do lie, with the deductions upon the same, the names of the founders and other things which your wisdoms shall think meet to be signified to us touching the state of every such house. And of all the premises to make unto us a certificate fair written in parchment, subscribed with your hands, with all goodly speed and diligence. Eftsoons desiring and praying you, and nevertheless commanding you, to use in the doings hereof, such a dexterity as may be to your discharges in conscience and answer to the special trust which we have reposed in you. Given under our signet at our Honour of Hampton Court, the 16th of January, in the 37th year of our reign.

to call before them the heads and officers of Colleges and houses in Cambridge;

to ascertain how their statutes are observed; what is the value of their possessions; and where they lie.

To return a certificate thereof with all speed.

16th January, 1545-6.

To our trusty and well-beloved Doctor Parker, Vice-chancellor of our University of Cambridge, and to our trusty and well-beloved chaplains Dr Redman and Dr May, and to every of them.]

[[2] Parker MS. CVIII. art. 83. Nasmyth's Catalogue.]

partly of wood sales: whereupon he said to the lords, that pity it were these lands should be altered to make them worse; (at which words some were grieved, for that they disappointed *lupos quosdam hiantes*). In fine, we sued to the King's majesty to be so gracious lord, that he would favour us in the continuance of our possessions such as they were, and that no man by his grace's letters should require to permute with us to give us worse. He made answer and smiled, that he could not but write for his servants[?] and others, doing the service for the realm in wars and other affairs, but he said he would put us to our choice whether we should gratify them or no, and bade us hold our own, for after his writing he would force us no further. With which words we were well armed, and so departed[1].

And promise to force them no further.

[1 From the following letter of Queen Katherine Parr, it seems that the University had applied to her to intercede for them with the King in this matter.

26th February 1545—6. Parker MSS. C. C. Coll. Camb. cvi. art. 200. p. 508. Copy.

To our right trusty, dear, and well beloved, the Chancellor and Vice-chancellor of my lord the King's Majesty's University of Cambridge, and to the whole said University there.

Your letters I have received, presented on all your behalfs by Mr Doctor Smith, your discreet and learned advocate. And as they be Latinly written, which is so signified unto me by those that be learned in the Latin tongue, so (I know) you could have uttered your desires and opinions familiarly in your vulgar tongue, aptest for my intelligence: albeit you seem to have conceived rather partially than truly a favourable estimation both of my going forward and dedication to learning, which to advance, or at the least conserve, you by your letters move me diversly, shewing how agreeable it is to me, being in this worldly estate, not only for mine own part to be studious, but also a maintainer and a cherisher of the learned state, by bearing me in hand that I am endued and perfected with those qualities and respects which ought to be in a person of my vocation. Truly this your discreet and politic document I as thankfully accept as you desire that I should embrace it. And for as much (as I do hear) all kind of learning doth flourish amongst you in this age, as it did amongst the Greeks at Athens long ago, I desire you all not so to hunger for the exquisite knowledge of profane learning, that it may be thought the Greeks' University was but transposed, or now in England again renewed, forgetting our Christianity, since their excellency only did attain to moral and natural things: but rather I gently exhort you to study and apply those doctrines as means and

XXV.

[JOHN MERE][2] TO DR MATTHEW PARKER.

February, 1547—8. Parker MSS. C. C. Coll. Camb. CVI. art. 152. p. 422. Orig.

RIGHT worshipful, it may please you to understand that the election was on Tuesday at 12 of the clock; and then coming to the schools, the regents all in manner appeared to be in sundry minds; but doctor Blyth coming with divers of his friends, and in the mean time proceeding to election, ye were chosen (as it may here appear by this scrutiny[3]) almost <small>Parker has been chosen</small>

apt degrees to the attaining and setting forth the better Christ's reverent and most sacred doctrine: that it may not be laid against you in evidence, at the tribunal seat of God, how you were ashamed of Christ's doctrine: for this Latin lesson I am taught to say of Saint Paul, *non me pudet evangelii;* to the sincere setting forth whereof (I trust) universally in all your vocations and ministries you will apply and conform your sundry gifts, arts, and studies, to such end and sort, that Cambridge may be accounted rather an University of divine philosophy than of natural or moral, as Athens was. Upon the confidence of which your accomplishment to my expectation, zeal, and request, I (according to your desires) have attempted my lord the King's Majesty, for the stablishment of your livelihood and possessions; in which, notwithstanding his Majesty's property and interest, through the consent of the high court of parliament, his highness being such a patron to good learning, doth tender you so much, that he will rather advance learning and erect new occasion thereof, than to confound those your ancient and godly institutions: so that learning may hereafter justly ascribe her very original, whole conservation, and sure stay to our Sovereign Lord, her only defence and worthy ornament: the prosperous estate and princely government of whom long to preserve, I doubt not but every of you will with daily invocation call upon him, who alone and only can dispose all to every creature. Scribbled with the hand of her that prayeth to the Lord and immortal God, to send you all prosperous success in godly learning and knowledge. From my Lord the King's Majesty's manor of Greenwich, the 26th of February.

KATERYN THE QUENE K. P.]

[2 From a comparison of the handwriting of this letter with that of Letter XIII., there can be little doubt that it was written by Mere.]

[3 The paper referred to is pasted below the letter in the MS.,

[JOHN MERE] TO DR MATTHEW PARKER.   [1547-8.

Vice-chancellor almost unanimously. His presence is desired in Cambridge.

unanimi consensu. Many long for your coming and most more wishing that ye will in any wise take it. Mr —[1] would had you to supper on Thursday, for it was a play; on Friday likewise a tragedy, and then very earnestly he wished you. He had at his drinking, which was with joles of fresh salmon, &c., doctors Redman, Glyn, Hatcher, Mr Sands, Grindal, the minor proctor, masters Pilkington, Christopherson, Gonell, Aylond[2].....

XXVI.

WILLIAM MAY TO DR MATTHEW PARKER.

13th March [1547—8[3].] Parker MSS. C. C. Coll. Camb. cvi. art. 184. p. 493. Orig.

Parker's device touching the order of the University looked for in London. His ill health a sufficient reason for his eating meat in Lent

MR VICE-CHANCELLOR, according to your promise we here look for your device touching the order of your University. And doubt you not but all things shall be done moderately and in due order. Your sickness is sufficient licence and dispensation for you to receive *absque scandalo* that meat which is most meet for you. Mr Mere, bearer hereof, can herein sufficiently instruct you. Thus fare you well. Written at London, the 13 day of March.

Your loving friend,

WILLIAM MEY.

To Mr Doctor Parker, Vice-chancellor of Cambridge, give these.

and is inscribed: "Forma scrutinii a⁰. 1547, 7⁰ Februarii de officio procancellarii." It bears the names of Dr Madew, master of Clare Hall, Dr Bill, master of St John's, Dr Parker, and Mr Ainsworth, master of St Peter's.]

[1 This name has been erased in the MS.]
[2 The rest of the letter is wanting in the MS.]
[3 Parker was Vice-chancellor in 1545, and again in 1548. (Dr Lamb's collection of Letters, &c. p. LXIX.) This letter seems connected with the royal visitation of the University of Cambridge, which took place in 1549, but was determined upon as early as the 4th April, 1548, (ibid. p. 102). Dr May, the writer of this letter, had been master of Queens' College, Cambridge. He was now one of the masters of requests to Edward VI., and in 1549 was one of the royal visitors of the University.]

XXVII.

ARCHBISHOP CRANMER TO DR. MATTHEW PARKER.

5th May, 1548. Parker MSS. C. C. Coll. Camb. cviii. art. 20. p. 111. Orig.

I COMMEND me unto you; signifying that the lord Protector, conceiving good opinion of your wisdom, learning, and earnest zeal which you bear to the setting forth of God's word among the people, hath, by the advice of the council, appointed you to preach one sermon at Paul's Cross in London, on Sunday, being the 22nd day of July next; not doubting but that you will purely and sincerely set out the holy scriptures, so as God's glory may be advanced, and the people with wholesome doctrine edified. These therefore shall be to require you to prepare yourself ready in the mean season to supply the day, time, and place to you appointed accordingly; foreseeing that you present yourself unto the dean of Paul's resiant at his house in Paul's church-yard, or unto his deputy there, the Saturday before noon that you shall preach, or at the least to signify then unto him by your letters, or some sure messenger, that you will not fail to preach the Sunday; because the Cross must in no wise be disappointed or destitute of a preacher. Thus heartily fare you well. From my manor of Lambeth, the 5th day of May.

Your loving friend,

T. CANT.

*To the right worshipful — Parker,
Vice-chancellor of Cambridge.*

XXVIII.

SIR JOHN CHEKE TO DR. MATTHEW PARKER.

7th June, 1548. Parker MSS. C. C. Coll. Camb. cxix. art. 26. p. 80. Orig.

MR DOCTOR, after most hearty commendations. I am as diligent in your behalf as I would be in mine own, and labour as sore that ye may think yourself to have found some kind of friendship at my hand, as I think indeed I have received at yours. When the commission is once come out, you and yours shall be the first to whom pensions shall be appointed, and for your part I trust so ordered that no pensionary better[1]. The time is not now long. Within this sevennight or little more, it is thought ye shall be dispatched. Wherefore ye need not much now to accumber yourself with any unquietness of delay, thinking that rateably ye shall be dispatched with the best and soonest. Fare ye well, the 7th of June. From Westminster.

Yours assured,
JOAN. CHEKE.

To the right worshipful Mr Doctor
Parker, Master of Benet College,
in Cambridge.

XXIX.

ARCHBISHOP CRANMER TO DR MATTHEW PARKER.

17th Feb. 1548—9. Parker MSS. C. C. Coll. Camb. CXIV. art. 130. p. 395. Orig.

I COMMEND me heartily unto you, signifying that my lord Protector's grace, having good opinion of your learned knowledge and godly zeal in the advancement of God's word, hath by the advice of the council specially appointed you to preach one sermon before the King's majesty's person, the third Sunday of Lent now coming[2]. Wherefore I pray you in the mean season to prepare yourself in a readiness for the purpose, and to repair unto the court against the day appointed to satisfy the office whereunto you are called accordingly. Thus heartily fare ye well. From my manor of Lambeth, this 17th of February, anno 1548.

Your loving friend,
T. CANT.

To my loving friend Doctor Parker,
Master of Benet College, in Cambridge.

[1 Parker had granted to him a pension of £40 per annum out of the revenues of Stoke]
[2 24th March, 1548—9.]

XXX.

BISHOP THIRLEBY OF WESTMINSTER TO DR M. PARKER.

4th March, 1548—9. Parker MSS. C. C. Coll. Camb. CXIV. art. 123. p. 389. Orig.

AFTER my right hearty commendations to you. Where my lord of Canterbury his grace hath appointed you to preach before the King's majesty the third Sunday of this Lent, and hath written unto you for the same purpose[3], and yet hath received no answer from you again; this shall be to desire you both to prepare yourself to accomplish his request, and also to advertise his grace by your letters of your determination herein. Thus I bid you heartily farewell. From Westminster, the fourth day of March, 1548.

Dr Parker is desired to prepare himself to preach before King Edward VI as directed by a previous letter.

4th March, 1548-9.

Your assured friend,

THOMAS WESTM.

To the right worshipful and my very loving friend master Doctor Parker, Master of Benet College, in Cambridge.

XXXI.

MARTIN BUCER TO DR MATTHEW PARKER.

Probably A.D. 1550. Parker MSS. C. C. Coll. Cantab. CXIX. art. 22. p 67. Orig.

S. D. PROFUIT mihi illa ad te, eximie D. Doctor, deambulatio, tametsi te non licuerit convenire. Volebam, si otium fuisset tibi, de communi professione nostra colloqui, et audire tuum consilium de rite moderandis meis prælectionibus. Prandendum hodie mihi est apud necessarium meum Scherbetum unde non longa via est ad tuum collegium. Si itaque vacaret D. T. de prandio, volente Domino, eum convenirem. De sumendo prandio apud te cum uxore die Mercurii, cum amicitiæ singularis sit beneficium non opus erat id a nobis orare. Si volet Dominus libenter tibi morem geremus et in hac re et in rebus verorum[?] officiorum. Opto D. Opt. valeas.

Bucer is desirous to confer with Parker, and to have his advice respecting the proper arrangement of his lectures. Will call on Parker in his college that evening, and he and his wife will accept Parker's invitation to dine with him on Wednesday.

M. BUCERUS, totus tuns.

Pereximio Theologo D. D. Mattheo Parkero, suo in Domino Patrono observando et charissimo.

[3 See preceding letter.]

XXXII.

MARTIN BUCER TO DR MATTHEW PARKER.

Probably A D. 1550. Parker MSS. C. C. Coll. Cantab. cxix. art. 22. p. 67. Orig.

Bucer thanks Parker for kindness and an invitation, which latter he would willingly accept, but that a German friend has come to him from London If there will be room for his friend he will come.

S. D. Summas habeo, vir clariss. D. T. gratias pro bona protectione[?] reditui meo et invitatione ad cœnam, quam libens inviserem si me non quidam bonus Germanicus, qui ad me Londino venit, remoraretur. Si ei tamen, ut umbræ meæ, locus sit, veniemus. Eruditus et humanus est...[1] diu regis minister fuit. Opt. vale.

Deditus tibi in Domino,

M. BUCERUS.

*Clariss. Theologo D. D. Parkero
patrono suo et amico summo.*

XXXIII.

MARTIN BUCER TO DR MATTHEW PARKER[2].

February, 1550—1. Parker MSS. C. C. Coll. Cantab. cxix. art. 23. p. 68. Orig.

Bucer solicits the loan of ten crowns, to be repaid in a month.

S. D. Oro D. T. clarissime D. Doctor, ut des mihi x. coronatos mutuo, uno tamen mense reddam, bona fide. Opt. vale.

D. T. deditiss. in Domino,

MARTINUS BUCERUS.
tamen peręgre scripsi[3].

*Clariss. viro D. D. Matthæo Par-
kero[4] domino ac fratri in
Christo charissimo.*

[1 A word here has baffled all attempts to decipher it.]
[2 The following words are written at the foot of the letter in Parker's hand: "Scriptum novissimum omnium quod scripsit D. Bucerus paulo ante mortem ejus."]
[3 Bucer died Feb. 28, 1550—51.]
[4 It is Barckero in the MS., but the address is not in Bucer's handwriting.]

XXXIV.

ARCHBISHOP CRANMER TO DR MATTHEW PARKER.

12th February, 1550—1. Parker MSS. C. C. Coll. Camb. cxiv. art. 124. p. 391. Orig.

I COMMEND me heartily unto you. And whereas the King's majesty, by the advice of his most honourable council, hath appointed you to preach one sermon before his highness' person at the court, upon Sunday the 22nd of March next coming, being the 6th Sunday in Lent, and hath commanded me to signify unto you his grace's pleasure in this behalf; this therefore shall be to require you to put yourself in a readiness in the mean time to satisfy the day and place to you appointed, according to the King's majesty's expectation, and not to fail in any wise. Thus heartily fare ye well. From my manor at Lambeth, the 12th of February, 1550.

Parker appointed to preach before Edward VI on the 22nd March then next.

12th February, 1550-1.

Your loving friend,
T. CANT.

To my loving friend Mr Doctor Parker.

XXXV.

SIR JOHN CHEKE TO DR MATTHEW PARKER.

9th March, 1550—1. Parker MSS. C. C. Coll. Camb. cxix. art. 25. p. 79. Orig.

I HAVE delivered the University letters to the King's majesty[5], and spoken with the lords of the council, and with my lord of Canterbury, for mistress Bucer. I doubt not but

Sir J. Cheke has spoken to King Edward VI, the

[[5] The rough draft of this letter is preserved, Parker MSS. C. C. Coll. Camb. cvi. art. 164. p. 461. After speaking in the strongest terms of the benefit conferred by King Edward on the University by Bucer's appointment to be professor there, and of the loss which they had sustained by his death, the University add: "Tum autem propter magnum amorem nostrum in excellentissimum virum D. Bucerum, optimam ejus uxorem, liberos et totam doctissimi hominis familiam Majestati tuæ commendamus. Huic egregio patre-familias orbatæ, liberalitatis tuæ munificentiam, Academiæ eruditissimo doctore destitutæ, prudentiæ tuæ subsidium, prostrati coram serenitate tua poscimus et efflagitamus."]

council, and archbishop Cranmer, on behalf of the widow of Bucer.

Honour done to itself by the University in the honour shewn to Bucer on his interment.

Bucer's excellent qualities

Parker's knowledge of him.

Bucer's books to be secured for the King, if he chooses to have them

Cheke's anxiety to serve Parker.

she shall be well and worthily considered[1]. The University hath not done so great honour to Mr Bucer, as honesty and worship to themselves, the which if they would continue in, as they cease not to complain, they might be a great deal better provided for than they think they be. But now complaining outright of all other men, and mending little in themselves, make their friends rather for duty toward learning than for any desert of the students, shew their good wills to the University. Howbeit if they would have sought other to recover or to increase the good opinion of men, they could not have devised wherein by more duty they might worthily be commended than in following so noble a man with such testimony of honour as the child ought to his father, and the lower to his superior. And although I doubt not but the King's majesty will provide some grave learned man, to maintain God's true learning in his University, yet I think not of all learned men in all points ye shall receive M. Bucer's like, whether ye consider his deepness of knowledge, his earnestness in religion, his fatherliness in life, his authority in knowledge. But what do I commend to you M. Bucer, who know him better, and can praise whom you know trulier. I would wish that that is wanting now by Mr Bucer's death, that men would by diligence and wisdom fulfil in themselves, and that they hear praised in others labour to obtain themselves; whereof I think ye be a good stay to some unbridled young men, who have more knowledge in the tongues than experience what is comely or fit for their life to come.

I pray you let Mr Bucer's books and scrolls unwritten be sent up and saved for the King's majesty, that he choosing such as shall like him best, may return the other without delay; except mistress Bucer think some other better thing to be done with them, or she should think she should have loss by them, if they should not be in her ordering.

I do not, Mr Parker, forget your friendship shewed to me aforetime, and am sorry no occasion serveth me to shew my good will; but assure yourself that as it lieth long and taketh root deep in me, so shall the time come, I trust, wherein ye shall understand the fruit thereof the better to endure and

[1 See a letter from archbishop Cranmer to mistress Bucer, Orig. Letters, Eng. Ref. First Series. No. XVI. p. 27. Park. Soc. See also No. CLXXX. p. 363 of the same volume.]

surelier to take place. Which may as well shortly be as be deferred, but good occasion is all. The Lord keep you, and grant the University so much increase of learning and godliness, as these causes may compel the unwilling men to be ashamed not to do for them. From Westmester, 1551. 5. Ed. the 9th of March.

<small>9th March, 1550-1.</small>

Yours assured,

JOAN. CHEEKE.

To his loving friend Mr D. Parker, Master of Benet College in Cambridge.

XXXVI.

BISHOP RIDLEY TO DR MATTHEW PARKER.

25th July, 1551. Parker MSS. C. C. Coll. Camb. cxiv. art. 133. p. 401. Orig.

MASTER Doctor, I wish you grace and peace. Sir, I pray you refuse not to take a day at the Cross: I may have, if I would call without any choice, enow, but in some, alas! I desire more learning, in some a better judgment, in some more virtue and godly conversation, in some more soberness and discretion. And he in whom all these do concur shall not do well to refuse (in my judgment) to serve God in that place; of the which number by cause I take you to be, therefore (leaving at this time to charge you with answering for the contrary to the King and his council) I must charge you to take a day, as ye will answer for the contrary on to Almighty God, at your own peril. If the day appointed be thought not commodious for you, I shall appoint another for it; but if I should discharge you for that place for the time hereafter, in good faith my conscience should accuse me, and tell me that I should rather go about to satisfy your request[2] (whom the truth is as your kindness hath bound me I would be glad to gratify) than to set forth God's cause. Thus fare ye well. From my house at London—and I pray you com-

<small>Ridley solicits Parker not to refuse to take a day at Paul's Cross.</small>

<small>His peculiar qualifications for that service.</small>

[2 Strype states that Ridley had sent to Parker, July 22, to ask him to preach at the Cross, but that he declined, and earnestly desired to be excused.]

46 MATTHÆUS PARKERUS ET GUALTERUS HADDONUS [1551.

Bulles desires to be commended to mistress Parker. mend [me] to mistress Parker[1], whom, although I do not know, yet for the fame of her virtue in God I do love—the 25 of July.

Yours in Christ,

NICOLAS LONDON.

XXXVII.

THE LORDS OF THE COUNCIL TO DR MATTHEW PARKER.

13th December, 1551. Parker MSS. C. C. Coll. Camb. cxiv. art. 15. p. 61. Orig.

Parker summoned to confer with King Edward VIth's council, and give his opinion in certain things touching the King's service. AFTER our hearty commendations. Whereas the King's majesty hath willed us to send for you to confer with you and take your opinion in certain things touching his highness' service: these are to pray you upon the sight hereof to put yourself in a readiness to make your repair hither unto us as soon as ye conveniently may for the purpose aforesaid. Whereof we pray you fail not, and so bid you farewell. *13th December, 1551.* From Westminster, the 13th of December, 1551.

Your loving friends,

WINCHESTER, NORTHUMBERLAND, J. BEDFORD, PENBROKE,

T. CHEYNE, W. CECILL.

To our loving friend Doctor Parker.

XXXVIII.

MATTHÆUS PARKERUS ET GUALTERUS HADDONUS BUCERI PUPILLORUM TUTORIBUS ET CURATORIBUS[2].

A D. 1551. Epistolæ Tigurinæ, Parker Societat. auspiciis editæ. 8vo. 1848. p. 239.

Bucer when dying, committed certain particulars of CUM D. Martinus Bucerus, optimæ memoriæ pater, quasdam ultimæ voluntatis particulas, moriens fidei nostræ com-

[1 Parker was married on 24th June, 1547, to Margaret, daughter of Robert Harleston, of Matsall in the county of Norfolk, gentleman.]

[2 The persons addressed were Ulric Chelius and Conrad Hubert. Letters from them relating to the administration of Bucer's estate

1551.] BUCERI PUPILLORUM TUTORIBUS ET CURATORIBUS. 47

miserit, et executores instituerit: nos omnibus adhibitis de rebus, quantum tempus et causa ferebant, tantum in eo progressi sumus, ut et muneribus nostris et conscientiis non dubitemus esse satisfactum. Quod si uberius vestræ dominationes cognoscere velint, ex separatis bonorum partibus inspectis facile intuebimini. Nunc vero quoniam illa vobiscum futura est, potestatem nostram in illam transfudimus: nec enim dubitamus quin et mater liberos amare velit, et uxor viri voluntatem supremam inviolate sit conservatura. Itaque illam una cum omnibus bonis, et toto hoc munere administrandi testamenti, vobis repræsentamus, et cum nos diligentiis nostris ad summum usi simus, vestræ subsequantur, et totam hanc optimi et excellentissimi viri D. Buceri voluntatem firmam et ratam in omnes partes custodiant: quod et nos fecimus, quantum potuimus, et vos idem facturos esse cognoscimus. Reliqua, si quæ per se consideranda sunt, in minutis rationibus apparebunt quas ad hoc ipsum perpolivimus; ut totam hanc rem, quantum festinatio uxoris D. Buceri sinebat, vobis explicatissimam relinqueremus. Valete in Christo, optimi domini. In Anglia, Cantabrigiæ, anno D. 1551.

his will to Parker and Haddon, and appointed them his executors.

They have transferred their authority to Bucer's widow, who is about to remove to Strasburgh, and they now recommend her and Bucer's estate to the care of the persons addressed, charging them to maintain Bucer's will inviolate

Such account is added as the suddenness of the departure of the widow will allow.

   Vestrarum dominationum amantes,

    MATTHÆUS PARKERUS,
    GUALTERUS HADDONUS.

 INSCRIPTIO.
Carissimis dominis Tutoribus et Curatoribus Pupillorum D. Martini Buceri. Argentorati.

Summa totalis ultra res non venditas nec æstimatas ut in dorso .. . . . 380 Lib. xx.

    IN DORSO.

Ratio eorum quæ non vendita sed domum revecta sunt.

Duo tapetia viridia. 2 longa pulvinaria plumis plena. Rubrum tegmen. Omnia vasa stannea ponderant xxiiii. lib. 5 ollæ æneæ. Ahenum magnum. 8 opercula cuprea. Mortarium. 3 vasa cuprea ad radendum apta. 2 ollæ cupreæ. 4 lecti superiores plumei. 3 cervicalia majora et 6 minora.

occur in Parker MSS. C. C. Coll. Camb. cxix. arts. 29 and 30, and in Epist. Tigurinæ, p. 241. The Parker MS. cxix. contains also a copy of Bucer's will, and several letters from his widow.]

4 pulvinaria. 5 tegmina. 2 rubra, reliqua viridia. 2 panni virides ad operienda scamna. 26 paria linteaminum. 20 mappæ. 21 manutergia. 30 mantilia. Nigræ cistæ 2 itinerationibus accommodata. 3 longæ togæ. 2 tunicæ interiores breviores, una pelle subducta. 2 paria caligarum. 3 diploides. Pallium.

XXXIX.

SIR JOHN CHEKE TO DR MATTHEW PARKER.

6th February, 1552—3. Parker MSS. C. C. Coll. Camb. cvi. art. 304. p. 609.

Regrets the lightness of young heads.

I AM sorry to see the lightness of young heads, who because they have attained to some learning be bold to abuse their wits, and pass the bounds of honesty. If learning teach not soberness to young men, obedience in subjects, honesty in all degrees, what should we do with learning, seeing we have knowledge enough of our self, without study and school, to do ungraciously? But as you shall not be the last that shall find such unthankfulness of unexperienced scholars, so have ye not been the first, and therefore do

Parker will do wisely in bearing soberly such headlong rashness.

wisely in bearing soberly such headlong rashness as overthroweth the user. I am glad again to see him called home, if he be truly called, and do not dissemble with necessity to overcome the time. But you shall easily perceive that by his demeanour and company, according whereunto you shall do well to order him.

letting all toward wits understand that when they go beyond learning to defame learning, they must not be favoured.

But you must let all toward wits understand, that when they go beyond learning to defame learning, that they must not be favoured for their own learning, but punished justly for other men's learning. Wherefore I am glad to see not only the success of this, but also trust it will be an example for other hereafter, how they presume too much on themselves, and venture further than their learning and wits can honestly lead them.

Trusts to commune with Parker in London.

The anchor of my suit resteth much in you, whereof I trust at London to commune with you. Thus with my wife's

1552-3.]   SIR JOHN CHEKE TO DR MATTHEW PARKER.   49

and mine hearty commendations to you and your wife, I bid you farewell in the Lord. From Cheekstoke, the 6th of February, 1552. 7 Ed. 6. 6th February, 1552-3.

Yours assured,

JOAN. CHEEK.

To the right worshipful Mr D. Parker, Dean of Lincoln, at Cambridge.

XL.

SIR NICHOLAS BACON, AFTERWARDS LORD KEEPER, TO DR MATTHEW PARKER.

9th December, 1558. Lambeth MS. 959. No. 29. Orig.

AFTER my right hearty commendations. These are to signify unto you, that for certain matters touching yourself, which I trust shall turn you to good, I would wish that you should repair hither to London, with as convenient speed as you can, where you shall find me at Burgeny-house, in Paternoster-row [1], if it be not over-long or you come. And if it chance that I be returned into Suffolk before your coming, then I would you should make your repair unto my brother-in-law, Sir William Cecil, the Queen's secretary, declaring unto him that I appointed you to wait upon him, to know his pleasure touching such matters as he and I did talk of concerning you. Thus wishing you well to do, I bid you heartily farewell. Written the 9th of December, 1558. By yours assuredly,
Lord Keeper Bacon requests Parker to repair to London "for certain matters touching himself."

If Bacon be absent on Parker's arrival, he is to repair to Sir William Cecil.

9th December, 1558.

N. BACON.

To the right worshipful and my very friend Mr Doctor Parker, give these, in haste.

[1 Burgeny or Bergavenny House, the London residence of the earls of Abergavenny, is described by Stowe as "one great house built of stone and timber" standing "at the north end of Ave Mary Lane." (Stowe's Survey, ed. Thoms, p. 127.) Sir Nicholas Bacon ultimately purchased and rebuilt Shelley House in Noble Street, Aldersgate, which was thenceforth named Bacon House. (Pennant's Lond. ed. 1813, p. 331.) Bacon's residence in Suffolk, afterwards referred to, was at Redgrave.]

4

XLI.

DR MATTHEW PARKER TO SIR NICHOLAS BACON.

Between 9th and 20th December, 1558. Lambeth MS. 959. art. 31. Orig. draft.

Acknowledges the receipt of Bacon's letter of 9th December, 1558.

RIGHT worshipful, after my duty of commendations. Whore of late I received your letters to this effect, that I should repair up unto you at London, upon occasion, as ye wrote, which may turn me to good, so judged by a late conference with the right worshipful Sir William Cecil, secretary to the Queen's majesty, of long time my special good friend and master. Ye shall understand that my

Parker in ill health.

quartane hath so much distempered the state of my health, that without apparent danger I cannot as yet commit myself to the adventure of the air, as by divers assayes I have attempted of late to my greater pain and further hinderance; whereupon, if your opportunity might so serve, I would most heartily pray your worship to signify so much. And further

He is of the same mind as when Sir John Cheke was desirous to do him good, as Bacon calls it.

yet in confidence of your old good heart to me, I would be a suitor to you, as I was once to Sir John Cheke, my entire good friend and patron, to the said Sir William Cecil, that where he was desirous, by his mediation, to do me good (as here you use to call it), even as I was then framed in mind, so am I at this day: I would be inwardly heavy and

He would be sorry if the favour of his friends procured him anything above his ability.

sorry that his favourable affection should procure me anything above the reach of mine ability, whereby I should both dishonest myself, and disappoint the expectation of such as may think that in me which I know is not; but specially I might clog and cumber my conscience to God-ward, before whom I look every day to appear to make mine answer, which I think, and as I trust, is not far off. Notwithstanding, though I would most fain wear out the rest of my life in private state, yet concerning that very small talent credited unto me, I would not so unthankfully to God ensue my quiet, that I could not be content to bestow it, so it were there whither my heart and conscience afore this time, and

He wishes for nothing more than the revenue of some prebend, so that he might occupy him-

daily yet doth incline me: I mean, to be no further abled, but by the revenue of some prebend (without charge of cure or of government) to occupy myself to dispense God's reverend word amongst the simple strayed sheep of God's fold, in poor destitute parishes and cures, more meet for my decayed voice, and small quality, than in theatrical and great audience: which walk and wish I would to be nigh the quarters where we both were born, by occasion whereof I might have opportunity to wait other-while on you at Redgrave, whither I have vowed my first journey, immediately upon my strength recovered, by the occasion of your friendly request of your letters ye sent me. And if I might be yet bolder with you, as I was with the said Sir John Cheke, to disclose my desire, of all places in England I would wish to bestow most my time in the University, the state whereof is miserable at this present, as I have had intelligence from time to time thereof. And if in any respect I could do service, as a weak member of the commonwealth, I think I might do it with them, having long acquaintance and some experience in the doings thereof; which judgment had the said Sir John Cheke towards me; and therefore to set me on work, had once, by the favour of the said Mr Secretary, procured to have me named to the worship [sic] of Trinity College, which yet chanced not to that effect, God otherwise determining the matter in his providence. But to tell you my heart, I had rather have such a thing as Benet College is in Cambridge, a living of twenty nobles by the year at the most, than to dwell in the deanery of Lincoln, which is two hundred at the least. Now, sir, ye may see herein yet my ambition in writing thus much; but I shall pray you to accept the circumstances, which ye may better insinuate to Mr Secretary than I dare be bold, by my rude letters, to molest his favourable goodness, or yet prescribe to your and his worship, wisdom and prudence. In conclusion, at the reverence of God, I pray you, either help that I be quite forgotten, or else so appointed, that I be not entangled now of new with the concurre [sic] of the world, in any respect of public state of living; whereby I shall have an unfeigned signification of your very good will to me indeed, and be bound to pray for you during my life.

Some of your scholars at Cambridge, enjoying the benefit of your liberal exhibition, have sent your worship now their letters; some be sick and absent.

Thus reposing the quiet of my mind, and having good hope in your friendliness to the considerations aforesaid, I wish you a full recovery of your health, and a continuance of God's grace and favour, with all your family.

Your beadsman to command,
M. P.

To the right worshipful and my singular good master and friend, Mr. Bacon, at Burgeny house.

XLII.

DR. MATTHEW PARKER TO SIR NICHOLAS BACON.

20th December 1558. Lambeth MS. 959. No. 31 b. Orig. Draft.

Excuses his long letter sent to Bacon at a time when he was unwell.

RIGHT worshipful, with my thankful duty of commendations. Hearing of your sickness still to occupy you, I was right heartily sorry that I molested you with so long a letter, into which fault, for that I will not fall again at this present, I shall use the fewer words. Sir, if I may know at what time I might in your return down, wait on your worship at Burgeny, or at Newmarket[1], I will by God's grace so appoint myself to be there first, the rather for that I would not give occasion to have your journey either protracted, or yet diverted out of the right line thereof. In the mean time I shall beseech God to restore your strength, that ye may the sooner be restored to the commonwealth, which in this apparent necessity of worthy persons, I fear, feeleth God's hand in this his visitation to be burdenous. I would wish ye were not much stirring abroad in the distemperance of the air, so contrarious to the state of men's bodies, once pierced with this insolent quartane, as experience sheweth. I think the spring-time as in natural respects must be expected, though Almighty God be bound to no time. Thus I heartily commend you to his gracious protection, this 20th of December.

Will meet Bacon either at Burgeny or at Newmarket.

20th December.

Your most bounden assuredly to command,
M. P.

[1 Parker probably continued up to this time still resident in that place of seclusion to which he retired during the reign of Mary. In March 1558-9 he had returned, as we shall see, to Cambridge.]

XLIII.

SIR WILLIAM CECIL TO DR MATTHEW PARKER.
30th December, 1558. Lambeth MS. 959. art. 30. Orig.

AFTER my hearty commendations. The Queen's highness, minding presently to use your service in certain matters of importance, hath willed me so to signify unto you, to the end you should forthwith, upon the sight hereof, put yourself in order to make your indelayed repair hither unto London; at which your coming up I shall declare unto you her Majesty's further pleasure, and the occasion why you are sent for; and hereof praying you therefore in no wise to fail, I bid you well to fare.

From Westminster, the 30th of December, 1558.

Your loving friend,
W. CECILL.

(margin: Parker summoned to repair to London forthwith on the Queen's service. 30th December, 1558.)

XLIV.

SIR NICHOLAS BACON TO DR MATTHEW PARKER.
4th January, 1558—9. Lambeth MS. 959. art. 31 a. Orig.

AFTER hearty commendations. These are to signify unto you, that ye may assure yourself, that you shall have anything that I can do for you touching the request of your letters, or any other matter being in my power. I do think that ye have received or this a letter from Mr Secretary, willing you to come up immediately, if your health will suffer, for certain weighty matters touching the Queen's service; so as I trust, by your presence, all things to your own contentation shall come the better to pass. If this letter be not come to your hands, and therewith you be not able to come, it shall be behoveful for you to signify so much, because I have been willed also to haste your coming up. Thus right heartily fare ye well. Written the 4th of January, 1558.

By yours assuredly,
N. BACON.

(margin: Bacon promises that Parker shall have anything he can do for him touching his request. He must come to town if his health will allow. 4th January, 1558-9.)

XLV.

DR MATTHEW PARKER TO SIR WILLIAM CECIL.
1st March, 1558—9. S. P. O. Domestic. Orig.

<small>Parker driven to Cambridge by inability to maintain a double charge elsewhere. He writes to Cecil, who has accepted the Chancellorship of the University, as to the practices of several of the Colleges to avoid the anticipated changes.</small>

RIGHT worshipful, my duty presupposed. Being hither driven by divers necessities, as not able by otherwhere dwelling to maintain a double charge, secret advertisement is brought on to me, which I thought meet to be put to your consideration, the rather now upon your acceptation of the highest office here for the stay of the University[1]. I hear that divers Colleges be much disordered, as well in their possessions as in other respects not so maintained as were left to them of late. They were awhile in fear by a visitation to be answerable; they have now gotten an intelligence of no visitation to be purposed. Upon full passing of the primacy they [gathered the sequel[2]]. Some masters be about to resign to their friends chosen for their purpose, peradventure to slide away with a gain. Queen Mary, immediately upon her quiet, gave out authority to the Chancellor (Bishop Gardiner). He forthwith sent his chaplain (Watson) with instructions to every College, and, as then I could gather, to report to him in what state every College stood in; and further, peradventure upon cause, to have the masters and others assured *de coram sis-*

<small>Sends him the precedents of Queen Mary's reign.</small>
tendo, et interim bene gerendo until a further order. The copies of these letters I send to your mastership[3], if ye desire

[[1] Sir William Cecil accepted the Chancellorship of Cambridge by a letter dated 19th February, 1558—9. See Peck's Desid. Curios. II. edit. 1779. The draft of the original letter, corrected by Sir W. Cecil, is in the State Paper Office.]

[[2] The words within brackets are supplied from Strype's Parker, Lib. I. chap. ix., the original being mutilated in this place. The meaning is, that on the passing of the act of supremacy, the masters of Colleges alluded to anticipated their ejection if they refused the oath of supremacy.]

[[3] The following are the copies of letters inclosed. These copies are both in the State Paper Office under their respective dates.

QUEEN MARY TO BISHOP GARDINER.

MARY THE QUEEN. Right Reverend Father in God, Right Trusty, and Right Well-beloved, we greet you well. And where amongst divers other inconveniences and misorders, brought in and set forth in that our University of Cambridge, one of the greatest and chief

to know the precedent. I would be loth in the first entry of your office Colleges should sustain hurt by any sleight, you

occasion of many of the said misorders, is, that without sufficient authority, only upon the sensual minds and rash determinations of a few men, the ancient statutes, foundations, and ordinances of the whole University, the Colleges, and other places of students, have been much altered, broken, and almost utterly subverted: whereby not only the last wills of many good men have been broken, and many wise, politic, and godly ordinances, confirmed by parliaments, and by sundry our progenitors, fondly and irreverently contemned, but the conscience of many honest men, which by their oaths were bound to the observation of the said statutes and foundations, have been much encumbered; and youth loosely and insolently brought up, to the great discredit of the University, and no small hinderance of the common wealth of all our realm.

We therefore, knowing it our bounden duty to Almighty God, to whose only goodness we acknowledge ourself called and placed in the royal estate of this realm, to travail by all the ways we may, that his glory and holy will being truly declared to all our subjects, he may of all sorts, in their several vocations, be reverently feared, served, and obeyed; have thought good for a beginning, to wish that the examples hereof may first begin in our Universities, where young men, and all sorts of students, joining godly conversation with their studies in learning, may after, as well by their doings as by their preachings, instruct and confirm the rest of our subjects, both in the knowledge and fear of Almighty God, in their due obedience towards us, our laws, and all others their superiors, and in their charitable demeanours towards all men. And because we know that where order is not kept, all things grow to confusion, we therefore have thought good to will and require you our Chancellor, and all others the heads and governors of the Colleges, and other houses, that both yourselves, for your own parts, do exercise your offices, and live, and cause all scholars, students, servants, ministers, and others living under you, of what sort, state, or condition soever they be, to live and frame themselves, their studies, conversations, and manner of living, in such form and order, as by the ancient statutes, foundations, and ordinances of that our University, and of the Colleges and others, is to you severally appointed, which statutes and foundations we will to be inviolably kept and observed, according to the ancient foundations and ordinances of the founders, and grants of our progenitors.

And therefore do eftsoons require and charge you our Chancellor, whom we do authorize by these presents for that purpose, to see the same well and truly observed, as you will answer for the contrary; notwithstanding any injunctions or new ordinances made, set forth, or delivered by any visitors or others sithence the death of our father of most worthy memory, King Henry the Eighth, (whom God assoyl,) or

not understanding the likelihood. The rest of the matter I commit to your prudent foresight. God grant so good luck of your election that the University may joy to be raised and restored, none otherwise than your zeal thereunto hath been long perceived, *ut amputetur malevolis omnis occasio improbitatis et querulationis. Primo Martii.*

1st March

Your bounden orator,

M. P.[1]

If your mastership shall intend any thing, D. Cole hath both counterpanes of the whole states of every college so found at the last visitation.

To the right worshipful Sir William Cecil, Secretary to the Queen's Majesty.

any other new device to the contrary thereof. Given under our signet at our manor of Richmond, the 20th of August, the first year of our reign.

BISHOP GARDINER TO THE UNIVERSITY OF CAMBRIDGE.

Doctissimis viris Vice-Cancellario et Senatui Cantabrigiensi.

Quam multæ causæ sint (viri doctissimi) quæ animum meum, ut ad vos hoc potissimum tempore accederem, permoverent, totidem fere occurrunt impedimenta, quæ corpus in vobis adsit, justissime prohibent. Interim autem, dum occasionem capto commodiorem, qua vos ipse inviserem; hunc Sacellanum meum, vobis non omnino ignotum, et mihi notissimum, cujus fidem perspectam et exploratam habeo, mandare volui, eidemque demandare, ut meo nomine referat, quæ vos ex me cuperem intelligere: cui ut credatis, oro, et bene valete. Londini ex ædibus meis, octavo calend. Septembr. 1553.

Vester Cancellarius,

Steph. Winton., Cancell.]

[[1] Indorsed in a contemporary hand, "1º Martii, 1559. Dr Parker to Mr Secretarie."]

XLVI.

DR MATTHEW PARKER TO SIR NICHOLAS BACON.

1st March, 1558—9. Lambeth MS. 959. No. 37. Orig. or Draft in Parker's hand.

RIGHT honourable, my duty presupposed. It is an old-said proverb, *ubi quis dolet, ibidem et manum frequenter habet*, beseeching you, for God's sake, the rather to bear the importunity of this my handwriting, supposing that this may be one of the last solicitations that I shall molest you with. Ubi quis dolet ibidem et manum frequenter habet.

Sir, your signification uttered to me at my first coming to you at London, concerning a certain office ye named to me, did hold me in such carefulness all my time of being there, with the recoursing [sic] of a dull distemperance set in my head by the dregs of my quartane and as yet not remedied, whereby I had no disposition to my book, beside some other displeasant cogitations concerning the state of this time, made me to have so little joy of my being at London, as I had never less in my life; most glad when my back was turned thereunto. But, to come nigher to my intent of writing, I shall pray to God ye bestow that office well; ye shall need care the less for the residue. God grant it chanceth neither on arrogant man, neither on fainthearted man, nor on covetous man. The first shall both sit in his own light, and shall discourage his fellows to join with him in unity of doctrine, which must be their whole strength; for if any heartburning be betwixt them, if private quarrels stirred abroad be brought home, and so shall shiver them asunder, it may chance to have that success which I fear in the conclusion will follow. The second man should be too weak to commune with the adversaries, who would be the stouter upon his pusillanimity. The third man not worth his bread, profitable for no estate in any Christian commonwealth, to serve it rightly. Parker had no joy of his visit to London. Importance of a right choice of an archbishop. Inconveniences if he should be an arrogant man, a fainthearted man, or a covetous man.

For my part, I pray God I never fall into his indignation, and wisdom it were not for a subject to deserve his prince's displeasure, and sorry would I be to discontent Mr Secretary and you; for whose worshipful favours I count myself more bound to pray to God, and to wish well to, than for all the men in the realm beside. I speak it sincerely, without flattery; for though I have little wit, yet I can discern betwixt Parker's anxiety not to discontent Bacon and Cecil:

men who delight to be flattered, and who not, though I would not consider how dishonest it were for me to use it. But, sir, except ye both moderate and restrain your overmuch good will in the former respects to me-ward, I fear, in the end, I shall dislike you both, and that your benevolences should by occasion of my obstinate untowardness jeopard me into prison; yet there shall I bear you my good heart, which I had rather suffer in a quiet conscience, than to be intruded into such room and vocation, wherein I should not be able to answer the charge to God nor to the world, wherein I should not serve the Queen's honour, which I would wish most heartily advanced in all her wise and godly proceedings; nor yet should I live to the honour of the realm, and so finally should but work a further displeasant contemplation to my good friends who preferred me.

This, this is the thing that make me afraid, my lord, though I passed not on mine own shame and rebuke; and therefore, by God's favour, and your good helps, I never intend to be of that order, better or worse, higher nor lower; *Non omnia possumus omnes, et tutissimum est ut quisque hanc artem exerceat in qua educatus, et ad quam natura homines formavit.* And as for other furnishments, I am too far behind. When I came first up to London I had thirty pounds in my purse, not ten shillings more, whereof I have wasted a good part; and if I were placed, as some of my friends wish to me, what would that do to begin or to furnish my household, &c.? I hear how the citizens of Norwich pray for the soul of their last bishop[1]; for when, upon his departure, they seized his goods, to answer his debts to them, straightway came the Queen's officers, and discharged them all, which yet were not able, for all his spare hospitality, to pay half that he owed.

Furthermore, to come to another consideration of a further imperfection, which I would have dissembled to you and others, but it cannot be, but must open it to you, my assured good master and friend, in secrecy, whose old good will maketh me the less abashed to be so homely with you at this time. In one of my letters I made a little signification of it, but peradventure ye did not mark it. Sir, I am so in body

[1] Dr John Hopton, chaplain to Queen Mary, Bishop of Norwich, 1554—1558.]

hurt and decayed, *coram Deo non mentior*, that whatsoever my ability were, either of worldly furniture or inward quality, and though my heart would right fain serve my sovereign lady the Queen's majesty, in more respects than of mine allegiance, not forgetting what words her grace's mother said to me of her, not six days before her apprehension, yet this my painful infirmity will not suffer it in all manner servings. Flying in a night, from such as sought for me to my peril, I fell off my horse so dangerously, that I shall never recover it; and by my late journey up, and my being there at London not well settled, it is increased to my greater pain. I am fain sometime to be idle, when I would be occupied, and also to keep my bed, when my heart is not sick. *What words Queen Anne Boleyn said to Parker about her daughter, not six days before her apprehension.*

This was one cause why I was importune to you for that room whereof I made mention in my former letters, by the which I might be abled, by the portion of that stipend, in this mine impoverishment to wear out my life tolerably, and should not by that be occasioned to come up to any convocations, as having no voice in that house; and peradventure being there, I might be a mean for the fewer matters of disturbance to come up to Mr Secretary, now chancellor there, to molest him more than should need, whose gentle affability might provoke some inconsiderate men not to regard his other greater affairs. And yet though I were so placed, I would not forswear London, or the court either, at times, as could stand with my ability and health of body, if my service could be any ways acceptable, and were agreeable to the proportion of my capacity. *Suitableness for Parker of a life passed at Cambridge.*

Sir, because I may not dissemble with you, I have told you all. Now do with me what ye will. I may be ashamed to spend so many words in a cause private of myself, but yet, because ye must be partner of some lack if I answered not the expectation, I could no less do but make you privy beforehand. I pray you think not that the prognostication of Mr Michael Nostre Dame reigneth in my head[2]. I esteem *Parker not influenced by prophecies of Nostradamus or any one else.*

[2 Nostradamus was believed to threaten the world with peculiar evils in 1559 and 1560. Parker probably specially alludes to a book, published about this time in English, by Day, and entitled "An excellent treatise, shewing such perillous and contagious infirmities as shall insue 1559 and 1560, with the signes, causes, accidents, and curation, for the health of such as inhabit the 7. 8. and 9. climate. Compiled

that fantastical hotch-potch not so well as I credit Lucian's book, *De veris narrationibus;* nor yet all other vain prophecies of Sonds more than I regard Sir Thomas Merys book of " Fortune's Answers upon the chance of three dice casting[1]." I would I saw no more cause to fear the likelihood of God's wrath deserved for dissolute life, to fall upon the realm, by the evidence of his true word, and by God's old practices; and yet no man considereth his ire already begun *dum non sinit viros dolosos dimidiare dies suos.* I shall pray to God to defend you and your family, and that ye may revolve in mind Christ's serious admonition, " *Quid proderit homini, si totum mundum lucretur, si animæ suæ detrimentum patiatur.*" Matt. xvi. Et, " *Non in abundantia cujusquam, est vita hominis ex hiis quæ possidet.*" Luke xii.

Sir, my duty of heart maketh me bold with you, not otherwise meaning before God, but thanking him many times that Mr Secretary and you may have the doings of things in this greedy world, and that ye have so good credit and ready access to the Queen's majesty to comfort her good inclination: whom I beseech the God of heaven to preserve with her council, yea, and with the seniority of her spiritual ministers also, against whom I see a great charge set before them, to overcome that must specially go through their hands by diligent watching upon the unruly flock of the English people, if they were not so much acloyed with worldly collections, temporal commissions, and worldly provisions. I speak this the rather in this respect which I thought good to put to your understanding. At my last being at London, I heard and saw books printed, which be spread abroad, whose authors be ministers of good estimation: the doctrine of the one is to prove, that a lady woman cannot be, by by Maister Michael Nostradamus, doctor in physicke, and translated into English at the desire of Laurentius Philotus Tyl. Mense Martil." (Herbert's Ames, II. 630).]

[[1] The reference seems to be to some book, popularly, but erroneously attributed to Sir Thomas More. He wrote or contributed to a book published with the title of " The Boke of the fayre gentylwoman that no man shulde put his truste or confydence in: that is to say, Lady Fortune: flateryngo euery man that coueyteth to have all, and specyally them that trust in her, she deceyueth them at laste," (12mo. Robert Wyer), but there is nothing in that book which justifies Parker's allusion.]

God's word, a governor in a Christian realm. And in another book going abroad, is matter set out to prove, that it is lawful for every private subject to kill his sovereign, *ferro, veneno, quocumque modo*, if he think him to be a tyrant in his conscience, yea, and worthy to have a reward for his attempt: *exhorrui cum ista legerem*[2]. If such principles be spread into men's heads, as now they be framed and referred to the judgment of the subject, of the tenant, and of the servant, to discuss what is tyranny, and to discern whether his prince, his landlord, his master, is a tyrant, by his own fancy and collection supposed, what lord of the council shall ride quietly minded in the streets among desperate beasts? what master shall be sure in his bed-chamber? It is the surest way for every man to serve God truly in his vocation, to deserve the rather his protection: and then both the devil and man, foreign and intestine, shall have their malices retorted upon themselves again. But thus goeth the devil about to dull the heroical stomachs of princely men to do good in their turn of time, to serve God and the commonwealth. They say that the realm is full of Anabaptists, Arians, Libertines, Free-will men, &c., against whom only I thought ministers should have needed to fight in unity of doctrine. As for the Romish adversaries, their mouths may be stopped with their own books and confessions of late days. I never dreamed that ministers should be compelled to impugn ministers. The adversaries have good sport betwixt themselves to prognostick the likelihood. Some protestants peradventure, perceiving how men nip them, to disable them to keep any learned men in house to confer with, to beat down these seditious sects, if any inconvenience for want of preaching shall fall, some may chance to say a verse of David's Psalter, *Lætabitque justus, cum viderit vindictam, et manus suas lavabit in sanguine peccatoris*, as not caring for their assurances, who abase them so low: and some peradventure have cast already their starting shifts, and make provision against all adventures. Well,

[2 Parker alludes to Knox's "First Blast of the Trumpet against the monstrous regiment of women," (16mo. Genev. 1558), Christopher Goodman's "How superior Powers ought to be obeyed of their subjects," (16mo. Genev. 1558), and other similar publications, sufficiently well known.]

I pray God all be conscience to God, that is sometime so pretended. Men be men, yea, after the school of affliction, men be men. Hypocrisy is a privy thief both in the clergy and in the laity. To make an end of such conference, which I would gladly have told you presently, but I could not wait so much leisure in you and opportunity; and loath I was to have begun my tale and not to have ended it by reason of interruption by others.

He would have conferred with Bacon on this subject, but could not wait his leisure.

But as for the principal occasion of my writing, howsoever it may dislike you, yet shall I evermore acknowledge my duty to you, yea, though now ye give me quite up. I reverence you so much, that I had rather ye disliked me utterly betimes, with your less repentance, rather than ye or other of my loving friends should bear any envy, or any displeasant unthankfulness, and so too late to repent for your commending of me of a persuasion in an appearance and not surely grounded, to be seen when experience should have shewed the trial. And therefore I write it to you in time again, after the signification of my very first letters to prevent you, for I know ye may with a few words remedy all the towardness yet concluded.

As to the archbishoprick. Parker will ever more acknowledge his duty to Bacon.

And think not, I pray your honour, that I seek mine private gain, or my idle ease. Put me where ye will else; and if, as far as my power of knowledge and of health of body will extend, I do not apply myself to discharge my duty, let me be thrust out again, like a thief. I thank God my conscience condemneth me not, that I have been aforetime any great gatherer; and now for the upholding of two or three years more of life, to heap unproportionably, I count it madness; and more than this purpose, by God's grace, I dare promise nothing: and as for such few folks which I may leave behind me, they shall not say by me, I trust, that happy be these children whose fathers goeth [sic] to the devil for their sake. Your lordship knoweth with what patrimony I began the world with, and yet have hitherto lived with enough; yea, when all my livings were taken from me, yet God, I thank him, ministered to me sufficiently above the capacity of my understanding or foreseeing. And thus commending your good lordship to that merciful governance, I pray your honourable wisdom to put this scribbling out of the way, from every man's sight and intelligence.

He does not seek gain or ease Anywhere but in the archbishoprick he will endeavour to do his duty

Right honourable, after my duty of commendations to your lordship, I am bold now to send to you a fancy of my head, expressed in these few leaves; which if I had compact in a letter, it would have seemed overlong, and being comprised in leaves, may appear to be but a very little book of one sheet of paper; which yet I so devised, upon consideration of your business, which will not suffer you to be long detained in matters impertinent, and therefore ye may turn in the leaf and read it at divers leisures, if your lordship shall vouchsafe the reading. And thus wishing you joy of heart, which I feel to be a great treasure in this world, as the want a grievous torment, I pray God preserve your honourable goodness, with my good lady your wife. If ye see ought in my quire worth reformation, ye know I am disciplinable, and have read, *quod meliora sunt vulnera diligentis, quam fraudulenta oscula odentis:* wherefore reserving mine unreasonable determination, as ye shall know, I shall yield myself whole [sic] conformable to your honour, *ubi, quomodo, quando, aliquid, vel tandem nihil.* Of an occasion lately ministered, I have sent my letters to Mr Secretary concerning another matter. *Primo Martii.*   1st March.

This letter written as a book in leaves, that Bacon may read it leaf by leaf at his leisure.

Your assured orator,

M. P.

XLVII.

SIR WILLIAM CECIL TO DR PORIE, VICE-CHANCELLOR, DR MATTHEW PARKER, AND MR EDWARD LEEDS.

21st March, 1558—9. Parker MSS. C. C. Coll. Camb. CXVIII. art. 22. p. 411. Orig.

QUONIAM absum ipse Academia, neque per cæteras occupationes meas, quod vos scitis, vacare mihi his rebus licet, non putavi alienum, quæ ipse propter absentiam procurare non possum, vicaria in illis opera vestra, qui præsentes estis, et diligentia uti. In quo peropportune accidit, vos mihi hoc tempore dari, quibus hanc causam committendo Academiæ curam quæ mihi credita est, non modo non negligere, sed optimam ejus rationem habere videri possum. Contentio nescio quæ de electione quadam inter Prefectum Collegii Reginæ

A dispute has arisen respecting an election

between the President and Fellows of Queens' Col. lege, Cambridge.
et Socios quosdam ejusdem, proximis his diebus exorta est. Huic sedandæ meam operam utraque pars multis verbis imploravit. Ego vero neque per absentiam possum, neque per

Both parties have intreated Cecil to put it to rest.
negotia licet mihi de hac re cognoscere. Nolo tamen committere, propter eam spem, quam Academia apud me deposuit, ut, aut innocentia alicujus injuste opprimatur, aut audacia

He requests Dr Porie and the others to determine the question, and restore peace to the University.
videatur defendi. Quapropter optimum esse duxi huic causæ vos dare cognitores, quos scio et propter solertiam vestram posse, et velle etiam propter bonitatem, eam ita statuere, ut, et Academia sibi pacem peperisse et hii qui litigarunt justitiam consecuti videantur. Dedi seorsum literas ad utramque partem quibus significavi sententiam illis in hac causa, a vobis esse expectandam. A vobis igitur magnopere contendo ut et istam litem diligenter audiatis, et quid in ea decernendum putetis mihi per literas vestras mature velitis renuntiare.

21 March, 1558.
Bene valete. Ex Aula, xxi° Marcii 1558.

Amicus charissimus,

GUL. CECILIUS.

To my assured loving friends Mr Doctor Porie, Vice-chancellor of the University of Cambridge, Mr D. Parker, and Mr Edward Leeds.

XLVIII.

SIR T. SMITH TO DR PORIE, VICE-CHANCELLOR, DR MATTHEW PARKER, AND MR LEEDS.

21st March, 1558—9. Parker MSS. C. C. Coll. Camb. cxviii. art. 23. p. 413. Orig.

Sir T Smith's regret that in the College in which he was educated and almost born, a controversy should have arisen.
ÆGERRIME quidem fero quod in eo collegio in quo primum educatus et quasi, ut ita dicam, fere natus fuerim[1], hæ sunt exortæ controversiæ; per quas si quidem leges et statuta collegii fuerint non ad æquum et bonum, sed at jus strictum exactæ, alteram necesse est partem exactum iri. Sed id me rursus consolatur quod ad vos ut audio refertur causa tota,

[1 According to Strype, Sir Thomas Smith entered at Queens' College in the 14th or 15th year of his age, and was made Fellow there when only 19 years old. See Strype's Sir T. Smith, pp. 6, 10. Oxf. 1820.]

qui componere potius per æquitatem, quam ad extremum eam intorquere velitis. Quid sentiam in tota causa, Gasconus amicus meus, qui idem et leges et statuta nostri Collegii novit, optime potest narrare. Vos oro ut æquum bonumque sectantes, id spectetis quod Collegium illud non imminuere, sed authoritate vestra possit augere. Bene valete. Londini xxi⁰ Martii. Anno Regni Elizabethæ primo.

Consoled by hearing that the whole matter is referred to such arbiters. His friend Gascon [Gascoyne?] is best able to give information respecting the laws and statutes of the College.

Amicus vester,
T. SMITHUS.

To the right worshipful and my loving friends, Mr Doctor Porie, Vice-chancellor of Cambridge, Mr Doctor Parker, and Mr Leeds.

XLIX.

DR EDMUND SANDYS TO DR MATTHEW PARKER.

30th April, 1559. Lambeth MS. 959. No. 41. Orig.

SALUTEM *in Christo.* Ye have rightly considered that these times are given to taking and not to giving, for ye have stretched forth your hands further than all the rest[2]. They never ask us in what state we stand, neither consider that we want; and yet in the time of our exile were we not so bare as we are now brought. But I trust we shall not linger here long, for the parliament draweth towards an end. The last book of service is gone through with a proviso to retain the ornaments which were used in the first and second year of King Edward, until it please the Queen to take other order for them. Our gloss upon this text is, that we shall not be forced to use them, but that others in the meantime shall not convey them away, but that they may remain for the Queen.

The times given to taking, not giving. Parker has lost more than any body. Condition of the returned exiles. King Edward's second Service-book 'gone through,' with a proviso to retain the ornaments. How that proviso construed.

After this book was past, Boxall[3] and others quarrelled with it, that according to the order of the scripture we had not *gratiarum actio;* "for," saith he, "*Dominus accepit*

Objections to the Service-book.

[2 During the reign of Queen Mary, Parker, being married, was deprived of all his preferments.]

[3 Dr Boxall, Dean of Peterborough, had been one of the Secretaries of State and of the Privy Council in the reign of Queen Mary.]

panem, gratias agit, but in the time of consecration we give no thanks." This he put into the Treasurer's head, and into Countie de Ferer's[1] head, and he laboured to alienate the Queen's Majesty from confirming of the act, but I trust they cannot prevail. Mr Secretary is earnest with the book, and we have ministered reasons to maintain that part.

Bill for supremacy is to pass. The bill of supreme government of both the temporalty and clergy passeth with a proviso that nothing shall be judged heresy which is not condemned by the canonical scriptures and four general councils. *The Queen on Mr Lever's suggestion will not take the title of supreme head.* Mr Lever wisely put such a scruple in the Queen's head that she would not take the title of supreme head. The bishops, as it is said, will not swear *Bill to restore the clergy to their livings.* unto it as it is, but rather lose their livings. The bill is in hand to restore men to their livings; how it will speed I know not. The parliament is like to end shortly, and then *The protestants forced to give up a confession of their faith, which is now in preparation.* we shall understand how they mind to use us. We are forced, through the vain bruits of the lying papists, to give up a confession of our own faith, to shew forth the sum of that doctrine which we profess, and to declare that we dissent not amongst ourselves. This labour we have now in hand and purpose to publish it so soon as the parliament is ended. I wish that we had your hand unto it.

Ye are happy that ye are so far from these tossings and griefs, alterations and mutations; for we are made weary *Parker must be removed ere long to a more large abbey.* with them. But ye cannot long rest in your cell. Ye must be removed to a more large abbey, and therefore in the mean time take your pleasure, for after ye will find but a little.

Marriage of the clergy to be winked at, not established by law. *Nihil est statutum de conjugio sacerdotum, sed tanquam relictum in medio.* Lever was married now of late. The Queen's Majesty will wink at it but not stablish it by law, which is nothing else but to bastard our children. Others [sic] things another time. Thus praying you to commend me to your abbesses I take my leave of you for the present. Hastily at London, April ult. 1559.

          Your,
            E. SANDYS.

To the right worshipful Master
 Doctor Parker, at Cambridge.

[1 The Count de Feria, ambassador from Spain.]

SIR WILLIAM CECIL TO DR MATTHEW PARKER.

5th May, 1559. Parker MSS. C. C. Coll. Camb. cxviii. art. 21. p. 409. Orig.

AFTER my very hearty commendations. Forasmuch as I am credibly informed that the two young men lately chosen to be fellows in the Queens' College be both forward in learning, and also well minded in the service of God, so as by their admission into the same house our common cause of religion shall no whit be impaired or hindered: and for that also I understand by Sir Thomas Smith that Mr Peacock, now President of the said College, is fully minded to give over his interest and title in the same to Dr May, which thing I like very well, I have therefore sent down my letters for their admission accordingly. And to the intent that as in the beginning of this matter I made you partaker of the pains for the understanding thereof, so finally to participate with you the determination of the same, I have sent you a copy of the said letters inclosed herein, whereby you shall perceive what I have done therein. I doubt not but as the young men by their admission shall think themselves benefited, so shall the other part who moved some doubt therein, by changing of the Master, avoid all such inconvenience as was supposed would have ensued; and they all together henceforth live in more quiet than hitherto they have done.

And thus I bid you heartily farewell. From the Court, the 5th day of May, 1559.

Your assured loving friend,

W. CECILL.

To my assured loving friend Mr Doctor Parker.

LI.

SIR NICHOLAS BACON TO DR MATTHEW PARKER.

17th May, 1559. Lambeth MS. 959. art. 32. Orig.

A resolution made in the Queen's presence that Parker should be Archbishop.

Parker's description of the required Archbishop in his last letter applies to himself.

THAT before this time I have not sent you answer to your last letters, the cause hath been for that I could by no mean understand to what end the matter mentioned in those letters would certainly grow unto: but perceiving this day, by a resolution made in the Queen's highness presence, that your friends shall very hardly deliver you of the charge written of in the same letters, I thought it good to make you privy thereunto; and therewith to advise you, to commit to the judgment of your friends your ability and disability to serve where and when you shall be called. If I knew a man to whom the description made in the beginning of your letter might more justly be referred than to yourself, I would prefer him before you; but knowing none so meet, indeed I take it to be my duty to prefer you before all others, and the rather also because otherwise I should not follow the advice of your own letter. The rest, which is much, I defer until our next meeting. It is like that, or it be long, you shall receive letters subscribed by me and others jointly. Thus right heartily fare you well. From the Court, the 17th of May, 1559.

Your assuredly,

N. BACON.

To the right worshipful and my very friend Mr Doctor Parker, give this.

LII.

SIR NICHOLAS BACON AND SIR WILLIAM CECIL TO DR MATTHEW PARKER.

19th May, 1559. Lambeth MS. 959. art. 33. Orig.

Parker is summoned to repair up to the Court.

AFTER our hearty commendations, these be to signify unto you, that for certain causes, wherein the Queen's Majesty intendeth to use your service, her pleasure is, that you should repair up hither with such speed as you conveniently may; and at your coming up, you shall understand the rest. Thus right heartily fare ye well.

From the Court, the 19th of May, 1559.

Your loving friends,

N. BACON.
W. CECILL.

To the right worshipful and our very friend Mr Doctor Parker, give these with speed.

LIII.

LORD KEEPER BACON AND SIR WILLIAM CECIL TO DR MATTHEW PARKER.

28th May, 1559. Lambeth MS. 959. art. 34. Orig.

AFTER our hearty commendations. Where before this time we directed our letters unto you, declaring thereby that for certain causes wherein the Queen's Majesty intendeth to use your service, you should repair hither with all convenient speed, whereof we have as yet received none answer: and, therefore, doubting lest by the default of the messenger, the letter be not come to your hands, we have thought good again to write unto you, to the intent you should understand her highness' pleasure is, that you should make your repair hither with all speed possible. Thus right heartily farewell.

From the Court, the 28th day of May, 1559.

Your loving friends,

N. BACON, C. S.
W. CECILL.

Parker is again summoned to Court with all speed possible.

LIV.

DR MATTHEW PARKER TO QUEEN ELIZABETH.

Probably June, 1559. Lambeth MS. 959. art. 35. Orig. Draft.

PLEASETH it your most honourable Majesty to be gracious lady to my poor suit, which at this time extreme necessity compelleth me to make, both in respect of my constrained conscience to Almighty God, as also in the regard of my duty which I owe to your noble estate and most high authority. So it is, most gracious and sovereign lady, where I have understanding of your most favourable opinion toward me, your grace's most simple subject, concerning the archbishoprick of Canterbury; in consideration whereof, I ought, and do, acknowledge my most bound duty, to be a faithful orator for your grace during my life. Yet calling to examination my great unworthiness for so high a function, which mine disability I might allege at length in particularity, but for molesting your grace's most weighty affairs, I am bold thus, by my writing, to approach to your high estate reverently on my knees, beseeching your honour to discharge me of that so high and chargeable an office, which doth require a man of much more wit, learning, virtue, and experience, than I see and perfectly know can be performed of me, worthily to occupy it to God's pleasure, to your grace's honour, and to the wealth of your loving subjects, beside many other imperfections in me, as well for temporal ability for the furnishing thereof as were seemly to the honour of the realm, as also of infirmity of body, which will not suffer me to attend on so difficult a cure, to the discharge thereof in any reasonable expectation.

And where, most gracious lady, beside my humble duty of allegiance to your princely dignity, I am otherwise, for the great benefits which sometime I received at your grace's honourable mother's benevolence (whose soul I doubt not but is in blessed felicity with God) most singularly obliged, above many other, to be your most faithful bedesman, both in thanking Almighty God for his fatherly protection hitherto over your noble person, and also furthermore to pray for the continuance of your fortunate reign in all godly prosperity; I am right sorry, and do lament within myself, that I am so basely qualified inwardly in knowledge, and outwardly in extern sufficiencies, to do your grace any meet service as I would wish could be acceptable, and to your grace's expectation: assuring your noble estate, that in any other smaller vocation, under the degree of such chargeable offices, and more agreeable to my infirmity, if it shall be so seen to your high wisdom, and merciful liberality, I shall endeavour myself to attend thereon to my uttermost power; referring yet myself wholly to your grace's pleasure, rather than by just allegatien of mine unworthiness the loyal duty of my faithful heart should be any ways suspected to your reverend Majesty. *but refers himself to the Queen's pleasure.*

Your Grace's poor subject,
MATTHEW PARKER[1].

LV.

LORD KEEPER BACON TO DR MATTHEW PARKER.

Probably June, 1559. Parker MSS. C. C. Coll. Camb. CXIV. art. 40. p. 125. Orig.

THE former resolution concerning you is now confirmed by a second, and if you be not already sent for to come hither, it will not be long or you shall. I meant before I understood thus much, to have had you this night at supper at my house, for the matter of your letters delivered to me by one that sued for a *ne exeat regnum*, which at my return to London he shall have; but being countermanded by the Queen, I must intreat you to take pain with my wife to pass away a shrewd supper. Written in haste from the Court by your assuredly, *A second resolution come to that Parker shall be Archbishop. One sued to the Keeper for a ne exeat regnum against Parker.*

N. BACON.

LVI.

ARCHBISHOP PARKER (ELECT) AND OTHERS TO THE UNIVERSITY OF CAMBRIDGE.

8th August, 1559. Peck's Desid. Curios. Lib. VII. No. 10. from a MS. of Roger Gale.

UNDERSTANDING that you be presently destitute of a preacher commonly called the University preacher, and considering the great necessity of that function, we have thought good with all convenient expedition to provide for the furnishing of that room. Wherefore we desire and likewise require *The office of University Preacher being vacant, the ecclesiastical commissioners order an immediate election.*

[1] The signature and the greater part of the preceding line are now lost. They are printed here as given in Burnet's Hist. Reform.]

you, that forthwith upon receipt of these our letters, you proceed to the election of such a learned and discreet person as may perform his duty in this case to the honour of the University and discharge of your conscience. And though we are loth to recede from the disposition and order of your honourable founders, yet in respect of extreme necessity (which in itself implieth dispensation with all laws) we will and do supply, with our authority, the lack of such degrees, as peradventure may want in such a person as you shall otherwise think meet for this room by your due consents; so that degrees of school shall in this case be no lack, in consideration of your small number and weak state (which God increase). And your good examples and discreet wisdoms we trust will herein be a good furtherance and great help.

From London, this eighth of August, 1559.

Your loving friends,
MATTHEUE, (*elect.*) CANT.
WALTER HADDON.
ROBERT HORNE.

LVII.

THE LORDS OF THE COUNCIL TO ARCHBISHOP PARKER AND BISHOP GRINDAL, ELECT.

24th August, 1559. Parker MSS. C. C. Coll. Camb. cxiv. art. 14. p. 53.

AFTER our very hearty commendations to your good lordships. Whereas Doctor Smyth[1], of Oxford, having prepared to have fled the realm into Scotland, hath been taken

[1 This Dr Smyth had been formerly "Master of Whittington College, and Reader of Divinity in Oxford." In Edward VIth's reign (1547), Cranmer persuaded him to recant at Paul's Cross the popish errors which he had professed publicly in the University, as well as by two books which he had written. In 1549, however, we find him violently opposing the Archbishop on the subject of the marriage of priests, and obliged to flee into Scotland to escape the consequences of his turbulence. Under Mary he conformed to the restored faith, and distinguished himself in the proceedings at Oxford against Cranmer, Latimer, and Ridley. The cause of the present letter was his refusal to take the oath of supremacy. His scruples were removed by the

in the north parts and sent hither unto us, we have thought good to send him to your lordships, praying the same to use such measures as you think meet to persuade him to be an obedient subject, and to embrace the doctrine established; whereunto if he shall shew himself conformable, then we pray you to signify the same unto us, to the end we may cause bands [sic] to be taken of him for his good continuance therein. Otherwise, if he be obstinate and will not shew himself as he ought, then we pray you to let us also understand from you the same, to the end order may be given for his further proceeding with, according to the laws. And thus we bid your good lordships right heartily farewell.

He is sent to Archb'shop Parker and Bishop Grindal, who are to use measures to induce him to conform.

They are to report the result to the Council with a view to further proceedings.

From Hampton Court, the 24th of August, 1559.

24th Aug. 1559.

Your Lordships' assured loving friends,

W. NORTH. ARUNDEL. F. BEDFORD.
F. KNOLLYS. W. CECILL.

To our very good lords, the Archbishop of Canterbury and the Bishop of London, elect.

LVIII.

ARCHBISHOP PARKER, ELECT, TO THE LORDS OF THE COUNCIL.

27th August, [1559.] Parker MSS. C. C. Coll. Camb. cxix. art. 42. p. 110. Draft.

PLEASETH it your honours to be advertised, that upon your letters sent to my lord of London and me, with the delivery of the party, Dr S——myth, whom they concerned, we spent some time with him in conference; and what partly by our allegations, and he more pressly weighing the form of the oath of the Queen's Majesty's supremacy by the exposi-

The Archbishop and Bishop Grindal have conferred with Dr Smyth, and he is contented to take the oath of supremacy.

[Archbishop and the Bishop of London, and himself and some others as his sureties, were bound for his future good conduct. Subsequently he contrived to get released from his bonds and fled to the continent. There are two letters of his to Parker (Parker MS. CXIX. art. 43), and on the margin of the first Parker has noted: 'Notwithstanding this earnest promise and bond, yet this good father fled into Paris. Such was his faith.' He was made Dean of St Peter's at Douay, and died in 1563. See Strype's Cranmer, Book II. c. 7, and Strype's Parker, Book I. c. 10.]

tion inserted in the injunctions, he is contented to take it, as he saith, with a full persuaded conscience: and saith further, that if he had so understood it afore, as he seeth cause at this present, he would never have departed from Oxford. And now, to some declaration of his conformity, I offered him to consider the form of subscription which we devised to be used in the order of visitations; whereunto he hath, as your lordships see, subscribed gladly. Now, it may please your honourable wisdoms to signify your further pleasure, how he shall be demeaned: and thus committing your honourable estates to the protection of Almighty God, with the assurance of my service and prayers, I cease further to molest your honourable affairs.

At Lambeth, this 27th of August.

Your humble orator,

MATTH. C.

LIX.

THE LORDS OF THE COUNCIL TO ARCHBISHOP PARKER, ELECT.

28th August, 1559. Lambeth MS. 959. No. 38. Orig.

AFTER our right hearty commendations to your lordship. By your letters of the 27th of this month, we understand at good length your travail taken with Doctor Smyth, for the which we heartily thank you. And forasmuch as it appeareth unto us both by your said letters and by the said Smyth's own subscription also, that he is brought to good terms of conformity, we pray your lordship to take good bonds of him for his repair unto Oxford, and there to make open declaration of this his conformity in open presence before the visitors there, unto whom we have directed our letters for that purpose, to the end that by this means other may the rather be brought to follow the said Smyth's example. And so we bid your lordship right heartily well to fare. From Hampton Court, the 28th of August, 1559.

Your lordship's loving friends,

E. CLYNTON.   W. CECILL.
THO. PARRY.   N. WOTTON.

LX.

THE LORDS OF THE COUNCIL TO ARCHBISHOP PARKER, ELECT.

7th September, 1559. Parker MSS. C. C. Coll. Camb. CXIV. art. 22. p. 77. Orig.

AFTER our very hearty commendations to your good lordship. Where one Anthony Atkins, fellow of Merton College in Oxford, having been called before the visitors there, hath not only refused the service set forth, but also used such lewd language as we have thought meet to commit him for the same to the Tower, the particularities of which his misdemeanour shall appear to your lordship in a schedule sent unto you herewith; we have thought good to pray your lordship to send at such time as you shall think convenient for the said Atkins unto you (wherein we have already taken order with the lieutenant that he shall be brought before you when you shall call for him), and to use with him such persuasions as your lordship thinketh meet, to move him to be conformable, and also to understand of the lord chief justice (if the attorney and solicitor be not at London) what his offence weigheth unto in law. And what you shall do herein we pray your lordship to signify unto us[1]. And thus we bid your good lordship right heartily farewell. From Hampton Court, the 7th of September, 1559.

Your good lordship's assured loving friends,

W. NORTH.
THO. PARRY. G. ROGERS. F. KNOLLYS.
WILLIAM PETRE, S. N. WOTTON.

[1 In a list of "recusants which are abroad and bound to certain places," printed by Strype in his Annals of the Reformation, under the date 1561, there occurs "Anthony Atkins, clerk, late of Oxford, to remain within the counties of Gloucester and Salop:" and in the margin is added, "A learned priest, very wilful." Strype's Annals, Vol. I. Part I. p. 412. 8vo. Oxf. 1824.]

LXI.

SIR NICHOLAS BACON TO ARCHBISHOP PARKER, ELECT.

9th September, 1559. Parker MSS. C. C. Coll. Camb. cxiv. art. 40. p. 125. Orig.

Bacon sends Parker the royal assent to his election as Archbishop.

I SEND your grace the royal assent, sealed and delivered within two hours after the receipt thereof, wishing unto you as good success therein as ever happed to any that have received the like. And as to the prolonging of my return,

Away from the court Bacon is like a bird "scaped out of the cage."

it fares by me as it doth by a bird that hath scaped out of the cage, which tasting the sweetness of liberty never returns unforced. Thus with thanks for your letter I leave any further to trouble you.

9 Sept 1559.

From Redgrave, 9th September, 1559, by your grace's assuredly,

N. BACON.

LXII.

THE LORDS OF THE COUNCIL TO ARCHBISHOP PARKER, ELECT.

23rd September, 1559. Parker MSS. C. C. Coll. Camb. cxiv. art. 25. p. 81.

Mathewe, vicar of Howe, co Kent, committed to the Marshalsea.

AFTER our very hearty commendations to your good lordship. Whereas one Mathewe, vicar of Howe in Kent, was for certain disorders in that his parish, committed by us a good time past to the Marshalsea, we have thought good to pray your lordship to send for the said Mathewe unto

The Archbishop to send for him, and set him at liberty if he be conformable.

you, and if you shall find him a conformable man and meet to be returned to his cure, and sorry also for his former fault, then we pray your lordship to cause him to be set at liberty and sent home to his benefice: otherwise, if he shall appear unto your lordship one not meet to be at liberty, then we pray your lordship to send him back to the Marshalsea, and to signify unto us what you shall do herein. And thus we bid your lordship heartily farewell. From Hampton

23 Sept. 1559.

Court, the 23rd of September, 1559.

Your good lordship's loving friends,

W. NORTH.   ARUNDEL.   THO. PARRY.
G. ROGERS.   F. KNOLLYS.   W. CECILL.

To our very good lord the Archbishop of Canterbury, elect.

LXIII.

THE LORDS OF THE COUNCIL TO ARCHBISHOP PARKER, ELECT.

27th September, 1559. Parker MSS. C. C. Coll. Camb. CIX. art. 3. p. 61. Orig.

AFTER our right hearty commendations to your good lordship. We by the advice of Mr Almoner have sent unto you the Bishop of Durham[1], desiring you to appoint a fit chamber for him and one man to attend upon him in your house near unto you; so that (at times to you seeming convenient) you may have conference with him in certain points of religion wherein he is to be resolved. And during the time he shall remain with you, to have a vigilant eye that no man have access unto him, but yourself and such as you shall appoint; and that he have meat, drink and all things necessary as to him appertain: for the which you shall be assured to be satisfied with thanks. And thus most heartily fare you well. From Hampton Court, the 27th of September, 1559.

The Arch. bishop to receive Bishop Tonstal into his house under restraint.

27th Sept. 1559.

Your Lordship's assured loving friends,

E. CLYNTON.   W. HOWARD.
THO. PARRY.   G. ROGERS.   F. KNOLLYS.   W. CECILL.

To our very good lord the Archbishop of Canterbury, elect.

LXIV.

SIR W. CECIL TO ARCHBISHOP PARKER, ELECT.

2nd October, 1559. Parker MSS. C. C. Coll. Camb. CIX. art. 5. p. 67. Orig.

MY good Lord, the contents of your yesterday's letters I have imparted to her Majesty and others of her Majesty's council. It is much liked the comfort that ye give of the Bishop of Durham's towardness, wherein I pray God ye be

Hope of Tonstal's towardness.

[1 Cuthbert Tonstal. Strype says of him that he "died in the Archbishop's house at Lambeth in November following (i. e. in November 1560), being eighty-five years of age. But before his death, by the Archbishop's means he was brought off from papistical fancies." Strype's Parker, B. I. c. x. p 94.]

not deceived. It is meant, if he will conform himself, that both he shall remain bishop and in good favour and credit; otherwise he must needs receive the common order of those which refuse to obey laws. Good my Lord travel herein as ye may with speed. 2 October.

2nd Oct. 1559.

Yours assuredly,

W. CECILL.

To the most Reverend Father in God the
Archbishop of Canterbury, elect.

LXV.

SIR W. CECIL TO ARCHBISHOP PARKER, ELECT.

5th October, 1559. Parker MSS. C. C. Coll. Camb. cix. art. 4. p. 65. Orig.

Tonstal's pension to be proportioned to his conformity.

My good Lord, the Queen's Majesty is very sorry that ye can prevail no more with Mr Tonstal, and so am I, I assure you; for the recovery of such a man would have furthered the common affairs of this realm very much. Her Majesty would that he should have liberty to send to Durham for discharge of his household. And further ye may say to him that I trust her Majesty will be pleased to appoint him some convenient pension in consideration of his reverend age, which shall also be the larger as his conformity shall give occasion.

I mean to send Mr Almoner in the afternoon to you with a determination of the Queen's Majesty concerning some good order for the placing of all the bishops now void in the realm, and other like promotions ecclesiastical, now void and in her Majesty's disposition. Things be more untoward than I can suddenly rectify, but by hope of God's goodness I comfort myself. And so take my leave.

5th Oct. 1559.

From Westminster, the 5 of October, 1559.

Your Lordship's assured friend,

W. CECILL.

To the most Reverend Father in God the
Archbishop of Canterbury, elect.

LXVI.

ARCHBISHOP PARKER AND OTHERS TO QUEEN ELIZABETH.

1559. Parker MSS. C. C. Coll. Camb. cv. art. 11. p. 201. Copy.

To the Queen's most excellent Majesty.

We knowing your gracious clemency, and considering the necessity of the matter that we have to move, the one doth encourage us, and the other compel us (as before) to make our humble petition unto your highness, and to renew our former suit, not in any respect of selfwill, stoutness, or striving against your Majesty (God we take to witness); for with David we confess that we are but as *Canes mortui aut pulices* in comparison: but we do it only for that fear and reverence, which we bear to the Majesty of the Almighty God, in whose hands to fall it is horrible; for it lieth in his power to destroy for ever, and to cast both body and soul into hell-fire; and lest in giving just offence to the little ones, in setting a trap of error for the ignorant, and in digging a pit for the blind to fall into, we should not only be guilty of the blood of our brethren, and deserve the wrathful *væ* and vengeance of God, but also procure to our reclaiming consciences the biting worm that never dieth, for our endless confusion. For in what thing soever we may serve your excellent Majesty, not offending the Divine Majesty of God, we shall with all humble obedience be most ready thereunto, if it be even to the loss of our lives; for so God commandeth us, duty requireth of us, and we with all conformity have put in proof. And as God through your gracious government hath delivered unto us innumerable benefits, which we most humbly acknowledge, and with due reverence daily give him thanks, so we do not doubt but that of his mercy he will happily finish in your Majesty that good work, which of his free favour he hath most graciously begun; that following the worthy examples of the godly princes which have gone before, ye may clearly purge the polluted church, and remove all occasions of evil. And for so much as we have heretofore at sundry times made petition to your Majesty, concerning the matter of images, but at no time exhibited any reasons for the removing of the same;

The writers are encouraged by the Queen's clemency, and compelled by the necessity of the matter to renew a former suit.

They doubt not that, under God, her Majesty will "clearly purge the polluted Church."

They have heretofore made petition concerning the matter of Images:

now, lest we should seem to say much and prove little, to allege consciences without the warrant of God's word, and unreasonably require that, for the which we can give no reason, we have at this time put in writing, and do most humbly exhibit to your gracious consideration those authorities of the Scriptures, reasons, and pithy persuasions, which as they have moved all such our brethren, as now bear the office of bishops, to think and affirm images not expedient for the church of Christ, so will they not suffer us, without the great offending of God, and grievous wounding of our own consciences (which God deliver us from), to consent to the erecting or retaining of the same in the place of worshipping. And we trust and most earnestly ask it of God, that they may also persuade your Majesty, by your regal authority, and in the zeal of God, utterly to remove this offensive evil out of the Church of England, to God's great glory, and our great comfort.

but without giving reasons for their removal, which they now adduce

REASONS AGAINST IMAGES IN CHURCHES.

Certain reasons which move us that we cannot with safe consciences give our assents that the images of Christ, &c. should be placed and erected in churches.

The words of the commandment

First, the words of the commandment, "Thou shalt not make to thyself any graven image[1]," &c. Exodi xx. And the same is repeated more plainly, Deuteron. xxvii., *Maledictus homo qui facit sculptile et conflatile etc. ponitque illud in abscondito. Et dicet omnis populus Amen*[2].

In the first place these words are to be noted, Thou shalt not make to thyself, that is, to any use of religion.

In the latter place these words, And setteth it in a secret place, for no man durst then commit idolatry openly.

So that, conferring the places, it doth evidently appear, that images both for use of religion and in place of peril for idolatry are forbidden.

God, knowing the inclination of man to idolatry, sheweth the reason why he made this general prohibition: *Ne forte errore deceptus adores ea et colas.*

This general law is generally to be observed, notwithstanding that peradventure a great number can not be hurt by them; which may appear by the example following.

[1] Exod. xx.   [2] Deut. xxvii.

The viith of Deuteron. God forbad the people to join their children in marriage with strangers, adding the reason, *Quia seducet filium tuum ne sequatur me*[3].

Moses was not deceived by Jethro's daughter, nor Booz by Ruth being a woman of Moab.

And yet for all that the general law was to be observed, "Thou shalt join no marriages with them." And so likewise, "Thou shalt not make to thyself any graven image, &c."

The ivth of Deuteronomy God giveth a special charge to avoid images, where it is written, "Beware that thou forget not the covenant of the Lord thy God which he made with thee, and so make to thyself any graven image of any thing which the Lord hath forbidden thee. For the Lord thy God is a consuming fire, and a jealous God. If thou have children and nephews, and do tarry in the land, and being deceived do make to yourselves any graven image, doing evil before the Lord your God, and provoke him to anger; I do this day call heaven and earth to witness that ye shall quickly perish out of the land which ye shall possess. Ye shall not dwell in it any long time, but the Lord will destroy you, and scatter you amongst all nations[4]," &c.

Note what solemn obtestations God useth, and what grievous punishments he threateneth to the breakers of the second commandment.

In the tabernacle and temple of God no image was by God appointed openly to be set, nor by practice afterward used or permitted, so long as religion was purely observed. So that the use and execution of the law is a good interpreter of the true meaning of the same.

If by virtue of the second commandment images were not lawful in the temple of the Jews[5], then by the same commandment they are not lawful in the churches of the Christians. For being a moral commandment, and not ceremonial, (for by consent of writers only a part of the precept of observing the Sabbath is ceremonial) it is a perpetual commandment, and bindeth us as well as the Jews.

The Jews by no means would consent to Herod, Pilate, or Petronius, that images should be placed in the temple at Hierusalem, but rather offered themselves to the death than

The Jews would rather die than assent unto images being placed in the temple.

---

[3] Deut. vii. [4].   [4] Deut. iv. [23—27].   [5] Exod. xx. [4].

[PARK. COR.]

to assent unto it[1]: who, besides that they are commended of Josephus for observing the meaning of the law, would not have endangered themselves so far if they had thought images had been indifferent in the temple of God; for, as St Paul saith, *Quid templo Dei cum simulacris*[2]*?*

God's Scripture against the use of images.
God's Scripture doth in no place commend the use of images, but in a great number of places doth disallow and condemn them.

Testimonies of the book of Wisdom.
They are called in the book of Wisdom the trap and snare of the feet of the ignorant[3].

It is said the invention of them was the beginning of spiritual fornication; and that they were not from the beginning, neither shall they continue to the end[4].

In the xvth chapter it is said, *Umbra picturœ labor*

[1] Joseph. Antiquit. Lib. XVII. cap. 8.; Lib. XVIII. cap. 5. et 15. ["κατεσκεύακεν δὲ ὁ βασιλεὺς ['Ηρώδης] ὑπὲρ τοῦ πυλῶνος τοῦ μεγάλου τοῦ ναοῦ ἀνάθημα καὶ λίαν πολυτελὲς, ἀετὸν χρύσεον μέγαν. κωλύει δὲ ὁ νόμος εἰκόνων τε ἀναστάσεις ἐπινοεῖν καί τινων ζώων ἀναθέσεις ἐπιτηδεύεσθαι τοῖς βιοῦν κατ' αὐτὸν προῃρημένοις. 'ὥστε ἐκέλευον οἱ σοφισταὶ τὸν ἀετὸν κατασπᾶν· καὶ γὰρ εἴ τις ἂν γένοιτο κίνδυνος τῷ εἰς θάνατον ἀνακειμένῳ, πολὺ τῆς ἐν τῷ ζῆν ἡδονῆς λυσιτελεστέραν φαίνεσθαι τὴν προτεθειμένην ἀρετὴν ὑπ' αὐτοῦ, τοῖς ἐπὶ σωτηρίᾳ καὶ φυλακῇ τοῦ πατρίου μελλήσουσι τελευτᾶν, διὰ τὸ ἀΐδιον τοῦ ἐπαινεῖσθαι φήμην κατασκευασαμένους ἔν τε τοῖς νῦν ἐπαινεθήσεσθαι καὶ τοῖς ἐσομένοις ἀειμνημόνευτον καταλιπεῖν τὸν βίον.'"
—Flavii Josephi Antiq. Jud. Lib. XVII. cap. 6. Tom. I. p. 843. ed. Havercampi, 1726.

"Πιλάτος δὲ . . . ἐπὶ καταλύσει τῶν νόμων τῶν 'Ιουδαϊκῶν, εἰσέφρησε προτομὰς Καίσαρος, αἳ ταῖς σημαίαις προσῆσαν, εἰσαγόμενος εἰς τὴν πόλιν, εἰκόνων ποίησιν ἀπαγορεύοντος ἡμῖν τοῦ νόμου . . . . οἱ δὲ ['Ιουδαῖοι] ἐπεὶ ἔγνωσαν, κατὰ πληθὺν παρῆσαν εἰς Καισάρειαν, ἱκετείαν ποιούμενοι ἐπὶ πολλὰς ἡμέρας, ἐπὶ μεταθέσει τῶν εἰκόνων . . . . πάλιν δὲ τῶν 'Ιουδαίων ἱκετείᾳ χρωμένων, ἀπὸ συνθήματος περιστήσας τοὺς στρατιώτας, ἠπείλει θάνατον ἐπιθήσειν ζημίαν ἐκ τοῦ ὀξέως, εἰ μὴ παυσάμενοι θορυβεῖν ἐπὶ τὰ οἰκεῖα ἀπίοιεν. οἱ δὲ πρηνεῖς ῥίψαντες ἑαυτοὺς, καὶ γυμνοῦντες τὰς σφαγὰς, ἡδονῇ δέξεσθαι τὸν θάνατον ἔλεγον, ἢ τολμήσειν τὴν σοφίαν παραβήσεσθαι τῶν νόμων, κ.τ.λ."—Ib. Lib. XVIII. cap. 3, pp. 875, 6.

"Πάντάπασι δὲ ὀλίγου χρόνου διελθόντος, Δωρῖται νεανίσκοι... Καίσαρος ἀνδριάντα κομίσαντες εἰς τὴν τῶν 'Ιουδαίων συναγωγὴν ἀνέστησαν. τοῦτο σφόδρα τὸν 'Αγρίππαν παρώξυνε, κατάλυσιν γὰρ τῶν πατρίων αὐτοῦ νόμων ἐδύνατο, ἀμελλητὶ δὴ πρὸς Πούπλιον Πετρώνιον, ἡγεμὼν δὲ τῆς Συρίας οὗτος ἦν, παραγίνεται, καὶ καταλέγει τῶν Δωριτῶν. ὁ δὲ οὐκ ἧττον ἐπὶ τῷ πραχθέντι χαλεπήνας, καὶ γὰρ αὐτὸς ἔκρινεν ἀσέβειαν τὴν τῶν ἐννόμων παράβασιν, τοῖς ἀποστᾶσι τῶν Δωριτῶν σὺν ὀργῇ τοῦτο ἔγραψε, κ.τ.έ."—Ib. Lib. XIX. cap. 6. p. 946.]

[2] 2 Cor. vi. [16].   [3] Sap. xiv. [11].   [4 Ib. xiv. 12, 13.]

sine fructu[5]. Item: "They are worthy of death, both that put their trust in them, and that make them, and that love them, and that worship them[6]."

The Psalms and Prophets are full of like sentences. *Of the Psalms and Prophets.*

And how can we then praise the thing which God's Spirit doth always dispraise?

Furthermore, an image made by a father (as appeareth in the same place) for the memorial of his son departed, was the first invention of images and occasion of idolatry[7]. *The first invention of images and occasion of idolatry.*

How much more then shall an image made in the memory of Christ, and set up in the place of religion, occasion the same offence?

Images have their origin and beginning from the heathen, and of no good ground[8]. Therefore they can not be profitable to Christians. Whereunto Athanasius agreeth, writing of images against the Gentiles, thus: ἡ τῶν εἰδώλων εὕρεσις οὐκ ἀπ' ἀγαθοῦ ἀλλ' ἀπὸ κακίας γέγονε, τὸ δὲ τὴν ἀρχὴν ἔχον κακὴν ἐν οὐδενί ποτε καλὸν κριθείη, ὅλον ὂν φαῦλον[9]. *Images have their origin from the heathen, and therefore can not be profitable to Christians.*

St John saith[10]: "My little children, beware of images." But to set them in churches, which are places dedicated to the service and invocation of God, and that over the Lord's table, being the highest and most honourable place, where most danger of abuse both is and ever hath been, is not to beware of them or to fly from them, but rather to embrace and receive them. *Saint John saith, Beware of them: but to set them in churches, and over the Lord's table, is not to beware of them.*

Tertullian, expounding the same words, writeth thus; *Filioli*, [inquit,] *custodite vos ab idolis. Non jam ab idololatria, quasi ab officio, sed ab idolis, id est, ab ipsa effigie eorum*[11]. *Tertullian on St John's words.*

Images in the church either serve to edify or to destroy: if they edify, then is there one kind of edification which the *Images in the church either edify or destroy.*

---

[5] Sap. xv. [4.]

[6 The words of Wisd. xv. 6 are: "Both they that make them, they that desire them, and they that worship them, are lovers of evil things, and are worthy to have such things to trust upon."]

[7] Sap. xiv. [15.]

[8] Euseb. Ecclesiast. Histor. Lib. VII. cap. 18. [ὡς εἰκὸς τῶν παλαιῶν ἀπαραφυλάκτως οἷα σωτῆρας ἐθνικῇ συνηθείᾳ παρ' ἑαυτοῖς τοῦτον τιμᾶν εἰωθότων τὸν τρόπον.—Euseb. Hist. Paris. 1659. Tom. I. p. 265.]

[9] Athanas. contra Gentes. [Op. Tom. I. p. 8 c. Paris. 1627.]

[10] 1 John v. [21].

[11] Tertull. de Corona Milit. [Opp. fo. Basil. 1528, p. 465.]

Scriptures neither teach nor commend, but always disallow: if they destroy, they are not to be used; for in the church all things ought to be done to edify[1].

A stumblingblock ought not to be laid before the blind, that is, the simple and unlearned people.

The commandment of God is: "Thou shalt not lay a stumblingblock or stone before the blind[2]."

And, "Cursed is he that maketh the blind wander in his way[3]." The simple and unlearned people, who have been so long under blind guides, are blind in matters of religion, and inclined to error and idolatry. Therefore to set images before them to stumble at[4], or to lead them out of the true way, is not only against the commandment of God, but deserveth also the malediction and curse of God.

The use of images is to the learned and confirmed in knowledge neither necessary nor profitable; to the superstitious, a confirmation in error; to the simple and weak, an occasion of fall, and very offensive and wounding of their consciences: and therefore very dangerous.

For saith St Paul: "Offending your brethren, and wounding their weak consciences, ye sin against Christ[5]." And, "woe be to him by whom offence or occasion of fall cometh. It were better that a millstone were tied about his neck, and he cast into the sea, than to offend one of the little ones that believe in Christ[6]."

An answer to the objection, that the offence may be taken away by sincere doctrine and preaching.

And where objection may be made that such offence may be taken away by sincere doctrine and preaching; it is to be answered, that that is not sufficient, as hereafter more at large shall be declared. And though it should be admitted as true, yet should it follow that sincere doctrine and preaching should always, and in all places, continue as well as images. And so, that wheresoever an image to offence were erected, there should also of reason a godly and sincere preacher be continually maintained: for it is reason that the remedy be as large as is the offence, the medicine as general as the poison. But that is not possible in the realm of England, if images should generally be allowed; as reason and experience may teach.

An argument from the custom of good magistrates.

As good magistrates, which intend to banish all whoredom, do drive away all naughty persons, especially out of such

---

[1] 1 Cor. xiv. [26].   [2] Levitic. xix. [14].   [3] Deut. xxvii. [18].
[4] Sap. xiv. [11]. Muscipulæ pedibus insipientium.
[5] 1 Cor. viii. [12].   [6] Matt. xviii. [6].

places as be suspected; even so images being *meretrices*, for that the worshipping of them is called in the prophets fornication and adultery, ought to be banished, and especially out of churches, which is the most suspected place, and where the spiritual fornication hath been most committed.

It is not expedient to allow and admit the thing which is hurtful to the greatest number. But in all churches and commonwealths, the ignorant and weak are the greatest number, to whom images are hurtful and not profitable.

And where it is commonly alleged that images in churches do stir up the mind to devotion, it may be answered that, contrariwise, they do rather distract the mind from prayer, hearing of God's word, and other godly meditations; as we read that in the council-chamber of the Lacedæmonians no picture or image was suffered, lest, in consultation of weighty matters for the common weal, their minds, by the sight of the outward image, might be occasioned to be withdrawn, or to wander from the matter.

The experience also of this present time doth declare that those parts of the realm which think, and are persuaded, that God is not offended by doing outward reverence to an image, do most desire the restitution of images, and have been most diligent to set them up again. Restitution therefore of them by common authority shall confirm them more in their error, to the danger of their souls, than ever they were before; for as one man writeth: *Nihil magis est certum quam quod ex dubio factum est certum.*

The profit of images is uncertain, the peril by experience of all ages and states of the church (as afore) is most certain. The benefit to be taken of them (if there be any) is very small. The danger ensuing of them, which is the danger of idolatry, is the greatest of all other.

Now to allow a most certain peril for an uncertain profit, and the greatest danger for the smallest benefit in matters of faith and religion, is a tempting of God, and a grievous offence.

PROOFS OUT OF THE FATHERS, COUNCILS AND HISTORIES.

First, it is manifest that in the primitive Church images were not commonly used in churches, oratories, and places of assembly for religion, but they were generally detested and abhorred, insomuch that the want of imagery was objected to the Christians for a crime.

Origen.	Origen reporteth that Celsus objected the lack of images[1].
Arnobius.	Arnobius saith also that the Ethnics accused the Christians that they had neither altars nor images[2].
Zephyrus.	Zephyrus, in his commentary upon the Apology of Tertullian, gathereth thus of Tertullian's words: *Qui locus persuadendi frigeret penitus, nisi perpetuo illud teneamus, Christianos tunc temporis odisse maxime statuas cum suis ornamentis, etc.*[3]
Irenæus.	Irenæus[4] reproveth the heretics called Gnostici, for that they carried about the image of Christ made in Pilate's time after his own proportion (which was much more to be esteemed than any that can be made now), using also, for declaration of their affection towards it, to set garlands upon the head of it.
Lactantius.	Lactantius affirmeth plainly, *Quod non est dubium quin religio nulla sit, ubicunque simulachrum est*[5]. If Christians had then used images, he would not have made his proposition so large.
Augustine.	Saint Augustine commendeth Varro the Roman in these words: *Quum Varro existimaverit castius sine simulachris*

[1] Contra Celsum, Lib. IV. [The following is perhaps the passage referred to: "Μετὰ ταῦτα δὲ ὁ Κέλσος φησὶν ἡμᾶς βωμοὺς καὶ ἀγάλματα καὶ νεὼς ἱδρύσθαι φεύγειν."—Contra Cels. Lib. VIII. c. 17. In Lib. VII. c. 62, these words of Celsus in reference to the Christians are quoted: "οὐκ ἀνέχονται νεὼς ὁρῶντες καὶ βωμοὺς καὶ ἀγάλματα." Opp. studio Carol. Delarue, Paris. 1733, Vol. I. pp. 755, 738.]

[2 In hac enim consuestis parte crimen nobis maximum impietatis affigere, quod neque ædes sacras venerationis ad officia construamus, non Deorum alicujus simulachrum constituamus, aut formam: non altaria fabricemus, non aras, &c.—Arnob. Disput. adv. Gentes, Lib. Sextus, ad init. libr., p. 189. Lugd. Batav. 1651.]

[3 The precise words of Zephyrus are, "Qui locus persuadendi frigeret penitus hoc tempore (quanquam ex abundantia hæc ad plebem dicta sunt) nisi perpetuo illud teneamus, Christianos tunc temporis odisse maximo statuas cum suis ornamentis, et in fundendis precibus quemlibet sibi angulum ut in cœlum suspicerent satis esse putasse." Tertulliani Opera. Paris. 1566. 8vo. Vol. II. p. 674.]

[4] Lib. I. cap. 24. [Gnosticos se autem vocant: etiam imagines quasdam quidem depictas, quasdam autem et de reliqua materia fabricatas habent, dicentes formam Christi factam a Pilato, illo in tempore quo fuit Jesus cum hominibus. Et has coronant, et proponunt eas cum imaginibus mundi philosophorum, &c.—Iren. adv. Hæres. Lib. I. cap. 24., sub fin., cap. p. 102. Oxf. 1702.]

[5] Divin. Institut. Lib. II. cap. 19. [cap. 18. Vol. I. p. 229. Lugd. Batav. 1660.]

*observari religionem, quis non videt quantum appropinquaverit veritati*⁶? So that not only by M. Varro's judgment but also by St Augustine's approbation, the most pure and chaste observation of religion, and nearest the truth, is to be without images. The same St Augustine in another place hath these words: *Plus valent simulachra ad curvandam infelicem animam quam ad docendam*⁷.

Ibid.

And upon the same psalm he moveth this question: *Quivis puer imo quævis bestia scit non esse Deum quod videt, Cur ergo spiritus sanctus toties monet cavendum quod omnes sciunt?*

Saint Augustine answereth: *Quoniam quum ponuntur in templis et semel incipiunt adorari a multitudine, statim nascitur sordidissimus affectus erroris*⁸. This place of St Augustine doth well open how weak a reason it is to say, Images are a thing indifferent in chambers, *ergo* in churches. For the alteration of the place, manner, and other circumstances, doth alter oftentimes the nature of the thing. It is lawful to buy and sell in the market, but not so in churches. It is lawful to eat and drink, but not in churches. And therefore

The alteration of the place, manner, and other circumstances, doth alter oftentimes the nature of the thing.

---

⁶ De Civit. Dei, Lib. IV. cap. 31. [Quapropter cum solos dicit [Varro] animadvertisse, quid esset Deus, qui eum crederent animam mundum gubernantem; castiusque existimat sine simulachris observari religionem, quis non videat quantum propinquaverit veritati?— Tom. v. p. 39 H. Paris. 1541.]

⁷ In Psal. cxiii. [Plus enim valent simulacra ad curvandam infelicem animam quod os habent, oculos habent, aures habent, nares habent, manus habent, pedes habent, quam ad corrigendam quod non loquentur, non videbunt, non audient, non odorabunt, non contrectabunt, non ambulabunt.—Tom. VIII. p. 285 E.]

[⁸ Quis puer interrogatus non hoc certum esse respondeat, quod simulachra gentium os habent et non loquentur, oculos habent et non videbunt, et cætera quæ divinus sermo contexuit? Cur ergo tantopere spiritus sanctus curat scripturarum plurimis locis hæc insinuare atque inculcare veluti inscientibus, quasi non hominibus apertissima sint atque notissima, nisi quia per speciem membrorum significat quam naturaliter in animantibus viventem videre, atque in nobis ipsis sentire consuevimus? Quanquam ut illi asserunt in signo aliquo fabrefacto atque eminenti collocato suggestu, cum adorari atque honorari a multitudine cœperit, parit in unoquoque sordidissimum erroris affectum, ut quoniam in illo figmento non invenit vitalem motum, credet numen occultum, effigiem tamen viventi corpori similem, seductus forma, et commotus authoritate quasi sapientium institutorum obsequentiumque turbarum, sine vivo aliquo habitatore esse non putat.—Tom. VIII. p. 285 A, B.]

saith St Paul: *An non habetis domos ad edendum ac biben-
dum? An ecclesiam Dei contemnitis*[1]*?* etc.

Many other actions there be which are lawful and honest
in private place, which are neither comely nor honest not only
in churches, but also in other assemblies of honest people.

Tertullian.   Tertullian saith he used sometimes to burn frankincense
in his chamber which was then used of idolaters, and is yet
in the Romish churches; but he joineth withal: *Sed non
eodem ritu, nec eodem habitu, nec eodem apparatu, quo agitur apud idola*[2]. So that images placed in churches and set
in honorabili sublimitate, as Saint Augustine saith, and
especially over the Lord's table, which is done, using the
words of Tertullian, *eodem ritu et eodem habitu*, which the
Papists did use, especially after so long continuance of
abuse of images, and so many being blinded with superstitious opinion towards them, can not be counted a thing indifferent, but a most certain ruin of many souls.

Epiphanius.   Epiphanius, in his Epistle to John Bishop of Hierusalem,
which epistle was translated out of the Greek by St Hierom,
being a likelihood that St Hierom misliked not the doctrine
of the same, doth write a fact of his own which doth most
clearly declare the judgment of that notable learned bishop
concerning use of images in churches. His words are
these: *Quum venissem ad villam quæ dicitur Anablatha, vi-
dissemque ibi præteriens lucernam ardentem, et interrogassem
quis locus esset, didicissemque esse ecclesiam et intrassem
ut orarem: inveni ibi velum pendens in foribus ejusdem
ecclesiæ tinctum atque depictum et habens imaginem quasi
Christi vel sancti cujusdam. Non enim satis memini cujus
imago fuerit. Quum ergo hoc vidissem, in Ecclesia Christi
contra authoritatem Scripturarum hominis pendere imaginem, scidi illud, et magis dedi consilium custodibus ejusdem loci ut pauperem mortuum eo obvolverent et efferrent,
etc.* Et paulo post: *Nunc autem misi quod potui reperire,
et precor ut jubeas presbyteros ejusdem loci suscipere velum
a latore quod a nobis missum est, et deinceps præcipere in
Ecclesia Christi istiusmodi vela, quæ contra religionem
nostram veniunt, non appendi. Decet enim honestatem*

---

[1] 1 Cor. xi. [22].

[2] De Coron. Milit. ["si me odor alicujus loci offenderit, Arabiæ
aliquid incendo, sed non eodem ritu, nec eodem habitu, nec eodem
apparatu, quo agitur apud idola." Opp. fo. Basil. 1528, p. 465.]

*tuam hanc magis habere solicitudinem, ut scrupulositatem tollat quæ indigna est Ecclesia Christi et populis qui tibi crediti sunt, etc.*³

Out of this place of Epiphanius divers notes are to be observed.

1. First, that by the judgment of this ancient father to permit images in churches is against the authority of the Scriptures, meaning against the Second Commandment: Thou shalt not make to thyself any graven image, etc.

[margin: Notes to be observed out of the above place of Epiphanius.]

2. Secondly, that Epiphanius doth reject not only graven and molten, but also painted images: forsomuch as he cutteth in pieces the image painted in a vail hanging at the church-door, what would he have done if he had found it over the Lord's table?

3. Thirdly, that he spareth not the image of Christ, for no doubt that image is most perilous in the church of all other.

4. Fourthly, that he did not only remove it, but with a vehemency of zeal cut it in pieces, following the example of the good king Ezechias, who brake the brazen serpent and burnt it to ashes.

5. Last of all, that Epiphanius thinketh it the duty of vigilant bishops to be careful that no such kind of painted images be permitted in the Church.

Serenus, Bishop of Massilia, broke down images and destroyed them when he did see them begin to be worshipped.

Gregory the First permitted images to be had, but with all earnestness did forbid them to be worshipped⁴.

Experience of the times since hath declared whether of these two sentences were better. For since Gregory's time,

[margin: Gregory the first.]

---

³ Epiphanius in epist. ad Jōhan. Episcopum Hierosolymit. [ad fin. epist., Opp. p. 631. Basil. 1542. "Præterea quod audivi quosdam murmurare contra me, quia quando simul pergebamus ad sanctum locum, qui vocatur Bethel, ut ibi collectam tecum ex more ecclesiastico facerem, et venissem ad villam, &c."]

⁴ Gregor. in registro Epist. [fol. ccccxiv. lib. vii. epist.] 109 [Paris. 1521. The title of the letter is: "Gregorius Sereno episcopo Masilinen. De imaginibus in ecclesiis non constringendis." The passage referred to is: "Præterea indico dudum ad nos pervenisse quod fraternitas vestra quosdam imaginum adoratores aspiciens, easdem ecclesiæ imagines confregit atque projecit: et quidem zelum vos ne quid manu factum adorari possit habuisse laudavimus; sed frangere easdem imagines non debuisse judicamus..... Tua ergo fraternitas et ea[s] servare, et ab earum adoratu populum prohibere debuit."]

the images standing, the West Church hath been overflowed with idolatry notwithstanding his doctrine. Whereas if Serenus's judgment had universally taken place, no such thing had happened. For if no images had been suffered, none could have been worshipped, and consequently no idolatry committed by them.

Histories and councils.

To recite the process of histories and councils about the matter of images would require a long discourse: it shall be here sufficient briefly to touch a few.

The East Church condemned and abolished images.

It is manifest to them that read histories that not only emperors, but also divers and sundry councils in the East Church, have condemned and abolished images both by decrees and example.

Valens and Theodosius.

Petrus Crinitus De Honesta Disciplina, libro IX.º ca. 9º, ex libris Augustalibus hæc verba transcripsit. *Valens et Theodosius Augusti Imperatores præfecto prætorio ad hunc modum scripsere. Quum sit nobis cura diligens in rebus omnibus superni numinis religionem tueri, signum Salvatoris Christi nemini quidem concedimus coloribus, lapide, aliave materia fingere insculpere aut pingere, sed quocunque reperitur loco tolli jubemus : gravissima pœna eos mulctando qui contrarium decretis nostris et Imperio quicquam tentaverint*[1].

Leo the third.

Leo the Third, a man commended in histories for his excellent virtues and godliness, who (as is judged of some men) was the author of the book *De re militari*, being translated out of the Greek by Sir John Cheke, and dedicated to your most noble father, by public authority commanded abolishing of images, and in Constantinople caused all the images to be gathered together on a heap, and burned them to ashes[2].

[1 "Sed libitum est verba ex libris Augustalibus referre: quo id totum melius innotescat, quoniam et Valens, &c." Fol. Paris, 1520. Lugd. 1585, pp. 278, 9.]

[2 Goldastus in his work entitled Imperialia Decreta de Cultu Imaginum (Franc. 1608, pp. 16—18) gives the following extracts from Leo's decree, published at Constantinople, A D. 726. "Joannes Damascenus in actis Stephani et sociorum ejus hæc ex edicto refert: Cum ad decimum jam Imperii annum Leo Isauricus Imperator pervenisset, accita et coacta Senatorum classe, absurdum illud et impium evomuit: *Imaginum picturas formam quamdam idolorum retinere,* inquiens, *neque iis cultum adhibendum esse, ne alioqui Dei loco imprudentes idola veneremur.* Et paulo post hæc ipsius Edicti verba: *Non autem huc spectat mea sententia, ut eæ prorsus deleantur, sed hoc aio, sublimiore loco eas collocandas esse, ne ore quisquam eas contingat, atque ita quo-*

Constantine the Fifth, his son, assembled a council of the bishops of the East Church, in which council it was decreed as followeth: "It is not lawful for them that believe in God through Jesus Christ to have any images, neither of the Creator nor of any creatures, set up in temples to be worshipped, but rather that all images by the law of God, and for the avoiding of offence, ought to be taken out of churches[3]."

Which decree was executed in all places where any images were, either in Greece or in Asia.

But in all these times the bishops of Rome, rather maintaining the authority of Gregory, than weighing, like Christian bishops, the peril of the church, always in their assemblies allowed images. And no marvel, for soon after Gregory's days they aspired to that supremacy which Gregory himself calleth antichristian, and therefore must needs defend the proposition then which they hold now, that the Church of Rome could not err.

Not long after, the bishops of Rome, practising with

dammodo rebus honore dignis contumeliam inferat." Goldastus subjoins several testimonies to the effect that Leo caused images to be burned. The following is one: "Regino Prumiensis Chronic. Lib. I. Anno DCLV. Leo Augustus ad pejora progressus est; ita ut compelleret omnes Constantinopolim habitantes, tam vi quam blandimentis, Sanctorum imagines deponere, et quascunque invenire potuit, in media civitate concremavit."]

[3 This Council was held at Constantinople in the year 754. "Its Acts and deliberations have all perished, or rather been destroyed by the patrons of image-worship; except so much of them as the Second Nicene Council saw fit to quote for the purpose of confuting them in their sixth Act." (Soames's Mosheim, Vol. II. p. 156, note.) The exact words above-cited have not been met with in the 6th Act of the Second Nicene Council, but the following quotations of the decrees of the Constantinopolitan Council taken from that Act are similar in substance: "ἅπαντες ἡμεῖς οἱ τὸ τῆς ἱερωσύνης ἀξίωμα περικείμενοι, ὁμοφώνως ὁρίζομεν, ἀπόβλητον εἶναι καὶ ἀλλοτρίαν καὶ ἐβδελυγμένην ἐκ τῆς τῶν Χριστιανῶν ἐκκλησίας πᾶσαν εἰκόνα ἐκ παντοίας ὕλης καὶ χρωματουργικῆς τῶν ζωγράφων κακοτεχνίας πεποιημένην." "Μηκέτι τολμᾶν ἄνθρωπον τὸν οἰονδήποτε ἐπιτηδεύειν τὸ τοιοῦτον ἀσεβὲς καὶ ἀνόσιον ἐπιτήδευμα. ὁ δὲ τολμῶν ἀπὸ τοῦ παρόντος κατασκευάσαι εἰκόνα, ἢ προσκυνῆσαι, ἢ στῆσαι ἐν ἐκκλησίᾳ, ἢ ἐν ἰδιωτικῷ οἴκῳ, ἢ κρύψαι, εἰ μὲν ἐπίσκοπος, ἢ πρεσβύτερος, ἢ διάκονος εἶεν, καθαιρείσθω· εἰ δὲ μονάζων ἢ λαϊκὸς, ἀναθεματιζέσθω, καὶ τοῖς βασιλικοῖς νόμοις ὑπεύθυνος ἔστω, ὡς ἐναντίως τῶν τοῦ Θεοῦ πραγμάτων, καὶ ἐχθρὸς τῶν πατρικῶν δογμάτων."—Harduin. Coll. Concil. Tom. IV. pp. 415, 417, Paris, 1714. See also Goldastus Imp. Decr. de cult. Imag. pp. 43, 44]

The second Nicene Council.

Thirasius, patriarch of Constantinople, obtained of Irene the empress (her son Constantine being then young), that a council was called at Nico, in the which the Pope's legates were presidents; which appeared well by the fruits. For in that council it was decreed that images should not only be permitted in churches, but also worshipped[1]. Which council was confuted by a book written by Carolus Magnus the emperor, the book yet being extant, calling it a foolish and an arrogant council[2].

Soon after this council arose a sharp contention between Irene the empress and her son Constantine, the emperor, who destroyed images. And in the end, as she had afore wickedly burned the bones of her father-in-law, Constantine the Vth, so afterwards unnaturally she put out the eyes of her own son Constantine the VIth.

About which time, as Eutropius writeth, the sun was darkened most terribly for the space of seventeen days, God shewing by that dreadful sign how much he misliked those kind of proceedings[3].

Never thing made more division or mischief in the church than the controversy about images.

To be short, there was never thing that made more division or brought more mischief into the church than the

[1] Concil. gen. To. 2. [Harduini Collectio Concil. Tom. IV. pp. 1—525. " Credentes in unum Deum in Trinitate collaudatum, honorabiles ejus imagines salutamus. Qui sic non habent, anathema sint ......Nos venerandas imagines recipimus. Nos qui non ita sentiunt anathemati subjicimus. His qui accipiunt sacræ scripturæ dicta adversus idola in venerandas imagines, anathema. Ei qui non salutat sanctas imagines, anathema, &c."—Tom. IV. p. 483. Paris, 1714.]

[2 The following is the Title of the book referred to: Opus inlustrissimi et excellentissimi seu spectabilis viri, Caroli Magni, nutu Dei, regis Francorum, Gallias, Germaniam, Italiamque, sive harum finitimas provincias domino opitulante regentis, contra Synodum, quæ in partibus Græciæ, pro adorandis imaginibus stolide sive arroganter gesta est. Item, Paulini Aquileiensis Episcopi adversus Felicem Urgelitanum et Eliphandum Toletanum Episcopos libellus. Quæ nunc primum in lucem restituuntur. Anno salutis M.DXLIX. 8vo. Supposed to have been printed at Paris by Bernard Torresano. The words "stolide sive arroganter" on this title-page are probably alluded to in the text.]

[3] Lib. de Rep. Rom. 23. ["Obtenebratus est autem sol per dies septendecim. Et non dedit radios suos, ita ut errarent naves maris, omnesque dicerent, quod propter obcæcationem Imperatoris sol obcæcatus suos radios retraxerit."—Eutropii Insigne volumen, quo Rom. Hist. Univ. describitur, &c., Lib. XXIII. p. 333. Basil, 1532]

controversy of images. By reason whereof not only the East Church was divided from the West, and never since perfectly reconciled, but also the empire was cut asunder and divided, and the gate opened to the Saracens and Turks to enter and overrun a great piece of Christendom.

The fault whereof most justly is to be ascribed to those patrons of images who could not be contented with the example of the primitive Church, being most simple, and sincere, and most agreeable to the Scripture, (for, as Tertullian saith, *Quod primum, verum; quod posterius, adulterinum*[4],) but with all extremity maintained the use of images in churches, whereof no profit or commodity did ever grow to the Church of God. For it is evident that infinite millions of souls have been cast into eternal damnation by the occasion of images used in places of religion. And no history can record that ever any one soul was won unto Christ by having of images.

To whom the fault is to be ascribed.

But lest it might appear that the West Church had always generally retained and commended images, it is to be noted that in a council holden in Spain, called *Concilium Eliberinum*, the use of images in churches was clearly prohibited in this form of words: *Placuit in Ecclesiis picturas esse non debere, ne quod colitur aut adoratur, in parietibus depingatur*[5].

The West Church has not always commended images.

But this notwithstanding, experience hath declared that neither assembling in councils, neither writings, preachings, decrees, making of laws, prescribing of punishments, hath holpen again[st] images to the which idolatry hath been committed, nor against idolatry whiles images stood. For these blind books and dumb schoolmasters (which they call laymen's books) have more prevailed by their carved and painted preaching of idolatry, than all other written books and preachings in teaching the truth and the horror of that vice.

Blind books and dumb schoolmasters prevail more than written books and preachings.

Having thus declared unto your Highness a few causes of many, which do move our consciences in this matter, we beseech your Highness most humbly not to strain us any further.

They beseech the Queen not to strain them any further.

---

[4] Contra Praxeam. [Opp. Tertull. fo. Basil, 1528, p. 418. The exact words are, " Quo peræque adversus universas hæreses jam hinc præjudicatum sit, id esse verum quodcunque primum: id esse adulterum quodcunque posterius."]

[5] Concil. Gen. To. 2. [Concil. Eliberit. in Concil. Stud. Labbei. Lut. Par. 1671—2, can. xxxvi. Tom. I. col. 974.]

further; but to consider, that God's word doth threaten a terrible judgment unto us, if we, being pastors and ministers in his Church, should assent to the thing which in our learning and conscience we are persuaded doth tend to the confirmation of error, superstition, and idolatry, and finally, to the ruin of the souls committed to our charge, for the which we must give an accompt to the Prince of pastors at the last day[1]. We pray your Majesty also not to be offended with this our plainness, and liberty, which all good and Christian princes have ever taken in good part at the hands of godly bishops.

nor to be offended with their plainness of speech:

Saint Ambrose writing to Theodosius the emperor, useth these words: *Sed neque imperiale est libertatem dicendi negare, neque sacerdotale, quod sentiat, non dicere*[2]. And again: *In causa vero Dei, quem audies, si sacerdotem non audies, cujus majore peccatur periculo? Quis tibi verum audebit dicere, si sacerdos non audeat*[3]*?*

These, and such like speeches of St Ambrose, Theodosius, and Valentinianus, the emperors did always take in good part; and we doubt not but your Grace will do the like, of whose not only clemency, but also beneficence, we have largely tasted.

but to refer this and other religious controversies to a synod of bishops.

We beseech your Majesty also in these, and such-like controversies of religion, to refer the discussment and deciding of them to a synod of your bishops, and other godly learned men, according to the example of Constantinus Magnus, and other Christian emperors; that the reasons of both parts being examined by them, the judgment may be given uprightly in all doubtful matters.

And to return to this present matter, we most humbly beseech your Majesty to consider, that besides weighty causes in policy, which we leave to the wisdom of your honourable councillors, the establishing of images by your authority shall not only utterly discredit our ministries, as builders of the things which we have destroyed, but also blemish the fame of your most godly brother, and such notable fathers as have given their lives for the testimony of God's truth, who by public law removed all images.

The almighty and ever-living God plentifully endue your Majesty with his spirit and heavenly wisdom, and long preserve your most gracious reign, and prosperous government

[1] Heb. xiii. [17]. 1 Pet. v. [4].
[2] Epist. li. 5, Epist. 29. [Op. Tom. III. p. 133. Basil, 1527.]
[3] Ibidem.

over us, to the advancement of his glory, to the overthrow of superstition, and to the benefit and comfort of all your Highness's loving subjects.

Amen[4].

[4 In the book entitled "The Hunting of the Romish Fox and the Quenching of Sectarian Firebrands... collected by Sir James Ware, Knight... and published by Robert Ware, gent." (Dublin. 1683. 8vo,) the consideration of the question respecting the removal of images from churches in England, is said to have been influenced by an important letter to archbishop Parker, of which we have not been able to find either the original or a copy. Its contents are thus stated: "This alteration[*] stirred up the malignity of several of the Romish clergy then lurking and wandering in that city; so that a *pia fraus* was contrived, purposely to calumniate and vilify her Majesty's endeavours for the reformation of the Protestant Church of England. There was one Richard Leigh, who had been formerly of the priory of that cathedral, who at this time undertook to work this intended fraud, or pretended miracle. The better to contrive this his purpose, he prepared a sponge, and the night before the Sunday following, (her Majesty's Vice-roy being to come to that cathedral with his attendants), this Romish impostor placed the same in a bowl of blood, to soak up the same. Early in the morning Richard Leigh came, and watching his opportunity, brought a stool with him to stand on, and in that cathedral there being an image of marble of Christ standing with a reed in his hand, and the crown of thorns carved on his head, he placed the sponge over the image's head, within a hollow of the crown; the sponge, being swollen and heavy with the blood that it soaked, begun to yield forth the same, which ran through the crevices of the crown of thorns, and truckled down the face of this image. The people did not perceive the same at the first; but whilst her Majesty's Vice-roy was at service, together with the archbishop of that diocese, Doctor Hugh Corwin by name, and the rest of that Privy Council, this impostor with his associates cried one to the other, 'Behold, our Saviour's image sweats blood!' several of the common people (wondering at it) fell down with their beads in their hands and prayed to the image. This report caused a number of people to gather together to behold this miracle; this impostor all the while saying, 'How can he choose but sweat blood whilst heresy is now come into his Church.' The news hereof disturbed the Lord of Sussex, the archbishop, and the rest of her Majesty's Privy Council of that realm: so that they hastened out of the quire, fearing some harm. When they came out, they beheld several people upon their knees, thumping of their breasts, crying out, *Mea culpa, mea maxima culpa*. Christopher Sedgrave, one of the aldermen, and mayor of that

Pia fraus concocted at the cathedral of Christ Church in Dublin, by Richard Leigh.

An image of the Saviour is made to sweat blood.

Consternation of the people.

[* The singing of the Litany in English in the cathedral of Christchurch in Dublin]

LXVII.

SIR FRANCIS KNOLLYS TO ARCHBISHOP PARKER.
13th October, 1559.   Parker MSS. C. C. Coll. Camb. cxiv. art. 224. p. 609.   Orig.

My good lord and reverend father in God, where as this bearer Edward Chamber hath been before the visitors at Abington (being in those parts beneficed), and hath been city, although he had been at English service, drew forth his beads and prayed with others before this image. Hugh, archbishop of Dublin, being displeased at this change, caused a form to be brought out of the choir, and then bade the sexton of that cathedral to stand thereon, and search and wash the image to see if it would bleed afresh; the sexton standing upon the form, and perceiving the sponge within the hollow of the image's head, cried out, Here's the cheat: which being brought down was shewn unto the idolizers, who were much ashamed, and some of them cursed Father Leigh and three or four others, who had been the contrivers of this cheat. The punishment that the archbishop inflicted on these impostors was, to stand upon a table with their legs and hands tied for three Sundays, with the crime written upon paper and pinned to their breasts. Afterwards they were imprisoned, and so banished that realm.

"The Sunday following Hugh archbishop of Dublin preached before her Majesty's Lieutenant and that Council, and before these impostors, who were placed on a table before the pulpit; choosing this text, 'And therefore God shall send them strong delusions, that they should believe lies.' 2 Thessalon. ii. 11. This text falling out so pat, and these impostors standing in the view of all the spectators, converted and reformed above an hundred persons of that city, who vowed they would never hear mass any more.

"The archbishop of Dublin wrote this relation, and to this effect, to his brother archbishop of Canterbury, Matthew Parker, who was at this time very joyful at the receipt hereof, by reason that the clergy were at this present debating whether the images should stand in the churches or no, the Queen herself being then indifferent whether to have images or to destroy them. This letter being shewed unto her Majesty, wrought on her to consent for throwing of images out of the churches, together with those texts of Scripture as the archbishop of Canterbury and other divines gave her for the demolishing of them.

"Upon the tenth of September, anno 1559, Hugh archbishop of Dublin caused this image to be taken down, although he had caused the same to be set up at his coming into that see, being formerly pulled down by his predecessor George Browne, in the reign of King Edward, which the said Hugh specifies in his letter to the archbishop of Canterbury" pp. 86—91.]

by them respited for his subscription until the 26th of this month, at what time they have appointed him to meet them at Windsor, I shall desire your lordship for charity's sake, that either you will now in this mean time travail with this bearer to satisfy his conscience your self, or else to appoint him to some learned man that may do the same, and against the said visitors come to Windsor, you will signify unto them your opinion for their dealing with him, as to your wisdom shall seem most convenient. And thus wishing you prosperity in all godliness, namely[1] in your good enterprise against the enormities yet in the Queen's closet retained[2], (although without the Queen's express commandment these toys were laid aside till now a late), I shall, with my hearty commendations, commit you and us all to the mighty protection of the living God. From the Court, 13th of October, 155[9.]

Sent to the archbishop, who is requested to travail with him for the satisfaction of his conscience as to subscription. Knollys wishes the archbishop all prosperity, especially in his enterprise against the enormities in the Queen's chapel.

Yours to command,
F. KNOLLYS.

To the right reverend Father in God, archbishop elect of Canterbury, give this.

LXVIII.

ARCHBISHOP PARKER, ELECT, AND FOUR OTHER BISHOPS ELECT, TO QUEEN ELIZABETH.

[About 15th October, 1559[3].] Parker MSS. C. C. Coll. Camb. cxxi. art. 30. p. 381.

MOST humbly sheweth your excellent Majesty, your lowly orators and loving subjects we underwritten, that like as your most noble father of immortal memory, King Henry the VIIIth, and your most godly and noble brother, King Edward the VIth, in their princely zeal which they bare to

Henry VIII. and Edward VI much tendered the advancement of

[1 i. e. especially.]
[2 A crucifix and lighted tapers, which Parker advised the Queen to remove, though without success.—Strype's Parker, Bk. I. c. 9. Vol. I. p. 92.]
[3 There is mention in this paper of the rents due at the last past Michaelmas, that is, doubtless, on the 29th September, 1559. The next paper, dated 26th October, 1559, distinctly alludes to this memorial, and is in the nature of an answer to it.]

learning by cherishing students and encouraging ministers.

the state of Christ's faith did much tender the advancement of learning by cherishing of students and encouraging of ministers, whereby they were the more able to do their duties to God, and to serve the necessity of the realm, by which their royal and princely affection they purchased perpetual fame and praise, as well within their own realms as throughout all Christendom: so we trust undoubtedly that your Grace, being endued with the benefits of knowledge far above any of your noble progenitors, will be inclined no less to the maintenance of learning for the setting forth of Christ's true religion, now for want of sufficient ministers in great jeopardy of decay. In respect whereof we trust that your Highness' gracious disposition will yet stay and remit this present alteration and exchange[1] (as we suppose in our consciences under reformation of your great wisdom), not meet to proceed for the inconveniences thereof now partly perceived like to ensue, and upon such good grounds and reasons as we could particularly describe in writing if your Highness' pleasure were to admit us to the declaration of the same.

The same is trusted of Queen Elizabeth.

And that she will therefore stay a proposed exchange which is thought not meet to proceed, for reasons ready to be stated.

Offer on behalf of the bishops of the province of Canterbury to give one thousand marks yearly for their lives in lieu of the proposed exchange.

And yet, lest we should appear not to consider your Highness' manifold and great charges daily sustained, in most humble wise we five underwritten, for us and the province of Canterbury, do offer to give unto the same yearly amongst us one annual pension of one thousand marks during our lives and continuance in the bishopricks for and in consideration of the exoneration of the said exchange.

If such offer is declined,

How be it, most gracious sovereign, as most obedient

[1 "The late parliament had made an act to enable the Queen upon the vacation of any bishoprick to convert the temporal revenues, or part thereof, unto herself, settling in exchange church-lands in lieu thereof, such as impropriations formerly belonging to monasteries dissolved and tenths, taking into her own hands good old lordships and manors for them. The inequality of which exchanges was, that to these impropriations were oftentimes considerable charges annexed by necessary reparations of houses and chancels, and yearly pensions payable out of them. And tenths would often fall short and be unpaid by reason of the poverty, or inability, or death of the poor curates and ministers. Nor could the bishops have any good title to them, it being doubtful whether they could be alienated from the crown, being by Act of Parliament given to it."—Strype's Parker, Bk. I. c. 9.]

1559.] BISHOPS ELECT, TO QUEEN ELIZABETH. 99

subjects in true and lowly allegiance of our hearts, we sue and pray, that if this our said supplication shall not be thought meet to take place, that yet your Highness would condescend favourably to peruse these our petitions following: which we be persuaded to be grounded upon natural equity, godly conscience, and good conformity for most part of them to the act passed. *(the Queen requested to consider the following petitions.)*

1. First, that the vicarages of impropried benefices appointed in exchange may be made just livings for the incumbents of the same. And that the chancels and mansion houses decayed might be considered by survey to some reasonable proportion of allowance in the exchange. *(That the vicarages of impropriated benefices, appointed in exchange be made just livings, and that chancels and mansion houses be repaired.)*

2. Item, that yearly pensions payable may be reprised out of the parsonages set over in exchange, and that yearly distributions, with the charges of church-books, &c., may be allowed such as the Injunctions bind the rectories withal. *(That yearly pensions payable, may be charged on the parsonages set over in exchange.)*

3. Item, that where the manred[2] with the manors is withdrawn from us, that we be not hereafter importably charged with the setting forth of men to war. *(That manred being withdrawn, the bishops be not charged with setting men for the wars)*

4. Item, that perquisites of courts and woods, sales and other such casual profits, may be parcels of the extent of the manors, and that consideration may be had for the equivalent recompence of the same, and that allowance may be made of procurations and synods payable at the visitations of personages impropriate, and also allowance for the mesne profits after the death of the incumbent to the next successor, so charged in the first-fruits and tenths, which mesne profits were translated by act of parliament from the bishop to the successor of the benefice from the death of his predecessor. *(That there be an equivalent compensation for perquisites of courts, &c.)*

5. Item, that fees to keepers of parks and woods not yet valued be not reprised out of the value of the manors, and that the said parks and woods may be also valued; and that corn, sheep, fowl, and fish, with carriages and other commodities, may remain for hospitality to the bishops. *(Also for parks and woods.)*

6. Item, that the patronage appendant to the manors *(That the patronage)*

[2 That is "man-rent," the obligation by tenure of personally serving the feudal superior in time of war, or of providing, as in the case of these bishops, a certain number of armed men as substitutes. The nature of man-rent is illustrated by a curious document printed in Scott's Border Minstrelsy; see his Poetical Works, II. 144. Edit. 1833.]

exchanged may be reserved to the bishop's see, and that the bishops of the new erected churches may give the prebends of those churches as in other is used, the rather to maintain learned men and preachers.

<small>*appendant to manors exchanged to be reserved to the bishops.*</small>

7. Item, if any of the tenths and rectories be evicted from us by order of law, that then recompence may be made.

<small>*That there be compensation for any tenths and rectories exchanged.*</small>

8. Item, that we may have remedy by law to recover the tenths denied or delayed, as well as when they were parcels of the revenues of the crown, before which assurance no exchange can reasonably pass.

<small>*That arrears of tenths may be recovered.*</small>

9. Item, that no rents be returned for spiritual possessions which be paid into the exchequer [nor] for annual rents temporal reserved *nomine decimæ*.

<small>*That no rents be returned for spiritual possessions.*</small>

10. Item, that bishopricks may be discharged of all arrearages, of subsidies and tenths, and other incumbrances passed in the days of the predecessors and in times of vacation, and that for the first year of our fruits-paying to be discharged of subsidy, as before time hath been used.

<small>*That bishopricks be discharged of arrears of subsidies, and during the first year of paying first-fruits.*</small>

11. Item, that it may please your Highness to continue the new erected sees founded upon great considerations by your noble progenitor the said King Henry, and that the benefice of Clyffe may be annexed to the see of Rochester, and from the see of Chester the benefice late annexed thereunto be not dismembered, in consideration of the exility of the bishopricks.

<small>*That the new erected sees be continued.*</small>

12. Item, we most humbly desire your Majesty that in consideration of our chargeable expectation, and for the burden of necessary furniture of our houses, and for the discharge of the great fees paid before, and at the restitution of temporalities, to suffer us to enjoy the half-year's rent last past at Michaelmas, and that our first-fruits may be abated and distributed into more years, for the better maintenance of hospitality: and that we may be put to our own surety at the composition of our fruits. Which gracious favour in the latter premises if your Highness do not shew towards us, we shall not dare enter our functions whereto your grace hath nominated us, being too importable else for us to bear. All which petitions, most redoubted sovereign lady, we make to your Highness, not in respect of any private worldly advancement or temporal gain (as God knoweth our hearts), but in respect of God's glory, Christ's faith and religion, your

<small>*That in consideration of the heavy expences of the bishops they be allowed to receive the half-year's rent due at the previous Michaelmas, and that first-fruits be abated and distributed over more years.*</small>

Grace's honour and discharge of your conscience to all the world, and for the honourable report of your nobility, and to the comfort of the realm[1].

Your Highness' most humble orators,

> MATTHUE, elect Cant.[2]
> EDM., elect London[3].
> RICHARD, elect Ely[4].
> WILL'MUS, elect Cicestren.[5]
> JOHN, elect of Hereford[6].

LXIX.

QUEEN ELIZABETH TO THE LORD TREASURER AND THE BARONS OF THE EXCHEQUER.

26th October, 1559. S. P. O. Domestic, VII. 19. Orig. Draft.

BY THE QUEEN.

RIGHT trusty and right well-beloved cousin and trusty and right well-beloved, we greet you well. Whereas the archbishop elect of Canterbury and the other elect bishops of London, Ely, Hereford, and Chichester remain unconsecrated[7], by reason that the exchange is not finished betwixt us and them, for certain temporalities, according to the power given us by a statute in the last Parliament, whereby we be informed the state ecclesiastical in the province of Canterbury and the rest of the said dioceses remaineth without government; our pleasure is that ye shall with all expedition proceed to finish the said exchange. And for that it is informed

The archbishop and other elect bishops remain unconsecrated, by reason that their intended exchange of temporalities with the crown remains unsettled.

The treasurer and barons

[1 This letter has no date. "It could not," says Strype, "be writ before August, in which month Parker's election was made by the Dean and Chapter of Canterbury." "In the contriving of this," he adds, "the Archbishop was chief, and the address, I suppose, was drawn up by his hand and head."]

[2 Archbishop Parker, elected 1 August, 1559, consecrated 17th December, 1559.]

[3 Bishop Grindal, elected 26th July, 1559.]

[4 Bishop Cox, elected 28th July, 1559.]

[5 Bishop Barlow, elected 1559.]

[6 Bishop Scory, elected 15th July, 1559.]

[7 The term "unconsecrated" only applies to the archbishop and the bishops elect of London and Ely. The other two elect bishops "being bishops before needed no consecration but were confirmed in their new bishopricks." Strype's Parker, Bk. II. c. 2, p. 126.]

are directed to finish the exchange with all expedition.

us, upon the behalf of the said five bishops, that ye have already in our name assigned for us certain of the temporalities of the said bishopricks, whereof part be such sort that

The exchange not to be so made as to deprive the bishops of lands reserved for the maintenance of hospitality,

the same truly shall not be able to keep their hospitality, being heretofore by their predecessors assigned and reserved for the same purpose, whereby the meaning of the act of parliament should be frustrate; we think it very convenient, and so are pleased, that ye should have consideration hereof,

or contrary to the favourable meaning of the act of parliament.

and extend nothing against them by this exchange contrary to the favourable meaning of the act of parliament, and that the exchange may be such as they may have in spiritualities an equal just value to the temporalities which shall be received from them; using therein such valuations as ye shall find hath been commonly answered to their predecessors upon their accounts. And, finally, our pleasure is that ye shall proceed to the accomplishing of this exchange with all speed possible, having consideration specially to forbear such things as tend to the help and maintenance of their hospitality, and to proceed to the like exchange with the rest of the bishopricks that be richly endowed, as York, Winchester, Durham, Bath, Sarum, Norwich, and Worcester, so as upon the election of men meet for those rooms the same may be placed with convenient speed.

Half a year's rent to be allowed to the archbishop and the bishops elect.

[1]And further, where there is answerable unto us at the feast of Michaelmas last past the whole year's revenue of the archbishoprick of Canterbury, the bishopricks of Hereford and Chichester; we be pleased that the bishops elect of the same shall have the moiety of the same, as of our reward, towards the maintenance of their charges. And where there is also to be answered to us but the one half-year's rent of the bishopricks of London and Ely, we be pleased likewise to grant such a quantity of the same, as shall amount to the moiety of the whole year's revenue of the same several two bishopricks.

And these our letters shall be your sufficient warrant and discharge in this behalf. Given under our signet at our palace of Westminster, the 26th day of October, in the first year of our reign[2].

[[1] This paragraph is wholly in the handwriting of Sir William Cecil.]

[[2] The result of this exchange, so far as related to the archbishoprick of Canterbury, is thus stated in a memorandum in Lam-

LXX.

THE LORDS OF THE COUNCIL TO ARCHBISHOP PARKER, ELECT.

2nd November, 1559. Parker MSS. C. C. Coll. Camb. cxiv. art. 26. p. 83. Orig.

AFTER our right hearty commendations to your good lordship. Whereas Peter Langrige and John Erle, late prebendary and peti-canon of the cathedral church of Winchester, do now remain in the prisons of the Bench and Marshalsea, where they be somewhat touched with sickness; we have given order, upon their humble suits, to the keepers of the said prisons that they shall be brought unto you, requiring you upon their coming to take bonds of them with sureties for their good behaviour and certainty of place of abode, in form as hath been formerly adjusted for others of their sort, and otherwise to use your discretions towards them. Thus fare you right heartily well. From Westminster, the second of November, 1559.

[margin: Peter Langrige and John Erle, prisoners for nonconformity, being in ill health, are sent to the Archbishop, who is to take their bonds with sureties, and release them. 2nd Nov. 1559.]

Your very loving friends,
PENBROKE.
W. HOWARD.
THO. PARRY. G. ROGERS. F. KNOLLYS. W. CECILL.
AB. CAVE. ED. SAKEVYLE.

To our very good lord the archbishop of Canterbury elect.

beth MS. 959, inserted in the printed life of Matthæus, in a copy of archbishop Parker's lives of the archbishops of Canterbury. The memorandum is in the handwriting of Sir John Parker, the archbishop's grandson: "When the said Matthew came to be archbishop, by virtue of an act of parliament, touching exchange of lands with Bishops, anno Reginæ Elizabethæ primo, there was taken from the See of Canterbury of the temporalities, consisting of manors, scites of priories, dominical lands, parks, &c., in Kent, Sussex, and Salop, to the clear yearly value of 1282$l.$ 6$s.$ 8$d.$, for which was returned over, in recompence, the tenths of the diocese of Canterbury, of 478$l.$ 10$s.$ 5$\frac{1}{4}d.$, and in parsonages impropriate 357$l.$ 15$s.$ 11$\frac{1}{2}d.$, and in annual rents 447$l.$ 9$s.$ 6$\frac{1}{2}d.$, so that by these valuations, the recompence was set down to exceed the lands taken by 34$s.$ 5$\frac{1}{4}d.$, as before in particulars is written. The Queen of her favour gave unto him of the Michaelmas rents, 1599, [sic, for 1559], 1235$l.$ 9$s.$ 7$d.$" The figures printed are those in the MS., but it is evident there is some slight mistake in them.]

[margin: Mode and nature of the exchange effected with the archbishoprick of Canterbury.]

LXXI.

SIR THOMAS PARRY AND SIR WILLIAM CECIL TO ARCHBISHOP PARKER, ELECT.

2nd November, 1559. Parker MSS. C. C. Coll. Camb. CXIV. art. 287. p. 795. Orig.

Mr Boxall to be deprived of his living if he refuses to take the oath of conformity

AFTER our right hearty commendations. The Queen's Majesty's pleasure is that ye proceed with Mr Boxall, whom we send unto you, according to the form of the statute and your commission, offering him the oath; which if he shall refuse to take, her Highness' pleasure is, ye then proceed to the deprivation of all his livings according to the tenor of the said statute, giving undelayed and sufficient order to other the commissioners of several circuits within the which any part or parcel of his livings lieth, that he be no more molested or troubled for not appearance, or any other cause whatsoever growing by reason of his said livings or their particular visitations, nor bound or driven to further answer for any matter rising by occasion thereof. Which her Highness' pleasure we pray and require you to put in execution as soon as ye conveniently may. And so we bid you right heartily farewell. From the Court, this second of November, 1559.

2 Nov. 1559.

Your loving friends,

THO. PARRY.   W. CECILL.

In proceeding with him, to have in remembrance what place he formerly held.

Postscript. We do also require you in proceeding with him to have in remembrance what place he hath had in this commonweal, and to have regard thereunto[1].

To my lord of Canterbury his good grace be these delivered.

[[1] This postscript is in the handwriting of Sir W. Cecil. Dr Boxall, as stated at p. 65, had been a Secretary of State, and one of the Privy Council during the reign of Queen Mary. He was also dean of Peterborough, Norwich and Windsor. Being a man of a mild and amiable disposition, he had abstained from all participation in the cruelties of the Marian period. It will appear hereafter that Archbishop Parker treated him with due consideration and courtesy.]

LXXII.

ARCHBISHOP PARKER, ELECT, TO SIR WILLIAM CECIL.

6th November, 1559. S. P. O. Domestic, 1559. Orig.

SIR,

We were this other day with the Queen's Majesty, in whose gracious words we took much comfort, but for the principal cause not yet fully resolved, and thereupon her Grace dismissed us, shewing to us that she would speak again with us as upon Saturday last, if she sent us so word, which her Highness have done. Therefore, because the matter is in good towardness, we would wish we were called for again to continue our humble supplication to the finishment and stay of that offendicle[2], the more speed would be had therein, for that some fear danger is like shortly to arise thereof, as by letters which this morning I have sent to my lord of London, at whose hands your worship may desire to have them, I perceive.

God keep us from such visitation as Knox have attempted in Scotland; the people to be orderers of things. Thus in most haste I commend you to God's good grace; this 6th of November.

Parker is much comforted by the Queen's gracious words on the subject of the removal of the crucifix from her chapel.

6 Nov. 1559.

Your orator,

MATTH. EL. CANT.

To the right honourable Sir William Cecil, Secretary to the Queen's Majesty.

LXXIII.

THE LORDS OF THE COUNCIL TO ARCHBISHOP PARKER AND THE REST OF THE ECCLESIASTICAL COMMISSIONERS.

9th November, 1559. Parker MSS. C. C. Coll. Camb. CXIV. art. 16. p. 55. Orig.

AFTER our very hearty commendations to your lordship. Where as Dr Carter and Dr Seggiswick having refused before our very good lord the Earl of Westmoreland and other commissioners in the north parts to receive the oath and

Dr Carter and Dr Seggiswick having refused the oath of supremacy,

[2 The "offendicle" here referred to was, in all probability, the crucifix in the Queen's chapel, the subject of the letter, No. LXVI.]

service by law established, were by them bound to appear personally before us; we have thought good upon their appearance here to send them to your lordship, praying you to proceed further with them according to the qualities of their faults and the laws provided in that behalf. Whereof we pray your lordship not to fail. And so we bid you heartily farewell. From Westminster, the 9th of November, 1559.

<small>Are remitted to archbishop Parker.</small>

Your lordship's assured loving friends,

W. NORTHT.   E. CLYNTON.   W. HOWARD.
THO. PARRY.   G. ROGERS.   F. KNOLLYS.   W. CECILL.
AB. CAVE.

To our very good lord the archbishop of Canterbury, elect, and the rest of the Commissioners.

LXXIV.

ARCHBISHOP PARKER, ELECT, TO SIR WILLIAM CECIL.

18th November, 1559.   S. P. O. Domestic.   Orig.

<small>Bishop Tunstall's executors.</small>

MY lord of Durh[am][1] hath one of his executors here, the other is in the [No]rth, where also is his testament. This executor saith that his mind was to be homely and plainly buried. Consider you whether it were not best to prescribe some honest manner of his interring, lest it might else be evil judged that the order of his funeral were at the council's appointment[2], not known abroad that the handling of it were only at his executors' liberality.

<small>His funeral.</small>

<small>His chief effects sealed up by the archbishop.</small>

I have sealed up two small caskets, wherein I think no great substance, either of money or of writings. There is one roll of books which he purposed to deliver to the Queen, which is nothing else but King Henry's Testament[3], and a book *Contra communicationem utriusque speciei,* and such

[[1] Cuthbert Tonstall, bishop of Durham, having refused to take the oath of supremacy, had been committed to the archbishop's house at Lambeth. He died there in November, 1559. Strype's Parker, Bk. I. c. 10, p. 94. See above Letters LXIII. LXIV. LXV.]

[[2] He was buried in the parish-church of Lambeth.]

[[3] Bishop Tonstall was one of the executors of King Henry VIII.]

matter. His body by reason of his sudden departure cannot be long kept. Thus Jesus preserve you. This 18th of November.

Your beadman,
M. EL. C.

To the Right Honourable Mr
Secretary.

LXXV.
ARCHBISHOP PARKER AND OTHERS TO THE PRESIDENT AND CHAPTER OF EXETER.

23rd December, 1559. Wilkins's Concilia, IV. 201, from Reg. Dec. et Cap. Exon. Lib. III. fo. 145.

AFTER our hearty commendations unto you. Whereas we the Queen's Majesty's commissioners are informed that her Highness's late visitors directed their letters to you for the reformation of certain disorders used in your cathedral church, which being of late sent, might peradventure be accepted of small force, because their commission in some part is determined; we have therefore thought good by these our letters to will and require you to obey, fulfil, and put in execution all and singular the causes mentioned in the said letter, and also quietly permit and suffer such congregation of people as shall be at any time hereafter congregated together in the said church, to sing or say the godly prayers in the morning, and other times set forth, used and permitted in this Church of England, to the laud and praise of his honour and glory, without any of your contradiction to the contrary, and that to be done in the most commodious and convenient place in the said church, whether it be in the choir or elsewhere; as you and every of you will answer to the same at his peril. And thus fare you well. From London, this 23rd of December, 1559.

Side notes: Letters of the Commissioners for visitation for reformation of disorders in the church at Exeter, confirmed by the Ecclesiastical Commissioners. The people to be allowed to assemble to sing or to say the prayers used and permitted in the Church of England.

Your loving friends,
MATTHEW CANT.   WILL. MEY.
EDM. LONDON.   THOMAS HUYCK[4].

To our loving friends, the president
and chapter of the cathedral
church of St Peter in Exon, and
to every of them.

[4] The circumstances which gave rise to this letter appear in Wilkins's Concilia, IV. 201, as derived from the register of the Dean and

LXXVI.

SIR WILLIAM CECIL TO ARCHBISHOP PARKER.

27th February, 1559—60. Petyt MS. Inner Temple, No. 47. fol. 379. Orig.

Recommendation for a Lent license to be granted to Sir Roger North.

It may please your grace, this bearer Sir Roger North, son and heir to the Lord North[1], being to me well known, hath, in consideration of his evil estate of health, and the danger that might follow if he should be restrained to eating of fish, prayed me to be mean to your grace to dispense with him therein: I doubt not but your grace shall of others also well understand how requisite it is for the preservation of his health that he be dispensed withal. And thus I take my leave of your grace. From Westminster, this 27th of February, 1559.

Your grace's to command,

W. CECILL.

Your grace seeth, notwithstanding my earnest conference with you in these matters, I am in probable cases moved to relent.

Chapter of Exeter. The Queen's visitors had enjoined upon the dean and chapter the reading of morning prayer in the choir, at six o'clock daily. The people attended the service "reverently" in great numbers, and "for their greater comfort and better stirring up of their hearts to devotion, appointed amongst themselves at every such meeting to sing a psalm, and all together with one voice to give praise unto God, according to the use and manner of the primitive church." The clergy of the cathedral deemed this practice to be an irregularity, and, as it was said, not only "scoffed and jested openly at the godly doings of the people," but "molested and troubled them," and "very uncourteously" forbade them the use of the choir. In a letter dated the 16th December, 1559, the Queen's visitors rebuked the president and chapter, during the vacancy of the deanery, for their opposition to the pious feelings of the people, "which of all others should most have rejoiced thereat, and should have encouraged the people to go forward," and the visitors charged the president and chapter to see that their vicars, and others their priests, should not only "leave their frowardness," but that they should "aid and assist the people in these their godly doings." The letter now printed was written by the ecclesiastical commissioners to enforce the directions of the Queen's visitors.]

[1 Sir Roger became the second Lord North on the death of his father, in December, 1564, and survived until December, 1597. (Dugdale's Baronage, II. 394.)]

LXXVII.

ARCHBISHOP PARKER TO DR NICHOLAS HEATH, DEPRIVED ARCHBISHOP OF YORK, AND OTHER DEPRIVED BISHOPS.

26th March, 1560. The Hunting of the Romish Fox, by Robert Ware. 8vo. Dublin, 1683. pp. 111—119[2].

IT is the pride, covetousness and usurpation of the bishop of Rome, and of his predecessors, which hath made the princes of the earth to defend their territories and their privileges from that wicked Babylon and her bishop; and whereas you and the rest of the late expulsed bishops have scandalized our reformed clergy within these her Majesty's realms, that we yield no subjection unto Christ and his Apostles, we yield more than ye fathers of the Romish tribe do; for we honour and adore Christ as the true Son of God, equal with his Father as well in authority as in majesty, and do make him no foreigner to the realm, as you members and clergy of the church of Rome do; but we profess him to be our only Maker and Redeemer, and ruler of his Church, not only in this realm, but also in all nations, unto whom princes and preachers are but servants; the preachers to propose, the princes to execute, Christ's will and commandments, whom you, and all that desire to be saved, must believe and obey, against all councils and tribunals who do dissent from his word, whether regal or papal.

The pride, &c. of the bishop of Rome has made the princes of the earth defend their territories from him.

The expelled bishops have scandalized the Reformed clergy by asserting that they yield no subjection to Christ and his apostles.

Controverted nature of the honour paid in the reformed Church to Christ.

The Apostles we reverence and obey, as the messengers from Christ, and do receive their writings with exacter obedience than Romanists do; for we will not permit, as Rome and her clergy do, any to dispense against the Scriptures.

The like of the reverence paid to the Apostles.

[2 Ware gives the following account of this letter. "Anno 1560. This year Matthew Parker having received from the expulsed archbishop of York and the rest of the popish bishops, a letter terrifying of the reformed bishops and clergy of the Church of England, with curses and other threatenings, for not acknowledging the papal tribunal; this worthy father, consulting with her Majesty and the Council, shewed the same with the following answer prepared upon the receipt thereof, which extremely pleased her Majesty, and the reformed party of her Council. After which her Majesty purged her Council from all suspected persons bending towards the bishop of Rome or his usurpations."—pp. 110—111.]

We will never say with Pighius[1]; "the Apostles wrote certain things, not that their writings should be above our faith and religion, but rather under."

The word of God is received by the Church of England from the Apostles, and the papal errors held in detestation.

We confess the Apostles were men allowed of God, to whom the Gospel should be committed, and therefore we receive the Word from them, not as the word of man, but as it is truly the Word of God; assuring ourselves it is God's power to save all who believe. Thus doth our Reformation detest your Romish errors and heinous presumptions, which makes your Romish writers and popes to add, alter, and diminish, nay also to dispense with the words that Christ himself spake, as well as the writings of the Apostles.

We own Councils called by the help of religious princes, but we own no subjection to papal tribunals.

We shall and do own such councils as the Church of Christ was wont to call, by the help of her religious princes; and do and shall own brotherly concord and communion, so long as they make no breach in faith or Christian charity; but as touching subjection and servitude, take ye heed lest ye commit treason against the laws of her Majesty's realms; for we owe them none. The blessed angels profess themselves[2] to be fellow-servants with the saints upon earth; what are ye or your bishop of Rome then, who (with your tribunals and jurisdictions) would be rulers and lords over the inheritance of Christ?

St Peter claimed no subjection. Witness St Cyprian.

Reverend sirs, consider how St Peter claimed no subjection; which St Cyprian, by these his words thus translated, saith: "Peter whom the Lord made first choice of, and on whom he built his Church, when St Paul after strove with him (for circumcision) did not take upon him, nor challenge any thing insolently or arrogantly, neither advanced he himself as chief, or like one unto whom emperors, kings or princes, should be subject[3]."

---

[1] Pig. Hierar. Lib. I. cap. 2. ["Non quidem ut scripta illa præessent fidei religionique nostræ, sed subessent potius." Col. 1538. fol. 6.]

[2] Rev. xxii. [9.]

[3 Cyprian ad Quirinum (Quintum) "Nam nec Petrus, quem primum Dominus elegit, et super quem ædificavit ecclesiam suam, cum secum Paulus de circumcisione postmodum disceptaret, vindicavit sibi aliquid insolenter aut arroganter assumpsit, ut diceret se primatum tenere et obtemperari a novellis et posteris sibi potius oportere."—Cypriani Opera, ed. Paris. 1726. p. 127.]

Because ye be so earnest with us of the Reformed Church of these her Majesty's dominions, for subjection to foreign tribunals, to confute you and your errors, pray behold and see how we of the Church of England, reformed by our late King Edward and his clergy, and now by her Majesty and hers reviving the same, have but imitated and followed the examples of the ancient and worthy fathers.   *The Church of England reformed by Edward VI, whose reformation is now revived*

Pray, sirs, resolve us, what tribunals did St Cyprian and the eighty bishops of Carthage acknowledge, when he said, *Christus unus et solus habet potestatem de actu nostro judicandi*: and again, *Episcopus ab alio judicari non potest*: and again he likewise saith, *Expectemus universi judicium Christi*[4] ?   *The reformation follows the examples of the fathers, St Cyprian.*

We further entreat you, before ye censure our Reformation and her Majesty, to collect what tribunals abroad did Polycrates, and the bishops of Asia with him, acknowledge, when he replied to the bishop of Rome, then threatening to excommunicate him and the rest of his bishops, *Non turbabor iis quæ terrendi gratia objiciuntur ?*

What tribunals did St Augustine and the two hundred and sixteen bishops acknowledge, when they decreed that none appealing over seas (to tribunals abroad) should be received to the communion within Africa; and when they repelled the bishop of Rome, labouring to please [place?] his *legates a latere* within their province, and willed him not to bring *fumosum seculi typhum*, that smoky pride of the world into the Church of Christ[5] ?   *St Augustine.*

Thus far have we imitated these fathers by our Reformation, and denying of unlawful demands, which be proud and usurpal of the bishops of Rome to demand from us of the clergy within these her Majesty's dominions: nay, not only them, but our predecessors the British bishops of old within   *We have imitated these Fathers and the old British bishops in our denial of the proud demands of Rome.*

[4 St Cyprian's Sentences in the Council of Carthage. "Habeat omnis episcopus pro licentia libertatis et potestatis suæ arbitrium proprium, tamque judicari ab alio non possit quam nec ipse potest alterum judicare. Sed expectemus universi judicium Domini nostri Jesu Christi, qui unus et solus habet potestatem, et præponendi nos in ecclesiæ suæ gubernatione et de actu nostro judicandi."—Cypriani Opera, ibid. p. 330.]

5 August. Concil. African. cap. 29 et 105. [Concil. Afric. cap. 6. in Crabb. Concil. Col. Agrip. 1551. I. 517.]

this realm; for what tribunals did they ever own, when Augustino came hither from Rome, when they replied, they owed him none, and would not be subject?

The English Reformers regret the separation of the deprived bishops.

I, and the rest of our brethren the bishops and clergy of the realm, supposed ye to be our brethren in Christ; but we be sorry that ye, through your perverseness, have separated yourselves not only from us, but from these ancient fathers, and their opinions; and that ye permit one man to have all the members of your Saviour Christ Jesus under his subjection: this your wilful opinion is not the way to reduce kings, princes, and their subjects to truth, but rather to blindfold them and the whole Church, and so lead them into utter darkness: for as Gregory saith, *Ecclesia universa corruit, si unus universus cadit*[1].

Opposition caused by the universal jurisdiction claimed by the bishop of Rome.

What was it occasioned the Romish writers to write against the Bishop of Rome? What was it caused Luther, Calvin, and other orthodox clergymen, to renounce Rome and her church, but this thing called the bishop of Rome's tribunal? Several learned men, from the first time that the Bishops of Rome began to demand tribute and to set up a tribunal, have written that that very thing caused these bishops to forget their Maker and also their Redeemer: yet by these your demands of us to own Rome and her tribunal, you forget your duties to God, with your father the bishop of Rome; for his usurping of a tribunal to make all nations subject to his beck, hath caused him and his successors ever since to forget the living God.

These bishops partake in the errors of the bishops of Rome.

Ye his followers and acknowledgers partake of this sin also, and have occasioned the bishops of Rome to fall into these errors; for ye have made it sacrilege to dispute of his fact, heresy to doubt of his power, paganism to disobey him, and blasphemy against the Holy Ghost to act or speak against his decrees: nay, that which is most horrible, ye have made it presumption in any man not to go to the devil

---

[1] Gregor. Lib. vi. Epist. 24. [The words of St Gregory are: "Scitis enim quanti non solum hæretici, sed etiam hæresiarchæ de Constantinopolitana ecclesia sunt egressi. Et ut de honoris vestri injuria taceam, si unus episcopus vocatur universalis, universa ecclesia corruit; si unus universus cadit. Sed absit hæc stultitia, absit hæc levitas ab auribus meis."—Greg. Opera, fol. cccxcvii. edit. Paris. 1518; p. 409. edit. 1533; p. 196. Vol. ii. edit. 1542.]

after him without any grudging: which is so shameful and so sinful a subjection, that Lucifer himself never demanded the like from his slaves in hell.

Consider therefore of these things; and it shall be the continual prayers of our reformed Church to convert ye all to the truth of God's Word, to obedience to your sovereign Lady Elizabeth our Queen, which in so doing ye glorify Christ, and the Eternal God which is in heaven, and is solely the chief and absolute ruler of princes.

Your faithful brother in Christ,
MATTHEW CANTUARIENSIS.

March 26, 1560.

LXXVIII.[2]

ARCHBISHOP PARKER TO WARHAM ST LEGER, ESQ.

April, 1560. Parker MSS. C. C. Coll. Camb. cxiv. art. 241. p. 662. Orig. Draft in Parker's hand.

IN my right hearty manner I commend me unto your worship, and thank you for your so friendly and ready remembrance of your money sent; which yet I would gladly have forborne for a longer time rather than ye should have had any damage by collecting it so instant upon your day. Ye have so gently used me from time to time in this first assay of your friendship, that ye have given me good cause to requite you, if it may lie in my power. And furthermore concerning you, that I have not forgotten your request for the preferment of that young gentleman of whom ye write; *(Acknowledgment of the receipt of money sent to the archbishop. The archbishop has not forgotten his request for the preferment of a young gentleman.)*

[2] This letter was written in reply to one from Mr Warham St Leger, or Sentleger, as he wrote his name, dated 12th April, 1560. (Parker MSS. cxiv. art. 240. p. 661,) in which he remitted the archbishop 30*l.*, the remainder of "fourscore and ten pounds," apparently money borrowed. Mr St Leger was the eldest surviving son of Sir Anthony St Leger, K. G., by his wife Agnes, niece of archbishop Warham. He succeeded to the family seat at Ulcombe, in the county of Kent, on the 12th March, 1558—9, on the death of his father, Sir Anthony, and was serving sheriff for Kent at the time when he wrote this letter. He was knighted in 1565, and was killed in Ireland in 1599. (Hasted's Kent, II. 423)]

[PARK. COR]

so that when he and you shall see your opportunity, I shall with right good will accomplish all that shall serve that purpose. And thus wishing you a full recovery of your distemperance[1], I commend you to the grace and protection of God as myself.

LXXIX.

BISHOP YOUNG OF ST DAVID'S TO ARCHBISHOP PARKER.

3rd May, 1560. Lambeth MS. 959. No. 41. Orig.

Thanks the archbishop for his friendly forewarning concerning his, the bishop's contemplated translation.

AFTER most humble commendations. It may please your grace to be advertised, that I have received your letters containing your friendly advertisement, or forewarning, concerning my settling where I am, or translating into other places; which thing well considered maketh me to think that one of mine acquaintance who hunteth much for his own further advancement, more than for my better settling, and much desireth my place, hath by his instruments practised therein and begun that thing. And some in authority, being my friends, hearing of such preferment towards me, and meaning

Thanks his friends for their good will, but although the other places are more honourable and much more profitable, he will not accept them.

good unto me, peradventure do set forward the same; unto whom, for their good will, I accompt myself most bounden. But for the matter, although the other places are more honourable and much more profitable than this wherein I am settled, I will in no wise for divers considerations accept them, otherwise than I shall be thereunto enforced upon mine allegiance, which I trust shall not happen unto me, considering my simple qualities and the great number of worthier men for those rooms and offices. I beseech your grace weigh the matter well, and stand my good lord therein; and Mr Gwynne, who hath Thomas Clement's prebend, upon communication had with him concerning that matter, having due consideration of your grace's pleasure and my Lord Keeper's in that behalf, is content to go from the same, so that he may have up his bonds entered for the first-fruits. I trust your grace or my Lord Keeper will help that to pass, considering he enjoyeth it not. If Mr Serjeant Rastell, or Mr Warner,

[1 He had excused himself from waiting on the archbishop in person, in consequence of having a fever.]

will bestow one hour with such diligence therein as they did many days for Clement, it would well come to pass without molesting of your grace. And thus resting for your pleasure and determination concerning your visitation, I commit your grace to the Almighty. From my house at Abergwillie, the third of May, 1560.

Your grace's to command,

THOMAS MENEVEN.

*To the most Reverend Father in
God, and my special good
Lord, my Lord of Canterbury,
his grace*[2].

LXXX.

ARCHBISHOP PARKER TO BISHOP GRINDAL.

27th May, 1560. Reg. Parker, I. fol. 220 b.

MATTHÆUS, permissione divina Cantuariensis archiepiscopus, totius Angliæ primas et metropolitanus, venerabili confratri nostro domino Edmundo, eadem permissione Londoniensi episcopo, vestrove vicario in spiritualibus generali officiali principali, sive commissario cuicunque, salutem, et fraternam in Domino charitatem. Licet compertum habeamus tam de jure, quam de laudabili ac diu legitimeque præscripta consuetudine, prædecessoribus nostris Cantuariensis sedis archiepiscopis, pro tempore successive existentibus, licuisse, ac nobis, qui Dei miseratione in eadem sede sumus collocati, prærogativa metropolitica sedis prædictæ licere, et liberum esse, universum populum sub finibus nostræ Cantuariensis provinciæ degentem ad voluntatis nostræ arbitrium visitare, et quos a via Domini, ac a vera pietate et religione deviantes invenerimus, ad debitam reformationis normam redigere et reducere; tamen cum aures nostræ non sine magno nostro dolore, crebris ac lachry- *It has been a prescriptive custom for the archbishops of Canterbury to visit throughout the province of Canterbury. But on account of the poverty of the clergy,*

[2 Sir John Parker, son of the archbishop, adds a note on the original MS.: "I could never find of any other bishop's letters to refuse a better bishoprick for worse, by his own accord." But bishop Young did not continue constant in his refusal. On the 27th January, 1560—1, he was translated to the see of York, in which he died on the 26th June, 1568.]

<small>and the complaint of the clergy and people, of the expence of such visitations, the archbishop has deferred his visitation to a more convenient time.</small>

mosis cleri nostræ Cantuariensis provinciæ clamoribus personuerunt ac personant, quod nedum clerus, sed et populus universus assiduis visitationibus ac procurationum exactionibus immodicis, ac cæteris oneribus ita premantur, ut, in maximum sui status ac ministerii scandalum, vix habeant quo victum et vestitum suos teneantur [*sic*]; nos igitur (sicuti tenemur) cleri ac ministrorum dictæ nostræ Cantuariensis provinciæ prementi necessitati obviare ex animo cupientes, ac quietem et tranquillitatem totius provinciæ nostræ, a comnium ubilibet in eadem degentium, præsertim in hoc tam negotioso anni tempore, summe curantes, visitationem nostram metropoliticam hujusmodi in et per totam provinciam nostram Cantuariensem inchoandam et exercendam usque in aliud tempus, quo eandem commodins exercere possimus, duximus deferendam. Et quia ad

<small>The archbishop has heard that several of his suffragan bishops propose to vis.t within their dioceses.</small>

nostrum nuper pervenerat auditum, quod nonnulli venerabiles confratres nostri provinciæ nostræ Cantuariensis episcopi suffraganei clerum et populum diœcesium snarum propediem visitare proponunt et intendunt, vobis, ac illis omnibus et singulis,

<small>Whereupon he forbids their doing so, under pain of contempt.</small>

ex causis prædictis, et aliis nos in hac parte specialiter moventibus, sub modo et forma subscriptis duximus inhibendum. Quocirca fraternitati vestræ tenore præsentium committimus et mandamus, quatenus, receptis præsentibus, cum omni qua fieri poterit matura celeritate, omnibus et singulis venerabilibus confratribus nostris, episcopis suffraganeis provinciæ nostræ Cantuariensis vice et auctoritate nostris inhibeatis, (quibus nos etiam tenore præsentium sic inhibemus); ne a tempore inhibitionis hujusmodi, eis aut eorum alieni in hac parte fiendæ ecclesias suas cathedrales, aut civitates vel diœceses suas, clerumve aut populum in eisdem degentem sive residentem visitare, seu visitari facere conentur, aut illorum aliquis conetur, sub pœna contemptus illis et eorum cuilibet infligenda, donec et quousque

<small>He also inhibits the bishop of London from attempting to visit under the same penalty.</small>

aliud a nobis habuerint in mandatis. Vobis etiam, confrater antedicte, tenore præsentium inhibemus, ac per vos officiariis et ministris vestris quibuscumque sic inhiberi volumus et mandamus, ne a tempore receptionis præsentium, ecclesiam vestram cathedralem, ac civitatem, vel diœcesim Londoniensem prædictam clerumque aut populum in eisdem degentem sive residentem visitare, seu visitari facere conemini, aut illorum aliquis conetur, sub pœna prædicta, donec et quousque alind a nobis habueritis in mandatis; salvis tamen vobis et illis, ac vestris et eorum officiariis, et ministris quibuscumque omnimodis jurisdictionis vestræ spiritualis et ecclesiasticæ exercitiis, in et per totas civitates et diœceses vestras respective (visitationibus ordinariis earundem duntaxat exceptis) præsentibus literis nostris inhibitoriis in aliquo non obstantibus. In cujus rei testimonium sigillum nostrum præsentibus apponi fecimus. Dat. vicesimo septimo die mensis Maii, anno Domini 1560, et nostræ consecrationis anno primo[1].

LXXXI.

THE LORDS OF THE COUNCIL TO ARCHBISHOP PARKER.

30th May, 1560. Parker MSS. C. C. Coll. Camb. cxiv. art. 30. p. 99. Orig.

AFTER our very hearty commendations to your good Lordship. Where there is presently void in the realm of Ireland the archbishoprick of Armagh and the bishoprick of Meath[2], the Queen's Majesty would have your Lordship to consider of some meet men to be preferred to the same, to the end that her Highness understanding from you who you think meet for this purpose, she may collate the same unto them accordingly. And thus praying your Lordship we may understand shortly what you shall do herein, we bid you right heartily farewell. From Greenwich, the 30th of May, 1560.

The archbishoprick of Armagh and bishoprick of Meath being vacant, the Queen desires Parker to recommend to her men meet to be preferred to those dignities.

Your good Lordship's assured loving friends,

W. HOWARD.
THO. PARRY.   G. ROGERS.
WILLIAM PETRE. S.[3]   ED. SAKEVYLE.

[1 There is on the archiepiscopal register (I. 220 b.) an entry of a special inhibition to the same effect as the above, dated on the 17th May, 1560, and addressed to John [Scory], bishop of Hereford.]

[2 The see of Armagh was filled up in 1562 by the nomination of Dr Adam Loftus, that of Meath in the year following, by the like nomination of Dr Hugh Brady. Ware's Works concerning Ireland, ed. Harris, I. 94. 156.]

[3 That is, "Secretary."]

LXXXII.

SIR WILLIAM PETRE TO ARCHBISHOP PARKER.

6th June, 1560. Parker MSS. C. C. Coll. Camb. cxiv. art. 214. p. 579. Orig.

Parker appointed on a commission to settle statutes for Christchurch, Oxford. The bishop of Ely understands the matter well.

IT may please your grace to receive hereinclosed a commission from the Queen's Majesty addressed to your grace and others for the consideration of the statutes for the college called Christchurch in Oxford. My Lord of Ely[1] understandeth well this matter, and although I be named in this commission, yet for that I shall not be able to attend, I pray your grace to take order therein with such others of this commission as be in London. I understand it is necessary and shall be a good deed. And thus I leave to trouble your grace. From Greenwich, this 6th of June, 1560.

Your grace's assured
to command,
WILLIAM PETRE. S.

LXXXIII.

SIR WILLIAM PETRE TO ARCHBISHOP PARKER.

14th July, 1560. Parker MSS. C. C. Coll. Camb. cxiv. art. 217. p. 587. Orig.

"Articles" transmitted from Germany, sent by the Queen to Parker for consideration. He is also to consider what answer should be given as to certain books which the writers desire.

IT may please your grace to receive herewith a letter and Articles[2] inclosed sent of late from certain learned men of Germany, which her Majesty prayeth you to consider, to the intent you may better make such speedy answer to the messenger as shall be convenient. And for the books which they desire, her Majesty also prayeth your grace to consider what may be meet to be answered therein, and to be at the Court to-morrow or upon Tuesday, where you shall by

[1 Bishop Cox, who had been dean of Christchurch.]

[2 Strype speaks of these as "Articles of Religion, as it seems" the object being "to propound an accommodation for union among all that professed the Gospel." After mentioning this letter of Petre he adds, "I am sorry I can give no more account of so material an occurrence." (Bk. II. c. 4. I. 176.)]

her Majesty understand her further pleasure herein. From Greenwich, this 14th of July, 1560.

Your grace's assured
to my power,
WILLIAM PETRE. S.

LXXXIV.

MARQUIS OF WINCHESTER[3] TO ARCHBISHOP PARKER.

17th July, 1560. Parker MSS. C. C. Coll. Camb. CXIV. art. 41. p. 127. Orig.

MY most hearty commendations remembered to your grace. These shall be to give you knowledge that having moved the Queen's Highness to have some preachers appointed in the bishopricks that be not filled, that is, York to have three, Durham two, and Winchester two, to be appointed, as I said to her grace, by the dean and chapter of every diocese; whereunto her Highness made answer, that I should take your grace's advice therein, and to accept such as ye should name to that charge; which I shall gladly do, and allow to every of them for their pains and charge between this and Michaelmas xl marks. And as your grace shall think best to be done herein, let me understand it by your letter; and I shall shew the Queen your grace's advice, and take her Majesty's resolute answer thereof, and proceed therein with your grace's letters to the parties the best I can[4]. Thus fare ye heartily well. Written the 17th of July, 1560.

Marginal notes: Has moved the Queen to have preachers appointed in the vacant dioceses. She wished Parker to be consulted and to nominate.

Your grace's loving friend,
WINCHESTER.

[3 Sir H. Paulet was Earl of Wiltshire, from Jan. 19th, 1550, to Oct. 12th, 1551. On the latter day he was created Marquis of Winchester.]

[4 Dr Bill, then dean of Westminster, wrote to the archbishop from the court, the 18th of July, 1560, on the same subject. "I spake," he says, "with Sir William Peters for preachers to be sent into such dioceses as lacked bishops. He answered that my Lord Treasurer [Lord Winchester] should take order with your grace, as well for the stipend as for the persons, supposing that there were certain prebendaries in Winchester able to supply that diocese if your grace

LXXXV.

LORD KEEPER BACON TO ARCHBISHOP PARKER.
24th July, 1560. Parker MSS. C. C. Coll. Camb. cxiv. art. 38. p. 123. Orig.

The Queen means to dine at Lambeth on Monday next.

I HAVE, since my coming to the Court, heard of Mr Peter that the Queen's Majesty meaneth on Monday[1] next to dine at Lambeth; and although it shall be altogether of her provision, yet I thought meet to make you privy thereto, lest, other men forgetting it, the thing should be too sudden. If this determination change[2] whilst I remain here you shall have word of it. Written in haste this 24th of July, 1560, by

your grace's assuredly,

N. BACON. C. S.

LXXXVI.

ARCHBISHOP PARKER TO BISHOP GRINDAL OF LONDON.
15th August, 1560. Grindal's Register. fo. 7.

Constrained by the great want of ministers, the bishops have admitted sundry artificers and unlearned persons to the ministry.

AFTER our right hearty commendations. Whereas, occasioned by the great want of ministers, we and you both, for tolerable supply thereof, have heretofore admitted unto the ministry sundry artificers and others, not traded and brought up in learning, and, as it happened in a multitude, some that were of base occupations: forasmuch as now by experience it is seen that such manner of men, partly by reason of their former profane arts, partly by their light behaviour otherwise

Such persons are very offensive to the people, and are thought to do more harm than good.

and trade of life, are very offensive unto the people, yea, and to the wise of this realm are thought to do great deal more hurt than good, the Gospel there sustaining slander; these shall be to desire and require you hereafter to be very cir-

liked them. And then two others to be appointed in to the North for the bishoprick should suffice, and those to be taken in the same country, if any notable preachers dwelled in those parts."—Parker MSS. C. C. Coll. Camb. cxiv. art. 308. p. 845. Orig.]

[1 Monday next after the 24th July, 1560, was the 29th.]

[2 The Queen dined at Lambeth on or about July 29th, on her way from Greenwich to Richmond. See Strype's Parker, Bk. II. c. 3. I. 171.]

cumspect in admitting any to the ministry, and only to allow such as, having good testimony of their honest conversation, have been traded and exercised in learning, or at the least have spent their time with teaching of children, excluding all others which have been brought up and sustained themselves either by occupation or other kinds of life alienated from learning. This we pray you diligently to look unto, and to observe not only in your own person, but also to signify this our advertisement to other of our brethren, bishops of our province, in as good speed as ye may: so that you and they may stay from collating such orders to so unmeet persons, unto such time as in a convocation we may meet together, and have further conference thereof. Fare ye heartily well. From our house at Lambeth, the 15th of August, by your loving brother,

Bishop Grindal is therefore required not to admit any to the ministry in future, except such as being of honest conversation, have also been exercised in learning, until the subject can be considered in convocation.

MATHEWE CANTUR.

LXXXVII.

THE LORDS OF THE COUNCIL TO ARCHBISHOP PARKER.

4th September, 1560. Parker MSS. C. C. Coll. Camb. cxiv. art. 23. p. 79.

AFTER our right hearty commendations to your good Lordship. Where Sir Edward Warner, Knight, lieutenant of the Tower, hath made request unto us that such prisoners as remain in his charge, having been committed from your Lordship and others for ecclesiastical causes, may be suffered to come together at their meals to two several tables; forasmuch as for our part we see no cause but that they may well enough so do, unless you shall know some occasion to the contrary, we have thought meet to refer the consideration thereof unto your Lordship, praying you, in case you think as we do, that the said prisoners may be suffered to come to two tables without inconvenience, that then you do by your letter signify unto the said lieutenant of the Tower[3] that he do suffer them so to do, prescribing nevertheless this

The Lieutenant of the Tower has desired permission for the prisoners committed for ecclesiastical causes to dine at two tables. The lords of the council remit the determination of the question to the archbishop.

[3 The archbishop's letter to the lieutenant of the Tower is printed, No. LXXXVIII.]

order unto him, that Dr Heath, Dr Boxall, Dr Pates, and Dr Feckenham, be admitted in one company to one of the tables, and to the other table, Dr Thirleby, Dr Bourne, Dr Watson, and Dr Turbervile[1]; or if you shall not think fit that this liberty be given, then may you signify unto us your opinion therein, to the intent we may answer the said lieutenant thereafter. And so we bid your good Lordship right heartily well to fare. From Windsor, the 4th of September, 1560.

Your good Lordship's assured loving friends,

W. NORTHT.   E. CLYNTON.
T. PARRY.   W. CECILL.
ED. SAKEVYLE.

LXXXVIII.
ARCHBISHOP PARKER TO SIR EDWARD WARNER, THE LIEUTENANT OF THE TOWER.

6th September, [1560.] Parker MSS. C. C. Coll. Camb. cxiv. art. 24. p. 80. Orig. Draft.

The archbishop had interfered to procure further liberty for the ecclesiastical prisoners in the Tower. The Council had referred the matter to the archbishop, who gives directions to the lieutenant of the Tower.

AFTER my right hearty commendations. Where upon my advertisement sent to certain of the Council concerning the further liberty of your prisoners, and for their most comfort to be associated together, ye shall understand that they have addressed their letters of answer again to me referring the order partly to my consideration. Whereupon if ye do conjoin at one table together Mr Doctor Heath, Dr Pates, Dr Feckenham, Dr Boxall, to be of one society, and Mr Dr Thirleby, Dr Bourne, Dr Watson, and Dr Turbervile, of an other, I think as this combination prescribed will not offend them, and as I trust may be done without inconvenience, so it may be your warrant, as knoweth Almighty God, who evermore preserve us all. At my house at Lambeth, this 6th of September.

Your loving friend.

[1 The persons enumerated were amongst the principal authorities of the preceding reign who refused to conform to the ecclesiastical changes under Elizabeth. Dr Heath had been archbishop of York and Lord Chancellor, Dr Boxall, Secretary of State, Dr Pate, bishop of Worcester, Dr Thirleby, bishop of Ely, Dr Bourne, bishop of Bath and Wells, Dr Watson, bishop of Lincoln, Dr Turbervile, bishop of Exeter, and Dr Feckenham, abbot of Westminster.]

LXXXIX.

ARCHBISHOP PARKER TO SIR WILLIAM CECIL.
16th October, [1560]. S. P. O. Domestic, 1560. Orig.

AFTER salutations in Christ to your Honour. This shall be instantly to desire you to make request to the Queen's Majesty that some bishops might be appointed into the North. You would not believe me to tell how often it is required of divers men's hands, and how the people there is offended that they be nothing cared for. Alas, they be people rude of their own nature, and the more had need to be looked to for retaining them in quiet and civility. I fear that whatsoever is now too husbandly saved will be an occasion of further expence in keeping them down, if (as God forfend) they should be too much Irish and savage: peradventure Terence counselleth not amiss: *pecuniam in loco negligere summum interdum lucrum.* I know the Queen's Highness's disposition to be graciously bent to have her people to know and fear God; why should other hinder her good zeal for money sake, as it is most commonly judged? If such as have been named to York and Durham be not acceptable, or of themselves not inclined to be bestowed there, I would wish that some such as be placed already were translated thither. And in mine opinion, if you would have a lawyer at York, the Bishop of St David's, Dr Young[2], is both witty, prudent, and temperate, and man-like. The Bishop of Rochester[3] were well bestowed at Durham, nigh to his own country; where their two bishopricks might be more easily provided for, and less inconvenience though they for a time stood void. And if to the deanery of Durham to join with him were Mr

[2 Dr Thomas Young, Bishop of St David's, was translated to the archbishoprick of York on the 27th January, 1560—1. Dr May, dean of St Paul's, had been nominated for that see, but died in August, 1560. Strype's Grindal, p. 38. fol. edit.]

[3 Dr Edmond Ghest, consecrated Bishop of Rochester, 24th March, 1558—9, was translated to Salisbury, 24th December, 1571, was born at Afferton, in Yorkshire. (Strype's Parker, Bk. II. c. 2. I. 127.) Dr Pilkington was appointed to the see of Durham on the present vacancy, 20th February, 1560—1.]

Skinner[1] appointed, whom I esteem learned, wise and expert, I think ye could not better place them. Now if either of them, or any of us all, should be feared to hurt the state of our churches by exercising any extraordinary patesing[2] for packing and purchasing, this fear might sure be prevented. We have old precedents in law practised in times past for such parties suspected, to be bound at their entry to leave the churches in no worse case, by their defaults, than they found them, and then, what would you have more of us? I have aforetime wearied you in this suit, and till I see these strange delays determined, I shall not cease to trouble your time. If ye hear me not for justice sake, for the zeal ye must bear to Christ's dear souls, importunity shall win one day I doubt not; for I see it hath obtained even *a judicibus iniquis, quanto magis a misericordibus.* Thus concluding, I shall offer my prayer to God that ye may find grace in your solicitations to the Queen's Majesty for the comfort of her people, and discharge of her own soul. At Lambeth, the 16th of October.

Your to my uttermost power,

MATTHUE CANTUAR.

*To the Right Honourable Sir William
Cecil, Knight, principal Secretary to
the Queen's Majesty.*

XC.

BISHOP SANDYS OF WORCESTER TO ARCHBISHOP PARKER.

24th October, 1560. Petyt MS. Inner Temple, No. 47. fol. 376. Orig.

My duty remembered, I thank your grace for your large letters; but I am often put to a doubtful interpretation by reason of your sundry dark sentences, hard to scan forth. As

[1 Ralph Skinner was appointed dean of Durham on this recommendation. He died in 1563. Strype's Annals, Bk. I. c. i. 515.]

[2 This word is clearly thus written "patesing." Circumstances in the life of Richard Pates, bishop of Worcester, during the reign of Queen Mary, render it any thing but uncharitable to inquire whether the word may not have contained an allusion to that prelate.]

I doubt not of equity at your hands, so have I at all times assured myself of your friendship.

In Northfolk and Arden's deprivation, truth is, I neither followed affection, nor sought my private gain. I was right sorry that they compelled me to do as they deserved I should do, and their displacing can no way profit me. Only I sought therein the vantage of Christ's church. They have bragged, but I never thought they should find so much favour at your hands. I know your nature in shewing of humanity, which I never misliked. And as I judge yours to be good, so I think ye will not utterly condemn all Germanical natures. For Germany hath brought forth as good natures as England hath. And if ye mean of us which were strangers in Germany for a time, sure I am there be some of us that be neither big-hearted nor proud-minded, but can in all simplicity seek the kingdom of Christ. And most sure I am that there be of us which have given you no offence, but have offended others in defending of you, and have favoured you and your authority so much as any your other friends have done. And for my part, I am right glad that ye know from whence it cometh that Canterbury is misliked. If ye know truly, sure I am I shall not be blamed. If ye follow suspicions, ye may easily be deceived. *Et si liceat pace et bona cum venia tua dicere, soles aliquando nimium in eam declinare partem.* And many probable collections may cause prudent men sometimes to conclude *indirectè*. As when ye think or suspect that my letters of answer written unto you were first expended by my Lord of London, and so sent down. Certainly he never see [*sic*] them. I have at no time so distrusted either your good will, or yet mine own wit, that I durst not write unto you without such perusing of my letters beforehand.

Truth is, I wrote a letter to my chancellor, which then was at London, requiring him to certify your grace fully concerning my visitation. The letter written unto you, whereof I made mention, was inclosed in his letter. He returned or the letter was delivered. His friend at London, to whose hands it came, sent down the letter again to my chancellor, and yours enclosed. This is most true. Neither was I at that time, neither am I at this time, either so delicate or soft in body, either so tender in ear, but that I could and can gladly receive *vulnera amantis*, yet methink *quod amantis est vulnerare delinquentes*, and not to burthen the blameless.

Sandys's visitation was with Parker's consent, and instead of being to his gain, was to his loss of £24.

For as concerning my visitation, wherewith your grace seemed so much offended, and that therein I sought my commodity, before I was lukewarm in place: first, I visited with your consent; I proceeded orderly, according to laws and injunctions; I innovated nothing; I was altogether led by laws; what sobriety I used, let the adversary report; I redressed, as I could, disorders, and punished sin; and my private gain was £24. loss; I gained only in doing some piece of duty, and that with my great travail; those sharp letters whereof I spake I have put out of the way, because I would neither hereafter see them, nor remember them.

Parker had accused him of seeking to win favour "against another day." His answer.

Where your grace burdeneth me, that I should think that men may do something to win a favour against another day; methink, I am sure, I wrote no such matter. That were too unadvised; for I am persuaded that neither you nor I shall find favour at that day. Ye bid me live and leave off talking. Sir, in my best life, I confess with Paul, *quod primus sum peccatorum*; yet I hope *quod nemo de me queri possit*, except malice overturn truth. I have *testimonium conscientiæ*, that my chief study is, that my life hinder not my preaching. And I trust my adversary cannot be so impudent as to open mouth against me. My Lord of Hereford and I be neighbours, and we often meet and confer by reason of council-matters here, and commissions directed unto us. I have brotherly monished him of such things as I saw in him, or heard of him; he hath promised, when occasion shall serve, to do the like to me.

State of the people in his diocese.

How his folks go I cannot well tell, but I assure you mine go so soberly and decently as they offend no piece of the Queen's Majesty's injunctions. For if I be under the yoke, such as pertain to me shall draw in the same yoke with me. And for my preaching and theirs, I trust it is altogether to edify and to win, using *obsecro*, and not *jubeo*. And I thank God the people hear me and believe me, and the chief comfort that I have is, that they universally favour me. I speak not of such as will never receive the truth, or favour honesty. And for the better utterance of the food for the soul, I am forced largely to feed the body. Without loaves people do not follow the word. I spend all and more. If I were on an even board, as I was at the beginning, such joy have I of

He is favoured by them.

Spends all the revenue from his see, and more.

this office, that I could wish to be dispatched; and I have often wrestled with myself in keeping it thus long. If God's cause were not, I should soon be at a point.

Sir, to make an end of my babbling, I shall pray you not to mislike or cut off a hearty well-willer without cause, but to continue my good lord and friend as ye were wont. *Quo amore te amavi, quibus verbis erga te usus sum, qua benevolentia te semper sum prosecutus, utinam æquè ipse scires, atque ille novit, qui abdita cordium scrutatur.* If I be any thing, I am yours, and that unfeignedly. And although ye have, as ye know, put me to sore pinches and danger of too heavy displeasure, yet could I never be persuaded that your good will was alienated from me. If I have been earnest in matters of conscience, I trust ye will not mislike me therein. When God's cause cometh in hand, I forget what displeasure may follow. In all other things, ye know, I could ever be guided by you. As I followed mine own conscience, so condemned I no others. Thus, as I thanked you for your long letters, I pray pardon for mine. The Lord Jesus preserve you to the great profit of his Church. At Hartlebury, October 24th, 1560.

Your grace's in Christ,
ED. WIGORN.

To the right honourable my Lord
of Canterbury his grace.

XCI.

ARCHBISHOP PARKER TO BISHOP GRINDAL OF LONDON.

18th November, 1560. Parker Reg. I. 225 a.

AFTER my right hearty commendations to your lordship premised. This shall be to desire and require you, for certain considerations conducent to the general reformation of the clergy of the province of Canterbury, to certify me on this side the first day of February next ensuing, or so speedily as you may conveniently, of the names and surnames of all and singular deans, archdeacons, chancellors, chaunters, and others having any dignity in your cathedral church, with all the prebendaries of the same. And also of all and singular parsons and vicars within your diocese; and how many of them be resident; and where the absent do dwell and remain; how many of them, as well of your cathedral church as of others beneficed in your diocese, be neither priests nor deacons; noting also the names of all such as be learned and able to preach; and which of them being already licensed do preach accordingly. And, finally, how many of them do commonly keep hospitality. And thus trusting of your lordship's good diligence herein, I wish you most heartily well to fare. From my manor of Lambeth, the 18th of November, 1560.

Your loving brother,
MATTHEWE CANT.

*To the right reverend father in God
the bishop of London*[1].

XCII.

ARCHBISHOP PARKER TO DR YALE HIS CHANCELLOR.

20th November, 1560. Parker Reg. I. fol. 225 a.

I COMMEND me unto you. And being informed that divers malicious persons, abusing as well their bishops, and their officers as others their ordinaries, do surmise untrue griefs and injuries to be done to them by their bishops and other ordinaries, and thereupon do appeal and get from you inhibitions and citations, to the great vexation and trouble both of their ordinaries, and also of their neighbours, the Queen's Majesty's poor subjects, and especially in causes of correction and reformation of their evil lives and manners. For the redress whereof, we will and charge you, that upon your acceptation of any such appeal, you cause an act to be made of it in the records of your court, specifying all circumstances thereof, and withal you take a corporal oath of all such proctors as shall exhibit the same, that as far as he doth

[1 "Memorandum, that there was sent a letter of this tenour to every bishop of the province of Canterbury." Another letter of a similar effect, with the addition of requiring the ages of the incumbents to be stated, occurs in Parker's Reg. I. 280 a.]

know or believe, the grief or cause pretended is true and just; causing also the same proctor to exhibit his proxy, and to make himself party to prosecute the same cause, as well as to appeal; so that if the party appealed be cited, and do appear at day and place appointed, that forthwith he be dismissed, with such charges as the law in that case doth bear, unless the party appealing then presently do prosecute his appeal with effect; and that in every one of your inhibitions you do appoint a reasonable day certain to the party appealing to prosecute his appeal; which if he then do not effectually, you to remit the cause again to the first court with charges reasonable, cutting off in all matters frivolous and frustratory delays, and finishing all causes with such expedition as in any wise the laws may suffer; any style or usage in any of your courts used to the contrary notwithstanding. And if these notes practised shall seem sufficient remedy for the said abuses, after a trial I would have you to frame the effect thereof in form of law, by me to be authorised for a perpetual rule to be observed in your courts. And thus fare you well. From my manor of Lambeth, the 20th of November, anno 1560.

To Mr Dr Yale, my chancellor and judge of my court of audience[2].

Marginal note: If appellants do not prosecute their appeals, the same to be dismissed with costs.

XCIII.

ARCHBISHOP PARKER AND OTHER BISHOPS TO QUEEN ELIZABETH.

Ascribed to A.D. 1560[3]. Petyt MS. Inner Temple, No. 47. fol. 542. Draft in Parker's handwriting.

Most redoubted Sovereign,

As our suit is simple, so in most lowly reverence we beseech your Majesty graciously to accept the same. We wish

[2 "Memorandum, that a letter of the like tenour was sent to Mr Doctor Weston, dean of the arches, of the same date." Park. Reg. I. 225.]

[3 It is very difficult to determine the exact date of this letter.

your Highness all manner benediction from God our heavenly Father, so to proceed in your godly enterprise as ye have blessedly begun and hitherto continued; doubting nothing in your earnest zeal to Godward, but that ye will bear in continual remembrance to advance his honour in your government, as he hath miraculously preserved your estate to restore again the sincerity of his religion. We shall pray to God, the God of hosts, to arm your princely heart with constancy in the same. We know how maliciously the adversary envieth your doings, how he compasseth subtilly to pervert your gracious affection to the same, [for Satan is no slugger, nor Judas no sleeper[1]]; but we trust, that he whose cause it is, and who hath begun this notable work in you, shall perform it to the glory of God, to your eternal fame and renown, to the establishing of your reign in all prosperity and wealth, and to the comfort of the whole Christian world, which, as may appear daily at eye[2], laboureth universally to be disburdened from that old tyrannical yoke, and to aspire to Christian liberty, which we now, by God's mercy and your authority, do peaceably enjoy. Only our care shall be to labour in our vocations, that this incomparable benefit of God be not turned in your subjects to carnal liberty. Our travail shall be the more comfortable herein to us, being assured of your Majesty's favour to continue towards our endeavours.

In trust whereof, according to our duty of vigilancy over your loving people, we have of late in our consultations devised certain orders for uniform and quiet ministration in religion. We trust your gracious zeal towards Christ's religion will not improve[3] our doings, though such opportunity of time hath not offered itself as yet to be suitors to your princely authority to have a public set synod to the full determination of such causes.

Some considerations would lead to the conclusion that it was written a little later than 1560, but it has been usually ascribed to that year, and the reasons to the contrary are not sufficiently demonstrative to warrant an interference with the old ascription.]

[1 These words are an addition in the handwriting of Bishop Cox.]
[2 At eye, i. e. at a glance.]
[3 To improve in the sense of *improbare*, to disapprove.]

Furthermore, most sovereign Lady, as in most loyal obedience and duty of allegiance to your Highness, we thought it our parts for our pastoral office, to be solicitous in that cause which all your loving subjects so daily sigh for and morningly in their prayers desire to appear to their eyes. Marriage we all wish to see your godly affection inclined to, whereby your noble blood might be continued to reign over us to our great joy and comfort, whereby the great fears of ruin of this your ancient empire might be prevented, the destruction of your natural-born subjects avoided. We cannot but fear this continued sterility in your Highness' person to be a great token of God's displeasure toward us. The greatest part of your most assured faithful subjects secretly rejoiceth with thanks to God, to see your reign hitherto so prosperous, the rather for the establishing of God's pure religion again amongst us, but all your natural subjects in general most effectuously do crave at your hand to see you entered into the blessed state of wedlock, whereby your Highness' establishment and their assurance might be fully concluded: the hollow-hearted subject feedeth his hope only in this delay. *Universal desire that the Queen should incline to marriage. Advantages which would result therefrom.*

We do not herein, right godly Lady, as counsellers in policy, but as Christ's ministers in vigilancy, *loquentes ad cor*, and burdening your Majesty's conscience in charity; which is a case incident to our ministry, evermore favourably heard of princes, and faithfully observed of pastors; that is to say, to regard the continuance of sincerity in doctrine, unity in common Christian charity, and safety of realms by godly succession in blood. For the which, with honour be it spoken, your Majesty hath to account before the just Judge, if ye pretermit the ordinary godly means appointed by God's wisdom uttered in his word. *The writers do not advise as counsellers in policy, but as Christ's ministers, and with true faithful hearts.*

Our affections of true heart toward your Majesty in this case of importance could utter many other weighty considerations, but that with words we will not be tedious to your prudent contemplation. But this we may say; until we shall see that fortunate day arise, we shall never repose ourselves to minister in our offices comfortably, in perfect joy and quiet of heart.

Thus beseeching your gracious disposition to interpret our true and faithful hearts, as we most sincerely before Almighty God mean the same, we shall continue to be your

Highness' daily bedesmen, the same eternal God to endue you with all grace, virtue, and honour. Amen.

Your faithful orators,

M. CANT.
E. LONDON.
R. ELY.

XCIV.

QUEEN ELIZABETH TO ARCHBISHOP PARKER AND OTHERS.

22nd January, 1560—1. Regist. Parker. Vol. I. fol. 215 a.

BY THE QUEEN.

ELIZABETH,

Most reverend father in God right trusty and right well-beloved, right reverend father in God right trusty and well-beloved, trusty and right well-beloved, and trusty and well-beloved, we greet you well. Letting you to understand, that where it is provided by act of parliament, holden in the first year of our reign, that whensoever we shall see cause to take further order in any rite or ceremony appointed in the Book of Common Prayer, and our pleasure known therein, either to our commissioners for causes ecclesiastical, or to the metropolitan, that then eftsoons consideration should be had therein. We therefore understanding that there be in the said book certain chapters for lessons and other things appointed to be read, which might be supplied with other chapters or parcels of scripture, tending in the hearing of the unlearned or lay people more to their edification; and that furthermore in sundry churches and chapels where divine service, as prayer, preaching and ministration of the sacraments be used, there is such negligence and lack of convenient reverence used towards the comely keeping and order of the said churches, and specially of the upper part, called the chancels, that it breedeth no small offence and slander to see and consider, on the one part the curiosity and

[marginal notes:]
It is provided by act of parliament, that the Queen may take further order in any rite or ceremony appointed in the Book of Common Prayer.

Wherefore, understanding that the chapters for lessons may be supplied with other chapters tending more to edification,

and that in sundry churches there is such lack of reverence towards their comely keeping as causeth offence,

costs bestowed by all sorts of men upon their private houses, and on the other part the unclean or negligent order and spare-keeping of the house of prayer, by permitting open decays and ruins of coverings, walls and windows, and by appointing unmeet and unseemly tables with foul cloths for the communion of the sacraments, and generally leaving the place of prayers desolate of all cleanliness and of meet ornaments for such a place, whereby it might be known a place provided for divine service; have thought good to require you, our commissioners so authorised by our great seal for causes ecclesiastical, or four of you, whereof we will you, Matthew, archbishop of Canterbury, Edmund, bishop of London, William Bill, our almoner, and Walter Haddon, one of the masters of our requests, to be always two, to peruse the order of the said lessons throughout the whole year, and to cause some new calendars to be imprinted, whereby such chapters or parcels of less edification may be removed, and other more profitable may supply their rooms; and further also to consider, as becometh, the foresaid great disorders in the decays of churches, and in the unseemly keeping and order of the chancels, and such like, and according to your discretions to determine upon some good and speedy means of reformation, and, amongst other things, to order that the tables of the commandments may be comely set or hung up in the east end of the chancel, to be not only read for edification, but also to give some comely ornament and demonstration that the same is a place of religion and prayer; and diligently to provide, that whatsoever ye shall devise, either in this or any other like point, to the reformation of this disorder, that the order and reformation be of one sort and fashion, and that the things prescribed may accord in one form as nigh as ye may; specially that in all collegiate and cathedral churches, where cost may be more probably allowed, one manner to be used; and in all parish-churches also, either the same, or at the least the like, and one manner throughout our realm: and further, we will that where we have caused our Book of Common Service to be translated into the Latin tongue, for the use and exercise of such students and other learned in the Latin tongue, we will also that by your wisdoms and discretions ye prescribe some good orders to the collegiate churches, to which

which have been permitted to have divine service in Latin. we have permitted the use of the divine service and prayer in the Latin tongue, in such sort as ye shall consider to be most meet to be used, in respect of their companies, or of resort of our lay subjects to the said churches, so that our good purpose in the said translation be not frustrated, nor be corruptly abused, contrary to the effect of our meaning. And for the publication of that which you shall order, we will and require you, the archbishop of Canterbury, to see the same put in execution throughout your province, and that you, with the rest of our commissioners before mentioned, prescribe the same to the archbishop now nominated of York[1], to be in like manner set forth in that province, and that the alteration of any thing hereby ensuing be quietly done, without shew of any innovation in the church. And these our letters shall be your sufficient warrant in this behalf. Given under our signet at our palace of Westminster, the two and twentieth of January, the third year of our reign.

> *To the most Reverend father in God, our right trusty and right well-beloved Matthew, archbishop of Canterbury; the Right Reverend father in God, our right trusty and well-beloved Edmund, bishop of London; and to the rest of our commissioners for causes ecclesiastical.*

XCV.

ARCHBISHOP PARKER TO BISHOP GRINDAL OF LONDON.

15th February, 1560—1. Parker Reg. Vol. I. fol. 228 a.

MATTHÆUS, permissione divina Cantuariensis archiepiscopus, totius Angliæ primas et metropolitanus, venerabili confratri nostro domino Edmundo, eadem permissione Londoniensi episcopo, salutem et fraternam in Domino charitatem. *The Queen has addressed* Cum serenissima domina nostra Elizabetha, Dei gratia Angliæ

[1 Archbishop Thomas Young, before mentioned, translated from St David's to York, 27th January, 1560—1.]

Franciæ et Hiberniæ regina, fidei defensor, etc. per literas suas missivas datas apud Westmonasterium 22do die mensis Januarii ultimo præterito, anno regni sui tertio, nobis ac fraternitati vestro[æ?], et allis commissariis suis ad causas ecclesiasticas decidendas per literas suas regias patentes magno sigillo Angliæ sigillatas deputatis et assignatis, inter alia dederit in mandatis, quatenus nos ad Dei optimi maximi gloriam illustrandam et ecclesiæ Anglicanæ honorem, et ad tollendum dissensiones et controversias inter subditos dictæ dominæ reginæ, et consensum veræ religionis firmandum, juxta tenorem cujusdam statuti in parliamento Angliæ tento apud Westmonasterium, anno primo regni ejusdem dominæ nostræ reginæ editi, quædam decreta sive ordinationes, correctiones, interpretatienes, seu reformationes conciperemus et faceremus ; ac nobis Matthæo, archiepiscopo Cantuariensi antedicto, per easdem literas suas missivas firmiter præcipiendo mandaverit, quatenus decreta, ordinationes, correctiones, seu reformationes prædictas in et per totam provinciam nostram Cantuariensem publicari et executioni demandari faceremus, prout in literis regiis missivis antedictis, (quarum tenores pro hic insertis haberi volumus,) inter alia latins continetur et describitur; Nos vero, affectantes ex animo ejusdem dominæ nostræ reginæ literis et mandatis obtemperare, volentesque pro nostro erga suam celsitudinem regiam officio demandatis et concreditis nobis a sua celsitudine negotiis omnem nostram curam et solertem adhibere diligentiam, fraternitati vestræ ex parte suæ regiæ majestatis firmiter præcipiendo mandamus, quatenus receptis præsentibus, cum omni qua poteritis celeritate et matura diligentia, ordinationes, correctiones, seu reformationes Kalendarii, simul cum tabulis præceptorum Dei, per nos et alios regios commissarios auctoritate et vigore dictarum literarum snarum regiarum missivarum, juxta formam statuti prædicti factas, conceptas, et stabilitas, quorum exemplaria in papiro impressa vobis, præsentibus annexa, transmittimus, omnibus et singulis venerabilibus confratribus nostris provinciæ nostræ Cantuariensis coepiscopis, et ecclesiæ nostræ Christi Cantuariensis suffraganeis publicetis et declaretis, eisque et eorum cuilibet ex parte dominæ nostræ reginæ firmiter præcipiatis, quatenus ipsorum singuli in suis cathedralibus ecclesiis, necnon civitatum et diœcesium snarum parochianis ecclesiis, ordinationes seu reformationes Kalendarii et tabulas præceptorum Dei prædictas, in

charging them to see that the same be inviolably observed.

omnibus et per omnia, juxta præscriptum literarum regiarum, inviolabiliter observari et perimpleri sedulo et accurate curent cum effectu, et fieri non postponant; sicque a vobis, frater charissime, in ecclesia vestra cathedrali, ac in et per civitatem et diœcesem vestram Londoniensem per omnia fieri et perimpleri volumus et mandamus. Datum in manerio nostro de Lambeth, decimo quinto die mensis Februarii, anno Domini 1560, et nostræ consecrationis anno secundo.

XCVI.

ARCHBISHOP PARKER TO LORD THOMAS HOWARD[1].

13th April, 1561. Parker MSS. C. C. Coll. Camb. cxiv. p. 165 b. Orig. Draft.

Application for a dispensation to allow a child of 13 or 14 years of age to hold a benefice, declined. The statute reserves "cases unwont" to the prince.

AFTER my hearty commendations to your Lordship. Concerning your request for the behoof of your servant, who desireth his child of thirteen or fourteen years of age to be abled by dispensation to take the cure of the rectory of Broadway, your Lordship shall understand that the statute made in the 21st of King Henry VIII. permitteth me not to dispense with any one to have cure of soul, being not at all within any order and being mere lay: for to dispense with such one to take benefice is one of the cases unwont, and appertaineth to the prince only; and if that this young student had a dispensation for the delay of his orders-taking, yet he were not freed with for his laity, and the bishop might repel him at his institution and so should [he] bestow his cost but in vain. Thus, being sorry that I cannot effectuously satisfy your Lordship's request in this matter, I wish your Lordship as well to fare as myself. At my manor, this thirteenth of April.

*To the right honourable and his loving
friend, the Lord Thomas Howard, be
it delivered.*

[1 Probably the second son of Thomas, first Viscount Howard of Bindon, and afterwards himself third Viscount Howard of Bindon, and K. G. (Dugdale's Baronage, ii. 274.)]

XCVII.

BISHOP RICHARD DAVIES OF ST ASAPH TO ARCHBISHOP PARKER.

18th April, 1561. Parker MSS. C. C. Coll. Camb. cxiv. art. 187. p. 515. Orig.

IT may please your good Grace to be advertised, that meaning with all expedition to have accomplished your Grace's advice and commandment touching my translation, I adventured, being scarce recovered (as now appeareth), to take my journey towards London, and after one day's labour I was cast down again by the way on Wednesday last, not able further to travel. Most humbly therefore beseeching your Grace that like as heretofore you have extended your gracious favour and goodness towards me, so now you would vouchsafe to weigh my case accordingly. My state of health is so doubtful that I can determine nothing but as God will. I fear the hasty proceeding of my successor[2] elect (not fully belike understanding my state) may be prejudicial not only to me but to us both, unless your Grace's wisdom do foresee the same, whereunto I refer the state of me and my matters to be further declared to your Grace by this bearer. Thus committing the same to the tuition of Almighty God. From Wrexham, the 18th of April, 1561.

The writer took his journey towards London in order to complete his translation, but was overtaken by illness on the way.

His successor in St Asaph proceeding hastily.

Your Grace's most humble,

RICHARD ASSAPHEN.

[2 Bishop Thomas Davies, who was not appointed until 2nd April, 1562, was this bishop's successor. It seems as if the successor elect here alluded to must have been some other person. The writer accomplished his translation to St David's on 21st May, 1561.]

XCVIII.

SIR WILLIAM CECIL TO ARCHBISHOP PARKER.
After 16th April, 1561. Parker MSS C. C. Coll. Camb. cxiv. art. 181. p. 506.
Orig.

Cecil sends a "merry simple request" of Cheney, afterwards

I BESEECH your Grace consider of this poor man's merry simple request[1]. Indeed it is not his shame to lack, and

[1 The request alluded to is contained in the following letter, on which the present letter of Sir William Cecil is indorsed:

RICHARD CHENEY TO MR SECRETARY CECIL.
16th April, 1561. Parker MSS. C. C. Coll. Camb. cxiv. art. 180, p. 505. Orig.

Because it pleased your mastership so gently to come and offer me your hand upon the leads at the Court, somewhat before Easter, these shall be most heartily to thank you, desiring you to be a help that more preachers may be sent abroad; for everywhere there is *messis multa sed operarii pauci, imo paucissimi*. I find a priest upon my 10*l*. benefice of Halford in Warwickshire, because I would go abroad and do some good where no preacher cometh. My priest hath 10*l*. out of my 10*l*. 10*s*., and I live there of the residue. I remember that when I preached before the Queen's Majesty rudely after the country fashion, I spake of the Queen's takers, but or I came home again from London then, they had taken a quarter of my wheat, which I would take money for if I might get it, and so would other poor men where I dwell. The hope whereof caused me to take my journey to Oxford, where I communed with certain learned men touching the true pronunciation of the Greek tongue, who stiffly defended the usual manner of pronouncing. Beware, learned masters, (said I) that while you wilfully go about to defend an untruth in this matter, you fall not into such an inconvenience as I once knew a bishop do. They would needs know how and wherein. I sat once (said I) at table with a bishop that did, as you now do, defend the untrue pronunciation of this Greek letter H. And after that I had declared many absurdities that followed thereof, I desired him to consider a few words written in the 27th of St Matthew. He immediately called for the New Testament in Greek. I appointed him a line or two in the place as before. He read, among other, these four words, Ἡλεὶ Ἡλεὶ λαμᾶ σαβαχθανὶ, making false Greek, but true English, pronouncing plainly *I lie, I lie*. Let this be a warning for you, learned masters, said I, for fear. There were in company then the Commissary, Doctor Babington, Doctor Wright, Archdeacon of Oxford, the Provost of Oriel College, with other. So we made an end of this matter merrily at the Bear, on the Annunciation-even last: and D. Babington gave me your old tutor's book of this matter, which I

therefore for God's sake let him be helped. I cannot with leisure do for him, but whatsoever your Grace will devise for me to do I will not forbear. Your Grace's at command.

W. CECILL.

Bishop of Gloucester, which he wishes Parker to consider, and let the writer be helped.

XCIX.

FLACIUS ILLYRICUS TO ARCHBISHOP PARKER.

22nd May, 1561. Parker MSS. C. C. Coll. Camb. cxix. art. 47. p. 127. Orig.

SALUTEM a Domino Jesu, unico piorum servatore. Amen.

Reverende in Domino Pater; cum statuissemus mittere istuc hominem idoneum accipiendorum veterum monumentorum gratia, quæ nobis R. M. ante annum per tuas literas pollicita est, putavi me etiam separatim aliquid ad T. V. Pat. scribere debere. Eo enim studio veterum monumentorum, præsertim quæ obscuratam Ecclesiæ veritatem illustrare, et pontificiam tyrannidem redarguere possint, ferer, ut non possim non instare ac urgere, ubi modo sese aliqua spes bene gerendæ in

A fit person sent over to receive certain ancient monuments promised him by the Queen through the archbishop.

never saw before, because I dwell in a corner where I see nothing; but I feel that I am worse by 40*l*. within this two years than I was before, such hath been my late gains. The cause hath been my gentle and loving friends, who have four or five times called me to London, and offering me a bishoprick; but I cannot think myself worthy so high a room; and as for the prebend of Westminster, it were more meet for one that would be resident upon it, as I intend not to be, and therefore I shall receive but 10*l*. by year. I began first in mine youth at the Court, but I intend to make an end in mine age at the cart, at my circumcised benefice. But what do I trouble your mastership with this homely letter in the midst of your weighty and manifold affairs? I trust you will bear with my rudeness and help me also, that where I lost 16*l*. by year before the Queen's Majesty's visitors at Aylesbury, and half a year's rent to boot, without recompence, I may somewhat be recompensed by your goodness, as my trust is. Or if your pleasure be that I only shall be a leeser [loser] in these days, that had more conference with the learned men of the contrary side in Queen Mary's time than many other had, I will hold me content with 40*l*. loss. Thus I bid your Mastership most heartily farewell. From Halford, in the south edge of Warwickshire, this 16th of April, 1561.

RYCHARD CHENY.

[*To the right honourable Mr Cecil, Secretary to the Queen's Majesty, at the Court, give this.*]

hac parte rei offerat, etiamsi minus decore id facere videar. Præterquam igitur quod et optamus et expectamus premissa monumenta, valde utile esset tuam Rev. P. id agere ut et istic in vestro regno et in Scotia, ex locis remotioribus et ignobilioribus, in certa quædam et illustriora comportarentur, omnes libri manuscripti et qui rariores esse existimarentur, aut etiam quorum nomina plane ignorarentur; quorum quidem non adeo infinitus esset futurus numerus, neque adeo immensos sumptus ea res postularet. Non etiam haberent quod civitates quererentur se libris spoliari, cum eis omnia impressa et etiam manuscripta monumenta patrum et aliorum scriptorum, quæ alioqui extant, relinquerentur. Quo vero eo facilius librorum historiæ ecclesiasticæ utilium conquisitio fieri possit, mitto indicem quendam quasi generalem. Baleus coram mihi narravit, se multa admodum vetera monumenta habere, quæ utile esset post ejus mortem in publicas bibliothecas regni retrahi, sicut et aliorum monumenta. Nam præterquam quod in privatorum ædibus facile, præsertim succedentibus indoctis hæredibus, intereant, et jam non sunt istiusmodi res, toti regno ac Ecclesiæ necessariæ, privati juris aut possessionis propriæ, sed publici. Utinam autem vacaret aliquando ipsi coram inspicere ac perlustrare omnes istic veteres codices, ut multas bibliothecas in Germania et Italia perspexi, sperarem me multa utilia vobis et nobis reperire; et inter alia etiam meum Catalogum Testium Veritatis egregie augere posse. Sed nec valetude, nec tempus, nec denique sumptus ad tantam peregrinationem et conatum suppetunt. Ut vero vicissim tuæ R. P. et Reg. M. meum humile studium ac officium declarem et probem, mitto muneri DISPUTATIONEM de Originali Corruptione et Libero Arbitrio ante annum coram nostris illustrissimis principibus habitam, contra quendam qui humanarum virium arbitrium potentiamque plane papistico more modoque extollebat, et Deo in conversione et renovatione cooperari volebat: qui quidem error nimia incrementa a morte Lutheri per quosdam in nostris Ecclesiis sumpsit. Quos in ea re secum sentire, Lovanienses in suo primo tomo, Lindanus et Osius in suis prolixis voluminibus, abunde testantur: tametsi id et res ipsa multo clarins loquatur. Quoniam etiam proxime tua ampl. indicavit Matthei Paris chronicon apud vos non reperiri, mitto excerpta ejus quæ dudum per quendam amicum fueram consecutus. Multa enim in hisce ipsis paucis compendio dicuntur, quæ a vestris hominibus legi utile est. Mitto etiam brevem indicem eorum quæ Reg. M. communicare possem, si ea habere cuperet et sumptus in descriptionem exemplarium quæ nobis relinquerentur facere vellet: neque enim prorsus velim hisce scriptis carere, quæ magno labore ac sumptu sum nactus. Curaveram olim, tempore Interim, cum omnes Germanicæ Ecclesiæ institutis cum Antichristo conciliationibus corruituræ videbantur, dedicari tuo antecessori meum librum De Fide; quem an unquam acceperit ignoro, ac forte nec tua quidem P. eum vidit. Quem ideo mitto, ut ea de illo suum mihi judicium, si modo ei vacaverit, perscribat. Cupio enim de tantis rebus eruditissimorum virorum judicia cognoscere. Hæc jam ad T. V. P. forte paulo prolixius perscripsi, quam ad tam occupatum tantæque dignitatis virum a me fieri decuisset, sperans eam benigne ac Christiane omnia in meliorem partem acceptaram esse.

Also a list of books he was ready to part with to the Queen.

Also sends his book De Fide.

Incidit vero adhuc aliquid quod tua C. benigne audiet. Johannem Tilium, Gallum, Episcopum Engolisinensem, qui edidit Canones Græcos cum suo nomine, et Caroli Magni, contra idolatriam imaginum non expresso suo nomine, procul dubio vel de nomine saltem nosti. Dicitur favere puriori religioni. Habet is multa vetera præsertim autem Concilia: forte haud difficulter ab eo tua P. descriptionem eorum exemplarium nancisci posset, et nostro huic instituto accommodare. Extant Romæ quidam boni codices, ut inclusa schedula testatur. Eos vos potentiores ac nummatiores haud difficulter per amicos describi curare possetis. Nos quidem eam rem exploravimus, sed sumptus, et tam potentes intercessores, ut res postulabat, habere nequimus. Tua vero Pat. publicæ utilitatis gratia, omnino aliquid ejusmodi conetur. Nam Anastasium extare valde prefecto operæ pretium esset. Dominus Jesus regat tuam V. P. suo Sancto Spiritu, ad gloriam nominis sui et Ecclesiæ utilitatem, Amen. Jenæ, 22 Maii, 1561.

John Tilius, bishop of Angoulesme, possesses many ancient Councils, of which probably Parker could obtain a description.

MSS. at Rome.

T. V. P. Stud.
MATTHIAS FLACIUS ILLYRICUS.

*Reverendissimo in Christo Patri ac
Domino D. Matthæo, archiepiscopo Cantuariensi suo Domino
plurimum colendo.*

C.
THOMAS SECKFORD TO ARCHBISHOP PARKER.
21st June, 1561. Parker MSS. C. C. Coll. Camb. cxiv. art. 251. p. 691. Orig.

The archbishop is requested to subscribe a presentation to a prebend in the cathedral of Norwich, in the Queen's gift.

MY very good Lord, it may like your Grace to understand that where a prebend is lately fallen void within the cathedral church of Norwich which is in the disposition of the Queen's highness; because I know that Mr Wendon, now archdeacon of Suffolk, is a very fit and sufficient person to receive the preferment thereof (as one of your Grace's own chaplains well know), I am therefore bold to pray your Grace to subscribe[1] your name to his bill of presentation. And I shall be glad, as heretofore I have been, to do your Grace any service that in me shall lie. From the Court, this xxi. day of June, 1561.

Your Grace's to command,

THOMAS SEKFORD[2].

To the most Reverend father and his singular good Lord, my Lord of Canterbury his grace.

CI.
QUEEN ELIZABETH TO ARCHBISHOP PARKER.
24th June, 1561. Regist. Parker. Vol. I. fol. 231 a.

BY THE QUEEN.

Necessity for rebuilding St Paul's.

MOST Reverend father in God, we greet you well. Although we know there needeth no means to provoke you to further the re-edifying of the church of St Paul's[3], in our city of London, being the same, both in respect of Christian religion and for the honour of our realm, a right necessary work to be finished and that with speed, whereby the use of

[[1] The word "subscribed" is written at the bottom of this letter, perhaps as a note of the archbishop's. But the appointment was a very improper one. Archdeacon Wendon was not in orders, and is described as going about in 1565 "in a cloak with a Spanish cape, and a rapier by his side." Shortly afterwards he betook himself to Louvaine, and was returned in 1576 in a list of "fugitives over sea contrary to the statute of 13 Eliz." Strype, Bk. II. App. No. I.]

[[2] Master of Requests to Queen Elizabeth.]

[[3] St Paul's was destroyed by lightning on the 4th June, 1561.]

prayer and divine service may be restored, and the fame and renown by such a work duly recovered, yet to join our authority with your devotion and good will, we do authorise you by way of any manner of usual or other good conference with the bishops of your province, and the principal members of the clergy thereof, to devise upon some contribution of money and relief to be levied and collected of the same clergy, wherein we mean neither to prescribe to you the manner of levying, nor the sum to be contributed, but refer the same to your wisdom, and the consideration of so great a work; and if you shall think meet to be informed therein, upon any special doubt, then to resort to our council, who in that behalf shall give you knowledge and advice of that which shall be convenient. Given under our signet at our manor of Greenwich, the 24th of June, the third year of our reign. *The archbishop authorised to collect a contribution from the clergy.* *And to resort to the Queen's council in case of any special doubt.*

*To the Right Reverend father in God
the archbishop of Canterbury.*

CII.

ARCHBISHOP PARKER TO BISHOP GRINDAL OF LONDON.

1st July, 1561. Regist. Parker. Vol. I. fol. 231 a.

AFTER my right hearty commendations unto your Lordship premised; having received the Queen's Majesty's letters, the tenor whereof I send to you herewith, I have thought good, for the better accomplishment of her Majesty's pleasure herein, to require your Lordship, that not only upon conference with the clergy of your diocese, you do resolve yourselves upon such reasonable imposition and contribution to be collected and answered of our said clergy, towards the re-edifying of the church of Paul's, as may seem correspondent to their several states and preferments in living; but also that you do with all convenient speed signify the tenor of the Queen's Majesty's said letters to the residue of the bishops of my province, requiring them to do the like in their several dioceses: doing your lordship further to understand that I think this rate to be the least that will be accepted, that the clergy of your diocese of London should *Bishop Grindal on conference with his clergy, to resolve on a contribution towards the rebuilding of St Paul's.* *Also to signify the tenor of the Queen's letter to the other bishops of the province of Canterbury, that they may do the like.*

The archbishop thinks the clergy of London should pay the twentieth part of their promotions, and those of other dioceses the thirtieth part.

pay and contribute the twentieth part of their spiritual promotions, and the clergy of every other diocese of my province, being not in their first-fruits, to pay the thirtieth part, and they which be in their first-fruits to pay only the fortieth part of their said promotions, according to the rate taxed in the Queen's Majesty's books; always provided, that stipendiaries and curates, and all such beneficed men which by order of the statute pay no first-fruits, be not in any wise charged herein, unless it be by your good persuasion; and that as well your Lordship for yourself, as also all other my brethren the bishops of my province, by your commandment, to send me your and their resolute order and answer herein with such convenient speed as you and they may. And thus fare you most heartily well. From my manor of Croydon, the first day of July, 1561.

Your loving brother,
MATTHEWE CANTUAR'.

To the right reverend father in God the bishop of London give these.

CIII.

ARCHBISHOP PARKER TO DR NICHOLAS WOTTON[1].

Shortly after 30th June, 1561.   Parker MSS. C. C. Coll. Camb. cxiv. art. 216. p. 283.   Orig. Draft.

Dr Wotton, dean of Canterbury, has recommended Mr Rush to be teacher in the grammar school at Canterbury.

My commendations presupposed to your honour. Where ye sent unto me this man Mr Rush to be considered for his ability and aptness to be teacher in the grammar school at

[1 The MS. is the rough draft of the archbishop's answer to Dr Wotton's letter to him, dated the last day of June, 1561, soliciting that Mr Rush might be appointed to the mastership of Canterbury school. It appears from Dr Wotton's letter, on the fly-leaf of which the archbishop's answer is written, that Mr Rush, after being educated for seven or eight years at Canterbury school, had been maintained by him at Oxford for seven years more, and had since been for seven or eight years a fellow of Magdalene College in that University. He ultimately became one of the Queen's chaplains, and a prebendary of Canterbury.   Strype's Parker, Bk. iv. c. 3]

Canterbury, I have some taste how meet he is by his letter written to me, the copy whereof I do send to you, referring the judgment thereof to yourself. And if ye will further send for Mr dean of Paul's to expend thereby how worthy he were to be commended for such a room, I think it would do well, as your honour and I wish for our honesties a convenient man in that room, such a one as might truly teach the youth the commodity², lest else it might chance them to unlearn again that hath been wrongly taught them. So would there be good advisement in the first admission. *Nam turpius ejicitur quam non admittitur hospes.* I have granted him my licence to preach, which office I think he will competently perform. And thus I commend you to Almighty God as myself.

CIV.

ARCHBISHOP PARKER TO THE SHERIFF OF OXFORD AND BERKS.

2nd July, 1561. Parker Reg. I. 231 b.

AFTER my right hearty commendations premised. Forasmuch as within the diocese of Oxford³ there is no convenient prison for such clerks convict as shall be committed to the custody of the ordinary, I have thought good to request your friendship in this behalf, that you will vouchsafe to permit such prisoners as shall be charged withal within the same diocese, to be safely kept in your common jail at Oxford; wherein like as you shall do me a friendly turn so will I be ready to requite the same upon occasion ministered. And thus fare you heartily well. From my manor of Croydon the second of July, 1561.

To the worshipful Mr Fabyan,
 sheriff of the county of Oxford
 and Berks, give these.

[² This and the preceding word have some appearance of being crossed out.]

[³ The see of Oxford was vacant from 1557 to 1567, and during that portion of the period which fell within the archiepiscopate of Parker, was administered by him.]

CV.

ORDER OF QUEEN ELIZABETH PROHIBITING THE RESIDENCE OF WOMEN IN COLLEGES.

9th August, 1561. Petyt MS. No. 47. fo. 373. Orig.

ELIZABETH R.

The Queen considering that the palaces and houses of cathedrals were built for societies of learned men,

THE Queen's Majesty, considering how the palaces and houses of cathedral churches and colleges of this realm have been, both of ancient and late time, builded and enclosed in severalty[1], to sustain and keep societies of learned men professing study and prayer, for the edification of the Church of God, and so constantly to serve the commonweal; and

and understanding that of late various occupiers thereof being married, keep private households with their families,

understanding of late, that within the houses thereof, as well the chief governors as the prebendaries, students, and members thereof, being married, do keep particular household with their wives, children, and nurses; whereof no small offence groweth to the intent of the founders, and to the quiet and orderly profession of study and learning within the same; hath thought meet to provide remedy herein, lest by sufferance thereof, the rest of the colleges, specially such as be so replenished with young students as the very rooms and buildings be not answerable for such families of women and young children, should follow the like example: and there-

her Majesty commandeth that no head or member of any college or cathedral, shall have his wife to abide with him therein,

fore expressly willeth and commandeth, that no manner of person, being either the head or member of any college or cathedral church within this realm, shall, from the time of the notification hereof in the same college, have, or be permitted to have, within the precinct of any such college, his wife, or other woman, to abide and dwell in the same, or to frequent

on pain of forfeiting all ecclesiastical promotions.

and haunt any lodging within the same college, upon pain, that whosoever shall do to the contrary shall forfeit all ecclesiastical promotions in any cathedral or collegiate church within this realm. And for continuance of this order, her Majesty willeth, that the transcript hereof shall be written in the book of the statutes of every such college, and shall be reputed as parcel of the statutes of the same. Given under

9th August, 1561.

our signet, at our town of Ipswich, the ninth of August, the third year of our reign.

[1 "Enclosed in severalty,"—i.e. so enclosed as to be in a state of complete separation.]

CVI.

ARCHBISHOP PARKER TO SIR WILLIAM CECIL.

11th August, [1561.] S. P. O. Domestic. Orig.

UPON hearing of a Diet for conference of learned men appointed in France[2], I wished that Mr Martyr, or Calvin, or both, could be procured thither; they were as able to stand in defence of a truth, assisted by him whose cause it is, as the adversaries striving against God, *et adversus Christum*, once should have any great cause to glory; *ista prima coitio si bene successerit, melius sperandum de cetero.* We be careful to re-edify a decayed temple, which is a good deed; if we all were as careful to help the re-edifying of so great a church as France is to Christ again, beside the commodity which should redound to that realm, it could not but turn to our own quiet at home, to have more friends in conjunction of religion; which is of more force to bind amity durable in men's hearts, than all extern worldly policies whatsoever. God grant that as God sheweth us of his part continual experience of his favour, we deserve not by our continual indurate negligence to be forsaken.

The examination of yonder lady of Lincoln[3] is returned, whereof I think ye have heard. In mine opinion, but that honour[4] is marvellously exalted, it were honourable to God she were chastised in Bridewell for example, and if my lord hath given her frailty any just occasion of forgetting her duty, he were well worthy to be thoroughly chidden, for his correction, of the council. But yet now, thus ceasing from this hot zeal, God preserve your affection still careful for promoting his word; which your pain will be once remembered *in resurrectione justorum.* Which God grant may be joyful to us all, though here we be in heaviness and affliction, by the

[2 A conference between Roman Catholics and Protestants was held at Poissy in August and September, 1561.]

[3 There was no Earl of Lincoln at this time. It does not appear to what particular "lady of Lincoln" the passage alludes.]

[4 The original has "honor honor is," &c.]

consideration of men's evil doings. At Lambeth, this 11th of
August.

Your [honour's] alway in Christ,

MATTH. CANTUAR.

I would God the Apology[1] had been scattered in France
before this conference had begun.

To the Right Honourable Sir William Cecil, knight, principal secretary to the Queen's majesty, at the Court.

CVII.

SIR WILLIAM CECIL TO ARCHBISHOP PARKER.

12th August, 1561. Petyt MS. No. 47. fol. 372. Orig.

The Queen offended with the clergy, on account of the indiscreet behaviour of those of Suffolk and Essex.

YOUR Grace shall understand, that I have had hitherto a troublesome progress, to stay the Queen's Majesty from daily offence conceived against the clergy, by reason of the undiscreet behaviour of the readers and ministers in these countries of Suffolk and Essex. Surely here be many slender ministers, and such nakedness of religion as it overthroweth my credit. Her Majesty continueth very evil affected to the state of matrimony in the clergy. And if [I] were not therein very stiff, her Majesty would utterly and openly condemn and forbid it. In the end, for her satisfaction, this injunction now sent to your Grace is devised[2]. The good order thereof shall do no harm. I have devised to send it in this sort to your Grace for your province; and to the archbishop of York for his; and to the Chancellors of the two Universities for their charge; so as it shall not be promulged to be popular.

She is very evil affected to the state of matrimony in the clergy.

For her satisfaction, the injunction before printed, No CV., has been devised.

[1 Jewel's Apology was written in the year 1561, and "sent to Secretary Cecil for his judgment and the Queen's approbation." (Strype's Parker, Bk. II. c. 6.) It was published in the following year.]

[2 See No. CV., printed, p. 146.]

The bishop of Norwich[3] is blamed even of the best sort for his remissness in ordering his clergy. He winketh at schismatics and anabaptists, as I am informed. Surely I see great variety in ministration. A surplice may not be borne here. And the ministers follow the folly of the people, calling it charity to feed their fond humour. Oh, my Lord, what shall become of this time?

The Lady Katharine Grey[4] is known to be big with child by the earl of Hertford. She is committed to the Tower, and he sent for home. She saith she is married.

I beseech your Grace devise of some meet master for St John's College in Cambridge[5], and write to me therein, so as I may shew your letter to the Queen's Majesty. From Smallbridge, 12th August, 1561.

Your Grace's at commandment,

W. CECILL.

*To the archbishop of Canterbury's
good grace.*

CVIII.

QUEEN ELIZABETH TO ARCHBISHOP PARKER.

22nd August, 1561. Parker MSS. C. C. Coll. Camb. cxiv. art. 7. p. 21.

BY THE QUEEN.

ELIZABETH R.

MOST reverend father in God, right trusty and right well-beloved, we greet you well. We hear that the fellows of our College of Eton next Windsor, without our assent, or without our pleasure therein by them sought, have chosen

---

[3 Bishop John Parkhurst, 1560—1575.]

[4 The stolen marriage of Katharine, sister of Lady Jane Grey, with Edward, Earl of Hertford, eldest son of the Protector Somerset, is a well known incident in the reign of Elizabeth. The Earl was at this time in France, but returned and shared his wife's imprisonment in the Tower.]

[5 The Mastership was vacant by the promotion of James Pilkington to the see of Durham, March 1560-1: it was given to his brother Leonard Pilkington.]

one[1] to be their provost, of whom there is dispersed very evil fame. And for that you and others have had heretofore commission to visit the same College, as a member of our College in Cambridge[2], which yet continueth: Our pleasure is, that you shall have good consideration hereof, and taking with you such other our commissioners as speedily may be had for such a purpose, repair to our said College and visit the state of the same: and to examine the authority of this rash election, and to make also a good scrutiny of the quality of this pretended provost, using the matter in such sort as whatsoever ye shall duly find in the said pretenced election not justifiable by law, or by laudable usage of that house, that the same be severely reformed, and the persons found therein faulty committed to receive due punishment. The rest of the order of that College we require you to see reduced to the best for the honour of Almighty God and increase of learning. And of your doing we require advertisement[3]. Given under our signet at Lea, the 22nd of August, in the third year of our reign.

To our most Reverend father in God,
our right trusty and right well-
beloved, the archbishop of Canter-
bury, primate of all England.

[[1] The provost whose election was complained of was Richard Bruerne, B.D., Hebrew Professor at Oxford. The election is said to have been tumultuous and irregular. The new provost prevented ejection by resigning.]

[[2] That is, King's College, Cambridge.]

[[3] Strype has printed some considerable extracts from the report made by Parker and his fellow commissioners, bishop Horne of Winchester, and Sir Anthony Cook (Strype's Parker, Bk. II. c. 7), which he professes to have derived from the original report in the "Paper Office." No such document can now be found in the State Paper Office, nor has it been discovered elsewhere. There are some minutes of the Visitation preserved, Parker MS. cxiv. art. 8. p. 23.]

CIX.

BISHOP COX OF ELY TO ARCHBISHOP PARKER.

— August, 1561. Petyt MS. No. 47. fol. 378. Orig. Draft.

SALUTEM in Christo. I received of late from your Grace by my lord of London, a copy of an edict from the Queen's Majesty concerning priests' wives not to remain in colleges or cathedral churches. Truly methinketh it very reasonable, that places of students should be in all quietness among themselves, and not troubled with any families of women and babes. But, when I consider, on the other part, concerning cathedral churches, I mused upon what ground or information that should be so ordained, forasmuch as it is not needful, but at this present very miserable, and sounding contrary to the ordinance of the Holy Ghost in the scriptures of God. In cathedral churches ye know the dean and prebendaries have large and several houses, one distant from another, and if their wives be driven out, I suppose ye shall seldom find in most of the churches either dean or prebendary resient there. It is also miserable, for that in some churches there is not past one or two there dwelling, and have small living beside their prebend. Now if their families be hurled out suddenly, it seemeth a poor reward for their preaching and godly travail hitherto. There is but one prebendary continually dwelling with his family in Ely church. Turn him out, doves and owls may dwell there for any continual housekeeping. It is miserable that the poor man's family should be turned out; and miserable that such a number of houses should be left desolate. God mercifully provided for his clergy among his people in Moses's time; neither married bishop, priest, nor Levite, was unprovided for living and house. Ye will say, that time was Jewish. Nay, God saw that such marriage was natural, and as St Paul saith, honourable, and to forbid or deface marriage is the doctrine of devils. And therefore the Holy Ghost gave a general rule to deacons, priests, and bishops, that they should be the husbands of one wife, keeping hospitality, bringing up their family virtuously; whereby they might be counted worthier for an higher government in Christ's Church. Albeit of late years, fond and blind devotion in the Latin Church hath marvellously perverted this godly ordinance, with forbidding that which God made free, and with separating of them whom God hath joined.

Methink, I can neither doubt nor distrust, but if the Queen's tender, merciful, and zealous heart towards God's truth were humbly and gently moved in this case, she would bear with my poor man, and some others this winter: and I trust would hereafter suffer two, three, or four, to remain in such vast cathedral churches, as have rooms plenty and several. What rejoicing and jeering the adversaries make! How the godly ministers are discouraged, I will pass over, and so leave you. Dominus Jesus, &c.

CX.

ARCHBISHOP PARKER TO BISHOP GRINDAL OF LONDON.

1st September, 1561.   State Paper Office, Dom. Eliz. Vol. xix. No. 41.   Copy or draft.

AFTER my right hearty commendations unto your good Lordship. Albeit of late receiving the Queen's Majesty's letters touching contribution and relief toward the re-edifying of the cathedral church of St Paul, to be levied and gathered of the clergy of my province, I, for the better accomplishment of her Majesty's pleasure in that behalf sent my letters unto your Lordship[1], and required you that upon conference with the clergy of your diocese of London, ye should resolve yourselves upon some reasonable contribution to be paid and conferred by them towards the re-edifying of the same church, and did you to understand what rate I thought were best; yet, forasmuch as in the proportion of the same rate, respect seemeth rather had to other dioceses of my province than to yours, whereas of congruence and reason your clergy, above others, ought to shew their benevolences in contributing to the re-edifying thereof, it being their cathedral and head church; I have therefore, upon due consideration thereof, thought it meet that all beneficed men within your diocese of

[1 See before, Letter CII. p. 143.]

London being not in firstfruits, of what value soever their benefices and spiritual livings be, shall pay and contribute the 20th part of their several promotions, and they which be yet in firstfruits, the 30th part of their spiritual livings, according to the rate and value taxed in the Queen's Majesty's books. And for curates and stipendiaries, because it is meet that every man which hath any living by the church, in your diocese especially, should according to his ability contribute in this behalf, I think the least rate that can be accepted at their hands is 2s. 6d. of every of them; the payment whereof, as it cannot much burthen them, being so small a sum, so it shall declare their good wills amongst the rest, to the furtherance of such a commendable work. Thus praying your Lordship with all convenient speed to put this in execution[2], I bid you most heartily well to fare. From my manor at Lambeth, the first day of September, 1561.

Marginal notes: Therefore all beneficed persons not in first fruits, should contribute the twentieth, and those in first-fruits the thirtieth of their spiritual livings. Curates and stipendiaries to contribute 2s. 6d. each.

Your loving brother,

MATTHEW CANTUARIEN.

CXI.

ARCHBISHOP PARKER TO ARCHDEACONS AND OTHER ECCLESIASTICAL OFFICERS[3].

1st October, 1561. Parker MSS. C. C. Coll. Camb. cxxii. art. 7. p. 3. Copy.

AFTER my hearty commendations. These shall be to desire and require you, for certain urgent considerations to

[2 The bishop of London communicated the contents of this letter to "the dean of Paules," in a letter dated the 6th September, a copy of which is contained in the same MS. whence we have derived the archbishop's letter. The bishop's letter to the dean had reference only to the "peculiar and exempted churches" within the dean's jurisdiction. Other letters were, no doubt, written to make the Queen's "pleasure," and the archbishop's "advice and commandment," known to the rest of the clergy.]

[3 Strype speaks of this as a letter to the archdeacons. There is nothing however in the MS. to shew to whom it was addressed, and the blank which has never been filled up in the original makes it probable that it was a form, copies of which were to be sent to

certify me, so speedily as you may, of all and singular parsons, vicars, and curates within your   , and how many of them be resident; and where the absent do dwell and remain; how many of them be neither priests nor deacons, noting the names of all such as be learned and able to preach; whether married or unmarried; of what degree; and which of them (being already licensed to preach) do preach accordingly; and finally, how many of them do commonly keep hospitality: and that your certificate in that behalf be conceived and made according to the form herein inclosed. And thus trusting of your diligence herein, I wish you well to fare. From my manor of Lambeth, the 1st of October, A°. 1561.

Your loving friend,
MATTHUE CANTUAR.

CXII.

THE LORDS OF THE COUNCIL TO ARCHBISHOP PARKER.

24th October, 1561. Parker MSS. C. C. Coll. Camb. cxiv. art. 20. p. 69. Orig.

William Rise sent to the archbishop that he may be instructed to recognise the Queen's supremacy.

AFTER our most hearty commendations to your good lordship. We send unto you by the bearer hereof, William Rise, who having been committed to the Tower for the breach of the Queen's Majesty's laws, and disturbing of the state divers ways, seemeth now unto us very humble in all respects, saving in the recognising of the Queen's Majesty's superiority by oath, according to the laws of the realm; and yet therein seemeth not unwilling to be instructed by some learned man; and because we would be glad he might be reduced to order therein, we have thought meet to pray your lordship to let him remain in your house between this and the 20th of November next, and to take some pains with him, as your commodity and leisure will serve, in procuring to instruct him and bring him to conformity by your good counsel and teaching.

various official persons, the space left being filled in with the word diocese, deanery, archdeaconry or the like as the case might be. See Strype's Parker, Bk. II. c. 5. See also above, Letter XCI.]

1561.] THE LORDS OF THE COUNCIL TO ARCHB. PARKER. 155

And of that you shall find to follow of your travel herein we pray you we may be advertised by the said time or before, to the intent that upon knowledge thereof we may cause such further order to be taken with him as shall be convenient[1]. And so we bid your lordship heartily farewell. From St James's, the 24th of October, 1561.

The archbishop to take some pains with him and advertise the Council of the result.

Your good lordship's most assured loving friends,

N. BACON, C. S.   WINCHESTER.   W. NORTHT.
E. CLYNTON.   W. HOWARD.
                                W. CECILL.
AB. CAVE.
WILLM. PETRE, S.   JOHN MASONE.

To our very good lord the archbishop of Canterbury.

CXIII.

THE LORDS OF THE COUNCIL TO ARCHBISHOP PARKER.

14th December, 1561. Parker MSS. C. C. Coll. Camb. CXIV. art. 18. p. 65. Orig.

AFTER our most hearty commendations to your good lordship. Understanding from you that William Rise heretofore committed to your custody is not yet persuaded to receive the oath appointed by statute for the acknowledging of the Queen's Majesty's authority: we have resolved that he shall be returned to the Tower, for which purpose we have

William Rise not having been persuaded to acknowledge the Queen's supremacy is to be returned to the Tower.

[1 On the fly-leaf of this letter is the following acknowledgment apparently in the archbishop's handwriting:

He acknowledgeth Queen Elizabeth, under God, to have the sovereignty and rule over all manner persons born within her realms, dominions, and countries, of what estate, either ecclesiastical or temporal, soever they be; so that no other foreign power shall or ought to have any superiority over the said persons spiritual or temporal.
WILLM. RICE.

Strype asserts upon the authority of this acknowledgment that the archbishop succeeded in bringing Rise to conformity, but he takes no notice of the second letter from the Council to the archbishop, the next in the present collection. Perhaps that letter with its order for his committal to the Tower induced Rice to make the above acknowledgment. See Strype's Parker, Bk. II. c. 9.]

written the letter inclosed to the lieutenant, praying your lordship to send the same together with the body of the said Rise unto him, of whose further custody your lordship is for this time discharged. And thus we bid your good lordship most heartily farewell. From Westminster, the 14th of December, 1561.

Your good lordship's most assured loving friends,

  N. BACON, C. S.
  PENBROKE.   E. CLYNTON.
  G. ROGERS.   W. CECILL.
  AB. CAVE.

To our very good lord the archbishop of Canterbury.

CXIV.

ARCHBISHOP PARKER TO SIR WILLIAM CECIL.

1561. Petyt MS. Inner Temple, No. 47. fol. 374. Parker's Orig. Draft.

Parker laments to perceive the Queen's feeling towards the clergy.

SIR, Yesterday, attending upon the Queen's Majesty to know if her Highness had any especial matter to appoint me, I perceived her affection to be such toward the state of her clergy that I can but lament to see the adversary so to prevail, who either envieth the quiet government of her time, which is now at a good point, with some labour and diligence of our parties, or else, who, under colours of dissimulations, labour to undermine the state of religion, and to intervert, or rather subvert, the Gospel of Christ and the liberty of his holy word. Whose devices I doubt not but he *qui habitat in cœlis deridebit et subsannabit in tempore. Nam Deus est qui custodit veritatem in seculum seculi.*

Was in a horror at words she spake concerning God's holy ordinance of matrimony.

I was in an horror to hear such words to come from her mild nature and christianly learned conscience, as she spake concerning God's holy ordinance and institution of matrimony. I marvelled that our states in that behalf cannot please her Highness, which we doubt nothing at all to please God's sacred Majesty, and trust to stand before God's judgment seat in a good conscience therewith, for all the glorious shine

of counterfeited chastity. And it is a wonder to me that her
Highness is so incensed by our adversaries, that all the world
must understand her displeasure against us. Whereby our
credits be little, our doings (God's service and hers) shall
take less effect among her subjects, to her own disquiet of
government. I never heard or read, but that all manner *Princes did ever use to cherish their ecclesiastical state.*
princes, as well Christian as profane, did evermore cherish
their ecclesiastical state, as conservators of religion, by the
which the people be most strongly knit together in amity,
their hearts stayed and won to God, their obedience holden
under their governors, and we alone of our time openly
brought in hatred, shamed and traduced before the malicious
and ignorant people, as beasts without knowledge to God-
ward, in using this liberty of his word, as men of effrenate
intemperancy, without discretion or any godly disposition
worthy to serve in our state. Insomuch that the Queen's *The Queen expressed a repentance that the clergy of that time [being married] had been appointed in office.*
Highness expressed to me a repentance that we were
thus appointed in office, wishing it had been otherwise.
Which inclination being known at large to Queen Mary's
clergy, they laugh prettily to see how the clergy of our time
is handled, and what equity of laws be ministered to our
sort. But by patience and silence we pass over, &c. and
leave all to God. In the mean time we have cause all to be
utterly discomforted and discouraged.

    Her Majesty moreover talked of other manner Injunctions
that shall hereafter follow. I trust God shall stay her heart, *She talked also of other Injunctions that were to follow.*
as his grace hath moved her to begin godly this good work
(which we take to be God's, and not *hujus seculi*) and so to
proceed, and so to finish. I doubt nothing, though these
œstus humani, conceived upon untrue reports, break sometime from her, that her Majesty will well advise her doings,
and will use Theodosius' days of deliberation in sentence-
giving, in matters of such importance. I would be sorry that
the clergy should have cause to shew disobedience, with
oportet Deo obedire magis quam hominibus. And what *The clergy will not shrink from def^ding Christ's verity.*
instillers soever there be, there be enough of this contemned
flock, which will not shrink to offer their blood to the defence
of Christ's verity, if it be either openly impugned, or secretly
suggilled[1].

    Alas, what policy is this? To drive out hospitality in

[1 Defamed. See p. 11, n. 1.]

cathedral churches, to drive out preachers in the head cities;
which being well instructed, the rest of the country is better
ruled in obedience. And to tarry in cathedral churches with
such open and rebukeful separations, what modest nature can
abide it, or tarry where they be discredited? Horsekeepers'
wives, porters', pantlers', and butlers' wives, may have their
cradles going, and honest learned men expulsed with open
note, who only keep the hospitality, who only be students
and preachers, who only be unfeigned orators, in open prayers,
for the Queen's Majesty's prosperity and continuance; where
others say their back pater-nosters for her in corners. The
extern discipline of this injunction might have been[1] so
ordered, that both abuses might have been reformed or prevented, and yet our estimation preserved for our office sake;
which, for my part, I would I had never entered, and may
rue the time to be the head, to whom resorteth daily and
hourly such complaints as I send you herewith[2], some copies
having of this argument, divers others. I have neither joy
of house, land, or name, so abased by my natural sovereign
good lady: for whose service and honour I would not think
it cost to spend my life; to the contentation of whose desire
and commandment I have earnestly travailed, or else some
things might peradventure have been worse. And where I
have, for the execution of her laws and orders, purchased the
hatred of the adversaries, and also, for moderating some
things indifferent, have procured to have the foul reports of
some Protestants, yet all things thus borne never discomforted
me, so I might please God and serve her Highness. But
yesterday's talk, with such earnest forcing that progresshunting Injunction made upon the clergy with conference of
no ecclesiastical person, have driven me under the hatches,
and dulled me in all other causes, mourning only to God *in
amaritudine animæ meæ, ut dicam cum Sara, "Peto, Domine, ut de vinculo improperii hujus absolvas me, aut certe
desuper terram eripias me*[3] ".

St Hierome's rhetoric recourseth to my mind, writing
Ad Oceanum in a cause not unlike : " *Nonne legisti ab apo-*

[1 " be," in orig.]

[2 Whose letter or complaint was enclosed does not appear. It may have been that from the bishop of Ely, printed before, No. CIX.]

[3 Tobit iii. 13.]

stolo, unius uxoris virum assumi in sacerdotium, et rem non tempora definiri? &c.... Qui sunt fidei candidati, ne uxores ducant, ne honesta jungant matrimonia, sed de republica Platonis promiscuas uxores, communes liberos habeant, immo caveant qualecumque vocabulum conjugis, ne postquam in Christo crediderint, noceat eis quod aliquando, non concubinas, nec meretrices, sed uxores habeant....Scriptum est, inquit, "Beatus vir cui non imputavit Dominus peccatum," arbitror quod possumus et nos huic cantico aliquid adjungere : beatus vir cui non imputabit Dominus uxorem...Num ignorabat apostolus tergiversationes nostras? Qui dixit "unius uxoris virum," ipse mandavit irreprehensibilem, sobrium, prudentem, ornatum, hospitalem, doctorem, modestum, &c. Ad hæc omnia claudimus oculos, solas videmus uxores[4]*."*
Et Augustinus, "Quod a Domino benedictum est, cur sordidum et contaminatum opus a quibusdam asseritur, nisi quia ipsi Deo manus quodammodo infertur?...Quando enim displicet opus, reprehenditur auctor....Deus dicitur loqui et dubitas? Deus benedixit et reprobas?...Quis audet Dei inventum reprobare, et quod nunquam alicui obfuit nisi adversario veritatis, &c.... Qua ergo ratione accusatur quod minime obesse probatur?...Et ut aliquid de apostolis dicatur, quod ad robur pertinet causæ, certe S. Johannes castimoniæ fuit custos, condiscipulus autem ejus, id est Sanctus Petrus, uxorem habuisse cognoscitur, et primatum ut acciperet inter apostolos non ei obstitit generatio filiorum? Quomodo ergo condemnandum putatur quod non impedit merita, &c.[5]*?"* St Augustine to the same effect.

Et Chrysostomus[6], *"Oportet episcopum unius uxoris, &c. Cur non dixit oportet episcopum angelum esse, nullæ humanæ infirmitati vitiove subjectum? Quia perpaucos hujusmodi inveniri fas erat, episcopis autem plurimis opus fuit, qui per singulas civitates magistri astituerentur. Sed Paulus alibi dicit, volo omnes esse sicuti et meipsum, id est, continentiæ, scilicet, ratione. Igitur, ne in angus-* Also St Chrysostom.

[4 Hieronymi Opera, Epist. ad Occanum, I. 411—424. edit. Vallars. Ven. 1766—1771.]

[5 Lib. Quæstion. Vet. et Novi Test. Augustini Opera, XVI. pp. 568—576. ed. Bassani, 1797.]

[6 In 1 Epist. ad Timoth. cap. 3. Hom. X. Opera, Basil, 1547. Tom. V. pp. 1480, 1481.]

tum nimis cam concluderet rem, si exactissimam virtutem expetisset, idcirco moderatiore admonitione maluit uti, ne ex desperatione perfectæ illius inveniendæ virtutis ecclesiæ sine episcopis essent, &c."

To conclude infinite such places with St Hierome, *Non sunt tanti virgines, quanti necessarii sunt sacerdotes*[1], whose affections with the honesty of the cause allowed in God's word, shall stablish my conscience with others, *ut portemus probrum Christi cum gaudio, respicientes in authorem et consummatorem Jesum, qui proposito sibi gaudio sustinuit crucem, confusione contempta.*

The clergy stablished by God's word and their own consciences will bear the reproach of Christ.

CXV.

JOHN FOX TO ARCHBISHOP PARKER AND BISHOP GRINDAL OF LONDON.

—— 1561[2]. Additional MS. Brit. Mus. 19,400. art. 50. Orig.

REVERENDISSIMO domino Matthæo Archiepiscopo Cantuariensi, et Domino Edmundo Episcopo Londinensi.

Reverendissimi in Domino antistites, salutem. Reperi nuper in registro ecclesiæ Londinensis, illustrem disputationem illam D. Cranmeri, D. Ridlei et D. Latimeri cum theologis Oxoniensibus, sub sigillo ejus universitatis et subscriptione notariorum per Hugonem Westonum et quosdam jurisconsultos exhibitam esse in æde convocationis, quæ primo Mariæ anno, sub Bonero episcopo, celebrata est. Continebantur præterea sub eodem sigillo et alia nescio quæ scripta, non indigna fortassis cognitione, si quo modo comparari possent. Nos hactenus in iis pervestigandis functi diligentia nostra sumus: ea quum nil profecit, opus est auctoritate vestra. Compellatus

Fox has lately found in the register of the bishop of London, that a certified copy of the celebrated disputation of Cranmer, Ridley, and Latimer at Oxford, was exhibited in the convocation house, 1º Mariæ.

[1 Hieronymi Opera, II. 291, edit. Vallars. Venet. 1766—1771.]
[2 The first English edition of the Martyrology was published in 1562. This letter having been written, as we may judge from the place whence it is dated, whilst some portion of that work was passing through the press, has been assigned to the year preceding. The copy of the Disputation to which this letter refers, was probably found and used by Fox. The very same copy is now Harleian MS. 3642.]

super ea re D. Incentus actuarius respondit, vel in manibus Boneri hærere ejus disputationis acta, vel penes reverendissimum dominum archiepiscopum Cantuariensem custodiri: prorsus sese habere negat. Atque sic habet hujus quidem negotii summa. Quod superest, faciet sublimitas vestra, ea in re quod videbitur, sive ansam hanc a me præbitam vobis arripiendam, sive negligendam potius existimetis. Mea sic quidem fert sententia, ut vix aliud esse putem, in quo reverenda vestra celsitudo vel piæ illorum memoriæ plus tribuere, vel publicis studiis impensius gratificari, magisve bonorum voluntati satisfacere poterit, quam si cura et auctoritate vestra, hæc quæ a doctissimis illis episcopis disputata gestaque sint e latebris aliquando vindicari posteritatique conservari queant. Opto præstantem reverentiam vestram diu in Christo florere quam felicissime. E pistrino nostro typographico. Vestræ celsitudinis in Christo observantissimùs,

Dr Incent states this copy is either in the possession of bishop Boner or of the archbishop of Canterbury.

The archbishop is appealed to for assistance in discovering a document which would so much conduce to the honour of those most learned bishops.

JOAN. FOXUS.

Reverendissimo D. Matthæo, archiepiscopo Cantuariensi, et D. Edmundo episcopo Londinensi.

CXVI.

SIR WILLIAM CECIL TO ARCHBISHOP PARKER.

1st January, 1561—2. Lambeth MS. 959. No. 36. Orig.

I HUMBLY thank your grace for a heap of things wherewith you have gladded me. First and last, your good will and opinion of me; secondly, your beneficial reward; thirdly, this last book, the Apology. Surely for my good meaning to further the cause of God's church, whereof you are a principal minister, I trust you doubt not; and if it were not for maintaining thereof, before God I this write, I would not contentedly abide in this service, to have a thousand pound a month.

If it were not for maintaining God's church, Cecil would not abide in his present service to have £1000. per month

This Apology[3] cometh to me in good season, as your

Publication of Jewel's Apology;

[3 Jewel's Apology, first printed in Latin, with the date of 1562. See a copy of the title-page prefixed to the reprint published by the Parker Society. Jewel's Works, Vol. III. 1848.]

published in good season.

Grace shall see by a letter received out of France this morning from our ambassador, which when you have read I beseech your grace to return. You may see how he would mingle policy and religion together. Surely he is wise and a good servant in this time.

Book negligently printed.

This book is negligently printed, and the margin would [sic] have had the common places marked. I mean to send five or six into France, and as many into Scotland. I forgat yesterday to send an acquittance, which herewith now I send. From Westminster, the first of January, 1561.

Your grace's at command,

W. CECILL.

CXVII.

ARCHBISHOP PARKER TO THE PROVOST AND FELLOWS OF ETON COLLEGE.

25th January, [1561—2]. Parker MSS. C. C. Coll. Camb. CXIV. art. 311. p. 853. Parker's Orig. Draft.

The archbishop recommends Mr Smith for election as a fellow of Eton.

WHEREAS understanding is given[1], that this bearer, Mr Smith, Master of Arts, is desirous to be placed in fellowship in your college, for that it lieth to your charge most specially to consider what meet persons ye should elect to join with you in the good governance of that house to the honour of God and to the expectation of the Queen's Majesty. This is therefore to present him unto your examinations to expend how meet he shall be for your company, praying you the rather at the contemplation of our letters to associate him unto your number if his qualities can agree with the order of your statutes. And thus I wish you well to fare. At Lambeth this 25th of January[2].

[1 The understanding alluded to is contained in a letter addressed by William Day, provost of Eton, to the archbishop, and in which his recommendation of "William Smith of Cambridge" is solicited. Parker MS. C. C. Coll. Camb. CXIV. art. 311.]

[2 The letter of the provost of Eton alluded to in the foregoing note is dated "23rd January, 1561."]

CXVIII.

SIR WILLIAM CECIL TO ARCHBISHOP PARKER.

—— January, 1561—2. Parker MSS. C. C. Coll. Camb. cv. art. 38. p. 363. Orig.

It may please your grace (by this included[3] you shall understand the matter) my lords pray your grace to cause the collection to be copied out with all speed, and to return the original with all speed to us, for my lords mean to return this original to the president of Wales, thereby to try out the writers, because their hands might be sought. January, 1561.

Cecil sends the archbishop a seditious paper to be copied and returned to the council.

Your grace's at command,

W. CECILL.

CXIX.

QUEEN ELIZABETH TO ARCHBISHOP PARKER.

12th February, 1561—2. Parker Reg. fol. 236 a.

Elizabeth, Dei gratia, Angliæ, Franciæ, et Hiberniæ regina, fidei defensor, etc. prædilecto nobis ac reverendissimo in Christo patri ac domino, domino Matthæo, miseratione divina Cantuariensi archiepiscopo, totius Angliæ primati et metropolitano, salutem. Volentes certis de cansis, qued barones nostri de scaccario

The Queen desiring that

[3 The document alluded to was, "a paper book cast abroad in the city of Chester," which the council of Wales, "considering that the same tended to sedition, and contained matters contrary to the Queen's Majesty's laws and proceedings set forth for religion," sent to the Privy Council. It consisted of a set of "Questions," which were afterwards answered by bishop Pilkington, and which are to be found, together with his answers to them, in the Parker Society's edition of his works, pp. 617, &c. They are there stated to have had the same author as the "Addition, with an Apologie to the causes of brinnynge, &c." and are appended to the bishop's Confutation of that Addition. They were however published, as appears from the date of this letter, some six months before the sermon which called forth the Addition was preached; St Paul's having been burned on the 4th, and the sermon preached on the 8th, of June, 1561. See Pilkington's Works, p. 481, notes. Park. Soc. Ed.]

the barons of the exchequer should be certified what hospitals and schools there are within the diocese of Canterbury, with the situations and possessions thereof.

per vos certiorentur, quot et quæ hospitalia et soholæ separatim fuerint infra diœcesim et jurisdictiones vestras Cantuarienses tam in locis exemptis quam non exemptis, et per quæ nomina eadem hospitalia et scholæ vocitentur et nuncupentur, quibusque in comitatibus et villis et parochiis illa et eorum quodlibet situantur et existant, ac quæ hospitalia eorundem separatim fundantur et usitantur, et possessiones eorundem expenduntur ad et pro subsidio et levamine pauperum; denique quæ schola aut scholæ earundem, vel possessiones et reventiones inde vel earundem alicujus, impræsentiarum sustentantur et manutenentur in diœcesi vestra prædicta, tam in locis exemptis et non

The archbishop is commanded to make a return thereof under his seal.

exemptis, una cum nominibus earundem, et illius uniuscujusque; Vobis mandamus, quod tam diligenti indagine scrutatis registris, et aliis archivis vestris præmissa tangentibus, quam aliis viis et modis, quibus maxime videritis expedire, quicquid inde inveneritis, prædictis baronibus nostris apud Westmenasterium a die Paschæ in unum mensem proximum futurum distincte, luculenter, et aperte, absque omissione aliqua, sub sigillo vestro authentico, in pergameno fideliter scriptum et redactum, certificetis, remittentes una cum dicto certificatorio vestro hoc breve. Teste Edwardo Saunders milite[1], apud Westmonasterium, duodecimo die Februarii, anno regni nostri quarto[2].

[[1] The lord chief baron of the exchequer, 1559—1577.]

[[2] The archbishop's return to this writ, made on the 3rd May, 1562, is printed hereafter under that date. Strype has presumed that a considerable delay intervened between the receipt of the writ and the archbishop's instructions to his commissary, or official, to prepare a return, which will be found under the date of 21st March, 1561—2, and has inferred from that circumstance, that the matter was "not over acceptable to the archbishop." But Strype has placed this writ in February 1561, not in 1561—2, and has not considered that such writs, when issued between term and term, were tested on the last day of the preceding term. The 12th of February, the day on which this writ bears teste, was the last day of Hilary Term, but the writ may have been issued some time after that day.]

CXX.

ARCHBISHOP PARKER AND BISHOP GRINDAL OF LONDON TO SIR WILLIAM CECIL.

13th March 1561—2. S. P. O. Domestic. Orig.

AFTER our right hearty commendations. We have thought it good to signify unto you, that it is very necessary the dean, prebendaries, and ministers of the church of Hereford were again under the rule and obedience of their bishop[3], as by letters of like authority from the late most famous prince, King Henry the Eighth, more plainly appeareth. May it therefore please you to be a mean to the Queen's Majesty for her Highness' letters to authorise the now bishop to visit the same church from time to time as occasion shall serve. Whereby that church shall be purged of many enormities, and God's glory greatly advanced. Thus we take our leave, committing you to God's protection. From Lambeth, this 13th of March, 1561.

Parker and Grindal solicit the Queen's authority for the bishop of Hereford to visit the cathedral of that city.

Your assured loving friends,
MATTHUE CANTUAR.
EDM. LONDON.

To the right honourable Sir William Cecil, knight, the Queen's Majesty's principal Secretary.

CXXI.

ARCHBISHOP PARKER TO MR NEVENSON, COMMISSARY OF THE CITY AND DIOCESE OF CANTERBURY.

21st March, 1561—2. Parker Reg. I. 236 a.

I COMMEND me unto you; and having received the Queen's Majesty's writ (the copy whereof I send you herewith), I will and require you, for the better accomplishment of her Majesty's pleasure therein, that within one month at the furthest next after Easter, you do certify me distinctly in writing, how many several hospitals and schools there be within my diocese of Canterbury, and the peculiar jurisdictions within the same,

The archbishop directs his official to prepare a return of hospitals and schools, in obedience to the Queen's writ, before printed, No. cxix.

[3 Dr John Scory, bishop of Chichester, deprived by Queen Mary, was bishop of Hereford from 1559 to 1585.]

and by what names the same hospitals and schools are called, according to the tenor and effect of the said writ. Thus trusting of your diligence, and that you will not fail herein, I wish you well to fare. From my manor of Lambeth, the 21st day of March, 1561.

CXXII.

ARCHBISHOP PARKER TO THE BARONS OF THE EXCHEQUER.

2nd May, 1562. Parker Reg. I. 237 b.

In obedience to the Queen's writ, before printed, No cxix., the archbishop returns an account of all hospitals and schools in his diocese.

HONORABILIBUS viris dominis baronibus curiæ scaccarii illustrissimæ in Christo principis et dominæ nostræ dominæ Elizabethæ, Dei gratia Angliæ, Franciæ, et Hiberniæ Reginæ, fidei defensoris, etc., et ejusdem curiæ thesaurario, ac cæteris in eadem a consiliis, Matthæus, permissione divina Cantuariensis archiepiscopus, totius Angliæ primas et metropolitanus, salutem in Domino sempiternam, ac fidem indubiam præsentibus adhiberi. Breve supradictæ dominæ nostræ reginæ præsentibus annexum nuper cum ea qua decuit obedientia, reverentia, et subjectione humiliter recepimus exequendum, cujus vigore pariter et auctoritate, habita diligenti inquisitione de et super contentis in brevi vestro prædicto, nomina omnium et singulorum hospitalium et scholarum infra diœcesim et jurisdictiones nostras Cantuarienses existentium, ac statum eorundem, quatenus per inquisitionem hujusmodi comperire et invenire potuimus, in schedula præsentibus annexa, describi fecimus et mandavimus. Et sic breve regium prædictum, quantum in nobis fuit aut est, debite sumus executi. In cujus rei testimonium sigillum nostrum præsentibus apponi fecimus. Datum in manerio nostro de Lambeth secundo die mensis Maii, anno Domini 1562, et nostræ consecrationis anno tertio.

The Lazar house of St Lawrence, by Canterbury.

Hospitale leprosorum sancti Laurentii juxta Cantuar.

It was first founded by one Hugo, the second abbot of St Augustine in Canterbury, and by the same first foundation there was appointed a relief for leprous people. And afterward there was appointed a woman under the name of a

prioress, and certain poor women called sisters, who [were]
there placed by the abbot of St Augustine for the time being,
having no certainty of the number of the sisters, and they
had the revenues of the house, which amounteth to xxxj *l.* by
the year; and the same is taxed, and payeth the perpetual
tenth. There be at this present only two poor sisters, and do
receive only forty shillings by year, paid by the farmer there.
The hospital is lamentably misused, by reason of a lease made
by the prioress and sisters of the said hospital to one Sir
Christopher Hales, Knight, which lease, as it is now said, is
come to one Mr Trappes of London.

Hospitale de Harbaldowne prope Cant.

The hospital of Harbaldown, near Canterbury.

It is of the foundation of the lord archbishop of Canterbury, and there be placed sixty poor people, men and women, and they have there corrodies by the lord archbishop for the time being, of perpetual alms. Item, They be not charged with the taxation of the tenths.

Hospitale sancti Johannis Baptistæ extra muros civitatis Cant.

Hospital of St John the Baptist, without the walls of Canterbury.

It is of the like foundation and order, that the hospital of Harbaldown is. *Referatur pro ulteriori declaratione ad reverendissimum.*

Hospitale pauperum sacerdotum civitatis Cant.

Hospital of poor priests, of the city of Canterbury.

It is of the foundation and patronage of the archdeacon of Canterbury. It was ordained for the relief of poor and indigent priests, and to be relieved of the revenues of the house. There is a master of the said hospital, *videlicet*, one Mr Bacon, a temporal man, who is not resident, neither maketh any distribution. The hospital house is marvellously in ruin and decay. It is taxed to the perpetual tenth, and payeth xxii*s.* x*d.* ob.

Hospitale in civitate Cant. vocatum Maynerd's Spittell.

Maynerd's Spittell, in the city of Canterbury.

It is of the foundation of the mayor and commonalty of the city of Canterbury, and they be endowed by their gift with as much lands and old houses as be worth by the year five marks, and not above. There be placed in the said hospital seven poor people, men and women, by the mayor and commonalty, and have no other relief besides the said revenues, but only the said five marks, and the alms of the town. They be not taxed to the tenth.

<small>Hospital of Estbridge, in Canterbury.</small>

Hospitale de Estbridge Cantuar.

It is of the foundation of the lord archbishop of Canterbury. There is a master presented by the lord archbishop, and is instituted and inducted, &c. It is appointed by the foundation, that the same should relieve poor people vagrant, that is to say, to have lodging and fire for a night, two, or three, at the good discretion of the master. There are competently furnished at this day eight beds for poor men in one chamber, and three beds in another chamber for women. And the people resorting are relieved according to the foundation in good reasonable order. The said hospital is taxed to the perpetual tenth, and payeth yearly xlvii$s$. xd. ob.

<small>Hospital of St Bartholomew, near Sandwich.</small>

Hospitale sancti Bartholomæi prope villam Sandwic.

It is of the first foundation of one Sir John Sandwich, Knight, and now of the foundation of the mayor and commonalty of the town of Sandwich. And by the said mayor there are placed, from time to time, the number of twelve brothers and four sisters, who are relieved only of the revenues of the said hospital, amounting to the yearly value by estimation of xl$l$. The said hospital is charitably used to God's glory, and the same surveyed, from time to time, by the mayor of Sandwich, and kept in godly order. It is not taxed to the perpetual tenth.

<small>Ellys's hospital, in Sandwich.</small>

Hospitale infra villam Sandwic. vocatum Ellys hospital.

It was first founded by one Thomas Ellys, and it is now of the foundation and patronage of the mayor and jurates of the same. There be placed, for term of life, eight brothers and four sisters, and they are relieved by alms and the revenues of the said hospital, amounting to xii$l$. by year. The hospital is very charitably ordered, and surveyed by the mayor. It is not taxed to the tenth.

Hospitale divi Johannis, vocatum St John's house of Sandwich.

This house is charitably founded, maintained, and provided by the mayor and jurates, and they have no possessions, and there are relieved twelve poor people, etc.

Hospitale sancti Bartholomæi prope Hythe.

It is of the foundation of Hamond, bishop of Rochester, in the time of Edward the Third. There are according to the foundation thirteen poor people, who are relieved by alms, and by the revenues of the said hospital, amounting to the sum of viii*l.* by year, with the charges. The said hospital is taxed to the tenth, and payeth vii*s.* ii*d.*

Hospitale sancti Johannis de Hith.

It is only founded, ordered, and charitably maintained by the jurates and commonalty of the said town, and there are kept, and daily maintained, eight beds for the needy poor people, and such as are maimed in the wars. The said hospital is endued with so much lands as do amount to vi*l.* by the year. It is not taxed to the tenth.

Domus pauperum apud Wye, vocata Le almshouse.

It is without any foundation, permitted, maintained, and upholden by Sir Thomas Kempe, Knight, only upon his charitable zeal; and there do live certain poor people of alms, &c. It is not charged with any tenth.

Domus leprosorum apud Bobbinge.

It is of the gift and foundation of George Clyfford, gent., of charity. There are harboured none but poor lazar people, who beg for their living. It is not charged with any tenth.

The declaration of schools within the diocese of Canterbury.

First, There is at Canterbury, within the metropolitical church there, a grammar-school by the Queen's Majesty's foundation. The schoolmaster hath by the year xx*l.*, the usher x*l.* It is not taxed nor charged with the tenth.

Wye.

Item, There is at Wye a grammar-school, of the Queen's Majesty's foundation, newly erected, *videlicet*, sithen the dissolution of the college there; and the schoolmaster receiveth yearly xiii*l.* vi*s.* viii*d.* It is not charged with the tenth.

Maidstone.

Item, There is a school erected by the charge of the mayor and commonalty of the town of Maidstone, and have purchased of the King certain lands, to that intent, amounting to ix*l.* vi*s.* viii*d.* It is not charged with the tenth.

Tenterden.

Item, There is a grammar-school at Tenterden, erected by certain parishioners there, who have of charity enfeoffed certain lands to the value of x*l.* by the year. And by the feoffment the schoolmaster is to be elected by the vicar there for the time being. It is not charged with the tenth

---

CXXIII.

ARCHBISHOP PARKER TO SIR WILLIAM CECIL.

[28th October, 1562[1].] S. P. O. Domestic. Orig.

Sir,

After my hearty commendations to your honour.

Parker having some weeks before had certain guests sent to him to be kept in secrecy, inquires whether it be the Queen's pleasure that he should still prepare a table for them, which he finds chargeable in this hard year. Hopes his house will not be made a hostry.

Where ye sent me certain guests, for four or five days to be used in secrecy, now well nigh four or five weeks ago; I would understand therefore whether it be the Queen's pleasure I should still prepare for them, being neither secret in themselves nor refusing open resort of others to their table, which I find in this hard year chargeable, as they look to be entertained; and although Mons. de la Haye be a right honest gentleman, yet other of his resorters and chamber-fellows be very nice, dainty, and imperious, as I am informed. I trust that your wisdom will consider that my house shall not be made an hostry for all times and for all comers which may live of themselves, and at times may betake to such entertained guests as necessity may require for the state of the realm. Otherwise I trust ye will not cause me to be

[1 The letter is indorsed, "28th October, 1562."]

* * I refer you * * *
* * * * * * * [2]
well conformable.
Your honour's always,
MATTH. CANTUAR.

To the right honourable Sir William
Cecil, knight * * *

CXXIV

ARCHBISHOP PARKER TO LORD KEEPER BACON.

[About November, 1562.] Parker MSS. C. C. Coll. Camb. cxiv. art. 223. p. 601.
Parker's own draft.

AFTER my right hearty commendations to your good lordship. This is to certify the same, that I and others have diversely travailed with Doctor Baxterville, partly for his conformity hereafter, and for some satisfaction of his oversight passed by him; and I am in good trust and opinion that he will unfeignedly shew himself a good obedient subject. Whereupon it may please your good lordship, the rather at the contemplation of my letters, to extend your favour to him for his further discharge, doubting not but he will see good cause to be a faithful orator for the Queen's Highness, and shew himself thankful to your honour and to others that hath procured him such a discharge[3]. And thus having nothing else to your lordship, I commend the same to the protection of Almighty God as myself.

[Marginal notes: The archbishop and others have travailed with Dr Baskerville, of whose conformity there is good hope. Parker recommends his "further discharge."]

[2 Mutilated.]
[3 The draft of this letter is written upon the fly-leaf of one addressed to the archbishop by "Richard Sackville," dated the 20th November, 1562. It appears from Richard Sackville's letter, that "Doctor Baskervyle" was received into favour "on his humble submission and promise not only of his own good conformity, but also hereafter to use his diligence and travail to bring others from their like error wherein he hath been in." (Parker MSS. C. C. Coll. Camb. cxiv. art. 222. p. 599.)]

CXXV.

SIR WILLIAM CECIL TO ARCHBISHOP PARKER.

23rd February, 1562—3. Petyt MS. Inner Temple, No. 47. fol. 573. Orig.

Sir William Cecil applies for a Lent licence for the Baron de la Ferte, one of the French hostages.

IT may please your Grace. Monsieur le Baron de la Ferte, one of the hostages here for the French King, requireth licence of the Queen's Majesty to eat flesh in his house this time of Lent; which although for order's sake I do not much allow, yet because he is one of those that is best affected to religion, and a stranger, I have thought good to recommend it to your Grace, praying the same that you will do herein that you shall think may conveniently be. And so I humbly take my leave. From Westminster, the 23rd of February, 1562.

Your Grace's humbly to command,

W. CECILL.

To my lord of Canterbury's Grace.

CXXVI.

SIR WILLIAM CECIL TO ARCHBISHOP PARKER.

27th February, 1562—3. Petyt MS. Inner Temple, No. 47. fol. 572. Orig.

Sir William Cecil applies for a restricted Lent licence for "the lord of Lethington," ambassador from Queen Mary of Scotland.

MY very good lord. The lord of Lethington, lately sent to the Queen's Majesty from the Queen of Scots, desireth to have the use of flesh this Lent. And because he is a stranger come in this charge, I heartily pray your Grace to consider of it, for his satisfaction therein. Marry I trust you will order it with as much restraint and limitation of days, with the manner thereof for himself and his only, as is meet for the example's sake. And so I bid your Grace heartily farewell. From the Court, the 27th of February, 1562.

Your Grace's at command,

W. CECILL.

I beseech your Grace be not too light-handed in licences to every person.

To my lord of Canterbury's Grace.

CXXVII.

ARCHBISHOP PARKER TO SIR WILLIAM CECIL.

Shortly after 14th April, 1563[1]. Petyt MS. Inner Temple, No. 47. fol. 326 b.
Original draft.

SIR,

In consideration of yesternight's talk, calling to remembrance [what] the qualities of all my brethren be in experieuce of our convocation societies, I see some of them to be *pleni rimarum, hac atque illac effluunt,* although indeed the Queen's Majesty may have good cause to be well contented with her choice of the most of them, very few excepted, amongst whom I count my[self]. And furthermore, though we have done amongst ourselves little in our own cause, yet I assure you our mutual conferences have taught us such experiences, that I trust we shall all be the better in governance for hereafter. And where the Queen's Highness doth note me to be too soft and easy, I think divers of my brethren will rather note me, if they were asked, too sharp and too earnest in moderation, which towards them I have used, and will still do, till mediocrity shall be received amongst us. Though toward them *qui foris sunt* I cannot but shew civil affability, and yet, I trust, inclining to no great cowardness, to suffer wilful heads to escape too easily. *Sed ista parerga.*

_{The archbishop thinks the experience of the recent convocation shews some of his brethren to be pleni rimarum, and unstable, yet the Queen has reason to be content with her choice of most of them.}

_{The Queen thinks the archbishop too easy, his brethren think him too sharp and earnest, which he shall continue to be until mediocrity be established.}

I have thought to use this kind of writing to my brethren already departed home, not to recite the Queen's Majesty's name, which I would not have rehearsed to the discouragement of the honest Protestant, nor known too easy, to the rejoice too much of the adversaries, *her* adversaries indeed. I had rather bear the burthen myself, to sustain the note of what they both will, than the good cause should be touched, like to [produce] much quiet obedience. Whereupon though I shall thus write, as having no warrant in writing, to stay full execution of the imperial laws, as it may be so far forced, yet if the jeoparding of my private estimation may do good, that the purpose itself be performed that the Queen would

_{He thinks of sending a letter in the inclosed form to his brethren who have gone home, to prevent their use of the Queen's name to the discouragement of Protestants, and joy of the adversaries.}

[1 This letter appears to have been written shortly after the rising of the parliament and convocation, the former of which rose on the 10th, and the latter on the 14th April, 1563.]

He requests Cecil's corrections of his draft

have done, it shall suffice, I think. If ye shall allow this device, I pray your honour to return it me again with your corrections as ye shall think meet[1].

CXXVIII.

ARCHBISHOP PARKER TO EACH OF HIS SUFFRAGAN BISHOPS.

Shortly after 14th April, 1563. Petyt MS. No. 47. fol. 324. Draft corrected by Sir William Cecil.

To my loving brother, &c. After my right hearty commendations to your lordship. This is upon good and deliberate considerations to require you, as also upon your obedience to charge you, to have a very grave, prudent and godly respect in executing the act of the establishment of the Queen's authority over her ecclesiastical subjects, late passed in this parliament[2]. And that if upon very apparent cause your lordship shall be as it were compelled, for the wilfulness of some of that sort, to tender the oath mentioned in the same act, the peremptory refusal whereof shall endanger them in *premunire*, that immediately upon such refusal of any person ye do address your letters to me, expressing the disorders of such one who is fallen into such danger, and that ye proceed not to offer the said oath a second time, until your lordship shall have my answer returned again to you in writing. Which upon your declaration of the behaviour of such wilful recusants, shall, I trust, extend to the punishment and abolishment of such corrupt members, if reason and clemency will not convince their wilful error and stubborn ignorance. Pray-

The archbishop urges prudence in the execution of the recent act for the establishment of the Queen's authority over her ecclesiastical subjects

Refusal of the required oath to be reported to the archbishop,

not to be tendered a second time without the archbishop's authority.

[1 The original is in some places so altered and interlined, that it is scarcely possible to read it with any certainty. The letter which follows is printed from the original draft here mentioned, as inclosed to Sir William Cecil. It was returned to the archbishop corrected by Sir W. Cecil, in his own hand.]

[2 This was the first act passed in the session of the parliament which had just closed. By the 4th section, the oath of supremacy was to be taken by all persons on ordination, and by the 5th section, the bishops were empowered to tender the oath to all ecclesiastics. A first refusal entailed the penalties of a premunire, and a second those of high treason.]

ing your lordship also not to interpret mine advertisement, as tending to shew myself a patron for the easing of such evil-hearted subjects, which for divers of them do bear a perverse stomach to the purity of Christ's religion, and to the state of the realm thus by God's providence quietly reposed, and which also do envy the continuance of us all so placed by the Queen's favour, as we be: but only in respect of a fatherly and pastoral care, which must appear in us which be heads of the flock, not to follow our own private affections and heats, but to provide *coram Deo et hominibus*, for saving and winning of others, if it may be so obtained. *[marginal: How this letter to be interpreted]*

And I also pray you to assure and persuade yourself, that this manner of my sudden writing at this time is grounded upon great and necessary consideration, for the weal and credit of us that are governors in the church under the Queen's Majesty, and yet for divers respects meet to be kept secret to yourselves, as I doubt not but your wisdoms will easily see and judge[3]. *[marginal: This letter to be kept secret.]*

CXXIX.

QUEEN ELIZABETH TO ARCHBISHOP PARKER.

16th May, 1563. Lambeth MS. 959. No. 47. Contemporary abstract.

ELIZABETH, &c. To all men, &c. Know ye that of our special grace, certain knowledge, and mere motion, and by the advice of our council, we have given and granted full autho-rity, power and licence, and by these &c. unto the most Reverend Father in God, Matthew archbishop of Canterbury, full authority &c., that he, during his life, may lawfully and without question, loss, damage, forfeiture, or other penalty, retain and keep in his service, from time to time, by way of retainers, over and besides all such persons as daily attend upon him in his household, and to whom he giveth meat, drink, livery, fee or wages, and also over and besides all such persons as shall be under him in any office, of any steward-ship, understewardship, baliffwick, keeper of park-houses, warrens, or other game of venerie, pheasants, partridges, and *[marginal: The Queen grants to the archbishop, that during his life he may retain in his service, over and above his customary servants,]*

[3 The last paragraph was added by Sir William Cecil]

forty persons, gentlemen or yeomen, to whom he may give his livery badge. other fowls of what kind soever, &c., the number of forty persons, gentlemen or yeomen, though they be tenants to us, or resiant within our honours, &c., to give at his pleasure his livery-badge or cognizance, &c., to do unto him their service, &c. The said persons to be reputed, taken and accepted, by virtue of this our grant and licence, to all instructions, constructions, and intents, as of the daily attendants on the said archbishop in his household, &c. Provided that this our grant shall not extend unto him to take or retain into his service any of our servants being named in our cheque-roll, nor any other being sworn or retained to serve us as our said servant, &c. And furthermore we have pardoned and released to the archbishop all and every trespass, act or acts of retainer heretofore had, or any contempt, violation, or forfeiture, &c. perpetrated or done sithence the first of January last past, contrary to any act of retainers, &c. In witness, &c., 16th day of May, in the 5th year of our reign.

not being persons entered on the cheque-roll of the Queen's servants.

CXXX.

BISHOP JEWEL OF SALISBURY TO ARCHBISHOP PARKER.

16th June, 1563. Lambeth MS. 959. art. 45.

Sends a Roman dispensation for one Harvee, a serving man, to hold a prebend, with request for the archbishop's opinion as to its legality.

AFTER my most humble commendations. Unless necessity forced me, I would be loth to trouble your Grace further, as knowing the troubles ye have already. Yet, forasmuch as your Grace is *sacra anchora* unto me and others, I shall humbly beseech your Grace to bear with me. The bearer hereof will exhibit unto your Grace a Roman dispensation under lead for one Harvee, prebendary of my church. I beseech your Grace to advertise me whether it will stand good in law or no, and whether the party may enjoy it, not having nor using priestly apparel, but in all respects going as a serving man, or no.

Case of Chafin, who had married two sisters, still before the delegates. Would they would decree

Chafin that hath married two sisters, upon his appeal from your Grace and me, hangeth still before the delegates, and, as much as I can perceive, is not likely to take any great hurt at their hands. I would they would decree it were lawful to marry two sisters, so should the world be out of doubt. As now it is past away in a mockery. D. Hewick promised me I should have it remitted with expenses.

Touching my last letters, and namely touching one * * charde, a person within my diocese, I beseech your Grace to shew me your advice accordingly, as I have humbly requested your Grace. Thus I beseech your Grace to tender my suits, and wish the same most heartily well to fare. From my poor house in Sarum, 16 Junii, 1563.

Your Grace's most humbly assured,
JO. SAR.

To the most reverend Father in God, my very good lord, my lord archbishop of Canterbury's grace, be these delivered.

CXXXI.

ARCHBISHOP PARKER TO SIR WILLIAM CECIL.

[Before Midsummer, 1563.] Lansd. MS. vi. art. 52. Orig.

SIR,

For that I intend by God's grace to visit my diocese shortly after Midsummer, thoroughly thereby to know the state thereof myself personally, and to take order among them; I would gladly the Queen's Majesty would resolve herself in our books of Homilies, which I might deliver to the parishes as I go[1], &c. And, for that I am altogether spoiled of my venison, I am compelled impudently to crave a couple of bucks at your hand, not as thinking that ye have any parks in Kent, but doubting not but that ye may with half a word to your friends soon speed my request; and as I crave of your honour, so I intend to assay my lord Robert[2], and other of my friends, to avoid the shame of my table, if I should not have to bid my neighbours to a piece of flesh, where most part of my brethren be better furnished in this provision than

[1 The second book of Homilies, which is here referred to, was settled at the convocation of January 1562—3, and was printed with the date of 1563. It remained unpublished, awaiting the Queen's approval, for many months]

[2 Lord Robert Dudley, afterwards Earl of Leicester.]

I am. And if I durst as boldly speak to the Queen's Majesty, for taking away my Broyle[1] in Sussex to recompense me with iii. or iiii. bucks in her park at Canterbury, as I did find grace in Queen Anne's favour in such like requests, I would offer my suit. Marry because I doubt in these days whether bishops or ministers may be thought worthy to eat venison, I will hold me to my beef, and make merry therewith, and pray for all my benefactors, &c.

Your honour must pardon importune beggars.

Your at all times,
MATTH. CANTUAR.

In fine, I wish your honour of much joy of God's good gift of late sent to you to cheer your family; *ecce sic benedicitur homo,* &c.

To the right honourable Sir William Cecil, knight, principal Secretary to the Queen's Majesty.

CXXXII.

THE LORDS OF THE COUNCIL TO ARCHBISHOP PARKER.
26th June, 1563. Additional MS. Brit. Mus. 19, 398. art. 44. Orig.

AFTER our very hearty commendations to your Grace[2]. Whereas we understand that according to such order as ye received from the Queen's Majesty, ye have directed your letters to all the bishops of your province for the levying of a contribution of the clergy within the same towards the re-edifying of the church of Paul's according to certain rates limited in that behalf, so it is that at this present the works of the said church, being one of the most notable monuments of this realm, which hitherto with great diligence and like success have been prosecuted, are now compelled to cease,

[[1] A park near Lewes in Sussex, which formerly belonged to the see of Canterbury.]

[[2] Struck out in the original, and "l" written over, as if intended for "lordship."]

1563.] THE LORDS OF THE COUNCIL TO ARCHB. PARKER. 179

and some part of the roof thereof to stand bare and uncovered, for want of lead and present money to sustain the charges of such a work, not only to the decay of the place uncovered, but also to some note and slander in the sight of the world; these are therefore to require your lordship forthwith, with all diligence, according to the rate of the book of tenths or subsidies to collect all the arrearages of the said contribution remaining unpaid, as well of all the dignities and prebends of your cathedral church as of all other spiritual promotions within your diocese of Canterbury, which for exility are not exempted from the said contribution by your former letters, and to pay the same unto the treasurers of the same works of Paul's at or before the first day of August next; taking such order for those that will deny or refuse the payment thereof according to the said rate before limited, as to your wisdom shall seem good. And thus we bid your grace right heartily well to fare. From Greenwich, the 26th day of June, 1563.

<small>The archbishop is therefore required to collect all arrears of the contribution towards the rebuilding,</small>

<small>and pay the same over to the treasurers before the 1st August next.</small>

Your good lordship's assured loving friends,

N. BACON, C. S.   W. NORTHT.
ARUNDEL.   PENBROKE.   R. DUDDELEY.
E. CLYNTON.   W. HOWARD.   F. KNOLLYS.
                                    W. CECILL.

To our very good lord the archbishop of Canterbury.

CXXXIII.

THE LORDS OF THE COUNCIL TO ARCHBISHOP PARKER.

<small>28th June, 1563. Parker MSS. C. C. Coll. Camb. CXIV. art. 19. p. 67.</small>

AFTER our right hearty commendations to your lordship. Forasmuch as the Queen's Majesty hath presently occasion to use the service of some discreet person, learned in the civil law, to be assistant unto the marshal of the town of Newhaven[3], for the ordering of such matters as may happen to

<small>The archbishop is desired by the Council to suggest some person learned in the civil law, to be sent to Newhaven</small>

[3 i.e. Havre de Grace, at this time in possession of the English under the Earl of Warwick, but besieged by the French. The marshal

fall in question there: we have thought meet to pray your lordship to think upon some fit person that for his wisdom and learning may be meet for this purpose, and to let us understand your opinion therein, to the end that the party whom you shall think meet for this service may be further communed withal and sent over to the said town with convenient speed, where he shall have such allowance and entertainment assigned unto him as shall be fit for one of his sort and haviour. And so fare your good lordship right heartily well. From Greenwich, the 28th of June, 1563.

Your good lordship's assured loving friends,

		W. NORTHT.
ARUNDEL.	PEMBROKE.	R. DUDDELEY.
E. CLYNTON.		W. HOWARD.
G. ROGERS.	F. KNOLLYS.	W. CECILL.

*To our very good lord, the archbishop
of Canterbury.*

CXXXIV.

THE LORDS OF THE COUNCIL TO ARCHBISHOP PARKER.

9th July, 1563. Parker MSS. C. C. Coll. Camb. cxxii. art. 9. p. 287. Orig.

AFTER our very hearty commendations to your good lordship. The Queen's Majesty, upon certain good considerations moving her to understand in some part the state of your diocese, hath commanded us to write unto your lordship with all speed possible, and thereby to require the same to make answer by writing distinctly to us of all these articles following:—

First, How many shires or counties your diocese doth contain, or into how many it doth extend?

Second, Into what manner of regiments the same is divided; whether the same be into archdeaconries, deaneries, or such like; and how many the same be, with their distinct names; who occupieth those rooms at this present; and where they are, to your understanding?

alluded to was Edward Randolph, the same whose humanity on the surrender of the town, is commemorated by Stowe in a passage in his Annales, ed. Howes, p. 656.]

Thirdly, What exempt or peculiar places are within the circuit of your diocese, where you have not full jurisdiction as ordinary, and what the names thereof be, and who hath the ordinary jurisdiction thereof at this present?

Fourthly, How many churches are within every such archdeaconry, deanery, or other regiment; which be parochial; how many of them have parsons, vicars, or curates; and where, as the parishes are so large as they have divers chapels of ease, which have or ought to have curates or ministers in them, to certify how many be of that sort in every such parish, with the names of the towns or hamlets where the same churches or chapels are so situate?

Fifthly, How many households are within every parish, or within any such member of any parish, that hath such churches and chapels of ease?

Sixthly, and lastly, Wheresoever any exempt places be within the circuit of your diocese, wherein you have no such jurisdiction, as you can presently make sufficient answer to these former Articles, her Majesty would that you should in writing copy out so much of the substance of these five former articles as shall seem convenient for the purpose, and with speed send to such persons as have the jurisdiction of those exempt places, or their deputies, residing next unto you, willing and commanding them in her Majesty's name forthwith to send distinct answers thereunto, to be sent either to yourself, or by you to be sent to us.

And because the greater part of these former Articles is such as we doubt not but ye are by means of your visitations able to cause sufficient certificate to be made unto us with speed, we require your lordship to use therein all the diligence that you can, and not to defer any time therein, but either by this messenger, or within two or three days at the farthest, to return us answer. And for some such part thereof as speedily you cannot certify, without conference had with your chancellors, commissaries, archdeacons, deans, or other inferior officers, our like earnest request is, that you do procure information thereof without delay of time; and to command in her Majesty's name the like to be done by all others, having, as above is said, any exempt jurisdictions; so as her Majesty may be amply and certainly satisfied herein.

And so fare your good lordship right heartily well. From Greenwich, the 9th of July, 1563.

    Your lordship's assured friends[1],
      T. NORFOLK.
 PENBROKE.   R. DUDDELEY.
         W. CECILL.

CXXXV.

ARCHBISHOP PARKER TO SIR WILLIAM CECIL.
23rd July, 1563. Lansd. MS. vi. art. 62. Orig.

AFTER my hearty commendations to your honour. Considering and understanding none otherwise but by common report of the same, in what state the realm now standeth in, molested universally by war, and particularly at London by pestilence, and partly here at Canterbury by famine, the people wanting their necessary provision, as is reported unto me, I thought it good upon my private consideration to call upon the mayor and his commonalty on Friday last, to meet with me at the cathedral church, where I did myself exhort them unto prayer, &c. And, for hereafter, have appointed them Fridays so to be used with prayer and preaching, and Mondays and Wednesdays in their parish-churches, prescribing that common prayer that was appointed in the Guise's time (altering a few words in the same). Sir, this I have done, not enjoining the like to the rest of my diocese, nor to the rest of my province, for want of sufficient warrant from the prince or council, whereof I do marvel that I have no advertisement. And although ye may say, we by our vocation should have special regard of such matter, yet because we be holden within certain limits by statutes, we may stand in doubt how it will be taken if we should give order herein; and therefore do not charge the rest of my diocese with injunction, as leaving them to their own liberty, to follow us in the city for common prayer if they will. If I had your

Marginal notes: The kingdom universally distressed by war, pestilence, and famine. — The archbishop has exhorted the corporation of Canterbury to prayer, &c, and appointed Fridays to be set apart for that purpose. — Marvels that he has received no advertisement of a general order, which he might communicate to the rest of his province. — Thinks such an order very necessary.

[1 Many of the original returns to these Articles are to be found in the Harleian MSS. That of archbishop Parker is in Harl. MS. 594. fo. 63.]

warrant, I would direct my precepts, as I think very necessary, to exercise the said public prayers. And thus, putting so much to your consideration, as I am sure otherwise fully occupied, I wish you the assistance of God in all good counsel. From my house at Bekesbourne, this 23rd of July, 1563.

Your honour's always,

MATTHUE CANTUAR.

*To the right honourable Sir William
Cecil, knight, principal Secretary
to the Queen's Majesty.*

CXXXVI.

SIR WILLIAM CECIL TO ARCHBISHOP PARKER.

1st August, 1563. Parker MSS. C. C. Coll. Camb. cxiv. art. 212. p. 575. Orig.

It may please your grace. Before I received a letter from you, I had of mine own head moved my lord of London to bethink himself of some formular of common prayer; who hath so done. Which I have as I could hastily perused, and for your grace's further authority I have procured you the Queen's Majesty's letter, which I send herewith to your grace, and wish that some haste were used, so it be well advised. *[marginal: Before the receipt of the archbishop's letter, Sir W. Cecil had moved the bishop of London to prepare a form of prayer, which he had procured to be sanctioned by the Queen's letter.]*

On Wednesday last a compact was made by my lord of Warwick, having authority so to do, to deliver Newhaven, with certain conditions of permission of the possession for us of eight days to carry away all our own[2]. This necessity the plague brought, which was inevitable. *[marginal: Newhaven surrendered by the Earl of Warwick.]*

Your grace's at command,

W. CECILL.

[2 The Earl of Warwick surrendered Newhaven under articles dated 28th July, 1563. Many English soldiers died there of the plague, and the infection was thought to have been brought thence into England.]

CXXXVII.

QUEEN ELIZABETH TO ARCHBISHOP PARKER.

1st August, 1563. Parker MSS. C. C. Coll. Camb. CXIV. art. 6. p. 15. Orig.

BY THE QUEEN.

ELIZABETH R.

MOST reverend father in God, right trusty and right well beloved, we greet you well. Like as Almighty God hath of his mere grace committed to us, next under him, the chief government of this realm and the people therein; so hath he, of his like goodness, ordered under us sundry principal ministers, to serve and assist us in this burden. And therefore considering the state of this present time, wherein it hath pleased the Most Highest, for the amendment of us and our people to visit certain places of our realm with more contagious sickness than lately hath been; for remedy and mitigation thereof we think it both necessary and our bounden duty that universal prayer and fasting be more effectually used in this our realm. And understanding that you have thought and considered upon some good order to be prescribed therein, for the which ye require the application of our authority for the better observation thereof amongst our people; we do not only commend and allow your good zeals therein, but do also command all manner our ministers ecclesiastical or civil, and all other our subjects, to execute, follow, and obey such godly and wholesome orders, as you, being primate of all England, and metropolitan of this province of Canterbury, upon godly advice and consideration, shall uniformly devise, prescribe, and publish for the universal usage of prayer, fasting, and other good deeds during the time of this visitation by sickness and other troubles. Given under our signet at our manor of Richmond, the 1st day of August, the fifth year of our reign.

It having pleased Almighty God to visit the realm with contagious sickness, it is thought that prayer and fasting ought to be more effectually used:

the Queen therefore commands general obedience to such orders thereon as the archbishop shall devise.

> To the most reverend Father in God our
> right trusty and right well beloved the
> archbishop of Canterbury and primate of
> all England[1].

[1 The form of prayer referred to in this letter is printed in the volume of "Liturgies and occasional Forms of Prayer, set forth in the reign of Queen Elizabeth," 8vo, 1847 (Parker Society), p. 478, and also in "The Remains of archbishop Grindal," 8vo, 1843, p. 81.]

CXXXVIII.

ARCHBISHOP PARKER TO SIR WILLIAM CECIL.

6th August, [1563.] Lansd. MS. vi. art. 66. Orig.

SIR,

HAVING received the Queen's Majesty's letters procured by your honour, for which I thank you, I received also therewith the formular of public prayer and fasting diligently devised by my lord of London[2], &c., and as it seemeth, perused by you, as your hand inspersed in divers parts doth testify. I received it on Thursday last, and returned it to the printer on this Friday morning, but yet being so bold to alter some parts thereof, not yet in substance and principal meaning, but in the circumstances: *videlicet*, because I see offence grow by new innovations, and I doubt whether it were best to change the established form of prayer appointed already by law in this alteration of prayer for a time, as the formular would infer all the whole service in the body of the church, which being once in this particular order devised, we do abolish all chancels, and therefore the Litany with the new psalms, lessons, and collects, may be said as Litany is already ordered, in the midst of the people; and to be short, I have no otherwise altered the book, but to make it draw, as nigh as can be, to the public book and orders used, &c. I wish that the collects had been shorter, and I fear the service to be too long for our cold devotions. Belike they meant to have the people to continue in prayer till four in the afternoon, and then to take their one meal; but all things agree not everywhere. Thus the Lord preserve your honour. At Canterbury, this 6th of August.

Your honour's assured,

MATTH. CANTUAR.

To the right honourable Sir William Cecil, knight, principal Secretary to the Queen's Majesty.

[2 Bishop Grindal.]

CXXXIX.

ARCHBISHOP PARKER TO SIR WILLIAM CECIL.

22nd August, [1563] Lansd. MS. vi. art. 70. Orig.

SIR,

BEING here and would be loth to be idle, and thereupon having consideration as well of these quarters for the common quiet among the people, as respecting the common service of the better sort toward the Queen's Highness and her affairs, I find them all in so good order that I do rejoice therein; as for my ecclesiastical persons, I deal with them indifferently, that I find also obedience in them. Now, Sir, with spying and searching I have found out by very credible information, among other things, in whose hands the great notable written books of my predecessor Dr Cranmer should remain, the parties yet denying the same, and thereupon despair to recover them, except I may be aided by the council's letters to obtain them. I pray your honour to procure their letters to authorise me to inquire and search for such monuments by all ways as by my poor discretion shall be thought good, whether it be by deferring an oath to the parties, or viewing their studies, &c. This opportunity of information being such, I would wish I could recover these books to be afterward at the Queen's commandment; I would as much rejoice while I am in the country to win them, as I would to restore an old chancel to reparation. Because I am not acquainted with the style of the council's letters in this case, I send you no minute, trusting that your goodness will think the labour well bestowed to cause the clerk of the council to devise the form. And thus, hearing of the likelihood of the plague to be in beginning in some places hereabout, and yet my own house, thanks be to God, in good quiet, I wish the Queen's family to be defended by God's hand. At my house from Bekesbourne, this 22nd of August.

The archbishop has found in whose hands certain books of archbishop Cranmer now remain.

He requests a council letter to enable him to procure the same. If he could recover them, to be afterwards at the Queen's commandment, he would as much rejoice as in restoring an old chancel.

Your honour's assured,

MATTHUE CANT.

*To the right honourable Sir William Cecil,
knight, principal Secretary to the Queen's
Majesty, at the Court.*

CXL.

SIR WILLIAM CECIL TO ARCHBISHOP PARKER.

25th August, 1563. MS. Reg. Brit. Mus. 7 B. xi. fol. 5. Orig.

MAY it please your grace, I thank the same for your letters. I am glad that you have heard of such hid treasures, as I take the books of the holy archbishop Cranmer to be; I have of late recovered of his written books five or six, which I had of one Mr Herd from Lincoln. Your grace writeth to have letters from the council, but to whom they should be written, or who the persons of whom the writings should be demanded, your grace's letter maketh no mention. And therefore, knowing no such earnestness here, or care of such matters, I forbear to press the council therewith, specially being not able to render them an account who hath the writings. But upon advertisement thereof I will not fail but procure such letters. From Windsor, where we are yet in health, thanked be Almighty God. On Tuesday the Spanish ambassador died here, within two miles, of a burning ague. 25th August, 1563.

Sir W. Cecil is glad that the archbishop has heard of such hid treasures as the books of holy archbishop Cranmer.

A council letter for obtaining shall be sent upon receipt of further information.

Your grace's at commandment,
W. CECILL.

CXLI.

ARCHBISHOP PARKER TO SIR WILLIAM CECIL.

27th August, 1563. Lansd. MS. vi. art. 71. Orig.

WHERE of late I made a request by letters to your honour, for the obtaining of the council's letters in that cause opened unto you, now I would be a suitor to the Queen's Majesty, by your favourable furtherance, for the behoof of the town of Sandwich, concerning her Highness' licence as well to the dean and chapter for their alienation, or rather a lease in fee-farm, of a rude acre of ground belonging to their church, whereon the town would build a grammar-school; Mr Manwood being so well disposed thereto, that he is fully determined to give to that foundation £20 by year *imperpetuum*

Parker solicits the Queen's licence for the dean and chapter of Canterbury to grant a lease in fee-farm of an acre of land in Sandwich, whereon the town proposes to build a school,

of his own possessions presently. The dean and chapter (whom I have particularly solicited) be well willing of their grant, staying only at the Queen's licence; the town itself wholly bent to the erection; Mr Manwood's land ready for assurance. The opportunity being such, I doubt not of the Queen's Majesty's good and gracious assent, as I have learned by experience by my own suit to her Highness for the recovery of the stipend of the schoolmaster at Stoke College, perceiving then her godly zeal to the furtherance of learning, yea in that case, where the stipend went out of her own coffers. This rare example of so godly foundation in Mr Manwood, a man of his vocation[1], who be commonly judged rather to employ all their abilities to their own posterities than to such common respects; and he being not without issue (and is daily like to have more), might have followed the common example, in leaving the gains of his time to his offspring; and therefore I would wish his purpose were favoured, both for example to others, as also to put away the common judgment which runneth upon such as be of his calling. I take it to be a motion of God, in consideration that we poor bishops be not now able to succeed our predecessors in their so liberal foundations. Now you, such as you be and as Mr Manwood is, must lay hand to the furtherance of such public endowments, or else ye be not like to leave to your successors which ye have received of your ancestors.

For that I would have a view, partly of the ground and situation thereof, and for other causes, I this last Sunday morning rode thither from my house, and was there by seven of the clock; the rather so soon, to prevent their civility of receiving (as the manner is), and partly to be present at their whole service. But in the first consideration they prevented me; for, though the morning was very foul and rainy, yet I found the mayor and his jurats ready at the town-gate to accompany me to my lodging, and so to the church, being men of honest civility, and comely grave personages of good understanding; their streets (as they might be for the

[1 Mr Manwood, afterwards Sir Roger Manwood, chief baron of the exchequer, a great benefactor to Sandwich. A licence was granted in conformity with Parker's application, and Manwood's free-school still exists.]

straitness of them) clean and not much savoury[2]; their service sung in good distinct harmony and quiet devotion; the singing men, being the mayor and the jurats, with the head men of the town, placed in the quire fair and decent, in so good order as I could wish. My auditory great and attentive to hear, and also to understand the Queen's pleasure in publication of the general prayer and fast: that I see not but the Queen's Majesty shall have of them good subjects and true orators. And furthermore, upon the erection of this school, her Highness shall have a number of young tender hands lift up in prayer for her Highness' prosperous reign.

The strangers there[3] being very godly in the Sabbath-day, and busy in their work on the week-day, and their quietness such as the mayor and his brethren have no causes of variances coming before them. As for other disorders reformable by ecclesiastical laws, I have before now deputed their minister (a grave learned man) to exercise (by mine authority) ecclesiastical censures, as he shall see cause, as hitherto little hath been spied. *State of the refugee strangers at Sandwich, and their church there.* *Parker allows their minister to exercise ecclesiastical censures*

By all the premises aforesaid considered, I mean to commend the town's request to the Queen's favour, so laudably behaving themselves as I see them, and partly to express to you some part of my joy which I have here by them in this outward corner of my diocese, and therefore I pray your honour help them. In so doing *mercedem reportabis a Domino in resurrectione justorum;* which God of his mercy make joyful to the Queen's Highness and to us all. From my house at Bekesbourne, this 27th day of August, 1563.

Your honour's assured,

MATTHUE CANTUAR.

To the right honourable Sir William Cecil,
knight, principal Secretary to the Queen's
Majesty, at the Court.

[2 Sandwich was at that time an important fishing-town.]
[3 Several hundred Walloon manufacturers, driven from their native country by the cruelty of the Spaniards, were permitted by Queen Elizabeth to take up their abode at Sandwich in 1561.]

CXLII.

LORD ROBERT DUDLEY TO ARCHBISHOP PARKER.

4th September, [1563] Parker MSS. C. C. Coll. Camb. cxiv. art. 61. p. 193. Orig.

The Queen having had "good hap" in hunting, sends the archbishop a deer killed with her own hand.

My Lord, the Queen's Majesty being abroad hunting yesterday in the forest, and having had very good hap beside great sport, she hath thought good to remember your grace with part of her prey, and so commanded me to send you from her Highness a great and a fat stag killed with her own hand[1]. Which because the weather was woght [sic] and the deer somewhat chafed and dangerous to be carried so far without some help, I caused him to be parboiled in this

which Leicester had had parboiled.

sort for the better preservation of him; which I doubt not but shall cause him to come unto you as I would be glad he should. So having no other matter at this present to trouble your grace withal, I will commit you to the Almighty, and with my most hearty commendations take my leave. In haste, at Windsor, this 4th of September.

Your grace's assured,

R. DUDDELEY[2].

To my very good lord the archbishop of Canterbury his grace.

CXLIII.

ARCHBISHOP PARKER TO LORD ROBERT DUDLEY.

6th September, [1563.] Parker MSS. C. C. Coll. Camb. cxiv. p. 193 b. Orig. draft.

After my right hearty commendations to your good lordship. Having received your letters expressing the Queen's

Parker's joy at the Queen's remembrance of him.

Majesty's gracious remembrance to her poor subject with part of her hunting in the forest, I was replenished with much joy at her favourable benevolence, wishing to her Highness all grace and felicity as in my prayer shall be unfeignedly remembered for her Highness, beseeching your lordship

[1 Originally written "bowe," which was afterwards struck out, and "hand" substituted. It has been printed "bow-hand."]

[2 Created Earl of Leicester 29 September, 1563.]

in my name to present to her Majesty my bounden duty of lowly thanks with better terms and more convenient words than I can well devise by my letters, wherein your lordship shall doubly bind me both for this kind of friendship, as also for that your lordship did so providently cause the deer to be preserved in season, if the whot [sic] weather would have permitted it. And thus offering your lordship my good heart, I commend the same to Almighty God as myself. From my little house at Bekesbourne, nigh to Canterbury, this 6th of September.

with acknowledgements to Lord Robert Dudley.

Your lordship's loving friend,

M. C.

To the right honourable my lord Robert Dudley of the Queen's Majesty's privy council.

CXLIV.

ARCHBISHOP PARKER TO SIR WILLIAM CECIL.

7th September, 1563. MS. Reg. Brit. Mus. 7 B. xi. fo. 3. Parker's draft.

WHERE I did write to your honour to procure the council's letters for the obtaining of certain ancient written books of the lord Cranmer, and belike did not express particularly either to whom these letters should be directed, or the persons of whom they should be demanded, your honour shall understand that the party to whom belongeth these books sued to me to recover them out of Dr Nevison's hands, in whose study the owner plainly avoucheth that he saw them with his own eyes there, and who did after that require them of him, being conveyed away from him the said owner, but the said Nevison denieth to have them. And I am persuaded he would do the same to myself, if I should de[mand] them, and thereupon desired to have the council's letters which he might the better regard, either directed to me to require them of him, or else to him to deliver them to me, being none of his own but usurped in secrecy, for the which I have made much long inquiry till now the party who oweth them denoted so much to me. I refer the consideration of this my desire, either to be satisfied by the means of such letters aforesaid,

Further particulars as to the MSS. of archbishop Cranmer, and the wishes of Parker respecting the same.

or else by yourself privately, as your gentle prudence shall think best. Indeed the matter is of earnest importance and need *** your help if gratitude * the said Nevison to me were not to seek[1].

Help forward Mr Manwood's good intent.
Finally, I pray your honour once again, help forward Mr Manwood's good intent, as conscience with the reason of your office may conveniently bear it. 7th September.

CXLV.

THE LORDS OF THE COUNCIL TO ARCHBISHOP PARKER.

15th September, 1563. Parker MSS. C. C. Coll. Camb. cxiv. art. 27. p. 87. Orig.

The lords of the council have acceded to the request of Dr Thirleby and Dr Boxall to be removed from the Tower to some place less exposed to infection of the plague.
AFTER our most hearty commendations to your good lordship. We have upon suit made unto us by the doctors, prisoners in the Tower, to be removed from thence to some other convenient place, for their better safeguard from the present infection of the plague, resolved that Dr Thirleby and Dr Boxall shall be placed in your lordship's house, in such convenient lodging as your lordship shall think meet, having each of them one servant to attend upon them. And

The archbishop to receive them into his house.
therefore we require your lordship to receive them into your house, and so to use them as is requisite for men of their sort, foreseeing that there be no other access or conference with them than you think meet, considering for what causes they be restrained from their liberty. And for the charges of their commons (during the time of their abode with you) we think good that they do satisfy your lordship for the same according to reason. And so we bid your good lordship most heartily farewell. From Windsor, the 15th of September, 1563.

Your good lordship's most assured loving friends,

F. BEDFORD. PENBROKE. R. DUDDELEY.
E. CLYNTON. W. HOWARD.
WILLIAM PETRE. S. F. KNOLLYS. W. CECILL.
N. WOTTON.

[1 The MS. has been a little cut in the binding. Perhaps this last passage should be read, "and need*ed not* your help if gratitude *in* the said Nevison to me were not to seek."]

CXLVI.

DR THIRLEBY, DEPRIVED BISHOP OF ELY, TO ARCHBISHOP PARKER.

16th September, 1563. Additional MS. Brit. Mus. 19, 398, art. 45. Orig.

Your grace knoweth the proverb, "an unbidden guest wotteth not where to sit." Although we be unbidden, yet we are not unappointed, Mr Boxall and I be assigned to remain with your grace, how long, or in what condition, I think you shall know by the lords of the Council's letter, which our keepers will bring with us. I mind to bring with me all my family of the Tower, that is, my man and my boy; for when I told my boy that I would leave him behind me, he made earnest suit to take him with me, saying, that he doubted not, since by your means he came to me into the Tower, that by your good contentation he might go with me out of the Tower. Therefore unless your grace shall command the contrary, I mind to bring him with me, although I alone should be comer enough to you. I doubt what ways we may come without danger of the plague to your grace, all the places in the way being so sore infected, yet they say need maketh the old wife to trot. I pray God to bring us well to you, and to preserve your grace to his pleasure. From the Tower, the 16th of September, 1563.

Your grace's to command,
THOMAS THYRLEBY.

To my lord of Canterbury
his grace.

CXLVII.

ARCHBISHOP PARKER TO DR THIRLEBY.

20th September, 1563. Additional MS. Brit. Mus. 19, 398. art. 46. Parker's original draft.

Sir, as an unbidden guest, as ye write, knoweth not where to sit, so a guest bidden or unbidden, being content with that which he shall find, shall deserve to be the better welcome. If ye bring with you your man and your young querister too, ye shall not be refused; and if your companion in journey can content himself with one man to attend upon him, your lodgings shall the sooner be prepared. Your best way were to Maidstone the first night, and the next hither. I would wish your coming were the sooner afore night, that such as shall come with you being once discharged of their charge, may return that night to Canterbury, two miles off, to their bed. And thus God send you a quiet passage: the 20th of September, 1563.

CXLVIII.

ARCHBISHOP PARKER TO SIR WILLIAM CECIL.

20th September, 1563.   Lansd. MS. vi. art. 75.   Orig.

I UNDERSTAND by letters sent to me from Dr Thirleby[1], that the council hath appointed himself and Mr Boxall to remain with me in house, under what conditions he writeth that I shall know by their letters, which their keeper shall deliver unto me at their repair hither, which is purposed upon Wednesday next. Pleaseth it your honour to signify to the honourable council, that I trust it may stand with their pleasure, if, for the fear that my household is in of them thus coming from a contagious air, I do place them in the town not far from my house here at Bekesborne, in an house at this present void of a dweller, till such time as they were better blown with this fresh air for a fourteen days. For their provision, I shall see to; and for jeopardy of the custody of their persons, I am surely persuaded of the one not to disappoint your expectations, as for the other I know not so well his nature; whereupon, if ought should chance in the mean time, till I receive them to myself, I trust the council will rather bear with me in avoiding the danger of infection as may be feared, than for their behoof endanger

[[1] Dr Thomas Thirleby was the bishop of Ely, deprived on the accession of Queen Elizabeth for refusing to take the oath of supremacy. He and Mr Secretary Boxall lived together in archbishop Parker's houses at Lambeth and Beaksbourne for several years. Dr Thirleby died at Lambeth on the 26th August, 1570, and was buried in the middle of the chancel of Lambeth church.]

my whole family. I mean not in respect of my own person to repine at such appointment, nor yet would I be thought slack to gratify mine old acquaintance (so far as my faith to God and his word, and mine allegiance to my prince and her government may bear with it), nor I mean not to allege the smaller room of my house already pestered, having not many under a hundred persons uprising and down-lying therein, beside divers of my family which for straitness of lodging be other where abroad; but if any peril should arise the country here would make much exclamation, for I see they be wonderfully afraid of all such as come from London. I thought it good therefore to signify thus much to your honour afore hand, praying the same to be a mean that my doings may be taken to the best. And thus I leave, wishing you God's favour as to myself, this 20th of September.

His house already contains nearly 100 persons, and the whole country is wonderfully afraid of infection.

Your honour's assuredly,
MATTHUE CANTUAR.

To the right honourable Sir William Cecil, knight, principal Secretary to the Queen's Majesty.

CXLIX.

THE LORDS OF THE COUNCIL TO ARCHBISHOP PARKER.

23rd September, 1563. MS. Reg. Brit. Mus. 7 B. xi. fol. 2. Orig.

AFTER our very hearty commendations to your good lordship. Being given to understand, that certain written books, containing matters of divinity, sometime belonging to archbishop Cranmer, your lordship's predecessor, are come to the hands of Dr Nevison, being very necessary to be seen at this time; we have somewhat earnestly written to the said Mr Nevison, to deliver those books unto your lordship. And like as we doubt not he will forthwith deliver the same unto you, considering they are for so good a purpose required of him, so if he shall deny the delivery thereof, we think meet that your lordship, by your own authority, do cause his study, and such other places where you think the said books do remain, to be sought: and if the same books may be

Written books of archbishop Cranmer in the hands of Dr Nevison are to be delivered to the archbishop.

If he refuse, his study to be sought, and the books to be taken into the archbishop's custody.

found, to take them into your lordship's custody[1]. And thus we bid your good lordship most heartily farewell. From Windsor Castle, the 23rd of September, 1563.

Your good lordship's most assured loving friends,

N. BACON, C. S.   W. NORTHT.   PENBROKE.
R. DUDDELEY.   E. CLYNTON.   F. KNOLLYS.
WILLIAM PETRE, S.   W. CECILL.

*To my lord of Canterbury's
good grace.*

CL.

BISHOP GRINDAL OF LONDON TO ARCHBISHOP PARKER.

3rd October, 1563.   Lambeth MS. 959. art. 43.   Orig.

The province of Canterbury troubled by the exaction of a remnant of the last subsidy.

PLEASE it your grace, your whole province is shrewdly troubled at this present by exacting a remnant of the last subsidy. There is a blind clause, which I understand not, in the grant of the said subsidy *an.* 4 *et* 5 *Phil. et Mariæ,* that if by exility or decay of benefices, &c. any arrearages be, they are to be answered the next year. I would that Doctor Bennett, Doctor Harvey, and such like that were then in the convocation, were called to expound their meaning.

The archbishop solicited to help to ease the province of this exaction.

If, because the Queen's Majesty, at your grace's suit, pardoned the components, that sum be now cast into the arrearages, it were an unreasonable matter. If your grace could help to ease your province it were well done. If your grace also sent for Godfrey, he might open some matter.

On Monday afternoon I intend to see your grace on my repairing hither from London. God keep your grace. 3rd October, 1563.

Your grace's in Christ,

EDM. LONDON.

[[1] The valuable volumes referred to, which are theological commonplace books of archbishop Cranmer, are now amongst the Royal MSS. in the British Museum, 7 B. XI. and XII. The letters here published relating to them are prefixed to the former of the two volumes.]

CLI.

ARCHBISHOP PARKER TO SIR GEORGE HOWARD.

[October, 1563.] Parker MSS. C. C. Coll. Camb. cxiv. art. 231. p. 625.
Orig. draft.

AFTER my hearty commendations to your worship. Having of late received your letters of commendation of Mr Beard, Vicar of Greenwich, for his diligence shewed there, I perceive further by your said letters, that he hath insinuated himself to your worship to be in good credit with me: and that therefore ye need not much to crave my help toward his preferment. Indeed, I think him to be studious, and by outward demeanour modest: and performing in deed so much as he seemeth in word to profess. I judge him worthy to be considered with competent living, but yet not meaning to advance him so far to place him by my letters of commendation as to that room he sued to me for, and thereupon so dismissed him, without my answer to you then, yet now have performed the same, praying your worship to take it in good part: wishing to you God's grace and his protection as to myself[2].

The archbishop thinks favourably of Mr Beard, vicar of Greenwich, but not so much so as to promote him to an office solicited for him by Sir George Howard.

CLII.

ARCHBISHOP PARKER TO SIR WILLIAM CECIL.

20th November, 1563. Lansd. MS. vi. art. 81. Orig.

IT may please your honour to understand, that I have great cause most humbly to give the Queen's Majesty thanks for the favour shewed toward my request for the preferment of my chaplain[3], and so likewise I heartily thank your honour

Preferment of the archbishop's chaplain.

[2 The draft of this letter is written under a letter from Sir George Howard to the archbishop, dated the 11th October, 1563. Sir George recommends his "friend" Mr Beard, whom he terms "our vicar of Greenwich," to the favour of the archbishop. He describes Mr Beard as having "used himself at Greenwich, like a godly, diligent, and learned pastor."]

[3 The preferment here alluded to was a prebend in Canterbury cathedral, vacant by the death of bishop Bale, and the person for whom it was obtained was Andrew Pierson, chaplain, almoner, and

Sir W. Cecil had written on behalf of his cousin, Barnaby Googe, who had entered into a contract of matrimony with a young gentlewoman, whose parents allege a pre-contract

for your instancy therein, as by your letters I understand; wherein ye write for your cousin and servant Barnaby Googe, to have his matter heard according to law and equity. Which matter as yesterday I have examined avisedly, having not only the young gentlewoman before me, to understand of herself the state of the cause, who remaineth firm and stable to stand to that contract which she hath made, as also her father and mother, whom I find the most earnest parents against the bargain as I ever saw. In fine, I have sequestered her out of both their hands into the custody of one

What the archbishop had done, and would do.

Mr Tufton, a right honest gentleman, until the precontract which is by her parents alleged for one Leonard's son, a pronotary, be induced; but they may give occasion to bring it into the Arches to spend money; howbeit I mean to dull that expectation, and to go *plane et summarie* to work, to spare expences, which rich Leonard and the wilful parents would fain enter, to weary the young gentleman, peradventure not superfluously monied so to sail the seas with them[1].

Bale's MSS. promised to the archbishop for money

Concerning the old antiquities of Mr Bale, I have bespoken them, and am promised to have them for money if I be not deceived.

Informality in the grant to the archbishop's chaplain.

Furthermore, as I was writing this letter of thanks to you, with the premises, was brought to me a donation by the Queen's Highness's great seal for my chaplain aforesaid; which being not in such order passed as both by law, custom, and statute of the house is required, I pray your honour most instantly to procure it to be agreeably reviewed. It will work a subversion of order in the church, and a breach of statute, besides other inconveniences which were too long to write. I would the clerks would better consider the order of such

one of the executors of archbishop Parker, a man whom he much patronized. The General Index to Strype furnishes references to his many employments and preferments.]

[1 Barnaby Googe was at this time in his 23rd year. The dedication of his first work, a translation of The First Three Books of the Zodiack of Life, by Palingenius, is dated "*decimo Martii anno Christi*, 1560, *ætatis nostræ* xx." (Brydges' Cens. Lit. ii. 212). During 1563 he published his collection of Eclogues, and was appointed a gentleman-pensioner to the Queen. Of Leonard, his opponent in this dispute, Strype says that John and Thomas Leonard had, in 1550, a grant of the office of Pronotary, or Clerk of the Crown, for certain counties, for their lives. (Strype's Parker, Bk. II. c. 17.)]

privy seals. I sent your honour an instrument of an institution used, immediately after the departure of the said Bale; but belike, and as it is reported, the Queen's Majesty had granted it two days before his departure, which little error peradventure also might be hurtful to the party to come into that prebend which was not void, although the great seal beareth date after the decease. But I pray your honour be not displeased to reform this instrument, that it may pass by presentation as it ought. Having thus much troubled your affairs, I commend your honour to God's grace as myself, this Saturday at night, being the 20th of November.

Bale's preferment granted by the Queen two days before his death.

Your honour's to my power,
MATTHUE CANTUAR.

To the right honourable Sir William Cecil, knight, principal Secretary to the Queen's Majesty.

CLIII.

ARCHBISHOP PARKER TO SIR WILLIAM CECIL.

[Ascribed to 1563.] Lansd. MS. vi. art. 89. Orig. in Parker's own hand.

I PRAY you lay not this aside, but rather bren it, read or unread, at your pleasure.

Sir, after my right hearty commendations. I cannot be quiet till I have disclosed to you, as to one of my best willing friends, in secrecy, mine imperfection, which grieveth me not so much to utter in respect of my own rebuke, as it grieveth me that I am not able to answer your friendly report of me before time, whereby, to my much grief of heart, I pass forth my life in heaviness, being thus intruded, notwithstanding my reluctation by oft letters to my friends, to be in such room which I cannot sustain agreeably to the honour of the realm, if I should be so far tried. The truth is, what with passing those hard years of Mary's reign in obscurity, without all conference or such manner of study as now might do me service, and what with my natural viciosity of overmuch shamefastness, I am so babished [sic] in myself, that I cannot raise up my heart and stomach to utter in talk

Parker's grief from a conscious self-insufficiency for his office.

His retired life in the hard years of Queen Mary's reign, has begotten in him a shame facedness, silence, and an inability

_{to deal with strangers.} with other, which (as I may say) with my pen I can express indifferently, without great difficulty. And, again, I am so evil acquainted with strangers, both in their manner of utterance of their speech, and also in such foreign affairs, that I cannot win of myself any ways to satisfy my fancy in such kind of entertainment, and ye know *caput artis est decere quod facias, et infeliciter eveniunt quæ tentes invita Minerva,* _{He entreats Cecil to help him to "shadow his cowardness."} *et satius dicunt qui confidentius audent.* Whereupon this is to require you, for all loves, to help me to shadow my cowardness till better may be, and to decline from me such oppertunities wherein I should work a lack to my promoters and a shame to myself.

_{He can manage his ecclesiastical business,} As for the ordering, overseeing, and compassing common matters ecclesiastical, in synod or out thereof, among mine acquainted familiar brethren, I doubt not but with God's grace and help of counsel to serve somewhat that turn within the realm; and there my stomach will stand by me, to do so far as these *exulceratissima tempora* will suffer or the unruly affections of men can be won; but if ye drive me out of this _{but beyond that can do nothing.} course, wherein I have only been brought up, as traded in a little experience of smaller matters at the university, ye shall drive me utterly out of conceit, and then can I do nothing. I perceive, what for bodily and painful griefs with which I am _{His infirmities and the business of his diocese occupy him entirely.} oft molested and vexed, not yet known or complained of to many folks, and partly with answering all such interpellations as be made to me from my brethren in the whole province in their causes of resolutions, and other such matters ecclesiastical, my study is done, my life belike must be spent *in actione,* wherein I am content to serve to my uttermost power, wishing yet *redemptionem corporis hujus* in respects aforesaid, rather than much joying in the delight of my state; wherein my desire is to please God, to serve my loving prince and natural country, and to content as I may my godly friends; and thus, praying your goodness to keep patience with me, in full confidence of your christian affection, *qui possit compati infirmitatibus aliorum,* I commend your honour to God as myself.

After I had thus far brought forth my letter, this came _{The bishop of Aquila having desired a conference on religious sub-} into my head as followeth. Where the bishop of Aquila[1] de-

[1 If this allusion be, as is probable, to the Spanish ambassador whose death is mentioned at p. 187, this letter must have been written some time before the 25th August 1563. See Hearne's Camden, I. 103.]

sired conference it were well he were satisfied; and as he doth prudently judge, that it might be sinistrally taken either me to go to him, or him to come to me, so I think for us to meet together at your house, it were neither good to your fame or mine; and strangely it would be construed among the light brethren in divers respects. Furthermore, ye know that he should come *præmeditatus*, and I *tanquam novus hospes* to his matters unprepared, and so the match the more unequal; besides that my books should not be nigh to me to avouch authority where it should need. If therefore your honour think it good that he were advertised to confer with me *scripto*, I would then be ready in answering him again *candide et succincte;* and this way my stomach and audacity would serve me, doubting not by God's help but to answer him reasonably with his own authors, for any alteration in religion stablished in the realm. And if in the end of our conference he would wish the originals of his writings to be remitted to him again, to avoid any suspicion that might run upon him amongst his own, it might so be, that none should know of our conference but yourself to be *honorarius judex* betwixt us. And thus with long writing I trouble your spare time, praying you to pardon all.

To the right honourable Sir William Cecil,
Secretary to the Queen's Majesty.

CLIV.

BISHOP GRINDAL OF LONDON TO ARCHBISHOP PARKER.

2nd January, 1563—4. Petyt MS. Inner Temple, No. 47. fol. 525. Orig.

I SENT your grace's books[2] yesterday to my lord of Ely, who returned me them this day with some notes of his opinion. It were good we had a time of some further conference.

If the communion be ministered in Paul's, it will be done so tumultuously and gazingly, by means of the infinite mul-

[2 A proposed form of thanksgiving for the diminution or cessation of the plague. See Liturgical Services of Q. Elizabeth, Park. Soc. ed. pp. 508—518.]

Inconvenience of a thanksgiving communion at Paul's.

titude that will resort thither to see, that the honesty[1] of the action will be disordered. And therefore I think it still good to remain in suspense till we talk with more.

God help your grace; 2ᵈ Januarii, 1563.

Your grace's in Christ,
EDM. LONDON.

I send your grace herewith also a temporal man's draft for two statutes to be considered.

CLV.

ARCHBISHOP PARKER TO SIR WILLIAM CECIL.

6th February, 1563—4. Lansd MS. VII. art. 59. Orig.

The archbishop's fears for the country in case of a French invasion.

AFTER my hearty commendations to your honour. Sir, I must request the same to be an instant mean (for special respect of our country here) to the Queen's Majesty and her Council. I assure your honour, I fear the danger, if it be not speedily looked to, will be irrecuperable. If the enemy have an entry, as by great considerations of our weakness and their strength, of their vigilancy and our dormitation and protraction, is like, the Queen's Majesty shall never be able to leave to her successor, that which she found delivered her by God's favourable hand.

Want of information.

Posts and letters with requests be sent, but little return is made, as I hear, and small aid and comfort cometh to my lord Warden, a good gentleman and meaneth honourably, but what can a man do more than may be done by a man almost destitute of men, money, and armour, &c.

Inability of the lord Warden to aid or comfort the people.

Disposition of Bale's prebend at Canterbury.

Furthermore, where I sued by mediation of your honour, to obtain Doctor Bale's prebend for my chaplain, and obtained it at the Queen's liberality[2], at what time of my suit I was certainly informed and persuaded that Mr Tamworth's advowson was for Mr Goodrik's prebend; now I perceive that it was general for the next avoidance, which being bestowed as before, doth prejudice the said advowson. Whereupon I beseech your honour, that ye would prefer the said advowson again to the Queen's Highness to have it renewed for the

[1 Honeste, Orig.]
[2 See before, Letter CLII., p. 197.]

next turn hereafter, which is no more cost, but her favourable grant to be the same that once was granted, to take place at the next turn, seeing it was of late otherwise at her free favour bestowed; wherein Mr Tamworth shall rejoice to have his grant take place, and I and my Chaplain cause to pray for your honour, not to suffer our possession to be reversed. And thus I commit your honour to God's protection this 6th of February, from my palace at Canterbury, 1563.

This afternoon is my lord Cobham[3] gone to Dover as a naked man, without strength of men.

I put it to your consideration what were best to be done with my two guests which ye sent me[4], in this time and country, in such vicinity; although I judge by their words that they be true Englishmen, not wishing to be subject to the governance of such insolent conquerors.

What to be done with the arch- bishop's guests on this fear of inva- sion

Your honour's assured,

MATTHUE CANTUAR.

To the right honourable Sir William Cecil, knight, principal Secretary [to] the Queen's Majesty.

CLVI.

ARCHBISHOP PARKER TO SIR WILLIAM CECIL.

20th January, [1563—4]. Lansd. MS. vii. art. 56. Orig.

SIR,

For that the country here is in much perplexity and fear, doubting what may follow of the preparation they hear of, made by the French, I thought good to write to your honour privately. How small so ever my skill is in such causes, I trust ye will bear with it, in respect of my zeal to my country. Indeed the fear riseth upon consideration that Dover Castle, Walmer and Deal Castles, Queenborough Castle, be as forsaken and unregarded for any provision, the country destitute of the lord Warden, or of a lieutenant to whom in such straits men might resort to; the people but feeble and unarmed, and commonly discomforted. This day I sent my

Alarm at a threatened French inva- sion

State of the castles on the coast.

[3 William Brooke, lord Cobham, was at this time lord Warden of the Cinque Ports.]

[4 Thirleby and Boxall, see Nos. CXLV—CXLVIII.]

Rumours in the isle of Thanet.

man into Thanet to Sir Henry Crisp, who standeth in much doubt. He hath understanding of a French pinnace to have searched as far as the Thames mouth, to know how the Queen's ships be appointed. He thinketh they be like to land in Sheppey, to keep the Queen's ships within the Thames, and not to come forth; whereupon they may be the bolder to arrive, &c.

He fears the wealthy people will remove from the country.

If the country be not comforted, I fear that some folks of wealth will be removing their household and substance, upon which example more may do the like. But that I repose my whole trust and confidence (next to God) in the Queen's Majesty's carefulness and your prudent foresight toward this quarter, I see no great trust in the furniture of men, munition, or artillery; I would else be carried with mistrusts of the worst, as other men be most commonly. I also

State of Dover.

sent another messenger to Dover to the lieutenant. The people in the town, as he reported, be amazed, and have their hearts cold, to hear of no preparation toward this feared mischief. Though you see fully all manner of proceedings and can note the furthest sequel of them, yet, in my opinion, it were not amiss, though some participation of advice pro-

Information needed, and more justices

ceeded into these quarters, to spread them abroad, to the stay of the people; for to whom to go, upon whom to stay, they know not. We have too few justices; betwixt Canterbury

Mr Edward Boyes recommended.

and Dover none. I would Mr Edward Boyes were one, whom I take to be an honest, staid gentleman, &c. Some of our justices go to the term, and a few remain. I pray your honour send me some information by this my servant, not for that I can see any ability in myself to do service that way, yet I could cause my neighbours to trust well, and cause

The archbishop's chaplains shall comfort the people in their sermons.

my chaplains to comfort the people in their sermons in the poor villages, and this is the best we can do in our skill. Beseeching God to assist the Queen's Majesty and all your circumspections, *ita maturare consilia vestra* that peace and verity may still reign amongst us in our days. From my house at Bekesborne, this 20th of January.

      Your honour's assured,

        MATTHUE CANTUAR.

To the right honourable Sir William Cecil,
 knight, principal Secretary to the
 Queen's Majesty, at the Court.

CLVII.

SCOTTISH MINISTERS TO ARCHBISHOPS PARKER AND YOUNG.

10th February, 1563—4. Parker MSS. C. C. Coll. Camb. cxiv. art. 209. p. 567. Orig.

MR JOHN SPOTTISWOOD, superintendant of the Lothian, M. John Knox and John Craig, ministers of Edinburgh, to the most Reverend fathers in God, the archbishops of Canterbury and Y[ork][1], desire the perpetual increase of the Holy Spirit, &c.

Because that in the general assembly of the Church of Scotland begun at Edinburgh the 25th of December 1563, and there continued certain days, after it [was] complained by our brother John Baron, minister of Christ Jesus his Evangile upon Anne Goodacre sometimes his wife, that he after great rebellion shewn unto him, and after divers admonitions given as well by himself as by others in his name, that she should in no wise depart from this realm nor from his house without his licence, hath not the less stubbornly and rebelliously departed, separated herself from his society, left his house, and withdrawn herself from this realm, as the said John's complaint more fully doth proport: the whole assembly, as well of the nobility as of the superintendants, ministers and commissioners of Churches, gave to us commandment and charge, as by this other act[2] your wisdom

In the general assembly held at Edinburgh, 25th December, 1563. John Baron complained that Anne Goodacre, his wife, in spite of admonition, had separated herself from him and departed the realm; whereupon the assembly directed the writers

[1] The edge of the original letter being much worn away, some words and letters are supplied from conjecture: these are inserted between [ ].]

[2] The following is the act alluded to, which is Parker MS. cxiv. art. 210. p. 569.

"At Edinburgh the 29th day of December, 1563. The same day anent the request and supplication given in the general assembly by John Baron, minister of the kirk of Cawston, bearing in effect how Anne Goodacre being his married wife, had of her own wickedness and evil counsel departed from his house here in Edinburgh, in June last bypast, without his licence (he being in the Calston, shortway from this town), towards the realm of England, notwithstanding his letters directed unto her, requiring and charging her to remain, notwithstanding also the requests of divers brethren to whom he also had written to request and charge her in his name to remain to his returning; not the less the said Anne had departed out of this realm

more clearly may perceive, humbly to request and pray you, whom God of his providence and mercy hath erected as principals in Ecclesiastical jurisdiction within the realm of England, that it would please you, and either of you, within your jurisdictions, to cause by public edicts, or else personally apprehended summon charge and warn, the foresaid Anne to compere before the said Superintendants, Ministers and Session of Edinburgh, in their Consistory, the sixtieth day after your summons. We therefore, in the name of the Eternal God, of his Son Jesus Christ, and as ye desire sin to be punished, and us your fellow-servants in Christ Jesus to serve you or any of you in the like case, most humbly require you to cause your edicts to be published in all such places as you know them to be exp[edient], charging the said Anne to compere before the Session of Edinburgh, in the accustomed place of their assembly, the 25th day of May next, to come to ans[wer] by herself and not by her procurator, to such crimes as shall

[marginal notes: to request the ecclesiastical authorities of England to summon the said Anne to appear in the consistory of Edin. burgh on the 60th day after summons. They therefore appeal to the archbishops to charge her to appear before the Session of Edinburgh on the 25th May then next, to an-]

towards England, to his great grief and heart's sorrow: and therefore most humbly requested the most honourable privy council there assembled, with the rest of the nobility, the superintendants, ministers, commissioners of provinces and kirks, to give unto him their advice, counsel, and direction, by what means he might be at liberty from the foresaid wicked woman, according to the precise rule of God's word, as at more length was contained in the said John's supplication. The assembly ordained letters to be directed to the archbishops of Canterbury and York, in name of the whole assembly, subscribed by the superintendant of Lothian, John Knox, M. John Craig, ministers of Edinburgh, and the scribe of the assembly, requesting them, *vicissitudinis causa*, that they should cause edicts to be proclaimed in either of their bounds, or personal citation to be executed against the said Anne Goodacre, that she should compere before the superintendant of Lothian and Session of the kirk of Edinburgh, the sixtieth day after their citation or edicts execution, by her self and not by her procurator, to answer to such things as the said John Baron, her husband, should lay to her charge, and further to answer as law will; with certification that if she compere not the said day and place, the said superintendant and session will proceed and minister justice against her at the said John's instance, according to God's word, &c. Given in the general assembly of the kirk of Scotland and fourth session thereof, day, year, and place foresaides.

Extracted out of the Register of the said general assembly by me, John Gray, scribe to the same; quilk I testify by this my subscription and signet accustomed.

Jn. Gray ———."]

be laid to her charge by her said husband and by us, for her rebellious departing, and other crimes that may be suspected to have ensued thereupon: with certification to her that if she compere not the said day and place, we will proceed and minister justice at [the] said John's instance according to God's word. Further, we most humbly desire you to remit to us, upon the expences of the said John, complainer, this our Act of the General Assembly, together with your edicts or summons duly executed and indorsed in authentic form. Which doing as we doubt not, you shall please the Eternal God and discharge that part of your godly office, so shall you bind us to the like or greater service, when soever it shall please you or any pastor within that realm to charge any of us. And thus we desire the Lord Jesus, that great and only pastor of the sheep, so to rule your hearts and ours that [we] with one mind and one mouth may unfeignedly seek the advancement of [his] name, the comfort of his troubled flock, the maintenance of virtue and suppression of vice, that it will so please him to bless our common labours in this his last harvest by the power of his Holy Spirit, that in the same his glory may be illustrated, his chosen edified, and our consciences discharged. Amen. From Edinburgh, the tenth of February, 1563.

swer to her husband, and also for her rebellious departure from the realm

Also to return to the writers this act with the summons of the archbishops indorsed thereon.

Your loving brethren in Christ Jesus and fellow-servants in his holy Evangile.

We understand that the wicked and rebellious woman, after her unlawful departing from her husband, remained for a season at York.

 M. JO. SPOTTISWOOD, Superintendant of Lotheane.
 JOHN KNOX, Minister of Christ Jesus his holy Evangill.
 JOHN CRAIG, Minister of Christ's Evangil.
    JN. GRAY.

CLVIII.

ARCHBISHOP PARKER TO SIR WILLIAM CECIL.

18th March, 1563—4. Lansd. MS. vii. art. 66. Orig.

AFTER my right hearty commendations to your honour. Whereas ye refer the consideration of my lord of St Asaph's[1]

[1 Dr Thomas Davies, bishop of St Asaph, 1562—1573.]

Cecil had referred to the archbishop the consideration of an application of the bishop of St Asaph for a licence to hold a living in commendam.

suit to me, how meet and convenient it were: I understand that to the maintenance of his hospitality it were needful for him to obtain so much favour for the *commendam* of his small benefices at the Queen's Majesty's hand, for her warrant to the faculties, which grace is such as commonly heretofore hath been granted, when livings were better and victuals cheaper. And though these *commendams* seem to

Its necessity

be a kind of appropriation, yet the inconvenience may be thought less than that the order of godly ministers in that

Poverty of the clergy.

function should be brought to contempt for lack of reasonable necessaries, which though before God it make no great matter, nor honest ministers need not to be abashed within themselves to expend no more than they may, yet the world looketh for port agreeable, and wise grave men think there is done already enough toward that state, for bringing super-

Urges the appointment of a bishop of Llandaff.

fluity to moderation, &c.

I trust ye do remember to prefer some one to the diocese of Llandaff[1], and also therewith to restore his house to him again. How little soever we do severally in our dioceses, it is a good stay in divers respects to the insolent affections of the people.

Fear of the plague.

I pray God to preserve the Queen's Majesty and her court, this variable time of God's visitation. It is feared here in Canterbury that the plague will take some root now in the spring, by reason that I am informed [there] are of late certain infected departed therein and more be in danger. Thus wishing to your honour God's favour and protection, I cease to write. From my house at Bekesborne nigh to Canterbury, this 18th of March, 1563.

Your honour's alway,

MATTHUE CANTUAR.

To the right honourable Sir William Cecil, knight, principal Secretary to the Queen's Majesty. At the Court.

[1 The reason of this request is not understood. Kitchen, bishop of Llandaff is said to have lived until 31st October, 1566, and it is not known that he was deprived of his see. No new bishop was appointed until 1567.]

CLIX.
ARCHBISHOP PARKER TO SIR WILLIAM CECIL.
14th April, 1564. S. P. O. Domestic, 1564. Orig.[2]

SIR,

WHERE of late was sent to me these letters enclosed[3], to such effect as your honour may perceive, for that I am in doubt how agreeable it were for me to satisfy such request, I am bold to pray your honour to impart your counsel to me, the rather for that it may seem to touch the state and order of the realm. *(The archbishop sends to Sir William Cecil the letter from Scotland before printed, No. CLVII., soliciting his advice thereon.)*

The request, in my opinion, is strange, for that this *vicissitudo* is used at the request of them which agnise one superior governor as subjects of one realm or empire; and is also used where the abode or continuance of the party to be called is certainly known, in whose territory the party continueth. And doubtful it is to me by what authority these requesters do exercise their conference, for they make no mention of their warrant or commission. And, further, I take that the party is not bound to obey any such commandment of the archbishops in England to appear in Scotland, the case as it is. And some doubt may rise whether they go about to practise a precedent by our assents to divorce the parties, and to license the innocent to marry again. Further, it may be considered how it may be taken at the Queen Majesty's hand for us to command any resiaunt within her dominions to appear before any foreign power out of the realm. Beside, that the example may be dangerous, if in evil times the like practice might be, and thereby to jeopard the indemnity of the godly where extreme princes be, or evil prelates reign, to desire to torment the poor Protestants. Now, if they require justice, it might as well here as there be ministered of us by the Queen's laws, which I trust do not much differ from God's word well understood. *(Objections suggested by the archbishop.)*

I am bold to write to your honour my fancies, whereto I yet do incline; notwithstanding ready to redress my cogi- *(But he submits to the judgment of the secretary.)*

[² Parker's original draft of this letter is Parker MS. cxiv. art. 211. p. 571.]

[³ The letter, No. CLVII, printed before at p. 205, with the inclosure appended as a note.]

[PARK. COR.]

tations, if your wisdom in respect of gratification of such neighbourhood as is now betwixt us (I mean England and Scotland) may think it convenient. If it were a matter private I would not trouble your other affairs, but seeing it may be drawn to a greater importance, I will stay till I may hear from you; praying you, as your opportunity will serve, to return your advice.

The archbishop has conferred with the lord Marquess thereon, who has promised his help.

I did of late in sum declare the cause to my lord Marquess[1] being here with me, who very honourably did answer that he also would help to some certain resolution at his repair to the Court. And thus I wish your honour all grace and felicity as to myself. From my house at Bekesborne, nigh to Canterbury, this 14th of April.

Your honour's alway,

MATTHUE CANTUAR.

To the right honourable Sir William Cecil, knight, principal Secretary to the Queen's Majesty. At the Court.

CLX.

THE MASTER AND WARDENS OF THE SKINNERS' COMPANY TO ARCHBISHOP PARKER.

7th May, 1564. Parker MSS. C. C. Coll. Camb. cviii. art. 65. p. 415. Orig.

Sir Andrew Judd having founded a grammar-school at Tunbridge and appointed the Skinners' Company governors.

WITH all humbleness. It may please your good grace to understand, that where one Sir Andrew Judd, late knight and alderman of the city of London, did appoint your humble beseechers, the master and wardens of the Company of Skinners in London, governors of a certain grammar-school in the town of Tunbridge, in the county of Kent, by the said Sir Andrew builded and erected, yet through sundry occasions much trouble hath for these four or five years happened to the said governors for the defence thereof in the Queen's Majesty's Court of Wards and Liveries: and in quieting thereof it is thus ordered by the master and council of the said Court of Wards and Liveries, that the said governors shall

the Court of Wards ordered them to stand to such

stand bound in a thousand marks to stand to the good order of your grace, and Mr Nowell, the dean of Paul's, for the

[1 Of Northampton, who was connected with Kent by relationship to lord Cobham.]

appointing of the rules and orders for the government of the said school and scholars there: and for the finishing thereof there are certain orders written and perused by the said right worshipful master dean of Paul's, as by his handwriting may appear, beseeching your grace to peruse the same according to your godly wisdom, and upon the allowing thereof to subscribe the same with your grace's hand[2], that thereby your humble beseechers may come to quietness. And thus your humble beseechers shall daily pray to God for the prosperous estate of your grace in honour long to continue. From London the seventh day of May, 1564. Your most humble beseechers.

Rules for its government as the archbishop and dean Nowell should appoint. Proposed statutes are therefore submitted to them.

by me WYLLM. FLETCHER.
by me THOMAS BANNESTER.
by me THOMAS ALLEN.
by me THOMAS STARKY.
by me JHON METCAWFFE.

*To the right honourable lord, the lord
archbishop's grace of Canterbury,
be this delivered.*

[2 The "orders" for Tunbridge school are preserved in the article immediately preceding this letter (Parker MS. CVIII. 64.) They exbibit a variety of alterations and additions both in the handwriting of Nowell, to whom they were first submitted, and also in that of Parker. At the end of them there are the autograph subscriptions of the dean and archbishop, and also a memorandum written by the archbishop. They are as follows:

"These articles, touching the school at Tunbridge, I have perused and do like them well.
ALEXANDER NOWELL.

These articles, perused, approved, and subscribed to, by the most reverend father in God, Matthue, archbishop of Canterbury, primate of all England and metropolitan, and by the right worshipful Alexander Nowell, dean of the Cathedral Church of S. Paul in London, the 12th day of May, in the year of our sovereign Lady Elizabeth, of England, France, and Ireland, Queen, defender of the faith, &c., the sixth.

Memorandum. That in the parliament in a^{o} domini 1572, et a^{o} Reginæ [?] Elizabethæ, 8 Maii, a^{o} 14 ejus, wherein passed an act for the better and further assurance of certain lands and tenements to the maintenance of the free grammar-school of Tunbridge, in the county of Kent; which statute is not in print."]

CLXI.

QUEEN ELIZABETH TO ARCHBISHOP PARKER.

14th May, 1564. Parker MSS. C. C. Coll. Camb. CXIV. art. 5. p. 13. Orig.[1]

BY THE QUEEN.

ELIZABETH R.

The Queen desiring that a French ambassador should be well received, has ordered the sheriff of Kent to conduct him from Dover to Greenwich.

MOST reverend father in God, right trusty and right well-beloved, we greet you well. Because we intend for the honour of us and our realm, and for the better increase of amity betwixt us and the French king, that an ambassador whom the said king sendeth to us, named Monsr de Gonour, of his privy council and order, should be well received and conducted to us, we have ordered that the sheriff of that county with the officers of our ports shall attend him at Dover, and that the said sheriff shall conduct him through the shire until he shall come to Greenwich.

She wills that the archbishop should receive the ambassador at Canterbury or Bekesbourn, and that he should be there lodged.

And nevertheless we will that he should be received by you at Canterbury, or if it shall be thought meeter, at your house at Bekesbourn, and there lodged, and so from thence the sheriff to take the charge of his conduction.

In so doing, the archbishop not to forget the place he holds in the church.

Wherefore we require you to have consideration hereof, and to use the said ambassador with all courtesy meet for the place that he holdeth, not meaning thereby that you should neglect the place that you hold in our Church, nor that you should receive him but at the entry of your church or house, nor to conduct him further than the limit of the said church or house. Given under our signet at our manor of Richmond, the 14th of May, the sixth year of our reign.

> To the most reverend father in God our
> right trusty and right well-beloved
> the archbishop of Canterbury.

[1 The original draft of this paper, in the handwriting of Sir William Cecil, is in the Domestic Correspondence in the State Paper Office.]

CLXII.

ARCHBISHOP PARKER TO BISHOP CHEYNEY OF GLOUCESTER[2].

[About the end of April, 1564.] Parker MSS. C. C. Coll. Camb. CXIV. art. 98. p. 315. Orig. Draft.

AFTER my hearty commendations to your lordship. Where I am sued unto by a certain honourable personage to extend my favour toward one Humfrey Delamore, parson of Kemisworth[3], that I would qualify him or else sustain him, in that his said benefice, which your lordship upon some suggestion seemeth to challenge to bestow otherwhere, this is to pray the same to tolerate the poor old man in his possession, belike not like long to continue by his sickly age in any of his small livings. Whereby I shall give you thanks, and also cease otherways to devise for his defence.

To my lord of Gloucester.

The archbishop being sued unto on behalf of one Humphrey Delamore, prays the bishop of Gloucester to tolerate the poor old man in his possession.

CLXIII.

ARCHBISHOP PARKER TO MR DRURY.

Probably about the end of April, 1564[4]. Parker MSS. C. C. Coll. Camb. CXIV. art. 99. p. 315. Orig. Draft.

MR DRURY, I commend me unto you. Where this bearer, farmer of a parsonage in Gloucestershire, sueth to

Mr Drury to judge of an application for union of certain benefices in Gloucestershire.

[2 The draft of this letter is written upon the blank leaf of a letter, dated the 27th April, 1564, and addressed to the archbishop by Edmund, lord Chandos, in which he prayed the archbishop's favour to the bearer, "who is like," continued lord Chandos, "to lose his benefice of Kemisford through suit of his enemies, unless your grace extend your favour to the poor man, in consideration that he is both an honest man, my poor neighbour, and also a favourer of true religion, being preferred to some of his livings by bishop Latimer, to whom also he was allied. And whatsoever the law is in his case I cannot determine, but this I am sure of, that it is pity to put a man of his years from his living." This letter is dated "from Bloundesden, my poor house, the 27th of April, 1564."]

[3 So written. It should be Kemisford as in lord Chandos's letter quoted in the note next above.]

[4 The draft of this letter is written upon the same leaf as the preceding addressed by the archbishop to the bishop of Gloucester.

have one other benefice and a chapel to be united together, this is to require you, if upon the understanding of the matter yo shall see cause to give out such an unition, to grant it.

Incent to search for the patron of Warehorn.

Furthermore, I would that Incent[1] should send me word, after search of his books, who is the patron of Warehorn. I gave it last belike by lapse.

CLXIV.

ARCHBISHOP PARKER TO SIR WILLIAM CECIL.

3rd June, 1564. S. P. O. Domestic. Orig.

The archbishop reports his reception of the French ambassador.

AFTER my right hearty commendations unto your honour. Although I know ye need not to be informed of the natural disposition of the Frenchmen, late made our friends, yet I thought it not amiss to write thus much unto your honour concerning these men, being here with me. Which though it be of no great importance, yet I had rather ye blamed my superfluity in writing, than of negligence to express my considerations. I note this gentleman, Mons. de Gonour, to be outwardly of a good gentle nature, and methink I espy that he hath schooled his young gentlemen attending upon him to note and mark not only the tract of our country, but also curiously to search the state of our doings [and] the order of our religion, as the most of them were very inquisitive therein. He coming unto me by Friday at two of the clock, and therefore had the longer day to spend, to give him some occasion of conference, after his reposing in his chamber, I walked in my garden under the sight of his eye, as talking familiarly with my neighbours the gentlemen of the country. He shortly after came down unto us into the garden, and brought especially with him the bishop of Constance, as interpreter betwixt us; who appeareth to be a good, soft-natured gentleman. The substance of

M. de Gonour of a good gentle nature.

His attendants very inquisitive.

He arrived on Friday at two o'clock.

Conferred with the archbishop, the bishop of Constance acting as interpreter.

Mr Drury, to whom it was addressed, filled from time to time many offices in connection with the ecclesiastical courts and transactions of his time. In 1562—3, he was the archbishop's "Commissary for the Faculties." Strype's Parker, Bk. II. c. xii.]

[1 John Incent, the archbishop's registrar.]

his inquisition was much for the order and using of our religion; the particularities whereof I discoursed unto him. He noted much and delighted in our mediocrity[2], charging the Genevians and the Scottish of going too far in extremities. *The subjects of their discourse.*

I perceive that they thought, before their coming, we had neither *statas preces*, nor choice of days of abstinence, as Lent, &c., nor orders ecclesiastical, nor persons of our profession in any regard or estimation, or of any ability, amongst us. And thereupon, part by word and partly by some little superfluity of fare and provision, I did beat that plainly out of their heads. And so they seemed to be glad, that in ministration of our Common Prayer and Sacraments we use such reverent mediocrity, and that we did not expel musick out of our quires, telling them that our musick drowned not the principal regard of our prayer. They were inquisitive of the abbeys suppressed: and after they knew they were converted to the maintenance of canons and preachers, both keeping hospitality and preaching God's word, and employed to the maintenance of grammarians and of beadmen, with other distributions to the poor villages yearly, with a portion also appointed to the repairing of the ways, &c., they wished the like to be universally concluded. *Services of the reformed church of England.* *Application of the revenues of the suppressed abbeys.*

They have also understanding of my prisoners here; and in that respect I noted unto them the Queen's clemency and mercy towards them, for the preservation of them from the plague, and for the distribution of them among their friends. They seemed to be grieved that they were so stiff not to follow the prince's religion. I do smell by them that the young gentlemen were well advertised to see to their behaviour within the realm. For understanding immediately upon their departure by mine officers of their behaviour, I could not charge them either with word or deed, or purloining the worth of one silver spoon: somewhat otherwise than I did doubt of before. *Drs Thirleby and Boxall.* *Behaviour of the ambassador's attendants.*

As I perceived them to be curious and inquisitive, so I appointed some of mine own to be as inquisitive with them, to understand their state in the country. Some of them were frank to note much more misery reigning amongst them than was commonly known abroad with us. And because they much noted the tract of this country in the fair plains and *Parker appointed some persons to inquire as to the state of France,*

[2 Moderation.]

and left his armoury open to observation.

downs so nigh the sea, and to mark the strength we were of, in a little vain brag (unpriestly ye may say) I thought good to have a piece of mine armoury in a lower chamber, nigh to my court, subject to their eyes; whereby they did see that some preparation we had against their invasion, if it had been so purposed. And so some of them expressed, that if a bishop hath regard of such provision, belike other had a more care thereabout. And so they talked, as I learned by them that were their companions.

He gave them a fish supper on Friday night,

For the days of our abstinence, I informed them that we were more religious in that point than they be; and though I made them a fish supper on Friday night, I caused them to understand that it was rather in the respect of their usage at home than for that we used so the Friday or other such fasting days, which we observe partly in respect of temperance and part for policy, not for any scrupulosity in choice of days.

and explained to them the state of our clergy

I signified unto them that we had both bishops and priests, married and not married, every man at his liberty, with some prudent caution provided for their sober contracting and conversation afterward; they did not disallow thereof. In fine, they professed that we were in religion very nigh to them. I answered that I would wish them to come nigher to us, grounding ourselves (as we do) upon the apostolical doctrine and pure time of the primitive Church. They were contented to hear evil of the pope, and bragged how stout they had been aforetimes against that authority. But I said, our proceedings here in England always were not in words, as in Edward the Third's days &c. the pope could never win again at our hands that then he lost in open field concerning provisions, &c.

Bishop of Constance intends to present to the Queen a French translation of the Epistle of Osorius.

Sir, the ground of their repair hither I know not certainly, but it may be that this ambassador may be a great stay in his country for the better supposing of us hereafter: what thereof may follow must be left to God. This bishop shewed me that he intended to present unto the Queen's Majesty Hieronimus Osorius' epistle, translated and printed by his procurement (as he said) into French[1]. I asked what

[1 The epistle of Hieronymus Osorius, bishop of Silvas, in Algarve, was a Latin letter addressed to Queen Elizabeth, with a view to her conversion to Roman Catholicism. Some statements in it were so offensive, that Haddon was encouraged, if not employed, to publish an

was his meaning? He answered, because it expressed so well the Queen's Majesty's graces and gifts, &c. I told him that I thought the Queen could take more pleasure to read it well in Latin than in French, and that so he might have better gratified the Queen's Highness with causing Mr Haddon's answer thereto to be translated, for oft copying thereof could be no pleasure to the Queen's Majesty, the matter being so bad. He had not heard of any answer thereto, and therefore I gave him a book for the ambassador and him to read by the way. If ye dislike the bishop's intendment ye may dissuade him.

Ye may think that I am either vainly idle, or that I think you have too much spare time, thus to trouble you. But I commit altogether unto your gentle consideration to gather of these things as ye think good. And thus avoiding further discourse, I commit you to God, as myself.

² The grief of a distempered head made me to indite my writing, as ye see. I would fain know what is meant or determined concerning my two guests sent to me, because I intend, God willing, now shortly to repair to Lambeth. This country is very dear to dwell in. This third of June. From my house at Bekesborne. <small>What is the archbishop to do with Thirleby and Boxall on his approaching removal to Lambeth?</small>

Your honour's always,

MATTHUE CANT.

To the right honourable Sir William Cecil, knight, principal Secretary to the Queen's Majesty, and of her Privy Council. At the Court.

CLXV.

THE LORDS OF THE COUNCIL TO ARCHBISHOP PARKER.

<small>23rd June, 1564. Parker MSS. C. C. Coll. Camb. CXIV. art. 28. p. 89. Orig.</small>

AFTER our right hearty commendations to your good lordship. We have received your letters containing the suit <small>The lords of the council</small>

answer. Osorius replied, and Haddon's rejoinder, left imperfect at his death, was finished by Foxe the Martyrologist.]

[² This concluding paragraph was written by Parker's own hand.]

have received an application that Mr Boxall for removal from Parker's house, on the ground of ill health. The misconduct of Dr Scott, late bishop of Chester, in absconding without regard to his sureties, disinclines the Council to comply with such request at present.

of Mr Boxall to be removed to some other place from your lordship's house, with the causes alleged on his behalf. And forasmuch as one Doctor Scott, sometime bishop of Chester, receiving favour upon his own bond and the bond of his friends, hath withdrawn himself, without regard had either of his own bond or the danger of his friends, and therein hath committed the act of contempt of the Queen's Majesty[1], a matter much noted and many ways evil reported unto us, we can not now therefore conveniently accord to Mr Boxall's suit, seeing the former lenity and gentleness used to others in his case hath so freshly wrought a lack of consideration in the person of the said Scott, which Mr Boxall being a wise man can consider; and so may your lordship hereby report unto him what doth move us to answer you in form as we do. Nevertheless, for the better preservation of his health, we pray your lordship (as we doubt not you will also of yourself) that he may be as much aided by benefit of place to lodge in your house, and by access of physicians when he shall need them, as shall be fit for remedy of health by your lordship's good considerations of him. And thus fare your good lordship right heartily well. From Richmond, the 23rd of June, 1564.

Your lordship's assured friends,
W. NORTHT.   R. DUDDELEY.
W. HOWARD.
G. ROGERS.   W. CECILL.

CLXVI.

WALTER HADDON TO ARCHBISHOP PARKER.

6th July, 1564. Parker MSS. C. C. Coll. Camb. cxiv. art. 242. p. 663. Orig.

Parker's former colleague has been reconciled to the Queen. Calfhill has preached an injudicious sermon in the royal presence.

VETUS Collega tuus et familiaris, vir consideratissimus, recens est cum Regina colloquutus, et quemadmodum spero plenissime reconciliatus. Calfhillus[2] coram Regina concionem habuit plane militarem, in qua tantum ex omni parte fuit offensionis, quantum nec ego libenter commemorare possum, nec tibi jucundum erit ad audiendum. Plus moderationis

[1 See Letter XIX. of this Collection, with the notes there.]
[2 This word is crossed out in the MS. apparently by a later hand.]

requirit Reginæ præsentia, venerationis aliquid amplius, et verecundiæ. Nunquam in illo loco quisquam minus satisfecit, quod majorem ex eo dolorem omnibus attulit, quoniam admodum est illis artibus instructus, quas illins theatri celebritas postulat. Sed nescio quomodo fastus optimorum ingeniorum fere pestis est nisi meditatione rerum celestium condocefiat. Nisi mansuetiores spiritus posthac concionatores ad aulam attulerint, metuo ne multum ex eorum temeritate damni religio sit acceptura.

De peregrinatione regali dies est indictus ad vicesimum hujus mensis, et itineris descriptio Stamufordiam versus est; sed est adhuc certi nihil. Regina prandet hodie cum D. Sackvillo. Nihil est aliud novi. Deus te servet, tuaque omnia. Pridie Nonas Julii, 1564°.

The 20th instant is fixed for the Queen to set out in the direction of Stamford.

Tuus beneficia[rius]
et benevolentissimus,
G. HADD^S.

CLXVII.

ARCHBISHOP PARKER TO LADY BACON[3].

—— 1564. Prefixed to "An Apologie or Answer in Defence of the Church of Englande, with a briefe and plaine declaration of the true Religion professed and used in the same." 8vo. Lond. 1564.

To the right honourable, learned, and virtuous Lady A. B., M. C. wisheth from God grace, honour and felicity.

MADAM,

ACCORDING to your request I have perused your studious labour of translation, profitably employed in a right commendable work; whereof for that it liked you to make me a judge, and for that the thing itself hath singularly pleased my judgment, and delighted my mind in reading it, I have right heartily to thank your ladyship, both for your own wellthinking of me, and for the comfort that it hath wrought me. But, far above these private respects, I am by greater causes enforced, not only to shew my rejoice of this your doing, but

The archbishop has perused lady Bacon's translation, which has pleased his judgment, and delighted his mind.

[3 Anna, wife of Sir Nicholas Bacon, and mother of Francis Bacon. She was the second of the learned daughters of Sir Anthony Cooke.]

also to testify the same by this my writing prefixed before the work, to the commodity of others, and good encouragement of yourself.

Bishop Jewel and the archbishop have perused the translation, and allowed it without alteration,

You have used your accustomed modesty in submitting it to judgment; but therein is your praise doubled, sith it hath passed judgment without reproach. And whereas both the chief author of the Latin work and I, severally perusing and conferring your whole translation, have without alteration allowed of it, I must both desire your ladyship, and advertise the readers, to think that we have not therein given any thing to

which has not proceeded from any dissembling affection for the translator,

any dissembling affection towards you, as being contented to wink at faults to please you, or to make you without cause to please yourself; for there be sundry respects to draw us from so doing, although we were so evil-minded, as there is no cause why we should be so thought of. Your own judgment in discerning flattery, your modesty in misliking it, the laying open of our opinion to the world, the truth of our friendship towards you, the unwillingness of us both (in respect of our vocations) to have this public work not truly and well translated, are good causes to persuade, that our allowance is of sincere truth and understanding. By which your

but of sincere truth and understanding.

travail, Madam, you have expressed an acceptable duty to the glory of God, deserved well of this Church of Christ, honourably defended the good fame and estimation of your own native tongue, shewing it so able to contend with a work originally written in the most praised speech; and, besides the honour ye have done to the kind of women and to the degree of ladies, ye have done pleasure to the author of the Latin book, in delivering him by your clear translation from the perils of ambiguous and doubtful constructions, and in making his good work more publicly beneficial; whereby ye have raised up great comfort to your friends, and have furnished your own conscience joyfully with the fruit of your labour, in so occupying your time; which must needs redound to the encouragement of noble youth in their good education, and to spend their time and knowledge in godly exercise, having delivered them by you so singular a precedent. Which your doing, good Madam, as God (I am sure) doth accept and will bless with increase, so your and ours most virtuous and learned sovereign lady and mistress shall see good cause to commend; and all noble gentlewomen shall (I trust) hereby be

By her labour on this work, she has deserved well of the Church of England, has defended her native tongue, done honour to her sex, and pleasure to the author.

allured from vain delights to doings of more perfect glory. And I for my part (as occasion may serve) shall exhort other to take profit by your work, and follow your example; whose success I beseech our heavenly Father to bless and prosper. And now to the end both to acknowledge my good approbation, and to spread the benefit more largely, where your ladyship hath sent me your book written, I have with most hearty thanks returned it to you (as you see) printed, knowing that I have therein done the best, and in this point used a reasonable policy; that is, to prevent such excuses as your modesty would have made in stay of publishing it. And thus at this time I leave further to trouble your good ladyship.

The archbishop has returned the book to lady Bacon, already printed, lest her modesty should have scrupled at publishing it.

M. C.

CLXVIII.

BISHOP PILKINGTON OF DURHAM TO ARCHBISHOP PARKER.

Probably A.D.1564. Parker MSS. C. C. Coll. Camb. cxiv. art.189. p. 519. Orig.

GRATIA et pax. Coming into Lancashire, divers honest men of Rachedale required me to commend to your grace George Hargreves to be their vicar. Your grace knew the same a minister long ago in Ely, if ye remember him. Surely the man is in years ancient, in manners blameless, in zeal earnest, in labour painful, in preaching of a good gift and knowledge. I cannot tell where ye should have a fitter man, out of the University, to take so great a charge with so small a living.

Recommendation of George Hargreves to be minister of Rochdale

There was one Wright, once of S. John's, now dwelling by Hadley in Suffolk, where he married D. Tailer's wife, and having a little benefice in an evil air, for recovering his health desired me to help to place him northward. My lord of London knows him well, and surely if he will take it (as I think he will not) he is as meet a man also. Another sort of the parish would have a young priest unlearned, and for nothing but friendship. These other two be fit men, and except ye know any better, ye may well bestow it on them; but surely all things considered, I think Hargreves the fittest man.

Also of one Wright as a fit man.

Among many other things that be amiss here in your
great cures, ye shall understand that in Blackburn there is
a fantastical (and as some think a lunatic) young man, which
says he has spoken with one of his neighbours that died four
year since or more. Divers times he says he has seen him, and
talked with him, and took with him the curate, the schoolmaster, and other neighbours, which all affirm that they see him
too. These things be so common here, and none of authority
that will gainsay it, but rather believe and confirm it, that
every one believes it. If I had known how to have examined
it with authority, I would have done it. It is too lamentable to see and hear how negligently they say any service
there, and how seldom. I have heard of the commission for
ecclesiastical matters directed to my lord of York, &c.; but
because I know not the truth of it, I meddle not. Your cures,
all except Rachedale, be as far out of order as the worst in
all the country. The old vicar of Blackburn, Roger Linney,
resigned for a pension, and now[1] Whalley has as evil a vicar
as the worst, and there is one come thither that has been
deprived, and changes his name, and now teaches school there,
of evil to make them worse. If your grace's officers lust
they might amend many things. I speak this for the amendment of the country, and that your grace's parishes might be
better spoken of and ordered. If your grace would, either
yourself or by my lord of York, amend these things, it
were very easy. One little examination or commandment to
the contrary would take away all these, and more.

The bishop of Man[2] lies here at ease, and as merry as
Pope Joan. The bishop of Chester[3] has compounded with
my lord of York for his visitation, and gathers up the
money[4] by his servant; but never a word spoken of any
visitation or reformation: and that, he says, he does of
friendship, because he will not trouble the country, nor put
them to charge in calling them together. I beseech you be
not weary of well-doing; but with authority and counsel

[1 Something has been here cut off the bottom of the page, but
whether it is a line of the letter or the address is uncertain.]
[2 Bishop Thomas Stanley, deprived by Queen Mary and restored
by Elizabeth; he died in 1570.]
[3 Bishop Downman, 1561 to 1577.]
[4 That is, the visitation fees.]

help to amend that is amiss. Thus, after my commendations I am bold boldly to write, wishing good to my country and the furtherance of God's glory. If Mr Hill had been at home, I would have written more particularly to him. God be merciful unto us, and grant *ut libere currat Evangelium*. *Vale in Christo. Cras profecturus Dunelmiam, volente Domino.*

Tuus, JA. Δυνελμεν.

To the honourable and reverend my lord archbishop of Canterbury.

CLXIX.

SIR WILLIAM CECIL TO ARCHBISHOP PARKER.

15th January, 1564—5. Petyt MS. Inner Temple, No. 47. fol. 65. Orig.

IT may please your grace. I do send herewith a form of a letter, which at the beginning to write the same I thought should have been meet for to have procured from the Queen's Majesty to your grace, but after that I had caused it to be new written, I misliked the same chiefly for length. But yet, before I would alter anything, I thought meet to remit it to your grace's consideration, praying the same to alter or abridge any part thereof. The next doubt I have is, whether the Queen's Majesty will not be provoked to some offence that there is such cause of reformation, and whether she will not have more added than I shall allow. Upon your grace's correction hereof I will follow your advice. 15th January, 1564.

Sir W. Cecil sends the archbishop the form of a letter from the Queen to his grace for his consideration. Cecil doubts whether it is not too long, and whether it will not offend the Queen to find that there is such cause for reformation.

Your grace's at command,
W. CECILL.

To my lord of Canterbury's good grace.

CLXX.

QUEEN ELIZABETH TO ARCHBISHOP PARKER.

25th January, 1564—5. Lansdowne MS. VIII. art. 6. Contemporary copy.

MOST reverend Father in God, &c. We greet you well. Like as no one thing, in the government and charge committed unto us by the favourable goodness of Almighty God, doth more profit and beautify the same to his pleasure and

Nothing in government conduces more to the pleasure of God, the

comfort of governors, and the weal of the people, than unity

acceptation, to our comfort and ease of our government, and, finally, to the universal weal and repose of our people and countries, than unity, quietness, and concord, as well amongst the public ministers having charge under us, as in the multitude of the people by us and them ruled; so, contrariwise,

Diversity in ministers or people must needs provoke the displeasure of God, be discomfortable to governors, and bring danger of ruin on the people

diversity, variety, contention, and vain love of singularity, either in our ministers or in the people, must needs provoke the displeasure of Almighty God, and be to us, having the burden of government, discomfortable, heavy, and troublesome; and, finally, must needs bring danger of ruin to our people and country. Wherefore, although our earnest care and inward

The Queen's earnest care has been that her realm should be governed by public officers and ministers following one rule,

desire hath always been, from the beginning of our reign, to provide that by laws and ordinances agreeable to truth and justice, and consonant to good order, this our realm should be directed and governed, both in the ecclesiastical and civil policy, by public officers and ministers following, as near as possibly might be, one rule, form, and manner of order in all their actions, and directing our people to obey humbly and live godly, according to their several callings, in unity and concord, without diversities of opinions or novelties of rites and manners, or without maintenance or breeding of any contentions about the same; yet we, to our no small grief

yet, to her grief she has heard, that

and discomfort do hear, that where, of the two manner of governments without which no manner of people is well ruled, the ecclesiastical should be the more perfect, and should give example and be as it were a light and guide to allure, direct, and lead all officers in civil policy; yet in sundry places of

for lack of regard of the primate and bishop,

our realm of late, for lack of regard given thereto in due time, by such superior and principal officers as you are, being the primate and other the bishops of your province, with sufferance of sundry varieties and novelties, not only in

there has crept into the church

opinions but in external ceremonies and rites, there is crept and brought into the church by some few persons, abounding more in their own senses than wisdom would, and delighting

open and manifest disorder, by diversity of opinions, and specially in rites and ceremonies

with singularities and changes, an open and manifest disorder and offence to the godly wise and obedient persons, by diversity of opinions and specially in the external, decent, and lawful rites and ceremonies to be used in the churches, so as except the same should be speedily withstand, stayed, and reformed, the inconvenience thereof were like to grow from place to place, as it were by an infection, to a great annoyance, trouble, and deformity to the rest of the whole body of the realm, and thereby impair, deface, and disturb Christian charity, unity, and concord, being the very bands of our religion; which we do so much desire to increase and continue amongst our people, and by and with which our Lord God, being the God of peace and not of dissension, will continue his blessings and graces over us and his people. And although we have now a good while heard to our grief sundry reports hereof, hoping that all cannot be true, but rather mistrusting that the adversaries of truth might of their evil disposition increase the reports of the same: yet we thought, until this present, that by the regard which you, being the primate and metropolitan would have had hereto according to your office, with the assistance of the bishops your brethren in their several dioceses, (having also received of us heretofore charge for the same purpose,) these errors, tending to breed some schism or deformity in the church, should have been stayed and appeased. But perceiving very lately, and also certainly, that the same doth rather begin to increase than to stay or diminish, We, considering the authority given to us of Almighty God for defence of the public peace, concord, and truth of this his Church, and how we are answerable for the same to the seat of his high justice, mean not to endure or suffer any longer these evils thus to proceed, spread, and increase in our realm, but have certainly determined to have all such diversities, varieties, and novelties amongst them of the clergy and our people as breed nothing but contention, offence, and breach of common charity, and are also against the laws, good usages, and ordinances of our realm, to be reformed and repressed and brought to one manner of uniformity through our whole realm and dominions, that our people may thereby quietly honour and serve Almighty God in truth, concord, peace, and quietness, and thereby also avoid the slanders that are spread abroad hereupon in foreign countries.

And therefore, We do by these our present letters require, enjoin, and straitly charge you, being the metropolitan, according to the power and authority which you have under us over the province of Canterbury, (as the like we will order for the province of York,) to confer with the bishops your brethren, namely such as be in commission for causes ecclesiastical, and also all other head officers and persons having jurisdiction ecclesiastical, as well in both our Universities[1] as in any other places, collegiate, cathedral, or whatsoever the same be, exempt or not exempt, either by calling to you from thence whom you shall think meet, to have assistance or conference, or by message, process, or letters, as you shall see most convenient, and cause to be truly understand [sic] what varieties, novelties and diversities there are in our clergy or amongst our people within every of the said jurisdictions, either in doctrine or in ceremonies and rites of the Church, or in the manners, usages, and behaviour of the clergy themselves, by what name soever any of them be called. And thereupon, as the several cases shall appear to require reformation, so to proceed by order, injunction, or censure, according to the order and appointment of such laws and ordinances as are provided by act of Parliament, and the true meaning thereof, so as uniformity of order may be kept in every church, and without variety and contention.

And for the time to come, we will and straitly charge you to provide and enjoin in our name, in all and every places of your province, as well in places exempt as otherwise, that none be hereafter admitted or allowed to any office, room, cure, or place ecclesiastical, either having cure of souls, or without cure, but such as shall be found disposed and well and advisedly given to common order; and shall also, before their admittance to the same, orderly and formally

[[1] The answer of the Vice-Chancellor of Cambridge, Richard Beaumont, Master of Trinity College, to the letter addressed to him by the archbishop, in accordance with the above requisition, is preserved, Parker MS. CVI. art. 337, p. 627. He states that he had called the Heads of Houses together, and requested them to make enquiry in their several Colleges and report to him; and he thus gives the result of the investigation: "All things touching the said three points are in good order, save that one in Christ's College, and sundry in St John's, will be very hardly brought to wear surplices, and two or three in Trinity College think it very unseeming that Christians should play or be present at any profane comedies or tragedies. But touching the substance of religion now generally agreed upon, I know none that impugneth any part thereof, unless it be two or three suspected papists, which yet lurk·in one or two Colleges, and shall, I trust, be revealed ere it be long." The letter is dated 27th Feb. 1564.]

promise to use and exercise the same office, room, or place, to the honour of God [and] the edification of our people under their charge, in truth, concord, and unity; and also to observe, keep, and maintain such order and uniformity in all the external rites and ceremonies, both for the Church and for their own persons, as by laws, good usages, and orders, are already allowed, well provided, and established. And if any superior officers shall be found hereto disagreeable, if otherwise your discretion or authority shall not serve to reform them, We will that you shall duly inform us thereof, to the end we may give indelayed order for the same; for we intend to have no dissension or variety grow by suffering of persons which maintain dissension to remain in authority; for so the sovereign authority which we have under Almighty God should be violate and made frustrate, and we might be well thought to bear the sword in vain. Superior officers found disagreeable to be reported to the Queen.

And in the execution hereof we require you to use all expedition that, to such a cause as this is, shall seem necessary, that hereafter we be not occasioned, for lack of your diligence, to provide such further remedy, by some other sharp proceedings, as shall percase not be easy to be borne by such as shall be disordered: and therewith also we shall impute to you the cause thereof. Expedition to be used in the execution hereof.

Indorsed. 25th January, 1564.

*To the archbishop of Canterbury,
from the Queen's Majesty.*

CLXXI.

ARCHBISHOP PARKER TO BISHOP GRINDAL OF LONDON.
30th January, 1564—5. Parker's Reg. I. 253 a.

AFTER my hearty commendations to your good lordship. Where the Queen's Majesty, the 25th day of this present month, addressed unto me her letters, very seriously and at great length discoursed, in her godly zeal much desirous to see unity, quietness, and concord amongst the public ministers of her realm, and the people of the same; and also declaring on the contrary part, that diversity, variety, and contention hath been very discomfortable and heavy unto her Highness; The archbishop has received the Queen's letter before printed, No. CLXX., which he recites.

which diversity being not redrest, must bring danger of ruin
to her people and country; the inconvenience whereof her
Highness foreseeing at the beginning of her reign, did therefore provide laws and ordinances to stay and knit her people
in unity, without diversities of opinions or novelties of rites
and manners, breeding but strife and contention; and that now
of late, for lack of regard of us, the bishops, notwithstanding
the earnest weight of words charged upon us by her Highness and the states of the realm, for due execution, sundry
varieties and novelties in opinions and in external ceremonies
and rites, by a few persons delighting in vain singularities
and changes be crept in, by whom Christian charity, the
band of good religion, is impaired and defaced, to the great
dishonour of Almighty God; and furthermore, where her
Highness hath oft heard, to her great grief, sundry reports
hereof, in which consideration yet her Majesty of her gracious
affection standeth in some mistrust that the adversaries of
truth might of their evil dispositions increase the said reports;
nevertheless, her Highness of late perceiving certainly that
the same misorders begin[1] rather to increase than to diminish; and further, her Highness, in consideration of her
authority given her of God for defence of concord and truth
in this Church of England, professing that she cannot endure
or suffer any longer these evils to proceed and increase in her
realm, hath certainly determined to have all such diversities
and novelties, against the laws, good usages, and ordinances of
the realm, to be expelled[2], and to have uniformity throughout
the whole realm, to the honour of God, to the unity of the
people, and so to avoid the slanders that are spread hereof in
foreign countries.

Whereupon her Majesty hath straitly charged me, according to such power and authority as I have under her, to have
consideration of the same in such form as by her said letters
is expressed, and to understand of every person having any
jurisdiction ecclesiastical, as well in both Universities, as in
other places exempt whatsoever, what varieties be used either
in doctrine or in ceremonies and rites of the Church, or in
the manners, usages, and behaviours of the clergy themselves, and to seek the reformation of the same.

[¹ Beinge, Park. Reg.]   [² Expressed, ibid.]

And, further, her commandment is, that none hereafter be admitted to any office or room ecclesiastical, but such as shall be disposed to follow common order, and shall also before their admittance orderly and formally promise to use themselves in truth, concord, and unity, and to keep such order and uniformity in all the external rites and ceremonies, both for the Church and their own persons, as by laws, good usages, and orders, already are provided.

Moreover, her Majesty expresseth her pleasure to be, none such as maintain disordered dissension to remain in authority, whereby her sovereign authority might be made frustrate, and might be thought to bear the sword in vain.

Finally, her Majesty straitly chargeth me to inform her Highness of all such as be not reformable, and to refer them to her further order; or else, for lack of my diligence herein, her Highness shall be compelled to provide further remedy, by some other sharp proceedings, as shall percase not be easy for them to bear. In which case her Highness also saith, that she shall impute to me the cause thereof.

These things thus considered, for the performing my duty to Almighty God, in declaration of mine allegiance and obedience to her princely authority, and to avoid her heavy indignation, I do by these my letters desire your lordship, and in her name straitly charge you, to expend and execute the premises; and also to signify the same with charge to the rest of our brethren in my province, that they inviolably see the laws and ordinances already stablished to be without delay and colour executed in their particular jurisdictions, with proceeding against the offenders by the censures of the Church &c., and such as be incorrigible to send up hither the causes and demerits of those persons; as they the said bishops to charge their inferiors having any jurisdiction, to do the same. And also, that you and they severally calling the most apt grave men to confer with in your and their diocese, to certify me what varieties and disorder there be, either in doctrine or in ceremonies of the Church and behaviour of the clergy themselves, by what names soever they be called. Which certificate to be returned by the last day of February next to come at the farthest. And that you and they thereof fail not, as ye and they will answer to the contrary at your and their peril. From my house at Lambeth, the 30th day of January, 1564.

Your loving brother,

MATTHEU CANTUR.

CLXXII.

JOHN FOX TO ARCHBISHOP PARKER.

7th February, 1564—5. Parker MSS. C. C. Coll. Camb. cxiv. art. 198, p. 537.

Fox applies to the archbishop for a renewal of his Lent licence.

SALUTEM et vitam in Christo æternam. Pro rara ac singulari hac naturæ tuæ mansuetudine, quæ semper mihi in te placuit, (Matthæe Episcoporum decus ac sidus eximium,) rogo etiam atque etiam sublimitatem tuam, ut hanc ipsam, quam superioribus his annis hactenus mihi concesseris quadragesimalem vescendi licentiam, hac etiam quadragesima renovare velis: eandemque ut quam diutissime mihi possis concedere, precor. Ita me amet Christus Dominus, nullum fere est cibi genus tam delicatum quod non fastidiat stomachi *His infirmities betoken that he shall not live long* mei delicatior infirmitas, etiam quum exquisitissima mihi parantur. Unde suspicor non valde longam mihi ætatem superesse[1]. *If the archbishop wishes his Fox to die, this Lent may despatch him, if he thinks his health valuable to the commonwealth, Fox begs that his necessity may be considered.* Si velis Foxum tuum mori cito, facile me conficiet hæc quadragesima. Sin putes salutem meam Christo et republica dignam, rogo amplitudinem et charitatem tuam, ut infirmitati meæ, vel necessitati potius (qua nulla esse major possit) in hac concedenda licentia concedat aliquid. Dominus Jesus mansuetissimam pietatem tuam diu nobis et reip. Christianæ superstitem esse velit. Lendini, 7 Februar.

Tuus in Christo,

JOA. FOXUS.

Reverendissimo D. Matthæo
archiepiscopo Cant.

[[1] Fox lived until 1587. This and other similar applications were occasioned by a recent enactment of the legislature, enforcing the Lent fast. Strype's Parker, Book II. c. 25.]

CLXXIII.

ARCHBISHOP PARKER TO SIR JOHN HOLT AND OTHERS, INHABITANTS OF ROCHDALE.

20th February, 1564—5. Parker MSS. C. C. Coll. Camb. CVIII. art. 73, p. 435.

AFTER my hearty commendations. Forasmuch as I have hitherto laboured, of good will and zeal which I bear to the youth of your parish and county, to procure a grammar-school to be erected and established within your parish, and for that it should take good effect, this is to pray your worships to be as helps to the finishing of the same; that is, one way, to consider by your prudence what the charges will amount to for the building of the school-house over and beyond the benevolences to be shewed of the parishioners there, and that I might be informed by your letters of the same as speedily as you could, thinking that if you would appoint two or three or four trusty men to be as overseers of the building there, and the fit placing of the said school, which as yet, I think, might be well set within some part of the vicar's ground, not much to his discommodity. And, further, ye shall understand that towards some help of the said building, I took order with Mr Byron that such money as remain in his hands unpaid to the vicar and curates there should be employed that way[2]. And further, whereas I sent a centre plat for length and breadth of the said school, and hearing now the likelihood of greater resort of scholars than I supposed, ye shall do well to extend it further in length than is proportioned; and as for either chimneys or plancher[3] to be at this time builded, for that it may amount to excessive charge, ye may spare that cost till that hereafter some good men of the division may increase the same with other furni-

[2 The rectory of Rochdale in Lancashire, which had come to the see of Canterbury by exchange with the crown in archbishop Cranmer's time, was let to Sir John Byron, one of the conditions being that he should pay the vicar a certain stipend. This he had neglected to do, and legal proceedings were consequently instituted against him by archbishop Parker. The matter, however, was subsequently arranged amicably, on condition of the payment named in this letter. See Strype's Parker, Book II. c. 26.]

[3 Plancher: planchier, cornice.]

tures belonging. And thus wishing you all to do well, I commend you to the grace of God as myself. At my manor of Lambeth, this xx. of February.

*To the worshipful and my loving friends
Sir Jo. Holt, knight, Charles Ratlif,
Charles Howel and Edward Butter-
worth, gentlemen, at Rochdale.*

CLXXIV.

ARCHBISHOP PARKER TO MR BYRON.

[— February, 1564—5.] Parker MSS. C. C. Coll. Camb. cviii. art. 74, p. 436. Orig. Draft.

The archbishop desires the erection of the school at Rochdale to go forward. He inquires what money is in the hands of Mr Byron to be employed that way, and what help may be expected from the parish.

AFTER my hearty commendations, gentle Mr Byron. For that I desire the school to go forward at Rochdale, I would be glad to hear from you, as well what sums ye have in your hands remaining of the stipend of the vicar and curates unpaid, which shall be employed that way, saving to the vicar now thereat from the time of his incumbency his portion due, as also what good help may otherwise be perceived of any of the parish and country agreeably to such expectation as I was partly put in by you and of others, whereby I shall the rather travail hereafter to extend further my good will to the same, and see cause to give you thanks accordingly. And thus, with commendations to Sir John Byron[1] your father, I commend you to the grace of God as myself.

Your friend,

M. CANT.

[[1] Sir John Byron, grantee of Newstead, and also the possessor of the old family seat of Clayton in Lancashire. The Mr Byron to whom this letter was addressed, was probably the fourth, but only surviving son of Sir John, himself knighted at a subsequent period, and grandfather of the first Lord Byron.]

CLXXV.

ARCHBISHOP PARKER TO SIR WILLIAM CECIL.
3rd March, [1564—5.] Lansd. MS. VIII. art. 1.

SIR,

I send your honour a book of articles, partly of old agreed on amongst us, and partly of late these three or four days considered, which be either in papers fasted on, as ye see, or new written by secretary hand. Because it is the first view, not fully digested, I thought good to send it to your honour to peruse, to know your judgment, and so to return it, that it may be fair written and presented. The devisers were only the bishops of London, Winchester, Ely, Lincoln and myself[2].

Parker sends a book of Articles for the judgment of Sir William Cecil.

This day in the afternoon we be agreed to have conference with Mr Sampson, Mr Humphrey, and four other of the ministers in London, to understand their reasons &c., if your honour will step over to us, as it please you.

A conference this day with Sampson and Humphrey at Lambeth.

To be prescribed in preaching, to have no matter in controversy in religion spoken of, is thought far unreasonable, specially seeing so many adversaries as by their books plentifully had in the court from beyond the sea, do impugn the verity of our religion.

To be prescribed to avoid matters of controversy in preaching is thought unreasonable

I pray you *in tota hac causa, ne nimium tendas funiculum;* and furthermore, I must earnestly pray your honour to obtain a private letter from the Queen's Majesty to my lord of London, to execute laws and injunctions; which he saith, if he be so charged, he will out of hand see reformation in all London; and ye know there is the most disorder, and

Letters solicited from the Queen to bishop Grindal, urging him to execute the laws and injunctions.

[2 The Articles here referred to are published by Strype in the Appendix to his Parker, Book II. No. xxviii. (Vol. III. p. 84, 8vo. ed.), under the title of "Ordinances accorded by the archbishop of Canterbury, &c., in his province." As afterwards altered and published under the title of "Aduertisments, partly for due order in the publique administration of common prayers and usinge the holy sacramentes, and partly for the apparell of all persons ecclesiasticall," they may be seen in Hearne's Camden, I. xxxii., and in Cardwell's Documentary Annals, I. 287. The bishops above alluded to as having assisted the archbishop in the compilation of these Articles were, Grindal, Horne, Cox, and Bullingham.]

then is the matter almost won thorough the realm. I pray
you earnestly, expeditely to procure these letters, for he is
now in a good mood to execute tho laws, and it will work
much more than ye would think &c. This third of March.

Your honour's,

MATTHUE CANTUAR.

*To the right honourable Sir William
Cecil, knight, principal Secretary to
the Queen's Majesty.*

CLXXVI.

ARCHBISHOP PARKER TO SIR WILLIAM CECIL.

8th March, [1564—5.] Lansd. MS. viii. art. 2.

SIR,

The archbishop sends to Sir William Cecil the Book of Ordinances subscribed by the bishops, that he may obtain the Queen's authorisation thereof.

I send your honour our book which is subscribed to by the bishops conferrers, which I keep by myself. I trust your honour will present it upon opportunity which ye can take in removing offences that might grow by mine imprudent talk. If the Queen's Majesty will not authorise them, the most part be like to lie in the dust for execution of our parties, laws be so much against our private doings. "The Queen's Majesty, with consent, &c." I trust shall be obeyed.

Racket stirred up by Withers, about the University windows.

I send you a letter sent to me of the racket stirred up by Withers, of whom ye were informed, for the reformation of the university windows, but I hear nothing done against him. My lord of Norwich[1] hath got him a commission to good purpose, *scilicet*. I have sent for him, but if you the council lay not your helping hand to it, as ye once did in Hooper's days, all that is done is but to be laughed at.

Sampson and Humphrey remain immovable

This afternoon came Mr Sampson and Mr Humphrey, which brought me my copies of Bucer and Martyr's letters, *sed illi antiquum retinent immobiles*. They would go home again to Oxford. I told them that they must tarry. If the Queen's Majesty, or you of the council, would send for them, ye may, or if my lord of Leicester, their chancellor, will proceed. I can do no good. Better not to have begun, except more be done. All the realm is in expectation. *Sapienti pauca.*

[1 Bishop Parkhurst.]

Your honour principally hath begun, *tua interest ut aliquid fiat*. If this ball shall be tossed unto us, and then have no authority by the Queen's Majesty's hand, we will set still. I marvel that not six words were spoken from the Queen's Majesty to my lord of London, for uniformity of his London, as himself told me; if the remedy is not by letter, I will no more strive against the stream, fume or chide who will. Thus the Lord be with you. For that I am not like to come to the sermon to-morrow, as in a grudge of an ague, I send thus to your honour. For pure pity I took home to dinner with me Mr dean of Paul's yesterday; he was utterly dismayed[2]. God send us of his grace. This 8th of March.

Your honour's,

MATTH. CANT.

To the right honourable
Sir William Cecil, knight.

CLXXVII.

SIR WILLIAM CECIL TO ARCHBISHOP PARKER.

14th March, 1564_5. Parker MSS. C. C. Coll. Camb. cxiv. art. 199, p. 547.

It may please your grace. The Queen's Majesty, at the humble suit of the warden of Winchester, is pleased to dispense with the scholars there, in like sort as she hath for the Universities of Cambridge[3] and Oxford, touching the observation of Wednesday made a fish-day by politic constitution. It may please your grace according to her Majesty's will so to give out your dispensation for the said College. And so I most humbly end. From Westminster, the 14th of March, 1564.

Your grace's humbly to command,

W. CECILL.

[2 A letter of dean Nowell, dated on this same 8th March, explains this allusion to a sermon of his, which gave offence to the Queen. See Strype's Parker, Bk. II. App. No. 29. (III. 94. 8vo. ed.)]

[3 The Cambridge dispensation was granted by Parker. A letter of thanks to him on that occasion occurs in Parker MS. cxiv. art. 202, and is printed in Strype's Parker, Bk. II. App. No. 32. It is dated *undecimo Calendas Decembris*, 1564.]

CLXXVIII.

ARCHBISHOP PARKER TO SIR WILLIAM CECIL.

24th March, [1564—5.] Lansd. MS. viii. art. 4.

SIR,

The archbishop regrets that Cecil stirred the question of uniformity, unless prepared to proceed with vigour

I would ye had not have stirred *istam camarinam*, or else to have set on it to some order at the beginning. This delaying works daily more inconvenience, *et obfirmatiores fiunt*. If it be purposed to have some of these earnest men afore the whole body of the council to the end only to be foul chidden, *verba tantum et præterea nihil* and I doubt whether it will work to a quietness, the deformities to be openly intreated. All men be not one man's children. If my lord of Leicester and your honour would consult with my lord keeper how to deal in this cause to do good and to pacify the Queen's Majesty, I think ye shall spend a piece of your afternoon well. If your honour shall think good to have my lord of London and me to meet you there at my lord keeper's, I leave it to your prudence. Peradventure your wisdoms shall take some occasions of our informations to treat this cause with less offence: for that we now know the whole state and complexion of the causes and the parties.

Suggests a meeting of lord Leicester and Cecil with the bishop of London and himself at the lord Keeper's

Withers is come to town.

Withers is come to me *cum magna confidentia, vultu senatorio*. I pray your honour send the complaint sent of him. I see not the best to send for disordered men hither, where, after they spy how the game goeth, *redduntur multo perfractiores*. I think that *non solum jam periculum vertitur in ritibus vestium tantummodo, sed omnium rituum in universum*, and therefore prudence would be taken.

Not only garments, but all rites are now called in question.

I pray your honour signify to me what ye think. This 24th of March.

Your honour's,

MATTH. CANT.

To the right honourable
Sir William Cecil, knight.

CLXXIX.

ARCHBISHOP PARKER TO SIR WILLIAM CECIL.

7th April [1565.] Lansd. MS. xix. No. 1.

SIR,

THE talk, as I am informed, is much increased, and unrestful they be, and I alone they say am in fault. For as for the Queen's Majesty's part, in my expostulation with many of them I signify their disobedience, wherein, because they see the danger, they cease to impute it to her Majesty, for they say, but for my calling on, she is indifferent. Again, most of them dare not name your honour in this tragedy, for many must have your help in their suits, &c. My lord of London is their own, say they, and is but brought in against his will. I only am the stirrer and the incenser. And my lord of Durham will be against us all: and will give over his bishopric rather than it shall take place in his diocese. Now my lord of Leicester, they say, shall move and obtain the Queen's Majesty, and this thing is now done in his absence, and Mr Cole is now at the Court in his hat and short cloak, which will overthrow all this attempt: and such twitell-twaytel there is much. For my part, I have and do *bona conscientia* whatsoever I do. I regard God's honour and the public quiet. I wish obedience to the Queen's Highness and to her laws: the greatest estimation her Highness can have amongst us. If this matter shall be overturned with all these great hopes, &c., I am at point to be used and abused: *nam scio nos episcopos in hunc usum positos esse.* We be the stiles over which men will soonest leap over. And if we be thus backed, there will be fewer Winchesters, as be desired. But for my part, so that my prince may win honour either by standing or relenting, I will be very gladly *lapis offensionis. Sed interim, cum Dominus sit mihi adjutor, non timebo quod mihi faciat homo.* And thus I am bold to open into your bosom such my weak cogitations; but truly not amazed nor danked; *fremat mundus, ruat cœlum:* and thus I beseech God to frame us all to his honour. This 7th of April.

Your honour's,
MATTH. CANT.

I would yet wish to understand what likelihood there might be of this great expectation.

*To the right honourable Sir W. Cecil,
knight, one of the Queen's Majesty's
privy council.*

CLXXX.

ARCHBISHOP PARKER TO SIR WILLIAM CECIL.

9th April, 1565. Lansd. MS. VIII. No. 46.

SIR,

The archbishop sends to Sir W. Cecil as Chancellor of Cambridge, some notes about licences to preach, granted by that University, which he considers to be informal, as not running in the name of the Chancellor.

According to your request, I return to you some part of my University notes concerning preaching. Your honour had need look to it, it will else grow to much inconvenience. I take all the licences hitherto in this form of Withers[1] to be naught, for they be not according to the laudable custom hitherto used. Your name as their Chancellor not prefixed (which authority ye were best to keep still: so may the better choice be made). And, to say a truth, seeing their letters patent be granted but agreeably to their privileges, &c., it is a weak hole for them, for that bull of *Episcopus Ostiensis* is long ago dead[2]. But for my diocese, except I see your name prefixed, they shall not be received.

I cannot tell what Mr Vice-chancellor's experience hath brought up to inform your honour more than those my notes declare. But they leave out of their licences such words as be in the bulla of *Hostiensis*, whereto their style doth allude.

I take it that though sometime the University seal goeth out by the name of the Vice-chancellor, yet it is not rightly

[1 See before, Letters CLXXVI. and CLXXVIII.]

[2 A bull of Julian, bishop of Ostia, addressed to bishop Fisher, Chancellor of Cambridge, whereby, under the authority of pope Alexander VI., the bishop of Ostia granted to the Chancellor power to license twelve preachers under the University seal. Strype's Parker, I. 383. 8vo. ed.]

done, for the incorporation is to the "Chancellor, masters, and scholars." Such style were fitter for the seal of office. And I think bishop Rochester, for the weight of the matter, would have it pass in his name, and I think not without some trial or credible information of the worthiness of the party. *Proper style of the University.*

In my opinion it were well done that they had a form prescribed of their licences, and so expressed in the proctors' book, and by a grace established, with the annulling of all licences passed before. *A form of licence should be prescribed.*

If they abuse so much the Queen's grant *te vivente* what will they do hereafter? All the ordinaries in their licences do insert such words: *quamdiu nobis placuerit, et dum laudabiliter te gesseris*, &c., and they simply hand over head admit all without revocation. The Lord be with you. This 9th of April, 1565.

Your honour's assuredly,
MATTH. CANT.

I pray you forget not Lewsam[3] advocation.

To the right honourable Sir William Cecil, knight, principal secretary to the Queen's Majesty.

CLXXXI.

ARCHBISHOP PARKER TO SIR WILLIAM CECIL.

[About Easter, 1565.] Lansd. MS. viii. art. 48.

Sir,

This appointment[4] of Sampson and Dr Humphrey is not appointed by me; by whom I know not; either by my lord of London or by my lord mayor. And if these solemn sermons should stay for want, now after so short a warning, it would raise a marvellous speech. I pray you advertise the Queen's Majesty. *Sampson and Humphrey appointed to preach at Paul's Cross either by the bishop of London or the lord mayor*

[3 Lewisham, co. Kent.]
[4 To preach at Paul's Cross. This letter probably alludes to sermons intended to be preached there at Easter 1565. It seems to have preceded the examination of Sampson and Humphrey on the 29th April, 1565, referred to in Parker's next letter. Easter Sunday in 1565 was the 22nd April.]

I think my lord of Rochester[1] will keep his day of preaching, for or else he would have sent me word in time to have provided some other; for I sent him word since he was hurt, and returned no nay to me, whereby I conclude that he will keep it.

I would Sampson and Humphrey had been peremptorily, at the first, put to the choice, either conformity or depart; but they abuse their friends' lenity, on whom they trust. God be with your honour.

Your honour's,

MATTH. CANT.

*To the right honourable
Sir William Cecil, knight.*

CLXXXII.

ARCHBISHOP PARKER TO SIR WILLIAM CECIL.

30th April, [1565.] Lansd. MS. VIII. art. 47.

SIR,

YESTERDAY I called on Mr Sampson and Dr Humphrey for conformity, and after some words of advertisement, I did peremptorily will them to agree, or else to depart their places. I shewed them these were the orders which they must observe; to wear the cap appointed by Injunction, to wear no hats in their long gowns, to wear a surplice with a non-regent hood in their quires at their Colleges, according to the ancient manner there, to communicate kneeling in wafer-bread.

In fine, they said their consciences could not agree to these orders, and they required some respite to remove their stuff. I answered, that I would signify their determination to the Queen's Majesty, and what time should be granted them to remove they should be informed. Mr Sampson declared, that by the death of Mr Bruerne, their receiver, there was a great sum of money of the College to be answered at the said Bruerne's hands. Mr Humphrey alleged, for that he had divers noblemen's sons, he trusted to have a time,

[1 Bishop Geste, 1559—1571.]

requesting much to be spared of the extremity of losing his living.

It may please your honour to inform the Queen's Majesty, to understand her pleasure how they shall be dealt with, whether to tolerate them or to provide others. As the deanery is at her Highness' disposition[2], and the presidentship of Magdalen[3] at the election of the College, upon what ground and how to proceed I am in doubt. If it be the Queen's Majesty's pleasure that I write letters to both Colleges, that they may not be reputed or accepted there in their rooms, or enjoy any commodity, I shall do her commandment. Resign I think they mean not; judicially to be deprived, against Mr Sampson my jurisdiction (after long pleading) might serve, yet so it cannot upon Dr Humphrey; but it is to be expended by the bishop of Winchester their visitor. As I may learn by your honour the Queen's pleasure I shall do, being right sorry that they be no more tractable.

Because I am not yet after my distemperance well settled, I come not personally, but write thus much to your honour, praying you to have your furtherance as may stand with the Queen's contentation and order of her laws. Thus God keep your honour in grace and health. This last day of April.

Cecil is requested to report their refusal to the Queen.

The archbishop will perform the Queen's pleasure; but is right sorry they are not more tractable.

Yours alway,

MATTH. CANT.

I was informed yesterday that Turner of Wells[4] hath enjoined a common adulterer to do his open penance in a square priest's cap. If it be true, this is strange toying with the prince's pleasure and injunctions. You of the council know what ye have to do.

To the right honourable Sir William
Cecil, knight, principal secretary to
the Queen's Majesty.

[2 The deanery of Christ Church, Oxford, held by Dr Sampson.]
[3 Oxford, held by Dr Humphrey.]
[4 Dr William Turner, dean of Wells, a well-known theological and botanical writer.]

CLXXXIII.

ARCHBISHOP PARKER TO BISHOP GRINDAL OF LONDON.
12th May, 1565. Parker Reg. I. 254 a.

The Queen is informed of divers indiscreet preachers;

AFTER my hearty commendations to your good lordship. For that the Queen's Majesty is informed of divers undiscreet preachers, who be thought to be licensed partly by my letters, partly by others of our brethren, of which preachers

whereupon more care is to be taken in choice of such as sue for licences.

divers have deceived our expectations; whereupon for the better instruction of her subjects, her Highness commanding the same, it is meet that we should take for hereafter a more diligent choice of such as shall sue for such licences. In the mean time, this is to pray and require your lordship to

Curates to suffer none to preach by virtue of the archbishop's licences dated before the 1st of April last past.

signify to the rest of our brethren in my province, to charge their curates to suffer none to preach in their cures by virtue of my licences bearing date before the first day of April last past; which order I find to have been used in my predecessors'

Such order was taken several times in archbishop Cranmer's days.

days, as in bishop Cranmer's I have to shew, who upon such occasion was compelled twice or thrice in his time to call in his licences before granted, with addition partly of certain clauses, and partly bonds not to disturb the state of religion stablished by public authority; notifying also that such as shall desire to be admitted by my licence or theirs, being

Licences will be renewed to meet persons.

meet for the same, shall be received again without any difficulty or any great charge for their licences, bringing in their old. Furthermore, this is also to require you, in the Queen's Majesty's name, that the officers of the ordinaries

No curate from another diocese to be admitted to serve without letters testimonial from his late ordinary

give charge, that no curate be admitted to serve, coming out of any other diocese, except he bring the letters testimonial from the ordinary where he did before serve. And also, that they be advertised that such ministers as be not of grave

Ministers not to let their benefices without consent of the ordinary.

and constant abode let not out their benefices without the consent of the ordinary, to foresee all unhonest parties, as divers have deceived the Queen's subjects in taking sums of money for their leases, and afterward dishonestly departed from their places, to a manifest fraud of their said farmers. From my house at Lambeth, this 12th of May, 1565.

Your loving brother,
MATT. CANTUR.

*To the right reverend father in God
and my loving brother, the bishop of
London, give these.*

CLXXXIV.

DR SAMPSON TO ARCHBISHOP PARKER.

3rd June, 1565. Petyt MS. Inner Temple, No. 47. fol. 323. Orig.

REVERENDISSIME, S. My humble thanks to your grace premised. By these letters inclosed your favourable commending of my cause to the chapter of Christ Church in Oxon is well witnessed to have had with them just regard. And now as my necessity compelleth me to crave further aid, so your facility to grant my last encourageth me to make this second request for the same. The honourable earl of Huntingdon[1] hath moved at my suit Mr Secretary, that, without assignment of place, I might go and abide at mine own liberty, where I may by seeking find some commodious settling for me and my poor family. He hath promised to become for me a favourable mediator herein to the Queen's Majesty, if that in this behalf he might receive from your grace some letter of commending this my humble suit to him, whereupon, as upon a meet ground, he might the better build his mediation to her Highness. I think my said lord of Huntingdon doth certify your grace of the truth hereof by this bearer. The equity of the thing and my urgent necessity considered, of their own condition, will move, I trust, your goodness to add this second salve to my misery, which I do humbly desire. The Lord Jesus direct you by his mighty Spirit to do in your calling that best pleaseth him. London, 3 Junii, 1565.

The archbishop's interference with Christ Church on behalf of Sampson has been favourably received.

The ear of Huntingdon has applied to the Secretary that he may be at liberty.

Cecil has promised to become Sampson's mediator if Parker will write on his behalf.

He is urgently intreated to do so.

Yours to command *in Domino,*

THO. SAMPSON.

To the most reverend father in God,
the lord archbishop of Canterbury.

[[1] Henry Hastings, third earl of Huntingdon of that creation, a well-known nobleman of strong protestant feelings.]

CLXXXV.
ARCHBISHOP PARKER TO SIR WILLIAM CECIL.
4th June, 1565. Petyt MS. Inner Temple, No. 47. fol. 322. Orig. Draft in
Parker's hand.

AFTER my right hearty commendations to your honour. Where I understand that Mr Sampson lieth still at suit for his favourable placing out at his own liberty, without note of committing him as prisoner to any place, your honour should do a right good deed in mine opinion to be suitor to the Queen's Highness for her favour therein. Her pleasure being thus executed upon him for example to the terror of others, might yet be mollified to the commendation of her clemency; whereunto her Highness is inclined both godly and naturally to all persons indifferently. And as your honour is the common refuge, to be a solicitor to the Queen's Majesty in our causes, so ye shall do a good act to continue herein. Which favour shewed, if it should be abused by the wilfulness of some fond heads, yet God's cause in reasonable men may be pitied. And thus, with the offer of my prayer, and most humble recommendations to the Queen's Highness, I take my leave of your honour. From my house at Canterbury, this 4th of June, 1565.

Marginal notes:
The archbishop thinks Cecil would do a right good deed to be suitor to the Queen for Sampson to be at liberty.
Such clemency, even if abused, will produce effect in reasonable men.

CLXXXVI.
ARCHBISHOP PARKER TO DR SAMPSON.
4th June, 1565. Petyt MS. Inner Temple, No. 47. fol. 323 b. Orig. Draft in
Parker's hand.

MR SAMPSON, after my hearty commendations. I am glad that my letters written in your behalf to the church took such effect as ye desired. And as ye have not deserved the same in your government (the contrary to my understanding), so again I have written my letters to obtain your other request: praying you *visceribus Jesu Christi* to salve again this great offendicle risen by your dissent from the course of the gospel. Remember what obedience so great liberty of the whole doctrine of Christ granted, requireth at our hands. I am persuaded that time and indifferent reading

Marginal notes:
The archbishop has complied with Sampson's request. He earnestly prays Sampson to conform.
Time and reading will

on your party, will give cause to join again to our communion; I mean not in doctrine, but in this matter of this ecclesiastical policy. And thus wishing you and all others well as to myself, I end my letters. Written at Canterbury, this 4th of June, 1565.

bring him again into the communion of the church of England.

CLXXXVII.
ARCHBISHOP PARKER TO THE EARL OF HUNTINGDON.
4th June, 1565. Petyt MS. Inner Temple, No. 47. fo. 322. Parker's Orig. Draft.

AFTER my right hearty commendations to your good lordship. I perceive your good zeal continue still towards poor afflicted men, as for whom your lordship do now write. Pity it is that the cause of Christ's religion is thus far hindered by timorous spiced conscience, although too wide conscience in the sinews of Christ's religion is not commendable. According to your desire I have written to Mr Secretary, moving him to be a mean to the Queen's Highness, which I trust he will be. And thus for want of time I cease to write any longer to your honour, which God long continue to your own heart's desire. From my house at Canterbury, this 4th of June, 1565.

I pray your lordship upon your occasion to commend me heartily to my lord of Leicester, with thanks for his warrants of late sent unto me.

Lord Huntingdon's zeal towards afflicted men still continues. Pity that religion is hindered by timorous spiced conscience. The archbishop has written to the Secretary as requested.

Desires to be commended to lord Leicester.

To the right honourable and my very good lord, the earl of Huntingdon.

CLXXXVIII.
ARCHBISHOP PARKER TO SIR WILLIAM CECIL.
[8th December, 1565.] Lansd. MS. VIII. art. 49.

I RETURN to your honour again your letters, by which may be understood[1] that ye have there ready to execute

Cecil, as Chancellor of Cambridge, has the ma-

[1 The orders for the enforcement of uniformity in clerical habits occasioned great dissension at Cambridge. The circumstances are fully detailed in Strype's Annals, I. cap. 44, and in his Parker, Book III. cap. 3. The present letter has reference to that dissension. So also has another letter, written five days afterwards, which occurs in the same

your orders of the best sort and of the most part, excepting a few Catilines, who by sufferance will infect the whole. Whereupon, where—King Edward's statutes stablished by his council delivered them by his visitors, the same now by the Queen's Majesty's visitors returned to them, your orders of late with consent of the body of the University, the Queen's Highness' pleasure sent to them by my letters—you their Chancellor, of the privy council and in such place and credit as ye be, will suffer so much authority to be borne under foot by a bragging brainless head or two, in mine opinion your conscience shall never be excusable. I pray your charity pardon my plainness. *Ex intimo corde, ex pura conscientia, coram Deo et Christo ejus*, I speak. We mar our religion; our circumspections so variable (as though it were not God's cause which he will defend) maketh cowards thus to cock over us. I do not like that the commissioners' letters should go to private Colleges, specially after so much passed. I must say, as Demosthenes answered what was the chief part in rhetoric, the second, the third; "Pronunciation," said he; so say I, Execution, execution, execution of laws and orders must be the first and the last part of good governance; although I yet admit moderations for times, places, multitudes, &c. And hereafter, for God's love, never stir any alteration, except it be fully meant to have them established; for or else we shall hold us in no certainty, but be ridiculous to our adversaries, contemned of our own, and give the adventure of more dangers; and thus ye must pardon my boldness. For mine own part I repose myself *in silentio, et in spe; et fortitudo mea Dominus*, howsoever the world fawneth or fumeth.

Yours in Christ our Lord,

MATTH. CANT.

To the right honourable Mr Secretary.

[MS. as the above (Lansd. MS. No. VIII. art. 50), but does not seem of sufficient importance to be printed in the text. It is addressed "To the right honourable Mr Secretary," and runs thus: "Sir, For that I think your honour to be in the midst of your doings for the University, I send you a private letter, which you may return again. I see there is strange delay amongst the wiser sort. Men be men. God keep your honour. This 13th of December. Your honour's alway, MATTH. CANTUAR."]

CLXXXIX.

BISHOP PARKHURST OF NORWICH TO ARCHBISHOP PARKER.

19th December, 1565. Parker MSS. C. C. Coll. Camb. cxiv. art. 172. p. 485. Orig.

MY duty premised unto your good grace. It may please the same to be advertised, that of late I have called before me Thomas Bateman and Cornelius Vanderstad, two of the strangers excommunicate at Sandwich by their minister there. They appear unto me to be very willing to be restored to the church again, and humbly to crave the benefit of absolution. Wherefore, if it might stand with your grace's pleasure either to absolve them by proxy, in respect of their great travel and charges, or else to permit me upon their humble submission (their follies acknowledged) to do the same, they were much bound unto your grace therefore: but in the mean season I have charged them not to repair to any place of common prayer with the rest of the congregation, nor yet to presume to the Lord's table, till I be further advertised of your grace's pleasure. And I have given the like charge to William Brand and Romanus de Backere, which pretend absolution, till I see their letters testimonial in that behalf[1]. *Two members of the Strangers' church at Sandwich excommunicated there, but then at Norwich, desire absolution. Bishop Parkhurst solicits the archbishop to absolve them by proxy, or permit him to do so. Two others charged to produce their letters testimonial of absolution.*

As touching the poor vicarage of North Elmham, I had conferred the same before the coming of your grace's clerk, unto one[2] Denny, being of mine own patronage, trusting therefore your grace will have consideration of this bringer some other way as shall seem to you best.

[[1] On the 9th Jan., 1566, a letter of thanks was written by the ministers and elders of the church of Sandwich to the archbishop, acknowledging that through the interposition of his authority, four excommunicate members of their church, two of whom were the above-named William Brand and Romanus de Backere, had been reconciled after public penance, and sundry others belonging to the same faction after the reading of a document, a copy of which is enclosed. The writers state that they had furnished these persons with a testimonial of their restoration, and also intimate that the disaffected at Sandwich were wont to resort to Norwich, and give trouble there. See Parker MS. cxix. arts. 83, 85, pp. 235, 241.]

[[2] There is a blank space here in the MS.]

248   BP PARKHURST OF NORWICH TO ARCHB. PARKER.   [1565.

North Flmham in the gift of the bishop of Norwich. He has received the part of the Bible appointed to him to revise.

I have received that part of the Bible appointed to me[1], and will travel therein with such diligence and expedition as conveniently I may. And thus I leave your grace to the protection of Almighty God. From Norwich, this 19th of December, 1565.

Your grace's most bounden,

JOHN NORWIC.

*To the most reverend father in God,
my very good lord, the archbishop
of Canterbury's grace.*

CXC.

ARCHBISHOP PARKER TO SIR WILLIAM CECIL.

29th December, 1565. S. P. O. Domestic. Orig.

SIR,

The archbishop has had much ado with the quarrels of Gonville Hall. Controversy between the master and Clarke and Dethick, compounded by Parker and Grindal.

I have had very much ado with the quarrels of Gonville Hall from time to time. The truth is, both parties are not excusable from folly. At the first controversy betwixt the master[2] and one Clarke and Dethick, my lord of London and I so compounded the matter, that we perceived it very needful to the quiet of that society to remove both Dethick and Clarke from their fellowships. Dethick, after a year, made suit to me to have a room again in the College. Upon his importunity I was importune upon the master to accept him, with condition of my promise that if by him any trouble should arise, I would take him from him again. Which pro-

Fresh controversy.

mise made me to receive him into my house, after this last expulsion by the master and more part of the company. From that they do appeal to your honour. I cannot see how rightly they can do it, or how your Vice-chancellor can deal in order with their College matters. The parties sued to me;

[¹ This was in preparation for the publication of what is called the Bishops' Bible, published in 1568. The portion of the work revised by bishop Parkhurst consisted of the apocryphal books of Ecclesiasticus, Susannah, Baruch, and Maccabees.]

[² The celebrated Dr Caius.]

I promised them to deal with the master to obtain of him more commodity than I take them worthy to have; only restitution to their fellowships I would not move. Wherein I see good cause; for if they be there, there will ever trouble arise. These fellows have divers drifts they shoot at, which I think good to be disappointed. I see the faction hath laboured very much in this matter. Although I see over much rashness in the master for expelling fellows so, so duly &c., he hath been well told of it, as well of my lord of London as by myself; and surely the contemptuous behaviour of these fellows hath much provoked him. The truth is, I do rather bear with the oversight of the master (being no greater than yet I see) in respect of his good done and like to be done in the College by him, than with the brag of a fend sort of troublous factious bodies. Founders and benefactors be very rare at these days; therefore I do bear the less with such as would (but in a mere triumph) deface him, and respect more that conquest than any quiet in the house; and the rather, for I think that if this matter be ended, there will arise no more trouble in such kind there, for the master hath firmly assured me to do nothing in such innovations, but partly with my knowledge and approbation first, and other of his friends. But undoubtedly in my opinion, *computans omnibus circumstantiis*, I think it nothing meet to have them restored again, what other commodities so ever they may have of favourable departing. If your honour will hear their challenges, ye shall hear such commerouse[3] trifles and brabbles, that ye shall be weary. And I would not wish particular Colleges (in these times) should learn to have, by forced appellations, a recourse to your authority as Chancellor, for the presidents' sake hereafter. And again, I would not have your time so drawn from better doings in the weighty causes of the realm. Scholars' controversies be now many and troublous; and their delight is to come before men of authority to shew their wits &c.; and I cannot tell how such busy sorts draw to them some of the graver personages to be doers, *an ex sinceritate et ex bona conscientia nescio*. My old experience there hath taught me to spy daylight at a small hole. Thus ye hear my fancy, which I pray your honour to take in good worth. To write much more my dull deaf head will not suffer me. I

[3 cumbrous.]

pray you if any offence be taken for my not oft attending, and to come over the reumatike Tempsis [1], answer for me. Thus God be with your honour, this 29th December, 1565.

Yours assuredly,

MATTH. CANT.

To the right honourable Sir William Cecil, knight, principal secretary to the Queen's Majesty.

CXCI.
BISHOP GESTE OF ROCHESTER TO ARCHBISHOP PARKER.

Probably A.D. 1565. Parker MSS. C. C. Coll. Camb. cxiv. art. 162. p. 465. Orig.

Bishop Geste returns the archbishop his copy of the book of Psalms which he has revised.

My duty humbly presupposed to your grace. These be to do the same to understand that, at the last, I have sent your grace your book again with such notes and advertisements that for my business I could well gather. I beseech your grace that when you have read them that I might have them again, for Mr Secretary would see them. If your grace will have me to amend them I am at your commandment. I will be with your grace upon Friday to know your mind and

Explains the Principles on which he had proceeded in his revision

to have the book. I have not altered the translation but where it giveth occasion of an error, as in the first Psalm at the beginning, I turn the preterperfect tense into the present tense, because the sense is too hard in the preterperfect tense. Where in the New Testament one piece of a Psalm is reported, I translate it in the Psalm according to the translation thereof in the New Testament, for the avoiding of the offence that may rise to the people upon diverse translations. Where two great letters be joined together, or where one great letter is twice put, it signifieth that both the sentences or the words be expounded together. Thus trusting that your grace will take in good part my rude handling of the Psalms, I most heartily bid the same well to fare in Christ.

Your grace's to his poor power,

[EDM. ROFFEN.[2]]

[[1] Thames.]
[[2] The signature is partly worn away. It is here supplied from

CXCII.
DEAN NOWELL TO ARCHBISHOP PARKER.
Probably about A.D. 1565. Parker MSS. C. C. Coll. Camb. CXIV. art. 328. p. 913.

My lord of London shewed me that he delivered a note of mine unto your grace touching Innocentius III. his judgment of consecration, that it should not be in these words, *Hoc est corpus meum*, but in some blessing going before; which the said Innocentius should say in his book *De officio Missæ, parte* 3, *cap.* 6, *vel* 4 *parte, cap.* 14[3]; and that Scotus in 4 *Sententiarum Distinct.* 8, *qu.* 3 should have the like. My lord of London told me, your grace had these books, and I would resort to your grace some time this day to be certified hereof, for I dare trust no report of the places of authors, unless I do myself see the originals, such wranglers have I to do with, and so unsure are men's notes of the place of the authors, by their fault, or the printer's. Thus ceasing to trouble your grace, I commend the same to Almighty God, who ever preserve your grace and all yours.

What Innocent III. is reported to have said respecting the words of consecration.

Scotus has the like.

Parker is said to have these books. Nowell will resort to his grace to be certified thereof; he can trust no report without seeing the originals.

Your grace's to command,
ALEXANDER NOWELL.

*To the right reverend father in God,
the lord archbishop of Canterbury
his good grace, give these.*

CXCIII.
ARCHBISHOP PARKER TO SIR WILLIAM CECIL.
4th January, 1565—6. Lansd. MS. VIII. No. 70.

SIR,

No sooner than yesterday, I was informed of certain articles charged upon Dr Caius, not only sounding and savouring atheism, but plainly expressing the same, with

Dr Caius is accused of Atheism.

the copy of this letter in Dugdale's Life of bishop Geste, (Lond. 8vo. 1840. p. 141). The book of Psalms was bishop Geste's part in the Bishops' Bible.]

[3 The words referred to by dean Nowell were used by bishop Jewel in his Reply to Harding's Answer. See the Parker Society's edition of Jewel's Works, I. 789.]

further shew of a perverse stomach to the professors of the gospel, of the which if I were credibly persuaded, I would take him *tanquam ethnicum et publicanum*, and would not vouchsafe him within my house.

There is a difference betwixt the frailty of a man's mutability, and a professing of plain impiety. Sir, in my opinion it were good if it can be indifferently testified before Mr Vice-chancellor, Dr Hutton, and one other indifferent man, so sent to by your letters to know a truth, so to suspend him, whatsoever order ye intend to take with the fellows of the house; and if it should fall out that they could be well testified, I would wish a better in his place to govern the house, and he to hold him in his foundership if he will. I like not the stones builded by such impiety &c.

At the first stir of this matter betwixt them[1], hearing what then they alleged, I saw good cause earnestly to blame the said Caius, blaming also the said fellows. But Caius was then so framed that he did commit the final end to my disposition. Whereupon I shall shew your honour what I intended, if the fellows had not proceeded from me as trusting to win the conquest of their restitution, which they perceived I would not grant. For I spied, so long as he was master there, and they fellows, there should be maintained but continual brawling, and the rather for that their appellation was not lawfully made, nor orderly prosecuted, and the drift was (as I judged) for Dethick to continue such stifflers[2] in the College of his pupils, to win him in time, by hook or crook, the master's room &c.

For the ending of their controversies, I thought good to cause a writing indented to be made betwixt them, whereby the fellows should appear willingly to depart from their fellowships, but yet to have one year's profit for their *ultimum vale*, to be borne for Spensor of Caius' own purse, for the other two of the College, and that the master should express to discharge them of the note of expulsion and the crime of perjury to their hindrance afterwards. And further, I meant within the compass of that year to have bestowed Dethick in some benefice, and the other two in some other

[1] See before, Letter CXC. p. 248.]

[2] Sticklers; an East Anglian form of the word. Forby's Glossary, II. 235.]

fellowships in other Colleges. But because they liked not of this as trusting of further friendship otherwhere, I gave them over.

My lord of Lincoln[3] desired me to be a suitor to your honour to obtain licence that his guest Mr Bourne[4] might be at his own house which he hath here in London, for the parliament time, being sufficiently bound to be quiet, and to return again with him or otherwise when the said bishop should repair home, because his own lodging here at Lambeth is too strait. If ye think that we by the commission may do it, we shall not wish it to be moved to the Queen's Majesty or the council, praying your honour to grant his desire. And thus I commit your honour to the grace of God as myself. This 4th of January, 1565.

Bishop of Lincoln wishes licence that Mr Bourne may be at his own house in London during parliament time, the bishop's lodging being too strait

Your honour's always,
MATTH. CANT.

To the right honourable Sir William Cecil, knight, principal secretary to the Queen's Majesty.

CXCIV.

ARCHBISHOP PARKER TO SIR WILLIAM CECIL.

24th January, 1565—6. Lansd. MS. viii. No. 73.

SIR,

I return to you your book again, and thank you for the sight thereof. I account it much worth the keeping, as well for the fair antique writing with the Saxon interpretation, as also for the strangeness of the translation, which is neither the accustomed old text, neither St Jerome's, nor yet the Septuaginta.

Thanks him for the sight of a Latin MS. of the Old Testament with a Saxon interpretation.

I had thought to have made up the want of the beginning of the Psalter, for it wanteth the first psalm, and three verses in the second psalm, and methought the leaf going before the xxvith psalm would have been a meet beginning

Beginning of the Psalms wanting.

[3 Bishop Bullingham, 1560—1570.]
[4 Dr Bourne, the deprived bishop of Bath and Wells.]

Lylye skilful in supplying wanting portions of MSS. Cecil has also a singular artificer of the same kind.

Parker rejoices in the preservation of such treasures.

before the whole Psalter, having David sitting with his harp or psaltery, *decachordo vel ogdochordo*, with his ministers with their *tubis ductilibus et cymbalis sonoris*, &c., and then the first psalm written on the back side: which I was in mind to have caused Lylye to have counterfeited in antiquity, &c., but that I called to remembrance that ye have a singular artificer to adorn the same, which your honour shall do well to have the monument finished, or else I will cause it to be done and remitted again to your library; in the riches whereof, *videlicet* of such treasures, I rejoice as much as they were in mine own. So that they may be preserved within the realm, and not sent over by covetous stationers, or spoiled in the poticaries' shops.

And thus I leave, wishing you to sing in our Lord, *in spiritu et veritate*, as ever David did, or as I wish to myself. This 24th of January, 1565.

Your honour's alway,

MATTH. CANT.

CXCV.

ARCHBISHOP PARKER TO SIR WILLIAM CECIL.

29th January, 1565—6. Lansd. MS. VIII. No. 74.

SIR,

I am about to devise for preachers in Lent before the Queen's Majesty. I perceive by some men's judgments I shall fail of divers, fearing the like sequel of reproof as is by insultation oft rehearsed of the adversaries. I would wish the dean of Paul's to be one: whom, if the Queen's Majesty shall not like after her accustomed manner to favour and to give him hearing, he shall be hardly entreated to occupy the place. I would your honour could understand the Queen's Highness' inclination: whereby I might thereafter move Mr dean at his being with me, whom I have invited to dinner on Thursday next.

The archbishop being about to fix the Lent preachers, wishes dean Nowell to be one, but he will not occupy the place unless the Queen will favour him, and give him hearing.

If the papists be angry (though in a flattery they dissemble to win), and the poor protestants discouraged, it will make an universal disliking, and kindle grudging and secret vain talking. *Tanti est in tam factioso seculo equabilita-*

tem servare. God bless her Highness long to reign over us *in pace et veritate.*

At my house, this 29th of January, 1565.

Your honour's always,

MATTH. CANT.

To the right honourable Sir William Cecil, knight, principal secretary to the Queen's Majesty.

CXCVI.

ARCHBISHOP PARKER TO THE DUKE OF NORFOLK[1].

[January, 1565—6.] Parker MSS. C. C. Coll. Camb. CXIV. art. 37. p. 117.
Parker's Original Draft.

AFTER my hearty commendations to your good grace. This is to signify to the same, that I have of very late writ-

[1] This is the reply to a letter addressed to the archbishop by the Duke of Norfolk from Norwich, on the 28th December, 1565, (MS. C. C. Coll. Camb. CXIV. art. 36, p. 115), in which he stated, "since my coming home the strangers hath been suitors to me for my letters to you for the having of a church, whereupon I talked with my lord bishop and others of the city, by whom I hear as well of their good order in religion, as also of their honest conversation, which I think my lord bishop hath satisfied you as well of that as their desire in the having a church, wherein I pray you stand their good lord; for here be churches, I know, that be void, that upon your letters to the bishop and the mayor they will take present order." The duke added in a postscript, "I have sent your grace a note of the like that was granted them in King Edward's days." There is also in the same volume of MSS. (CXIV. art. 170, p. 481), a letter from the bishop of Norwich to the archbishop on the same subject, dated 27th December, 1565, in which he states that "the minister of the strangers with the whole congregation are petitioners to be admitted to some church within the city, where they may resort to hear the word of God, according to their former manner in the town of Sandwich." The bishop adds that he had moved Mr Mayor therein, and found him "somewhat strange," which occasioned his application to the archbishop. The strangers alluded to were refugees from the Low Countries, a portion of those who settled at Sandwich. They were assigned a church in Norwich, which they still occupy.]

The archbishop has written to the bishop of Norwich to grant the strangers a vacant church in Norwich, where they have some store.

His ordinary authority will suffice to arrange with them as to their forms of prayer and discipline.

ten my letters to my lord of Norwich to grant unto the strangers a vacant church within the city, wherein I think they have some store; and have further requested his lordship to know your pleasure and advice, whereby the citizens may be the sooner induced to this desire; and then his ordinary authority shall suffice to take order with them, as well for the form of their public prayers, as otherwise for the state of religion, and for their discipline whereby that church may live in the more perfect quiet, wishing that they might be persuaded to recede as little as might be from common order of prayers and administration of the sacraments, as is used by authority in the realm. And if hereafter any cause shall be seen for any further help of my party it shall be ready at all times, as God knoweth, to whose merciful tuition I recommend your grace as heartily as myself.

CXCVII.

BISHOP SANDYS OF WORCESTER TO ARCHBISHOP PARKER.

6th February, 1565—6. Parker MSS. C. C. Coll. Camb. cxiv. art. 155. p. 453. Orig.

Bishop Sandys returns a portion of the Bible sent to him for perusal, with his corrections and marginal notes.

His advice as to the proper course of proceeding in the revisal of the translation.

MY duty remembered. According unto your grace's letters of instructions I have perused the book[1] you sent me, and with good diligence (having also conference with some others) considered of the same in such sort I trust as your grace will not mislike of. I have sent up with it my clerk, whose hand I used in writing forth the corrections and marginal notes. If it shall please your grace to set over the book to be viewed by some one of your chaplains, my said clerk shall attend a day or two to make it plain unto him how my notes are to be placed. In mine opinion your grace shall do well to make the whole Bible to be diligently surveyed by some well learned before it be put to print, and also to have skilful and diligent correctors at the printing of

[1 The books of Kings and Chronicles were revised by bishop Sandys for the Bishops' Bible.]

it, that it may be done in such perfection that the adversaries can have no occasion to quarrel with it. Which thing will require a time, *sed sat cito si sat bene*. The setters forth of this our common translation followed Munster too much, who doubtless was a very negligent man in his doings, and often swerved very much from the Hebrew. Thus trusting that your grace will take in good part my travails wherein wanted no good will, I commend the same to the grace of the Almighty God. From my house at Worcester, this 6th of February, 1565. Our translators followed Munster too much.

Your grace's in Christ at command,

ED. WIGORN.[2]

CXCVIII.

ARCHBISHOP PARKER TO SIR WILLIAM CECIL.

7th February, 1565—6. Lansd. MS. VIII. art. 76. Orig.

SIR,

I SEND you here these letters inclosed to consider. Loth I would be, after so long tarriance for Llandaff, the Queen's Majesty should be deceived, and her good people not well appointed. Although Doctor Lewes, and two or three other such, have informed me of him[3], which caused me to write as I did; and these letters have stayed me to think for instruments of his *commendams, &c.* Marry, as for Bangor, if the Queen's Majesty had sought a great way to supply that room there were not a fitter than this Mr Hewet, whom I know myself, and dare upon mine own credit to commend, rather than The archbishop sends letters which throw doubt on a person recommended for the bishoprick of Llandaff.

Mr Hewet a fit person for the bishoprick of Bangor; not so Dr Ellis, recommended by the earl of Pembroke.

[2 Bishop Sandys of Worcester, 1559—1570. A fragment of another letter from bishop Sandys to archbishop Parker occurs in Parker MSS. C. C. Coll. Camb. CXIV. art. 157, p. 455. It reads thus: "My duty remembered. With humble thanks for the book you sent me, whereof I like very well. The writer hath learnedly travailed in it, and the setting forth of it cannot but do good. Your grace should much benefit the church in hastening forward the Bible which you have in hand. Those that we have be not only false printed, but also give great offence to many by reason of the diversity in reading...." The remainder is lost.]

[3 The person alluded to was Dr Hugh Jones, ultimately bishop of Llandaff. This appears from a future letter.]

Doctor Ellis, having been aforetimes sheriff of the shire, neither being priest nor having any priestly disposition. I had rather for my party dissent from my lord of Pembroke's request, than to commend a doubtful man to the Queen's Highness, on whom, as yet persuaded, I would be loth to lay my hands on. He may otherwise do good service. And thus I thought good in time to put to your consideration the premises, wishing your honour God's assistance as to myself. From my house at Lambeth, this 7th of February, 1565.

Your always in Christ,
MATTHUE CANTUAR.

To the right honourable Sir William Cecil, knight, principal secretary to the Queen's Majesty; at the court.

CXCIX.

ARCHBISHOP PARKER TO SIR WILLIAM CECIL.

12th February, 1565-6. Lansd. MS. VIII. art. 77. Orig.

SIR,

The archbishop has received Cecil's request for firewood, to be supplied to salt-works in Kent, in which he had an interest. How the archbishop has complied with it.

My lord of Pembroke's secretary and your servant Mownt were with me with your letters requesting timber and firewood for your salt-works, as may be borne. I have satisfied your request for part, and have this morning taken order who shall attend upon him, and to have forty oaks and twenty or thirty acres of wood. The rest ye may be sped at Mr Dean's and Mr Rolfe's. I doubt not but you have well considered the likelihood of the matter. I shall wish it good success, better than I do know the like took place

How such salt answered in Norfolk.

about a thirty years past in my country, about Walsingham side, from whence came to Norwich by cart great plenty, so that the price of the bushel fell from 16d. to 6d. But after experience they ceased of their buying, and fell to their old salt again, three pecks whereof went farther than a bushel of that white fair fine salt.

Fears the public will suffer from the destruction of wood which will ensue.

If the wood in Kent should be much wasted with such salt-making, as it hath been by Dover pier, and otherwhere by saltpetre making, and then planting many strangers about the sea-coasts, having good store of them at Sandwich and Norwich, it would be doubted of, what good would come to the commonwealth thereby.

But if Almighty God giveth it good success in that country, and then if the Queen's Majesty of her princely liberality, and my lords the gainers would convert part of that gain to the repairing and maintaining of Dover haven, that were indeed to the great honour and wealth of the realm.

And thus, your honour, see my bolt for the love I bear to the country. Thus wishing to your honour as much grace from God as to myself, I take my leave. At my house in Lambeth, this 12th of February, 1565.

Your always in Christ,

MATTH. CANT.

To the right honourable Sir William Cecil,
knight, principal secretary to the Queen's
Majesty.

CC.

ARCHBISHOP PARKER TO SIR WILLIAM CECIL.

12th February, [1565—6]. Lansd. MS. VIII. art. 78. Orig.

I AM about to make ready the instrument of Hugh Jones' *commendam* to be at Llandaff, notwithstanding the last letters sent to your honour: for I yet hear better of the party. Since which time I have conferred with some wise men partly of the same country; who in respect of good to be done there in that diocese, they wish no Welshman in Bangor. They band so much together in kindred, that the bishop can do not as he would for his alliance sake. I am desired of some well affected of that country to have a visitation, and to set order there, such as whosoever should come to the bishoprick should be fain to prosecute it. I hear that diocese to be much out of order, both having no preaching there, and pensionary concubinary openly continued, notwithstanding liberty of marriage granted. If I thought the Queen's Majesty would allow her own chaplain Mr Herle to be placed there hereafter, I would join him with some others learned to go through the diocese; and I think Mr Herle to be a grave priestly man, and should well furnish the office with *commendam* of his livings which he hath now, though he should give over Manchester, where he now can have little rest.

At present warden of Manchester.

If it would please your honour to send me some little signification of your mind in these causes, I would frame myself thereafter. I am now instantly sued unto to have such a commissary there as can be proved to keep openly three concubines, as men of good reputation offer to prove.

Cecil's "old master," Mr Marley's dispensation shall be sped.

Your old master Mr Marley's dispensation shall be sped accordingly after the accustomed manner; so hath other dispensations been beforetimes stayed in the Chancery, and to be as warrant to us to pass the *faculties* according to the statutes, otherwise doubted of whether they be available against quarrellers in any other prince's days. Jesus be with you. This 12th of February.

Your honour's alway,

MATTH. CANT.

To the right honourable Sir William Cecil, knight, principal secretary to the Queen's Majesty.

CCI.

ARCHBISHOP PARKER TO SIR WILLIAM CECIL.

26th February, 1565—6. Lansd. MS. VIII. art. 80. Orig.

SIR,

Dean Nowell so occupied against Dorman, that he prays to be discharged from preaching this Lent.

MR DEAN of Paul's, for that he is thoroughly occupied against Dorman[1], hath long before now prayed to be discharged this Lent, and so he is like to be. Whereupon Mr Dean of Exeter[2] shall supply to-morrow, the rather for that

[1 Dorman was one of the answerers to bishop Jewel. In 1565 he published a book entitled "A Proof of certain Articles in Religion denied by Mr Jewell." Nowell replied in the same year with "A Reproof of a book entitled 'A Proof, &c.'" Dorman immediately rejoined with a "Disproufe of M. Nowelles Reproufe," and Nowell was now busy in the preparation of an answer entitled "A Continuation of the Reproof of Mr Dorman's Proof," published in 1566]

[2 Dr Carey, dean of the Queen's chapel and also of Exeter.]

Mr Gibbes hath foully defamed him to be altogether unlearned. Indeed he hath been very sick of late, but yet I trust he shall occupy the day: because I hear not the contrary from him; and if all chances should so hap, I have appointed my chaplain Mr Bickley[3] to be ready, for all such wants, as well of him as other: for I have sent to divers, but they return me no answer whether they shall come or no. *Dean Carey to supply his place.* *Mr Bickley appointed to preach.*

I have altered but a few of your first bill, but removed Mr Perne[4], and appointed either my lord of Ely[5] or Peterborough[6] to occupy one day. And thus I commit your honour to God's good grace as myself. *Other appointments.*

I think, all things accounted, I shall allow your judgment for Bangor toward Mr Robinson[7]; whom the country doth much desire, and be much afeard either of Ellis or Hewett; very stout men, so only commended, and *præterea quoad mores episcopales nihil.* This 26th February. *The archbishop acquiesces in Mr Robinson for Bangor, in preference to Ellis or Hewett.*

Your honour's,
MATTH. CANT.

To the right honourable Sir William Cecil, knight, principal secretary to the Queen's Majesty.

CCII.

ARCHBISHOP PARKER AND BISHOP GRINDAL TO SIR WILLIAM CECIL.

9th March, 1565—6. Lansd. MS. viii. art. 82. Orig.

BEING informed by this bearer John Bodley, that upon his late suit to you for the renewing of his privilege with longer term, for the reimprinting of the late Geneva Bible[8] *Cecil has referred to the archbishop and bishop an application by Bodley*

[3 Warden of Merton College, Oxford, and afterwards bishop of Chichester, 1585—1596.]
[4 Master of Peter House, Cambridge.]
[5 Bishop Cox.]   [6 Bishop Scambler.]
[7 Nicholas Robinson, bishop of Bangor, 1566—1584.]
[8 The Geneva translation of the Bible was first printed in 1560—1, under the authority of a special licence from Queen Elizabeth to Bodley, which gave him the sole privilege of printing that translation

for a privilege for reim-printing the Geneva b[ible].

by him and his associates set forth, you suspended to give your furtherance until you had heard our advice.

So it is, that we think so well of the first impression, and review of those which have sithence travailed therein, that we *They recommend that a further term of 12 years be granted to him.* wish it would please you to be a mean that twelve years' longer term may be by special privilege granted him, in consideration of the charges by him and his associates in the first impression, and the review sithence sustained. For though one other special Bible for the churches be meant by *It will not at all hinder the Bible intended to be set forth for the churches.* us to be set forth, as convenient time and leisure hereafter will permit: yet shall it nothing hinder, but rather do much good, to have diversity of translations and readings. And if his licence, hereafter to be made, go simply forth without proviso of our oversight, as we think it may so pass well enough, yet *They will take order that no impression shall be published without their concurrence.* shall we take such order in writing with the party, that no impression shall pass but by our direction, consent, and advice. Thus ending we commend you to Almighty God. From Lambeth, this 9th of March, 1565.

Your in Christ,

MATTHUE CANTUAR.
EDM. LONDON.

To the honourable Sir William Cecil, knight, principal secretary to the Queen's Majesty.

CCIII.

ARCHBISHOP PARKER TO SIR WILLIAM CECIL.

12th March, 1565—6.   Lansd. MS. VIII. art. 83. Orig.

SIR,

The archbishop's perplexity by reason of want of support in his endeavours to procure uniformity. I AM much astonied, and in great perplexity to think what event this cause will have in the proceeding to an end. Where I have endeavoured myself to enforce the Queen's Majesty's pleasure upon all my brethren, and have desired

for seven years from 8th Jan. 1560—1. It seems doubtful whether Bodley's privilege was renewed at this time as advised in this letter. See Anderson's Annals of the Eng. Bible, II. 324; Strype's Parker, Bk. III. cap. 6. I. 413, 8vo. ed.]

that others should not hinder such proceedings by secret aiding and comforting, I see my service but defeated: and then again otherwhiles dulled by variable considerations of the state of times, and of doubtfulness in discouraging some good protestants if this order should be vehemently prosecuted. I have stayed upon such advertisements; but I alway perceived much hurt might come of such tolerations (the parties hardened in their disobedience), and at the last the Queen's Majesty's displeasure, to see how her commandment take little effect, where yet order for all other men's apparel, and laws for abstinence, so much forced and well set to, may induce an obedience, howsoever a great number may be offended; and therefore they who think that disorder of our state were as soon reformed if we had like helps, seem to me to speak reasonably. I have written to the Queen's Majesty, as you see. I pray your honour use your opportunity. And where once this last year certain of us consulted and agreed upon some particularities in apparel (where the Queen's Majesty's letters were very general), and for that by statute we be inhibited to set out any constitutions without licence obtained of the prince, I sent them to your honour to be presented; they could not be allowed then, I cannot tell of what meaning; which I now send again, humbly praying that if not all yet so many as be thought good, may be returned with some authority, at the least way for particular apparel: or else we shall not be able to do so much as the Queen's Majesty expecteth for, of us to be done. And surely if I draw forward, and others draw backwards, what shall it avail, but raise exclamations and privy mutterings against your honour and against me, by whom they think these matters be stirred? I see how other men get their heads out of the collar, and convey the envy otherwhere. But undoubtedly I cannot but think the Queen's Majesty is unworthily dealt with, thus to be resisted. And yet I see the wilfulness of some men such, that they will offer themselves to lose all, yea, their bodies to prison, rather than they will condescend. And if I should this attempt, and have no more warrant and help, I might, after much stirring, do little in the end, but hurt. I have written and written oft, that a few in London rule over this matter.

For the sermons at the Spital, some persons appointed

shall be disappointed, and others placed, as is promised me. Mr Dr Cole and Mr Peny were named there*, but I dare not adventure to commend them for conformable; and thus sending this messenger to your honour, whom I have made privy of my doings, I cease further to write. Saving that I must say this much more, that some lawyers be in opinion, that it is hard to proceed to deprivation, having no more warrant but the Queen's Majesty's only word of mouth.

I have been answered by some certain, since my return home, that some of your preachers preached before the Queen's Majesty without tippet, and had nothing said to them for it.

This letter, if your honour think it tolerable, I pray you seal it up and deliver it. I hope by the bearer to hear some good answer. This 12th of March.

Your honour's alway,

MATTH. CANT.

Sir, in our book of articles, the fourth chapter, littera K, we made the pain sequestration, and not deprivation. For that much depriving with new fruiting, will be taken *in malam partem*.

*Yesterday the lord mayor sent me such word: this day came the chamberlain and another from him to signify that it would be hard to get any other; and therefore they wished to have those two, with the bishop of Durham[1] or Mr Beaumont[2]. I told them the Queen's pleasure resolutely, and if they would seek to her Majesty to be dispensed with, I could not assure them to speed, and so left them to their consultation, charging them yet that they should not suffer the days to be unoccupied, so to derive an envy and muttering against their sovereign[3].

> To the right honourable Sir William Cecil,
> knight, principal secretary to the Queen's
> Majesty.

[1 Bishop Pilkington.]
[2 Master of Trinity College, Cambridge.]
[3 This paragraph was added as a postscript, with reference to the passage relating to Dr Cole and Mr Peny.]

CCIV.

BISHOP DAVIES OF ST DAVID'S TO ARCHBISHOP PARKER.

19th March, 1565—6. Parker MSS. C. C. Coll. Camb. CXIV. art. 175. p. 493. *Orig.*

PLEASETH it your grace to be advertised that I received that piece of the Bible which your grace hath committed to me to be recognised, the fourth day of March last; and your grace's letters dated the sixth of December, I received eight days before I received the portion of the Bible. I am in hand to perform your request, and will use as much diligence and speed as I can, having small help for that or for the Welsh Bible. Mr Salisbury[4] only taketh pain with me. *The bishop has received the portion of the Bible assigned to him for revision.*

For all such old monuments as we had, Mr Secretary hath them two years ago; some he had of Mr Chanter, and some of me, which we had of our own store; but in the library of St David's there is none at all. He had of me *Giraldus Cambrensis*, a Chronicle of England the author unknown, and *Galfridus Monumetensis*. What books he had of Mr Chanter, I do not remember. One notable story was in the Chronicle; how after the Saxons conquered, continual war remained betwixt the Britons (then inhabitants of the realm) and the Saxons, the Britons being Christians, and the Saxons pagans. As occasion served they *Secretary Cecil had all the bishop's "old monuments" two years ago. None in the library of St David's. A notable story contained in the Chronicle sent to secretary Cecil,*

[4 The "Mr Salisbury" mentioned in this and a subsequent letter (p. 271) was, according to his own account of himself, "a seeker for antiquities." He has been thought to be the same person who was afterwards bishop of Man, but the bishop's christian name was "John," whilst that of Salisbury the antiquary was "William." Strype says that a William Salisbury was joined with J. Waley, in a patent for the exclusive printing of Bibles and religious books in Welsh, for the term of 7 years. (Annals, cap. xxxvii. I. ii. 88, 8vo. ed.). His reputation as an antiquary having become known to archbishop Parker, he sent to bishop Davies an ancient MS., requesting his opinion of it with that of Mr Salisbury. The bishop's report will be found in the present letter; Mr Salisbury's occurs in the same volume of Parker's MSS. (CXIV. art. 174, fol. 491). He took great pains upon the subject, and framed an alphabet from the characters used in the MS., but was unable to decipher them. In his answer Mr Salisbury sent the archbishop facsimiles of certain characters used in various fragments of ancient charters of donation in the possession of the bishop of St David's.]

sometimes treated of peace, and then met together, communed together, and did eat and drink together. But after that by the means of Austen the Saxons became Christians in such sort as Austen had taught them, the Britons would not after that neither eat nor drink with them, nor yet salute them, because they corrupted with superstition, images, and idolatry, the true religion of Christ, which the Britons had reserved pure among them from the time of king Lucius.

proving the purity of doctrine in the British church before St Augustine

As for the quire of strange charects, Mr Salisbury doth declare unto your grace how little we could do in it. Because I found in this one word ' Sion' two letters like, and yet not placed both together, as 'i' and 'o' is in 'Sion,' I gave it over, committing it to Mr Salisbury.

A MS. in strange characters reported upon by Mr Salisbury.

Pleaseth it your grace now to understand the state of Llandewibrefy. The earls of Pembroke and of Leicester have written to me four letters in the behalf of Mr Bowen, and they themselves have presented him by a vowson which assuredly is counterfeit and void of truth, having to it neither the bishop's hand (which he never omitted, so far as hitherto I have seen of his writings, to add to his seal), nor chanter or canons' hands; yea, the chapter seal seemeth by such sodering and patching as it hath, to be artificially set to, and taken from some old writing. When I received the earls' three former letters, I stayed to answer till I might understand of Mr Gwynne's consent to surrender up his collation, thinking to use a way both to gratify the earls and avoid prejudice by accepting of a counterfeit vowson, that is, the incumbent's consent attained, to give it by my collation to the disposition of the earls. At the return of the incumbent, I could not get him to give over, for he thought his title good, and Bowen's vowson nought. In this doing cometh the fourth letter of the earls jointly in one, marvelling of the delay, accusing me of injustice, suspecting me of practice meeter to be left to me to consider of, than to be expressed. I have answered to the earls, together with the earl of Arundel, which also wrote one letter, at length declaring what I meant to do if I had been at liberty, and what I meant to stand in, that is, the counterfeit vowson; signifying unto them my simplicity and true dealing afore God and man, which if it please them to try, I shall never be confounded. I do also signify unto them (as I do now to your grace),

Earls of Pembroke and Leicester have presented to Llandewibrefy upon a counterfeited grant of a former bishop;

which not being concurred in by the bishop he is accused by the earls of injustice and sinister dealing.

that there is another vowson exhibited unto me in behalf of Samuel Farrar, son to bishop Farrar, martyr, granted seven years before Bowen's vowson by the said bishop, his hand and seal being to the same, and the chapter seal fair, confessed by my lord of York's grace, having not only *primam et proximam*, but also *quamcunque unam advacationem*. Which although I am not at liberty to admit, partly because of my former collation, and partly because of a *caveat* entered for the title that the earls doth defend, yet in conscience I cannot work nothing to the prejudice thereof, which I should do if I should and might admit the earls' title. Mr Doctor Aubrey and others, insatiable cormorants in my diocese, using Bowen for an instrument that should have *nomen sine re*, do work all this, and so odiously set me forth, because they have not all their will, that I, whose innocency God doth know, am by their report made the wickedest man alive. I have poured my complaint unto your grace because I have not many places of refuge. Almighty God preserve your grace. 19 Martii, 1565. Your grace's to command,

RICHARD MENEVEN.[1]

CCV.

ARCHBISHOP PARKER AND BISHOP GRINDAL TO SIR WILLIAM CECIL.

20th March, 1565-6. Lansd. MS. VIII. art. 86. Orig.

AFTER our right hearty commendations to your honour. This is to signify that we have consulted how to proceed, whereby we may have your allowance or disallowance. We have conferred with some learned in the law, in what degrees to treat this matter.

1. First, we mean to call all manner of pastors and

[1 Richard Davies, bishop of St David's, 1561—1581. Joshua, Judges, and Ruth, were the books of the Bible the translation of which underwent his revision.]

curates within the city of London, to appear before us at Lambeth in the chapel there, and to propound the cause, and say something to move them to conformity, with intimation of the penalty which necessarily must ensue against the recusants.

2. To inquire of every one whether he will conform

2. Item, after the general propositions made (as afore) to the whole number, we intend particularly to examine every of them, whether they will promise conformity in their ministrations and outward apparel, stablished by law and Injunction, and testify the same by subscriptions of their hands.

3. To suspend such as refuse to promise conformity, and sequester their livings.

3. Item, it is intended presently to suspend all such as refuse to promise conformity in the premises, and also to pronounce sequestration of their ecclesiastical livings from after the day of our Lady next, being now at hand. And after such sequestration, if they be not reconciled within three months, to proceed to deprivation of their livings by due form of law.

4 A confirmation of the sarcenet tippet to those who wear it under statute 24 H VIII

4. Item, we may make an infymacion[1] for the sarcenet tippet, to such as may wear it by act of Parliament, anno 24 H. VIII., and to none other, if this shall be thought good.

5. Very many churches will be destitute for service at Easter.

5. In fine, we think very many churches will be destitute for service this Easter, and that many will forsake their livings, and live at printing, teaching children, or otherwise as they can.

What tumult may follow, what speeches and talks be like to rise in the realm, and presently in the whole city by this,

They trust the Queen will send some person in authority to join the two bishops.

we leave it to your wisdom to consider. We trust that the Queen's Majesty will send some honourable to join with us two, to authorize the rather her commandment and pleasure, as your honour signified unto me was purposed. And thus, praying you to consult with whom your wisdom shall think most meet, that we may be resolved; and that on Friday, the

Parties summoned to appear on the next Saturday.

parties summoned for their appearance on Saturday following at one of the clock, order may be taken. Or else after those two holy days[2] on Tuesday at afternoon, at furthest. And thus

[1 Confirmation.]

[2 Sunday, the fourth Sunday in Lent, and Monday the 25th March, Lady-Day. The 20th, on which this letter was written, was Wednesday. It appears from subsequent letters, that the meeting was finally appointed for Tuesday the 26th March.]

we bid your honour well to fare. From my house at Lambeth, the 20th of March, 1565.

Your loving friends,

MATTHUE CANTUAR.
EDM. LONDON.

To the right honourable Sir William Cecil, knight, principal secretary to the Queen's Majesty.

CCVI.

ARCHBISHOP PARKER TO SIR WILLIAM CECIL.

25th March, 1566. Lansd. MS. ix. art. 33. Orig.

SIR,

I AM in good hope that to-morrow my good lords, my lord keeper, my lord marquess, and your honour, will be here, which will work a thorough establishment of order: to avoid hereafter any longer delaying of all our parties. If I might surely trust thereto, I would so prepare an evil dinner against your coming, or else I would have more assistance with my lord of London and myself. I pray your honour let me be informed by this my messenger whereto I may trust. And thus I bid your honour well to fare as myself, in all grace and virtue. This our Lady-day.

Hopes lord keeper Bacon, marquess of Northampton, and Cecil, will attend the meeting at Lambeth on the morrow.

Your loving friend,

MATTH. CANT.

To the right honourable Sir William Cecil, knight, and principal secretary to the Queen's Majesty.

CCVII.

ARCHBISHOP PARKER TO SIR WILLIAM CECIL.

26th March, 1566. Lansd. MS. ix. art. 35. Orig.

SIR,

I MUST signify to your honour what this day we have done in the examination of London ministers. Sixty-one promised

Results of the conference with the

conformity; nine or ten were absent[1]; thirty-seven denied, of which number were the best, and some preachers; six or seven convenient sober men, pretending a conscience, divers of them but zealous, and of little learning and judgment. In fine, we did suspend them, and sequester their fruits, and from all manner ministry, with signification that if they would not reconcile themself within three months, then to be deprived. They shewed reasonable quietness and modesty, otherwise than I looked for. I think some of them will come in when they shall feel their want, specially such as but in a spiced fancy hold out; some of them no doubt were moved in a conscience, which I laboured by some advertisements to pacify, but the wound is yet green; it is not felt as I think it will hereafter. Some of them alleged they were in fruits, and would have had some toleration or discharge of payment; I answered, I could not so dispense, and left them to their own suit. Thus your honour hath all worth the writing. I pray your honour move my lord of London to execute order. My lord of Ely did write me a letter, wherein he did signify, that if London were reformed, all the realm would soon follow, as I believe the same.

This 26th of March, 1566.

Your honour's alway in Christ,

MATTH. CANT.

To the right honourable Sir William Cecil, principal secretary to the Queen's Majesty.

CCVIII.

ARCHBISHOP PARKER TO BISHOP DAVIES OF ST DAVID'S.

28th March, 1566. Parker MSS. C. C. Coll. Camb. CXIV. art. 176. p. 495.
Draft in Parker's hand.

Salutem in Christo. I thank your lordship for your return of answer to my former letters, which I do consider

[1 Amongst the absentees was Miles Coverdale. His letter of excuse addressed to Dr Robinson, the archbishop's chaplain, for the

accordingly, and shall not molest you for hereafter, seeing *for pains taken with* your store is otherwhere bestowed. I pray you thank Mr *the ancient MS* Salisbury, whose full writing his conjectures I like well; and as for decyphering my quire in such a strange charect, it shall be reserved to some other opportunity to be considered. As for those charects wherein some of your records of *The characters transmitted in facsimile by Mr Salisbury are the old Saxon. The archbishop has those in his house who well understand them.* donations be written, whereof he sent a whole line written, it is the speech of the old Saxon, whereof I have divers books and works, and have in my house of them which do well understand them.

Now concerning your benefice for which your lordship *understand them. As to the conflicting claims to Llandewibrefy, the archbishop advises the bishop to follow right and equity, and commit his credit to God* have so many letters and requests, whose requests for that you do not out of hand gratify (which, as ye write, of justice and without prejudicing of others ye cannot do), in my judgment in such suits I would wish your lordship to follow right and equity, and make your answer accordingly: which if it will not be received, commit your credit to God, *et veritas liberabit*. What though ye shall be strangely reported, *conscia mens recti famæ mendacia ridet*. And better shall ye finally satisfy wise men, noble men, and rightwise men, by a constancy to truth and justice, than to be tossed up and down at pleasures of others (for the time so informed) *expertus loquor*, and therefore I so write, of my goodwill toward your lordship, which I do commit to the tuition of Almighty God as myself. From my house at Lambeth, this 28th of March, 1566.

CCIX.

ARCHBISHOP PARKER TO SIR WILLIAM CECIL

28th March, 1566. Lansd. MS. ix. art. 36. Orig.

I PRAY your honour to peruse this draft of letters, and *The Book of Advertisements and draft of a letter to be sent therewith, sent to Cecil for his correction.* the Book of Advertisements[2] with your pen, which I mean to send to my lord of London. This form is but newly printed, information of the archbishop, is in the Lambeth MSS. 959, art. 58, and has been printed in the edition of his Remains, published by the Parker Society, p. 532.]

[2 The letter inclosed is printed at p. 272. The Book of Advertisements has been mentioned at p. 233, Letter CLXXV.]

and yet stayed till I may hear your advice. I am now fully bent to prosecute this order, and to delay no longer, and I have weeded out of these articles all such of doctrine, &c., which peradventure stayed the book from the Queen's Majesty's approbation, and have put in but things advouchable, and, as I take them, against no law of the realm. And where the Queen's Highness will needs have me assay with mine own authority what I can do for order, I trust I shall not be stayed hereafter, saving that I would pray your honour to have your advice to do that more prudently in this common cause which must needs be done.

The Queen will have Parker assay what he can do for order by his own authority.

Some of these silly recusants say now that they thought not that ever the matter (in such scarcity of ministers) should have been forced, and some begin to repent; and one of them was with me this day to be admitted again to his parish, and now promiseth conformity, whom I repelled till I had him bound with two good sureties of his own parish, and so I have, and he now saith that there will come more to that point, whom I will so order. For as for the most part of these recusants, I would wish them out of the ministry, as mere ignorant and vain heads. The sooner (as I think) this determination be known abroad, the sooner shall the speech cease, and the offence assuage, and more peace and order to follow. Thus Almighty God keep your honour in all grace, as myself. From my house at Lambeth, this 28th of March, 1566.

Some of the recusants begin to repent.

For the most part they are mere ignorant and vain heads.

Your honour's assuredly,

MATTHUE CANTUAR.

To the right honourable Sir William Cecil, knight, one of the Queen's Majesty's privy council.

CCX.

ARCHBISHOP PARKER TO BISHOP GRINDAL.

28th March, 1566. Regist. Parker. I. fol. 256 b.

The bishop knows what offence is taken at the want of uniformity in service and apparel.

RIGHT well beloved brother, after my right hearty commendations in our Saviour Christ. Whereas you do well know what offence is taken, for that divers and sundry of the state ecclesiastical be so hardly induced to conformity in administration of public prayers and sacraments, and in outward apparel agreeable, in regard of order, for them to wear, notwithstanding established and other orders and ordinances prescribed in the same; in which disorder appeareth (as is commonly interpreted) a manifest violation and contempt of the Queen's Majesty's authority, and abusing her princely clemency, in so long bearing with the same without execution of condign severity for their due correction, if the laws were extended upon them. And whereas the whole state of the realm, by act of Parliament openly published, doth most earnestly in God's name require us all to endeavour ourselves, to the uttermost of our knowledge, duly and truly to execute the said laws, as we will answer before God. By the which act also we have full power and authority to reform, and punish by censures of the church, all and singular persons which shall offend. And whereas also the Queen's most excellent Majesty, now a year past and more, addressed her Highness' letters enforcing the same charge, the contents whereof I sent unto your lordship in her name and authority, to admonish them to obedience, and so I doubt not but your lordship have distributed the same unto others of our brethren within this province of Canterbury; whereupon hath ensued in the most part of the realm an humble and obedient conformity, and yet some few persons, I fear more scrupulous than godly prudent, have not conformed themselves; peradventure some of them for lack of particular description of orders to be followed, which as your lordship doth know, were agreed upon among us long ago, and yet in certain respects not published. Now for the speedy reformation of the same, as the Queen's Highness hath expressly charged both you and me, of late being therefore called to her presence, to see her laws executed, and good orders decreed and observed, I can no less do of my obedience to Almighty God, of my allegiance to her princely estate, and of sincere zeal to the truth and promotion of Christian religion now established, but require and charge you, as you will answer to God, and to her Majesty, to see her Majesty's laws and injunctions duly observed within your diocese, and also these our convenient orders described in these books at this present sent unto your lordship. And furthermore, to transmit the same books with your letters (according as hath been heretofore

[PARK. COR.]

used) unto all others of our brethren within this province, to cause the same to be performed in their several jurisdictions and charges. And where we have of late the 26th day of this present month of March, called before us, according to the Queen's Majesty's commandment in this behalf signified, all manner of parsons, vicars, and curates, serving within the city of London, and have commanded divers of them in [sic] their obedience, who have considered their duties in this behalf; so have we also from this day forth suspended all ministers expressly refusing conformity, from their public ministration whatsoever, and have also denounced sequestration of all the fruits of their livings so long time as they shall remain in this disobedience; signifying further, that if within the space of three months from thence next ensuing this advertisement, either any of them do attempt to offend in the like disobedience, and be therefore convicted by the notorious evidence of the fact, or shall continue without reconciling of themselves, and promising and subscribing their conformity to the laws and orders agreeable, to be then deprived *ipso facto* of all their spiritual promotions; in which case it may be lawful in due order of law to all patrons and donors of all and singular the same spiritual promotions, or any of them, to present or collate to the same, as though the person or persons so offending were dead; after which like sort all other ordinaries, after notice given unto all persons within their jurisdictions of the laws, injunctions, and other orders established for the same conformity, I think will follow in order the same example; whereby we trust all contention and just offence amongst the Queen's subjects may at the last be suppressed, peace and quietness in unity of doctrine and uniformity of extern behaviours recovered, the Queen's Majesty's authority reverenced, her laws obediently regarded, to the promotion of the truth of the gospel, and to the glory of Almighty God; to whom for this time I commit you in all grace and virtue as myself. From my house at Lambeth, the 28th day of March, 1566.

Your loving brother,
MATTHEW CANTUAR.[1]

[[1] A letter to the same effect addressed to the Dean of Bocking is entered on Parker's Register, r. 257, and similar letters to the incumbents of other peculiar jurisdictions within the province of Canterbury.]

CCXI.

ARCHBISHOP PARKER TO SIR WILLIAM CECIL.

3rd April [1566]. Lansd. MS. ix. art. 37. Orig.

WHERE your honour would be informed of the preachers of these sermons of solemnity, ye shall understand, that for Good Friday shall the dean of Exeter; the Monday, Dr Beaumont; the Tuesday, one Mr Young, chaplain to my lord of London; for the third day my lord mayor sent to me praying to me to obtain of Mr Becon (who they hear shall preach at the cross this next Sunday) to supply that day. I promised that I would move him to satisfy their desire, or else the day like to be void, for possibly they can get none other. I said that I would rather than the day should be void, to raise a speech, that Mr Beaumont should divide his Monday matter to Wednesday; and hitherto I can signify no more. *Easter preachers at Paul's Cross*

I am complained to that Crowley[2] and his curate gave a great occasion of much trouble yesterday in his church, for expelling out of his church divers clerks[3] which were in their surplices to bury a dead corse, as customably they use, and as they say my lord of London did before prescribe them to wear surplices within the churches. To-morrow we intend to hear the cause, and if we find the deserts of them to be such as they gave such occasion of tumult in a people so gathered together, I trust the Queen's Majesty nor the council shall think any severity in us, or lack of prudence, in considering the time. Thus in our Lord I bid your honour well to [fare], this third of April. *Complaint made to the archbishop of Crowley and his curate, for turning out of his church divers clerks, attending a funeral habited in surplices.*

We provide as we can for some parishes destitute, but [cannot] supply the most part vacant. Some be peevish, some froward, [some] fearful, and some would fain slip in with honesty: to whom we [shew] such affability as we may, not yet suffering our authority and constancy to seem to fear, or to be more desirous of them than we move them to their *State of feeling in various parishes.*

[2 Incumbent of St Giles's, Cripplegate; remembered as a poet and a printer, as well as a divine.]

[3 It seems from the next letter that the persons meant were choristers.]

own commodity, but specially to the people's quiet, to obedience of laws, &c., and we have conferred to that end.

Your honour's in haste, as ye see, written,

MATTH. CANT.

To the right honourable Sir William Cecil, knight, one of the Queen's Majesty's privy council, and principal secretary to her Highness.

CCXII.

ARCHBISHOP PARKER TO SIR WILLIAM CECIL.

4th April, [1566]. Lansd. MS. ix. art. 38. Orig.

Account of the doing of the ecclesiastical commissioners with Crowley and deputy Sayer

IF your honour have leisure to hear of our doing with Crowley this afternoon, and with one Sayer the alderman's deputy, and the singers. We found that Crowley quarrelled first with the singing men for their "porters' coats," and said, that he would shut the doors against them, and so far was the deputy charged with such words. In the examination of Crowley fell out many fond paradoxes that tended to ana-

Crowley's opinions tending to those of the anabaptists

baptistical opinions, to have a motion in conscience to preach in his church (being not deprived) without extern vocation, and saying, as pastor he would resist the wolf if he can, meaning the surplice man. We asked, whether he would resist a minister so sent to them? He said, that till he was discharged, his conscience would so move him, whereupon he desired to be discharged. I seeing his desire, I did even presently discharge him of his flock and parish. Then he

He desired to be deprived by order of law.

fled to this, that he would be deprived by order of law; which I told him was to say, that he would be deprived, and yet not deprived. He seemed that he would have had the glory to be committed to prison, rather than he would grant to suffer such a wolf to come to his flock, but I dulled his glory.

Is charged to keep his house, and the deputy bound for their appearance.

But yet, for some severity, and in suspense, we charged him to keep his house, and bound the deputy in one hundred pounds to be ready at calling when the Queen's council should call for either of them, to judge of their doings. The deputy seemeth to be an honest man, yet peradventure too much leaning from the surplice; he protested that he threatened the singing men to set them fast by the feet, if they would break the peace. By his tale there was a fond uproar among them, but the singing men shrank away, and they then fell to quietness with shrewd stomachs. Peradventure your honour may think we have done too little, but yet the suspense and secret prison is some terror, and I doubt that few will think it too much. And so, at length, my lord of London and I dismissed them all with our Advertisements, in their obedience. I pray your honour pardon the babbling. This 4th of April.

Your honour's alway,

MATTH. CANT.

To the honourable Sir William Cecil, knight, principal secretary to the Queen's Majesty.

CCXIII.

ARCHBISHOP PARKER TO SIR WILLIAM CECIL.

[12th April], 1566. Lansd. MS. ix. art. 39. Orig.

SIR,

I RECEIVED your letters yesterday afternoon, sitting in commission with Doctor Lewes, Mr Osbourne, and Dr Drurie, about brabbling matters, as this whole week I have done, and fully tired with the importunity. And whereas I was minded to have come this day unto the court, my health faileth me that I cannot, but am compelled to keep my bed.

Your honour desireth to know whether there were six hundred persons ready to the communion, and came unto a church, and found the doors shut. These reporters make *ex musca elephantem*. My lord of London can best answer for his own jurisdiction; but this I can say, that where I have sent divers days three and four of my chaplains to serve in the greatest parishes, what for lack of surplice and wafer-bread, they did mostly but preach. And one of my chaplains serving the last Sunday[1] at a parish, and being informed that divers communicants would have received, the table made all ready accordingly, while he was reading the passion, one

Cecil had written to know whether 600 persons came to a church to communicate and found the doors shut.

One of Parker's chaplains serving a parish last Sunday made ready the

[1 7th April, the sixth Sunday in Lent.]

man of the parish drew from the table both cup and the wafer-bread, because the bread was not common, and so the minister derided, and the people disappointed. And divers churchwardens to make a trouble and a difficulty, will provide neither surplice nor bread. As for mine own peculiars, fourteen or fifteen be all in order. Some did refuse, but now they be induced, and they be counted sortly learned with the best of them, as one Cole of Bow church, and one Beddell of Pancras. And I can do no more, nor can promise any more; my age will not suffer me to peruse all the parishes. And I have meetly now called on my lord of London, who is younger and is nigher them, and have vacant priests in his church, and he did send me word by his letters on Wednesday at night, that there should need but preachers, for other might be appointed to serve the cures. And, for the supplying of the cures, your honour knoweth that my lord of London and I in our letters jointly signified that there would be many parishes unserved[1], and many speeches would arise, and much resistance would there be. And such difficulty did my letters unto the Queen's Majesty signify. And at my first speech with the Queen's Highness (being the second Sunday in Lent[2]) I answered, that these precise folk would offer their goods and bodies to prison, rather than they would relent. And her Highness willed me to imprison them.

As for Crowley's imprisonment into his own house, I have signified unto your honour by my former letters, and my lord of London who was with me sitting can shew you of his behaviour, that I could do no less. For the mayor sent unto me to examine the cause of a stir moved by him in his church; and he answered plainly that he would not suffer the wolf to come to his flock; and therefore to stay his resisting we committed him. The next Sunday I sent Mr Bickley to preach in his parish, and they heard him quietly, and a minister thither sent was received with his surplice, &c.

All this week I have little assistance of my lord of London because of this day sermon, and he may be now spoken unto to see to his charge. I have talked with new coming preachers to London, moving to sedition, and have charged them to silence. I have some in prison, which in this quarrel fell to open blows in the church. And yesterday I have had

[1 See before, p. 268.]   [2 The 10th of March, 1565—6.]

many of my lord of London's parishes' churchwardens and others, and have perused their doings; and must I do still all things alone? I am not able, and must refuse to promise to do that I cannot, and is another man's charge. I do but marvel that I must be charged to see and judge of all preachers in London, and the care committed unto me only, as though the burden must be laid on my neck, and other men shall draw backward. All other men must win honour and defence, and I only shame to be so vilely reported. And yet I am not weary to bear, to do service to God and to my prince; but an ox can draw no more than he can. *"Must I do all things alone?"*

It is no great inconvenience though some parishes want in London. London is no grange. They may go otherwhere. But these precise men, for all their brag of six hundred communicants, do profess openly, that they will neither communicate nor come in the church where either the surplice or the cap is, and so I know it is practised. To all other particulars of your letters I have before written my letters, and ye have my lord of London who can tell you of them all. Surely this matter is strangely handled. God send us of his grace; whereunto I commend your honour as myself. *These precise men profess that they will not come to a church where the surplice or cap is.*

This Good Friday, 1566.

MATTH. CANT.

To the right honourable Mr Secretary.

CCXIV.

BISHOP DAVIES OF ST DAVID'S TO ARCHBISHOP PARKER.

24th April, 1566. Parker MSS. C. C. Coll. Camb. CXIV. art. 173. p. 489. Orig.

I MOST humbly thank your grace for your comfortable letters of the 28th of March last[3], wherein I found such grave godly counsel, that if I had been far weaker than I was, yet was it able to make me strong to go forward in all true and upright dealing. I found also in the same letters experience of the truth of that which the wise man saith, *vena vitæ os justi*[4]. *Thanks for letter of 28th March.*

[3 See before, p. 271.]   [4 Prov. x. 11.]

Well forward with the revision of his portion of the Bible.

I am well forward in the recognising of that part of the Bible that your grace hath committed unto me[1]. I will by the help of God finish it with as much speed as I can. I bestow for the performance of the same all such time as I can spare from such affairs as will suffer no delays.

Proceedings respecting Llandewibrefy.

Mr Gwynne the bearer hereof hath his hands full to answer for Llandewibrefy, whereof I wrote to your grace afore. *Quare impedit* is intended of the one part, and the office for the Queen's Majesty to make it a college of the other part; which office is now brought in, as I am advertised, to Mr Osbourn's office, and is so imperfect and insufficient in law, that it would be easily avoided if it were not that every title, be it never so simple, shall be taken to the best for the Queen. Beseeching your grace to help the suit of this bearer in the church's behalf as occasion may serve. Thus Almighty God preserve your grace. From my house at Abergwylly, the 24th of April, 1566.

Your grace's in Christ to command,

RICHARD MENEVEN.

CCXV.

ARCHBISHOP PARKER TO SIR WILLIAM CECIL.

28th April, 1566. Lansd. MS. ix. art. 40. *Orig.*

SIR,

It is the Queen's pleasure to have the order for uniformity go forward.
Parker utterly despairs without further aid.

THE Queen's Majesty willed my lord of York to declare her pleasure determinately to have the order to go forward. I trust her Highness hath devised how it may be performed. I utterly despair therein as of myself, and therefore must sit still, as I have now done, alway waiting either her toleration, or else further aid. Mr Secretary, can it be thought, that I alone, having sun and moon against me, can compass this difficulty? If you of her Majesty's council provide no otherwise for this matter than as it appeareth openly, what the sequel will be *horresco vel reminiscendo cogitare.* In King Edward's days the whole body of the council travailed in Hooper's attempt. My predecessor, Dr Cranmer, labouring

The council interfered in the cases of Hooper and Farrar. How can Parker alone hope to succeed?

[1 See before, p. 267, n. 1.]

in vain with bishop Farrar, the council took it in hand; and shall I hope to do that the Queen's Majesty will have done? What I hear and see, what complaints be brought unto me, I shall not report; how I am used of many men's hands. I commit all to God. If I die in the cause (malice so far prevailing) I shall commit my soul to God in a good conscience. If the Queen's Majesty be no more considered, I shall not marvel what be said or done to me. If you hear and see so manifestly as may be seen, and will not consult in time to prevent so many miseries, &c., I have and do by this presence [sic] discharge my allegiance, duty, and conscience to you in such places as ye be. I can promise to do nothing, but hold me in silence within mine own conscience, and make my complaints to God, *ut exsurgat Deus et judicet causam istam: ille, ille qui comprehendit sapientes in astutia ipsorum.* Thus God be with your honour. Almighty God preserve the Queen's Majesty. This 28th of April, 1566.

Malice against him

He has discharged his conscience towards Cecil.

He can promise nothing but to keep silence.

Your honour's in Christ,

MATTH. CANT.

To the right honourable Sir William Cecil, knight, one of the Queen's Majesty's privy council.

CCXVI.

BISHOP COX OF ELY TO ARCHBISHOP PARKER.

3rd May, 1566. Additional MS. Brit. Mus. 19,400. art. 18. Orig.

Salutem in Christo Jesu. I thank your grace for your sundry letters. Your grace's last I received by Jugg, one of the Queen's Majesty's printers, wherein I perceive your travail and zeal, and some grief that things proceed not rightly, which is too much to be lamented for such respects as your grace with other considereth rightly. *Quod Dominus dixit Josuæ, hoc tibi dictum puta:* "*Confortare et esto robustus. Noli metuere et noli timere quoniam tecum est Dominus Deus tuus, &c.*" Time and truth shall put folly to flight. *Interim, modis omnibus enitendum, ne nostra heroina frangatur animo aut offendatur ad verrucas paucorum, ac*

That things proceed not rightly is too much to be lamented.

Be not afraid.

Time and truth shall put folly to flight.

Fears lest the Queen and mild be disgusted. The fanaticism of protestants is mad, but that of papists is worse than a plague. It pays that the Bible is well forward. The burden will rest on Parker. The translation should be into common English words, and should be uniform.

interea ad multorum tubera conniveat. Male sanus est nostrorum zelus, at papistarum deliria quavis peste nocentiora. I trust your grace is well forward with the Bible[1] by this time. I perceive tho greatest burden will lie upon your neck touching care and travail. I would wish that such usual words that we English people be acquainted with might still remain in their form and sound, so far forth as the Hebrew will well bear. Inkhorn terms to be avoided. The translation of the verbs in the Psalms to be used uniformly in one tense, &c. And if ye translate *bonitas* or *misericordia*, to use it likewise in all places of the Psalms, &c. God send this good travail a blessed success, *et Dominus Jesus pietatem tuam nobis diutissime servet incolumem.* From Somersham, 3 Maij, 1566.

Your grace's assured,
RICHARD ELY.

CCXVII.

DR WALTER HADDON TO ARCHBISHOP PARKER.

27th May, 1566. S. P. O. Domestic, 1566. Orig.

The writings of the nonconformists have made their way into the Low Countries. It is astonishing that they should so openly disparage their prince, and oppose authority in things indifferent. Every age inherits the errors of its predecessors.

Etsi non placet ad te sine argumento scribere, tamen inanes tibi potius literas mittam quam nullas, quoniam in altero mea culpa est sane nulla, in altero esse fortasse potest aliqua. Video tibi negotium ab ecclesiasticis quibusdam exhiberi, nam usque ad has regiones quædam illorum scripta permanaverunt, partim solato [sic] sermone comprehensa, partim versiculis coagmentata; quibus mirum est principi tam aperte detrahi et communem optimarum constitutionum authoritatem convelli[2], præsertim cum res ipsas, ut sunt, arbitrarias esse confiteantur. Sed nimirum talis omnium temporum conditio fuit, ut suos secum errores importaverint; testis est illa princeps omnium Ecclesia quam Dominus noster Jesus Christus et deinde Apostoli administraverunt, quæ suos Iscariotas et Simones Magos habuit: itaque nos, in quos exitus sæculorum incurrerunt, recusare non possumus quin zizania cum triticis

[1 The four Gospels and the Acts of the Apostles were revised by bishop Cox.]
[2 MS. 'combelli.']

in Ecclesia nonnunquam occurrant. Diabolus in omnia se vertit, ut omnes ad se illiciat. Tu, bona conscientia fretus, publicam authoritatem et Ecclesiæ concordiam tuere sicut facis, et officio perfunctus de successu refer ad Deum, in cujus manu non solum corda principum inclusa sunt, sed etiam populorum omnium. Cum huc descenderemus, magni de rebus novis susurri; nunc rursus obmutuerunt. Vale. Brugis, sexto Calendas Junias, 1566.

Tuns deditissimus,

GUALT. HADDON.

*To my honourable very good lord, my
lord's grace of Canterbury.*

margin: Parker is encouraged to persevere, leaving the result to God.

CCXVIII.

ARCHBISHOP PARKER TO SIR WILLIAM CECIL.

5th June, 1566. S. P. O. Domestic, 1566. Orig.

WHEREAS my lord of Sussex did write unto me to have my recommendations to your honour of his chaplain Mr Rush for the obtaining of a prebend in Canterbury church[3], I thank you that ye did something refer his suit to my contentation, for having such in that society of whom I might rejoice. I have now good hope of this man, that if your honour do commend him to the Queen's Majesty he shall honestly deserve that favour, I trust, in that behalf; for he is studious, and by reading shall come to good constancy of judgment. I see his quality of utterance to be ready and apt, and as I hope he shall do good service in that church hereafter. I would wish I had no worse hereafter obtruded to me than he is like to be.

I send your honour letters sent me from Mr Haddon[4],

margin: The Earl of Sussex on the request of Cecil wishes Parker's recommendation of Mr Rush to a prebend in Canterbury. He is studious, and ready of utterance.

margin: Sends a letter from Haddon,

[3 Perhaps the same person mentioned in Letter CIII., printed at p. 144. In a letter amongst the Parker MSS. (CXIV. art. 55. fol. 171), the earl of Sussex requested the archbishop to recommend the same person, then become Dr Rush, for the deanery of York. This was on the 7th February, 1566—7.]

[4 The letter preceding this.]

from which Cecil may see the activity of the nonconformists. It justifies the answer given to them. Fears what will ensue if greater severity be not used, and personages of reputation do not express greater discontent. The bishop of London feels by experience the marks and bounds of these good sprites, which but for him might have been suppressed five or six years ago. The Queen had thought that the answering would only breed contention.

by the which ye may see how they ply their matters; so that I think yet no cause of repentance given, that some answer is made them, as well in respect of our own honesty (who do wear this apparel) as in regard of the cause as it toucheth both the prince and the realm. And surely, sir, if there be not some more severity extended, and some personages of reputation expressing a more discontentation toward such disorderly doings, it will breed a cease one day in governance. And now my lord of London by experience feeleth and seeth the marks and bounds of these good sprights, which, but for his tolerations &c., had been suppressed for 5 or 6 years ago, and had prevented all this unquietness now taken, and both his reputation better saved and my poor honesty not so foully traduced. Thus trusting that the Queen's Majesty is put out of doubt (that the answering might breed but contention) by your good solicitation to urge how necessary it is that her good subjects should be healed again which are wounded by their fond preaching and writing, I commend your honour to the tuition of God, as myself. From my house at Croydon, this 5th of June, 1566.

Your honour's assuredly,

MATTH. CANT.

To the right honourable Sir William Cecil, knight, principal secretary to the Queen's Majesty.

CCXIX.

ARCHBISHOP PARKER TO DR WALTER HADDON.

[About 6th June, 1566] Petyt MSS. Inner Temple, No. 47. fol. 327.
Parker's draft.

Receipt of letter, No. CCXVII.

I HAVE received your letters, wherein *et amice et graviter*, you do both comfort my travail taken in the stablishing of order and concord in our church, as ye do godly admonish me to go on to do mine office, and to refer the success thereof to God. As I am alway persuaded to receive apt letters elegantly written which cometh from your pen, so I rejoice to see in you so much grave Christian philosophy. Ye may well marvel of the boldness of these men ecclesiastical, advancing themselves so far to insult against the prince, and public authority of laws, &c., and not to be ashamed to put their fancies in public print. Lamentable it is that some of these light heads be much comforted of such whose authority should be bent to repress them. The boldness of their book imprinted caused some examination to be set forth, which here I send you to expend[1]. Indeed all things be not so answered as their writing deserved, but yet more was considered what became such which hath taken in hand to make answer, than what they deserved. And I am deceived if a little be not enough to satisfy wise and learned men in these controversies. And thus signify to you, that with the assistance of the Queen's Majesty's council we have dispersed a few of the heads of them, some to the bishop of Winchester, some to Ely, and some to Norwich, to school them, or else at the least to have them out of London, till we see cause to restore them their liberty. I commend you to God, with my commendations to my lord Montague, to Mr Dene, and to Dr Abre[2].

At Croydon this * *

These light heads comforted of some in authority.
Sends a printed answer to their book.
A little is enough to satisfy wise and learned in this controversy.
A few of the heads dispersed amongst the bishops of Winchester, Ely, and Norwich.

CCXX.

ARCHBISHOP PARKER TO LORD ABERGAVENNY[3].

27th June, 1566. Parker MSS. C. C. Coll. Camb. CXIV. art. 80. p. 253.
Parker's own draft.

AFTER my hearty commendations to your good lordship. Concerning the demand of your letters claiming a right in the

[1 The books referred to were, "A Declaration in the name and Defence of certain Ministers in London," put forth by the nonconformists, and a reply entitled, "A Brief Examination, for the time, of a certain Declaration lately put in print in the name and defence of certain ministers in London refusing to wear the apparel prescribed by the laws and orders of the Realm."]

[2 Aubrey.]

[3 This letter is in reply to one written to the archbishop from "Earydge the 20th day of June," and signed "Henry a Burgauenny." The writer states: "having a good title unto the stewardship of the liberties of Canterbury, as parcel of mine inheritance, this may be to

office of stewardship of my liberties, as I would have wished to have heard before this time your claim, whereby I might have the sooner resolved your lordship, so upon this sudden, in the very end of the term, your letters coming to me to Croydon, being thereby the further from my counsel, I am not ready to make your lordship such answer as were meet, peradventure. But I will confer with my counsel, and thereupon return my answer to your lordship so shortly as I may by God's grace, which I wish to your lordship as to myself. From my said house at Croydon, this 27th of June, 1566.

Your lordship's loving neighbour,
MATTH. CANTUAR.

CCXXI.

ARCHBISHOP PARKER TO MATTHIAS FLACIUS ILLYRICUS, JOHN WIGAND, AND MATTHIAS JUDEX.

18th July, [1566[1]]. "Conspectus supellectilis epistolicæ et literariæ manu exaratæ, quæ exstat apud Jo. Christophorum Wolfium, pastorem ad D. Cathar. Hamburgensem." Hamburgi. 8vo. 1736. pp. 6—9.

PERQUAM mihi grata est, religiosi viri, hæc pia humanitas vestra, qua redditi mihi sunt nuper a vobis per fidum quendam nuntium commentarii vestri, unde faciliorem mihi vestro

require your lordship that I may have it at your grace's hands according to my right. Therefore I would be very loth to bring any suit against your grace, or against any of yours, if I may have it otherwise, for I am determined to see what the law will say unto it." Parker MSS. C. C. Coll. Camb. CXIV. art. 77. p. 245. The writer was Henry Nevill, baron Bergavenny, 1535—1586.]

[[1] It is very difficult to determine the date of this letter. Bale died 27th September, 1563: it cannot therefore be earlier than 1564. But the place of date does not agree with what is known of Parker's movements in the July of that or the following year. It does agree with them in 1566, in which year it is therefore placed, but with considerable doubt, especially as there is reason to think that Matth. Judex, one of the persons to whom it is addressed, was not then alive. But the same reason applies to any other year after Bale's death. Either the archbishop was not informed of the death of Judex, or the address, which is stated, not copied, by Wolfius, was inserted without due consideration.]

nomine dedistis defensionem: siqui posthac falso doctrinam, quam profitemini, calumniabuntur. Quam quidem doctrinam et fidem vestram, quomodocunque ex parte cunctis non placet: tamen aperte profiteor, ingenue vos sincereque fecisse, qued tam plene, tam cumulate, tam sine omni fuco et ambiguitate mentem et sententiam vestram indicastis. Quibus tamen opinionibus vestris diligenter consideratis, non possum non dolere, quod aliqua sit in præcipuis religionis controversiis inter nos dissensio, utrosque præsertim instructos una scripturæ regula, uno etiam animi ardore duetos, et restituendi veritatem, et a finibus Christi ecclesiæ quam procul exterminandi omnem errorem et mendacium. O quanta hic occasio lapsus præbetur bonis! Quantum hic probriis et maledictis ab hostibus vexatur ipsa evangelii restitutio! Utinam quidem alter alteri, sedatis affectibus, patienter magis et attente auscultare vellet, et neuter ita faveret sententiæ ut faceret hanc publicam religionis causam, materiam gloriæ, ambitionis, dissensionis! *Regrets that there is any dissension between parties both of whom accept the Scriptures as their rule.*

Quod ad præcipuam illam causam attinet, ob quam venit domesticus vester tabellarius, ad vos scilicet deferendi causa ejusmodi veterum commentaries, quales obtinere a nobis speravistis; cognoscite, quo diligentior fui, ut desiderio vestre hac ex parte plene satisfacerem; vel potius, ut laborem, quem ad magnum universæ Christianæ ecclesiæ commodum sumitis, juvarem: eo infelicius mihi res ex animi mei sententia adhuc successit: et ubi reposueram maximam spem nanciscendi quod cuperem, ibi jam omni prorsus spe privor. Atqui posteaquam plurimos plurimis, et locis et viris, frustra misissem nunties, tandem animarer ad recuperandum D. Balei libros, quos (ut dicebatur) spes esset acquirendi, si periculum ipse facerem: didici igitur tandem, inquisitione facta, ad cujus manus post ejus fugam ex Hybernia hi pervenere. Quorum cum ingens acervus ad me perferebatur, reperi haud dubie nullos, mea sententia, vel dignos vetustate vel argumenti ad vestrum institutum commodi ac utilis. Quos tamen cum vidisset vester Nigerus, una cum meis et aliorum complures, multum juvare posse dicebat. Habet igitur, hac conditione, ut intra annum transmittantur. *With regard to the special business of their messenger, that of taking over to them materials for their commentaries, Parker has failed in his desire of helping them. After many inquiries he procured some of Bale's MSS., but in his judgment not of any value. Their agent desired to have them, and they have therefore been delivered to him on loan for a year.*

Qued si sit apud vos nostræ nationis scriptorum tam locuples quasi instrumentum et apparatus quam mentio fit in vestro catalogo, arbitror superesse vobis multo plures de nostris *If they possess all the English writers mentioned in their catalogue,*

quam sint rursus in toto Angliæ regno, quorum sit apud nos certa intelligentia atque cognitio: sive hoc sit, qued quidam volunt gratificari vobis in hoc utili conatu, et ex privata quadam offensione non respiciunt publicum ecclesiæ bonum, sive qued quidam hæc se possidere neminem conscium esse velint. Atque ita, ut canis in præsepi, nec ipsi fruuntur, nec ex his fructus ad alios redire sinunt. Reginæ porro Majestatis bibliotheca non ea possidet, per quæ hoc munus, qued exigitur, præstare queat, id qued mihi retulit is qui illius curator et custos præficitur. Atque ita se res habet ut vestræ petitioni, sicuti vellem, non satisfaciam, licet (priusquam experientia eram edoctus) certo credidi me vestram causam plus juvare potuisse. Certe Academiæ, et quæcunque fuerunt religiosorum ædificia, prius diripiebantur quam animadvertebatur quantum incommodi rediturum esset ecclesiæ Christi ex hac librorum clandestina direptione et jactura. Papistæ autem nihil exhibebunt: penes quos (fertur) cum essent hujusmodi monumenta, quæ vel maximam doctrinæ suæ partem labefactarent, bonos quosdam authores commisere igni, invidentes mundo horum inspectionem, id qued mihi constat de Vigilii[1] libris quibus sic abusi sunt.

Plura scripsissem de his rebus, et de hoc tam molesto onere, attamen fructuoso, quod suscipitis in componenda hac historia, nisi quod, partim morbo partim aliis rebus sic impedier, ut his cogitationibus libere, quod cuperem, vacare non concedatur. Sunt qui in historia vestra authorum quorum vos nudam tantum commemorationem facitis, ipsa verba recitata esse desiderant. Quod etsi in historia tam grandi sit laboriosum, et viris multæ lectionis usum non præbet; tamen initiatis non nihil lucis sit allaturum, et contra maledicos magni etiam futurum momenti. Sed huic deinceps prospicere sit vestræ prudentiæ cogitatio. Mitto vobis viginti angelatos, significationem grati mei erga vos animi, quam boni consulatis rogo. Interim precor ut adsit vobis Sanctus Dei Spiritus, perpetuus adjutor conatus vestri. In Christo valete, 18 Julii, Croidoni.

Vestri studiosus,
MATTHÆUS CANTUAR.

[1 Vigilius, an African bishop of the sixth century. His works were published under the editorship of Chifflet, in 1665, 4to.]

CCXXII.

ARCHBISHOP PARKER TO SIR WILLIAM CECIL.
22nd July, 1566. S. P. O. Domestic, 1566. Orig.

Sir,

According to the Queen's Majesty's pleasure and your advertisement, you shall receive a form of prayer[1], which after ye have perused and judged of it, it shall be put in print and published immediately. It may be that some prayer of thanks be added, or else inserted in the preface some short advertisement, to give God thanks for our so long restful peace, which is an argument that may justly upbraid, peradventure, our ingrate forgetfulness. As ye like or dislike we shall proceed. Thus God preserve the Queen's Majesty with her whole Court, and send a prosperous return home hither again.

The archbishop sends a form of prayer for the preservation of Christian countries invaded by the Turks.

From my house at Croydon, this 22nd of July, 1566, at 4 of the clock afternoon.

Your honour's alway,

MATTH. CANT.

To the right honourable Sir William Cecil, knight, principal secretary to the Queen's Majesty, and one of her privy council.

[Indorsed by successive postmasters.]

R^d at Waltham Cross, the 23rd of July, about 9 at night.
R^d at Ware, the 23rd of July, at 12 o'clock at night.
R^d at Croxton, the 24th of July, between 7 and 8 of the clock in the morning.

[1 "A form to be used in common prayer, every Sunday, Wednesday, and Friday, through the whole realm: To excite and stir all godly people to pray unto God for the preservation of those Christians and their countries that are now invaded by the Turk, in Hungary or elsewhere. Set forth by the most reverend father in God, Matthew, archbishop of Canterbury, by the authority of the Queen's Majesty." See it in "Liturgical Services set forth in the reign of Queen Elizabeth," Parker Society, p. 527.]

CCXXIII.

ARCHBISHOP PARKER TO SIR WILLIAM CECIL.

26th November, 1566. S. P. O. Domestic. Orig.

SIR,

The archbishop understanding that Chichester deanery has been bestowed upon Dr Curteys, solicits that a prebend in his cathedral be granted to Mr Curteys or Mr Bickley.

I UNDERSTAND that the Queen's Majesty hath bestowed Chichester deanery upon Mr Curteys, whereof I am glad, not knowing whether the prebend in my church be granted, which I would wish either to Mr Curteys for his better furniture, or else to Mr Bickley, who hath done service and is ready to continue, and is both honest and well-learned. If it be otherwhere purposed, yet I would it should pass, not by collation but by presentation, as it ought by order and statute.

The Bible distributed among divers men. He is desirous that Cecil should revise one of the Epistles.

Sir, I have distributed the Bible in parts to divers men. I am desirous, if ye could spare so much leisure either in morning or evening, we had one Epistle of St Paul or Peter or James of your perusing[1], to the intent that ye may be one of the builders of this good work in Christ's Church, although otherwise we account you a common paterne[2] to Christ's blessed word and religion. Thus God keep your honour in health. From my house, this 26th of November.

Your honour's,

MATTH. CANT.

To the right honourable Sir William Cecil, principal secretary to the Queen's Majesty.

CCXXIV.

ARCHBISHOP PARKER TO SIR WILLIAM CECIL.

21st December, [1566]. S. P. O. Domestic. Orig.

SIR,

Asks the loan of the Book of Articles, presented to Elizabeth by the Marian exiles on

I PRAY your honour to cause your clerk to seek up the Book of Articles which were subscribed by all the professors of the gospel newly arrived from beyond the sea, which book was presented to the Queen's Majesty; I would gladly have it

[1 Sir William Cecil does not appear to have complied with this request.]

[2 Patron.]

for two or three days, and then I would not fail to return it again. *their return to England.*

The world is full of offences and displeasure contained. As yesterday, certain of us the bishops were with the Queen's Highness, and belike informed that some of us have put in the bill of religion into the parliament[3] without knowledge or assent of her Highness, as we were bidden to ask of them my brethren, and so to report again[4]. For my party, I knew nothing thereof, in the Nether House how it came in, nor heard it read in the Upper House, and so most of my brethren do answer for any knowledge thereof. Your presence with the Queen's Majesty wanteth; whereby her Highness may be the more disquieted with informations, although graciously her Highness uttered that she would give no light credence to reports, and lamented much the dulness of praying in her court and of fasting; and I added, the great negligence of having God's word the last Sunday. Her Majesty is not disliking of the doctrine of the book of religion, for that it containeth the religion which she doth *The Queen has been informed that some of the bishops put the bill of religion into the parliament without her knowledge. She does not dislike the doctrine of*

[3 The bill here alluded to was for confirmation and subscription of the Articles of 1562—3. It will be found mentioned in the next letter.]

[4 The answer returned seems to have satisfied the Queen that the bishops had not introduced the bill in question, as appears from the following letter:

DR YOUNG, ARCHBISHOP OF YORK, TO ARCHBISHOP PARKER.

27th December, 1566. Parker MSS. C. C. Coll. Camb. cxiv. art. 142. p. 421. Orig.

It may please your grace to be advertised that yesterday I was with the Queen's Majesty, and returned answer of our doings by her commandment, with our brethren the bishops, and also excused your absence by reason of your sickness; wherewith her Highness seemed to be satisfied. I moved also the other matter (whereof we talked upon Friday) touching open signification, &c., but that would not be, as I shall declare unto your grace to-morrow in the parliament-house, at which time this session shall end, as it is now determined and pronounced by her Majesty. I have also sent unto your grace by my servant the bearer the £vii. allotted for my portion.

From Canon Row, this Sunday, at 3 of the clock, the 26th of December, 1566.

Your grace's loving brother,

THO. EBOR.]

the book, but the manner of putting forth openly profess, but the manner of putting forth the book. Thus I cease, wishing your honour full restitution of your health, of joy and quiet of mind, constancy to endure in patience, with rightwise Lot. *Is enim oculis et auribus justus cum habitaret inter illos, quotidie animam justam iniquis illorum factis excruciabat. Sed dabit Deus olim hiis meliora; et novit Dominus pios e tentatione eripere, &c.;* to whose merciful protection I commend your honour as myself. From my house, this 21st of December.

Your honour's alway,
MATTHUE CANTUAR.

To the right honourable Sir William
Cecil, knight, one of the Queen's
Majesty's privy council.

CCXXV.

ARCHBISHOP PARKER AND OTHER BISHOPS TO QUEEN ELIZABETH.

24th December, 1566[1]. S. P. O. Domestic. Orig.

TO THE QUEEN'S MOST EXCELLENT MAJESTY.

Most humbly beseecheth your most excellent Majesty, your faithful, loving, and obedient subjects, the archbishops and bishops of both the provinces within this your Majesty's realm, whose names are hereunder written; that it would please your Highness, according to your accustomed benignity, to have gracious consideration of their humble suit ensu-
A bill lately passed the ing:—Whereas a bill[2] hath lately passed in your Majesty's

[1 It appears from a draft of this paper in the Library of St John's College, Cambridge, which contains various interlineations by archbishop Parker, that it was "Exhibited to the Queen's Majesty, the 24th Dec. a°. 1566."]

[2 The bill here alluded to is described by Dewes as a "Bill with a Little Book printed in the year 1562, (which was the fourth or fifth year of her Majesty's reign) for the sound Christian religion." It was brought into the House of Commons on the 5th December, 1566, and passed on the 13th. On the next day it was taken up to the House of Lords, where it was stayed by the commandment of the Queen, who considered that the initiation of a bill affecting religion by the commons was an infringement of her ecclesiastical supremacy. The

lower house of parliament concerning uniformity in doctrine, and confirmation of certain Articles agreed upon by the whole clergy of this your Majesty's realm in the late convocation called together by commandment of your Majesty's writ accustomed, and thereby holden in the fifth year of your Majesty's most happy reign: which bill was lately exhibited to your Highness' upper house of parliament, with special recommendation as well at the first delivery thereof, as again of late by recommendation renewed from the said lower house, and thereupon was once read in the said upper house: so it is that we understand that the further reading of the said bill in your upper house is stayed by your Majesty's special commandment. Whereupon we your Highness' humble and faithful subjects think ourselves bound in conscience as well to the sacred majesty of Almighty God, as in respect of our ecclesiastical office and charge toward your Highness and loving subjects of your realm, to make our several and most humble suit unto your Majesty, that it may please the same to grant that the said bill, by order from your Majesty may be read, examined and judged by your Highness' said upper house, with all expedition; and that if it be allowed of and do pass by order there, it would please your Majesty to give your royal assent thereunto. The reasons that enforce us to make these humble petitions are these. First, the matter itself toucheth the glory of God, the advancement of true religion, and the salvation of Christian souls, and therefore ought principally, chiefly, and before all other things, to be sought. Secondly, in the book which is now desired to be confirmed, are contained the principal Articles of Christian religion most agreeable to God's word publicly sithens the beginning of your Majesty's reign professed, and by your Highness' authority set forth and maintained. Thirdly, divers and sundry errors, and namely such as have been in this realm wickedly and obstinately by the adversaries of the Gospel defended, are by the same Articles condemned.

bill was afterwards revised and carried in 1571, by stat. 13 Eliz. c. 2. Judging from that statute, it would seem that the object of the bill was to enforce subscription of the Articles of 1562—3, which constituted the "Little Book" referred to in Dewes's account of the act, and the "Book" alluded to in this and the preceding letter. See Dewes's Journals of Parliament, pp. 132, 133.]

<small>4th It shall be a means to establish unity</small>

Fourthly, the approbation of these Articles by your Majesty shall be a very good mean to establish and confirm all your Highness' subjects in one consent and unity of true doctrine, to the great quiet and safety of your Majesty and this your realm: whereas now, for want of a plain certainty of Articles of doctrine by law to be declared, great distraction and dissension of minds is at this present among your subjects, and daily is like more and more to increase, and that with very great danger in policy, the circumstances considered, if the said Book of Articles be now stayed in your Majesty's hands,

<small>5th The prelates beseech the Queen to consider the matter as one who must give account of her office.</small>

or (as God forbid) rejected. Fifthly, considering that this matter so narrowly toucheth the glory of God, the sincerity of religion, the health of Christian souls, the godly unity of your realm, with the utility thereof, and the dangers on the contrary, we thought it our most bounden duties, being placed by God and your Highness as pastors and chief ministers in this Church, and such as are to give a reckoning before God of our pastoral office, with all humble and earnest suit to beseech your Majesty to have due consideration of this matter, as the governor and nurse of this Church, having also an account to render unto Almighty God, the King of kings, for your charge and office. Thus, most gracious Sovereign Lady, your said humble subjects, moved with the causes above rehearsed, besides divers others here for brevity sake omitted, beseech your most excellent Majesty, that this our petition may take good effect, as the weightiness of the cause requireth, and that before the end of this present session of parliament. And we, according to our most bounden duties, shall daily pray to God for the preservation of your Majesty in honour, health, and prosperity, long to reign.

  MATTHUE, ARCHB. OF CANT.
  THO. EBOR. ARCHBUSSHOPPE.
  EDM. LONDON. N. LINCOLN.
  JA. DURESME. RI. MENEVEN.
  ROB. WINTON.
  WILLMUS. CICESTREN.
  JO. HEREF. THOMAS COVEN. & LICH.
  RICHARDE ELY. WILL. CESTREN.
  ED. WIGORN. THOMAS ASSAPHEN.
    NICOLAUS EPUS. BANGOR.

CCXXVI.

RICHARD GRAFTON TO ARCHBISHOP PARKER.

Ascribed to A.D. 1566. Parker MSS. C. C. Coll. Camb. cxiv. art. 339. p. 953.
Orig.

THESE are to certify your grace, that concerning my book of Guido[1], I have sought for it but I cannot find it; but to my remembrance I delivered it to Mr Keyes[2], to whom also I will send for it, and your grace shall shortly see it. *Book of Guido cited by Grafton in his Chronicle*

And for the matter of Lucy, that Eleutherius sent Eluanus and Meduinus unto him that his Britons might receive the faith of Christ; concerning their two names they are added by Mr Keyes, but where he found it I know not, but I will learn of him and certify your grace[3]. The rest of the story of Lucy is in Fabian[4], in his III. book and lix. chapter. *Mission of Fleutherius to Lucius.*

And for the man that your grace moved me of for the alteration of the place of the book; so soon as I came from your grace I went home to his house, who dwelleth right at the back gate of my lord of London's house, and there I was answered by his wife that he is abroad in the country, she knoweth not where, neither can she tell when he will return. But, enquiring further, I have learned, that he being accused to have been the beadle and gatherer together of a number to sundry places to hear mass, he was sent for to the commissioners, and thereupon is fled and gone; but I think it will not be long but I shall hear of him. His name is Robert Caley, printer[5]. And no farther to trouble *Robert Caley the printer absconded to avoid arrest, for gathering together a company to hear mass.*

[1 Guido, that is, Guido de Columna, is referred to by Grafton in his Chronicle.]

[2 "Caius, the antiquarian, I suppose." Strype's Parker, Bk. III. c. 14.]

[3 The archbishop's question seems to have had reference merely to the names given to the pretended papal missionaries, said to have been sent to the imaginary king Lucius. The names here stated are assigned to them by Geoffrey of Monmouth, whence Mr Keyes, or Caius, no doubt derived them.]

[4 Fabyan's Chronicle, p. 38. edit. 1811.]

[5 Robert Caley's printing was confined to the reign of Queen Mary. During that time he printed several well-known works of Gardiner, Feckenham, Harpsfield, and other divines in favour with the court. Herbert's Ames, II. 828.]

your grace, these are most humbly to beseech the same that if any of my copy be perused, though it be the less, yet that this bringer may receive the same, because the printers stay for lack of copy. And thus God Almighty long prosper and preserve your grace.

Your grace's humble orator,
RICHARD GRAFTON.

*To the right reverend father in God,
my lord archbishop his grace of Canterbury.*

CCXXVII.
ARCHBISHOP PARKER TO THE WARDEN OF ALL SOULS' COLLEGE, OXFORD[1].

5th March, 1566—7. Gutch's "Collectanea Curiosa," II. 274, from the Archives of All Souls' College.

Information having been given of plate of a superstitious fashion reserved in All Souls' College, the archbishop moved the warden to melt it into a mass for the future use of the College,

WHEREAS having information of certain plate reserved in your College, whereat divers men justly be offended to remain in such superstitious fashion as it is of, I moved you, Mr Warden, to declare to the company of that fellowship, for avoiding all suspicion of superstition, that the said plate should be defaced, put into some mass, for your house, whereof it may have need hereafter, and so safely to be conserved in your treasury; for that I have not heard what you have done, by these my letters I do require you to make

he now requires him to return an inventory of their plate and vestments,

a perfect inventory containing the form and fashion of the said plate, and also the number and fashion of their vestments and tunicles which serve not to use at these days; and if any of their company peremptorily deny to do as is reasonably requested, then you to send up their names and reasons

with the names of any fellows of the College who refuse to concur in what is reasonable.

whereon they stand, and that the said persons, two or three of them, if there be so many, to come up with the said causes and reasons to know further discretion in the same matter; and this I require you to do without further molestation, which else may ensue. And so I bid you farewell. From my house at Lambeth, this 5th of March, 1566.

Your friend,
MATTHEW CANT.

[1 Dr Richard Barber, Warden of All Souls, 1565—1571.]

CCXXVIII.

ARCHBISHOP PARKER AND OTHERS, TO THE WARDEN AND FELLOWS OF ALL SOULS' COLLEGE, OXFORD.

26th March, 1567. Gutch's "Collectanea Curiosa," II. 275, from the Archives of All Souls' College.

AFTER our hearty commendations. Whereas understanding is given that you do retain yet in your College divers monuments of superstition, which by public orders and laws of this realm ought to be abolished as derogatory to the state of religion publicly received, part whereof be in this schedule inserted[2] expressed: this is therefore to will you, [and] in the Queen's Majesty's name to command you, immediately upon the next repair of any common carriage, or otherwise at your own advice; that you send up hither unto us at Lambeth, wholly and entirely, every thing and things in this present schedule annexed, to be presented to the Queen's Majesty's commissioners; whereby we may take such order and direction therein as shall appertain to your honour, to the fulfilling of the Queen's laws and orders, and to our discharge and yours: willing that you Mr Warden, within ten days after the receipt of these letters, do repair up with some copy of your statutes, and bring with you Mr Humph. Brookesby and also Mr Foster, to the intent we may have their reasons for better information and for satisfying of their consciences, if it may be. Willing you all and every one of

[2 The "Schedule" ran as follows:
"Three mass-books, old and new, and two portuisses.
Item, 8 grailes, 7 antiphoners, of parchment and bound.
Item, 10 processionals, old and new.
—, 2 hymnals.
—, an old manual of prayer.
—, an invitatory book.
—, 2 psalters in * * and one covered with a skin.
—, a great pricksong book of parchment.
—, one other pricksong book of vellum, covered with a hart's skin.
—, 5 other of paper, bound in parchment.
—, the founder's mass-book, in parchment, bound in board.
Item, in Mr Mills's hand, an antiphoner and a legend.
Item, a portuisse in his hand, in two volumes, a manual, a mass-book, and a processional."]

you not to fail hereof, as you will answer to the contrary at your peril. And thus we bid you well to fare. At Lambeth, 26 Mar. 1567.

Your loving friends,

MATTHEW CANT.
EDMUND LONDON.
F. KNOLLS.
A. CAVE.

CCXXIX.

DR JOHN CAIUS TO ARCHBISHOP PARKER.

8th April, 1567. Parker MSS. C. C. Coll. Camb. cxiv. art. 293. p. 815. Orig.

In most humble manner my duty considered. Of late I sent your grace your book of Oxford[1] by Mr Dethick, together with a letter shewing such duties as Mr Dethick received here and none[?] did pay. Now I send you by Dr Pory the answer to the said Oxford hook, desiring your grace most heartily not to let it be copied at any man's hand, for that it is not yet so planned as I would have it, and trust of more matter at your grace's hand. Your grace's judgment I much desire, and Mr Haddon's and Mr Secretary Cecil's, who be men of wit and skill, and close also if your grace so require them. Your man Mr Joscleyn I fear will shew it to everybody, and give out copies *ante maturitatem*, and do little good in it himself. I beseech your grace re-

[1 A small work entitled "Assertio Antiquitatis Oxoniensis Academiæ," written by Thomas Caius, Registrary of the University of Oxford, and presented by him to the Queen. A copy of it appears to have come into Parker's hands through Cecil, and as it contained some reflections upon the sister University of Cambridge, the archbishop forwarded it to Dr John Caius, the celebrated antiquary, and Master of Caius College, Cambridge, with a request that he would vindicate the honour of his University. The result was the drawing up and publication of his book "De Antiquitate Cantabrigiensis Academiæ," the rough draft of which was sent up, with the above letter, for the archbishop's inspection. See Strype's Parker, Bk. III. c. 18.]

member what I wrote to you in that matter heretofore. I am
sorry that the book is no better written for your grace. I
have so much business that I myself cannot write, nor scantly
have leisure to confer it with the original; and young men
now-a-days be so negligent, that they care for nothing. I
beseech your grace therefore to pardon it, and to think that
my desire is that it should be much better than it is, if well it
could be brought to pass *in tantis negotiis;* trusting to give
your grace one in print, if upon the reading thereof your grace
shall think it worthy the printing[2]: for as your grace said,
it is troublesome writing out of copies, and commonly they be
depraved in writing. I wholly commit it to your grace's
pleasure, and trust no man shall see it until I hear further of
your grace's pleasure. View it again I would before it
should be printed, for that many things be roughly left for
want of leisure, and haste to satisfy your grace. In the
order of the prelates I submit myself unto your grace as well
as in other things. The names of the noble men I know not,
which were requisite to be known, as hereafter at more
leisure I mind to do. Because all things should be the
readier to your grace I have put to every *pagina* his number. If anything your grace will note, the number is ready
to tell the place. If anything your grace will have altered,
note it *seorsum* for avoiding diversity of styles. Some things
that your grace thought best should be put out, were by the
writer put in before I was aware, and therefore remain, but
so that what your grace will have done with them shall be
done. I would have put them out again but for blotting the
book and disgracing the same to the eye. I have not bound
it as is meet for your grace, because I would your grace by
the rudeness thereof should have no pleasure to shew it to
others but those who I desire should see it. I shall desire
your grace to save it well, and that I may have it again
when your grace have done, for that the original is not so
good as it, nor so plain, for many things amended since it
was last written, which for want of leisure I could not
transfer into the original. And thus submitting not only my
book, but myself also unto your grace, I shall pray God for

[2 The book was printed in the next year, 1568, without the
author's name. Archbishop Parker's copy, probably the presentation
copy promised above, is in the Library of Corpus Christi College.]

your prosperity and long health to your pleasure[1]. From Cambridge, this 8th of April, 1567.

By your grace's own

CAIUS.

To the right honourable and my singular good lord, my lord's grace of Canterbury.

CCXXX.

ARCHBISHOP PARKER AND OTHERS TO THE WARDEN OF ALL SOULS' COLLEGE, OXFORD.

19th April, 1567. Gutch's "Collectanea Curiosa," II. 277, from the Archives of the College.

Order for J. Mallocke and three other fellows of All Souls' to appear forthwith before the ecclesiastical commissioners, to answer such matters as shall be brought against them.

AFTER our hearty commendations. For divers weighty causes us specially moving, we do will and command you in the Queen's Majesty's name, all excuses and delays set apart, that immediately upon receipt of these presents you will and command by authority hereof in the Queen's Majesty's name, J. Mallocke, R. Braye, bachelor of law, Rob. Franklin, and Steph. Brill, fellows of your house, that they and every of them do forthwith upon such monition given, personally appear before us or other our colleagues, her Highness's commissioners appointed for causes ecclesiastical, at Lambeth, to answer unto such matter as shall there be brought against them and every of them, and that after their appearances there to be made, they do from time to time attend and not depart without our special licence; and hereof we require you not to fail. Given at Lambeth, 19 April, 1567.

Your friends,

MATTHEW CANT.
EDM. LONDON.
THO. YALE[2].

[1] On the fly-leaf of this letter the archbishop has written the following note:

"Parliamentum tentum tempore Regis Rich. 2^i. apud Cantabrigiam, ut in carta Regis Henr. VI. apparet in libro M^i. Mere, fo. 23. b.

Et hoc apparet factum a^o. 12 Rich. 2^i. a^o. 1388, ut in registro W^i. Courtney, archiep^i. fol. 286. At hic archiepiscopus hospitatus est in do^o. Carmelorum, Cant., 14 Octob^s."]

[2 On the 23rd April, 1567, Richard Barber, LL.D., John Mal-

CCXXXI.
LORD LEICESTER AND SIR WILLIAM CECIL TO ARCHBISHOP PARKER.

Probably about the middle of the year 1567. S. P. O. Domestic. Draft corrected throughout by Sir William Cecil.

AFTER our right hearty commendations to your grace. Whereas we understand that the lady St Loe, widow[3], having retained a schoolmaster in her house, named Harry Jacklocke, Richard Bray, Bachelors of Laws, R. Foster, A.M., and R. Skrimsham, student of law, appeared before archbishop Parker, Walter Haddon, Thomas Yale, and William Danvers, LL.D., who made the following order: "That upon their returning home unto All Souls' College, the said Richard Barber then shall call the whole fellowship then present within the College together, and upon the common consent of all, or the greater part of the said fellowship, so gathered, shall cause to be defaced and broken such church-plate as is in their College or custody, appertaining to the use of the church or chapel, except six silver basons, with their ewers or crewets, one tabernacle gilt with two leaves set with stones and pearls, two silver bowls, a silver rod, and three processionals. Item, that they send up to the said commissioners their two books of the Epistles and Gospels, reserving unto themselves the images of silver of the same defaced in manner aforesaid." The warden was also enjoined to charge all fellows who were discontented with this order to appear before the commissioners within ten days, and "from time to time to cause every of the said fellowship or College misreporting or gainsaying this order to appear before the said commissioners within ten days."—Gutch's Collect. Curios. II. 279.]

The lady St Loe having retained Harry Jackson of Merton College, Oxford, as tutor to her son, finds that she has been slandered by the said tutor.

[3 The lady St Loe, to whom this letter relates, was the celebrated founder of the noble families of Cavendish and Newcastle, and the builder of Hardwick and Chatsworth. She was daughter of John Hardwick, of Hardwick, in the county of Derby. Her first husband was Robert Barley, of Barley, in the same county. She was married secondly to Sir William Cavendish, by whom she had a large family. Her third husband, to whom she was married in 1559, was Sir William St Loe, captain of the guard to Queen Elizabeth. The slanders of Mr Jackson did not prevent her marrying, as a fourth husband, George, Earl of Shrewsbury, whom she survived. Sir William St Loe died soon after the year 1565, and in 1567 the Earl of Shrewsbury became a suitor for the hand of the wealthy widow, (Retrosp. Rev. 2d Ser. II. 325.) Their marriage took place probably soon after 9th February, 1567—8; certainly before October, 1568. As the slander of Mr Jackson seems to have related to a pretended contract of matrimony (see note below), this enquiry may have had some connection with the intended marriage between Lady St Loe and the Earl of Shrewsbury.]

The archbishop is to call Jackson before him, and examine the matter.

son, sometime a scholar of Merton College in Oxford, for the teaching and bringing up of her son, findeth herself much troubled and disquieted with certain slanderous reports which he hath, as we are informed, published of her abroad. And for that the said lady hath always been known and reputed of honesty, virtue and good fame, these be to pray your grace, upon such information as this bearer shall give you on the said lady's behalf, to call him before you, and to cause the matter to be fully heard and examined with that speed that may be, either by yourself (if your leisure may serve) or by calling some such as the Queen's Majesty's solicitor, Mr Onssley, and Mr Peter Osborn of the exchequer, or such other of the ecclesiastical commissioners as you shall think meetest, that the said lady's good fame may be preserved, as we think she hath deserved. And if it shall be duly proved that the said Jackson hath unjustly defamed her, to her reproof and discredit, then we pray your grace to provide that he may receive such open and meet punishment as he shall deserve[1]. For surely such kind of slanders as we have heard that he hath reported are not to be overpassed without some notable punishment[2].

[1 His punishment was further enforced by the following letter to the archbishop of Canterbury, the draft of which is also in the State Paper Office:

"Whereas we be informed that you, with others, which you have called unto you, have diligently examined the slanderous pretended contract, devised in subtle and infamous wise, by one Henry Jackson, against our [trusty] and wellbeloved servant the lady St Lowe, who [hath] lived in our court and to the world in very good [repute] and credit. And because it is meet that for example such a slanderous device should not escape, but be severely punished, we will and require you (calling so many of our commissioners for the ecclesiastical causes as you shall think meet, informing them of the truth of the case as it is, and as by examination you find) to proceed forthwith to the extreme punishing of the said Henry Jackson, by any manner of corporal coercion, chastisement, or punishment, openly or privately, as to your discretions upon the examinations of the truth of the cause shall be thought by you most convenient. Wherein our pleasure is, you shall use all convenient speed that you may, that our said servant may be restored to her good name and fame. And these our letters shall be your sufficient warrant for the doing thereof. Given, &c."]

[2 In an indorsement, which is very much defaced by damp, this paper is said to be a "copy of the Earl of Leicester and the Secretary's(?) letter to the archbishop of Canterbury for the lady St Loe."

CCXXXII.

ARCHBISHOP PARKER TO ——.

3rd July, 1567. Parker MSS. C. C. Coll. Camb. CXIV. art. 322. p. 889.
Parker's Orig. Draft.

I AM complained unto by Jane Grigby, wife of Justinian Grigby, who was bound by recognisance to cohabitate with this wife, and to renounce the company of one Thomas Pegson and his wife, which neither, as I am informed, is observed. Whereupon to avoid the further trouble and charge of the parishioners coming up hither, I would ye sent for such as can make faith in their depositions upon their oaths, which when ye have returned I shall proceed accordingly. I would also ye enquired how reasonably this his wife useth herself, and if she be not in fault of the breach of this order. And thus fare ye well. From my house at Lambeth, this third of July, 1567[3].

The archbishop has been complained to by Jane Grigby against Justinian Grigby. To avoid trouble and charge, the person addressed is to send for such persons as can make depositions on oath, on which the archbishop will proceed.

CCXXXIII.

ARCHBISHOP PARKER TO SIR WILLIAM CECIL.

12th August, 1567. S. P. O. Domestic, Orig.

SIR,

EXPECTING the Queen's pleasure by your letters in what particularity I might deal with the bishops and deans of cathedral churches, I have information from Canterbury church and of the dean there[4], of whom so great information was made, that he had sold and divided such a huge quantity of plate worth 1000 pound, and vestry ornaments, &c. It is no great marvel though Pope Hildebrand's sprite walketh furiously abroad to slander the poor married estate, seeing

The dean of Canterbury accused of having sold and divided £1000. of plate and vestry ornaments.

The mention of Mr Onssley, that is, Onslow, as the Queen's solicitor fixes the date of the letter as being subsequent to 27th June, 1566, which was the day of his appointment.]

[3 This letter was written in consequence of an application to the archbishop by archdeacon Thomas Cole, dated from out of Essex, 28th June, 1567, and made at the instance of "divers gentlemen in Kent," and especially of a brother of the woman's husband, who were anxious to see the woman righted. Parker MS. CXIV. Art. 321, p. 887.]

[4 The dean to whom this letter relates was Dr Thomas Godwin, afterwards bishop of Bath and Wells. He was instituted to the deanery on 10th March, 1566—67. Todd's Deans of Canterbury, p. 35.]

credit is so ready to believe the worst; *sed qui habitat in cælis irridebit eos.* The broken plate and bullion found in the church he with consent of all the chapter have converted to the church use only, not one penny divided, partly for a stock, as most necessary, partly in buying some plate for the furnishing of the common table; the whole was sold came but to £243. 11s. 6d., the rest which remaineth is not worth half an hundredth mark: and this is all they have. As for church stuff, nothing stirred, but such as it is, is rotting in their custody, of no great value. Peradventure it might be said Mr dean Wotton would never have done so much, forsooth this plate had been sold by his and the common consent, if some men of the chapter would have granted thereto; and as for dividends of plate and copes beforetimes, Dr Wotton had his portion as large as any other had, and at his house was reserved some plate as portion of that old dividend had betwixt them. Mr Thomas Wotton may be asked. There was not left in the church at my coming the tenth penny of the plate and ornaments which were left there at Mr Dr Wetten's coming thither. I would it were indifferently credited to understand, whether the married sort or the virginal pastors had done most spoil in the church; though fault have been in both.

And as for All Souls' College plate, is turned whole and reserved as bullion among them, their church-books only turned out of the way. There may be roaring and rooking in the realm by new devised visitations, but I fear it will work but a disquiet in the commonwealth. I would we all proceeded in godly quiet, with thanks to God for our peace: wonders doth no good, and yet meet to stop covetous bellies. Surely they love not the Queen's Majesty sincerely that still do beat into her head such untrue tales, to bring all her clergy to such a known displeasure without cause. *Deus misereatur nostri, &c., ut cognoscamus, &c.* Thus God keep your honour in all grace and health as myself. This 12th of August.

Your honour's,
M. CANT.

*To the right honourable Sir William
Cecil, knight, principal secretary
to the Queen's Majesty.*

CCXXXIV.

SIR WILLIAM CECIL TO ARCHBISHOP PARKER.

12th September, 1567. Parker MSS. C. C. Coll. Camb. CXIV. art. 218. p. 589.

It may please your grace to receive my humble thanks for your care taken in the discreet advice given to me concerning the appeasing of the unprofitable rash controversy newly raised, upon the article of the descent of Christ to hell[1]. *Thanks for advice how to appease a controversy.*

I am much troubled with the Queen's Majesty's earnestness to have certain commissioners in the whole realm to inquire of the waste of the whole clergy[2]; for so she is also much thereto enticed. I do what I can [to] delay the execution, fearing that hereby the clergy shall receive great blemish in opinion; and so I mean to defer it as I can. *The Queen is enticed to appoint commissioners to inquire of waste committed by the clergy.*

From my house in Westminster, the 12th of September, 1567.

Your grace's at command,
W. CECILL.

To the most reverend father in God,
the archbishop of Canterbury's
good grace.

CCXXXV.

ARCHBISHOP PARKER TO SIR WILLIAM CECIL.

5th October, 1567. S. P. O. Domestic, Orig.

Sir,

I have considered the contents of your letters, and think that it is graciously considered that the bishop of Oxford[3] elect should have a helper, a coadjutor in his such impotency. *The bishop of Oxford elect should have a coadjutor in his impotency.*

[1 Cecil was concerned in the matter as Chancellor of the University of Cambridge, where the controversy arose.]

[2 That is, the waste that some of the clergy were said (by their enemies, according to Strype) to make in church-property by long leases, &c. In 1571 an act of parliament was passed to prevent the evil.]

[3 Bishop Hugh Curwen, or Coren, elected to the see of Oxford, 26th September, 1567. He lived only until October in the following year.]

[PARK. COR.]

As for such as be named by him, the first two and the third man whom your honour nameth, I cannot much allow of them, being, I fear, of such inclination that neither they will serve God in good religion nor do their duty to the prince; their contemplations be otherwhere set. I must say to you, that it is my daily prayer for such not to be put in place of coadjutors. And as for the other three, they have no such livelihood of their own to be put to such travail, and therefore not to be stayed for the purpose as it is intended. It were the best that this coadjutor were *ad omnem effectum coadjutor*, as well to preach as to confirm children, and to give orders in that diocese, if any such could be found. Where your honour writeth that his election is orderly passed with the Queen's Majesty's royal assent, so I think it will not be forgotten that he must come hither by himself or his procurator, before he be stablished; for both order and law and the King's letters patents in the erection of that church and bishoprick, exempteth him not, either from oath or profession to the see of Canterbury; for his election, or rather postulation, is but to be presented to the Queen's Highness to have her royal assent, and after that to be sent hither for his confirmation in the jurisdiction spiritual. The archbishop of York so passed, and the bishop of Chichester, Hereford, and St David, went that way. Thus your honour hath mine opinion; committing the same to the tuition of God as myself, this 5th of October, 1567.

Your honour's alway,

MATTH. CANT.

To the right honourable Sir William Cecil, knight, principal secretary to the Queen's Majesty.

CCXXXVI.

SIR ROBERT WINGFIELD AND OTHERS TO ARCHBISHOP PARKER.

27th October, 1567. Parker MSS. C. C. Coll. Camb. cxiv. art. 237. p. 647. Orig.

Our humble commendations and duties remembered unto your grace. Great necessity doth occasion us to write unto you for one Master Lawrence, a late preacher, of whom we have good experience both for his modesty, faultless life, and sound doctrine; who hath been well exercised amongst us this five or six years with great diligence. He commonly preached twice every Sunday; and many times on the working days if there chanced any marriages or funerals: and that he did of his own charge, never taking anything, as his enemies cannot accuse him neither of that nor yet of anything else justly worthy of reproach. And so we testified unto your grace's visitors, and desired them that he might continne his preaching still, for we knew very well that we should have great need of him. And now we see it more evident, for here is not one preacher in a great circuit, viz. from Blythburgh to Ipswich, which is twenty miles distant and ten miles in breadth along by the sea-coast; in the which circuit he was wont to travel.

Thus we have thought good to certify your grace of the necessity of our country, and the diligence and good behaviour of this man, trusting that your grace will either restore him again, or else send us some other in his room, the which we most heartily desire, commending the same to Almighty God, who preserve your grace. Dated the 27th of October, aº 1567.

Your grace's to command,

ROBERT WINGFELD.   WYLLYAM CANNDYSH.
WYM. HOPTON.   THOMAS FELTON.
        THOMAS COLBYN, of Beckles.
        THOMAS PLAYTER[1].

*To the right reverend father in God and
our good lord, the lord archbishop of
Canterbury his good grace.*

[[1] Above these signatures there is pasted on, apparently from another letter, "Your grace's at commandment, Ro. Hopton."]

Side notes: One master Lawrence, for five or six years a preacher near Ipswich, has been removed by the archbishop's visitors. He was diligent and of good character. He was the only preacher in a circuit of 20 miles by 10. The writers pray that they may have him restored, or some other preacher provided.

CCXXXVII.

ARCHBISHOP PARKER TO BISHOP GRINDAL OF LONDON.
Before November, 1567. Parker Regist. I. 260 a.

Bishop Grindal to certify the names of all persons having spiritual promotion within his diocese,

AFTER my right hearty commendations unto your lordship premised. These shall be to desire and require you, for causes good and urgent, to certify me in writing distinctly, on this side the first day of the next Michaelmas term, the names and surnames, degrees, and reputed age of all and singular, as well your dean, archdeacons, dignities, and prebendaries within your cathedral church, as of all and singular others any ways beneficed, or having any spiritual promotion

how many resident, where the absents dwell, how many ministers or deacons, and how many no priests or deacons, also how many be learned, how many preachers, and how many keep hospitality

within your said diocese, and how many of them be resident upon their said spiritual promotions, and where and in what place and calling the absents do dwell, how many of all such be ministers or deacons, and how many no priests or deacons; noting also who, and how many of the foresaid be learned, and able to preach, and how many be licensed thereto, and by whom they be so; and finally, how many of them do keep hospitality upon their benefices within their said diocese, with a like note of all vacant benefices, and the names of such as do receive the fruits thereof. Thus not doubting your lordship's speedy diligence herein, I wish you well to fare. From my manor of Lambeth, this, etc.

CCXXXVIII.

ARCHBISHOP PARKER TO SIR GILBERT GERRARD.
31st December, 1567. Parker MSS. C. C. Coll. Camb. cxiv. art. 259. p. 717.

The archbishop, on Sir G. Gerrard's re-

AFTER my hearty commendations. I satisfied your desire[1] to write to the company of Merton College not to proceed against Mr Latham in deprivation without I understood the

[1 In Parker MS. cxiv. art. 256. p. 711, there is a letter from Sir Gilbert Gerrard, who then filled the office of attorney-general, to the archbishop, dated 29th December, 1567, on behalf of Latham, to which this is an answer. Latham had been a fellow of Merton, "divers years," and desired to continue in his fellowship without entering into any profession, which was contrary to the statutes.]

cause. All the fellows of the house, one[2] excepted, have *quest, had written to Merton College not to deprive Mr Latham without reporting to him the cause They answered by accusing him of various crimes.* written to me, that they be able to charge him with crimes worthy expulsion, amongst which they offer to prove one not worthy to be named. I willed their messengers not to deal that way against him to the disabling of him otherwise, and if they could prove his perjury, I remitted them to themselves; I would not intermeddle. But I think Mr Latham should do most for himself to enjoy his dispensation of taking orders, and so keep reasonable countenance in honesty, than to stand to the uttermost. And better it were he gave place of his own accord, than to depart with the note of expulsion. *Mr Latham had better retire of his own accord.* And thus imparting my advice, as I did to himself privately, I commit your worship to God's grace as myself. This last of December.

Your loving friend.

CCXXXIX.
ARCHBISHOP PARKER TO LADY BACON[3].
6th February, 1567—8. Petyt MS. Inner Temple, No. 47. fol. 59. Parker's Draft or Copy.

MADAM,

My hearty salutations to your ladyship presupposed, *in Christo servatore et judice.* I understand that ye use otherwhiles to be a good solicitor to my lord your husband in the causes of the poor for justice, &c., and I doubt not that ye remember the Christian duty ye bear to him, as well in respect of conscience to Almighty God, as for his honourable estimation and fame to the world; *et hoc est esse, juxta divinam ordinationem, vere adjutorium salutare coram Adam datum a Deo, tempore vanitatis nostræ.* Upon which ground I thought good, now in the end of the term, after my lord's angry business nigh defrayed, to write a few words to you. To my lord I perceive I may not write, except they be *placentissima;* and therefore I shall stay my hand. My lord, as by his few lines written to me in answer to my friendly letters, doth say he hath conceived that he thought not to have heard at my hands before I had spoken with *Lady Bacon a good solicitor to her husband in the causes of the poor. The archbishop therefore applies to her, as he may not write to the lord-keeper, from whom he has received a hard answer, sent*

[² The MS. leaves it uncertain whether this word is 'one,' or 'none.']

[³ See before, Letter CLXVII. p. 219.]

himself: and not so contented, but sent me a hard answer in word by my man yet extern to us both, whom I wished not to have known any inkling of our private dealings; so privately, I say, written of my party, that I tell you the truth, *coram Deo servatore meo*, the talk not opened nor conferred within any signification to my yoke-fellow, though yet, I trust, not so great a day-body and without God's fear, but can consider both reason and godliness. Yet I have kept my grief within myself from her: not as to have you think that such a matter were to be much regarded, howsoever it be taken of such two as we may be esteemed, but that I have used friendship toward my lord in all points, whatsoever he conceiveth. But I am sorry he can so soon conceive displeasantly against me, not deserved, I say, and to abide thereby not deserved. For I meant not only prudently, but christianly, godly, and friendly, howsoever it be taken. The testimony of my conscience shall make me take this his storm quietly to Godward, rather offering him in my prayers to God, than careful of any submission as having offended, which I intended not, as faulty[1].

In his conceiving, as he writeth, for to have suspended my such writing, till I had heard from him, or spoken with him, &c., ye shall understand that the party who came up with the duke's grace's letters, resorted to me a little before dinner, and shewed me in his talk, that he was appointed to come again that afternoon, to have received his letters to the duke's grace in answer, &c. Whereupon I thought the time present such as that, before he should write to his grace, to put to his wisdom and consideration so much as I did write. For, after that time, it had been too late to speak with himself, who at that afternoon had no leisure, if I had come to him; and yet sending my letters by that messenger, nor making him privy of the sending, &c.

But, concerning the matter itself, forsooth, I am sure I did so reasonably write, that if he had been the prince of the realm, or I but his chaplain, I might have written privately, as I did. And where he findeth lack in me that I did so write, peradventure I might find some lack in him for not staying his displeasure till he had known what great cause I had to write, yea much more than I did write, both in con-

[1 fawtie, in Orig.]

science and in good love of friendship. Madam, be not offended with my plainness, as though I would make comparison with him. I know his office, I know his gifts of God, and his place, and yet may Matthew Parker write privately to Nicholas Bacon in matter of good friendship without offence. In all humility of heart I will not stick to submit myself to his page of his chamber, and will be admonished by him in reason, though he were mine enemy; and again, in doing mine office to God, and my duty of friendship to them whom I will sincerely love and honour. I will not be abashed to say to my prince that I think in conscience, in answering to my charging. As this other day I was well chidden at my prince's hand; but with one ear I heard her hard words, and with the other, and in my conscience and heart, I heard God. And yet her Highness being never so much incensed to be offended with me, the next day coming by Lambeth bridge into the fields, and I according to duty meeting her on the bridge, she gave me her very good looks, and spake secretly in mine ear, that she must needs countenance mine authority before the people, to the credit of my service. Whereat divers of my arches then being with me peradventure marvelled, &c. Where peradventure somebody would have looked over the shoulders, and slyly slipt away, to have abashed me before the world, &c.

But to enter the matter of late. I sent my visitors into Norwich, Dion's country and mine, to set order and to know the state of the country, whereof I heard, of credible and of worshipful persons, that Gehazi and Judas had a wonderful haunt in the country, that *Quid vultis mihi dare?* had so much prevailed there among the Simonians, that now to sell and to buy benefices, to fleece parsonages and vicarages, that *omnia erant venalia.* And I was informed the best of the country, not under the degree of knights, were infected with this sore, so far that some one knight had four or five, some other seven or eight benefices clouted together, fleecing them all, defrauding the crown's[2] subjects of their duty of prayers, somewhere setting boys and their serving-men to bear the names of such livings. Understanding this enormity, how the gospel was thus universally pinched, to the discouraging of all good labourers in God's harvest, I meant to

[2 'cr.' in Orig.]

On the visitation it was presented that the lord keeper had set a mere lay body as a prebendary in the cathedral there, and that he had another prebend lay at home, both of whom denied Parker's authority over them, and refused to appear

inquire of it, &c. In such inquisition was presented at Norwich, that my lord had set a serving man not ordered, a mere lay-body, in the face of the whole city, to be a prebendary of the church there, and that he had another at home at his house, another prebendary; and bearing themselves great under my lord's authority, despised mine, to be at the church's visitation, &c.

The visitors reported these circumstances to Parker, who communicated them to Bacon, who did not remember the names of the persons alluded to.

This matter hath been long tossed among that people of these two places thus used, which I knew not of till my visitors came home again, and inquiring of them first of the cathedral church, &c., I was informed of these two, of whom I told my lord himself what was spoken, who not remembering their names, I ceased of talk, and yet he seemed not well content that they should not do their duties. My commissioners, unknowing to me, when they were at the church, charged the dean &c. to pay them no rent of their prebends till they had shewed good cause to me of their absence.

The visitors charged the dean to make no payments to them till they shewed good cause for their absence. Smythe, one of them, applied to Parker, who after hearing the facts, advised him to resign his prebend upon a pension

After the visitation, Smythe, one of them, came thither and was denied his money, and after came one of them to me for a letter of release. When I perceived what he was, and perceiving that yet he had honest learning, I moved him to enter order to avoid the speech of the world, and not to live so contrary to laws, and so to honest that small number of the church besides, being but six prebendaries though they were all at home, where one could hardly be spared, not so well as in churches where be forty or fifty prebends. After many words he answered me, that though he had been brought up in some profane learning, yet in scripture he had no knowledge, and thereupon would not enter into the ministry. He thereupon asked further my counsel. ¶ told him that I thought it best for him, for the necessity of life, after his service spent with my lord, reserving some pension, to resign it to such an one as were able to do good in that church. He told me that certain had offered him well, but he liked not their judgments.

He consequently agreed to gratify the whole city by resigning to Mr Walker, who was desired to continue there for his gift of preaching, which he could not

In fine, he thought good to gratify the whole city and to resign it to Mr Walker, who was desired for his gift of preaching to continue there in the city, and so to be from the danger of *non residens* from a little benefice he hath in the country, whither he must be fain else to go and leave the city destitute; for such kinds of informations be now readily made and heard in the King's Bench, as I heard this other day of a very honest man keeping at his greater benefice a very good house, is charged with *non residens* by a promoter from his less benefice, not yet far off from his other, for every month's absence £10.

Otherwise do, for fear of an information for non-residence.

This Smythe had my letters of release to the dean, to receive his payment after what time he resigned his prebend upon a pension of £5 assured by the church. Upon which vacation the duke's grace did write to my lord in Mr Walker's favour. This party travelled hither with his letters, but he could not be admitted. The cause was answered that Smythe was bound to my lord to pay £5 pension of his prebend to a sister's son of my lord's studying at Cambridge. The party told me that my lord made the answer himself, and that was the let. When I heard it, I was sorry to hear it of him, *qui fœnum habet in cornu*, as I think it will be in the green-yard[1] a common-place shortly of the preachers there. I excused the matter as well as I could, who told me the usage of this kind of doing in all the country, and marvelled that they which favour the gospel should so use it, with divers words more, whereby I gathered the sequel what was like to follow of his repulse.

Thereupon Parker gave Smythe his release to the dean, and the duke of Norfolk applied to the lord-keeper on behalf of Mr Walker. The keeper refused to confirm the arrangement, because Smythe was bound to him to pay £5 per annum out of his prebend to a sister's son of the keeper's, studying at Cambridge.

Walker reports the refusal to Parker,

In this very article of time, retaining this Walker at dinner in my house of purpose, I in dinner-time did write to my lord my letters, only to put the matter to his wisdom and consideration, without any of the hard circumstances of the cause, how it was like to be taken, saving only of my lord of Norfolk's pleasuring, &c., who I am sure would have taken it thankfully to have sped, and so made it known amongst his friends in the city, which should have, I doubt not, promoted the credit of the gospel, for his grace to be the motioner and bringer into the church and into that city such a preacher, whereby the people of the city might have received joy and gladness, and the enemies of the gospel disappointed of their triumphing on that preacher, if he had sped at the duke's request, &c.

who keeping Walker to dinner, writes to the keeper to put the matter to his wisdom and consideration, but in vain.

But all this would not serve, for the messenger said, this £5 pension was the stop and let, &c. Marry, he told me, that my lord would answer the duke's grace that he should be sure of the next vacant room when it chanced there. I

All he would do was to promise that the duke should have the next vacant prebend

[1 The 'green-yard' was a place near the bishop's palace at Norwich, where sermons were commonly preached.]

pray God send my lord many joyful years to continue both in life and in office, till that day and time, but I think this offer would have been taken in time, and I wish I had borne this £5 pension of mine own purse, that the common slanderous speech might have been stayed, where I fear it will by this doing be further wondered at. But it may be said, "Let such as talk of it remedy it if they can." Oh, madam, God is the rewarder of all good doings, and reformer of all disorders. I see this country so much without remorse of conscience in this outrage, that the stones will speak of it, if it be not reformed.

[margin: Parker wished he had taken the £5 pension upon himself, that the slanderous speech which this incident occasioned might be stayed.]

If my lord be angry with me for my plainness, I fear not Almighty God. *Deus, ultionum Deus,* will be content. Yea, and he will ask account of me, if I hold my peace, when both my lord and I shall stand dreadfully before his chancery, and therefore I will not so covet the favour of man to displease God.

[margin: If Bacon be angry with Parker's plainness, he fears not God will be content.]

And surely, Madam, I could no less do of tender heart to his estimation. And loth would I be that his example should be alleged for divers spoilers in that country of the ministry, the office of man's salvation, the office of Christ's crucified mysteries, howsoever the carnal princes of the world do deride God *et omnia sacra. Sed qui habitat in cœlis irridebit eos.* For God's love, Madam, help you, *tanquam una caro cum viro tuo, sed ambo Christi membra charissima,* to help to eliminate out of his house this offendicle, *ut ne ponat maculam in gloria senectutis suæ. Labi et falli humanum, sed perseverare durum.* I will not write that I hear reported, nor will credit all tales. Fie on the world, to carry God's good, elect, and principal members of his kingdom, so to be drowned in the dregs of this mortality, not to regard these so chief causes. What shall be hoped for in friendship, if the advertising of one another in true faithful friendship, and to Godwards, shall stir up enmity and disliking? Let the blind world say, "*Suaviora sunt fraudulenta oscula odientis, quam vulnera diligentis.*" Let the wise man say contrary, "*Quam meliora sunt vulnera diligentis, quam fraudulenta oscula odientis.*" I am jealous over my lord's conscience, and over his honourable name. It may become my office to himward, though he be great in office, to hear the voice of a poor pastor; for there is one which saith, *Qui*

[margin: What shall be hoped for if true friendship stirs up enmity?]

vos audit, me audit; qui vos spernit, me spernit; qui vos tangit, tangit pupillam oculi mei; as contemptible soever the vain world esteemeth us. I have alway joyed in my lord, alway honourably reported him. I have in good places, and before the most honourable, compared him with More and Audeley for their eloquence, wit, and learning in law; with bishop Goodrick for his sincerity towards justice. Although they all had their faults, which God keep from my lord and me; the first imbrued with papistry; the second *omnino passim et ab omnibus;* the third a dissembler in friendship, who used to entertain his evil-willers very courteously, and his very friends very imperiously, thinking thereby to have the rule of both, whereby he lost both. For while his evil-willers spread how he would shake up his acquaintance, they gathered thereby the nature of his friendship toward his old friends; and therefore joyed not much of his glorious entertaining, and his friends indeed joyed less in him, for such his discouragement that they felt at his hands. *Expertus loquor, &c.*

Now what will be judged of many of the world, which peradventure love neither of us, if it may be heard, how we two, in that place that we be in by God's providence and the Queen's favour, both professing God's verity as we do, so long conjoined as we have been, now to fall at square, so nigh to fall into our earthly pit, he to contemn me, I to be dulled in my contentation toward him? What will this work in the commonwealth, and specially if it should break out, upon what ground this grief is conceived and taken? I would be loth to break friendship with any mean body, much less with my lord; and yet either king or Cæsar, contrary to my duty to God, I will not, nor intend not, God being my good Lord. It is not the solemnity or commodity of mine office that I so much esteem: I was sorry to be so accumbered, but necessity drave me; and what fate shall thrust me out, *susque deque fero.* I am grown now into a better consideration by mine age, than to be afeared or dismayed with such vain terriculaments of the world. I am not now to learn how to fawn upon man, *cujus spiritus in naribus ejus;* or that I have to learn how to repose myself quietly under God's protection against all displeasure of friends, and against all malignity of the enemy. I have oft said and expended that verse,

Cadent a latere tuo mille, &c. In this mind I trust to live and die. Here I will not answer as a Paynim did to a Paynim, *Cur habeam cum pro principe, qui me non habet pro senatore.* But while I live I will pray for my lord, that all grace and good fortune may assist him in himself and in his posterity; and shall be as glad and ready to the duty of godly friendship to him, if it may be reasonably taken, as any one whatsoever with whom he is best pleased and least provoked with, as any one that fawneth most upon him for his office sake, or for his virtue, to my power.

And thus reposing myself *in bona et constante conscientia* in this brittle time, I commit your ladyship to God, as myself. Because ye be *alter ipse* to him, *unus spiritus, una caro,* I make you judge, and therefore I transmit the very copy of my letter sent to him, to expend the rather of my writing, whereby ye may take occasion to work as God shall move you. And thus I leave. From my house at Lambeth, this 6th of February, 1567.

Your friend unfeigned in Christ,

MATTH. CANT.

Sends a copy of his letter to Bacon.

CCXL.

SIR HENRY SYDNEY TO ARCHBISHOP PARKER.

3rd March, 1567—8. Parker MSS. C. C. Coll. Camb. CXIV. art. 104. p. 331. Orig.

Sir Henry Sydney moves the archbishop for a Lent licence for his son Philip.

I THANK your good grace most humbly for my great cheer yesterday, and signify the same that the chiefest matter wherein I had to move your grace was for a licence to be granted to my boy Philip Sidney[1], who is somewhat subject

[1 The future Sir Philip Sydney was born on the 29th November, 1554. This letter contains one of the earliest notices of him. The mention of Dr Cooper as his tutor is a new fact in his biography. It was probably Dr Thomas Cooper, subsequently bishop of Lincoln, and afterwards of Gloucester, the translator of Lanquet's Chronicle, compiler of the Thesaurus, and author of the Admonition in reply to Martin Marprelate; he was also one of Parker's executors and preached his funeral sermon. A letter from him to archbishop Parker occurs in Addit. MS. Brit. Mus. 19, 398, art. 42. It is without date, but accompanied some controversial composition which had been previously submitted to Sir William Cecil, perhaps the manuscript of

to sickness, for eating of flesh this Lent, for which I then forgot to speak unto you; and have therefore now thought good to desire your grace to grant unto him the said licence in what sort may seem best unto you, so as he may have with him Mr Doctor Cooper, who is his tutor. And thus I humbly take my leave. From Durham House, this Wednesday the third of March, 1567. Your grace's most humble to command,

H. SYDNEY.

CCXLI.

ARCHBISHOP PARKER TO FREDERIC III. ELECTOR PALATINE.

25th March, 1568. Parker MSS. C. C. Coll. Camb. cxix. art. 5. p. 10. Orig. draft.

FUIT apud me, illustrissime princeps, a te missus Dominus Immanuel, consiliarius tuus, vir admodum probus et doctus, mihique ex diuturna olim consuetudine ita cognitus: a quo et accepi humanissimas Celsitudinis tuæ literas[2], pro quibus ingentes habeo gratias. Insuper didici quanta sis cura et

Has received a letter from the elector Palatine, sent by Parker's old acquaintance, Tremellius

the little book entitled "An Answer in defence of the truth against the Apology of Private Masse," published London, 1562, 16mo. (See Wood's Athenæ, ed. Bliss, I. 612.) Another letter from Cooper to Parker occurs in Parker MS. cxiv. art. 306. p. 839. It bears date 4 Jan. 1568, and relates to some appointment lately received by the writer through Parker's influence with the Earl of Leicester. Possibly this was the Vice-Chancellorship of Oxford, which the Earl of Leicester, Chancellor of the University, bestowed upon Dr Cooper. See Strype's Parker, Book IV. c. 4, and App. No. XC. III. 295. 8vo. ed.]

[2 The letter referred to remains amongst the Parker MSS. (cxix. art. 4. p. 9,) and is dated 12th February, 1567—8. It commends to Parker Emmanuel Tremellius, who was about to visit England on the business of the Elector Palatine. The prince alluded to was Frederic III., a great friend to the Protestants both in France and the Low Countries. Tremellius was an old acquaintance of Parker; see note under a letter from him to Parker, dated 16th September, 1568. There are three other MSS. of his in the Parker collection; an early letter to Parker in cxix. art. 91; a bond given by him on receiving a grant of a prebend "in ecclesia Argentina," cviii. art. 61; and a translation by him of the Epistles to the Galatians and the Ephesians from the Syriac into Latin, cccxl. art. 1.]

Thanks God for the elector's zeal for the gospel.

solicitudine ut evangelium Christi apud multa Europæ regna e maximis superstitionum tenebris jam collucens, adhuc magis ac magis ad vituperationem omnium eorum qui ei male favent, vigeat. Pro hac eximia amplitudinis tuæ virtute ac generosa erga Christum constantia Deo gratias agimus, quantum possu-

Has given attention to his affairs, and will always do so

mus maximas. Jam pro virili dedimus operam (ut semper dabimus) grato officio non deesse rerum tuarum procurationi, ubi opus fuerit, ad quæ vestra meum equidem officium requiri valde jucundum mihi fuit, utcunque forte eventus non sit secutus secundum expectationem. Hoc igitur in presenti

Will pray to God to give his highness in the midst of his troublesome affairs, that peace in which he and all promoters of the gospel may rejoice.

nobis superest, ut a Deo semper assiduis precibus vestro nomine contendamus ut rebus turbulentis eam pacem det quo vestra Celsitudo cum omnibus evangelii fautoribus plurimum et nunc et perpetuo gaudeat; quod quidem minime dubitamus cum jam ejus causa agitur.

Lambethi prope Londinum, 25° Martii, anno Christi 1568.

Tuæ celsitudini deditissimus,

MATTHÆUS CANTUAR.

CCXLII.

ARCHBISHOP PARKER TO SIR WILLIAM CECIL.

29th March, [1568.] Lansd. MS. x. art. 41. Orig.

Sir,

For the next Wednesday sermon was doctor Bullingham[1]

Arrangements for Paul's Cross.

prepared, for Mr Freke[2] had given it over to me by his letters afore, and now I hear that the dean of Paul's is appointed thereto; whereupon I mean that the said doctor Bolingham shall supply Good Friday in the stead of the bishop of Winchester[3]; whose health will not suffer him.

I understand ye bear your favour to Mr Blont the

Mr Blont recommended for a benefice.

bearer of this. I pray you further him to this benefice; I trust he will behave himself honestly: I like his learning well, whom I have heard now twice to judge of him. It is doubt whether the incumbent be dead, but is like, as I hear, shortly.

[1 Afterwards bishop of Gloucester and Bristol.]
[2 Afterwards bishop of Rochester, and subsequently of Norwich.]
[3 Bishop Horne.]

Sir, where the Queen's Highness will reserve Canterbury prebends for her chaplains, it shall be as it please her; but I pray your honour to consider how the church standeth, that foreigners and noblemen passing that way, may find convenient number at home to offer them a dinner, &c., for if many of them should be absent and have their whole profits, as many of late have obtained, the rest should be too much hindered in their hospitality, and therefore will make them to absent themselves, as upon this occasion some of them be now about to depart. They hear that doctor Nevison will sue for his whole profits absent, and Mr Freke will do the like; which I would think not expedient. Mr Sentleger, Mr Boleyn, and Mr Dorel be thus preferred, which is enough and too much. I put this to your consideration.

From my house, this 29th of March.

Your honour's alway,

MATTH. CANT.

To the right honourable Sir William Cecil, knight, principal secretary to the Queen's Majesty.

CCXLIII.

AMBROSE EARL OF WARWICK TO ARCHBISHOP PARKER.

3rd May [probably 1568.] Parker MSS. C. C. Coll. Camb. cxiv. art. 58. p. 183.

My very good lord, after my hearty commendations. Whereas this bearer, my servant, hath printed divers of my lord of Salisbury his book touching the Defence of the Apology of England[4], the charge whereof will turn to his great hinderance if he may not utter them; this shall be heartily to pray your good grace the rather for my sake, if you shall so think it meet, to grant an injunction, for the speedier sale of them, that every minister may be bound to have one. In

[4 The Defence of the Apology was first published in 1567. The date "Anno 1567, 27 Octobris" stands upon the title-page. The book was printed by Henry Wykes.]

doing whereof your grace shall pleasure the poor man very much, and I, ceasing at this present any further to trouble the same, commit you to the keeping of Almighty God. From the Court, the 3rd of May.

Your grace's most assured to command,
A. WARWICK[1].

CCXLIV.

ARCHBISHOP PARKER TO THE WARDEN OF ALL SOULS' COLLEGE, OXFORD.

12th May, 1568. Parker MSS. C. C. Coll. Camb. cxiv. art. 265. p. 731. Parker's draft.

Parker writes on behalf of a widow of an old tenant of All Souls' College, to procure for her a renewal of a lease.

MR WARDEN, whereas I am informed that where of late ye were with Mr Heneage[2] signifying to him that the farm which hath been so loud sued for is now in division, and that ye informed him you would not stand against his friend, neither direct nor indirect. This is therefore once again to request you and other of the company to shew your good wills unto this said gentlewoman, the rather for that she offereth more commodity to your College than other doth[3], and for that she is contented to accept it as ye yourself shall

[[1] The signature together with the two preceding words is by a different hand, perhaps that of the earl himself, the rest of the letter being written by an amanuensis.]

[[2] Sir Thomas Heneage, who at this time had written to the archbishop in favour of Mrs Foster, a widow, who had been lessee of the farm of Salford, under All Souls' Coll. Oxford. The lease had now fallen in, and she was desirous of obtaining a renewal, whereas the College meditated dividing the farm and letting it pass into other hands. Sir Thomas's letter, which is dated 11 May, 1568, is in Parker MS. cxiv. art. 263. p. 725.]

[[3] Sir T. Heneage writes: "The poor widow is content to take it at their hands as they will let it, paying double her accustomed rent for the whole farm, or else as much as she doth now pay for the one half thereof, and as much money as hath been accustomed to be paid for the fine of the whole, although it be but a reversion for fourteen years that they can make any grant of at this time." A second letter of his to the archbishop on the same subject, dated 30th May, 1568, is in Parker MS. cxiv. art. 264. p. 727.]

think it most meet for the advancement of your farm and of your tenants there. And being therefore thus advertised of your inclination, I have thus written my letters as aforetimes. And thus I bid you well to fare. From my house of Lambeth, this 12th of May.

Your loving friend.

CCXLV.

QUEEN ELIZABETH TO ARCHBISHOP PARKER.

13th May, 1568. Lansd. MS. xciv. art. 19. Contemporary Minute compared with Parker Reg. I. 270 b.

BY THE QUEEN.

MOST reverend father in God, right trusty and right well beloved, we greet you well. Forasmuch as we do understand that there do daily repair into this our realm great numbers of strangers from the parts beyond the seas, otherwise than hath been accustomed, and the most part thereof pretending the cause of their coming to be for to live in this our realm with satisfaction of their conscience in Christian religion, according to the order allowed in this our realm; and doubting lest that among such numbers, divers may also resort into our realm that are infected with dangerous opinions contrary to the faith of Christ's church, as anabaptists and such other sectaries, or that be guilty of some other horrible crimes of rebellion, murder, robberies, or such like, committed by them in the parts from whence they do come; to which kind of people we do no wise mean to permit any refuge within our dominions. Therefore we do will and require you to give speedy order and commandment to the reverend father in God the bishop of London, and all other ordinaries of any places where you shall think any such confluence of strangers to be within your province, that without delay particular special visitations and inquisition be made in every parish for this purpose requisite, of all manner of persons being strangers born, of what country, quality, condition, and estate, they be, with the probable causes of their coming into this our realm, and the time of their continuance, and in what

(marginal notes: Great and unusual repair of strangers into England, some of whom may be infected with dangerous opinions, contrary to the faith of Christ. The archbishop is ordered to direct the bishop of London and other ordinaries, to make various inquiries respecting all strangers, especially as to the churches to which they resort)

sort they do live, and to what churches they do resort for exercise of their religion, with such other things requisite in this case to be understand for the worthiness of their continuance in this our realm: and thereupon to cause perfect registers to be made and so to continue, and to give advertisement to our justices and ministers of our lay power to proceed speedily to the trial of such as shall be found suspected of the foresaid crimes, or otherwise that shall not be conformable to such order of religion as is agreeable with our laws, or as is permitted to places specially appointed for the resort of strangers to the exercise of religion in the use of common prayer and the sacraments; and in all other things we will and require you to use all good diligence and provision by the means of the bishops and ordinaries under you, as well in places exempt as otherwise, that no manner of strangers be suffered to remain within any part of our dominions in your province, but such as shall be known or commonly reported to be of Christian conversation, and meet to live under our protection, according to the treaties of intercourse betwixt us and other princes our neighbours.

No manner of strangers to be suffered to remain in the Queen's dominions, but such as be of Christian conversation.

Given under our signet, at our manor of Greenwich, the 13th day of May, 1568, the tenth year of our reign.

CCXLVI.

ARCHBISHOP PARKER TO SIR WILLIAM CECIL.

21st May, 1568. Lansd. MS. x. art. 47. Orig.

SIR,

UPON consideration of our brittle time of tarriance, *dum sumus in mundo operemur bonum, et opera illorum sequuntur illos, &c.* I pray your honour to help in this cause, which I would have craved your counsel in, if this day had taken in the Star Chamber. The purpose is contained in the letter herein inclosed[1]. My desire is that they might be penned in such form as that my lords of the council would subscribe to them, that they might be delivered to the justices at their next meeting, trusting that it will do good; the charge

Cecil is solicited to help in a cause explained by an inclosed paper.

[1 The following note is written upon the letter: "For the making of the river to Canterbury navigable."]

will amount to fifteen hundred pounds, as is thought: which is too great, except they be aided. As your honour shall think good so shall my servant attend your pleasure. And thus I pray God preserve your honour in grace and health, this 21st of May.

Your honour's in Christ,

MATTH. CANT.

To the right honourable Sir William Cecil, knight, principal secretary to the Queen's Majesty.

[margin note: The assistance of the council is solicited for an undertaking that will cost £1500]

CCXLVII.

ARCHBISHOP PARKER TO BISHOP GRINDAL OF LONDON.

24th May, 1568. Parker Reg. I. 270 b.

AFTER my right hearty commendations unto your good lordship premised. Whereas I have of late received the Queen's Majesty's most honourable letters missive, the true tenor whereof hereafter ensueth: "Most reverend father in God," &c., [as before printed, No. CCXLV. p. 321.] These shall be therefore in the Queen's Majesty's name to will and require your lordship, that having regard (as I doubt not but you will) to the execution of the Queen's Majesty's said letters within your own diocese, you do also forthwith signify the tenor thereof to all and singular my brethren, the other bishops and other ordinaries within my province, where you shall think any confluence of strangers to be; willing and commanding them, and every of them, in the Queen's Majesty's name, without delay to cause the tenor of her Majesty's said letters to be executed through every of their several dioceses and jurisdictions, as well in places exempt as not exempt, as to them and every of them shall appertain. And thus I bid your lordship most heartily well to fare as myself. From my house at Lambeth, the 24th of May, 1568.

[margin note: The archbishop has received the Queen's letter of 13th May, 1568, as before printed, No ccxlv. p 321. He therefore requires the bishop of London to execute the same, and to signify the tenor thereof to the other bishops of the province of Canterbury.]

To the right honourable and my loving brother, the bishop of London, give these.

CCXLVIII.

ARCHBISHOP PARKER TO THE WARDEN OF ALL SOULS' COLLEGE, OXFORD.

1st June, 1568. Parker MSS. C. C. Coll. Camb. cxiv. art. 265. p. 729. Parker's Draft.

Parker writes again, urging the College to comply with the recommendation on behalf of Mrs Foster

I AM much ashamed to write so oft in a matter belonging to your College, but that I see they be worshipful that be suitors to you and may do your College pleasure if they be gratefully considered; and also for that this gentlewoman, Mrs Foster, desireth nothing to the College hinderance, but much to the advancement of the same, as offering forty mark but for a part of that she sueth for, and threescore pound for a fine[1]; so that as I have been alway answered, your tenants may be preferred as you list yourself, which hitherto hath been made the chief stay for not granting. Whereupon for that your friends hath been fed with hope of their reasonable request by the doubtful and variableness of your answers, I would now at the conclusion give you counsel to protract the time no longer, so to drive the poor gentlewoman and her friends to be at further charge, as she hath sustained hitherto the charge well nigh of forty pounds so that your College might have been preferred, and she at less charge, whereof I pray you have consideration. And thus I bid you well to fare. From my manor at Croydon, this first day of June, 1568.

Your loving friend.

CCXLIX.

ARCHBISHOP PARKER TO SIR WILLIAM CECIL.

11th June, [1568]. S. P. O. Domestic, 1568. Orig.

SIR,

Parker solicits for his steward a lease of a farm of the Queen's in Suffolk, formerly let at £4, but now at £50 per annum.

WHEREAS Mr Colby, my steward, a gentleman of a very honest nature and grateful to his friends, would fain be a suitor to the Queen's Highness by your mediation, for a farm lying just to a piece of his land in Suffolk; which farm was once let (as he saith) for four pounds yearly, but now drawn up

[1 On the back of this draft the archbishop has noted: "Mistress Foster offereth £lx fine and xl mark rent, for £xx before; leaving almost two third parts for the tenants."]

to the yearly rent of fifty pounds, which yet for the commodity of the nighness he would be glad to be farmer there and pay that rent. He seemeth to be abashed to crave your favour by himself, but he can consider by whom he is pleasured with thankfulness. Sir, I see so much honesty in him that I cannot less do but commend his suit to you, referring yet this and all other such requests to your wisdom and discretion.

I am much careful for the success that may rise to the Queen's person and the realm by the arrival of the Scottish Lady[2]. I fear *quod bona Regina nostra auribus lupum tenet.* I trust in God ye have amongst yourselves well consulted. God grant the event of your counsel to be prosperous. As it cannot be but that many eyes be set wide open upon the Queen's Highness, to note her behaviour and governance, so, in mine opinion, nothing hath chanced externly to her Majesty wherein her prudence shall be more marked and spied; which God rule to his glory and to her own safeguard, whereto my prayer shall bend.

<small>Parker's fear on the arrival of Mary Queen of Scots in England.</small>

It had become me to have done my duty of coming to the Court, but, in good faith, I carry about me such a casual body, vexed with the stone, that I cannot do as I would. Thus I wish to your honour all felicity in God. From my house at Croydon, this 11th of June.

Yours in Christ,

MATTH. CANT.

To the right honourable Sir William Cecil, knight, principal secretary to the Queen's Highness, and one of her privy council; at the Court.

CCL.

ARCHBISHOP PARKER TO SIR GILBERT GERRARD[3].

21st June, [1568]. Parker MSS. C. C. Coll. Camb. cxiv. art. 258. p. 715. Parker's Draft.

I MARVEL much that the fellows of Merton College should be so much grieved with one order we made for three only

<small>Marvels that the fellows of Merton College are dissatisfied</small>

[2 Mary Queen of Scots, landed at Workington on the 16th May, 1568.]

[3 Sir Gilbert's letter, to which this is an answer, is dated from London, June 21st, 1568. It is in Parker MS. cxiv. art. 258. p. 713.]

with a recent order, that there should be three priests within the College. priests to be within the College, whereunto they be all form[sic] by statute, and amongst the number of twenty of them that not three are disposed to serve the realm in that holy ministry, but would in idle pleasures wear out their lives. I cannot of conscience favour them therein. And of late hearing of a bye-statute they had, that none of the younger fellows might be priests, I dispensed with them in that statute, whereby they might the better come to their number of three. They ought all to be   [1] and so the nigher to be divines.

One physician tolerated for the reading of Linacre's lecture. There is one physician amongst them tolerated for the reading of Linacre's lesson within their house, which else should be to the more shame of the house if outward students should read it. I am sorry that Latham[2] should deceive mine expectation to abhor the ministry, being one of the ancients, to give good example to the house; but because I hear their warden shall shortly come home[3] he shall take order amongst them. I think ye should be Latham's better friend to move him to the ministry, for whom ye might soon provide. And I am sorry that this matter being of this congruence I cannot pleasure your request as else I would.

Evils that will ensue if there be no preachers. Surely, Mr Attorney, if there be no preachers to maintain Christ's religion, to move the subjects' hearts in persuasion of obedience to the prince, and the tenants to their landlords, neither Westminster Hall will long continue nor outward force will rule the matter: in which consideration methink, where founders hath bestowed their cost to bring them up that way, to deceive God and the world, I think it not reasonable. And thus, pinched at this time with a shrewd fit of the stone, I wish you God's grace and health as to myself. From my house at Croydon, this 21st of June.

Your loving friend.

[1 A word here has baffled all attempts to decipher it.]

[2 The bearer of the letter of Sir Gilbert Gerrard to the archbishop. Latham now professed to be studying for the law. See before, Letter CCXXXVIII.]

[3 Mann, the warden, had been sent as the Queen's ambassador into Spain.]

CCLI.

ARCHBISHOP PARKER TO SIR WILLIAM CECIL.

4th July, [1568]. S. P. O. Domestic. Orig.

SIR,

I WOULD pray your honour to peruse and to correct these letters[4], which may be again engrossed, and if some of the council will subscribe to them, I trust it will turn to some good. The princes beforetimes, as Henry the 3d in his 31st

The archbishop sends a letter to be signed by the council.

[4 The letter alluded to related to the preservation of ancient writings. It exists in the following form in Parker MS. CXIV. art. 12. p. 49: "Whereas the Queen's Majesty, having like care and zeal as divers of her progenitors have had before times for the conservation of such ancient records and monuments, written of the state and affairs of these her realms of England and Ireland, which heretofore were preserved and recorded by special appointment of certain of her ancestors, in divers Abbeys, to be as treasure-houses, to keep and leave in memory such occurrents as fell in their times. And for that most of the same writings and records so kept in the monasteries are now come to the possession of sundry private persons, and so partly remain obscure and unknown: in which said records be mentioned such historical matters and monuments of antiquity, both for the state ecclesiastical and civil government. Whereupon we of the Queen's Majesty's privy council, knowing her express pleasure in the same, have thought good to write these our letters to all and singular her subjects within her realm of England, to notify her pleasure: which is, that the most reverend father in God and our very good lord the archbishop of Canterbury should have a special care and oversight in these matters aforesaid. And thereupon we will and require you, that when the said archbishop shall send his letters, or any of his learned deputies, having these our letters, and requesting to have the sight of any such ancient records or monuments written, being in your custody, that you would at the contemplation of these our letters gently impart the same. Not meaning hereby, in the use of such books for a time, to withdraw them from your right and interest unto them, but after a time of perusing of the same upon promise or hand, to make restitution of them again safely into your hands, to be safely kept hereafter, so as both when any need shall require resort may be made for the testimony that may be found in them, and also by conference of them the antiquity of the state of these countries may be restored to the knowledge of the world. In which your doing ye shall not only shew yourself grateful subjects to the Queen's Majesty, your natural prince, but also shall minister friendly occasion to us to give you thanks, as opportunity shall serve, in any of your causes, as may rise upon the report of the said

year, caused all the chronicles to be searched concerning the superiority over Scotland; they were by certain delegates perused and drawn in articles, reporting the books where they were. It were good such records should remain, &c. In story it is reported that the prince of the realm by right is not *Dominus Hiberniæ*, but *Rex Hiberniæ*. It were pity such records should be spoiled. If ye think this motion good, I am content to set some of my men in work; and if this opportunity be not taken in our time, it will not so well be done hereafter. Thus I wish your honour grace in good, and good success in your journey, and a good successor in York[1].

From my house at Croydon, this 4th of July.

Your honour's evermore in Christ,

MATTH. CANTUAR.

To the right honourable Sir William Cecil, knight, principal secretary to the Queen's Majesty.

CCLII.

THE LORDS OF THE COUNCIL TO ARCHBISHOP PARKER.

5th July, 1568. Parker MSS. C. C. Coll. Camb. cxiv. art. 31. p. 101. Orig.

AFTER our right hearty commendations to your good lordship. Where of late we caused divers gentlemen of Cheshire to be committed to ward for their disobedience in

archbishop. And thus we bid you well to fare. From Howard Place, the seventh of July, 1568.

N. BACON, C. S.	T. NORFFOLKE.	W. NORTHT.
R. LEYCESTER.	W. HOWARD.	
		W. CECYLL."

There is both a printed and written copy of the above letter amongst the Parker MSS. The latter may perhaps be the original, though the signatures have been cut off. The former has the following attestation subscribed: Facta collatione hujus scripti cum originali, in custodia suprascripti reverendissimi patris existente, per me Johannem Incent, notarium publicum, ejusdem reverendissimi patris registrarium principalem, concordat cum eadem. J. INCENT.]

[1 Archbishop Thomas Young died 26th June, 1568.]

refusing to answer upon their oath before the bishop of Chester unto such matter and articles as was objected against them: albeit all the rest of the said persons have since that time, upon their humble submission and offer to reform themselves and to answer unto the said articles before the said bishop, been set at liberty, and sent down to him for that purpose into that country; yet Sir John Southworth only amongst the rest refusing to follow that order, hath been still continued in ward hitherto. And forasmuch as he now also in the end hath submitted himself, and offered to answer upon his oath unto the said articles, as by his said submission (the copy whereof we send unto you herewith) you may at better length perceive, and only desireth that he may not be compelled to do the same either before the said bishop of Chester, or before the archbishop of York (now deceased), upon some mistrust which it seemeth he hath conceived that he should not find such indifference at the said bishop's hands as were convenient; we have thought meet to pray your lordship to call the said Sir John Southworth before you and the rest of the commissioners for causes ecclesiastical, and upon his corporal oath to examine him, and cause him to answer unto such matter as shall be herewith sent you. Which if you shall find him to do willingly and obediently, as by his submission he offereth, we pray your lordship we may be advertised thereof by your letters, to the intent that if we shall find sufficient cause thereto, we may be means unto the Queen's Majesty for his further enlargement. And of his doings and behaviour, together with his depositions, and the whole circumstance of that shall have passed in this his cause before you, we pray your lordship we may receive full certificate in due form from you, to the intent we may cause the same to be notified unto the said bishop of Chester, which for divers good considerations we think very necessary. And so we bid your good lordship right heartily well to fare.

From Greenwich, the 5th of July, 1568.

Postscript. We suppose it shall be well done that your lordship and the rest of the commissioners do deal with the said Sir John Southworth only for his answering unto the matters that are already objected against him[2], thinking it

[2 The charges against him will be seen in the form of submission appended to the next letter, p. 330. He at first refused, but better that for other things touching his conscience he be rather procured to be won by persuasion and good information than by process or other open manner of dealing.

Your good lordship's assured loving friends,

NORFFOLK.   W. NORTHT.
H. LEYCESTER.   E. CLYNTON.   W. HOWARD.
                                                                W. CECILL.

To our very good lord the archbishop of Canterbury.

CCLIII.

ARCHBISHOP PARKER TO THE LORDS OF THE COUNCIL.

14th July, [1568]. S. P. O. Domestic. Orig.

Sir John Southworth has been before the

It may please your honours to understand that this day, being the 14th of July, I have had Sir John Southworth here with me, according to your lordships' order. I offered him the form of submission prescribed by your honours[1]; he afterwards consented to sign the submission. In the next year (1569), however, he was taken up and committed to the custody of the bishop of London, and afterwards of the dean of St Paul's. See Strype's Parker, Bk. III. c. 19.]

[1 The form of submission which was returned attached to Parker's letter, is as follows:

"The submission of Sir John Southworth, knight, made the — of July, 1568.

"Where I, Sir John Southworth, knight, forgetting my duty towards God and the Queen's Majesty, in not considering my due obedience for the observation of the ecclesiastical laws and orders of this realm, have received into my house and company, and there relieved, certain priests, who have not only refused the ministry, but also in my hearing have spoken against the present state of religion established by her Majesty and the states of her realm in parliament; and have also otherwise misbehaved myself in not resorting to my parish-church at common prayer, nor receiving the holy communion so often times as I ought to have done: I do now by these presents most humbly and unfeignedly submit myself to her Majesty, and am heartily sorry for mine offences in this behalf, both towards God and her Majesty. And do further promise to her Majesty from henceforth to obey all her Majesty's laws and ordinances set forth by her Majesty's authority in all matters of religion and orders ecclesiastical, and to behave myself therein as becometh a good, humble, and obe-

refused to submit himself to any such subscription; his conscience cannot serve him in most points of that order. He offereth to promise not to receive or sustain any such disordered persons as heretofore he hath sustained and holpen. He further seemeth to desire that he may be suffered to live according unto his conscience, and desireth much to have licence to go over sea. The consideration of all such suits I refer to your honourable wisdoms, which I beseech God to assist to do what may please him and may be safety to the Queen's Highness and to the state of the realm. From my house at Croydon, this foresaid 14th day of July.

archbishop, but refused to subscribe the submission tendered to him.

He desires licence to go over sea.

Your honours' to command,
MATTHUE CANTUAR.

To the most honourable my very good lords, the lords of the Queen's Majesty's privy council. Be it delivered. At the Court.

CCLIV.

ARCHBISHOP PARKER TO SIR WILLIAM CECIL.
19th August, [1568]. S. P. O. Domestic. Orig.

SIR,

AFTER my hearty commendations. I am informed that one of my brethren late bishop of Chichester[2] should be departed. If [sic] when the Queen's pleasure shall be to appoint another, I pray you remember her chaplain Mr Curteys to

Bishop of Chichester departed. Mr Curteys the Queen's chaplain,

dient subject, and shall not impugn any of the said laws and ordinances by any open speech, or by writing or act of mine own, nor willingly suffer any other in my company to offend therein, whom I may reasonably let or disallow; nor shall assist, maintain, relieve or comfort any person living either out of this realm without the Queen's Majesty's licence, or within this realm, being commonly known to be an offender against the said laws and orders now established for godly religion, as is aforesaid. And in this doing I firmly trust to have her Majesty my gracious good lady, as hitherto I and all other her subjects have marvellously tasted of her mercy and goodness."]

[2 Bishop William Barlow, bishop of Chichester, 1559—1568. The person recommended by the archbishop, Dr Richard Curteys, was ultimately appointed to the vacant see, but not until April 1570.]

recommended for the vacant see.

that office. The choice is not great otherwhere, and he being an honest learned man, I would trust that he should well supply it, to God's honour, and to the Queen's contentation. He is now but a poor man and wanteth living; his age is competent. I would be loth it should fall upon one such body as, I am informed by his friends, make suit for it.

Complaints of the bishop of Gloucester.

We of this order learn by experience what rule Gloucester[1] maketh in his people. He is so old that he would bring his people to his contemplations, which he laboureth to do, but spyeth that he shall never, and thereupon wisheth he were discharged, which he hath pretended a long time. But he meaneth another thing. At this very present time I have little else to write, and must make an end the sooner, for the unreasonable rheum and catarrh that hath this four or five days unreasonably reigned upon me. From my house at Lambeth, this 19th of August.

Your honour's loving friend,

MATTH. CANTUAR.

To the right honourable Sir William Cecil, knight, principal secretary to the Queen's Majesty. At the Court.

CCLV.

IMMANUEL TREMELLIUS TO ARCHBISHOP PARKER.

16th September, 1568. Parker MSS. C. C. Coll. Camb. cxiv. art. 300. p. 827. Orig.

Tremellius understands from letters of the bishop of London, that his letters sent by ambassadors from the churches in Flanders had not been delivered. His great regret.

REVERENDISSIME Domine, patrone benignissime. Ex literis reverendissimi Londinensis intelligo meas literas tuæ celsitudini non esse redditas, quas per Flandricæ ecclesiæ secundes legates miseram. Ob quam rem sane vehementer doleo. Videor enim vestrarum celsitudinum et beneficiorum immemor omnia silentio sepelivisse. Cum tamen re vera nec oblitus sim, nec unquam oblivioni sim traditurus, ego summopere cupio ut C. T. jubeat inquiri de memoratis Flandricæ ecclesiæ secundis legatis, et cognoscat quid de illis literis egerint, quas

[1 Bishop Cheney, see before, pp. 138, 213.]

a me ad C. T., ad Dominum Londinensem et ad D. Henricum Knollium perferendas acceperunt. Nam eos Londinum tuto pervenisse audio.

Libri mei præter expectationem meam adhuc servantur a typographo: ita ut ab eo deceptus alios nolens deceperim. Promittit quidem intra sex septimanas prodituros esse libros sed nescio num toties deceptus credere et aliis promittere audeam. Cum prodierint non committam ut erga C. T. habear ingratus. Uxor C. T. reverenter salutat et immortales habet gratias. Rogat etiam una mecum ut C. T. dignetur optimam dominam una cum utroque filio nostris verbis salutare. In hoc mercatorum strepitu plura scribere non possum, et C. T. oro ut brevitatem boni consulat. Data occasione scribam copiosius. Deus ac Pater cœlestis tuam celsitudinem cum tota familia quam diutissime incolumem conservet. Francofurdi, 16 Septembris, 1568. Raptim.

His books still delayed in the press.

As soon as they are published he will shew himself grateful to Parker. Kind messages from his wife to Parker, his wife and sons.

T. celsitudini addictissimus,

IMANUEL TREMELLIUS[2].

Reverendissimo D. D. Matthæo Parkero, archiepiscopo Cantuariensi et totius Angliæ primati, domino ac patrono meo clementissimo. Lambeth. in Anglia[3].

CCLVI.

ARCHBISHOP PARKER TO SIR WILLIAM CECIL.

22nd September, [1568]. S. P. O. Domestic. Orig.

SALUTEM *in Christo.* Sir, I have received your letter, and shall perform that your desire concerning Mr Welles, when he cometh to me or any of his factors. I hear his knowledge and honesty to be well reported.

Mr Welles.

[2 Tremellius was a converted Jew; a very learned man. During the reign of Edward VI. he and his wife were received with great favour in England. He was for several years teacher of Hebrew at Cambridge, and at that place Parker became acquainted with him. On the accession of Mary, Tremellius retired to the continent, and at the date of this letter was professor of Hebrew at Heidelberg.]

[3 Note by the archbishop: *rec.* 20 *Novemb.* 1568.]

The revision of the English Bible completed.

So after much toil of the printer, and some labours taken of some parties for the setting out and recognising of the English Bible, we be now come to a conclusion for the substance of the book. Some ornaments of the same be yet lacking; praying your honour to bear in patience till it be fully ready.

The archbishop means to present the first copy to the Queen as soon as he hears she has come to Hampton Court.

I do mean, by God's grace, if my health will serve me better than it is at this time, to present the Queen's Highness with the first, as soon as I can hear her Majesty to be come to Hampton Court, which we hear will be within eight or nine days, which God prosper, and send to your honour grace and health as I wish to myself. From my house at Lambeth, this 22nd of September.

Your honour's loving friend,
MATTH. CANT.

To the right honourable Sir William Cecil, knight, principal secretary to the Queen's Majesty. At the Court.

CCLVII.

ARCHBISHOP PARKER TO SIR WILLIAM CECIL.

5th October, [1568]. S. P. O. Domestic. Orig.

SIR,

Parker's health is such, that he dare not adventure to present the new edition of the Bible to the Queen:

AFTER my right hearty commendations; I was in purpose to have offered to the Queen's Highness the first-fruits of our labours in the recognising the Bible, but I feel my health to be such that as yet I dare not adventure. Whereupon for that I would not have the Queen's Highness and your honour to be long delayed, nor the poor printer, after his great charges, to be longer deferred, I have caused one book to be bound as ye see, which I heartily pray you to present favourably to the Queen's Majesty, with your friendly excuse of my disability in not coming myself.

he therefore sends a copy for Cecil to present,

with a letter to the Queen, of which he sends a copy

I have also written to the Queen's Majesty, the copy whereof I have sent you[1], the rather to use your opportunity of delivery, if your prudence shall not think them tolerable.

He also sends a note of those who

And because I would you knew all, I here send you a note to signify who first travailed in the divers books[2],

[1 The letter inclosed is printed No. CCLVIII. p. 337.]
[2 The following is the List of the Revisers of the several books

though after them some other perusing was had; the letters *first travailed in the several* of their names be partly affixed in the end of their books; *books,*

inclosed in this letter, and still remaining with it in the State Paper Office:

The sum of the Scripture . . .⎫
The Tables of Christ's line . .⎪
The Argument of the Scriptures .⎬ M. Cant. [Abp Parker.]
The first Preface into the whole Bible⎪
The Preface into the Psalter . .⎪
The Preface into the New Testament⎭

Genesis⎱ M. Cant. [Abp Parker.]
Exodus⎰

Leviticus⎱ Cantuariæ. [? Andrew Pierson, prebend of Can-
Numerus⎰ terbury.]

Deuteronomium} W. Exon. [Bp Alley.]

Josuæ⎫
Judicum⎪
Ruth⎬ R. Meneven. [Bp Davies.]
Regum, 1, 2.⎭

Regum, 3, 4.⎱ Ed. Wigorn. [Bp Sandys.]
Paralipomenon, 1, 2.⎰

Job .⎱ Cantuariæ. [?Andrew Pierson, prebend of Can-
Proverbia⎰ terbury.]

Ecclesiastes⎱ Cantabrigiæ. [Andrew Perne, Master of Peter-
Cantica .⎰ House, and dean of Ely.]

Ecclesiasticus⎫
Susanna . .⎬ J. Norwic. [Bp Parkhurst.]
Baruc . .⎪
Maccabeorum⎭

Esdras .⎫
Judith . .⎬ W. Cicestren. [Bp Barlow.]
Tobias .⎪
Sapientia .⎭

Esaias . .⎫
Hierimias .⎬ R. Winton. [Bp Horne.]
Lamentationes⎭

Ezechiel⎱ J. Lich. and Covent. [Bp Bentham.]
Daniel⎰

Prophetæ⎱ Ed. London. [Bp Grindal.]
minores⎰

Matthæus⎱ M. Cant. [Abp Parker.]
Marcus⎰

Lucas⎱ Ed. Peterb. [Bp Scambler.]
Johannes⎰

Though after them there was some other perus-ing. With the ob-servations in his first letters sent to the revisers by Cecil's ad-vice.

which I thought a policy to show them, to make them more diligent, as answerable for their doings. I have remembered you of such observations as my first letters sent to them (by your advice) did signify[1]. It may be that in so long a work things have scaped, which may be lawful to every man, *cum bona venia,* to amend when they find them; *non omnia*

Acta Apostolorum ⎱ R. Eliensis. [Bp Cox.]
Ad Romanos . . ⎰

1 Epistola Corin. } D. Westmon. [Dr Gabriel Goodman.]

2 Epistola Corin.
Ad Galatas . .
Ad Ephesios .
Ad Philippenses.
Ad Collossenses
Ad Thessalon. .   } M. Cant. [Abp Parker.]
Ad Timotheum .
Ad Titum . .
Ad Philemon .
Ad Hebreos . .

Epistolæ Canonicæ ⎱ N. Lincoln. [Bp Bullingham.]
Apocalipsis . . ⎰

This list does not entirely agree with the letters of their names partly affixed "by the revisers" at the end of their books. Those letters are as follows: At the end of Deuteronomy, W. E. ; of the Second Book of Samuel, R. M. ; of the Second Book of Chronicles, E. W.; of Job, A. P. C.; of Psalms, omitted in the archbishop's enumeration just printed, T. B.; of Proverbs, A. P. C. ; of Song of Solomon, A. P. E. ; of Jeremiah, R. W. ; of Daniel, T. C. L. ; of Malachi, E. L. ; of the Second Book of Maccabees, J. N.; of the Acts of the Apostles, R. E. ; of Romans, R. E. ; of 1st Corinthians, G.G.]

[1 Observations respected of the translators:

First, to follow the common English translation used in the churches, and not to recede from it but where it varieth manifestly from the Hebrew or Greek original.

Item, to use sections and divisions in the texts as Pagnine in his translation useth, and for the verity of the Hebrew to follow the said Pagnine and Munster specially, and generally others learned in the tongues.

Item, to make no bitter notes upon any text, or yet to set down any determination in places of controversy.

Item, to note such chapters and places as contain matter of genealogies, or other such places not edifying, with some strike or note, that the reader may eschew them in his public reading.

Item, that all such words as sound in the old translation to any

possumus omnes. The printer hath honestly done his diligence; if your honour would obtain of the Queen's Highness that this edition might be licensed and only commended in public reading in churches, to draw to one uniformity, it were no great cost to the most parishes, and a relief to him for his great charges sustained. The psalters might remain in quires, as they be much multiplied, but where of their own accord they would use this translation.

<small>The printer should have a licence for the sole sale of this edition, which should be commended for reading in churches.</small>

Sir, I pray your honour be a mean that Jugge only may have the preferment of this edition; for if any other should lurch him to steal from him these copies, he were a great loser in this first doing. And, sir, without doubt he hath well deserved to be preferred: a man would not think that he had devoured so much pain as he hath sustained. Thus I wish your honour all grace, virtue, and health, as to myself. From my house at Lambeth, this fifth of October.

<small>Jugge only ought to have "the preferment of this edition"</small>

Your honour's loving friend,
MATTHUE CANTUAR.

To the right honourable Sir William Cecil, knight, principal secretary to the Queen's Majesty, and one of her privy council, be it delivered.

CCLVIII.

ARCHBISHOP PARKER TO QUEEN ELIZABETH.

[5th October, 1568.] S. P. O. Domestic. Copy inclosed in the preceding.

After my most lowly submission to your Majesty, with my hearty rejoice of your prosperous progress and return. Pleaseth it your Highness to accept in good part the endeavour and diligence of some of us your chaplains, my brethren the bishops, with other certain learned men, in this new edition of the Bible. I trust by comparison of divers translations put forth in your realm, will appear as well the workmanship of

<small>Presents to her Majesty the new edition of the Bible.</small>

offence of lightness or obscenity, be expressed with more convenient terms and phrases.

The printer hath bestowed his thickest paper in the New Testament, because it shall be most occupied.]

Workmanship of the printer and circumspection of the revisers.

the printer, as the circumspection of all such as have travailed in the recognition. Among divers observations which have been regarded in this recognition one was, not to make it vary much from that translation which was commonly used

No unnecessary alteration.

by public order, except where either the verity of the Hebrew and Greek moved alteration, or where the text was, by some negligence, mutilated from the original. So that I trust your loving subjects shall see good cause in your Majesty's days to thank God and to rejoice, to see this high treasure of his holy word so set out as may be proved (so far forth as mortal man's knowledge can attain to, or as far forth as God

Prays that it may be licensed for reading in churches.

hath hitherto revealed) to be faithfully handled in the vulgar tongue; beseeching your Highness that it may have your gracious favour, licence, and protection, to be communicated abroad, as well for that in many churches they want their books and have long time looked for this, as for that in certain places be publicly used some translations which have not been laboured in your realm, having inspersed divers prejudi-

Parker's additions.

cial notes, which might have been also well spared. I have been bold in the furniture with few words to express the incomparable value of this treasure. Among many things

This only a necessary treasure.

good, profitable, and beautiful ye have in possession, yet this only necessary; whereof so to think and so to believe maketh your Majesty blessed, not only here in this your governance, but it shall advance your Majesty to attain at the last the bliss everlasting, which after a long prosperous reign over us, Almighty God send you, as certainly He will, for cherishing that jewel which He loveth best, of which is pronounced that, *Quomodocunque cœlum et terra transibunt, Verbum tamen Domini manebit in eternum.* God preserve your Highness in all grace and felicity.

CCLIX.

ARCHBISHOP PARKER TO MR SERJEANT MANWOOD[1].

Probably 1568. Parker MSS. C. C. Coll. Camb. cxiv. art. 279. p. 769.

AFTER my hearty commendations. To the answer of

[1 Manwood was appointed serjeant on 23rd April, 1567. His letter, to which this is an answer, bears date 4th January.]

your letters[2] I would now pray you to refer the gift of this benefice, after my first gratifying to your request, to my own disposition. I would some such a one as might do more good in that quarter. I was deceived in that lease confirming, which were meet to be dissolved, if law would bear it[3]. Declines an application for the gift of a benefice to a particular person. Wishes one who would do more good.

If you will gratify (as of your own procuring) your usher and there presently to dwell, I shall be content.

And thus wishing you many good years, I leave you to God.

To my worshipful friend
Mr Serjeant Manwood.

CCLX.

ANTONIUS CORRANUS TO ARCHBISHOP PARKER.

16th January, 1568–9. Parker MSS. C. C. Coll. Camb. cxiv. art. 334. p. 935.

S. P. per Christum unicum servatorem, &c.

INTELLEXI, presul præstantissime, liberos tuos discere Gallicum idioma, studium certe generosa juventute dignum, præsertim hoc nostro tempore quo sæpe sæpius cum exteris hominibus versari coguntur; etiam illi qui a negotiis maxime abhorrent. Hanc ob causam illis mitto duos libellos[4] Gallico Has understood that Parker's children learn French,

[2] The letter alluded to is in Parker MS. cxiv. art. 278. p. 767. It is a request from Serjeant, afterwards Lord Chief Baron, Manwood—the same person who is mentioned before (p. 187) in connection with his foundation of Sandwich School—for the living of Old Romney, in Kent, to be given to Nicholas Jones, his brother's son-in-law, for whom he had asked it on the last occasion of its being void, but had been refused on the ground that his relative was neither in holy orders nor of any University. He hopes now for better success because Jones has been for two years studying at Cambridge.]

[3 Serjeant Manwood in his letter says: "The thing is by lease conferred by your grace, let out for seven years, or thereabout, to come, at the clear yearly rent of £10."]

[4 The books alluded to were: "Epistre et amiable Remonstrance d'un Ministre de l'Evangile de notre redempteur Jesus Christ envoyée aux Pasteurs de l'Eglise Flamengue d'Anvers, lesquelz se nomment de la Confession d'Augsbourg, les exhortant à concorde et amitié avec les autres Ministres de l'Evangile." 12mo. 1567; and "Lettre envoyée a la Maiesté du roy des Espaignes, &c. nostre sire; par laquelle un sien treshumble subject lui rend raison de son departement du Royaume d'Espaigne, et presente à sa Majesté la confession des principaux poinctz de nostre Religion Christienne: luy monstrant les griefves

he therefore sends them two French books written by him, as a thankoffering to the church at Antwerp, in which he first officiated as a minister Favour and liberality shewn to the foreign strangers by bishop Grindal

sermone a me conscriptos in gratiam Antuerpiensis ecclesiæ, in qua pastoris munere fungi cœperam, cum novæ istæ tragœdiæ exortæ fuerunt. Tu, vir præstantissime, pro tuo candore, hoc munusculum tuis liberis missum æqui bonique consules. Conveni hisce diebus D. Episcopum Londinensem, et pro sua erga me et alios peregrinos humanitate, singulis trimestribus aliquot coronatos mihi daudos statuit. Ego certe cuperem aliqua in re vobis ac vestro regno inservire posse, sed quando non datur facultas, animi propensionem atque affectum erga vos suscipietis. Servet te Deus incolumem, presul amplissime, suique Spiritus dona tibi magis ac magis adaugeat ad gloriam suam. Vale. Londini, 16 Januarii, anno 1568.

Tibi ex animo deditissimus,
ANTONIUS CORRANUS[1] HISPALLENSSIS.

Amplissimo presuli, D. archiepiscopo Cantuariensi, D. mihi plurimum observando.

CCLXI.

QUEEN ELIZABETH TO ARCHBISHOP PARKER.

17th January, 1568—9. Parker MSS. C. C. Coll. Camb. cxiv. art. 10. p. 43. Orig.

By the Queen.

Elizabeth R.

Most reverend father in God, right trusty and right well-beloved, we greet you well. Where we are informed that   [2] Newton, one of the prebendaries of

persecutions qu'endurent ses subjets du Pais bas pour maintenir la dite Religion et le moyen duquel sa Majesté pourroit user pour y remeder." 12mo. 1567.]

[1 Antonio del Corro, a learned Spaniard, preacher to the Spanish congregation in London, and afterwards divinity reader in the Temple. See Strype's Parker, Bk. III. c. xx.; Strype's Grindal, Bk. I. c. xiii.; Wood's Athenæ, ed. Bliss, I. 578; and a letter of Parker, dated 17 March, 1574—5, printed hereafter.]

[2 A blank is left here in the MS. The Christian name of the deceased prebendary was Theodore. Strype's Parker, Bk. II. c. ii. Among the Parker MSS. cxiv. art. 11. p. 45, is a letter from lord Leicester which relates to this transaction. It appears that the deceased and the dean of Winchester were brothers of Frances, wife of William Brook, lord Cobham, and that the new arrangement was

that our cathedral church of Canterbury, is lately departed out of this world to God's mercy, we let you wete that for certain considerations us specially moving, we have resolved to bestow the said prebend now void upon our well-beloved doctor Newton, now dean of Winchester, and brother to the late prebendary deceased. For which purpose if the same be merely of our own gift, we shall cause our presentation or other grant to be hereafter made forth in form accustomed. But in case it be in your gift and disposition, we require you to be content to bestow it upon him at this time, and for recompense thereof we are pleased, and by these our letters do promise you, that you shall have the preferment of the next prebend after this that shall happen to fall void there of our gift, to bestow upon whom you will. Given under our signet, at our honour of Hampton Court, the 17th day of January, the 11th year of our reign, 1568.

A prebendary of Canterbury, named Newton, being dead, the Queen has resolved to bestow his prebend upon Dr Newton, dean of Winchester. If it be in the Queen's gift, a presentation will be made in form accustomed; if in Parker's, he is required to bestow it upon Dr Newton, on a promise of having the Queen's next presentation that shall fall void.

*To the most reverend father in God our
right trusty and right well-beloved
the archbishop of Canterbury, metropolitan of all England.*

CCLXII.

ARCHBISHOP PARKER TO SIR WILLIAM CECIL.

22nd February, [1568—9]. S. P. O. Domestic. Orig.

Sir,

This poor plain man cometh to me and signifieth, that by the counsel of a stranger whom he hath kept in his house, and by his own cost and industry, [he] hath found out the making of brimstone, whereof he bringeth an assay; and saith further that the stuff where he gathereth it, on the shore of Whitstable, is so fat, that it will yield so well that it will rise to a good commodity, and nothing so chargeable as hath been somewhere proved to be. I thought it good to send him first to your honour to understand the cause; praying you to deal

Parker sends to Cecil a poor man, who has discovered the making of brimstone from stuff gathered on the shore at Whitstable.

made by the Queen "at the suit of lady Cobham," and was urged upon Parker by lord Leicester as an opportunity of pleasing not only the Queen, but lady Cobham, and "sundry the friends and kinsfolks" of the dean.]

with the simple man, that he may be well relieved for his truth. Thus I commit your honour to God's tuition as myself. From my house, this 22nd of February.

Your honour's alway,
MATTHUE CANTUAR.

To the right honourable Sir William Cecil, knight, principal secretary to the Queen's Majesty, and of her privy council.

CCLXIII.
ARCHBISHOP PARKER TO THE BAILIFFS OF LYDD.
25th March, [1569]. Gent. Mag. Vol. LXXIV., p. 1190, from Orig. then in the possession of Robert Cobb, Esq., of Lydd.

Dr Hardiman, vicar of Lydd, is to be required to depart the town, and if he is troublesome, to be apprehended and brought to Parker.

WHEREAS I understand that Dr Hardiman is yet among you, by whose behaviour as you have been much slandered and evil edified[1], so I doubt of his quietness to ensue among the parishioners there; whereupon this is to require you to command him immediately to depart your town, and not to make his resort thither to the further disquiet of the town. And if you, Mr Bailiff, shall perceive any trouble by him, I require you, in the Queen's Majesty's name, to apprehend him, and cause him to be brought hither to make his answer. Seeing that he hath dishonoured God, and abused his vocation, and hath much misused my favour long borne to him, specially in respect to the commodities and profits of you all,

[[1] In the same place whence this letter has been derived, there is a long letter from the "bailiffs, jurats, commons, churchwardens, and sworn sidesmen" of Lydd, appealing to the archbishop in reference to "the evil disposition, lewd behaviour, and ungodly incontinent life of John Hardyman," D.D., their vicar. They accuse him "first and principally" with having "denied his wife (whom he daily keepeth) to be his own wife, but hath said she is the wife of one John, late his man," and that he married her for fear of Parker's displeasure. There were other charges of personal incontinency and profligacy. This letter of the bailiffs and jurats is said to have been dated in August, 1568. It does not appear what immediate notice Parker took of their application.]

being my neighbours and of my diocese, I account him worthy of no further toleration. And thus I bid you well.

From my house at Lambeth, this 25th of March.

Your loving friend,

MATHUE CANTUAR.

To my loving friends, Mr Bailiff of the town of Lydd, and to the Jurats of the same.

CCLXIV.

ARCHBISHOP PARKER AND OTHER ECCLESIASTICAL COMMISSIONERS TO SIR WILLIAM CECIL.

13th April, 1569[2]. Lansd. MS. x. art. 48.

SIR,

THE last term informations were given unto us, as commissioners to the Queen's Highness for causes ecclesiastical, of divers misdemeanours as well in manners as in doctrine in the society of Benet College, alias Corpus Christi in Cambridge; for examination whereof we directed our letters of commission to the Vice-chancellor and some others the heads of the University; who then seemed somewhat to stay the execution of our said commission, fearing (as they said) to prejudice their privileges; whereupon Mr Vice-chancellor sent his letters by their bedell to you, whom then it pleased therein to be informed by our opinions, which then we signified unto you by our letters, the copy whereof, word by word, is herein inclosed[3], which as resolution you returned to

Information given to the ecclesiastical commissioners of disorders in Corpus Christi College, Cambridge.

They issued a commission to visit, the lawfulness of which was doubted.

[2 The date of 13th April, 1568 is assigned in a contemporary indorsement, but it appears from the inclosure that the letter was written shortly after the 4th January, 1568—9.]

[3 The inclosure runs as follows: "It may please you to be advertised, that our opinion is, that the Queen's Majesty's commission for causes ecclesiastical doth extend and may be executed upon persons resiant within either of the Universities, or within any other privileged place within the realm, by virtue of the words 'in places as well exempt as not exempt.' And that the Vice-chancellor of the University of Cambridge, and others which are joined with him in commission from the commissioners here, may safely, without prejudice of the liberties of the same University, proceed to the execution of the said commission. Yet, notwithstanding, we think it not amiss, for avoid-

the Vice-chancellor by the bedell. Afterward, we having intelligence that the Vice-chancellor proceeded not to the execution of our said commission, we revoked the same, and advocated the said cause to our own examination; to the debating whereof the most part of the said society, being parties to the said matter, voluntarily appeared at Lambeth and submitted themselves to be ordered. One Stallard, Bachelor of Art, and principal party in the said business, remaining still at Cambridge, we sent for, by our letters and commandment, the execution of the which our commandment the Vice-chancellor stayed, commanding the said Stallard not to appear before us, and withal withstood a search for suspected books by us decreed to be made in the said College, removing such as we had appointed for the same, and caused a search to be by such and in such manner as he devised, unsealing the door that we for that purpose caused to be sealed; which his doings the said Vice-chancellor answereth by his letters, alleging it never heard that any extraordinary and foreign authority had intermeddled to call any from the University; which his doings, and terms, we marvel not a little at, having in fresh memory our continual proceedings in this commission since the first time of it, and that we have from time to time called, as occasion served, out of both the Universities, and have had always to this present, appearance, humbly, without any denial or contradiction, and have done therein (as we trust) good service to God, the Queen, and the realm, removing by authority of our said commission, out of both Universities, divers stubborn papists, and head adversaries of God's true religion, to the number of forty and more, and some of them sent to us by order of the privy council, as may appear by our records.

ing all scruples, that the said Vice-chancellor and the others associate with him do declare by protestation, that their meaning in the executing of the said commission is not to prejudice any the liberties of the said University, but only to shew their obedience unto the authority of the Queen's Highness committed to the said commissioners. From Lambeth, this fourth of January, 1568. MATTH. CANTUAR. EDMUND LONDON. THO. YALE. THO. WATTES.

To the right honourable Sir William Cecil, knight, one of the Queen's Majesty's privy council, and Chancellor of the University of Cambridge.]

The denial of which authority now, after so long time, in the Universities, we take it too much to prejudice the credit of our said former doings, and to derogate the authority of the Queen's Highness' commission committed unto us by authority of parliament; yet for that the Vice-chancellor for his year and time is your deputy, before any ways we call him in question for his doings, we thought it convenient to make your honour privy thereof, and to expect your further mind herein at our next meeting, which we hope shall be upon Monday next at Lambeth. And thus we commend you to Almighty God.

       MATTHUE CANTUAR.
       EDM. LONDON.
       THOMAS YALE.
       WILLM. DRURYE.

To the right honourable Sir William Cecil, knight, one of the Queen's Majesty's privy council, and Chancellor of the University of Cambridge.

CCLXV.

ARCHBISHOP PARKER TO BISHOP GRINDAL OF LONDON.

6th May, 1569. Parker Reg. I. fol. 278 a.

AFTER my hearty commendations unto your good lordship premised. I have of late received (as your lordship knoweth) commandment from the Queen's Highness, and her honourable privy council, to take order for a certain view to be had, and with speed certified, of armour to be provided by the clergy of the province of Canterbury, according to the proportion and rate prescribed and used in the time of the reign of the late King and Queen, King Philip and Queen Mary, which rate and proportion is to these letters in a schedule annexed[1]; these are to will and require your lord-

The archbishop has received commandment for a view to be had of the armour provided by the clergy, according to the annexed rate, prescribed in the time of Philip and Mary;

[1 The schedule was as follows:

"Whereas the lords of the Queen's Majesty's most honourable privy council have given commandment for the provision of armour and other furniture by the clergy of this realm, according to such order and rates as was used in the time of the late King Philip and

wherefore the bishop of London is required to give order for the same.

ship to give order, as well to the clergy of your own diocese, for the ready performance of the same, as also to signify the said commandment to the residue of my brethren the other bishops of my province of Canterbury, willing and commanding them, and every of them forthwith to accomplish her Highness' said commandment in every their several dioceses and jurisdictions, as to them and their bounden duties appertaineth, and the same view by them and every of them so taken according to the said rate and proportion, speedily to certify unto me at Lambeth, with the names, surnames, and promotions of all that, according to the said schedule, be chargeable with any such provision. And thus I bid your

certifying the names of persons chargeable with such provision.

Queen Mary, the several rates and order then used in that behalf are hereafter particularly specified; videlicet:

That every one of the clergy having lands, or possessions of estate of inheritage of freehold, shall provide and find, and be chargeable with, armour, horses, and other furniture, in such sort, and in manner and form, as every temporal man is charged by reason of his lands and possessions, by virtue of the statute made in the fourth and fifth years of the reigns of the late King Philip and Queen Mary.

Item, That every one of the said clergy, having benefits, spiritual promotions or pensions, the clear value whereof, either by themselves or joined together, do amount to the clear yearly value of xxx*l*. or upwards, shall be bound and charged to provide, have, and maintain armour, and other provision requisite, according to such proportion and rate, as the temporality are bound and charged by the said statute, by reason of their moveable goods.

Item, If any of the clergy of this realm have both temporal lands and possessions, and also spiritual promotions, he shall be charged with armour and other provision according to the greatest rate of one of them, and not with both.

Observations in rating of the proportion of armour.

I. First, The bishop to rate himself amongst the temporality for lands.

II. Secondly, To rate the dean and prebendaries, as the temporality, for goods from xxx*l*. upwards.

III. Item, To rate the whole diocese in like sort.

IV. Item, To account such as be resident within the diocese under the sum of xxx*l*, and yet having benefices or pensions elsewhere, to make up the same sum or upwards, to be rated there among the supplies.

V. Item, To rate every incumbent where he is resident, and every ordinary chaplain not resident, in the diocese where he serveth."

lordship most heartily well to fare as myself. From my house at Lambeth, the 6th of May, a thousand five hundred threescore and nine[1].

CCLXVI.

ARCHBISHOP PARKER TO THE DEAN AND CHAPTER OF YORK.

16th May, 1569. Parker Reg. I. fol. 278 b.

AFTER my most hearty commendations premised. Whereas in the time of the late King Philip and Queen Mary there was a certain proportion and rate prescribed and used, for armour to be found and maintained by the clergy of this realm of England, which rate and proportion is mentioned and described in a schedule therein inclosed, I have of late received commandment from the Queen's Majesty and her honourable privy council, for a certain view to be had, and with speed certified, of the said armour to be provided by the clergy of my province of Canterbury according to the rate and proportion contained in the schedule above mentioned; wherein like as I have given order for the due and speedy accomplishment of the Queen's Majesty's said commandment throughout my province, so I thought convenient to give you advertisement thereof; wishing you to have due regard for the like view to be had, and with all convenient speed certified, throughout the province of York, where you have charge and jurisdiction during the vacation of the archiepiscopal see there; and the same view so taken to certify to the honourable privy council with speed convenient. And thus I bid you most heartily well to fare. From my house at Lambeth, the 16th of May, 1569.

In time of Philip and Mary, a proportion prescribed for armour to be maintained by the clergy.

The archbishop has received commandment for a view of the said armour within his province.

Having given order for the same, he recommends the dean and chapter, the archbishoprick being vacant, to do the same for the province of York,

and to certify to the privy council.

[1 A similar letter, without the schedule annexed, was addressed by the archbishop to the commissary general of the diocese of Chichester, dated the 19th May, 1569. Park. Reg. I. 193 a.]

CCLXVII.

ARCHBISHOP PARKER TO SIR WILLIAM CECIL.

18th May, [1569]. Lansd. MS. xi. art. 54. Orig.

SIR,

Godfrey's account of benefices taxable to armour.

I HAVE perused Godfrey's book for benefices of xxx *li.* and upward taxable to the provision of armour; the rate is of small importance to that which shall be certified from every ordinary, beside that it is in many respects imperfect. For some taste I send your honour a view of mine own diocese, which is like to be my certificate; some considerations I have added, to express what is to be followed, and have sent to some of my brethren (where I think it will be taken) some copies for their better expedition, not as prejudicing their own inventions, but shewing mine if they like it: if any thing were to be further considered, if you inform me I shall follow it.

Lever complains of the state of Sherborne Hospital.

Mr Lever[1] sheweth his grief in the evil ordering of the house: it were pity that the church, being so far off, should yet be out of good order. He saith that he hath complained to the bishop, but it is not considered. Thus I wish your honour God's grace as to myself. From my house, this 18th of May.

Your honour's alway,

MATTH. CANT.

To the right honourable Sir William Cecil, knight, principal secretary to the Queen's Majesty.

CCLXVIII.

ARCHBISHOP PARKER AND BISHOP GRINDAL OF LONDON TO THE VICE-CHANCELLOR AND HEADS OF HOUSES AT CAMBRIDGE.

20th May, 1569. Strype's Annals, I. ii. 86, on the authority of Rev. T. Baker, B.D.

Understanding the affection of the University to

UNDERSTANDING of the good and godly affection that divers of your University bear to the knowledge of the He-

[1 Thomas Lever, the celebrated preacher. Notwithstanding his nonconformity he retained the mastership of Sherborne Hospital until his death. The bishop to whom complaint was made was Pilkington.]

brew tongue, wherein originally for the more part was written the word of God; to the gratifying of the same, as we have in our former letters commended our trusty and well-beloved Rodolphus Cavallerius, otherwise called Mr Anthony, so now we send him unto you; a man whom we have aforetime not only known in the same University[2], but also have seen good testimony of his learning in the said tongue; and having more experience of his good zeal to exercise his said talent toward all such as be desirous to be partakers of the same; whereupon this is to pray and require you to accept him as his worthiness for his learning and diligence, as we trust, shall deserve; whereby you shall not only yourselves receive the fruit to your own commendations, but also give us occasion to devise for your further commodity, as Almighty God shall move us, and our ability upon any occasion shall further hereafter serve. And thus wishing to you the grace of God to direct your studies to his glory and to the profit of the commonwealth, we bid you all heartily well to fare. From Lambeth, this 20th of May.

the knowledge of Hebrew,

the archbishop and bishop send them Rodolphus Cavallerius,

praying them to accept him as his learning and diligence shall deserve.

Your loving friends,
MATTHUE CANTUAR.
EDM. LONDON.

To our loving friends Mr Vice-chancellor of Cambridge, and the heads of the same.

[2 Anthony Rodolph le Chevalier, the person alluded to, was a French protestant, celebrated for his knowledge of Hebrew. He came to England several times as a refugee. On the first occasion, which was during the reign of Edward VI., he taught Hebrew at Cambridge, and was also French tutor to the princess, afterwards Queen, Elizabeth. This letter refers to the period of his second residence in England. In consequence of the recommendation contained in it, he appears to have been again appointed to teach Hebrew at Cambridge. There we find him on the 5th of September, 1569, on which day he wrote a letter (which is preserved, Parker MS. CXIX. art. 87. p. 243) to the archbishop, complaining amongst other things of his stipend being diminished. He shortly afterwards returned to his native country; but escaping a third time, on the occasion of the massacre of St Bartholomew, he died at Guernsey, when again on his way to England, in 1572.]

CCLXIX.

ARCHBISHOP PARKER TO SIR WILLIAM CECIL.

3rd June, [1569]. Lansd. MS. xi. art. 57. Orig.

SIR,

The Queen purposes to supply the vacant bishopricks

IN mine opinion the Queen's Majesty hath done graciously to purpose to furnish the places now vacant of her watchmen; the times be dangerous, and require prudent, speedy, and vigilant foresight. Once at the request of my lord of Leicester, when the Queen's Majesty was at Hampton Court, I tituled to him my phantasy, from the which I do not much disagree at this time, except that where I doubted how

Aylmer recommended for London

Mr Aylmer could be accepted, I passed him over; but I think certainly the Queen's Highness should have a good, fast, earnest servitor at London of him, and, I doubt not, fit for that busy governance, specially as these times be, when papists (the Queen's mortal enemies, pretend what men will) have

Bishop Grindal for York

gotten such courage; and I think my lord of London as fit for York, a heady and stout people, witty but yet able to be dealt with by good governance, as long as laws can be executed and men backed. If the Queen's Highness and her realm will be well served she must bear with some manners

Men cannot be angels, but the clergy are disciplinable, and soon reformed.

of men; men cannot be angels; and yet I trust disciplinable, and soon reformed (I speak of our sort), if they be reasonably considered of in themselves, and not by others' gay reports, for the most part unanswered. If it were sufficient to accuse, who should be innocent? To discourse particularly the cause of my judgment toward these other parties, it were too long; but, generally, for that I think them meet in such considerations as move me, but as the Queen's Majesty shall allow in

Mr Curteys does better at court. Mean chaplains hardly thought of.

them all. Mr Curteys might do better to be nigher to serve the court, than as yet to be removed far; it is hardly thought of, so mean chaplains to be toward the prince &c. Thus I cease, commending your honour to God's tuition, with my most humble acknowledging my duty of commending the Queen's Majesty to God in my prayers. From Croydon, this 3rd of June.

Your honour's always,

MATTHUE CANTUAR.

To the right honourable Sir William Cecil, knight, principal secretary to the Queen's Majesty, and one of her privy council.

CCLXX.

ARCHBISHOP PARKER TO SIR WILLIAM CECIL.

1st July, 1569. Lansd. MS. XI. art. 59. Orig.

SIR,

WHEREAS this other day at the Arches a question was moved, whether Mr Tilney might be dispensed with, and doubt was made who might do it, your honour saying that the Queen's Majesty may do as much as the pope, and saying further, that I might do it, and why not the Queen &c.? *On a question upon a dispensation, the secretary said the Queen might do as much as the pope; the archbishop might dispense.*

For that your honour should not mistake my words, either to arrogate to myself above my measure, or to derogate the Queen's Majesty's authority, which in all respects, as God and laws may bear, I would as well have defended as I would wish mine own life regarded, whereupon I thought good to put to your consideration (privately) some of my cogitations. I will not dispute of the Queen's absolute power, or prerogative royal, how far her Highness may do in following the Roman authority, but I yet doubt, that if any dispensation should pass from her authority to any subject, not advouchable by laws of her realm made and stablished by herself and her three estates, whether that subject be in surety at all times for afterward: specially seeing that there be parliament laws precisely determining causes of dispensations. Wherein, *Why not the Queen?* *Parker doubts whether if a royal dispensation pass to a subject in any case not warranted by law, the subject be secure at all times.* as I have heard say, King Henry himself did use that authority in some of his own private causes. The prince may dispense *in omnibus casibus insolitis*, where the archbishop's authority is shut up by the words of the statute. If these cases had their right course, the prince may grant them, but yet by a warrant to the office of Faculties, under that law to pass. And whereas somebody may say, that the bishop of Canterbury can dispense, I think for myself, I take some heed not to extend my sleeve beyond mine arm, nor to use much ready talk *in medio magnatorum*, which make me to sit sometime mute and hear others; and yet I think to this day I have not absolutely granted any *casus insolitus*, if they be weighed, but leave them to my prince, as I ought. It is one thing to discuss what is done, in order or out of order, and commonly hand over head, and what is safely and surely done by warrant of law. During the prince's life who will doubt of anything that may pass from that authority? But the question *Parker is careful not to extend his sleeve beyond his arm.* *During the prince's life who will doubt of any*

is, what will stand sure in all times, by the judgment of the best learned? And here I am offended with some lawyers, who make the Injunctions of the prince in her own life not to be of such force as they make a Roman law written in the same or like case; *exempli causa,* I urge the Injunction upon all ministers, when their case come in question, whether they be capable of any ecclesiastical living, if they marry not in such due form as yet I think is godly prescribed, specially if the words of the Injunction (which were once a disjunctive but by the printer made a copulative, *viz.* that the parties marriable must be so allowed by two justices of the peace or [and] by the ordinary). It is said to me, that the omission or contempt of this maketh them not incapable. Marry if there be any Roman law that forceth deprivation, then is the danger seen, but not afore.

Sir, I think these lawyers keep but their old trade, and not regard much the imperial laws of the prince, and yet these new cases of marrying have no other direction in law beforetimes, but by Injunction for this present time. But I enter now a sea of perplexities, and give your honour occasion to think in such emergents, and thereby to pray you to take in good part and plain sense, that I did bluntly speak this other day to you before my lord-keeper, as, at that sudden, wanting time and place to have opened further my mind; and in such narrow points to tread in, I am ready to be informed to judge otherwise, if I may see reason and learning to lead me.

I think I make you weary. God keep you in all grace as myself. From my house, this first of July.

Your honour's assuredly,

MATTHUE CANTUAR.

CCLXXI.

ARCHBISHOP PARKER TO SIR WILLIAM CECIL.

9th August, [1569.] Lansd. MS. xi. art. 62. Orig.

Sir,

I am still sued unto by the printer Binneman to entreat your honour to obtain for him a privilege for printing two or three usual books for grammarians, as Terence, Virgil, or Tully's Offices, &c. He feareth that he shall sustain great loss of his printed books of the lottery. I think he should do this thing aptly enough, and better cheap than they may be bought from beyond the seas, standing the paper and goodness of his print; and it were not amiss to set our own countrymen on work, so they would be diligent, and take good correctors. He hath brought me a little piece of his workmanship in a trial, which he desireth to be sent to your honour, to see the form and order of his print. *(printing two or three school books, which the archbishop recommends.)*

I wrote to you in my last letters to borrow, but for a week or two, your book of Matthew Paris' story. I would be loth to be importune, but I would turn it to the commodity of our own country; as for in other works every man is doing, but these are but in few men's hands, and be testimonies not to be lost, and time would be taken. *(Wishes for the loan of Matthew Paris.)*

I had thought that the Queen's Majesty would have resolved in the appointing of the vacant rooms before her progress. There cannot be too many watchmen, which Latimer was wont to say; and that there is one diligent watchman ever resident, which never ceaseth to walk about for his preys[1]. What an infamy hath he stirred now up of Cambridge, for that unnatural filthiness there too much known and blazed abroad, in this great liberty of marriage! Good men lament, the adversary laugheth. I hear that Fulke's head shall be stroken, and made master of that house, &c.[2] *(Thought the Queen would have filled up the vacant bishopricks. Latimer's sayings. Devilish works at Cambridge.)*

I am at this day occupied with all the wits I have, to persuade to Gerard Danet and his sister-german, that their contracting for man and wife, and having had two children betwixt them, and she now great with the third, that it is sin to be repented of. Thus the devil locketh up men's hearts in outrage. Before God, I know not what to do with them, and how to deal. I would I had your counsel. I examine as secretly as I can, and yet it is abroad. I have spent a whole afternoon with the sister, but all in vain. They have continned this ten or twelve years. Six year ago I thought I had won the brother in secret communication from his lewdness, and so he promised me, but it falleth out otherwise. I marvel *(Case of marriage of brother and sister-german.)*

[1 Prayes, in Orig.]
[2 See Strype's Parker, Bk. III. c. xxiii.]

of their mother. Thus this watchman the devil watcheth and wandereth, &c., to shame God's word, to shame their house, &c. God preserve your honour in all grace, and defend us all from the assaults of the enemy. From my house, this ninth of August.

Your honour's alway,

MATTH. CANT.

*To the right honourable Sir William Cecil,
knight, principal secretary to the Queen's
Majesty.*

CCLXXII.

SIR WILLIAM CECIL TO ARCHBISHOP PARKER.

24th September, 1569. Parker MSS. C. C. Coll. Camb. cxiv. art. 213. p. 577. Orig.

The Queen has solicited Parker to be favourable to Sir Henry Lee, in a cause referred to him. Cecil desires the same favour for Sir Henry Lee as his old friend, whom he heartily loves.

It may please your grace. Although I know that upon the Queen's Majesty's motion by her Majesty's favourable letters to your grace in the behalf of Sir Henry Lee, knight[1], you will shew him all manner of favour in a cause referred to your grace, that reasonably may; yet to shew to your grace how heartily I do love Sir Henry Lee for many good causes, I am bold to cause mine own letters to wait upon those of her Majesty, and do most heartily beseech your grace to let it appear by his end in this cause, that if her Majesty's letters had not provoked your favour towards him, as I know they shall, as far as reason will permit your grace, yet mine might have had such grace of commendation for him, being my dear friend, as he should think that I am in that credit with your grace, that he and others think me to be. And so assuring myself at all times, I end.

From Windsor, the 24th of September, 1569.

Your grace's at command,

W. CECILL.

[1 Sir Henry Lee, of Quarendon, in the county of Bucks, K. G., a great favourite of Queen Elizabeth.]

CCLXXIII.

THE LORDS OF THE COUNCIL TO ARCHBISHOP PARKER.
6th November, 1569. Petyt MS. Inner Temple, No. 47. fol. 48. Orig.

AFTER our very hearty commendations to your good lordship. The Queen's Majesty of late in conference with us upon the state of this her realm, among other things meet to be reformed, is moved to think, that universally in the ecclesiastical government the care and diligence, that properly belongeth to the office of bishops and other ecclesiastical prelates and pastors of this church of England, is of late years so diminished and decayed, as no small number of her subjects, partly for lack of diligent teaching and information, partly for lack of correction and reformation, are entered either into dangerous errors, or into a manner of life of contempt or liberty, without use or exercise of any rites of the church, openly forbearing to resort to their parish-churches, where they ought to use common prayers, and to learn the will of God by hearing of sermons, and consequently receive the holy sacraments. Of the increase of which lamentable disorders her Majesty conceiveth great grief and offence, and therefore hath expressly charged us to inquire the truth hereof by all good means possible, and to provide speedily for the reformation and remedy hereof. Whereupon, according to her Majesty's charge, and as we find it very requisite of our own duties, as well towards Almighty God, as to her Majesty and our country, we have entered into a further consideration hereof; and though we find a concurrency of many causes, whereupon such general disorders and contempts have of late years grown and increased, (the remedy whereof we mean to seek and procure by as many other good means as we can) yet certainly we find no one cause hereof greater, nor more manifest, than an universal oversight and negligence (for less we cannot term it) of the bishops of the realm, who have not only peculiar possessions to find, provide and maintain officers, but have also jurisdiction over all inferior ministers, pastors, and curates, by them to inquire, or be informed, of these manner of contempts and disorders, and by teaching and correction to reform them; or if the offenders should for any respect appear incorrigible, thereof to make due informa-

[margin: The Queen is moved to think that the care of bishops and pastors is so diminished, that no small number of her subjects forbear to resort to their parish-churches.]

[margin: The lords of the council, upon consideration,]

[margin: find no one cause hereof more manifest than the universal negligence of the bishops.]

tion to her Majesty, as the supreme governor under God of the whole realm. And surely though we know that some of the bishops of the realm are to be more commended than some other for preaching, teaching, and visiting of their dioceses, yea and for good hospitality and other good examples of life, yet at this time doubting that a great part of the realm in sundry places is touched with the infection of these disorders, though some more, some less, and (as we fear) no bishoprick fully free: we have therefore necessarily concluded to notify to every one of the bishops alike this her Majesty's carefulness and desire to have her realm herein reformed, and for that purpose at this present to seek the understanding of every diocese in certain points hereafter following. [And] therefore we will and require your lordship, in her Majesty's name, that first [ye will] earnestly conceive and thankfully allow of this her Majesty's godly d[isposition], and next that you do circumspectly, and as quietly as you may (with [out any] manner of proceeding likely to breed public offence), enquire, or [cause to be] enquired by such as are faithful officers and not dissemblers, what [persons] they be, and of what quality, degree, and name, that have not of late t[ime] resorted to their parish-churches within your diocese, or have not used the [common] prayers according to the laws of the realm, or have not at [usual] times received the holy sacrament; and how long they have [forborne]. And further also we require to be advertised, what ecclesiastical public officers you have under your lordship in your diocese, who they be, what their names and degrees, ordained to see to the execution of the laws and orders of the church. Likewise what preachers you have properly for the more part conversant with yourself in household, and what other preachers residing abroad in your diocese, and what ecclesiastical livings every of them hath, with the values thereof, or what other stipends they have, wherewith they have any maintenance or sustentation to continue in their functions. Likewise, we require you by authority of these our letters to confer with the dean and chapter of your cathedral church, and with the heads of any other collegiate church in your diocese, or with any other persons having any peculiar jurisdiction within your diocese, and cause them to certify distinctly by writing, what number of prebendaries, canons, and preachers they have which do reside within the said churches and jurisdictions, and how many do not reside, and how many of them do use and not use to preach, and what be their names and degrees, and in like sort the names and degrees of them that have any sustentation in their churches to preach, and yet do not reside nor do preach. And likewise we desire to be advertised what churches or places ordained to have common prayer, are by any means presently void of curates, and in whose default the same happeneth, and in what sort you think the same may be best remedied. And whilst you shall be occupied in the inquisition hereof, wherein we would have you use all good diligence, we heartily and earnestly require your lordship, as you will be accounted worthy of your calling, to employ all your care and industry in procuring more diligent preaching and teaching within your diocese, as well by yourself as by all others having the gift to preach, and therein to use all charitable means by diligent instruction and faithful teaching and example of life, to stay the good, faithful and obedient subjects in their duties, and to induce and persuade others to return from their disorders and errors, so as all parties may observe their duties in the public and open service of Almighty God according to his ordinance, and as by the common order of the realm is for God's honour established. And whatsoever your lordship shall think meet and needful to be granted or devised for your further assistance, thereof to advertise us, whom you shall find ready to aid and satisfy you as far forth as we shall find in our powers reasonable, either by ourselves or by means to her Majesty, whom we perceive earnestly disposed to have the glory of God increase, by the due reverence of all her subjects in his service, according to his blessed word and commandment. And thus we bid your good lordship well to fare. From Windsor, the 6th of November, 1569.

What number of prebendaries, canons, and preachers, in Cathedral and collegiate churches.

What churches are void of curates, and by whose default.

The archbishop to use all care in procuring more diligent preaching.

And what he thinks necessary for his further assistance therein, to advertise the council, who will aid to their power.

Your lordship's loving friends,

N. BACON, C. S.   W. HOWARD.
F. BEDFORD.   R. SADLER.
E. CLYNTON.   F. KNOLLYS.
W. NORTHT.   WA. MILDMAY.
R. LEYCESTER.   W. CECILL.

Postscript. We pray your lordship not to delay the answering to us with speed the names of the recusants to come to church, without delaying for the rest, and to procure the like certificates of these matters from the bishopricks of Chichester and Oxford now vacant, and to that end to send them a copy of these our letters, with special charge to see the same accomplished.

CCLXXIV.

ARCHBISHOP PARKER TO SIR WILLIAM CECIL.

8th March, [1569—70]. Lansd MS. xii. art. 35. *Orig.*

SIR,

Dr Porey desires to resign his prebend at Westminster to Mr Aldrich, his successor in the mastership of Corpus Christi College, Cambridge, which the archbishop recommends.

WHERE I have this two or three years moved Dr Porey to resign up his mastership, whom I found always very loth so to do, yet with calling on I so persuaded him since Christmas, that he was content, and went down to that effect, looking that he should have returned again to Lambeth, &c. I perceive now that his joy is gone, and maketh means to resign up all his livings, as well Westminster as Lambeth, having no more, and seemeth to be content (as by his letters to me) he would resign up Westminster prebend to his successor in his mastership at Cambridge, Mr Aldrich, senior proctor, whom I know to be an honest young man, learned in all the tongues, and also in French and Italian, and is I trust like to do service in the realm hereafter; whereupon if it would please your honour to prefer this resignation to the Queen's Majesty with favour, I doubt not but it should be well bestowed. I have

He has also sent to lady Stafford to speak a good word, if Cecil approves.

sent to my lady Stafford, that if your honour shall like of it, she may also for the love of her son, who is in that College, speak some good word, but yet not without your favour and contentation. I have been judged to look to be his executor, as though I stayed him in his mastership in hope of such expectation. The truth is, he is but a poor man, and in good faith I look not to be advantaged five shillings by him, nor shall be either his executor or supervisor, if God should take him to his mercy; but he may live and spend all he hath as far as I know. Thus the Lord preserve you in all grace and goodness. From my house at Lambeth, this 8th of March.

Your honour's always in Christ,
MATTHUE CANTUAR.

To the right honourable Sir William Cecil, knight, principal secretary to the Queen's Majesty.

CCLXXV.

ARCHBISHOP PARKER TO SIR WILLIAM CECIL.

30th March, [1570]. Lansd. MS. LXIII. art. 80.

WHEREAS your honour wrote to me your thanks for Sir Henry Lee[1], I have to give you thanks for your gentle acceptation of my good will. When the Queen's Majesty wrote to me in his favour, and your honour followed in the same request, I could no less do, of duty to her Highness and of humanity towards you, [than?] to do as I have done; and yet ye may be sure not against justice (I trust), nor against my conscience; only supplying by equity where extremity of law might have moved matter, &c. *(Sir William Cecil had thanked the archbishop for some favour conferred on Sir Henry Lee.)*

Where your honour writeth to me to have mine opinion for the successor of my lord of London[2], although I have boldly written my judgment, yet at this present I think this: that her Majesty can have none of such as be in place of bishops to begin new game again for fees and fruits, and therefore I think, except it were the bishop of Hereford[3], in respect for changing one misery for another, else he or any other would not take it; for as the poet saith, *Negotiorum vim qui sibi velit comparare, navem (Londinensem), &c. Hæc duo comparate.* Beside that most of them be not fit for that place. For though many of them be too weak to *(Successor to the bishop of London. No bishop will take it except the bishop of Hereford. Nor is any one of them fit for that station.)*

[1 See Letter CCLXXII. p. 354.]
[2 Bishop Grindal was elected archbishop of York 11th April, 1570. His promotion had no doubt been determined upon before the date of this letter.]
[3 Bishop John Scory, 1559—1585.]

use themselves in such popularity, yet I think divers of them not to be able to use their place and the time, with their easiness of nature, as were convenient. Although, surely, sir, I must needs say of them, they be as notably well learned and well occupied as any prince in Europe hath. As for the dean of York[1], whom I take to be a very honest, quiet, and learned man, so I think him not meet for that place. As for Mr Provost of Eton[2], in all respects I think him meetest for that room, and I think the Londoners would take him better than the dean of Westminster[3], whom though I judge to be a sad grave man, yet in his own private judgment peradventure too severe.

<small>Dean of York not meet.</small>

<small>Provost of Eton the meetest.</small>

<small>Dean of Westminster too severe.</small>

As for Oxford bishoprick, Mr Cooper[4] as dean cannot have it, nor the University can well forbear him. Mr Westfaling[5] is a wise sober man, but because he is but a prebendary and not master of a College, he is peradventure the less meet, because the bishoprick wanteth a house. And for that Mr Bickley[6] is master of a house and keepeth thereby a port of worship, I think he would well serve the turn, and I know that he is disciplinable, and will be ruled by counsel, and is of his nature both sincere and stout enough, and apt to govern. I speak not this of partiality because he is my chaplain, for I do but hurt him howsoever the world take such things for great preferments, but I weigh more my duty to the Queen's Majesty in her service, and to the commonwealth, than the respect of men's quiets, &c. But this is an odious argument of writing in such comparisons, but I know to whom I write.

<small>Bishoprick of Oxford, Mr Cooper cannot have. Mr Westfaling has no house.</small>

<small>Mr Bickley would well serve the turn.</small>

Certainly her Majesty should do prudently to be at a point in these two matters, the delay whereof will work more displeasure to the see of York than she heareth of. I am now preparing to repair into Kent, mine own diocese, where I have not been a good while, and I am looked for, and I trust shall do some service there. If these persons, which are to be

<small>Inconvenience of delay.</small>

[1 Matthew Hutton, 1567—1589.]
[2 William Day, 1561—1595.]
[3 Gabriel Goodman, 1561—1601.]
[4 Thomas Cooper, dean of Christ-church, 1567—1570.]
[5 A canon of Christ-church, Oxford, 1561—1585; bishop of Hereford, 1585—1601.]
[6 Thomas Bickley, warden of Merton College, Oxford, 1569—1585.]

confirmed some, and some to be consecrated, were to be placed here, it would save them much charge, or else they must come to me to Canterbury[7]. I pray your honour to obtain the licence and favour of her Majesty hereunto. I know no particular matter to hear of her Highness why I should much need to come personally. And thus I wish your honour as well in God as myself. From my house at Lambeth, this 30th of March.

Your honour's assured,
MATTHUE CANTUAR.

To the right honourable Sir William Cecil, knight, principal secretary to the Queen's Majesty, and one of her privy council.

CCLXXVI.

ARCHBISHOP PARKER TO SIR WILLIAM CECIL.

1st April, [1570]. Lansd. MS. xii. art. 80. Orig.

SIR,

IF I had known so much particularity in the Faculty matter, as I am now informed, I should have written more particularly, where to general words I wrote but generally, but yet offered my book particularly to be viewed, which also shall be recorded, and sent so soon as time will serve. You shall understand that Brooks coming to me for the prebend of Ricall in York church, I shewed difficulty to him, unless my lord of London could be contented. The said Brooks signified unto me that my lord of Leicester sent him to me for my hand, and said that his honour would prefer it to the Queen's Majesty, and said also, that my lord of London favoured him in that suit, whereupon I subscribed. I afterward learned that my lord of Leicester should tell him, that her Majesty had appointed it to the bishop's devotion, and I thereupon rested, &c. After that, I was informed that this Rycall was granted in vowson to one Mr Hamond of York-

Brooks applied to the archbishop for Rycall prebend, in the cathedral of York. He referred the applicant to the bishop of London.

Rycall granted to Mr

[7 Archbishop Grindal was confirmed in the see of York on the 22nd May, 1570, in the cathedral at Canterbury.]

shire, which known, my lord of London earnestly requested me not to grant my dispensation to any child, and shortly after, Mr dean of York wrote to me in these form of words: " I understand that suit shall be made to your grace by one Mr Hamond of Yorkshire, that his son, a boy of tender age, and little learning and discretion, may be dispensed withal to receive a prebend in this church that was Dr Spencer's, called Ricall. The prebend is a very good one, and meet for a preacher. This country is much destitute, and standeth [in] need of preachers. The father that sueth for it is a great rich man, and *filius hujus seculi*. Therefore I beseech your grace let him not abuse your authority to bring his purpose to pass, and then, I doubt not, but it shall be bestowed upon a preacher." Shortly after were delivered me letters from a certain nobleman to grant my dispensation for the said child, yet honourably written thus, "if you shall think it meet." I stayed of my grant. And if your honour think that noblemen must be thus satisfied, I refer it to your conscience. Noblemen must, and I trust will, be answered with reason. If any would not, I refer all to Almighty God, who is the true nobleman indeed; and if any nobleman hath found anything, I would he well viewed the seal, whether it be not counterfeited, for I know what I have done. And if I be sifted never so narrowly, yet shall it not be found that I have given dispensations of ecclesiastical livings to bishops' sons, neither six, nor three, to my remembrance.

And whereas in your letters which your honours of the privy council in the Queen's Majesty's name have earnestly required us, "and we will be accounted worthy of our calling, to employ all our care and industry in procuring more diligent preaching and teaching, in staying the obedient subjects in their duties, and to induce others from their disorders and errors, to the service of Almighty God, and to the good governance of the realm[1]:" methink seeing your nobilities do agree to God in this request, we should satisfy you especially; as for all others, *cadant a latere tuo mille et decem millia, &c.; ad me non appropinquabit. Sunt enim quidam, quos si quid juves pluma levior gratia, si quid offendas plumbeas iras ge*[*runt*]. Good Mr Secretary, take

[1 See letter of 6th November, 1569, printed before, No. CCLXXIII. p. 357.]

no grief, as these words were written to you; but I write *coram Deo in amaritudine animæ meæ*, doubting not but that your honour hath far better contemplations. I have a long time offered in convocation to my brethren to procure the dispatchment of this offensive court. I have signified the same to your honours. For I have more grief thereby than gain, and I would it were wholly suppressed, as reason and statute would bear withal, or else committed to some other, that could do it with better discretion, as I am sure there are many, for so divers profess in their open sermons, and utter the same in their private letters. But I know you be never without business for the state of the commonwealth, to whom we shall join our aid, though not in great doings, but yet in earnest prayers that you may have God in your eyes, howsoever some noblemen will be men. And therefore here I cease, wishing your honour to God as myself. From my house at Lambeth, this first of April.

Parker has long offered in convocation to get rid of the offensive Court of Faculties.

Divers profess to be able to manage it better.

Your loving friend in our Saviour,
MATTHUE CANTUAR.

I should have written this letter myself, but being acrased, my head would not bear it. And for that ye should be informed of all specialties, I have sent Dr Drury, who hath been my officer for these nine years.

*To the right honourable Sir William
Cecil, knight, principal secretary to
the Queen's Majesty.*

CCLXXVII.

ARCHBISHOP PARKER TO SIR WILLIAM CECIL.

3rd April, [1570]. Lansd. MS. xii. art. 79. Orig.

SIR,

YOUR honour shall be advertised, that where this afternoon or to-morrow I was minded to have taken bond of Bomelius shortly to have departed the realm, according to such purpose as hath been a good time in me toward him, and not disliked by certain of her Majesty's council, as Sir

The archbishop being minded to take bond of Bomelius to depart the realm, he has inclosed the letters.

564   ARCHB. PARKER TO SIR WILLIAM CECIL.   [1570.

to Parker, which are sent to Cecil for examination.

William Fytzwilliams told me from my lord-keeper and from you; to prevent this my doing, this Bomelius this morning sent his wife to me with these letters enclosed[1]: and because the contents be of high importance, I thought it the best to send him to your honours of the council, where ye may examine him most sufficiently. What he hath to say I know not, but I fear that the devil is busy in mischief. It were good ye knew it, and the more I suspect malice, hearing but yesterday of a mischievous intended practice (if it be true) for poisoning of her Majesty's ships in the ordinance and victual. I see Judas *non dormit*, and some spite hath reached to myself, but this last term, where *quidam filii Beliall* did gouge my poor barge in divers places in the bottom, that if it had not been spied, I was like to have drenched in the midst of the Thames (no great loss, yet of such one as I am); but I would have been sorry my family to have perished, or that such *incircumcisi Philistei* should have gloried to insult, with *ubi est Deus eorum, &c.* I shall pray still to God for the protection of you all. If this man's secrecy be but an astrological experience or prediction, it is the less, but I fear further of some conspiracy. Before Easter I gave him liberty to be an open prisoner in the King's Bench, where before he was a close prisoner, but I charged the keeper that he should practise no more upon the Queen's subjects. Whether any practitioner hath resorted to him (as many have a wonderful confidence in him and in his

Holes bored in the bottom of Parker's barge

If Bomelius's secret be but an astrological prediction, it is the less.

Great popular confidence in his magic.

[1 Bomelius, a foreign physician and astrologer, acquired great reputation in London, but rather amongst the people than at court. His letter on the present occasion, which is still preserved (Lansd. MS. XII. art. 84), professed to disclose some evil impending over England. Sir William Cecil, instead of having the man before the privy council, as suggested by Parker, wrote to him for further information. On the 7th April, 1570, Bomelius replied by sending a judgment upon the Queen's nativity, and a portion of a book written by himself, in which he endeavoured to shew that great changes happened in kingdoms every 500 years, and argued danger from the lapse of that period since the Norman Conquest. Cecil, thinking perhaps that his astrology was not more accurate than his chronology, took no further notice of his predictions, whereupon at the end of a month he wrote again (Lansd. MS. XII. art. 73) wishing for a licence to transfer his services to Russia, which was probably granted.]

magic) I know not. What he hath to utter ye may learn. *Sub omni lapide scorpio latet,* yet of *timidi mater non flet.* I am thus bold, peradventure more suspicious than I need; but I refer all to your wisdom. From my house, this third of April.

Your honour's in Christ,
MATTHUE CANTUAR.

To the right honourable Sir William Cecil, knight, principal secretary to the Queen's Majesty, and one of her privy council.

CCLXXVIII.

ARCHBISHOP PARKER TO SIR WILLIAM CECIL.

4th May, 1570. S. P. O. Domestic. Orig.

SIR,

I UNDERSTAND by the warden of Manchester College[2], who being very weary to continue that College with such incumbrance as he hath had thereby, and hath no hope to be relieved hereafter of his trouble, except he betrayeth that college with giving over a lease of the best land it hath, and he being now desirous to relinquish it to her Majesty's disposition, to be converted to some College in Cambridge, who might hereafter send out some preachers to inhabit that quarter, and also by the rest of the revenue maintain some students. If it please your honour to move her Highness to this alteration, I think you should do a good deed; and where you were brought up for the first beginning of your study in St John's College, I think you should shew yourself a good benefactor, to turn this land thereto, with what condition of order as might seem best to your wisdom. And thus wishing you as much grace to Godward as to myself, I commit you

[2 The warden was a Mr Herle, mentioned before in Parker's letter of the 12th February, 1565—6. (p. 259.) His conduct as warden was inquired into some years afterwards, and was not thought altogether blameless. See Strype's Parker, Bk. IV. c. ii.]

to his protection. From my house at Canterbury, this fourth of May.

Your loving friend in God,
MATTHUE CANTUAR.

To the right honourable Sir William Cecil, knight, principal secretary to the Queen's Majesty, and one of her privy council.

CCLXXIX.

ARCHBISHOP PARKER TO SIR WILLIAM CECIL.

26th May, [1570].   S. P. O. Domestic.   Orig.

Sir,

The archbishop whilst remedying disorders in his diocese, has been sued to by Keyes, formerly the sergeant porter.

After my right hearty commendations. Where I am in travailing here about divers disorders in my diocese, specially of those persons that live either incontinently or in fashion of a divorce asunder from their wives, there was offered unto me a suit from him that was sometime serjeant porter. In his letters, the copy whereof I send your honour[1],

[1] The letter which was enclosed ran as follows: "Most reverend father in God. For that all men are bound, which any kind of way is troubled in conscience, to seek all means possible for the ease thereof, hath moved me at this time to trouble your grace, protesting before God he lives not that hath a more unquiet conscience than I have. God of his mercy make your grace a mean to persuade that the Queen's Majesty may extend her mercy towards me, that according to God's law I may live. I trust your grace will take it in good part that I am here constrained by conscience to charge you, I being one of your flock, to say that you are bound in conscience to move the Queen's Majesty and the honourable council that I may live according to the laws of God with my wife. I will here omit what great grief it is to me to have occasion to make this suit to your grace, I being under so gracious, so merciful, and so godly a prince, and have written so many letters to this end, and have opened my case sundry times to the honourable council. Alas, what shall I say or think? Sure I must think that her grace doth not know that we are man and wife. Here I might allege divers sentences out of God's book to move your grace, what danger it is to a Christian man's soul to live from his wife, nor I dare not here say what danger they do run

wherein he chargeth me, as of my pastoral office, to help for redress of his case. Whereupon this is to pray your honour in the way of conscience to move the matter to the Queen's Highness, whereby her Majesty may have godly consideration and prudent respect for her policy[2]. I trust her Highness will graciously consider the quiet of her poor subject's conscience, as may stand with God's law, the respect whereof maketh me to be a solicitor, as my duty bindeth me.

Furthermore, in searching for disordered persons, I am informed of one gentleman, called Culpepper, who hath married the sister of Leonard Dacres, the rebel[3], and whether into at God's hand that doth keep man and wife asunder; for I do know that all Scriptures are so well known to your grace, that it were mere folly for me to take upon me to recite any. Also I do omit to open the whole circumstance of my marriage, for that I do think it is not altogether unknown to your grace, I being twice examined before my lord of London; but so sure as there is a living God, so sure we be man and wife before him. I fear I am too tedious to your grace, wherefore I will end, desiring God of his mercy to put into the Queen's Majesty's heart, by your grace's means, that if my long imprisonment and punishment, which hath been almost five years, be not thought sufficient for my presumptuous act, that I might live the rest of my life in prison with my wife, according to God's law; which to do, God is my judge, only for conscience sake I had rather do, than to live with this liberty that I now have. Thus, leaving to trouble your grace any further at this time, I wish you long life, with much increase of honour, most humbly beseeching your grace to give me leave to wait upon you to utter my troubled conscience at large by mouth; and if this be not a truth which I have written to your grace, I wish to be punished in example of all others. From Sandgate Castle, this 7th of May, 1570. One of your grace's poor and humble flock, to command during life, THOMAS KEYES."]

[[2] Thomas Keyes, the sergeant porter of Queen Elizabeth, who is here alluded to, was the person who married Lady Mary Grey, sister of Lady Jane Grey. He, as Sir William Cecil remarked, "was the biggest" and she "the least" person of all the court. (Lansd. MS. CII. art. 66). The fate of Keyes subsequent to his marriage has been unknown to the writers upon that period. They do not seem to have even known his christian name correctly.]

[[3] Leonard Dacres, "Dacres of the crooked back," as he was termed by Mary Queen of Scots, was an active participator in the rebellion of 1569. He was the second son of William Lord Dacre of Gillesland. After an unsuccessful endeavour to defend Naworth

you have taken order with him I know not; but hearing that he maketh away his things to make as much money as he can, and doubting of the sequel, being otherwise noted not to receive the communion, I have at all adventures sent for him to appear. If he do allege any order taken of him by the council, then I shall the sooner dismiss him, or else I will have him bound to be forthcoming.

is making away his things, and does not receive the communion. Parker has sent for him.

I am here stoutly faced out by that vain official who was declared to have slandered Mr Morris and some justices of the peace, and purpose to examine the foul slander of Morris, according to the request of your letters. The official seemeth to discredit my office, for that I am but one of the commission, and have none other assistants here; and therefore it would do good service if the commission I sued for to be renewed were granted. There be stout words muttered for actions of the case, and for dangerous premunires, and specially tossed by his friends, papists only, where the better subjects do universally cry out of his abuses. If I had some advice from you I should do the better. And thus wishing your honour God's grace as to myself, I commit the same to his protection. From my house at Canterbury, the 26th of May.

Parker is outfaced by a vain official.

Your honour's loving friend in Christ,

MATTHUE CANTUAR.

To the right honourable Sir William Cecil, knight, principal secretary to the Queen's Majesty, and one of her privy council.

CCLXXX.

ARCHBISHOP PARKER TO SIR WILLIAM CECIL.

25th August, [1570]. S. P. O. Domestic. Orig.

SIR,

AFTER my hearty commendations in Christ. I should have written to your honour afore this time, but it hath pleased Almighty God, whose will is always the best and

It has pleased God to offer

Castle, he fled into Scotland, and thence to the Low Countries, where he died in 1573]

must be obeyed, to offer unto me some matter of patience[1], and foolish frail nature troubleth me yet so, that I have much ado with myself to gather my wits and memory together; but I thank God that yet it hath pleased his mercy to suffer my poor faith to prevail against natural considerations, and my hope to bear quietly the wants of my small household commodities.

the archbishop some matter of patience

The cause of my writing is partly of the motion of the friends of Mr Dr Thirleby, who (as himself desireth) would wish in this his great sickness to be removed from my house to his friends, for better cherishing and in hope of his recovery[2]. I would grant no further but the choice of three or four large chambers within my house, except you can agree thereto, and for this cause this messenger cometh to your honour to know the Queen's Majesty's pleasure; which understanded, in circumstances as they shall be prescribed, so they shall be followed, if it please Almighty God to continue me any further in life, having somewhat ado to keep myself upon my foot. I thought by his presence (being both of us much of an age) to learn to forsake the world and die to God; and hereto I trust to incline myself, what length or shortness of life soever may follow.

Dr Thirleby in his great sickness seeks to be removed to his friends.

I fear the recovery of the bishop of London[3], who as I hear is fallen back to his fits again.

The bishop of London dangerously ill.

Mr Wattes and I in our conference seemed to wish these persons in the new necessary commission[4]; I call it necessary, for I hear now of late of more massing than hath been heard of this seven years. Ye may allow of these or of any other whom your wisdom shall think meet either to remove or to add. And thus I beseech your honour to have most humbly my commendations of prayers to her Majesty, wishing the

Suggestions for a new commission.

[1 Mrs Parker, the archbishop's wife, died on the 17th August, 1570. She was interred in the Duke's, that is the Duke of Norfolk's chapel, on the north side of old Lambeth church.]

[2 Dr Thirleby died on the 26th August, the day after the date of this letter.]

[3 Bishop Sandys, the new bishop of London, translated from Worcester 2nd June, 1570.]

[4 Probably the ecclesiastical commission. "These persons" seems to refer to some inclosed list of persons. No such list has been found.]

[PARK. COR.]

same a prosperous return with all her court, and to you with your whole family God's favour and protection as to myself. From my house at Lambeth, this 25th of August.

Your honour's alway in Christ,

MATTHUE CANTUAR.

To the right honourable Sir William Cecil, knight, principal secretary to the Queen's Majesty, and one of her privy council.

CCLXXXI.

ARCHBISHOP PARKER TO SIR WILLIAM CECIL.

2nd November, 1570. S. P. O. Domestic. Orig.

SIR,

I PRAY you let me use your favour and counsel. In the late commission for causes ecclesiastical, one clause escaped in the writing, as in this libel[1], which I must needs impute to myself and writers: and with your help I would cause it to be new written, if your honour would obtain that it might be signed by her Majesty's hand. As for the great seal, may soon be put to. In this renovation I would wish Mr Day, provost of Eton[2], to be a commissioner for some causes necessary, and also would wish Mr dean of Westminster[3] to be of the quorum, and so might Thomas Bromley[4] and Thomas Wilbra-

Suggestions for alterations in the ecclesiastical commission. Provost of Eton, dean of Westminster, Thomas Bromley and Thomas Wilbraham, esqs, proposed as commissioners.

[1 The following was the clause above referred to: "to be one, that then you, or three of you as aforesaid, shall have full power and authority to order and award such punishment to every offender, by fine, imprisonment, or otherwise by all or any of the ways aforesaid, and to take such order for the redress of the same, as to your wisdoms and discretions, or three of you, whereof you the said archbishop of Canterbury, or you bishops of London, Winton, Ely, Rochester, Chichester, and Dovor; or you the said Anthony Cooke, Thomas Smith, Henry Neville, Thomas Goodwin, Walter Haddon, Thomas Seckford, Gilbert Gerald, David Lewis, Thomas Yale, and Thomas Wootton, &c."]

[2 Dr William Day, provost of Eton, dean of Windsor, and ultimately bishop of Winchester, 1595—1596.]

[3 Dr Gabriel Goodman, dean 1561—1601.]

[4 Afterwards lord-chancellor.]

ham[5], esquires. And because Mr Marven of Chichester diocese is written "Marten," and no such body, I would have him more truly written, which they say, in the commission, cannot be altered but in the Queen's presence. And finally, I would think good some proviso were in the end, that neither Winchester commissioners, Chichester commissioners, or of Canterbury, should deal in causes out of their dioceses, to avoid confusion amongst us, if the Queen's pleasure were so expressed. If these particularities may be thought good unto your honour, upon your answer I would cause the book to be new written again and sent you, to use your opportunity especially to the Queen's Highness. And thus God preserve your honour. From my house at Lambeth, this second of November.

Your honour's evermore in Christ,
MATTH. CANT.

To the right honourable Sir William Cecil, knight, principal secretary to the Queen's Majesty, and one of her privy council.

CCLXXXII.

ARCHBISHOP PARKER TO QUEEN ELIZABETH.

27th December, [1570.] S. P. O. Domestic. Orig.

Most humbly submitting myself to your excellent Majesty, I crave your pardon of this my boldness, praying your Highness not be offended with my plainness herein uttered, which I open in most secret wise to yourself in conscience, by Almighty God, to whose sacred Majesty at his fearful and reverend judgment we all shall once stand. The insufficiency of my speech, the weakness of my mind, have hitherto stayed me, not in person to say much, partly in consideration of mine own unworthiness, and partly in fear of displeasure, whereunto willingly and wittingly I would not fall, to win the whole realm. I have very seldom purged myself to your Highness of whatsoever information hath been made, refer-

Solicits pardon for his boldness

Insufficiency of speech and weakness of mind have stayed him from saying much in person.

[5 A distinguished lawyer, at this time attorney-general of the court of wards.]

ring mine innocency to Almighty God, and to your good nature and credit, wherein I have reposed myself quietly.

Has been informed that it has been taken unkindly that his counsel alleged his title to the wood of Longbeach.

I have been informed that some unkindness might have been thought in me, for that my learned counsel hath (by commandment) opened before your Highness' officers what could be alleged for the title of that unlucky wood of Longbeach. O Madam! I never meant to shew any wilfulness or ingratitude to your Highness, of whom I have received all that I have (as God knoweth), in heart. I was called into your court of exchequer (after three or four years' quiet possession, serving the country there with wood of the fall of forty or fifty pounds by year, as hath been used by my predecessors) to answer by what title I have holden the same. I never meant, as God knoweth my conscience, to make havoc thereof, to improve it to the benefit either of wife or children (if it hath been so judged), but to reserve and to

Meant to restore it to the disposition of the crown.

restore it again to the disposition of the crown, or in extreme necessity for casualty of fire falling on some of my houses, to use somewhat to the re-edifying, as certain of your officers hath known my purpose.

The truth is, your Highness may be, I fear, compassed

When he first came into Kent, he prayed Sir Richard Sackville to be a mean to procure him a lease of Charing, the house of his predecessors.

therein; as once I saw the likelihood. It pleased Sir Richard Sackville, when I was at my first coming in Kent, to come to me as to visit me; he moved to communication, and I, as an unexpert man, prayed him to be a mean to your Highness that I might be your farmer and tenant in rent to the house of Charing, sometimes my predecessors', being decayed and very ruinous, which I would have repaired; and being as it were in the midst of the diocese, I would sometimes have dwelt there, to the stay and comfort, I trust, of that stout people of that country, as, at this day, God be praised, the whole shire is both quiet, reverently obedient, and in conscience ready to serve both in body and goods, and I trust will so continue.

He procured a lease for himself, and intended to set up iron mills.

He upon the disclosing of my desire, to prevent me, sued to your Highness for the lease thereof to himself, and charged your Highness with some reparations, and intending, as I was credibly informed, in this wood, being very nigh to that house of Charing, to erect up certain iron mills; which plague, if it should come into that country, I fear it would breed much grudge and desolation; to the avoidance whereof, my friends and learned counsel advised me to shew my interest, being called thereto; not minding by this speech (most gracious lady) to gainsay your pleasure or title, either in this or in anything that your Highness hath given me, whereof I answer the fruits, the tenths, and subsidies, which came to my see (as they inform me) by several value, and being no member of the manor of Westwell, which is of the rent of £20 by year, now in this late exchange, among other things of the sum of one thousand pounds, recompensed in a rectory of £20 by year.

To prevent him, Parker was advised to shew his interest, not to gainsay the pleasure of the crown.

And whereas your Majesty may be informed that the late exchange is but penny for penny, some wise men think, that of four or five hundred marks which might be increased, your revenues not augmented so many shillings; although now I hear that by the lease that may be of this wood, a better rent is advanced to the crown, which yet if it had pleased you, might have been much more to your possessions beneficial, if it had been so sought; except your Highness meaneth of your princely liberality this way to advance the service of some other of your subjects so beneficially, whereunto I am ready to submit myself in all that I have in any title whatsoever: protesting here before your Highness, knowing your pleasure, myself and all I have to be at your commandment, to tarry or to forego the vocation your Highness hath called me unto, better content for myself to live with the tenth part, than with the whole, if it may be to the glory of God, and to the honour and quiet governance of your realm. And whether in this place, wherein your Highness hath set me in (more lamenting mine unworthiness than rejoicing in the solemnity thereof) I have had too much worldly joy, God knoweth, bearing yet all manner of griefs and obloquies for doing justice and your commandment with very good will; at which place some learned, some of other private respects, do so much bear at, that they conclude plainly in doctrine and hold in affection, *quod archiepiscoporum nomina simul cum muneribus suis et officiis sunt abolenda;* which practice when they have brought about (as in your Majesty's time of your gracious consideration I doubt not of), that this room should be either too low abased or quite abolished, I think your Highness' council should have too much ado, beside their other great affairs, in staying of the unruliness of some part of the ministers for religion, and in some others of the laity

Parker is ready to tarry or forego his vocation at the Queen's pleasure.

His office much objected to, and desired to be brought low, or abolished.

for their insolent living, and standing the insatiableness of many patrons in the giving of their benefices in these times, considering the wonderful impoverishment of the most of the clergy, partly by the great and interminable exactions of these arrearages for tenths and subsidies, many paid afore by their predecessors, and yet called for again, even from your father's days. I see them in such extreme poverty, that, of pure conscience, I am driven to forbear of my ancient rights to ease them of their burthens, for the better maintenance of Christ's holy religion, which as it may be choked with overmuch in unconscionable men's hands, so it will fall to ground amongst beggars, which shall set their whole care and force of mind, not to study but to live, which at this day experience sheweth it; as in your University of Cambridge not two men in the whole able or willing to read the lady Margaret's lecture, although preachers they have many, but I fear divers of small consideration.

Thus praying your Majesty, at the reverence of God, patiently to hear these words of your poor priest and well-meaning chaplain, referring altogether to your grace's contemplation, as I see how Almighty God worketh in your heart far above much wisdom of the world, whose Majesty in you thus oftentimes appearing, I do reverence with lowly humility, referring all to your divine prudence, how, in what, or when your Highness will have me obedient, *secundum Deum et Jesum Christum servatorem nostrum;* to whose fatherly protection I will never cease in prayer to commend your Majesty in soul and body; which God long preserve, Amen. From Lambeth, this 27th of December.

Your Majesty's most bounden orator,
MATTHUE CANTUAR.

To the Queen's most excellent Majesty.

CCLXXXIII.

ARCHBISHOP PARKER TO SIR WILLIAM CECIL.
8th January, 1570—1. Petyt MS. Inner Temple, No. 47. fol. 53. Parker's draft.

SIR,

WHERE upon the return of my lord of London[1] from the court we had communication of the communion bread, and he seeming to signify to me that your honour did not know of any rule passed by law in the Communion-book that it may be such bread as is usually eaten at the table with other meats, &c.; I thought it good to put you in remembrance, and to move your consideration in the same. For it is a matter of much contention in the realm: where most part of protestants think it most meet to be in wafer-bread, as the injunction prescribeth; divers others, I cannot tell of what spirit, would have the loaf-bread, &c. And hereupon one time at a sessions would one Master Fogg have indicted a priest for using wafer-bread, and me indirectly for charging the wafer-bread by injunction: where the judges were Mr Southcoots and Mr Gerrard, who were greatly astonied upon the exhibiting of the book. And I being then in the country, they counselled with me, and I made reasons to have the injunction prevail. *A question having arisen as to the proper character of the communion-bread, the archbishop reminds Sir W. Cecil that*

First, I said, as her Highness talked with me once or twice in that point, and signified that there was one proviso in the act of the uniformity of Common Prayer, that by law is granted unto her, that if there be any contempt or irreverence used in the ceremonies or rites of the Church by the misusing of the orders appointed in the book, the Queen's Majesty may, by the advice of her commissioners, or metropolitan, ordain and publish such further ceremonies, or rites, as may be most for the reverence of Christ's holy mysteries and sacraments, and but for which law her Highness would not have agreed to divers orders of the book. And by virtue of which law she published further order in her injunctions both for the communion-bread[2], and for the placing of the *the Queen has power to ordain new ceremonies or rites, if there be any irreverence or misuse of those existing.*

And by virtue of that power she made the order about communion-bread in the Injunctions.

[1 Bishop Sandys.]
[2 Queen Elizabeth's Injunctions of 1559 directed, that the sacramental bread should be similar to the "singing cakes, which served for the use of the private mass," but "somewhat bigger."]

tables within the quire. They that like not the injunctions force much the statute in the book. I tell them that they do evil to make odious comparison betwixt statute and injunction, and yet I say and hold, that the injunction hath authority by proviso of the statute. And whereas it is said in the rule, that "to take away the superstition which any person hath or might have in the bread and wine, it shall suffice that the bread be such as is usually to be eaten at the table with other meats, &c.;" "it shall suffice," I expound, where either there wanteth such fine usual bread, or superstition be feared in the wafer-bread, they may have the communion in fine usual bread: which is rather a toleration in these two necessities, than is in plain ordering, as is in the injunction.

How the rubric "it shall suffice," was construed by Parker.

This I say to shew you the ground which hath moved me and others to have it in the wafer-bread; a matter not greatly material, but only obeying the Queen's Highness, and for that the most part of her subjects disliketh the common bread for the sacrament. And therefore, as her Highness and you shall determine, I can soon alter my order, although now quietly received in my diocese, and I think would breed some variance to alter it. I hear also that in the court you be come to the usual bread. Sir, the great disquiet babbling that the realm is in in this matter maketh me thus long to babble, and would be loth that now your saying or judgment should so be taken as ye saw a law that should prejudice the injunction.

People dislike common bread for the sacrament.

In the court they be come to the usual bread.

Sir, I thank your honour for your prudent secrecy, that you did use toward that party that laboureth to know who did write letters to the Queen to signify such innovation. He saith he is promised to know, &c. It would breed but unkindness, and therefore I left him in his suspense, as in my last long letter I would I had spared one word written which might work unkindness, but that I say your wisdom will rather make charity than break it.

If this unhandsome weather, or my casual body, shall defer the longer my duty of coming to the Queen, I pray you ease it with some word. And thus God make you strong. This 8th of January.

CCLXXXIV.

ARCHBISHOP PARKER TO SIR WILLIAM CECIL.

21st January, [1570—1.] S. P. O. Domestic. Orig.

I AM ashamed to write thus oft to your honour, though necessity driveth me; but hereafter I will write seldomer. Whereas her Highness and your honour would have had some apt speech concerning that question: *an principibus sit potius resistendum quam obediendum in rebus adiaphoris?* I am informed that no such matter was applied. I fear *quod aliquid monstri alunt et suas res agunt.* I doubt *quod quia magis diligunt gloriam hominum quam gloriam Dei, timent plebem, nam palam de illo loqui nolunt propter metum Judeorum, et propter Phariseos non confitentur, &c.* If this matter be thus begun, and slily with a flourish passed over, I think it will breed that inconvenience that Mr Mullyns (as I am informed) should openly tell the precisians that her Highness' sword should be compelled to cut off this stubborn multitude, which daily groweth. Your honour moved me to write to him, and so I did, as here I send you the copy; you can tell how well he followed your counsel or mine; but surely, Sir, it is a matter of great importance; and thus I leave the contemplation thereof to your wisdom. I see how I may be heard amongst them in their sermons before her Majesty this Lent. I would your honour would return their names, but I trust that which one will not, one other shall, for it is high time. This 21st of January.

Your honour's in Christ,

MATTHUE CANTUAR.

To the right honourable Sir William Cecil,
  knight, principal secretary to the Queen's
  Majesty, and one of her privy council.

[Side notes: The Queen and Cecil would have had notice taken of a question as to obedience to the prince, probably reported to have been argued amongst the Puritans. Parker is informed that no such matter was applied, but he looks upon the precisians with great sp'cion. The Queen will be compelled to cut off this stubborn multitude.]

CCLXXXV.

ARCHBISHOP PARKER TO SIR WILLIAM CECIL.

2nd February, 1570—1. Petyt MS. Inner Temple, No. 47. fol. 54 b. Parker's draft.

Dr Bullingham's preaching.

The Queen should have the best.

SALUTEM *in Christo*. I was glad to hear of your good recovery: God grant it may long [sic]. Sir, this other day Dr Bullingham[1] preached in my chapel in my hearing, whom I take to be an honest true-meaning man; but because I did credit others much commending him, I once preferred him before her Majesty, but I intend hereafter not to do so again. I would her Highness had the best. In him I perceive neither *pronunciationem aulicam* nor *ingenium aulicum*; not meet for the court; and therefore I appointed Dr Young of Cambridge[2] to supply his room, and warned he is; and what will fall out for the other I yet know not, because they may alter their days; and therefore send I your honour another copy when your pleasure shall be so to use it. The bishop of Galloway[3] have sent to me to speak with me. I have appointed to-morrow, though not fully recovered. I think on Monday or Tuesday, if your honour think it so good, I mind to come to the court. And thus in our Lord I desire your honour well to fare as myself, and fully to be recovered. From my house, this second of February, 1570.

Your lordship's always in Christ,

M. C.

CCLXXXVI.

ARCHBISHOP PARKER TO SIR WILLIAM CECIL.

6th February, 1570—1. Petyt MS. Inner Temple, No. 47. fol. 50b. Parker's draft.

SIR,

Sends form of sacramental bread, formerly appointed by bishop Grindal and the archbishop.

As you desired, I send you here the form of the bread used, and was so appointed by order of my late lord of London and myself, as we took it not disagreeable to the injunc-

[1 Afterwards bishop of Gloucester, 1581—1598.]

[2 Master of Pembroke Hall; bishop of Rochester, 1578—1605.]

[3 One of the Scottish commissioners for the release of Mary Queen of Scots]

tion. And how so many churches hath of late varied I cannot tell; except it be the practice of the common adversary the devil, to make variance and dissension in the sacrament of unity. For where we be in one uniform doctrine of the same, and so cut off much matter of variance which the Lutherans and Zuinglians do hatefully maintain, yet because we will have some matter of dissension, we will quarrel in a small circumstance of the same, neither regarding God in his word, who earnestly driveth us to charity, neither regarding the love and subjection we should bear to our prince, who zealously would wish the devout administration of the sacrament, nor yet consider what comfort we might receive ourselves in the said sacrament, if dissension were not so great with us. Sir, I pray, help to pacify it, whether by proclamation or by any other way, as in wisdom of governance you see sometimes things must be forced or remitted.

Being in unity of doctrine as to the sacrament, we will quarrel in a small circumstance of the same.

Pray help to pacify it.

And because you may not nor cannot reasonably be idle, yet you must for a better health remit your earnest business, and thereupon I send you here a trifle which I found out writ in old French. It is marvel but that you have seen it, notwithstanding I think everybody hath not.

A publication of a trifle found by the archbishop writ in old French.

But, sir, as I came yesterday from you I was informed that one nobleman in England should impute it to my doing that the cross is brought into the chapel again, so that I perceive they will load me with envy; but certainly I never knew of it, nor yet in good faith I think it expedient it should be restored. And therefore I think *est modus in rebus, &c.*, not too much to exasperate my heart.

Parker falsely accused of bringing back the crucifix to the Queen's chapel.

And thus I commit your honour to God as myself, this 6th of February, 1570.

CCLXXXVII.

THE LORDS OF THE COUNCIL TO ARCHBISHOP PARKER AND LORD COBHAM[4].

17th February, 1570—1. Parker MSS. C. C. Coll. Camb. cxiv. art. 29. p. 95. Orig.

AFTER our hearty commendations to your lordships. Where the Queen's Majesty hath determined for divers neces-

[4 Lord warden of the cinque ports; see before, p. 203.]

The Queen having determined to hold a parliament next April.
sary great causes concerning the state of the realm to have a parliament holden at Westminster this next April, and for that purpose her Majesty's writs are directed to the sheriffs of every shire to cause proclamation thereof to be made, so as there may be knights chosen in every shire, and citizens and burgesses in every city and borough, according to the laws and good customs of the realm: upon some deliberation had by her Majesty with us concerning the due execution hereof, her
has called to remembrance
Majesty hath called to her remembrance (which also we think to be true) that though the greater number of knights, citizens, and burgesses for the more part are duly and
that in many places consideration is not had to choose persons able to give good information and advice.
orderly chosen; yet in many places such consideration is not usually had herein as reason would, that is, to choose persons able to give good information and advice for the places for which they are nominated, and to treat and consult discreetly upon such matters as are to be propounded to them in their assemblies. But contrariwise that many in late parliaments (as her Majesty thinketh) have been named, some for private respects and favour upon their own suits, some to enjoy some immunities from arrests upon actions during the time of the parliaments, and some other to set forth private causes by sinister labour and frivolous talks and arguments, to the prolongation of time without just cause, and without regard to the public benefit and weal of the realm; and therefore her Majesty being very desirous to have redress herein, hath charged us to devise some speedy good ways for reformation hereof at this time, so as all the persons to be assembled in this next parliament for the cities, shires, and boroughs, may be found (as near as may be) discreet, wise, and well-disposed according as the intention of their choosing ought to
For remedy whereof
be. And therefore, as we have thought meet to give knowledge hereof to such as we think both for their wisdoms, dispositions, and authorities in sundry counties in the realm can and will take care hereof, so have we for this purpose made
the archbishop and lord Cobham are directed to confer with the sheriff and principal persons in counties and boroughs.
special choice of your lordships, requiring you in her Majesty's name to consider well of these premises, and to confer with the sheriff of that shire of Kent by all such good means as you shall think meet, and with such special men of livelihood and worship of the same county as have interest herein, and in like manner with the head officers of cities and boroughs, so as by your good advice and direction the per-

sons to be chosen may be well qualified with knowledge, discretion, and modesty, and meet for those places. And in so doing your lordships shall give just occasion to have her Majesty herein well satisfied, the realm well served, and the time of the assembly (which cannot be but chargeable with long continuance) to be both profitably and speedily passed over and ended, and finally the counties, cities, and boroughs well provided for. And so we bid your lordships heartily farewell. From Westminster, the 17th of February, 1570.

so that by their good advice and direction, the persons to be chosen may be well qualified.

Your lordships' assured loving friends,

N. BACON, C. S.	W. NORTHT.
T. SUSSEX. F. BEDFORD.	R. LEYCESTER.
E. CLYNTON.	W. HOWARD.
JAMYS CROFT.	W. CECILL.

To our very good lords the archbishop of Canterbury and the lord Cobham.

CCLXXXVIII.

ARCHBISHOP PARKER TO LORD BURGHLEY[1].

4th June, 1571. Petyt MS. Inner Temple, No. 47. fol. 35. Parker's draft.

SIR,

I HAVE considered what your honour said to me this day concerning St Augustine's authority in the Article[2] in the first original agreed upon; and I am advisedly still in mine opinion concerning so much wherefore they be alleged in the article; and for further truth of the words, besides St Austen, both he in other places, and Prosper in his "Sentences wrote of Austen" (*Senten.* 338 and 339), doth plainly affirm our opinion in the Article to be most true, howsoever some men vary from it.

Authority of St Augustine properly referred to in the Article.

Sir, I am about to spend this week in examination of

Is about to spend the

[1 Sir William Cecil was created Baron Burghley on 25th February, 1570—1.]

[2 The allusion is to the 29th Article, which was now printed for the first time. The passage referred to as in St Augustine will be found in his *Tract. in Joan. xxvi. Opera, Tom.* IX. *col.* 230. *Ed. Basil.* 1569, and those in Prosper, in *Sententiæ ex operibus D. August. Ed. Paris.* 1671. p. 128.]

^{week in examination of Goodman, Lever, and other puritans.} Masters Goodman, Lever, Sampson, Walker, Whiborne, Gouff, and such others. I would be glad that the bishops of Winton, Ely, Worcester, and Chichester, being all commissioners, join with me. My lord of Sarum hath promised to stand by me. I doubt whether the bishop of London would deal with me to that effect to suspend them, or deprive them, if they will not assent unto the propositions inserted. Howsoever the world will judge, I will serve God, my prince, and her laws, in my conscience, as it is high time to set up it [sic], and yet I would be glad to be advised, to work prudently, rather to edification than destruction.

Book of Discipline.
If it will please her Majesty to grant our Book of Discipline, I will labour to put it in print for further instruction. *Si non placet, faciet Dominus quod bonum est in oculis suis.* For my part, I am at a point in these worldly respects, and yet shall be ready to hear *quid in me loquatur Dominus.* And thus committing your honour to Almighty God, I wish you the same grace as I would have myself. From Lambeth, 4th of June, 1571.

CCLXXXIX.

ARCHBISHOP PARKER AND OTHER ECCLESIASTICAL COMMISSIONERS TO CHURCHWARDENS AND OTHERS NOT TO SUFFER UNLICENSED PERSONS TO MINISTER.

7th June, 1571. Parker MSS. C. C. Coll. Camb. cxxi. art. 37. p. 481. Orig.

To all and every the Queen's Majesty's officers, churchwardens[1], sidemen, swornmen, and others, having any government or oversight for the time being, of or in any church, chapel, or parish within the province of Canterbury.

Where the Queen's Majesty being very careful for the good government of her realm and dominions in all godly and wholesome religion agreeable to the word of God; and being very desirous to have both the laws and orders well and faithfully observed and her loving subjects reposed in godly quiet, concord, and unity, and specially in matters of

[1 'Churchwarden' in MS. In this and other places some obvious corrections have been made from the printed copies. Parker MSS. cvi. art. 298, and cxxi. art. 36.]

religion: We undernamed, of her Majesty's commission ecclesiastical with other our associates, as our duty is, advisedly considering her good zeal worthy to take place, to the honour of God, and the godly quiet of her subjects, have thought good to signify thus much, and also to charge you and every of you whom it may concern. And therefore we will and require you, and in the Queen's Majesty's name straitly charge and command you and every of you, that in no wise ye suffer any parson or minister to minister any sacrament, or say any public prayers, in any your churches, chapels, or other place appointed for common prayers, in any other order, manner, or sort, than only according to the prescription of the book of Common Prayers and the Queen's Majesty's laws published in that behalf. And that in no wise ye suffer any person publicly or privately to teach, read, or preach in any the said churches, parishes, chapels, private houses, or other places, unless such be licensed to preach, read, or teach, by the Queen's Highness' authority, the archbishop of Canterbury his licence, or by the licence of the bishop of the diocese. And that he be such a minister as is licensed to preach after the first of May last, and not removed from the ministry by us, or any other lawful authority. And that you have a diligent care in the accomplishment of this her Highness' service and pleasure by us thus to you declared, as you and every of you will answer to the contrary. Given at Lambeth in the county of Surrey, the 7th of June, in the year of the reign of our sovereign lady Elizabeth[2] &c. the thirteenth.

No parson or minister to be suffered to minister any sacrament, or say public prayers, except according to the Book of Common Prayer. Nor any person to be suffered to teach, read, or preach, without a licence dated after the 1st May last.

MATTHUE CANTUAR.   EDWINUS LONDON.
  ROB. WINTON.   RICHARDE ELY.
  NIC. WIGORN.   RIC. CICESTREN.
GABRIELL GOODMAN.   THO. BROMLEY.
THOMAS WYLSON.   G. BROMLEY.
PET. OSBORNE.   THO. YALE.
RYCHARDE WENDESLEY. JOHN MERSHE.

[2 "by the grace of God of England, France, and Ireland, Queen, Defender of the Faith, &c." in printed copy.]

CCXC.

ARCHBISHOP PARKER TO LORD BURGHLEY.

17th June, 1571. Lansd. MS. xiii. art. 67. Orig.

The Inns of Court, reduced to better order about religion two years ago, do now again grow very disordered.

RIGHT honourable, whereas I am credibly informed that the houses of court being about two years sithence reduced to better order concerning religion, by means of a decree or ordinance made by your lordship and others the lords in the Star Chamber, touching the correction of the same houses for sundry their contempts and obstinacy in that behalf, do now of late grow again very disordered and licentious in over bold speeches and doings touching religion, used by some of the same houses without controlment, which happeneth (as I take it) for want of due execution and observation of your lordships' said decree and ordinance, the same not having been so effectually and severely considered of by the ancients and governors of the same houses as were convenient. These are

Cecil is requested to obtain a letter thereon from the council in the form inclosed.

therefore to desire your lordship to obtain a letter of the effect here inclosed[1] from my lords of the council to the commissioners ecclesiastical; and by virtue thereof, and of the commission, I hope there will be some better order and reformation therein to the furtherance of religion. And so I bid your lordship most heartily well to fare. From Lambeth, the 17th day of this present June, 1571.

Your lordship's assured in Christ,

MATTHUE CANTUAR.

CCXCI.

THE LORDS OF THE COUNCIL TO ARCHBISHOP PARKER AND BISHOP SANDYS OF LONDON.

17th June, 1571. Petyt MS. Inner Temple, No. 47. fol. 38. Contemporary copy or draft.

Order in the Star Chamber for expulsion of sundry of

AFTER our hearty commendations. There was an order taken in the Star Chamber about two years sithence[2] by the

[1 See the next document.]
[2 The order was dated 20th May, 1569. A copy of it is in the

lords of the privy council, your lordships, the judges, and others there, for the putting out of commons, expulsion, and reformation of sundry the corrupt and perverse sort in religion, in the inns of court, and for the restraint of that sort to be preferred to the degrees and callings there. Whereupon letters were directed from us to the benchers and governors of the same houses for the execution thereof accordingly, as by the said order and letters more at large appeareth. Nevertheless we are now of late credibly informed, that the said benchers and governors have been somewhat remiss and careless in the execution of the said order and letters, and chiefly in that they have sithence received again certain persons there thereby expulsed or put out of commons, and preferred othersome to degrees and callings there, contrary to the true meaning of the said order and letters. *The perverse sort in religion from the inns of court.* *The benchers have received back again some of those thereby expelled, and preferred others.*

We do hereby require your lordships, that you and such others of the commissioners ecclesiastical there as your lordships shall think most meet, will carefully peruse and consider the said order, and thereupon to call before you such of the benchers or governors of the said houses as you shall think fittest and best affected in religion, and by their good advice and furtherance to search and sift out the manner of the execution, breach, and observation of the said order and letters, and thereupon to take such order, as well for the reformation of that that hath or may be done contrary to the true meaning of the said order, as also to make such further order and orders against the corrupt and obstinate sort, both in the said houses of court, and also in the houses of chancery, as to your good considerations shall from time to time be thought convenient. Wherein as occasion shall serve, upon your advertisement, our good assistance shall be always ready in that behalf. And so fare you heartily well. From Westminster, the 17th day of June, 1571. *The archbishop and bishop to call before them such of the benchers as they shall think fittest, ascertain the facts, and make such further order as they shall think convenient.*

Your loving friends, &c.

same volume of MSS. whence the present document is derived, fol. 47. Six persons were ordered by it to be excluded from commons.]

CCXCII.

QUEEN ELIZABETH TO ARCHBISHOP PARKER.
20th August, 1571. Petyt MS. Inner Temple, No. 47. fol. 50. Orig.

BY THE QUEEN.
ELIZABETH R.

The Queen having required the archbishop to have good regard to the preservation of uniformity in divine service,

MOST reverend father in God, right trusty and right well-beloved, we greet you well. Where we required you, as the metropolitan of our realm, and as the principal person in our commission for causes ecclesiastical, to have good regard that such uniform order in the divine service and rules of the church might be duly kept, as by the laws in that behalf is provided, and by our Injunctions also declared and explained; and that you should call unto you for your assistance certain of our bishops, to reform the abuses and disorders of sundry persons seeking to make alteration

and he having proceeded therein with the help of the bishops of Winchester and Ely, the latter bishop has now repaired to his diocese.

therein; we understanding that with the help of the reverend fathers in God, the bishops of Winchester and Ely, and some other, ye have well entered into some convenient reformation of things disordered, and that now the said bishop of Ely is by our commandment repaired into his diocese, whereby you shall want his assistance: we minding earnestly to have a perfect reformation of all abuses, attempted to deform the uniformity prescribed by our laws and Injunctions, and that none should be suffered to decline either on the left or on the right hand from the direct line limited by authority of our said laws and Injunctions, do earnestly by our authority royal will and charge you, by all means lawful, to proceed herein

Whereupon the Queen wills Parker to proceed as he has begun, and directs him to send for the bishops of London and Sarum, and to charge them to assist him, until the month of October.

as you have begun. And for your assistance we will, that you shall, by authority hereof, and in our name, send for the bishops of London and Sarum[1], and communicate these our letters with them, and straitly charge them to assist you from time to time, between this and the month of October, to do all manner of things requisite to reform such abuses as afore are mentioned, in whomsoever ye shall find the same. And if you shall find in any of the said bishops (which we trust ye shall not) or in any other whose aid you shall require, any remissness to aid and assist you, if upon your

[1 Bishops Sandys and Jewel. The latter died on the 23rd September, 1571.]

admonition the same shall not be amended, we charge you to advertise us; for we mean not that any persons, having credit by their vocation to aid you, should for any respect forbear, to become remiss in this service, tending to the observation of our laws, injunctions, and commandments. Given at our manor of Hatfield, the twentieth day of August, in the 13th year of our reign.

To our most reverend father in God, our right trusty and right well-beloved the archbishop of Canterbury, metropolitan and primate of all England.

CCXCIII.

ORDER OF HENRY EARL OF ARUNDEL FOR SUPPLY OF DEER TO ARCHBISHOP PARKER.

22nd August, 1571. Lambeth MS. 959. art. 1. Orig.

DELIVER unto the most reverend father in God, my very good lord the archbishop of Canterbury, upon his grace's letters, such and so many deer of season in winter and summer yearly, as his grace shall write for[2], and this shall be your sufficient warrant therefore. And if it shall please him to hunt at any time, I will you make him such game as ye would do unto me. Fail not hereof as ye tender my pleasure. At Nonsuch, the 22nd of August, 1571.

The archbishop to have as many deer of season out of Nonsuch Park as he shall write for, and if he will hunt, game is to be made him.

Your master,
ARUNDELL.

To Robert Gavell, keeper of the great park at Nonsuch, and to Roger Marshall, and to one of them, and all other keepers of the park of Nonsuch for the time being.

[2 On the back of this warrant, granted by Henry Fitzalan, the last Earl of Arundel of that family, the archbishop has written the following form of letter to be used on these occasions: "Whereas it hath pleased my very good lord the Earl of Arundel, in his honourable liberality, as by the letter of his own handwriting may appear, to grant unto me, Matthew, archbishop of Canterbury, such deer as

CCXCIV.

ARCHBISHOP PARKER TO ———

16th December, [probably 1571[1]]. Harleian MS. 6990. art. 49. Orig.

Thanks for kindness to the archbishop's lances at York.

AFTER my right hearty commendations to your good lordship, with like thanks for the great favour and gentleness shewed unto my poor lances at York, being right glad that your lordship is prosperously returned. And whereas I have been long in requiting your good will in bestowing this written story upon me, I send the same story to your lordship in print, somewhat more enlarged with such old copies as I had of other of my friends, praying your lordship to accept

Sends a book, partly printed from a MS. lent by the person addressed.

shall be written for by me the said Matthew; this is to pray you to appoint to this my messenger a ——— of this season, wherein ye shall do me thankful pleasure. At Lambeth, this — in the year of our Lord God —

M. C.

To my loving friend the keeper of the park at Nonsuch, or to his deputy there.]

[1 Three circumstances are stated in this letter which lead towards a conclusion as to its date and the person to whom it was addressed, but do not fix either of them: 1. The favour and gentleness shewn to the archbishop's "poor lances" at York. This probably refers to the military service of the archbishop's tenants by knight's service in the army of the south, sent to York to assist in suppressing the rebellion of 1569. 2. The person addressed is one who "prosperously returned" from the north. The southern army was under the command of the Earl of Warwick and Lord Clinton. Lord Hunsdon was in London at the time the rebellion broke out, but posted down in all haste to his command at Berwick. The Earl of Sussex, who had the command in chief of the Queen's army, had been for sometime resident at York. 3. The person addressed had lent the archbishop a MS., which he returned with a copy in print "somewhat more enlarged with such old copies as I had of other of my friends." This may have been the Chronicle of Matthew Paris, published in 1571. That book was "enlarged" from several MSS., and especially from a MS. lent to the archbishop by Henry Earl of Arundel. MSS. were also lent him for that publication by Sir Henry Sydney, Edward Aglionby, and Sir William Cecil, but no peer has yet been found mentioned as the lender of a MS. on that occasion, except the Earl of Arundel, who certainly was not at York in 1569.]

it in good part. And thus I wish your lordship as well to prosper in all grace and goodness as myself. From my house at Lambeth, this 16th of December.

Your lordship's loving friend in Christ,

MATTHUE CANTUAR.

CCXCV.

ARCHBISHOP PARKER TO BISHOP PARKHURST OF NORWICH.

2nd January, 1571—2. Parkhurst Epp. Camb. Univ. Libr. MS. Ee II. 34. art. 39. fol. 66 b. Copy.

SALUTEM in Christo. Where your lordship writeth that you would know mine opinion, partly for certain preachers which be in your country; I take it, that neither your lordship nor myself can, without great partiality, set them awork to trouble the commonwealth, and the state of good religion, whatsoever they talk. And therefore you may use your authority as you think good, not meaning to write in their favour. *[The archbishop replies to a question as to licensing certain preachers.]*

And whereas you find by experience that some parishes will not be brought out of their own parishes, being able to find a sufficient curate, I think they speak reason. For it is not intended by our canons that everything should be so precisely kept, but for the most part, and as occasion of edification should require. And thus I wish your lordship a prosperous year following. From my house at Lambeth, this 2nd Jan. *[It is intended by the canons that everything shall be kept as edification shall require.]*

Your loving brother,

MATTHUE CANTUAR.

CCXCVI.

ARCHBISHOP PARKER AND OTHER ECCLESIASTICAL COMMISSIONERS TO THE DUCHESS OF SUFFOLK.

13th January, [1571–2.] Petyt MS. Inner Temple, No. 47. fol. 507. Orig.

The ecclesiastical commissioners having sent for one Brown, chaplain to the duchess of Suffolk, she would not suffer him to come to them, claiming that he resided in a privileged place.

WHEREAS upon just cause, and according to the trust that her Majesty hath put us in, we sent for one Brown, your grace's chaplain[1] (as he saith), by a messenger of her Majesty's chamber appointed for that purpose; we are given to understand that your grace would not suffer him to come unto us, alleging a privileged place for his defence. Our commission extendeth to all places, as well exempt as not exempt, within her Majesty's dominions, and before this time never by any called into question. We are persuaded that your grace knowing the authority of our commission, and how straitly we are charged to proceed in redressing disorders, will not stay your said servant, contrary to the laws of this realm, but will send him unto us to answer such matter as he is to be charged withal. We would be loth to use other means to bring him to his answer, as we must be forced to do, if your grace will not like hereof. Thus we bid your grace heartily farewell. From Lambeth, this 13th of January.

Your loving friends,

GABRIELL GOODMAN.   MATTHUE CANTUAR.
RICHARDE WENDESLEY.   ED. LONDON.
 B. MONSON.

To the right honourable the duchess of Suffolk, her grace.

[1 The person mentioned is said by Strype (Book IV. chap. 6,) to have been Robert Brown, the originator of the sect called Brownists. Strype erroneously supposed, on the authority of this letter, that Brown was domestic chaplain to the duke of Norfolk. It would seem from the address that it was to the well-known duchess of Suffolk, Katherine, widow of Charles Brandon, that the person sent for stood in that relation.]

CCXCVII.

ARCHBISHOP PARKER TO LORD BURGHLEY.

19th May, 1572. Lansd. MS. xv. art. 34. Orig.

SIR,

BECAUSE your lordship writeth to me in secret, and be your own secretary, so I write again. This case of murder is not only lamentable and detestable, but *ominosum.* I have marked the state of this neutral government. I look for no other end but that is very likely. I have framed myself to be carried away with the floods, when they shall arise. This Machiavel government is strange to me, for it bringeth forth strange fruits. As soon is the papist favoured as is the true protestant. And yet forsooth my levity doth mar all. When the true subject is not regarded but overthwarted, when the rebel is borne with, a good commonwealth, *scilicet.* When the faithful subject and officer hath spent his wit to search, to find, to indict, to arraign, and to condemn, yet must they be kept still for a fair day to cut our own throats. Why is Barker[2] &c. spared, &c.? Is this the way to rule English people? But it deserveth to be counted clemency. O cruelty, to spare the professed enemy, and to drive to the slaughter herself and her best friends! O subtle dissimulation of the enemy! For myself, I shew you truly, I delight not in blood. Yea, if I had not been so much bound to the mother, I would not so soon have granted to serve the daughter in this place, and if I had not well trusted to have died or this time, your honours should have sent thrice for me before I would have returned from Cambridge. Alas, my lord, ye see and have seen a long time what they seek. Think you that men mark not your governance? Think you not that it is perceived that when her Majesty hath truly determined and spoken, ye overthrow not what is purposed? Let us be quite out of estimation, and of no credit, and let us (if we can make anything to colour others) be objected to envy, be put to peril, yea, cast away. Think you, that this way you among yourself shall escape? O my lord, is it glory, riches, or life that I seek in

[2 Barker was one of the witnesses whose examinations brought to light the treason of the duke of Norfolk. He was a gentleman in the duke's service.]

this cause, that I now in this age dissemble and stand in fear, and not of God, *qui potest et animam et corpus perdere in* *gehennam?* No, I could be better content to live for myself with one man only than with forty. I see and hear of the market-folks only how the game goeth. I must needs reverence your great pains, wit, and diligence; I must needs confess the princely heart of her Majesty; but I fear *qui te beatum dicunt ipsi te decipiunt.* I see honour and glory is daily sought, I pray God send plenty thereof; but I see that this cause is supernatural, in God's hand, his wrath is deserved, &c. *Ille Deus in cujus manu sunt corda principum* will arise, and in the mean time harden her heart to work his purpose, and deserved vengeance of us and of our posterity. For the earnest zeal, and for my manifold duties' sake, I fear her Highness shall be strangely chronicled, and I would it were amended. I have and will pray, nought else can I do, but *in silentio et in spe* continue. One thing in this hurly-burly I pray your honour to let me speak to you. I am informed credibly, that in your letters, some of them, ye profess that ye be at your wits' end. Sir, howsoever it be, let the world know no such thing. Some friends be not secret. Blaze they will to win credit. Now or never we must set out a good countenance, and surely so I comfort such faithful as come lamentably dejected to me. We shall never be at peace and quiet till that *homo peccati* have that is justly deserved. *In mora periculum.* French princes will dissemble and deceive to win their purposes. *Det Deus tibi intellectum, &c.* I pray you, my lord, be not angry with me: *nam aliquando et olitor opportuna loquitur.*

(*Indorsed*) 19th May, 1572.

CCXCVIII.

ARCHBISHOP PARKER TO BISHOP BARNES OF CARLISLE.

22nd May, 1572. Parker MSS. C. C. Coll. Camb. CXIV. art. 144. p. 422.

SALUTEM *in Christo.* Upon the receipt of your letters[1] concerning your young man to be a notary, I use this

[[1] The draft of the present letter of the archbishop is written

order, to refer the ability of any such to one or two of the arches to judge of them; which I did enjoin your man, who coming to me without any such testimony, I remitted him again to your lordship. What cause I have to deal circumspectly in that court I could sh[ew] you but for length. And thus being glad otherwise [to] pleasure you, I commit your lordship to God as myself. From my house at Lambeth, this 22nd of May.

On application to the archbishop to appoint any one to be a notary, he refers the applicant to one or two of the arches to judge of his ability.

CCXCIX.

ARCHBISHOP PARKER AND OTHERS TO LORD BURGHLEY.

31st May, 1572. Parker MSS. C. C. Coll. Camb. cxviii. art. 39. p. 637. Orig.

YOUR honour requested us two archbishops, the bishop of London, and the bishop of Ely, to peruse the bill of complaint of the young men against their elders, masters of Colleges, &c. We have deliberately conferred their objections, answers, and replies, which we now send to your lordship herewith, besides that we heard both the parties challenging the one the other at full. In fine, we perceive, by due consideration, that the meaning of the proctors is, to find many matters amiss in the new statutes, for the which they seek reformation. We think that the statutes as they be drawn may yet stand, and no great cause why to make any alteration. We think also that these younger men have been far overseen to seek their pretended reformation by disordered means, and namely in going from College to College to seek subscription of hands, without the licence of the Vice-chancellor, &c. The consideration whereof for some satisfaction or reconciliation, we refer to your order and wis-

Lord Burghley referred to the subscribers the complaints of the young men of Cambridge against the masters of Colleges.

They perceive that the proctors desire to find many things amiss in the new statutes, but are of opinion that there is no great cause to make any alteration. The young men have sought reformation by disordered means.

upon the letter of the bishop of Carlisle here alluded to. It is dated from "the Rose Castle in Cumberland, the 14th May, 1572." The person recommended was Edward Brakinbury, "kinsman and servant" to bishop Barnes. One of the archbishop's appointments of a notary, dated 10th February, 1573—4, is entered in the Register Book of the parish of Buckland Newton near Cerne in Dorsetshire. The oath to be taken by the notary is recited in the appointment.]

dom. And thus we commend your lordship to the grace of God. From Lambeth, the last of May, 1572.

Your lordship's in Christ,

MATTHUE CANTUAR.
EDM. EBOR.
ED. LONDON.
RICHARD ELYE.
NIC. BANGOR[1].

CCC.

ARCHBISHOP PARKER TO LORD BURGHLEY.

2nd July, [1572.] Lansd. MS. xv. art. 35. Orig.

SIR,

Begs for the liberty of lord Henry Howard.

I AM called upon to write to your lordship to obtain liberty for my lord Henry[2], which he much desireth; whereupon seeing the parliament is now at a stay, I pray you be a mean to her Majesty that he may have his desire. And thus I wish your lordship well to fare in Christ. This second of July.

Your honour's loving friend,

MATTHUE CANTUAR.

To the right honourable and my very good lord, the lord of Burghley.

[[1] The signers of this report were archbishops Parker and Grindal, with bishops Sandys, Cox, and Nicholas Robinson.]

[[2] Lord Henry Howard, second son of the celebrated earl of Surrey, and brother of Thomas Howard, fourth duke of Norfolk, the duke who was executed on the 2nd June preceding the date of this letter. Lord Henry was ultimately created earl of Northampton, by which title he was well known in the reign of James I.]

CCCI.

ARCHBISHOP PARKER TO LORD BURGHLEY.

8th July, [1572.]   Lansd. MS. xv. art. 36.   Orig.

SIR,

I WOULD come to the court to sue to the Queen's Majesty, if I knew what day I might most opportunely do it, in this case following. Now, at the last, with much diligence of conference and long debating, we have finished the book of statutes as may concern the cathedral churches newly erected. There is set out, for brevity's sake, first, the titles of the statutes. Secondly, the words inserted in our commission. Thirdly, imperfections and reformations, with a doubt to be resolved. Then the body of the statute, which may be diversely considered to divers churches in their private statute. If it please your lordship, or any other whom it shall please the Queen to appoint, to peruse that which is set down, and with some reformations as you shall think expedient, and so the book returned, we shall now, in the Queen's absence, cause every particular book to be written with some fair hand in parchment, and so to sue to her Highness at her return from progress for her hand-subscription, that it may pass the great seal; of which doing we have a precedent of the statutes of Durham church, sealed with the great seal, and signed with Philip and Mary's hand. And also we have prepared a book ready of the old statutes by King Henry's time, if any man will compare the same. Thus, desiring to have your advice before the Queen's Majesty's departing[3], I thought good to write so much. And thus God preserve your good lordship. From my house at Lambeth, this 8th of July.

If your lordship desireth any further notice, I send this my chaplain, who was present at all these doings.

Your lordship's loving friend in Christ,
MATTHUE CANTUAR.

*To the right honourable and my very good
lord, the lord of Burghley.*

[3 This was the year of the Queen's visit to Kenilworth.]

CCCII.

ARCHBISHOP PARKER TO LORD BURGHLEY.
17th August, 1572. Lansd. MS. xv. art. 38. Orig.

AFTER my right hearty commendations to your honour. I received your lordship's letters wherein ye signify to me that one Mr Wood had brought to your honour letters from divers of the best credit of that University, for the couveniency of his placing in physic in All Souls' College. Furthermore, that the young man hath informed you that he was with me since my letters written to your honour, and said that, upon his allegations, I should not mislike his cause so much as before, upon former information. The truth is, this man was not with me, nor made such allegation, but a pupil of his shewed me a copy of certain letters written by the warden, when he was neither warden nor fellow, that touched the honesty of the said Wood, whereupon I signified to the messenger, that I liked not the childishness of him to write such a vain letter, as one of them was, and thereupon I required either the same Wood, or himself, to come to me again, and I would hear better the cause, for that the warden was then in town, and was purposed to have resolved the cause (as at that time I shewed his pupil my disliking). But I never heard of either of them both till your honour had sent me your last letters. Indeed the said Wood is stept in a manifest perjury, to sue for any dispensations against the founder's ordinance, willing them all to be inclined to be priests, and at convenient time to take the same order. They be so much offended now with the ministry that of forty such fellows in the house, there are but two priests, and whether this be a good example to the University for men to run in open perjuries, and whether it be good to the governance that so few priests and preachers (specially in the University) should be, I leave that to her Majesty's consideration and your wisdom. If her Highness will take it upon her conscience to break such ordinance, I refer it to her Majesty. Beside this cause touched, I see more inconveniences that will follow, both in this and in other Colleges, if this be won by importunity; but as for myself, I cannot bear with it in reason, praying your lordship not to be offended with this my writing. And thus wishing her Majesty and you all to return well home again, I commit your honour to God as myself. From my house at Lambeth, this 17th of August, 1572.

Your lordship's loving friend,

MATTHUE CANTUAR.

*To the right honourable my good lord,
the lord treasurer of England, give these.*

CCCIII.

ARCHBISHOP PARKER TO LORD BURGHLEY.

25th August, [1572]. Lansd. MS. xv. art. 39. Orig.

SIR,

For all the devices that we can make to the contrary, yet some good fellows still labour to print out the vain "Admonition to the parliament[1]." Since the first printing it hath been twice printed, and now with additions, whereof I send your honour one of them. We wrote letters to the mayor and some aldermen of London to lay in wait for the charects, printer, and corrector, but I fear they deceive us. They are not willing to disclose this matter.

"Admonition to the parliament" twice reprinted.

Furthermore, this other day was brought me a popish bull in Spanish, printed, which, as I am informed, a certain Spaniard as he was going to his execution drew out of his bosom, as long worn there, by the which he had confidence that he should never come to such death, and cried brute of them that brake promise with him, and furthermore required of the people there, that if any were present that could instruct his conscience to die better to God-ward, that his soul might be in better surety of salvation, he earnestly requested it. This bull being thus taken up, was, at the last, brought to me, although I do not well remember in what parts beyond the seas this execution was done. I have

A bull in Spanish brought to the archbishop, of which he relates the history he had heard.

[1] The "Admonition," generally ascribed to Cartwright, but probably the composition of various authors. For an account of several editions of it, see Herbert's Ames, III. 1631—2]

delivered this bull to be secretly translated by a trusty body, which when it is once performed, I will send it over to your lordship, doubting whether you have seen it.

Recommends the warden of All Souls' to lord Burghley's favour.

I pray your honour be good to this honest young man, the warden of All Souls' College. In the cause of that College, as of certain other of that University, I did write as I think convenient. And thus I wish your honour as well to fare in Christ as I wish to myself. From my house at Lambeth, this 25th of August.

Your honour's loving friend in Christ,

MATTHUE CANTUAR.

To the right honourable and my very good lord, my lord treasurer of England. At the Court.

CCCIV.

ARCHBISHOP PARKER TO LORD BURGHLEY.
16th September, 1572. Lansd. MS. xv. art. 42. Orig.

SIR,

Return of recusants to the council.

ACCORDING to our careful duty, we have returned answer to the council of such things as be demanded; and as for to certify the names and qualities throughout the realm, of all such papists as do not like the religion, it were an infinite

Increase of papists.

matter. I marvel what it mean that they grow so fast; whether it be of private maintenance, or for that they be exasperated by the disordered preachings and writings of some puritans, who will be never at a point, I know not; but cunningly they be encouraged of some persons that pretend otherwise. They shoot not at us only, but at you all; and if our spoil would serve them, I would not be long to resign up to them. I have heard say, that when cardinal Lorrain saw our Prayer-book in Latin, or in French, he should answer, that he liked well of that order, "if," saith he, "they would go no further." I beseech God to hold his hand over

If "that desperate person"

us. If that only desperate person[1] were away, as by justice

[1 The allusion seems to be to Mary Queen of Scots.]

soon it might be, the Queen's Majesty's good subjects would be in better hope, and the papists' daily expectation vanquished. I pray God ye bring home her Majesty well, and yourself with her. They be full of spite and secret malice. Their imps be marvellous bold, and flock together in their talking-places, as I am informed, rejoicing much at this unnatural and unprincely cruelty and murder. I have intelligence of some that will not spare to utter their rejoices, and of long have they looked for such slaughter at home; and some of their books written I have gotten, wherein they go about in large writing to set out their desire, and make their conclusion, *quod heretici morte sunt plectendi.* I may not prescribe mine opinion in things of policy, but I fear that when papists be so bold, and full of armour, they may mean much hurt and mischief. In dead Queen Mary's days, and these be not like, when this statute was made, they were in number almost all papists. The Philistines used in their policy[2] that none of the Israelites should have any weapon, but only Saul and Jonathas; *caverant enim Philistini, ne forte facerent Hebrei gladium aut lanceam, &c.* To mine own self, such papists as come to me will not be aknown but to dislike these cruel and viperous murders, but I learn by other inferiors how they triumph. God send us of his grace to protect his little flock. There be many worldlings, many counterfeits, many ambidexters, many neutrals, strong themself in all their doings, and yet we which ought to be *filii lucis,* want our policies and prudence. *"Non putâram!"* is the fool's experience; and if *piscator ictus semel sapit,* what shall come of us, who after such striking as is now used, shall not be left alive *ut sapiamus?* God's will be done: and I beseech God send to the Queen's Majesty *aures ut audiat, cor docile et benignum ut intelligat,* and to be advertised by the trustiest of her council to provide in time, and not to drive long such matters of reformation. If Almighty God oft and oft calling upon us, and shewing his favourable countenance from time to time, and yet we will *in securitate despicere omne consilium ejus &c.,* then I fear that which doth follow, by the prophecy of wise Solomon, *ego quoque in interitu vestro ridebo, et subsannabo cum vobis id quod timebatis advenerit, &c.* as followeth. Thus I wish her Majesty prosperously to

were away," the good subjects would be in better hope.

Rejoicings at the massacre of St Bartholomew.

The papists should be disarmed.

[2] 1 Reg. 13. D. [1 Sam. xiii. 22.]

return soon, to yourself God's good protection, and to you all *spiritum fortitudinis, &c.* From my house, this 16th of September.

Your lordship's loving friend in Christ,

M. CANT.

To the righ[t honourable] and my very good lord, the lord treasurer of England. At the Court.

CCCV.

ARCHBISHOP PARKER TO LORD BURGHLEY.
[6th October, 1572.] Lansd. MS. xv. art. 43. Orig.

SIR,

I WROTE to your honour private letters *in amaritudine animæ, et in insipientia mea.* I trust ye do not procure me any displeasure for them, and, before Almighty God I speak it, no creature in earth knoweth of this, or for that my par-

Parker believes in Cecil's attachment to the Queen, whatever subtilty there be in others.

ticular writing to you. I have that persuasion that ye love her Highness, and wish her preservation, whatsoever subtle respects be in some others. The truth is, as well for Almighty God's commandment, for that she is now my prince,

Last words of Anne Boleyn concerning her to him being her poor countryman

as for the last words that ever her Majesty's mother spake to me concerning her, being her poor countryman, I have as much cause to wish well to her Majesty as any other whatsoever, and so will I be, whatsoever cometh of it. If I be in any error, I can be glad to be otherwise advertised, to change my fearful opinion toward her; and, sir, because I hear one other thing, I will open it to your lordship, and do with it

Examination of a person at Dover.

what ye think best. I am, I think, credibly informed, that the mayor of Dover brought up a strange body to be examined, of whom I hear, that because your lordship could have no leisure (as I am sure ye be carefully and thoroughly occupied) ye committed the examination to Mr Somner and to this mayor, and he hath it in writing, that this villain should

His slanders against the Queen.

utter most shameful words against her, *viz.* that the earl of Leicester and Mr Hatton should be such toward her, as the matter is so horrible, that they would not write down the words, but would have uttered them in speech to your lordship if ye could have been at leisure; furthermore he should say, that a brother of his in Calais should affirm that within this winter he trusted to hear of so many throats cut here in England as be reported to be in France; and he should say, "What make ye of the persecution of Queen Mary?" for within this twelvemonth, he doubted not but that Henry's bones, and mistress Elizabeth's too, should be openly burned in Smithfield. And further I hear that this party is yet delivered, and sent home to London again, to the rejoice of his friends. Sir, if this be true, God be merciful to us; I can say no more. As Mardocheus, I hear and understand, which I pray God turn to her honour, but I cannot do any less in conscience, but to unburden myself, and pour it into your bosom, and her Majesty willeth me to write still to you. God defend her Majesty, and all her trusty friends.

To the right honourable my lord treasurer,
be it delivered.

(*Indorsed,*) 6th October, 1572.

and anticipation of troubles in England.

CCCVI.

ARCHBISHOP PARKER AND OTHER ECCLESIASTICAL COMMISSIONERS TO BISHOP PARKHURST OF NORWICH.

9th October, 1572. Parkhurst Epp. Camb. Univ. Libr. MS. Ee. II. 34. art. 89. fol. 90. Copy.

SALUTEM *in Christo*. Ye shall understand that we are credibly informed of one Mr Cotton, gentleman, (who married of late Sir Roger Woodhouse's daughter) abiding within six miles of Norwich (whose father being a knight, and dwelleth in Kent), that the said younger Cotton should be a man very evil disposed. Whereupon this is to require you, and in the Queen's Majesty's name charge you, to search his house suddenly, to see what books unlawful or armour he hath in store; and thereof to make an inventory, and to stay them, and to send him up, or to take a bond of him for his appearing before us the Queen's Majesty's commissioners[1]. And

Mr Cotton the younger reported to the commissioners as very evil disposed.

The bishop of Norwich is to search his house suddenly.

[1 There is in the same MS. (art. 90. fol. 90 b.) bishop Parkhurst's answer to the above letter, in which he says, that having discovered

hereof fail you not. And thus we bid your lordship well to fare as ourselves. At Lambeth, this 9th of October, 1572[1].

Your loving brothers,
MATTHUE CANTUAR.
ROBT. WINTON.
RICHARDE WENDESLEY.

CCCVII.

ARCHBISHOP PARKER TO BISHOP SANDYS OF LONDON.
29th October, 1572. Regist. Parker. II. fol. 73 a.

Sends the bishop of London a special form of prayer for the time.

MATTHÆUS, providentia divina Cantuariensis archiepiscopus, totius Angliæ primas et metropolitanus, venerabili confratri nostro domino Edwino, eadem permissione divina Londinensi episcopo, salutem, et fraternam in Domino charitatem. Cum nos librum quendam precum publicarum, intitulatum, "A form of common prayer to be used, and so commanded by authority of the Queen's Majesty, and necessary for the present time and state. 1572, vicesimo septimo Octobris[2]," de mandato illustrissimæ dominæ nostræ reginæ componi ac imprimi et publicari fecimus; nos igitur, librum prædictum in et per totam provinciam Cantuariensem debitæ executioni demandari volentes, librum ipsum præsentibus annexum vobis

where Cotton lodged, he took his journey thither, and "found the said Mr Cotton very sick of a tertian ague, in the house of one Francis Downes, gentleman, of East Tuddenham, who is of like evil disposition touching religion." The bishop adds: "he confesseth himself to be a papist, and saith he is not ashamed thereof: for anything I can perceive, he is a fit instrument to take any enterprise in hand." Parkhurst inclosed an inventory of the books and weapons found in Cotton's chamber. The former he judged "of no great importance, saving the book of the prophecies." As however Cotton was too ill to be removed, and could find no bail, being a stranger in those parts himself, and his friend Downes being in London, the bishop bound him in his own recognizances. The consequence was, that he absconded, and baffled all attempts for his apprehension. See Letters CCCVIII. and CCCXVII. of this collection.]

[1 There is a note at the foot: "Received 13 October, at night."]

[2 The form referred to is published in the Liturgical Services of the reign of Queen Elizabeth, (Parker Society), 1847. 8vo. p. 540.]

1572.]   ARCHB. PARKER TO BP SANDYS OF LONDON.   403

transmittimus publicandum, volentes ac fraternitati vestræ firmiter injungendo mandantes, quatenus vera exemplaria libri prædicti universis et singulis venerabilibus confratribus nostris dictæ provinciæ nostræ Cantuariensis, cum ea qua fieri poterit matura celeritate transmittatis, seu transmitti faciatis; eisque ex parte nostra injungatis, quibus nos etiam tenore præsentium sic injungimus, quatenus eorum singuli in singulis diœcesibus eorundem coram decano et capitulo cujuslibet ecclesiæ cathedralis, ac archidiaconis et clero suæ diœcesis, prout ad eos et eorum quemlibet pertinet, librum prædictum debite publicent, et ab omnibus quos concernit, observari, et debitæ executioni demandari procurent, sive sic publicari et observari faciant cum effectu. Et præterea, fraternitati vestræ ut supra injungimus, quatenus librum prædictum in et per diœcesim vestram Londinensem, prout ad vos attinet, debite et effectualiter publicari et executioni demandari faciatis, prout decet. In cujus rei testimonium sigillum nostrum præsentibus apponi fecimus. Datum in Manerio nostro de Lambeth, vicesimo nono die mensis Octobris, A. D. 1572, et nostræ consecrationis anno decimo tertio.
^(marginal notes: to be published and observed throughout the province of Canterbury, and through the bishop's own diocese of London.)

CCCVIII.

ARCHBISHOP PARKER TO BISHOP PARKHURST OF NORWICH.

2nd November, 1572.   Parkhurst Epp. Camb. Univ. Lib. MS. Ee. ii. 34, art. 95. fol. 95.   Copy.

SALUTEM *in Christo*. I have received two books, and the lewd book of prophecies. As for Cotton[3] himself, he is not yet come up, whereof we do marvel. I would be loth to hear, for not binding him with sureties, he should scape away. I pray your lordship devise some way to foresee the same. You shall do well in mine opinion, by all means you can, inquire of such unordered persons papistically set, not coming to prayers according to the laws, nor bearing goodwill unto the religion received; which must not be proved by surmises, but by their deeds, words, or letters. And if you signify them to us, we shall have consideration of them. You shall also do well to signify what good men of countenance ye have, able to be in grand commission for examining and

[3 See Letter CCCVI. p. 401.]

ordering of such contemners. And thus, having else nothing, I commit your lordship to God, as myself. From my house at Lambeth, this second of November, 1572.

Your loving brother,

MATTHUE CANTUAR.

marginalia: What men fit to be in commission for ordering recusants.

CCCIX.
ARCHBISHOP PARKER TO LORD BURGHLEY.
5th November, 1572. Lansd. MS. xv. art. 44. Orig.

YOUR honour may understand how partially I have dealt betwixt these two persons, partly by their bills, and mine arbitrament, which I send to your honour to consider of, the length whereof grieveth me to send to you, otherwise occupied more profitably; and but for the satisfaction of her Majesty I would not have troubled you. This complaint cometh not from that old simple man, but from that covetous merchantman (Levers), who claimeth the farm; which if he could have got, he did not much regard Mr Willoughby's possession, as his own notes to me written do testify. Secondly, because he allegeth that he is my kinsman; the truth is, he is no more my kinsman than the man in the moon. My consideration was, for that the benefice hath been shamefully ordered before time in his incumbency; the town being of a great people bordering upon the seal, and many times unserved, and at my metropolitical visitation there, more exclamation was made than of any in Norfolk or Suffolk; the chancel quite down, the vicar's house almost decayed, which yet Mr Willoughby made a promise and a pretence to me, that he would build them up again though it should cost him an hundred pounds or more, in which respect I did labour for his restitution, long before his late complaint, till I heard all these words were but wind. But of late, in respect of partial favour I bare him, for that he was sometime in council with Queen Anne, I delivered him from all manner charges

marginalia: The course taken by the archbishop on an arbitration between Levers and Willoughby, committed to him by the Queen.

marginalia: Levers allegeth that he is the archbishop's kinsman no more so than the man in the moon.

marginalia: The matter relates to a benefice on the Coast, which has been much neglected.

marginalia: Willoughby formerly in council with Queen Anne Boleyn.

[¹ The place alluded to was Aldborough, in Suffolk. A paper under the archbishop's signature, illustrative of the affairs of Dr Willoughby, is attached to the present letter. Dr Willoughby is described in it as "so childish" as to "have spent £4 for painting of a pulpit."]

of dilapidation, and suffered his farmer (Levers) to go away with the whole year's rent, and have awarded him ten pounds yearly pension for two years, wherein the fruits are to be paid, and the house to be recovered, and, after that two years, fourteen pounds by year, as much as ever he received; and now hearing of the desire of the country to have one learned among them, this man being well learned, a bachelor of divinity, and a good preacher, and purposeth daily to dwell among them, I took it to be a good discharge to the Queen's Majesty's conscience to have such a man to be preferred and continued in that populous fisher-town. If this my doing be not thought reasonable, I refer it to her Majesty's consideration, in which regard I reserved a clause in the arbitrament.

Furthermore, where your honour did write to me for serjeant Lovelace to be my steward of liberties, the truth is, that he was with me sithen Justice Manwoed was placed[2], to whom I did grant my good will for his friend, and the said Lovelace being long with me never made mention of that matter, but to one of my servants, saying yet to him, that he should not long enjoy the office though he obtained it, for that he thought shortly to be otherwise placed. Furthermore, if it were free in my hand, yet I doubt to accept him for mine officer of that (though he be and hath of long time been of my council, and quarterly paid him his fee), seeing he is steward of the liberties of the church. Thus wishing to her Majesty God's good protection, and to your honour his assistance, I commit you to the same as myself. From my house at Lambeth, this 5th of November, 1572.

Serjeant Lovelace recommended to the archbishop by Burghley, as steward of his liberties.

Your lordship's assured in Christ,

MATTH. CANT.

CCCX.
ARCHBISHOP PARKER TO LORD BURGHLEY AND THE EARL OF LEICESTER.
7th November, [1572.] Lansd. MS. xvii. art. 53. Orig.

I RECEIVED your lordships' letters in the behalf of Mr John Stowell, whereby it appeareth that he hath misinformed

[2 Manwood, afterwards lord chief baron, was appointed a justice of the Common Pleas on the 14th October, 1572.]

Particulars of case of John Stowell, accused of cohabiting with a person as his wife, a former wife being alive.

your lordships in some part of the state of his cause. For the matter why he was convened before me and others her Highness' commissioners, was the public offence that was given by him to the country where he dwelleth, for cohabiting with a gentlewoman as his wife, his former wife being on live, and as I am informed by my officer of the Arches, he is called to that court by his former wife, to shew cause why she ought not to be restored unto him; and yet before him he utterly denieth to make present answer whether he be married or no to the gentlewoman with whom he dwelleth, and now he refuseth to answer us of the commission, except we will deliver his articles against him in writing, having a week to deliberate thereof before now. And for his such refusal, he was by me and others the commissioners appointed by order to prison before the receipt of your lordships' letters. And thus, for my part, I am right sorry, for that he seemeth to be a protestant, that we should be compelled in him to restrain this foul disordered doing, to avoid further example. From my house at Lambeth, this 7th of November[1].

Your lordships' loving friend in Christ,

MATTHUE CANTUAR.

To the right honourable my good lords, the lord treasurer and the earl of Leicester.

CCCXI.

ARCHBISHOP PARKER TO LORD BURGHLEY.

8th November, 1572. Lansd. MS. xv. art. 46. Orig.

Offence between lord Leicester and the archbishop.

YOUR lordship shall understand that I have written to my lord of Leicester, praying your good lordship to help to pacify him if he be offended. Verily, my lord, I desire, as it may please God, to be in favour with such noble personages as be in service toward my lady and mistress and specially be favoured of her Majesty, in whom she is contented and

[1 See Letter CCCXL. p. 447, and note 3.]

pleased, and howsoever my rude nature may seem otherwise, yet I would fain use the same.

We should have written to your lordships before now of the answer [to] the letters which your lordships of the council sent to us with the packet of letters sent from beyond the sea. My lord of London took upon him to pen the letters, and so we have rested a good time, but yet they come no[t] forward. We have examined divers parties, and find no great matter. The book of Ireland's history[2] we obtained, which here I send to your lordship, which your honour may communicate to my lord of Leicester, for it is dedicated to him; and if this Campion could be reclaimed or recovered, I see by this wit, that he were worthy to be made of. And thus I wish your good lordship heartily well to fare, with my thanks that your lordship took my scribbling in so [good] part. From my house, this 8th of November.

Letters sent by the council to be examined by the archbishop and bishop of London.

Campion's History of Ireland.

The writer worth reclaiming.

Your lordship's loving friend,

MATTHUE CANTUAR.

To the right honourable, and my very good lord, the lord treasurer of England.

CCCXII.

ARCHBISHOP PARKER TO LORD BURGHLEY.
13th November, 1572. Lansd. MS. xv. art. 47. Orig.

SIR,

I COMMEND me heartily to your lordship, thanking the same for your friendly admonition brought unto me from you by Mr dean of Westminster[3]. And where ye send me word that some men think I am carried with Mr Yale[4], in good faith the truth is not so; for when I know and can resolve the matter myself, I take none of his coat to be my counsellers, but I will follow the counsel of them that fear God. And though he chanced to be one of the commission this other day, I was nothing incensed against Mr Stowell, but

Reply to the notion that Parker allows his judgment in ecclesiastical causes to be stayed by Mr Yale.

Case of Stowell.

[2 The History of Ireland, written by Campion. The MS. is in the Cotton Library, Vitellius F. ix. It was published in 1633 by Sir James Ware.]

[3 Dr Gabriel Goodman.]   [4 The archbishop's chancellor.]

took advantage of his counsellor's words which was, if he should answer directly to our demands: viz. whether he was married to the second or not, it might have been a prejudice to him in the Audience Court, which maketh me now to defer the matter a while before your message came, whose counsel I prepose to follow, although distemperance, wherewith I am now grieved, doth compel me not to hear such causes. I desired Mr dean to be here to-morrow at afternoon, when we would wish Stowell to come afore us, to defer the cause. And I will send to my chancellor that he shall also cease in his court for a time; which I do the rather for that I would not have you, which be supreme justices, suspected as though we durst not for your letters request to deal in justice.

Lord Leicester's anger with the archbishop.

And whereas I at your good counsel did write my letters to my lord of Leicester to pacify him with true information, I understand by him that delivered my letters that he is so much offended that he would not once vouchsafe (being at leisure) to read my letters, but put them up in his pocket. If the first untrue information, heard with one ear, weigh so deeply in credit that the other ear will not hear the answer, then I can say no more. I will refer myself to God, but will do as justice, prudence, and honesty shall bear me at length.

Stowell's offers of £100 and £200 if the archbishop could but be mollified.

I understand that the party hath letters from my lord of Bath[1] of comfort, who informed me first in this matter. I have his note by me, and therefore marvel the more, and would gladly see these letters. I perceive the matter is very hotly taken, and Stowell careth not what to spend so he may have his fair lady; for as one informed me yesternight, he is offered a hundred pounds, and another of my house two hundred pounds, to mollify me in this case. I told the hundred pounds man that I rather wished it molten in his belly, than justice either by me or any of mine should be so bought and sold. But surely, my lord, what is lawful in this case I will not dispute; but if this man, or any other, should procure in this common wealth *quare expedit*, and so to be countenanced out the realm should have such a blow thereby, that our posterity shall judge of us that money and mastership worketh all with us in our time. And though we be nothing and outcasts among the puritans and their great

[1 Bishop Gilbert Berkeley, 1560—1581.]

fautors, a shrewd sort of them; as long as God shall suffer me in this office, I will still anger them and grieve them in such matters as they work unjustly. Thus I commend your honour to the grace of Almighty God as myself, this 13th of November.

Your lordship's alway in Christ,

MATTH. CANT.

To the right honourable, and my good lord,
the lord treasurer.

CCCXIII.

ARCHBISHOP PARKER TO LORD BURGHLEY.

22nd November, [1572.] Lansd. MS. xv. art. 49. Orig.

SIR,

MR dean of Westminster coming to me yesternight with your messages, moved me partly to write unto your lordship or to the council, how we proceeded in matters of commonwealth, and partly signified your desire and counsel for the answering of Saunders' book, &c. I had thought that your honour had understanding of all these causes, and I am sure I have spoken and written to you particularly of most of these things, so that I feared to weary you with multiplicity of matters, or doubted whether we might be judged to care more for our private defences and estimations, partly against the puritans and partly against the papists, than upon good zeal of the quiet governance of the Queen's people. And to write to the lords of the council in such particularities (some being affected as the report goeth) I thought it no prudence.

As for Saunders' book[2], brought in by one Andrewes, I knew your pleasure at sundry times, at the parliament chamber. As for the puritans' book, I signified by letters how they multiplied them by secret printing. As for the answer of Saunders' babbling book, I see few men either able or willing; not for the invincibleness of it, but for the huge

Dean of Westminster has moved the archbishop to write to Burghley about Saunders's book.

Few men able to answer Saunders's book on account of its size.

[2 "De visibili Monarchia Ecclesiæ, Lib. VIII." printed at Antwerp in 1571.]

volume; and I think the bishop of Sarum's book for English men have written sufficiently. And as for common matters in Latin, partly Germans and partly others have largely answered. So that their leisure may suffer them to write what they will, and yet will never be answered, though we had leisure to tend upon it. I with other the commissioners took order with every such bookseller as sell books in England, to bring their inventories first before they sell them, which being bound thereto I think they do. Among their books I found half a score of these traitorous books of Saunders; I distributed almost all of them, except one or two to such men whom I thought meet to peruse them. I sent to the bishop of Ely one, who hath done most to my remembrance, for he hath read over the long book, *qui vel Fabium delassare valeat.* He writeth his judgment that the book is not so strong but that it may be answered; he hath divided it into certain parts, and wisheth such men and such to take it in hand. And this is all, except that to assay the judgment of the greatest learned man (so thought) in England, viz. Mr Deering, I delivered him four or five quires of the first part of the book, which he returned to me again, but in such sort confuted, as too much childishness appeared.

As for the puritans, I understand how throughout all the realm, among such as profess themselves protestants, how the matter is taken: they highly justified, and we judged to be extreme persecutors. I have seen this seven year how the matter hath been handled on all parts. If the sincerity of the gospel shall end in such judgments, I fear you will have more ado than you shall be able to overcome. They slander us with infamous books and libels, lying they care not how deep. You feel the papists, what good names they give you, and whereabouts they go. We have sought as diligently as we can for the press of these puritans, but we cannot possibly find it. The more they write, the more they shame our religion; the more they be applauded too; the more be they comforted. Our bearing and suffering, our winking and dissembling, have such effects as now we may see everywhere to be fallen out. Yet here I cease, for troubling of your honour's great affairs too much. I pray God all doings be good policies of such as be thought most politic. I commit myself to God, as your honour to his good protection. From my house at Lambeth, this 22nd of November.

Your lordship's assured in Christ,
MATTHUE CANTUAR.

*To the right honourable, and my very good
lord, the lord of Burghley, lord treasurer
of England.*

CCCXIV.

ARCHBISHOP PARKER TO LORD BURGHLEY.

13th December, [1572.] Lansd. MS. xv. art. 50. Orig.

WHERE your lordship sent unto me by Mr dean of Westminster your desire to have Saunders' book answered, your honour shall understand that I have taken care thereof and laboured certain men which be at good leisure to do somewhat. And for a shew to be first sent out to the reader, both English and strange, I have appointed the confutation of so much as concerneth the honour and state of the realm, the dignity and legitimation of our prince, with just defence of king Henry's honour, queen Anne's, and partly your own, as by name you be touched, viz. *a pag.* 686 unto *pag.* 739. I have committed it to Mr Dr Clerk, who is of late doctor of law at Cambridge, and for his more estimation I have honested him with a room in the Arches, who shall I doubt not but sufficiently deal in the matter, and he shall not want my advice and diligence. As for some particular matters which be not known to me, I trust to have your counsel. Furthermore, to the better accomplishment of this work and other that shall follow, I have spoken to Day the printer, to cast a new Italian letter, which he is deing, and it will cost him forty mark, and loth he and other printers be to print any Latin book, because they will not here be uttered, and for that books printed in England be in suspicion abroad.

Now, sir, Day hath complained to me, that dwelling in a corner, and his brethren envying him, he cannot utter his books which lie in his hand, two or three thousand pounds' worth, his friends have procured of Paul's a lease of a little shop to be set up in the church-yard, and it is confirmed; and what by the instant request of some envious booksellers, the mayor and aldermen will not suffer him to set it up in the church-yard, wherein they have nothing to do, but by power. This shop is but little, and low, and leaded flat, and is made at his great cost, to the sum of forty or fifty pounds, and is made like the terrace, fair railed and posted, fit for men to stand upon in any triumph or shew, and can in nowise either hurt or deface the same. And for that you of the council have written me, and other of the commission, to help Day, &c., I pray your lordship to move the Queen's Majesty to subscribe her hand to these or such letters, that all this intendment may the better go forward, wherein your honour shall deserve well both of Christ's church, and of the prince and state, &c. I pray your lordship respite the said Dr Clerk in that work which we have spoken to him for, that this may be the sooner done. And thus God preserve your honour in better health than I in a naughty body feel in this hard winter. At Lambeth, this 13th of December.

Your honour's loving friend,
MATTHUE CANTUAR.

CCCXV.

ARCHBISHOP PARKER TO LORD BURGHLEY.

21st December, [1572.] Lansd. MS. xv. art. 52. Orig.

Sends the first part of the answer to Saunders for Burghley's consideration.

CONCERNING the first entry against the foul talk of Saunders, I send it to your lordship to consider of, praying you, if ye think so good, to return your allowance or disallowance, how ye judge of this beginning, and whether the writer shall go forward, or in what sort. Else I have nothing to write to your honour, but wish the same all grace of God as to myself. From my house at Lambeth, this 21st of December.

Your honour's in Christ,
MATTHUE CANTUAR.

To the right honourable my good lord the lord treasurer, be it delivered.

CCCXVI.

ARCHBISHOP PARKER TO LORD BURGHLEY.
25th December, 1572. Lansd. MS. xv. art. 54. Orig.

WHERE your lordship wisheth some particular informations against such as have had commissions against the clergy, as of sir R. Bagnal, &c., who stand upon their justification, and, as ye write, be importune to be let loose again; indeed you term it rightly and aptly " to be let loose," for there could not have been devised a more extreme way to scourge the poor clergy as to set such loose to plague them. If it be true that I hear, they be marvellous vicious. They do so that I fear her Majesty shall not be judged to do that which is *regium* or *pium*. Alas, howsoever the faults be justly plagued, howsoever the state brought in her time to despite the poor ministers of the gospel, yea, and good preachers extremely dealt with, will this turn to honour, after the fruits, tenths, subsidies of late most liberally granted, after the arrearages of tenth, of subsidies from king Henry's days required and extorted, and some of these sums and arrearages twice and thrice discharged, and now, after all this, such pastimes to be procured? I do not so much lament the misery and beggaring of the poor priests, as I do most heartily bewail to see this manner of handling under her Majesty's merciful governance, whom I desire of all other to be graciously reported. But, as I have done, I keep in my contemplations. God send us all of his favour, *ut in fine sit honorificum, &c.* At leisure I may fortune write what I hear, if at the least way be meant such stay and redress.

Your lordship writeth that you guess the writer's pen was holden by my hand. The truth is, that neither he nor any other in such an argument shall want either my head or heart, or yet any of my collections; but surely the writer is a pithy man, and apt to deal in such a cause. Though he be young, yet I doubt little of him, whom I send to your lordship to hear your advice. My lord of Leicester feareth his judgment, but I doubt not this labour shall both betray him and stay him for hereafter. He hath written one quire more, which at leisure ye may read and peruse; peradventure in reading some words thereof, as in the 17th page, ye may think he hath mine information, but before God that trait was only of himself; and though that in private and secret letters to you alone I do write of such manner Machiavel governance, as hearing sometime wise men talk, yet I like not this particular charge or application in this so open writing, nor by mine advice shall not be inserted.

He has handled the divorce well.
He hath handled the divorce in mine opinion well, and, as stories may instruct most in English, except you know any more particularities to be added for the more confirmation.

The Queen once told Parker of a bull in which the marriage of Henry and Anne Boleyn was confirmed Parker searched for it in vain. Has Burghley found it?
Indeed one time her Majesty secretly told me of a pope's bull, wherein king Henry's marriage with queen Anne was confirmed. She willed me to seek it out. I did so amongst mine old registers, and others whom I thought might have it. I did it as secretly and as prudently as I could, and to mine own self, but I could not hear of it; for if I had, I would have informed her Highness again thereof. If ye have found it, it would serve well to amplify the falsehood of the pope, and disprove this loving writer, Saunders. And I made your honour once privy of a little discourse, both of history and of statute-law, to let the world understand what provision have been

Defence of the prince against the pope in old time.
beforetime made to avouch the prince's liberties against the pope's usurpation: and I think it not amiss to be here entreated, and but that the eloquence of the writer can hardly be brought to set down the barbarous and strange terms of some laws, yet I would wish the matter to be forced, and the law-terms, terms of art, to be holpen by circumlocutions. I pray your honour say something to him in this argument.

Parker unlucky in his suits to the Queen.
I had thought to have uttered a small suit that should not be either in honour hurtful, nor to her purse chargeable, but that I am so unlucky and unfortunate to win anything for myself or for my friends, that I will hereafter crave little, as I have not much used importunity in such causes this dozen years, although most of my predecessors have had things of more importance granted them, by the prince's favour in their time; but I will hold me within my bounds, and take the times as they be, and will yet do my duty in conscience, and serve to my uttermost power, till the day of my dissolution. And thus, wishing to your honour your heart's ease in this your great felicity ye be in, I commit the same to Almighty God as myself. But for tediousness I would have written more, but I cease.

As I was writing this letter, this Christmas morn, this inclosed was sent to me. I will make not any gloss of it. I refer it to your prudence. At my house, this Christmas-day, 1572.

Your honour's always in Christ,

MATTHUE CANTUAR.

*To the right honourable, and my good lord,
the lord treasurer, be it.*

CCCXVII.

ARCHBISHOP PARKER TO BISHOP PARKHURST OF NORWICH.

2nd January, 1572—3. Parkhurst Epp. Camb. Univ. Libr. MS. Ee. ii. 34. art. 103. fol. 100, b. Copy.

I AM sorry for your journey that it was so painful unto you for the stay of Mr Cotton, who, as I am informed, is now gone[1]. I would have been glad if your lordship could have certified me where he abideth; and if hereafter it cometh to your knowledge, I pray you so to signify. *Mr Cotton has absconded.*

Concerning the names of the persons which be in commission you may defer them till the parliament, which is also deferred till April. I have else little more to write unto you; but wishing you health, and many good years yet to come. From my house at Lambeth, the second of January, 1572. *The Commission for Norwich diocese may be deferred till parliament assembles in April.*

If your lordship or your chancellor would make a collection for such extremities as late have been executed upon the clergy, by certain extraordinary visitors, it would do very well, and I pray you so to do.

Your lordship's brother,

MATTHUE CANTUR.

[[1] See Letter CCCVI. above.]

CCCXVIII.

ARCHBISHOP PARKER TO THE EARL OF SUSSEX.

9th January, [1572—3] Cotton MS. Vespasian F. xii. fol. 189. Orig.

Sends a list of suggested Lent preachers for the Queen's approval.

IT may please your good lordship, after my hearty commendations to the same, to understand, that I send here unto you the names of such preachers as may serve the Queen's Majesty this Lent, which your lordship may signify unto her Highness, to know her pleasure, whom she will accept, and whom she will reject. And, for that your lordship may have store of persons named to supply such rooms as her Highness shall mislike, I have in another paper to yourself written other names. Your lordship may think that I do this somewhat too soon, but I pray you to consider that some of these may alter their rooms according to their business and health. And when her Highness is resolved, if it please your lordship to signify her pleasure unto me, I shall do further accordingly. And thus I commend your good lordship to the tuition of Almighty God as myself. From my house at Lambeth, this 9th of January.

Your lordship's assured in Christ,
MATTHUE CANTUAR.

To the right honourable my very good lord the earl of Sussex, one of her Majesty's privy council, and lord chamberlain in her Court[1].

CCCXIX.

ARCHBISHOP PARKER TO BISHOP PARKHURST OF NORWICH.

24th February, [1572—3][2]. Parkhurst Epp. Camb. Univ. Libr. MS. Ee. ii. 34. art. 121. fol. 109. Copy.

The archbishop has been moved to ask the

SALUTEM *in Christo.* I am moved by one of my good lords of the council, and also requested by this gentleman,

[1 The Earl of Sussex was appointed Lord Chamberlain in 1572.]
[2 Parkhurst's answer to the above letter, and that of 3rd March, (No. CCCXX. p. 417), is dated 7th of March, 1572. It is in the same

Mr Christopher [?] Heydon's son and heir, that your lordship and your officers would commend the late bishop of Sarum's last book to be had in the rest of the parish-churches within your diocese, wherein they be not. I was glad to hear of his good affection, and even so commend the same to your good zeal, doubting nothing of the favour you bear to the author, and much less to the matter. And thus, yet desirous to hear of the gentleman Mr Cotton[3], I commit you to God as myself. From my house at Lambeth, this 24th of February.

bishop of Norwich to commend Jewel's answer to Harding to be had in such churches of his diocese wherein it is not. He does so accordingly.

Your lordship's brother,

MATTHUE CANTUAR.

CCCXX.

ARCHBISHOP PARKER TO BISHOP PARKHURST OF NORWICH.

3rd March, 1572—3. Parkhurst Epp. Camb. Univ. Libr. MS. Ee. ii. 34, art. 122. fol. 109. Copy.

Salutem in Christo. I received a letter, dated the 23rd of February, which specifieth of certain letters that I should

Bishop Parkhurst has mentioned the receipt of

MS. art. 123. fol. 109, b. He says: "Touching the bishop of Sarum's work, as I have singular cause to allow as well as of the author as of his works, so do I conjecture that the placing of such controversies in open churches may be a great occasion to confirm the adversaries in their opinions, that having not wherewith to buy Harding's books, shall find the same already provided for them; where like unto the spider sucking only that may serve their purposes, and contemning that is most wholesome, will not once vouchsafe to look upon the same. This is but my fear only, and therefore till I shall hear further from your grace I do not think it good to move the same to the diocese, otherwise at the two next Octaves after Easter the same shall be commended, as your grace have advised."]

[3 There is in the same MS. (art. 129. fol. 112, b.) a letter from Parkhurst to the archbishop, in which he states that he has discovered that one Sir Peter Kilburn, living in the precincts of the cathedral at Norwich, is a friend of Mr Cotton's, and that he has accordingly had him examined. He incloses copies of his answers to the archbishop, and asks his advice as to further proceedings both in this case and in that of an old woman in Stowmarket, "that taketh upon her by words of conjuration, and such other unlawful means, to cure all manner of diseases."]

[PARK. COR.]

write to your lordship, touching a collection to be made of the clergy of your diocese, thereby to set them free from the extremity of the late visitors, &c. And further ye write, that some certain sum were set down [sic], and then you would move your commissioners in their circuits to propound the same to the clergy, and so to return answer, &c. I pray you to send me up those letters, and remember by whom they were delivered. For they have shamefully abused my name to you; for I never meant to write such letters, as I am sure I have not done. But belike some forgery is devised of such good fellows as at this last day of the Star Chamber were examined and sent to the Fleet, and [made] answerable to all such of the clergy as have been extorted by them. I pray your lordship to stir in this matter, and send me word so soon as you can. And thus I bid you well to fare as myself. From my house at Lambeth, this third day of March, 1572.

Your loving brother,

MATTHUE CANTUAR.

Postscriptum. I could wish your letters were better sealed.

CCCXXI.

ARCHBISHOP PARKER TO LORD BURGHLEY.

12th March, [1572—3.] Lansd. MS. XVI. art. 27. Orig.

SIR,

I BESEECH your honour, with my most humble duty, to have me commended to her Majesty, certifying that I do not purpose any such new attempts in [the] state of my poor governance, but that I will take first her Majesty's advice, of herself or from your lordship. There is no such dispensation meant, and I am of that opinion that *sermo datur cunctis etc.* Words may not now be used, but doings. It is (by too much sufferance) past my reach and my brethren. The comfort that these puritans have, and their continuance, is marvellons; and therefore if her Highness with her council (I mean some of them) step not to it, I see the likelihood of a pitiful commonwealth to follow; *Deus misereatur nostri.* Where Almighty God is so much English as he is, should not we requite his mercy with some earnesty to prefer his honour and true religion. In mine opinion it is prudently purposed not to call out of their countries such as must serve the state. Wonderful expectations there be of this next parliament. And whereas they say, that we, the bishops, sued to her Highness that the nether house shall not deal in such matters of religion, but now they say they stand in better hope. If your honour knew how we be bearded and used, ye would think strange that we should be thus dealt with in so favourable a governance; and but that we have our whole trust in God, in her Majesty, and in two or three of her council, I see it will be no dwelling for us in England.

<small>Wonderful expectations of the next parliament</small>

I beseech your honour to wait your opportunity to move her Highness in my suit. Surely it is the best in all respects, if the truth of information might take place; I mean for the alteration of my houses. I do not mean any one penny advantage to myself, but to the commodity of the see, if it shall stand in any tolerable estate.

I would remove some part of an old, decayed, wasteful, unwholesome, and desolate house at Ford, to enlarge the little house I have at Bekesborne, where, as well for the foreign friend as for the foreign enemy, I would think it needful and requisite, and to repair my palace with some better lodging. I think it honest, and yet I would leave houses enough to such as should have the oversight of my grounds there. If it please her Majesty I would make a deed of gift of it to her Highness, and then her Highness might grant it again to me and to my successors. The corner thereof and soil is such as I think no man will have any delight to dwell there, if he have any other place nigher the church. And thus committing the same to her Majesty and to your discretion, I cease, and so continuing in patience and prayer, ready to do what I can in service, solitary, as I can, wearing out my time, with rejoices otherwhiles when I hear of good success to herself and to her realm, I commit you to Almighty God as myself, this 12th of March.

<small>Parker's desire to take down a portion of the house of his see at Ford, to enlarge his own house at Bekesbourne, which he offers to give to the Queen for the use of the see.</small>

Your assured in Christ,
MATTHUE CANTUAR.

I have now found matter of that bull of the King's marriage[1], and send your honour some more quires, and within two or three shall make an end.

*To the right honourable the lord Burghley,
high treasurer of England.*

CCCXXII.

ARCHBISHOP PARKER TO LORD BURGHLEY.

9th April, [1573]. Lansd. MS. xx. art. 59. Orig.

SIR,

Sharp message sent from Burghley to Parker respecting his supposed want of liberality to strangers.

To answer a sharp message that Mr Dr Wilson saith you willed him to say to me concerning certain strangers. For lack peradventure of information your lordship is offended. Thus standeth the case. I am not greatly slack to my uttermost ability to provide for strangers, whose state I have always pitied; *Deus novit.*

His answer. What he had done for count Montgomerie and the French ministers.

As for count Montgomerie[2] and those ministers of France exiled, I did not only procure by collection a good portion, but also gave them of my own purse a large and an honest portion amongst them, which I have not yet much blazed, nor intend not; let other men delight in their *Gloria Patri,* I will do but what I can quietly.

What for an Irish bishop.

I saw a letter that your lordship should send to the bishop of London, that we should provide for an Irish bishop. The truth is, one Irish bishop came to me, whom I retained at my table, and gave him certain crowns.

What for Alexander Citolini.

The Italian, Mr Alexander[3], upon your letters I retained him both friendly and gently. I think he cannot

[1 See p. 414.]
[2 A French protestant who fled into England after the massacre of St Bartholomew.]
[3 Alexander Citolini, a learned and accomplished Italian, who fled from his native country on account of his religion. His distinguished friends in England do not seem to have kept him from falling into great pecuniary distress. See Strype's Parker, Bk. IV. c. xxii. and Lansd. MS. XVII. art. 6.]

say the contrary. I gave him also certain French crowns. I received him at my board, and otherwhiles in my hall, when he cometh. I offered him also his entertainment within my house, and to provide him things necessary. My lord of Bedford and himself refused it, as not convenient. I signified unto him that the Queen's Majesty might give him the next advowson of a prebend in Canterbury church, but your lordship liked not that. As to him, I did promise my diligence in the same. I also have written for him to certain of my brethren for some prebends, but I hear not that they have any void yet. I wrote to the bishop of Ely for him for a prebend in his church. He writeth unto me that he hath sent up one to you for him, for the next voidance. Also I am contented that he may have one of the prebends which I give in Canterbury church for the advowsons of the same till they fall.

Furthermore, one Malachias, sometime an Irish bishop[4], who hath been long in prison, wherein I know that he gave papistical council to some of my folks, coming to visit them, but now he saith he is returned from papistry, and saith you favour him, and that you are about to give him an Irish archbishopric. He came to me to require a plurality, but I told him it should be a *commendam* that he must sue first for at the Queen's hands, and I would give him my fees, and dismissed him, and gave him an honest piece of gold. If you knew the truth of my ability, you should see I do as much as I can. I am no gatherer, nor will be, whatsoever they prate abroad. - *Coram Deo non mentior*, I am compelled to borrow every half-year before my money cometh in, for my own expences. Excepting a little money that I have to bury me, I have no superfluity; *sed hæc domestica, &c.*

<small>What for one Malachias, an Irish bishop.</small>

As I was thus writing Mr Alexander Citolinus came to dinner; not sitting with myself, for that I am distempered and keep my chamber, he dined in the hall. After dinner I sent him word of the advowson of that prebend that the bishop of Ely should give him, and I caused him to be asked whether he would go with me into Kent; he made no grant thereto, but would first commune with you or my lord of Bedford.

<small>Citolinus had come in to dinner whilst he was writing.</small>

[4 See two letters respecting this person printed in Strype's Parker, App. LXXXVII. and LXXXVIII.]

Thus I commend your lordship to the tuition of Almighty God. From my house at Lambeth, this 9th of April.

Your lordship's loving friend in Christ,
MATT. CANTUAR.

To the right honourable, my lord
treasurer of England.

CCCXXIII.
ARCHBISHOP PARKER TO LORD BURGHLEY.
25th April [1573]. Lansd. MS. xvii. art. 28. Orig.

SIR,

I THOUGHT it good to signify to your honour concerning that young gentleman the lord Stourton[1], with whom both I and some of my chaplains have diligently conferred and friendly have entertained. I perceive the young nobleman is of no reading, but yet dependeth of some of his old corrupt instructions. In my conference I did much (peradventure *satis et nimium pro imperio*) lay before him his unkindness to the Queen's Majesty, to steal away from her governance in such sort, and charged him with unnatural affection toward his country to withdraw his such aid as he might do to it, &c.; saying that if her favour were not the more, he might be utterly undone, &c.[2]; and in this respect he perceiveth his own folly and great oversight, promising that hereafter he will be better advised and better take heed. He feareth much that her Highness is in great displeasure with him, and fain would he have pardon, and desireth much to hear some comfortable words that he may understand of her Highness' mercy and clemency, howsoever his foolish youth (as he saith) hath overseen himself. I promised him to write to such effect, and he gathereth some comfort because he was no

Marginal notes: The young lord Stourton is of no reading. Parker's conferences with him.

[1 John, Lord Stourton, eldest son of Charles, Lord Stourton, executed in 1557 for the murder of the Hartgills. He was committed to the custody of the archbishop for an attempt to quit the kingdom without the Queen's licence.]

[2 In consequence of the crime committed by his father, this young gentleman, termed by courtesy a lord, could not regain his family position except by the favour of the Queen. He was restored in blood by act of parliament in 1575. He died in 1588.]

longer kept in prison or committed more sadly. He was a while very stiff, and could not hear of the disabling of his religion, and of the reasonableness of ours (established as I tell him by public authority, howsoever some friends pretending the love of it go out of the way), so that I could not persuade him to come to our daily prayer in my chapel with my household, but now he relenteth, and seemeth to be ready to hear and read, and thinketh in some things otherwise than he hath done; and this day I have a promise of him that he will come to my common prayers both now and hereafter. I have good trust in his nature, and I think it pity *linum fumigantem extinguere.* I see honesty in him, for when I charge him much that his schoolmaster, now in the Marshalsea, Mr Williams, had been his instructor upon whom he dependeth, he seeketh utterly to excuse him and commendeth him, and sorry he were he should be hardly intreated for his sake, as not guilty more than when he spake to go over with him he agreed; as Terence saith, *Pecuniam in loco negligere, maximum interdum lucrum,* so I think, *Summum jus, non aliquando exigere, summum interdum lucrum,* as methinketh her Majesty is altogether inclined that way, and yet in necessary severity I doubt not her Majesty will do like a prince. And thus you knowing this case, order it as ye shall think best, praying your lordship that I may hear of some information to instruct or to comfort my guest, and to hold him yet in some suspense for all doubts. Thus I commend your honour to God's good tuition, as myself. From my house, this St Mark's day.

At first very stiff in religion.

Now he promises to come to Parker's daily prayers in his chapel.

Excuses Mr Williams, his instructor.

Your lordship's at all requests in Christ,
MATTH. CANT.

To [the right] honourable, my [very] good lord, the lord treasurer; at the Court.

CCCXXIV.

ARCHBISHOP PARKER TO LORD BURGHLEY.

27th April, [1573]. Lansd. MS. XVII. art. 29. Orig.

SIR,

I KNOW you have much business. My lord Stourton desireth much to hear some words from the Queen's High-

Lord Stourton wishes to be placed with his uncle, lord Derby

ness. His suit is, also, to be placed with his uncle, my lord of Derby[1], the rather for that he understandeth that I am going into Kent, if God will. Furthermore, I would be glad to know how you be resolved with the hook I sent to your

Ford House

honour concerning the translation of Ford House. For some distemperance I feel in me I write the less, wishing to your honour God's grace and good health. This gentleman is he that is appointed to attend upon the lord Stourton, whom the rather I send, if peradventure your lordship would question with him. From my house at Lambeth, this 27th of April.

Your lordship's friend in Christ,
MATTH. CANT.

The fame goeth that some Bagnol or some Druets shall by commission search out a *melius inquirendum*. I can say no more, but *Deus misereatur nostri. Est modus in rebus*[2].

To the right honourable my very good
lord, the lord treasurer.

CCCXXV.

ARCHBISHOP PARKER TO LORD BURGHLEY.

9th May, 1573.   Lansd. MS. xvii. art. 31.

SIR,

The archbishop sends to lord Burghley, first, a transcript of a treatise of Gervase of Tilbury;

THERE came to my hand a treatise written by Gervasius Tilburiensis, who was sometime treasurer of the exchequer; and while I doubted whether your lordship had seen the said book or no, I thought it not unmeet for your office to cause it to be copied, and sent to your honour.

second, Lambard's Perambulation of Kent, not yet published;

I have joined thereunto (which I am sure ye have not seen) a description of the county of Kent, written and laboured by an honest and well-learned observer of times and histories, which he sent to me to peruse, to correct and amend, and so to be under the reformation of some whom

---

[1 Lord Stourton's mother was Anne, daughter of Edward Stanley, third earl of Derby. The uncle referred to was Henry, who succeeded as fourth earl of Derby in 1572.]

[2 See before, Letter CCCXVI., p. 413.]

he judgeth to be conversant in histories, not meaning to put it abroad till it had suffered the hamber[3] of some of his friends' judgments, and then at further deliberation peradventure to set it forth: which book, although I have no commission to communicate it, I refer it, either to shew you, as I think ye be not unwilling in such knowledges to be partaker, and thus present it to your correction and amendment when your leisure can serve you. In the meantime I pray your lordship to keep it to yourself. As I have made this author a judge of some of my small travails, whereof I send you this one bound by my man, I am not minded to suffer them abroad in this quarrelous and envious world. I think the rather we both used this foresight, to suppress our labours in *nonum annum*, as Horace counselleth, rather than to suffer an undigested and tumultuous collection to be gazed on of many folks. Indeed, because neither my health nor my quiet would suffer me to be a common preacher, yet I thought it not unfit for me to be otherwise occupied in some points of religion; for my meaning was, by this my poor collection thus caused to be printed (and yet reserved to myself) to note at what time Augustine my first predecessor came into this land, what religion he brought in with him, and how it continued, how it was fortified and increased, which by most of my predecessors may appear, as I could gather of such rare and written authors that came to my hands, until the days of King Henry the VIIIth, when the religion began to grow better, and more agreeable to the Gospel. You may note many vanities in my doings, but I thought it not against my profession to express my times, and give some testimony of my fellow-brothers, of such of my coat as were in place in her Majesty's reign, and when I was thus placed; and though ye may rightly blame an ambitious fantasy for setting out our church's arms in colours, yet ye may relinquish the leaf and cast it into the fire, as I have joined it but loose in the book for that purpose, if you so think it meet, and as ye may, if it so please you, (without great grief to me) cast the whole book the same way. Which book I have not given to four men in the whole realm, and peradventure shall never come to sight abroad, though some men, smelling of the printing it, seem to be very desirous cravers of the

[3 hammer (?)]

same. I am content to refer it wholly to your judgment, to stand or to fall. To keep it by me I yet purpose, whiles I live, to add and to amend as occasion shall serve me, or utterly to suppress it and to bren it. And thus, making your lordship privy to my follies, and for that I have within my house in wages, drawers and cutters, painters, limners, writers, and bookbinders, I was the bolder to take mine occasion thus *equitare in arundine longa*, so spending my wasteful time within mine own walls, till Almighty God shall call me out of this tabernacle, which I pray God may be to his glory, and my soul-health; I say, *ut obdormiam in Domino, et requiescam in pace, in spe resurrectionis cum Christo servatore meo;* which I beseech Almighty God to send to her Majesty after this transitory travel, *post longitudinem dierum;* as I wish the same to your honour as for myself.

Her Highness is justly offended with this dissolute writing[1], and intendeth a reformation, which, if it be not earnestly laboured on your parties which be supreme judges, long ago called on, I fear ye shall feel Muncer's commonwealth attempted shortly. It must needs follow whereof Sleidan writeth in his history, if the law of the land be rejected, if the Queen's Majesty's injunctions, if her chapel, if her authority be so neglected, if our book of service be so abominable, and such paradoxes applauded to. God send us of his grace. I fear our wits be infatuated, *ut Deus in plenitudine temporis supplicium sumat.* I have forgotten myself to write thus long to your honour. God keep you, this 9th[2] of May.

Your honour's in Christ,
MATTH. CANT.

If these books had been sooner finished your honour should have had them sooner.

To the right honourable, my good lord,
   the lord treasurer of England.

[1 The allusion is to the writings of the puritans. See Strype's Parker, Bk. IV. c. xxiv.]

[2 In the margin is written by the archbishop "14th," to which day it is probable, from the postscript, the sending of this letter was delayed.]

CCCXXVI.

ARCHBISHOP PARKER TO LORD BURGHLEY.
5th June, [1573]. Lansd. MS. XVII. art. 34. Orig.

Sir,

Since I came from the Star Chamber this letter inclosed[3] was brought unto me. I trust ye will proceed, and I know they be but cowards. If ye give over, ye shall hinder her Majesty's governance more than ye be aware, and much abase the estimation of your authorities. Before God, it is not the fear I am in of displeasing, but I would wish her Majesty safety and estimation, and in that I am careful as one well-willing, and therefore am more busy than peradventure I need to be; but yet I shall pray to God that all things may prosperously proceed. And thus I cease. I would not long trouble your other affairs. This 5th of June.

Your loving friend in Christ,
MATTHUE CANTUAR.

Urges lord Burghley to proceed. They [the puritans?] be but cowards.

To the right honourable, my very good lord, the lord treasurer of England.

CCCXXVII.

ARCHBISHOP PARKER TO LORD BURGHLEY.
15th June, [1573]. Lansd. MS. XVII. art. 35. Orig.

Sir,

I do now write to her Majesty to inform her Highness what I have done for the deanery of the Arches, also informing her Majesty concerning Mr Aldrich of Cambridge, for whom I laboured so much to have him preferred, in whose discommendation (upon information) your honour once did write to me. Now he hath stout heart against me, and his friends will obtain to get the Queen's dispensation, that he may continue master in Benet College without his degree, as an head precisian in despising of the degrees of the university, and a great maintainer of Mr Cartwright. I moved him to consider of his duty to the realm, &c.; but I fear all in vain. His friends be come up to obtain his dispensation, and to

Sends a letter to the Queen respecting the appointment of Dr Clerk as dean of the Arches.

And a dispute with Mr Aldrich, master of Benet College.

[3 The letter inclosed is now Lansd. MS. XVII. no. 34. It is from Whitgift to the archbishop. See it in Strype's Parker, Book IV. ch. 24.]

procure him to be a chaplain either of my lord of Leicester, or of Sir Ralph Sadler, to outweigh me, and to deface me; for he will be no more my chaplain. His friends say it may be easily done to get such chaplainship, for they say I am out of all credit and favour, &c. If your lordship know my meaning (I trust honest and indifferent) toward that college, and how I have favoured him and his brother-fellow there, I doubt not but Almighty God will allow of my sincere meaning, howsoever I am requited unkindly, never meaning one penny commodity to myself, or to any of mine. I were loth to trouble your honour with many words, because the rather for that I send your honour the copy of my letters I write to her Majesty. I trust in your carefulness to the commonwealth ye will duly consider of all doings, for we shall once make answer, in our considerations, to Almighty God. And thus God preserve you in grace, honour, and virtue, this 15th of June.

Your orator in Christ,
MATTH. CANTUAR.

*To the right honourable, my good lord,
the lord treasurer of England, be it
delivered.*

CCCXXVIII.

ARCHBISHOP PARKER TO QUEEN ELIZABETH.

[15th June, 1573]. Lansd. MS. xvii. art. 35. Copy inclosed in the preceding letter to Lord Burghley.

PLEASETH it your most excellent Majesty. Since my return home to Lambeth, I willed Dr Clerk to remove him from the room of the deanery of the Arches. He immediately said, that he had as lief forego his life, for thereby he should be utterly undone, as now neither able to procure, being so discredited, &c. This morning he came again to me with the same intent. Then I told him that it was your Majesty's pleasure he should depart. He answered with all submission, that he trusted in your clemency and justice, that he might have your favour with the right of the law; and said moreover, that Dr Yale and Dr Weston were as young as himself was, when they were preferred, and that he is of thirty-six or thirty-seven in years, and had spent all his life in study.

Moreover, if it may please your Majesty, I understand that great suit is to be made to your Highness for your dispensation, in a case of perjury, for one Mr Aldrich, a troublous precisian, to continue master of Benet College, otherwise called Corpus Christi College, notwithstanding his oath, whereunto he is bound by the statute to proceed bachelor of divinity within three years of his election, which he hath not done; whereupon, and for other grievous complaints made against him in his evil government, I advised him to depart quietly, and make his friends to favour the president of the college, the oldest therein now, to have him chosen, as he himself and all his fellows of the house have resigned up their whole interest by their subscription to me for mine interpretation, and as the said Aldrich hath divers times written to me, and spoken the same, that he will do anything that I should move him in this matter. But now he saith he will stand utterly against me, and some of his friends be come up to sue to your Majesty for letters of dispensation; and they say in jest that I am pope of Lambeth and of Benet College, and that I am out of all credit and of no reputation, and that they will sue to some great man of the council to accept him as chaplain, to outface me, and to beard mine authority. Your Majesty seeth this cause how it lieth. I trust in your singular prudence and wisdom, that this inconvenience may be prevented, and my singular hope, next to God, is in your Majesty's favour, as mine endeavour shall be alway to serve your Highness, and to pray for you, as in many respects I am bound. If your Majesty knew this whole matter as it is, I trust ye will not suffer such a scholar or his friends to triumph over your chaplain, to the confounding of your governance.

CCCXXIX.

ARCHBISHOP PARKER TO QUEEN ELIZABETH.
19th June, [1573]. Lansd. MS. xvii. art. 35. Orig.

It may please your excellent Majesty to understand, that this day Mr Dr Clerk being with me at Lambeth, I dealt

his office, he answered that he would much rather yield up his life.

with him again according to your Highness' pleasure, for the rendering up of his patent and interest in the office of deanery of the Arches, and, as at the first, so now, finally, with all humility, he prayed me to receive this his last answer, namely, that much rather would he render up his life than his office; for besides that he should thereby be altogether undone, his living being thus taken from him, he should also so greatly and utterly be defaced and discountenanced, by being thus pronounced by your Majesty's own mouth insufficient, as the same once put in ure against him, never might he more shew his face, not only in the Arches, where his only profession and whole means of living consisteth, but also must likewise banish himself even from all other places and company of credit. He

He hopes he may enjoy the benefit of the law.

humbly prayed, therefore, that at the least he might enjoy the benefit of the law, as all other your Majesty's subjects ever have done; for inasmuch as he possessed and was vested in the said office, not only by patent from me during pleasure, but also (since the death of Mr Dr Weston) by my grant and promise of a new patent to be made to him during life, he affirmeth that neither in equity in respect of his patent during pleasure, nor yet in justice in respect of my grant and promise made during life, his said office and living without great and important causes may be taken from him; and to such causes as either are or can be objected against him, he craveth therein no manner of favour to be shewed unto him,

Challenges trial of his competency.

but that some public trial of his sufficiency may be made, as well for the proof of his learning and his ability in years, as also for the commendation of his honest and modest sort of life; and if he shall not in any one of these be disproved, then, saith he further, that as he doth assure himself how your Majesty will by no means take from him the benefit of law, which hitherto your Highness did never yet deny to any, so seemeth he also in most humble sort to say, that in all the actions of his life he hath ever most carefully sought the honour and service of your Majesty, and namely in this last

His labours against Saunders, which are commended by the archbishop.

labour of his against Saunders, wherein I must needs witness with him, that surely he shewed himself a most dutiful and careful subject towards your Highness; and though he acknowledgeth that whatsoever he hath done, shall do, or can do, is but the least part of his bounden duty towards your Majesty, yet he hopeth, that, of your grace, you will please to accept the same as a mean, so assuredly to conserve him in your Majesty's favour, as that he may never be pronounced by your Majesty unworthy of that whereof the archbishop of Canterbury, and also the laws of the realm, both have and do allow him as worthy and capable, being (to conclude) the first reward and living that ever yet he obtained in recompense of all his study and learning, in which he hath now spent the course and travail of his life by the space of these twenty years past; having also refused (as he telleth me) in Angiers the stipend of three hundred crowns yearly to be a public reader there, only in respect, as he dutifully affirmeth, of the great bond and desire he hath ever had and shall have to serve your Majesty.

Thus far have I only signified to your Majesty the effect of Mr Dr Clerk's declaration unto me, wherein, as near as I can, I have forced myself to lay before your Highness the effect of Mr Clerk's very words and speeches to me, the consideration of which, the more it entereth into me, the more it moveth me to make humble suit to your Majesty; first, to have respect of him who surely having deserved your Majesty's favour shall by this mean be brought to his utter undoing and defacing; secondly, that if your Majesty will needs proceed so severely against him, that yet (forsomuch as he is orderly and lawfully vested in the possession of the said office, and hath and do sit in place of judgment there,) his accusers may by public trial prove his insufficiency; and though it hath been rarely or never seen (as I think) that one thus placed by the archbishop of Canterbury, hath been brought in question and after long time displaced, yet this kind of justice may seem to satisfy; thirdly, if neither respect of him nor his cause may move your Highness, that yet your Majesty will have some respect and consideration of me, and of that place whereunto your Highness hath placed me, and pleased to call me to; in which if I, whom your Majesty will have to possess jurisdiction over so many other bishops, shall yet be reproved in the choice of one of mine own officers, a thing that in the meanest bishop that is was never yet impugned, surely it cannot be but unto the see itself a great derogation, and unto me no small discredit and rebuke, and yet not so much discredit to me, as in the end it shall prejudice to your Majesty's service, I and my doing being thereby brought into contempt, and that by those which are or should be to me as the foot is to the head; wherein surely your Majesty shall give too great an encouragement unto them, and peradventure in greater matters hereafter to oppone themselves against me, and so, consequently, I shall not be able to serve your Majesty as I would, and as my duty is. Last of all, if I can by no means satisfy your Majesty, then must I end with this; that as I do willingly submit both myself and all that I have to your Highness, as from whom it was first and wholly derived, so I do likewise yield up this cause unto your Highness, to deal and do therein as your good pleasure shall be, trusting that your Majesty will never lay on me so heavy a burden as to make me the instrument of his displacing whom for good respects I have already placed; or that I should remove him as unworthy whom in my conscience I do think very worthy, and do judge very few or none of them which would so fain have me dejected worthy or meet, as I dare stand to the proof, or that I should take that office from him, which by my word I have faithfully promised and given to him; or, last of all, I to be the doer of his utter discredit and undoing, who in my knowledge both hath dutifully served your Majesty and the realm; which extremities as I cannot consent, neither for mine own conscience' sake before Almighty God, nor yet with the reasonable credit of that place I do possess, so my humble suit is, that your Majesty will never require it of me, but rather, if needs, your Highness will in this sort proceed, to assign the displacing of him to such other as shall please your Majesty. And so most humbly I take my leave of your Highness: wishing in my prayer to Almighty God your long and prosperous reign over England, and that the great grace wherewith Almighty God hath blessed you, with the goodness of your own nature and conscience, be not drawn to other men's several affections. From Lambeth, this 19th of June.

Your Highness' most bounden and obedient chaplain,

MATTHUE CANTUAR.

To my sovereign good lady the Queen's most excellent Majesty.

CCCXXX.

ARCHBISHOP PARKER AND OTHER ECCLESIASTICAL COMMISSIONERS TO THE VICE-CHANCELLOR OF CAMBRIDGE.

5th July, 1573. Lansd. MS. XVII. art. 38 b. Copy inclosed in letter of archbishop Parker to Lord Burghley of 15th July, 1573.

MR VICE-CHANCELLOR, after our hearty commendations. Although our commission in causes ecclesiastical doth sufficiently authorise us to deal with any of her [Majesty's] subjects, and to call them before us, as well in places exempt as not exempt, as we have aforetimes used to do, and at this day do, as well by the said commission as also by appointment of the Queen's council, as of late we did for some fellows and scholars in the University of Oxford, and as we have done beforetime as well there as in the University of Cambridge, whereby we doubt not we have rooted out some corrupt members that else were like to have troubled the whole estate; yet, because we being for the more part sometime of this University, and zealous to the same, we for precedent sake have thought it good to write first unto you, requiring and commanding you in the Queen's Majesty's name to send up unto us one Thomas Aldrich, master of art in Corpus Christi College, otherwise called Benet College, and to have him bound with sufficient sureties to make his personal appearance here before us and other our colleagues at Lambeth, immediately upon the receipt of these our letters; whereof we pray you not to fail. He to answer to such objections as shall be propounded unto him, and not to depart without our special licence thereunto. And thus we bid you heartily well to fare. And furthermore, we give you thanks for the transmitting of the acts done before you concerning William Clarke, the 6th of December, and the first of July, 1573.

From Lambeth, this 5th of July, 1573.

M. CANT.
R. WINTON.
W. FLETWOOD.
R. WENDESLEY.

[PARK. COR.]

CCCXXXI.

ARCHBISHOP PARKER AND BISHOP SANDYS TO ONE OF THEIR BRETHREN OF THE ECCLESIASTICAL COMMISSION.

6th July, 1573. Petyt MS. Inner Temple, No. 47. fol. 518. Contemporary copy.

<small>The church assaulted by false brethren, who under colour of reformation, seek the ruin of learning and religion.</small>

SALUTEM *in Christo*. These times are troublesome. The church is sore assaulted; but not so much of open enemies, who can less hurt, as of pretensed favourers and false brethren, who under the colour of reformation seek the ruin and subversion both of learning and religion. Neither do they only cut down the ecclesiastical state, but also give a great push at the civil policy. Their colour is sincerity, under the countenance of simplicity, but in very truth they are ambitious spirits, and can abide no superiority. Their fancies are favoured of some of great calling who seek to gain by other men's losses. And most plausible are these new devices to a great number of the people, who labour to live in all liberty. But the one, blinded with desire of getting, see not their own fall, which no doubt will follow; the other, hunting for alteration, pull upon their necks intolerable servitude. For these fantastical spirits, which labour to reign in men's consciences, will, if they may bring their purposes to pass, lay an heavy yoke upon their necks.

<small>They attack both ecclesiastical and civil polity.</small>
<small>They are favoured by some of great calling.</small>

<small>They seek a popular state.</small>

In the platform set down by these new builders we evidently see the spoliation of the patrimony of Christ, a popular state to be sought. The end will be ruin to religion, and confusion to our country. And that you may the better perceive how these fancies are embraced, and like to take effect, except in time they be met withal, here inclosed we have sent unto you certain articles taken out of Cartwright's book, and by the council propounded unto Mr Deering, with his answers to the same, and also a copy of the council's letters written to Mr Deering, to restore him to his former reading and preaching, his answer notwithstanding, our advices never required thereunto. These proceedings puff them up with pride, make the people hate us, and magnify them with great triumphing, that her Majesty and the privy council have good liking of this new building, which hitherto, as we think, in no Christian nation hath found any foundation

<small>The writers have sent articles out of Cartwright's book, with Deering's answers to the same, and the council's letter restoring Deering to his reading and preaching.</small>

upon the earth, but is now framed upon suppositions, full of absurdities and impossibilities, in the air. We are persuaded that her Majesty hath no liking hereof, howsoever the matter be favoured by others.

The Queen hath no liking hereof.

But forsomuch as God hath placed us to be governors in his church, hath committed unto us a care and charge thereof, and will one day require a reckoning at our hands for the same; it shall be our duties to labour, by all means we can, to see sound doctrine maintained, gainsayers of the truth repressed, good order set down and observed; that the spouse of Christ, so dearly redeemed, may by our ministry be beautified. These perilous times require our painful travails; and seeing that God's cause is brought into question, and the church many ways troubled, we must with good courage stand to the defence thereof, and resist the underminers. We here bear a heavy burden and incur many dangers and displeasures, but nothing shall be grievous unto us, if we may do good to his church. We doubt not but that you are like affected, and bear a burden in mind with us. We have made a special choice of you, whom for good learning, prudent counsel, and godly zeal, we love and reverence, and have thought it good to put you in remembrance of these matters, and withal to require you to consider of these things, and to be prepared against our next meeting, which we think will be shortly, to say unto the same as may most tend to the glory of God, good of his church, maintenance of his gospel, establishing of decent and good order, to the edifying of his people, and to the repressing of all gainsayers. Thus thinking it convenient that you should keep these matters secret to yourself, we commend you to the good direction of God's Holy Spirit. From Lambeth, this 6th of July, 1573.

The church being troubled, we must resist the underminers.

They therefore put the person addressed in remembrance of these matters, and require him to be prepared to speak upon the same.

   Your loving brethren,

      MATTHUE CANTUAR.
      ED. LONDON.

CCCXXXII.

ARCHBISHOP PARKER TO LORD BURGHLEY.

15th July, [1573]. Lansd. MS. xvii. art. 38 b. Orig.

SIR,

As the Queen is going into Kent, Parker is busy preparing to go thither.
IT may please you, now certainly understanding the Queen's Majesty's progress to hold into Kent, and so to Canterbury, that I am now altogether preparing to go thither, to make my houses ready against her Majesty's coming. And for that ye may be called on to declare the tract of the shire, besides other such books as I sent to your lordship for the same purpose, I now join one other treatise concerning Dover. Whether your lordship have it or no, I know not; but in such points I had rather be too busy than too slow in participating my trifles.

Sends a book about Dover.

Aldrich and the fellows of Corpus Christi submitted the questions concerning the College to the archbishop. But Aldrich has now appealed to Burghley as Chancellor of Cambridge.
I understand that Aldrich's matter is come before you. Both he and all the fellows by their subscriptions referred the whole matter to my hearing, for all such causes as concern that College. I think it had been better for him and the College causes, to have been ended by me in commission; for I do know more than the whole University doth; whose privileges yet I did not mean to hurt, as by this my letter written to the Vice-chancellor[1] you may perceive. But when this jurisdiction is so daintily looked on, I fear it will turn to the hurt both of the whole University, and specially to the utter undoing of that poor College. Surely, sir, his insolency is too great. The childish maliciousness for his vain tales, and his with his brother's ingratitude to me, besides their manifest precisianship, is too intolerable. Your lordships of the council committed the hearing of the matter concerning some of St Jobu's College in Oxenford of late to our commission, as alway the Queen's authority hath been used to the commodity of both Universities, although yet in Oxenford they have an ecclesiastical commission besides, &c. I would things were so reformed as may tend to the quiet government of the realm, otherwise I do not much care for any jurisdiction. And thus I commit your good lordship to the tuition of

Aldrich's insolence is too great.

[1 The letter before printed, dated 5th July, 1573.]

Almighty God as myself. From my house, this 15th of July. -

    Your loving friend in Christ,
      MATTHUE CANTUAR.

*To the right honourable, my good lord,
the lord treasurer of England.*

CCCXXXIII.

ARCHBISHOP PARKER TO LORD BURGHLEY.
18th July, [1573]. Lansd. MS. xvii. art. 39. Orig.

SIR,

 I THANK you for sending of your letters, which I return again unto your lordship. As for the letter which so doth charge you, the truth is, in mine opinion, the man hath more zeal than wit or wisdom, or yet learning, and therefore I take his weighty advertisements to be but *fulgur ex pelvi*. Surely if this fond faction be applauded to, or borne with, it will fall out to a popularity, and as wise men think, it will be the overthrow of all the nobility. They be not unwise or unskilful men that see the likelihood. We have to do with such as neither be conformable in religion, nor in life will practise the same. Both papists and precisians have one mark to shoot at, plain disobedience; some of simplicity, some of wiliness and stubbornness. I marvel what prudence it can be, first to hew thus at us, and certainly yourself will shortly follow.

Comments on a letter which contained a charge against Burghley.

The puritan faction deemed democratic

 Now I fear that my lord Cobham is come out of Kent to signify that the measles and the pox reign at Canterbury, and the plague at Sandwich. What it may mean I cannot tell. I was never in better readiness to go to Canterbury than at this time. My wine, beer, and other provision be appointed and sent thither; but if I knew her Majesty should not go, I would yet stay the cost of my carriage; for as in fifteen years it should rejoice me to see her Majesty at my house at Cantuary (for I weigh not so much the cost), so would I be loth to have her person put in fear or danger.

Sickness reported in Kent.

Parker's preparations to receive the Queen.

 I have read over also the Vice-chancellor's letters, &c.,

Letters about the appeal to Burghley by Corpus Christi College

and perceive they have their whole trust in your honour, as much caring for their liberties, which in good faith I would were preserved as gladly as any of them all would. And though your authority be now worthily to be regarded, yet I fear a president will rise after you that shall not be able to do as you can, and I think her Majesty's commission may stand and help their privileges. I do not care who hath the hearing of the controversy, so the College be saved, and lewd and monstrous governance escape not away unreformed. It is but sleight, and their cloak to shroud them in, to claim other men's hearings. The matter is too long to be set out in particularities. I read their childish letter, wherein I perceive but homely invention, yet they insinuate that our authority by commission might (*in dicta causa*) bear over a truth; as though we have not to consider in this world our upright dealing, and forget that we be subject to the talks of those irritable precisians at Cambridge. Indeed Thomas Aldrich himself, with all the fellows' subscriptions, in February last, wrote and referred that matter to me only, and acknowledged me to be most fit to decide this controversy, which they touch for the sense of that statute (of the master's continuance). Some of those five fellows hath and do now live of my purse daily, and yet craftiness can pervert their senses. If I knew her Majesty should not go into Kent, I

Parker would like to be present at the hearing of the controversy.

would then desire your honour that I might be at the hearing of these controversies, and yet would I tarry one week longer to do good to my old nurse the College. There be many more controversies, whereof I am now informed, than the doubt of one statute. I would the Vice-chancellor and one of the heads more were with us in your name to hear the matter debated. His insolency would soon appear. Mr Vice-chancellor might soon be entreated, for he useth to come up, because his wife is here; one other of the heads might come up with him. Mr dean of Westminster and I might hear and report to your honour, because the heads claim your honour or the Vice-chancellor their visitors. I have set out all the words of the statute which may concern this authority. Mr Aldrich and one other of his faction might come up with him. The president of the house and one more of the fellows against him might also come up, to prosecute their complaints. Sir, meet it is it were ended, for it is a mere factious matter,

and will continue the precisians and all others at variance, for
the most part of the heads be against Aldrich. He hath but
one head with him, and though there be subscribed five
fellows in their letter, yet there be seven against him. It is
pity Mr Whitgift should be one to come up, because he is
occupied about his book. Yourself, sir Anthony Cook, myself, the bishop of Winchester, be yet their visitors, for the
commission of visiting is not yet revoked; first, I and Dr
May did conciliate the old statutes and reformed them in
King Edward's day and visitation, and then your lordship,
Mr Cook, the bishop of Winchester, Dr Haddon, and I, subscribed to a reformation, or supply again of those statutes,
and put to the Queen's seal.

This Thomas Aldrich resigned up his prebend at West- *Aldrich having resigned a prebend in Westminster.*
minster into the Queen's hands, about February last, and so
it remaineth. I have been so much ashamed of his negli- *Parker recommends Mr John Still, B.D., in his place.*
gence in that Westminster church, being laboured for by me,
that now I would Mr John Still, bachelor of divinity, were in
his [place], who is both wise, discreet, and learned, and of
good credit in London. Do in it as ye think good, for I
never intend to return the resignation (which I have by me)
of that prebend to his use, whosoever may have it.

I have also caused the book of Dover to be examined *Book of Dover.*
again and reformed, which here I return again to your honour,
the last part whereof, *De warda castri, &c.*, I had in an
old ancient book. I perceive by your letter that my lord of *Lord Leicester still grieved. Perhaps Parker is too sharp.*
Leicester is yet grieved, but I refer it to God. It may be
that I am too sharp. Indeed I mean well (as the surgeon
doth in administering his corrosive), and am not trained up in
the courtly eloquence, and I perceive the court is now altered
from that that I once knew it in. Well, God be merciful to
us all, that we may spend our lives to please him. *Cetera
valeant.* Now that I see the length of my letter I am
ashamed, but you can soon defray a babbling letter. From
my house, this 18th of July.

Your evermore in Christ,
MATTH. CANTUAR.

To the right honourable, my good lord,
the lord treasurer of England.

CCCXXXIV.

ARCHBISHOP PARKER TO LORD BURGHLEY.

23rd July, 1573. Lansd. MS. xvii. art. 40. Orig.

SIR,

Doubts as to the mode of determining the controversy about Corpus Christi College.

I HAVE received your letters, and perceive in what doubtfulness you be, whether such matters as are to be objected against Aldrich, both spiritual and temporal, and for causes of religion, may be heard by the Queen's Majesty's commissioners by prerogative of her Majesty, by authority metropolitical, by their own desires referring the interpretation of the college statute to me, which now he goeth from, or whether all and singular these matters must be heard by the Chancellor or Vice-chancellor, and only within the university; and being in doubt whether your honour will have me to come unto you, in what sort. I would be glad to attend upon you, if no prejudice or hurt to our commission might grow, in yielding to them of the University more than is needful: whose privileges yet I would be as glad to maintain as any of them. The causes of his disproving be many moe than I signified unto you, as shall fully appear, either by my declaration, if your honour will have me come unto you, as your prudence at this time shall think it expedient, or by some other which I shall send, as this my messenger,

Dr Acworth, Parker's messenger to Burghley.

Dr Acworth[1], can somewhat say for information. And thus holding myself in suspense, till I know your further pleasure, I commit you to God as myself. From my house at Lambeth, this 23rd of July, 1573.

Your loving friend in Christ,

MATTH. CANT.

*To the right honourable, my good lord, the
lord treasurer of England.*

[[1] Dr Acworth, who had at one time been public orator of Cambridge, was the author of one of the answers to Saunders, published in this year, 1573. He is also reported to have assisted Parker in the compilation of his Antiquitates.]

CCCXXXV.

ARCHBISHOP PARKER TO LORD BURGHLEY.
27th July, [1573]. Lansd. MS. xvii. art. 41. Orig.

Sir,

Hearing that her Majesty goeth to Mr Thomas Wootton's, where your lordship may fortune to be, and calling to my remembrance that I think you have not the preface before the Topographical Discourse of Kent, which the author purposed to dedicate to the said Mr Wootton, I thought it good to send it to your honour[2], to put you in remembrance not to be acknown to him that you have it from me, and the rather for that his desire was to participate it unto me, to have mine advice in the book, and not to publish it abroad; for that the author doth repute it to be imperfect, and worthy of further reformation. Keyes, my messenger yesterday to your honour, brought me no resolution for my guest the lord Stourton how he shall be used. And thus I wish your lordship health in this cold and wet progress. From my house at Lambeth, this 27th of July.

Sends preface to Lambard's Kent.

No answer yet for lord Stourton.

Your lordship's loving friend in Christ,
MATTHUE CANTUAR.

*To the right honourable, and my very good
lord, the lord treasurer of England.*

CCCXXXVI.

ARCHBISHOP PARKER TO LORD BURGHLEY.
17th August, 1573. Lansd. MS. xvii. art. 44. Orig.

Sir,

Gladly would I do all the service I could to the Queen's Majesty and to all her nobles, with the rest of her most honourable household. I have no other counsel to follow, but to search out what service my predecessors have been wont to do. My oft distemperance and infirmity of body maketh me not to do so much as I would.

Arrangements for the reception of the Queen at Canterbury.

[2 It still remains attached to this letter, but the signature "W. Lambard" has been defaced.]

The Queen's lodging.

If her Majesty would please to remain in mine house, her Highness should have convenient room, and I could place for a progress-time your lordship, my lord Chamberlain, my lord of Leicester, and Mr Hatton, if he come home: thinking that your lordships will furnish the places with your own stuff. They say mine house is of an evil air, hanging upon the church, and having no prospect to look on the people, but yet I trust the convenience of the building would serve.

Burghley's lodging.

If her Highness be minded to keep in her own palace at St Austin's, then might your lordships be otherwise placed in the houses of the dean, and certain prebendaries. Mr Lawes, prebendary, would fain have your lordship in his convenient house, trusting the rather to do your lordship now service, as he did once in teaching a grammar-school in Stamford by your appointment. Mr Bungey also would be glad to have your lordship in his lodging, where the French cardinal lay: and his house is fair and sufficient. Mr Pierson would as gladly have your lordship in his fine house, most fit for your lordship, if you think so good.

Custom on receiving the Queen into Canterbury.

The custom hath been, when princes have come to Canterbury, the bishop, the dean and the chapter, to wait at the west end of their church, and so to attend on them, and there to hear an oration. After that, her Highness may go under a canopy till she cometh to the midst of the church, where certain prayers shall be said, and after that, to wait on her Highness through the quire, up to the traverse next to the communion-table, to hear the even-song, and so afterwards to depart to her own lodging.

Parker suggests that she should attend the cathedral and receive the communion on Sunday, and afterwards dine at his house

Or else, upon Sunday following, if it be her pleasure, to come from her house of St Austin's by the new bridge, and so to enter the west end of the church, or in her coach by the street. It would much rejoice and stablish the people here in this religion, to see her Highness that Sunday (being the first Sunday of the month when others also customably may receive), as a godly devout prince, in her chief and metropolitical church openly to receive the communion, which by her favour I would minister unto her. *Plurima sunt magnifica et utilia, sed hoc unum est necessarium.* I presume not to prescribe this to her Highness, but as her trusty chaplain shew my judgment. And after that communion it might please her Majesty to hear the dean preach, sitting either in her traverse, or else to suffer him to go to the common chapter, being the place of sermons, where a greater multitude should hear. And yet her Highness might go to a very fit place, with some of her lords and ladies, to be there in a convenient closet above the heads of the people to hear the sermon. And after that I would desire to see her Highness at her and mine house for the dinner following. And, if her Highness will give me leave, I would keep my bigger hall that day for the nobles and the rest of her train. And if it please her Majesty, she may come in through my gallery, and see the disposition of the hall in dinner-time, at a window opening thereinto. I pray your lordship be not offended though I write unto my lord of Sussex, as lord Chamberlain, in some of these matters as may concern his office.

I am in preparing for three or four of my good lords some geldings, and if I knew whether would like you best, either one for your own saddle, or a fine little white gelding for your foot-cloth, or one for one of your gentlemen or yeomen, I would so appoint you. And thus trusting to have your counsel, as Mr dean cometh purposely for the same, I commit your honour to God's tuition as myself. From my house at Bekesborne nigh to Canterbury, this 17th of August, 1573.

He is preparing horses for some of the lords, what kind of horse will Burghley like to have?

Your lordship's assured in Christ,

MATTHUE CANTUAR.

Postscriptum.—I thank your honour for your letters ye sent to me by Mr Aldrich, and that ye regard mine estimation in this cause, wherein it is wonderful (as I hear say) how this fond young man hath dealt. He would needs resign over his room, rather than to be deprived, and so he remaineth hereabout, but brent child dreadeth the fire, and therefore I cannot tell how to take him or believe him.

Aldrich desires to resign, rather than be deprived.

*To the right honourable, his very good lord,
the lord Burghley, high treasurer of
England.*

CCCXXXVII.

LORD BURGHLEY TO ARCHBISHOP PARKER.
11th September, 1573. Petyt MS. Inner Temple. No. 47. fol. 347. Orig.

IT MAY PLEASE YOUR GRACE.

Lord Burghley sends a book containing some attack upon himself and the lord-keeper, with request to know the archbishop's opinion thereon.

You shall see how dangerously I serve in this estate, and how my lord-keeper also, in my respect, is with me bitten with a viperous generation of traitors, papists, and I fear of some domestic hidden scorpions. If God and our consciences were not our defence and consolation against these pestilential darts, we might well be weary of our lives. I pray your grace read the book, or so much as you list, as soon as you may, and then return it surely to me, so as also I may know your opinion thereof. When your grace hath done with this, I have also a second smaller, appointed to follow this; as though we were not killed with the first, and therefore a new assault is given. But I will rest myself upon the Psalmist's verse; *Expecta Dominum, viriliter age, et confortetur cor tuum, et sustine Dominum.* From my lodging at Mr Pierson's, 11th September, 1573.

Your grace's at command,

W. BURGHLEY.

To my lord of Canterbury's grace.

CCCXXXVIII.

ARCHBISHOP PARKER TO LORD BURGHLEY.
11th September, 1573. Petyt MS. Inner Temple. No. 47. fol. 348. Orig. draft.

SIR,

The archbishop thinks the attack upon Burghley not worth an answer.

I RETURN to your lordship your mad book again. It is so outrageously penned, that malice made him blind. I judge it not worth an answer. Some things were better put up in silence, than much stirred in. Your conscience shall be your testimony to Almighty God. It is no new matter for such as take pain for the good governance of the commonwealth to be railed on. In my opinion they be very comfortable words which be uttered by our Saviour Christ, who once shall be our Judge; *Beati estis cum probra jecerint in vos homines, et dixerint omne malum adversum vos, mentientes et propter me; gaudete et exultate: sic enim persecuti sunt prophetas qui fuerunt ante vos.* In these and like words I for myself repose my heart's quietness. Beseeching Almighty God with his Holy Spirit to comfort your mind in these blasts of these devilish scorpions. *Conscia mens recti mendacia ridet, &c.* From my house at Canterbury, this 11th of September, 1573.

Your assured in Christ,

MATTH. CANT.

[margin: Christ's comfortable words to those who are reviled untruly.]

CCCXXXIX.

ARCHBISHOP PARKER TO LORD BURGHLEY.

3rd November, 1573. Lansd. MS. xvii. art. 51. Orig.

Sir;

Upon a word your honour gave out yesterday, to have us understand about your subscriptions, how careful ye be for our state ecclesiastical, I must tell you secretly I doubted whether I might smile or lament, to think that you would so offer it to our contemplations. The truth is, though we be quite driven out of regard, ye had need look well to yourself. The devil will rage, and his imps will rail and be furious. He can transform himself into *angelum lucis.* I saw before I came first to Lambeth, and so wrote my fancies to some one of the noble personages of this realm, my contemplation that I then did see and read, and now is practised, and will every day, I fear, increase. When Lucian in his declamation *Pro tyrannicida,* shall speak for his reward in destroying a tyrant, howsoever Erasmus and More play in their answering to it, and then consciences of men shall be persuaded (and that under the colour of God's word) that this act is meritorious, what will come of it, think you? I doubt not ye call to remembrance of a word once uttered by a Scottish gentlewoman (as I am informed), that though Fenton[1] be dead, yet there be more Fentons remaining, &c.

[margin: The archbishop's fearful anticipations of the course of public events.]

[1 The allusion probably is to Felton, who published the pope's bull for the deposition of Elizabeth, by affixing it to the gate of the

I will not write of that of which I have no full proof of; it is neither *tutum* nor *sanum.*

Repairs of Bekesborne.
If your lordship would comfort me with her Majesty's grant, I would yet assay to amend Bekesborne building. At my last being at Canterbury, keeping my visitation in the church, &c., I saw high time by injunctions to prevent evil.

The necessity for statutes for the regulation of cathedrals.
I saw high time for her Majesty to procure the safety of such foundations by sending to them statutes under her seal. I have caused them to be done, and would offer them if they should not hang too long in your hands. Furthermore, I saw there and otherwhere, by experience and partly by report, that her Majesty's needful ecclesiastical commission is foully abused, and would be redressed. I pray your lordship think not amiss of my meaning, which to you secretly I disclose.

Caution as to appointments to St A·aph and Norwich.
All is not gold that glittereth. Look well whom you do admit into Asaph[1], and into that poor decayed room of Norwich[2], that you be not beguiled. Many things be spoken of us, and how they be credited God knoweth; and many things be deserved, and some things are untrue. The world is subtle. And thus drawing to an end, I bid your lordship heartily well to fare as myself. At Lambeth, the third of November, 1573.

Your honour's evermore in Christ,

MATTHUE CANTUAR.

*To the right honourable, and my very good
   lord, the lord treasurer of England.*

residence of the bishop of London. He was executed in 1570. The Scottish lady referred to was doubtless the Queen of Scots.]

[1 The see of St Asaph became vacant in September, 1573, by the death of bishop Thomas Davies. Bishop William Hughes succeeded on the 11th December, 1573. His conduct in the see fully justified the warning of the archbishop.]

[2 Norwich was still occupied by bishop Parkhurst, who survived until 2nd February, 1574—5. The vacancy alluded to was that of the deanery.]

CCCXL.
ARCHBISHOP PARKER TO LORD BURGHLEY.
7th November, [1573³?] Lansd. MS. xvii. art. 52. Orig.

SIR,

UPON view of your letters, I shortly after addressed these my letters, which to-morrow in the morning I had appointed one of my men to bring to your lordships. Concerning the discourtesy of us in committing the party to prison, ye may think if it please you, that we meant neither any lack of duty, nor convenient consideration, if ye knew the whole cause, whatsoever be informed your honour. And if we should be discouraged to do justice, for fear of any informer's talk, we had a warm office. We are not so brute, that we cannot consider of such men's requests as it becometh us. Mr dean of Westminster, Mr Yale, Mr Hamond and Mr Wendesley thought it, with me, no less cause than to commit him. And thus, without further writing, I shall wish to your honour all manner of grace. From my house late, at Lambeth, this night, this 7th of November.

Replies to some complaint against the ecclesiastical commission for committing some one to prison.

Your lordship's at reasonable commandment,

MATTH. CANT.

CCCXLI.
ARCHBISHOP PARKER TO LORD BURGHLEY.
9th November, 1573. Lansd. MS. xvii. art. 54.

SIR,

MY lord of Lincoln's[4] man was with me this day, and according to his request I could no less do but send unto your honour, as your lordship may see here by his own copy. I refer the matter to your wisdom. I would prog-

Letter from the earl of Lincoln.

[³ This letter is indorsed with the date of 1573, and is bound up in the Lansdown Collection amongst the letters of that year. These circumstances occasioned its being so placed in this volume, but upon further consideration, it seems probable, that it referred to the imprisonment of Stowell and was written in 1572. In that case the letter alluded to as being inclosed was the one before printed No. CCCX., p. 405.]

[⁴ Edward Clinton, twelfth baron Clinton, created earl of Lincoln 4th May, 1572.]

Reparations of Bekesborne.

nosticate nothing. And thus, if I knew her Majesty's contentation, I would prepare toward the reparations of Bekesborne, meaning to do while I live as though I should live ever, and yet I trust, being ready in all the storms of the world, to depose this tabernacle to-morrow. Doubting not but your lordship is so framed for both *bonam famam et infamiam, per convicia et laudes,* to go forward in your vocation, as God hath placed you. Leaving your honour to the tuition of Almighty God, as myself. From my house at Lambeth, this 9th of November, 1573.

Your lordship's in Christ,

MATTH. CANT.

If your lordship would send me the book that I took your honour at Canterbury, which I did intend to my lord keeper, I would thank you.

*To the right honourable, my very good lord,
the lord treasurer of England.*

CCCXLII.

ARCHBISHOP PARKER TO LORD BURGHLEY.

11th November, 1573. Lansd. MS. xvii. art. 55. Orig.

SIR,

Further letter on behalf of lord Stourton He comes to chapel, and behaves himself modestly and orderly at table.

MR ARUNDELL sheweth me that your lordship thought it necessary that I should write unto your honour in some commendation of the lord Stourton. You shall understand that I can testify of his coming into my chapel with the rest of my household, and that he giveth ear to the lessons there read, and beareth such sermons as are made there. I see him modestly behaving himself and orderly at my table, according to his degree so used by me. Thus much I do testify, praying you to be good lord to him for his further liberty, if you shall think it so good. And thus I commend your honour to the tuition of the Almighty. From my house at Lambeth, this 11th of November.

Your lordship's loving friend in Christ,

MATTHUE CANTUAR.

*To the right honourable, my good lord,
the lord treasurer of England.*

CCCXLIII.

ARCHBISHOP PARKER TO LORD BURGHLEY.

13th November, [1573]. Lansd. MS. XVII. art. 56. Orig.

SIR,

THIS morning came the warden of the printers, Harrison, and brought me one other book in quires, and told me that one Asplyn, a printer to Cartwright's book, was, after examination, suffered again to go abroad, and taken into service into Mr Day's house, and purposed to kill him and his wife, &c. And being asked what he meant, he answered, "The spirit moved him;" so that they be all taken and in prison, as he told me. Since I sent to your lordship this messenger, this he told me. I cannot yet learn that the book is new printed since queen's Mary's days[1]; but I have set this Harrison and other awork to search out more. Thus God preserve your honour, this 13th of November.

One Asplyn, a printer of Cartwright's book, attacks Day the printer and his wife.

Your lordship's in Christ,

MATTH. CANT.

To the right honourable, my lord treasurer of England.

CCCXLIV.

ARCHBISHOP PARKER TO LORD BURGHLEY.

15th November, 1573. Lansd. MS. XVII. art. 58. Orig.

SIR,

IF grace, I trust, and zeal in the queen's quieter government, and some affection to my native country moved me not, I would not at this time commend any man to any room. I see her Majesty and yourselves to be in deliberation best to appoint for the deanery of Norwich. If Mr Still were not my chaplain, I would say that he were as meet a man in all respects as I know in England. I know that people, how

Mr Still stongly re commended for the deane. y of Norw ch.

[1 Strype says (Parker, Bk. IV. c. xxxiv.) that this "seems to have been Goodman's book;" that is, the volume entitled "How superior powers ought to be obeyed of their subjects," by Christopher Goodman, printed at Geneva, 1558, 12mo.]

[PARK. COR.]

they be disposed and inclined; they would have one learned and gracious to them to stay them. If I wished not well to my country, I would be loth to bestow him, or to spoil him in that place there. The church is miserable, and hath but six prebendaries, and but one of them at home, both needy and poor; of which, some of those six I know to be puritans; Chapman, of late displaced by the bishop of Lincoln; Johnson cocking abroad, with his four several prebends (as they say) in new-erected churches, both against statute and his oath. Indeed this Still is a young man, but I take him to be better mortified than some other of forty or fifty years of age. I have been of late shamefully deceived by some young men, and so have I been by some older men. Experience doth teach. The world is much given to innovations; never content to stay to live well. In London our fonts must go down, and the brazen eagles, which were ornaments in the chancel and made for lectures, must be molten to make pots and basins for new fonts. I do but marvel what some men mean, to gratify these puritans railing against themselves, with such alteration where order hath been taken publicly this seven years by commissioners, according to the statute, that fonts should not be removed. Answer is made that they be but trifles, *sed hœ nugœ seria ducunt.* I were loth to blame any man, but I have sent and sent again, and spoken too, and yet cannot be received. As for the ecclesiastical commission, I see it is foully abused, and if it be not reformed by a new, it will work inconvenience. Papistry is the chief wherein we should deal, and yet the clamorous cry of some needy wives and husbands do compel us to take their matters out of their common bribing courts, to ease their griefs by commission. I am sorry to write so much, but I think that an hungry, scraping, and covetous man should not do well in that so decayed a church; and yet how your lordships be resolved I cannot tell. Thus I humbly commend her good Majesty, and all you, to God's blessed tuition. From my house at Lambeth, this 15th of November, 1573.

Your evermore in God,

MATTH. CANT.

To the right honourable, my very good lord,
    the lord treasurer of England.

CCCXLV.

ARCHBISHOP PARKER TO BISHOP SANDYS OF LONDON.

24th November, 1573. Petyt MS. Inner Temple. No. 47. fol. 508.
Contemporary Copy.

AFTER my right hearty commendations to your lordship. Forasmuch as the Queen's Majesty being very careful and desirous, that one uniform order in the celebration of divine service and ministration of the sacraments should be used and observed in all places of this her Highness' realm and dominions, according to the Book of Common Prayer set forth by public authority and her Majesty's Injunctions, without alteration or innovation, hath not only divers and sundry times heretofore, and likewise now of late, signified her Highness' pleasure unto me therein, with straight commandment to see the same duly executed. But also, for the better execution thereof, hath of late caused the lords of the privy council to give in commandment on her Majesty's behalf to every of my brethren the bishops of this her realm, to give speedy order for the due execution of the premises in every of their several dioceses and jurisdictions, to the intent that her Highness may be truly certified, as well of the accomplishment of her pleasure in that behalf, as also what obedience is used by her subjects, as well of the clergy as also of the laity, touching the said uniformity. I have thought good to will and require your lordship, not only with all convenient speed to cause diligent inquisition to be made throughout your own diocese and jurisdiction, how her Majesty's said pleasure and commandment in this behalf is observed, but also to publish the contents of these my letters to all the rest of my brethren the bishops of my province, willing and requiring them and every of them, forthwith to cause the like inquisition to be made through their several dioceses and jurisdictions, and that you and they do make certificate to me thereof on this side the feast of the Nativity of our Lord God next coming, together with the names and surnames of all such, as well of the clergy as of the laity, as shall obstinately refuse to shew themselves conformable herein. And thus I bid your lordship heartily well to fare. From my house at Lambeth, this 24th of November, 1573.

Your loving brother,
M. CANT.

To the reverend father the bishop of London.

CCCXLVI.

ARCHBISHOP PARKER TO MR JOHN BOYS[1].

5th December, 1573. Original in the possession of the Rev. Samuel Simpson, M.A., Douglas.

Since the death of Edward VI, the palace court of Canterbury has been neglected on account of a contention for the stewardship of the liberties, which is ended by the death of the duke.

WHEREAS the keeping of the palace-court hath been, since the death of king Edward the Sixth, much neglected, through contention for the stewardship of the liberties, as well in the time of my predecessor the cardinal, as ever since my coming to the bishoprick, the cause whereof is now removed by the attainder of the duke. Therefore, as well for the saving of my royalties and privilege, as for that my tenants shall not be thereby brought in bondage to hold of the Queen's Majesty;

Therefore for preservation of the privileges of the archbishoprick Mr Boys is willed to hold such court annually, calling before him all such as hold of the palace of Canterbury by knight service.

these are to will you, that once yearly you hold a court at my palace of Canterbury, calling before you, according to the accustomed usage, all such as hold of my palace by knight-service, taking of them such accustomed fine as there ought to be paid for suit of court. And if any shall refuse to pay, these are to will you that you distrain such for the whole suit due in my time, which is fifteen shillings. The not doing service may be prejudicial to me, and a great charge and burden to my tenants, which otherwise in time will be drawn to hold of the Queen's Majesty. Fail you not service. The fifth of December. From my house at Lambeth.

Your loving friend,
MATTHUE CANTUAR.

*To my loving friend Mr John Boys,
    steward of my liberties.*

[1 This letter bears an impression of a seal containing the arms of the archbishop as given in the books of the Parker Society. Round the arms is the following legend: "Mundus transit et concupiscentia ejus; ætatis suæ 70."]

CCCXLVII.

ARCHBISHOP PARKER TO LORD BURGHLEY.

30th December, 1573. Lansd. MS. xvii. art. 60. Orig.

SIR,

FOR that Almighty God (whose pleasure is always most to be regarded and obeyed) hath mercifully visited your body with sickness, I doubt not but that ye have *unctionem Spiritus Sancti internam,* to accept it patiently as frail nature can bear it. I am persuaded *quod hæc momentanea carnis afflictio æternum et immensum gloriæ pondus operabitur;* and though that in respect of yourself it were the very best ye continued still your desire to be dissolved *et esse cum Christo,* yet for the commonwealth's sake, I doubt not, ye be indifferent to say with that ancient man, *Si populo tuo, O Domine, adhuc sum necessarius, non recuso laborem;* so that ye may be able to believe with St Paul, who saith, *Quod mihi vita Christus est,* if ye live, and if ye be dissolved, to affirm that his further saying, *Et mori lucrum.* Thus, not minding to trouble your honour with long writing, I commit your good recovery to Almighty God in my prayers, whereof I do partly hear, and thank his mercy. From my house at Lambeth, this 30th of December, 1573.

Letter of consolation written to Cecil on occasion of a severe illness.

Your assured orator in Christ,

MATTHUE CANTUAR.

To the right honourable, and his good lord, the lord treasurer of England.

CCCXLVIII.

ARCHBISHOP PARKER TO LORD BURGHLEY.

Probably A.D. 1573. Lansd. MS. xvii. art. 93. Orig.

WHY I am not readier to report the prudence and policies of Mr Cartwright in his book[2], these reasons move me:

[2 The book of Cartwright here alluded to, and the pages of the first edition of which are referred to in the following page, was

1. *First*, I am a principal party, and an offendicle to him.

2. *Secundo*, he is so well applauded to, that howsoever he disliketh the act of throats' cutting, or of breaking men's necks, he delighteth to apply both terms to archbishops and bishops.

3. *Tertio*, he saith and affirmeth, that besides our names we have almost nothing common to those which have been in elder times, of whom he saith some had not an halfpenny to bless them with, and thinketh that if our fat morsels were employed to the maintenance of the poor, of the ministers, and on universities, the heat of this disputation and contention for archbishops and bishops would be well cooled. And he is much offended with the train they keep, and saith that three parts of their servants are unprofitable to the filling of the church and commonwealth. And he is very angry with their furniture of household.

4. *Quarto*, he thinketh no archbishop to be needful in these times, except he were well assured that he would pronounce the truth of every question which shall arise, and of this if he be assured, then it will make his mastership to be more favourable to the archbishops than presently he is; and saith that the office of commissioner is not permitted by God's word to him.

Sir, because you be a principal councillor I refer the whole matter to her Majesty and to your order; for myself I can as well be content to be a parish-clerk as a parish-priest. I refer the standing or falling altogether to your own considerations, whether her Majesty and you will have any archbishops or bishops, or how you will have them ordered.

And because you may see in some private respect *quamvis in insipientia mea* I must boast, although *testimonium conscientiæ* were enough, to shew unto you privately how the archbishop of Canterbury spendeth the living that her Majesty hath committed to his trust; if other men could do better, I am pleased to be private.

entitled "A Replye to an Answere made of M. Doctor Whitegifte againste the Admonition to the Parliamente." 4to. pp. 224.]

Expences yearly by the archbishop of Canterbury.

First, to the poor. — In certain yearly rent for two hospitals, clx^{li}.
Besides other almose, relief of prisoners, decayed persons, &c.

To ministers, &c. — In certain yearly stipends, ccxxxvij^{li}. xiij^s. iiij^d.
Beside the relief of strangers learned, as others. — T. Cartwright, pag. 98, 89.

To scholars and schools. — In foundation of six scholars, xviij^{li}; of two fellows, xij^{li}; yearly for ever, &c. Besides exhibitions to scholars of Cambridge and Oxford, and founding of a grammar-school in Lancashire.

To repair churches and highways. — Reparations of thirteen chancels, of five mansion-houses, and certain farms; erecting of an highway in the university of Cambridge to the schools. — W. Turner, in his Hunting of the Wolf.

Subsidies, free rents, new-year's gifts, and other such resolutes . . . cccc^{li}.
Annuities and fees . . cccc^{marks}.
Liveries, c^{li}. Wages, ccl^{li}. . cccl^{li}.
Household fare . . . xiij$^{c.\ li}$. or xiiij$^{c.\ li}$.

Over and beyond

Apparel, armoury, bedding, hangings, linen, plate, pewter, books, &c. Physic, journeying, ferriage, carriage, suits in law, christenings, marriages, necessaries for offices, stable with his furniture, arrearages, loss of rents, &c.

CCCXLIX.

ARCHBISHOP PARKER TO THE VIDAME OF CHARTRES.

13th January, 1573–4. Prefixed to Marlorat's Thesaurus, fol. Lond. 1574.

VOLUNTATEM ac consilium istius optimi ac industrii viri Domini Feuguerii[2], in hoc suo Thesauro conflando, nos ac

[1 Printed about 1554. The author was the dean of Wells before mentioned. See before, p. 241, and Wood's Athenæ Oxon. Bliss's Ed. (I. 361).]

[2 The work to which this letter was prefixed was entitled "Pro-

nobiscum ex fratribus nostris nonnulli diligenter admodum consideravimus. Atque hoc quidem statuimus, illius viri industriam summis laudibus dignam esse, et ab omnibus amplectendam: ipsumque opus cunctis pastoribus et ecclesiæ ministris apprime utile ac pernecessarium videri. Deus O. M. Dominationem tuam quam diutissime servet incolumem. Lambethi, idibus Januariis.

Dominationis tuæ bonus amicus,
MATTHÆUS CANTUAR.

CCCL.

ARCHBISHOP PARKER TO MR MATCHETT[1].

25th March, 1574. Parkhurst Epp. Camb. Univ. Libr. MS. Ee. ii. 25. art. 199. fol. 154. Copy.

He is to go to his ordinary, and shew him that the Queen will have vain prophesyings suppressed.

You shall go unto my lord your ordinary, and shew him that the Queen's Majesty willed me to suppress those vain prophesyings. And thereupon I require him in her Majesty's name immediately to discharge them of any further such doing. And so, &c.

Your friend,
MATTHUE CANTUR.

pheticæ et Apostolicæ, id est, totius divinæ ac canonicæ Scripturæ, Thesaurus, in locos communes rerum, dogmatum suis divinis exemplis illustratorum, et phraseon scripturæ familiarum, ordine alphabetico digestus. Ex Augustini Marlorati adversariis a Gulielmo Feuguereio in codicem relatus." Lond. 1574. fol. It stands in the book with the following title: "Reverendissimi ac Domini Cantuariensis de hoc opere ad clarissimum heroa Vidamium Carnutensem judicium." John de Ferriers, the Vidame of Chartres, was a French protestant who fled from his native country after the massacre of St Bartholomew.]

[1 This is only an extract, and not the entire letter. It is thus prefaced in the MS.: "These lines were taken out of a letter sent from my lord of Canterbury his grace to Mr Matchett, parson of Thurgarton, xxv[to] Martii, 1574."]

CCCLI.

ARCHBISHOP PARKER TO BISHOP PARKHURST OF NORWICH.

17th May, 1574. Parkhurst Epp. Camb. Univ. Libr. MS. Ee. ii. 34. art. 211. fol. 160 b. Copy.

SALUTEM *in Christo.* I understand that you have received certain letters to continue that exercise that is used in your diocese, contrary to that commandment that the Queen's Majesty willed me to send to all my brethren of the province. I pray you signify unto me what their warrant is[2]. And where I wrote unto you that her Majesty would have those vain exercises suppressed, you would have further information from me what was meant, whether all exercises should be suppressed, or else such as your discretion should count vain, and none other[3]. Good my lord, be not offended; it is one

[margin: What is the warrant of those who withstand the Queen's command?]
[margin: Reply to Parkhurst's inquiry whether only "vain" prophesyings]

[2 On the 6th of May, the bishop of London, together with Sir F. Knollys, Sir T. Smith, and Sir W. Mildmay, members of the privy council, wrote to bishop Parkhurst that they had heard that there were in Norfolk "certain good exercises of prophesying, and expounding of Scriptures," of which "some, not well minded towards true religion and the knowledge of God," spoke evil; and they accordingly require the bishop, "that so long as the truth is godly and reverently uttered in this prophesying, and that no seditious, heretical, or schismatical doctrine, tending to the disturbance of the peace of the church can be proved to be taught or maintained in the same, that so good a help and mean to further true religion may not be hindered and stayed, but may proceed and go forward to God's glory, and the edifying of the people." On the 28th May, bishop Parkhurst wrote back to the bishop of London that before the receipt of the letter of 6th May written by him and the three other privy councillors, the archbishop's command to stop the prophesyings had reached him through Mr Matchett (Letter CCCL., p. 456); and that since that time the archbishop had written to him (the letter in the text of 17th May) to know on what warrant certain persons had enjoined him to permit such exercises to continue. He asks his brother bishop's advice how he is to satisfy both his metropolitan and the privy councillors. Both letters are in the same MS. as that in the text; arts. 206, 207. fol. 158 b, and 159.]

[3 On 2nd April bishop Parkhurst wrote to the archbishop that he had seen his letter to Mr Matchett, an extract of which is printed No. CCCL., and was anxious to know whether he meant "the abuse of some vain speeches used in some of those conferences, or else gene-

<small>should be suppressed.</small> of my old griefs, that I have sometimes written unto you in such letters as I have sent, which your friends have seen, which have given you counsel to stand upon the word "vain." It is pity we should shew any vanity in our obedience.

<small>Communion bread; of what kind it should be.</small> You would needs be informed by me whether I would warrant you either loaf-bread or wafer-bread, and yet you know the Queen's pleasure. You have her injunctions, and you have also the service-book; and furthermore, because I would deal brotherly with you, I wrote in my last letters, how I used in my diocese for peace sake and quietness. I would your lordship and other were nearer, to hear what is said sometime. And thus for this time I bid you fare well as myself. From my house at Lambeth, this 17th of May.

Your lordship's brother,
MATTHUE CANTUAR.

CCCLII.

ARCHBISHOP PARKER TO THE EARL OF SUSSEX.

12th June, 1574. Harleian MS. 6991. art. 41. Orig.

My very good lord, perceiving by Mr Cooke, your lordship's chaplain, that by some words of the letter lately sent <small>Mr Yate to be placed in c·stody of the earl of Sussex, either to be brought to conformity, or proved to be unworthy the earl's favour</small> from me to your lordship touching Mr Yate, it might be construed that your lordship had not so free a disposition in using of him as was expected, this shall be to certify your lordship that my meaning both then was and now is, that your lordship, according to the speech had between you and me in the Star Chamber, should have him sent you, and that by your approved discretion he should be ordered as to you seemed good, until such time as he were either reduced to some conformity, or uttered himself to be the man not worthy that favour which he now findeth by your lordship's means.

rally the whole order of those exercises;" giving it as his own opinion that if not abused, such exercises "have and do daily bring singular benefit to the church of God, as well in the clergy as the laity." The letter is in the same MS. as that in the text, art. 201. fol. 155.]

And thus I commit your good lordship to God. From my house at Lambeth, this 12th of June, 1574.

Your good lordship's assured friend,

MATTHUE CANTUAR.

To the right honourable, my very good lord, the earl of Sussex.

CCCLIII.

ARCHBISHOP PARKER TO BISHOP PARKHURST OF NORWICH.

14th June, 1574. Parkhurst Epp. Camb. Univ. Libr. MS. Ee. ii. 34. art. 214. fol. 161 b. Copy.

I RECEIVED your letters wherein you shew your conformity to the Queen's commandment uttered by me[1]. And though that Mr William Heydon maketh a great stir in your diocese, and as I am informed reporteth untruly of me, I

Suppression of prophesyings, and Mr Heydon's great stir.

[1 In the same MS. (art. 209. fol. 159 b.) is a copy of the letter referred to, in which the bishop says that the letter from "certain of good place and great credit" about which the archbishop had enquired (see p. 457), was written "not by the way of warrant, but as giving advice," and that, notwithstanding that advice, on understanding the Queen's commandment through the archbishop, he had already himself stayed the prophesyings in some places, and commanded his officers to suppress the same throughout the diocese. The bishop's letter bears date vi^{to} Junii, 1574, and there is (art. 208, fol. 159) the bishop's letter of the 7th of June to his chancellor, requesting him to signify to every of the bishop's commissaries "that they in their several circuits may suppress" the prophesyings. There is also a letter (art. 212. fol. 161) from the bishop of Rochester to the bishop of Norwich, dated 13th June, 1574, in answer to an enquiry made by Parkhurst, "whether the like commandment be generally given through this province." The answer is: "I must tell your lordship that I hear of no such commandment, neither in London diocese, neither yet in mine, nor elsewhere: but my lord of London, I, and others, have taken such order, that no man within any of our diocese in any matter of controversy shall have anything to do. And so by this means the exercise is continued, to the comfort of God's church, [and] increase of knowledge in the ministry without offence. And so I doubt nothing but it shall do within your diocese, if your lordship observe the like order."]

think he were best to be a little colder in his zeal. And, my lord, be not you led with fantastical folk. I thank you for your informations. Beliko your records are not of any long time. I mean not to desire your lordship not to take counsel, but not to take such young men to counsel, as when they have endangered you, they cannot bring you out of trouble. Of my care I have to you and to the diocese I write thus much.

<small>Communion bread; loaf-bread not to be commanded or winked at.</small> And as for their contention for wafer-bread and loaf-bread, if the order you have taken will not suffice them, they may fortune hereafter to wish they had been more conformable: although I trust that you mean not universally in your diocese to command or wink at the loaf-bread, but, for peace and quietness, here and there to be contented therewith. And as for the imprudent dealing of my chaplain for the further notifying of the Queen's pleasure, you shall understand that that was but a second addition to my former letters for the same, to require you to be mindful. And whereas aforetimes I have written to your lordship in the favour of Mr Reade (which by his report you have always favourably considered), so I pray you now extend still your good will, if in case he be your officer for the registership, which I trust he will honestly discharge. And thus I bid your lordship heartily well to fare. From my house at Lambeth, 14 Junii.

Your lordship's brother,

MATTHUE CANTUAR.

CCCLIV.

ARCHBISHOP PARKER TO LORD BURGHLEY.

19th June, 1574. Lansd. MS. XIX. art. 7. Orig.

SIR,

<small>Have devised to lay in wait for Undertree.</small> WE have devised, before your letters came, to lay in wait for Undertree, and I trust we shall have him if it be possible; and he shall be appointed to be at my house secretly, or at Mr Steward's on the water-side, and as soon as we have the possession of him, we shall immediately send your honour

word, to do and follow that ye shall think good. And thus the Lord give us all grace. From Lambeth, this 19th of June, 1574.

Yours in the Lord,
MATTH. CANT.

*To my [very good] lord, the [lord].
treasurer.*

CCCLV.

ARCHBISHOP PARKER TO LORD BURGHLEY.
19th June, 1574. Lansd. MS. xix. art. 6. Orig.

SIR,

IF this matter be not effectuously with severity ordered, farewell your assurance with all your posterity, and farewell the quiet governance of her Majesty and her safety. I have had leisure enough a great while to perpend some men's words and proceedings. This deep, devilish, traitorous dissimulation, this horrible conspiracy, hath so astonied me, that my wit, my memory, be quite gone. I would I were dead before I see with my corporal eyes that which is now brought to a full ripeness, whereof I gave warning a great while ago, if I had been heard. If the detector be not honourably considered and safely protected (whom yet I never saw), all will be naught. I fear some to have lain in her bosom, that when opportunity shall serve will sting her. Ware of too much trust. Why was King Henry the VIIth accounted so wise a man, and esteemed to have knowledge in astronomy, but that he would hear and be close? If they mean to destroy her nigh friends in such sort (and that in conscience), what mean they to herself? *Det Dominus spiritum sapientiæ et intellectus contra hos spiritus pestiferos, et Deus misereatur nostri &c.* If at the last these and sure [such?] fellows do escape, *posteriora erunt pejora prioribus.* God save your lordship, and send you of his grace. God knoweth it is not myself, or any thing I have, I care for. Well! God be with your honour.

Urges Burghley to deal severely with the parties in a supposed traitorous conspiracy.

Reason of the reputation for wisdom acquired by Henry VII.

(*Indorsed*) 19th June, 1574.

*Archbishop of Canterbury by Mr Winsloo,
upon the discovery of a conspiracy.*

CCCLVI.

ARCHBISHOP PARKER TO LORD BURGHLEY.

23rd June, [1574]. Lansd. MS. xix. art. 8. Orig.

SIR,

Undertree not yet taken. Letter from him inclosed. Belike these men be hasty judges.

To answer your letter I could not till I came home from the Star Chamber, for that my steward is as earnest as he can be, yet with prudence, occupied. I thought, because I saw him not since yesterday, that he obtained him, but I understand that on Friday Un.[1] goeth toward the Isle, and then I surely trust he shall be stayed, unknown to him. I send you the letter which Un. wrote to him this morning. Belike these men be hasty judges, to condemn men before they examine their defects; but *qui habitat in cœlis irridebit eos.* And thus I pray you pacify her Majesty's desire; *sat cito si sat bene.* This 23rd of June.

Your honour's assured in Christ,

MATTH. CANT.

Sir, the craving of this money now was more of the steward's offer to further him in his journey than of his own accord.

To the honourable, my very good lord, the lord treasurer.

CCCLVII.

ARCHBISHOP PARKER TO LORD BURGHLEY.

26th June [1574]. Lansd. MS. xix. art. 9.

SIR,

Parker solicits that the council should give some recommendation to an exposition of the Sunday Lessons by the bishop of Lincoln.

WHERE there is, by the diligence and labour of the bishop of Lincoln, "A Brief Exposition of such Chapters of the Old Testament as usually are read in the church at Common Prayer on Sundays, set forth for the better help and instruction of the unlearned[2]," I think this his book to be profitable

[1 Undertree; see before p. 460.]

[2 The book, of which the archbishop here quotes the title, was published in 1573. London. 4to. The bishop of Lincoln alluded to was Dr Thomas Cooper, mentioned before at p. 316.]

for instruction and necessary for the unlearned minister, but most to the poor subjects, who are certainly to be informed by the stability of this doctrine. And thereupon, if your lordship will signify the same unto her Majesty's council, that they would give some commendation thereunto, I suppose it would do well; the rather for that the simpler the doctrine is to the people, the sooner may they be edified, and in an obedience reposed. And thus I bid your lordship heartily well to fare. From my house at Lambeth, the 26th of June.

Your lordship's assured loving friend,

MATTHUE CANTUAR.

To the right honourable, my very good lord, the lord Burghley, lord treasurer of England.

CCCLVIII.

ARCHBISHOP PARKER TO LORD BURGHLEY.

26th June, 1574. Lansd. MS. xix. art. 10. Orig.

SIR,

I AM not, nor have been a great while, pleased that Un.[3] make such delays, notwithstanding I think these things must be borne; and as for your disliking that ye were made privy, and thereupon ye state to be sorry thereof, in good faith I think the matter is such as men must not only spend their credit, rather than their lives. Ye may be sure all that may be possibly done is and shall be done, and by message from Un.[3], this night he shall be spoken with, either by hook or crook; and, sir, ye know we meant no gain thereby, but to put it to your consideration, which your lordship may take therein, and do what ye shall think best. Thus the Lord be with your honour. 26th June, 1574.

<small>Undertree not yet taken, but will be that night by hook or by crook.</small>

Your lordship's assured in Christ,

MATTH. CANT.

To my very good lord, the [lord] treasurer.

[3 Undertree.]

CCCLIX.

ARCHBISHOP PARKER TO LORD BURGHLEY.

30th June, 1574. Lansd. MS. XIX. art. 11.

SIR,

Results of the examination of Undertree and others

I AM glad and thank God that this matter falleth out at length thus, especially because I trust the realm is not yet corrupted with such sprites as were feared, which was my greatest grief, and made me most astonied; 2. That your honour and such others (meaning well) need not to stand in much doubt, and that God will protect his; 3. That innocent men be purged by this examination, and friends be still the same. It standeth now to your honourable wisdoms to use this matter, that the searchers to their great cost, charge and travel, be not discouraged. I noted the council's letters wisely written, yesterday sent me, for enlarging of Bonham and Stonden. I doubt not but ye will use it well; and yet seeing ye have that principal and subtle party, let him be well examined, let him write, as his pen will serve him too readily. I fear somewhat that he taketh all upon himself. I marvel that Brown's letters, so many, should be counterfeited ever with one hand. I would wish that lewd scrivener which counterfeited Bonham's hand should pay of his charges in prison, and Stonden, by his means only apprehended, were considered. If this varlet be hanged (as it is pity such one should remain in a commonwealth to abuse so many honourable and honest should escape) I would think it well; if the party, as the earl of Bedford, be so minded that he should bear displeasure. He hurteth himself, and now he hath a warning. Ye be not like hereafter to have some men careful as they have hitherto been. I send your honour my fond but plain cogitation. As for myself, and others with me, I am able to say, we meant honourably to God, carefully to her preservation, and dutifully to your estates and the state public. I am so much troubled with the stone, and now I fear the strangury, &c., that I am sorry to be *onus terræ;* but with prayer and as occasion will serve, I will still do, *dum interim simus in hoc tabernaculo, dissolvi cupientes.* God

Bonham and Stonden to be discharged.

Parker would think it well if the varlet (Undertree) were hanged.

preserve your honour. From my house, this last of June, 1574.

Your assured in Christ,

MATTH. CANT.

*To the right honourable, and my good lord,
the lord treasurer.*

CCCLX.

ARCHBISHOP PARKER TO LORD BURGHLEY.

13th August, [1574]. Lansd. MS. xix. art. 12. Orig.

SIR,

I HAD rather you understood a truth by my report in such matters wherein I am a doer, than by the uncertain speech of the court. I have travailed much by myself alone, for want of other commissioners, to try out a possession, which was very earnestly believed, and set forth and by print recorded and spread, without licence. The two printers whereof with others that sold those pamphlets were committed to prison. And if I had my will, I would commit some of the principal witnesses to prison, to learn them hereafter not to abuse the Queen's Majesty's people so boldly falsely and impudently. After I had by divers examinations tried out the falsehood, I required Sir Rowland Hayward and Mr Recorder of the city to be assistant with me, who heard the wench examined, and confessed and played her pranks before them. We had the father and the mother, by which mother this wench was counselled and supported, and yet would she not confess anything. Whose stubbornness we considering sent her to close prison at Westminster gate, where she remaineth until her daughter and another maid of Lothbury have openly done their penance at Paul's Cross, as it is ordered[1].

Parker reports the result of a pretended possession of a girl examined before him.

The girl was set on by her mother. She not confessing is sent to the gatehouse.

The girl and a companion to do penance at Paul's Cross.

[1 The daughter alluded to was named Agnes Bridges, and the maid of Lothbury, Rachel Pinder, the former of the age of twenty, the latter of eleven or twelve. They performed penance on the 15th August, before all the congregation at Paul's Cross, the preacher reading their confessions. (Stow's Chron. ed. Howes, p. 678).]

I am so grieved with such dissemblers that I cannot be quiet with myself. I do intend, because these books are so spread abroad and believed, to set out a confutation of the same falsehood. The tragedy is so large that I might spend much time to trouble your honour withal. But, briefly, I have sent to your lordship a copy of the vain book printed, and a copy of their confessions at length. And thus knowing that your lordship is at the court, I thought good to send to you, wishing her Majesty and all you waiting upon her a prosperous return. From my house at Lambeth, this Friday the 13th of August.

Books published upon the subject

Your lordship's loving friend,
MATTHUE CANTUAR.

*To the right honourable my very good lord,
the lord treasurer of England.*

CCCLXI.

ARCHBISHOP PARKER TO THE EARL OF SUSSEX.

2nd October, 1574. Lambeth MS. 1168. No. 12. Orig.

AFTER my right hearty manner, I commend me unto your good lordship, rejoicing much that it hath pleased Almighty God so well to prosper her Highness's journey into the west country, and so fortunately returned again with her whole household. My duty were, as my desire is, to wait upon her Majesty, which I would gladly do, but that the plague is so much stirring, partly in London and partly in Lambeth, so that divers of my servants and household have had their children and servants of late departed of the plague, whom I do sequester out of my house for a time. I would not be bold to approach so near her Highness in this state that my household is of, till I knew her Majesty's contentation, beseeching your good lordship (with my most humble duty of offering my prayer and service) to know her pleasure. Thus, sending my servant for that purpose, I beseech your honour to let me be informed; and so commend

Queen's return from her progress

Plague being in London and Lambeth, Parker sends his servant to know if he may wait upon her Majesty

your lordship to God as myself. From my house at Lambeth, this second of October.

Your lordship's loving friend,
MATTHUE CANTUAR.

To the right honourable and my very good lord, the earl of Sussex, lord chamberlain to the Queen's Majesty, at the Court.

(*Contemporary Indorsement.*)
B. of Canterbury, 2d October, 1574.

CCCLXII.

ARCHBISHOP PARKER TO THE EARL OF SUSSEX.
7th October, [1574]. Cotton MS. Titus B. ii. fol. 302 a. Orig.

I RECEIVED your honourable letters, answering my request to know her Majesty's pleasure. I have great cause to acknowledge my bounden duty of thanks and readiness of service to her Highness for her Majesty's special favour so to consider of me her poor chaplain. And furthermore I have to give your good lordship my hearty thanks, for your friendly declaration to her Majesty of my letters, in such good sort as I perceive your honour hath done. And if that I can do your lordship any pleasure or service, I pray you be bold of me, as of your assured well-willer. And thus Almighty God preserve your honour to his pleasure. From my house at Lambeth, this seventh of October.

<small>Thanks for the Queen's answer to the request in his last letter, and to the earl for his friendship.</small>

Your lordship's assured friend,
MATTHUE CANTUAR.

(*Contemporary Indorsement*)
7° October, 1574.—The B. of Canterbury.

CCCLXIII.

ARCHBISHOP PARKER TO LORD BURGHLEY.
23rd November, 1574. Lansd. MS. xix. art. 14. Orig.

AFTER my right hearty commendations to your good lordship. I will do the best I can to other of my Cambridge

<small>Will do his best to contribute to some increase</small>

of living for the Hebrew reader at Cambridge.

brothers, to contribute some increase of living to that Hebrew reader, and as soon as I have obtained I will inform your honour, or else signify the same to Mr Vice-chancellor of that University.

The archbishop publishes Alfred's life.

Concerning that rude pamphlet which I promised your honour, because I send but this morning one book to her Highness, I would her Highness should have the first, and put it to her pleasure. This last addition of Alfred's life[1] I have added to such stories as before I sent to my lord Arundel, which yet being so homely, I would not have done if his lordship had not seemed to desire it. I send your lordship one which is but meanly bound, as to certain others of my good lords I purpose to send the like. And thus I wish your lordship well to fare in all things as myself. Because her Majesty is come secretly to my lord of Leicester, I know not whether I might offer myself to her Highness; but this

As soon as his book finished he purposes to journey to the Queen at Hampton Court.

week as soon as my book prepared for her Highness were finished, I purposed to journey to her at Hampton Court. The correcting of it, and the binding and printing, hath stayed me thus long only. And thus I again wish you God's good Spirit as to myself. This 23rd of November, 1574.

Your loving friend,

MATTH. CANT.

I pray your lordship purpose the same books your lordship intended to be sent them of Cambridge; that will do them good, and be an honest testimony that ye love learning.

I think all other men's books are now delivered and bestowed.

To the right honourable, my very good lord, the lord treasurer of England.

[1 The book alluded to was Asser's life of Alfred, printed by Day (fol. 1574), in types purposely cast, at the expence of the Archbishop, to represent the characters used in Anglo-Saxon MSS. The Archbishop also contributed a preface.]

CCCLXIV.

ARCHBISHOP PARKER TO DR ROBERT NORGATE[2].

25th November, 1574. Miscel. Letters, &c. No. 43. Parker's printed Lib. C. C. Coll. Camb. Orig. draft.

I UNDERSTAND that men would be glad to have your houses, and that ye may make of them xx*l.*, which is not agreeable to your charges. Notwithstanding because St Andrew's-day is so nigh[3] at hand, and for that they do mean to enter by that day, I think you may suffer them to come in, but you do well to grant them as yet no leases. And methink you write they will be contributory to pay according to the rate. *Parker thinks that some persons who would be glad to become tenants of the college may be admitted, but not to have leases as yet.*

I marvel that I hear not from Henry Maynard, by whom I returned certain books to your college, as Homer in Greek, &c. When he is come home I shall more certainly write unto you. Thus I bid you well to fare. From my house at Lambeth, this 25th of November, 1574. *He marvels that he hears not from Henry Maynard*

CCCLXV.

ARCHBISHOP PARKER TO LORD BURGHLEY.

9th January, [1574—5]. Lansd. MS. xix. art. 60. Orig.

SIR,

IT may please your good lordship to understand that Mr Dean of Westminster brought unto me a vain young strip- *The dean of Westminster brought to the archbishop Thomas Cartwright's brother, a lunatic.*

[[2] This letter is in answer to one from Dr Norgate, master of Corpus Christi College, Cambridge, in which he says: "I have talked further with those men who are suitors to take our new buildings by lease;" and after stating the terms to which they consented, adds: "wherefore I pray your grace to let me have understanding of your grace's pleasure herein by the carrier this week if it may be, because some of them would remove hither before St Andrew next, at which time their quarter-day do expire for those places where now they do dwell." Miscel. Lett. No. 43. Parker's printed Lib. C. C. Coll. Camb. Orig.]

[[3] See preceding note.]

ling, being Thomas Cartwright's brother, so simple and fond that I think not meet to present him or his matter to you of the council. And where he should say in his frenzy that he is rightful heir of the lands in this realm, and that the Queen's Majesty keepeth them in his right, with such other words spoken to Mr Dean, I thought it good for such vain talk to commit him to the gatehouse at Westminster, and purpose to take order with young Martin and other his friends by their bonds to have him kept at their charges, either at Bridewell, or Bedlam, or else in some other prison, or at home in their own houses, till his wits come again to himself, and also for his forthcoming. His wit is so foolish and so simple that I thought this to be a good way, the rather because his brother, and such precisians, should not think that we deal hardly with this young man, being in this foolish frenzy, for his brother's sake, whose opinions have so troubled the state of the realm, that ye had need make much of some of the clergy to beat out of the commons' heads that which is beaten in.

<small>Committed to the gatehouse at the charge of his friends.</small>

And, sir, in mine opinion where there is very great talk for terrible things to be contrived the next parliament against the clergy, as specially for a *melius inquirendum*, as they call it, I trust the Queen's Highness meaneth not so to be induced to win a little increase of revenue, to lose in the end ten times more. *Quod satis est sufficit.* Take away a few of the clergy which specially be appointed to preach before her Highness, and I take the rest to be but a simple sort.

<small>Terrible things to be contrived in the next parliament against the clergy.</small>

Furthermore, where your honour sent me word by my steward that I should have the next advowson granted in Ely unto you, at my calling on of the bishop for some relief of Alexander Citolinus[1] (although I purpose not to bestow the whole upon him, but upon some ecclesiastical person), I pray your lordship send it me by this messenger.

<small>Benefice promised to the archbishop in Ely for relief of Citolinus.</small>

As concerning the examination of the papists in such sort as your last letters signified unto us, we shall do as opportunity will serve. And thus I wish your preservations in God,

<small>Examination of papists.</small>

[[1] See before, p 420, note 3.]

to his glory and your own soul's health. From my house at Lambeth, this 9th of Jannary.

Your lordship's loving friend in Christ,

MATTHUE CANTUAR.

To the right honourable the lord Burghley, lord treasurer of England, my very good lord.

CCCLXVI.

ARCHBISHOP PARKER TO PETER DATHENUS.

24th January, 1574—5. Parker MSS. C. C. Coll. Camb. cxxii. art. 13, p. 437.
Parker's draft.

GRATIAS summas ago, domine Petre Dathene, qued meum munusculum tibi, Illustrissimi principis D. Frederici comitis palatini Rheni[2] sacrique imperii electoris legato, in singularis mei tam in illum quam in teipsum amoris signum et indicium nuper missum, tanta benevolentia susceperis. Magnique vicissim ego facio numisma illud in quo imago illius tam vere percussa et expressa est. Id quod inter maximi apud me pretii monumenta quæ mihi gratissimam eorum quos amo atque venerer memoriam referre solent, diligenter custodiendum reponam, et illius principis honore et humanitate etiam urbanitateque tua. Illi a Deo felicia cuncta, animumque (de quo non dubito) in religione christiana constantem deprecor, tibi vero ipsi pietatem et ardorem. Precor etiam ut in precibus tuis quotidianis mei memoriam habeas, sicut et ego tui. Dominus et conatus hic tuos secundet, et felicem illis transactis in patriam reditum concedat. Saluta meis verbis Illustrissimum principem et comitem Fredericum[3], meosque apud eum amices, precipue autem Emannuelem Tremelium ejusque

[2 See before, p. 317.]
[3 Count Frederick, son of Lewis VI. and grandson of Frederick III. He was afterwards the Elector Palatine Frederick IV., and father of Frederick V., who married Elizabeth, daughter of our king James I.]

_{him, especially Emmanuel Tremellius and his wife.} conjugem¹. Vale, ex ædibus meis Lamothe, nono kal. Februarii, 1574.

Tuus in Christo bonus amicus,

MATTHÆUS CANTUARIENSIS.

Charissimo in Christo, fratri D. Petro Datheno, illustrissimi principis Frederici comitis palatini Rheni præcipuo legato.

CCCLXVII.

ARCHBISHOP PARKER TO LORD BURGHLEY.

18th February, [1574—5]. Lansd. MS. xix. art. 65. Orig.

SIR,

_{The earl [of Leicester] purposes to undo the archbishop.} I AM credibly informed that the earl is unquiet, and conferreth by the help of some of the examiners to use the counsel of certain precisians I fear, and purposeth to undo me, &c. But I care not for him. Yet I will reverence him because her Majesty hath so placed him, as I do all others toward her. And if you do not provide in time to dull this attempt, there will be few in authority to care greatly for your danger, and for such others. They will provide for themself, and will learn by me in my case how to do. I was informed by a wise man, that a conspiracy of us was purposed if the parliament had gone forward. At whom they shoot, God knoweth all. If I, led with the vehement words of the first statute (before I was in place), how archbishops and bishops be charged as we would answer before God, &c. (which words I have put to his consideration advisedly), if I set forth that religion which I know in conscience is good and confirmed by public authority; if I do the Queen's commandment, for which the precisians hate me; what is meant, but to go over the stile where it is lowest? Beware of cunning; all _{For himself he cares not three points.} is not gold that glittereth. As for myself I care not three points. For, if I should lie in prison for doing a point of justice with charitable discretion, I will rejoice in it. Whatsoever wealth or commodity may stand in my office, I desire it not

[¹ See before, p. 333.]

for myself. I wrote my letters to him, and did for charity move one other of the greatest parties of them to conscience; but not in a submission (as some of the crew take it and report it), for I have neither offended him nor them (except I was careful for your safeguard and he peaceably again writing to me), yet I understand what is purposed against [me]; for religion's sake, I take it. And do you think that they know not what religion y[ou] be of, and what ye do therein? In talk (as I am informed), you be accompted the dean of Westminster. It must be of some policy that I neither write nor oft come to the court. I like not these dialogues, these treatises, these French books, &c.

I feel some displeasure in some that be towards me, as where they keep in the King's Bench an honest old man, a very good and modest preacher, and sometime my almoner, whom I sent home to his benefice to do good, and yet in extremity of law, against all conscience, in the Court of Requests condemned and persecuted for the love of me, of such whom I specially made, and who at this day have the most part of their living by me; a matter picked partly of covetousness and mere malice, and so favoured. But this matter is too long to write of. He hath lien there ever since Hallowmas, in a nasty prison, chargeably, and rotting among the worst; who shall be there still, before I will serve their turns. I may not work against precisians and puritans, though the laws be against them. Know one and know all. *An old man persecuted on account of his love of Parker.*

I trust her Highness with your advice will take good heed, and specially for providing of such as shall govern the dioceses. I like well my neighbour at Westminster, the dean there, to be at Norwich, whose sad and sure governance in conformity I know. I set not one halfpenny by the profit of the diocese for any procurations or jurisdictions; for at my last metropolitical visitation there I had never a penny of them, but the visitors spoiled all; and I spent £20 of mine own purse, to have that diocese well visited, and yet no good done, and the country exclaiming, and some varlets purchased (as I am informed) £20 yearly by their bribing, whom some of my visitors belike used, but I knew not of it till all was done. I am a fool to use this plainness with you in writing; but though I have a dull head yet I see, partly by myself and partly by others, how the game goeth. *Recommends the dean of Westminster for the bishoprick of Norwich.* *His cost in making a thorough visitation of that diocese.*

<small>Toys out his time</small>

I toy out my time, partly with copying of books, partly in devising ordinances for scholars to help the ministry, partly in genealogies, and so forth; for I have little help (if ye knew all) where I thought to have had most. And thus, till Almighty God cometh, I repose myself in patience. At my house, this 18th of February.

Your in Christ,

MATTH. CANT.

To the right honourable, and his very good lord, the lord treasurer of England.

CCCLXVIII.

ARCHBISHOP PARKER TO ARCHBISHOP GRINDAL OF YORK.

17th March, 1574—5. Petyt MS. Inner Temple, No. 47. fol. 22. Orig. draft in Parker's hand.

<small>Case of a person who has exercised spiritual jurisdiction without ordination. He shall not escape by faculty</small>

SALUTEM *in Christo.* Where your grace hath written unto me[1] that you think that it will fall hardly with him[2] who hath exercised spiritual jurisdiction these 15 or 16 years, and thereupon you writ to stay, if any suit should be made for him to escape by faculty; your grace shall understand that seeing you have sent me warning of it in time, I do not intend to gratify his friends thereby, nor yet to favour the suit that might be made unto me out of Carlisle, &c.

<small>Complaint of increase of sects not true</small>

Where you are informed that there is great complaint of certain sects, as one chattered at the cross openly that such a deformity was in Cambridgeshire, which thing I searched out and found these news to be enviously uttered, who talked his pleasure of that bishoprick of Ely which he looketh to enjoy, and hath laid wagers of his deposition, as I am informed, and that he will give Somersham house to him that sueth for it;

<small>Libeller of bishop of Ely.</small>

[1 This letter is in reply to one dated 4th March, 1574—5, which is in the same volume of Petyt MSS. as the answer, fol. 21. It has been printed in the "Remains of Archbishop Grindal." (Parker Society) 1843. 8vo. p. 353.]

[2 Grindal, in his letter alluded to in the last note, mentions this person as named Lowther.]

which this man will not do, and therefore it hath brought him much displeasant report. As for his min * * * that is said of him, for keeping of household, I leave it to God and his own conscience, but as for this chatterer, I am informed credibly by letters that he should report very ill words of me spoken to him from your successor. For the matter itself I do not care three chips for aught that can be proved in * * allegiance, doing it so faithfully and prudently as I did, and would do the same again if I knew no more than I did at that time.

Concerning the information of her Majesty coming into your country, it is like to be true. As for my doing, that shall not need to be an example to your grace, being yet as you write in your fruits, and having no more there yearly revenue growing unto you; but I think verily your good will will be taken, as her Highness did very lovingly accept my service. I met her Highness as she was coming to Dover upon Folkestone Down, the which I rather did, with all my men, to shew my duty to her, and mine affection to the shire, who likewise there met her. And I left her at Dover, and came home to Bekesbourne that night: and after that went to Canterbury to receive her Majesty there: which I did, with the bishops of Lincoln and Rochester, and my suffragan, at the west door. Where, after the grammarian had made his oration to her upon her horseback, she alighted. We then kneeled down, and said the Psalm *Deus misereatur*, in English, with certain other collects briefly; and that in our chimmers and rochets. The quire, with the dean and prebendaries, &c. stood on either side of the church, and brought her Majesty up with a square song, she going under a canopy, borne by four of her temporal knights, to her traverse placed by the communion board: where she heard even-song, and after departed to her lodging at St Augustine's, whither I waited upon her. From thence I brought certain of the council, and divers of the court, to my house to supper, and gave them fourteen or fifteen dishes furnished with two mess at my longer table, whereat sat about twenty; and in the same chamber a third mess at a square table, whereat sat ten or twelve: my less hall having three long tables well furnished with my officers, and with the guard, and other of the court. And so her Majesty came every

Queen dined in his great hall with the council, corporation, &c

Sunday to church to hear the sermon; and upon one Monday it pleased her Highness to dine in my great hall throughly furnished with the council, Frenchmen, ladies, gentlemen, and the mayor of the town with his brethren, &c.; her Highness sitting in the midst, having two French ambassadors at one end of the table, and four ladies of honour at the other end. And so three mess were served by her nobility; at washing her gentlemen and guard bringing her dishes, &c. Because your grace desireth to know some part of mine order, I write the more largely unto you.

Application against Corranus, who was thought to be preaching erroneous doctrine in the Temple.

Furthermore concerning these sectaries, Mr Alvey came unto me to have my counsel how to deal with Corranus, reader in the Temple[1], whom his auditory doth mislike for affirming free will, and speaking not wisely of predestination, and suspiciously uttering his judgment of Arianism, for the which I hear some wise of his said auditory to forsake him; and more than this, saving for the common precisianship in London, I hear of no sects, although being this other day at

Her Majesty disliked Deering

the court her Majesty disliked Deering's reading, &c. Where I was, partly to answer the dean of Norwich and his chapter upon a rotten composition, wherein yet their predecessors did

Dispute between the archbishop and the dean and chapter of Norwich.

confess that *sedibus vacantibus* I have all the jurisdiction which the bishop hath *sede plena*, and yet they deny it me. By this old composition they should claim no more but to have one of three *de suo gremio*, only in time of visitation and examining of the comptes found in the same; and they have appealed into the chancery very fondly, and go about to deface my jurisdiction, whereof Dr Steward is custos. They have not yet their commission, which I purpose to answer if it come so far. Her Highness also would have my judgment

Mr Blethin, the new bishop of Llandaff. Whom Parker recommended for Norwich.

as well for the bishoprick of Llandaff as for Norwich, and to the first is Mr Blethin preferred[2], and for the other I signified specially, not prejudicing any others, my testimony of the dean of Westminster, Dr Piers, and Dr Whitgift[3]. How

[1 See before, p. 339.]

[2 William Blethin, prebendary of York, was elected bishop of Llandaff, 13th April, 1575. He died bishop of that see 15th October, 1590.]

[3 None of the persons recommended were appointed to the see of Norwich on this vacancy, although two of them were shortly after raised to the episcopal bench. Dr Piers, dean of Christchurch, was

it shall be God knoweth. And thus, inditing in my bed at leisure, I babble the more with you, and bid you heartily well to fare in Christ as myself. Lambeth, 17th Martii, 1574.

Concerning the book *De Disciplina*[4], I sent it to Mr Elmer, thinking that he would have taken the pains to have answered it, but he sent me his letters that he cannot deal therein, and yet keepeth my book still, which I had much ado to get. It is done, and I have it by me, which is handled indifferently well, notwithstanding I will use more judgment before I put it out. As for the earthquake I heard not of it, nor it was not felt of here. *Dominus est; faciat quod bonum est in oculis suis.*

Aylmer declines to answer the book "De Disciplina."

CCCLXIX.

ARCHBISHOP PARKER TO LORD BURGHLEY.

11th April, [1575]. Lansd. MS. xx. art. 60.

DOMINE vim patior, responde pro me. I trust that this shall be one of the last letters which I shall write unto your lordship, the rather for that I am now stricken with mine old disease more sharply than ever I was. It may be, that whereas I have a great while provided for death, yet God will peradventure have me continue a while to exercise myself in these contemplations of grief; *Domini voluntas fiat.* In your absence now from the court I have travailed with her Majesty for the bestowing of the bishoprick of Norwich. I have named unto her, at her commandment, three, that is, the dean of Westminster, Dr Piers, and Dr Whitgift. Amongst them all I have preferred for learning, life, and governance, the dean of Westminster, not because he is towards your lordship, whom I credibly hear that you named, or for any displeasure that I bear to my lord of Leicester's

Parker's illness.

Bishoprick of Norwich.

He specially recommends the dean of Westminster.

successively bishop of Rochester and Salisbury, and Whitgift was appointed to Worcester before his elevation to the archbishopric. The present vacancy in Norwich was filled by the translation of bishop Freke from Rochester.]

[4 A puritanical treatise upon church-government, attributed to Walter Travers.]

chaplains, or to her Majesty's almoner, of any envy to his person; but surely, sir, I speak it afore God, seeing I see her Majesty is affected princely to govern, and for that I see her in constancy almost alone to be offended with the puritans, whose governance in conclusion will undo her and all others that depend upon her, and that because I see him and very few else, which mean to dull that lewd governance of theirs, I am therefore affected to him; whereof yet I make him not privy. For surely, my lord, I see and feel by experience that divers of my brethren partly are gone from me, partly working secretly against me, for the satisfying of some of their partial friends; but I see men be men.

<small>The Queen charged the archbishop for his visitation of Winchester diocese. The bishop was told that he had sifted his clergy, and put a thorn in his foot.</small>

Her Majesty this other day, when I was at Richmond at her commandment, suddenly charged me for my visitation. I think I know from whence it came, and who did inform one nobleman to open it unto her: but I say, and say again, that my visitation in Winchester diocese (which was the device of the bishop) wrought such a contentation for obedience, that I do not yet repent me of it, though the bishop be told that his clergy was sifted, and the thorn was put in his foot; but he will so pluck it out that it should be so in other men's feet that they should stamp again, as I am credibly informed. The Isle of Wight and other places of that diocese be now gone again from their obedience. If this be a good policy, well, then let it be so. If this be a good policy, secretly to work overthwartly against the Queen's religion stablished by law and Injunction, as long as they so stand, I will not be partaker of it.

Her Majesty told me that I had supreme government ecclesiastical; but what is it to govern cumbered with such subtlety? Before God, I fear that her Highness' authority is not regarded, so that if they could, for fear of further incon- <small>The objectors would change the Queen's government.</small> venience, they would change her government; yea, yours and mine, how cunningly soever we deal it. And surely, my lord, whatsoever cometh of it, in this my letter I admonish you to look unto it in such sincerity as God may be pleased, or else He will rise one day and revenge his enemies. Does your lordship think that I care either for cap, tippet, surplice, or wafer-bread, or any such? But for the laws so established I esteem them, and not more for exercise of contempt against law and authority, which I see will be the end of it, nor for any other respect. If I, you, or any other named "great papists," should so favour the pope or his religion that we should pinch Christ's true gospel, woe be unto us all. Her Highness pretendeth in the giving of her small benefices, that for her conscience sake she will have some of us, the bishops, to commend them; and shall her Majesty be induced to gratify some mortal man's request (*qui suas res agit*), and be negligent in the principal pastor of so great a diocese, wherein peradventure her authority is utterly contemned? And yet we must reform such things as most part of gentlemen be against. As for my part, I set as much by my living, bigger or less, or nothing. But if this be not looked unto, I will plainly give over to strive against the stream.

[margin: Burghley and himself termed "great papists."]

This great number of anabaptists taken on Easter-day last may move us to some contemplation. I could tell you many particularities, but I cease, and charge your honour to use still such things as may make to the solidity of good judgment, and help her Majesty's good government in princely constancy, whatsoever the policy of the world, yea, the mere world, would induce. To dance in a net in this world is but mere vanity. To make the governance only policy is mere vanity. Her princely prerogatives in temporal matters be called into question of base subjects, and it is known that her Highness hath taken order to cease in some of them. Whatsoever the ecclesiastical prerogative is, I fear it is not so great as your pen hath given it her in the Injunction, and yet her governance is of more prerogative than the head papists would grant unto her. But I cease, and refer all things to God, in whom I wish you continued to his pleasure. I am compelled thus to write, lying in my bed, by another man's pen, but I doubt not so chosen that you shall not need to doubt. From my house at Lambeth, this 11th of April.

[margin: A number of anabaptists taken on Easter-day.]

[margin: The Queen's ecclesiastical prerogative not so great as attributed to her by Burghley in the Injunctions.]

Sir, I am not much led by worldly prophecies, and yet I cannot tell how this old verse recourseth oft to my head;
Fœmina morte cadet, postquam terram mala tangent.

[margin: Old verse which runs in his head.]

Your lordship's assured friend in Christ,
MATTH. CANT.

*To the right honourable, my very good
   lord, the lord treasurer.*

APPENDIX.

The parts printed in Italics are by a different (probably a later) hand.

No. I.

Anno Dni. 1504. 6 Augusti, lra. G. et F., MATTHÆUS PARKER natus Norwici in parochia Sancti Salvatoris: et in parochia Omnium Sanctorum prope Fibrig gates enutritus, et educatus in parochia S. Clementis juxta fibrig,

SUB

GULIELMO patre, qui vixit ad a^m Dni. 1516, et ad a^m ætat. suæ 48;

ALOYSIA matre, quæ vixit ad a^m Di. 1553. et ad a^m ætatis suæ 83.

Edoctus
- In legendo 1.
- In scribendo 2.
- In cantando 3.
- In gram^a 4.

a
1. Thoma Benis, Theol. bacc. rector[e] S. Clementis, et partim Richardo Pope, presbytero.
2. Willmo. Priour, clerico ecclesiæ Sancti Benedicti.
3. W^o Love, presbytero / R. Manthorp, clerico } S. Stephani { duris præceptoribus.
4. Willmo. Neve, commodo et benevolo pedagogo.

A^o
1522. 8 Septembr. circa a^m ætatis meæ 17. missus Cantabrigiam, *opera Mri. Bunge parochi Sancti Georgii, sed sumptibus matris*, in Colleg. Corporis Christi, sub tutore R^o Cowper, Artium m^{ro}. sed parum docto, edoctus in dialectica et philosophia, partim in hospitio Divæ Mariæ, partim in collegio [Corporis] Christi.

1522. Mense Martii. Electus Bibliotista Col. Corporis Christi.

1525. Admissus Bacchal. in Artibus.

1526. 22 Decemb. Factus subdiaconus sub titulis Barnwelli, et Sacelli in campis Norwici.

1527. 20 Aprill. Factus Diaconus.

1527. 15 Junii. Factus presbyter.

1527. 6 Septemb. Electus in socium Collegii Corporis Chri.

1527. 3 ——— Creatus magister in artibus.

1533. Dominica prima Adventus incepi officium prædicandi
{ Grancet^r. 1
Beche. 2
Ecclia. Benedci. 3
Madingley et 4
Barton. 5 } *Dominica Adventus.*

A°
1535. 30 Martii. Vocatus in aulam Annæ Reginæ.
1535. 14 Julii. Factus bacchal. theologiæ.
1535. 4 Novembr. Promotus ad decanat. de Stoke Clare, per Annam Reginam. A° Hen. 8^l. 27.
1537. 1° Martii. Vocatus ad aulam Regis, et factus Capellanus Hen. 8^l.
1538. 1° Julii. Creatus Professor Theologiæ.
1542. 27 May. Præsentatus ad rectoriam de Ashen in Essex.
1541. 28 Octobr. Installatus in 2 prebendam Ecc. Elien. per collacionem. Hen. 8^l.
1544. 4 Decembr. Electus in magistrum Collegii Corporis Chri.; per lras. commendatitias Hen. 8^l.
1544. 30 April. Resignavi rectoriam de Asshen.
1544. 1° Maii. Presentatus ad rectoriam de Birlingham, Norf.
1544. 25 Januar. Primo electus ad officium Vicecanc. Cantab.
1545. 22 Septembr. Presentatus ad rectoriam de Landbeche.
1547. 1 April. Deposui decanatum de Stoke ex vi statut. Parliamenti.
1548. 7 Febr. Secundo electus ad officium Vicecancel. Cantab.
1550. primo Octobr. Resignavi rectoriam de Birlingham. *S. Andreæ.*
1552. primo Junii. Presentatus ad prebendam de Coringham. } *per illust. Principem Edwardum sextum.*
1552. 8 Junii. Nominatus ad Decanatum de Lincoln.
1552. 9 Julii. Installatus in prebendam predictam.
1552. 30 Julii. Electus in decanum Lincoln.
1552. 7 Octobr. Installatus in decanatum in propria persona.

1553. Decembris. Resignavi officium Magisterii Collegii Corporis Christi Laurentio Moptyd, quem ipse necessitate quadam delegeram Successorem meum.
1554. 2 Aprilis. Privatus præbenda mea in ecclia. Eliensi; et privatus rectoria mea de Landbech; ad quam eccliam. presentandum procuravi Willmum. Whalley, Canon. Lincoln. quem elegi successorem meum; et institutus fuit 30 Septemb.
1554. 21 Maii. Spoliatus fui decanatu meo de Lincolne; sic, eodem die, prebenda mea de Coringham in eadem ecclia. Ad quam presentatus fuit Mr. Georgius Perpoynt, vi advocationis ejusdem, mihi(?) concessæ per Epum. Lincoln. J. Tailor. Decanatus conferebatur Fran° Malet, D. Theo. per M. Reginam.

Postea privatus vixi, ita coram Deo lætus in conscientia mea, adeoque nec pudefactus, nec dejectus, ut dulcissimum ocium literarium, ad quod Dei bona providentia me revocavit, multo majores et solidiores voluptates mihi pepererit, quam negociosum illud et periculosum vivendi genus unquam placuit. Quid postea obventurum sit nescio; sed Deo, cui cura est de omnibus, qui olim revelabit occulta cordium, meipsum totum, piamque et pudicissimam uxorem meam, cum duobus charissimis filiolis meis, commendo. Eundemque Deum optimum maximum precor, ut ita in posterum infractis animis portemus probrum Christi, quo semper meminerimus hic non esse nobis civitatem manentem, sed inquiramus futuram, gratia et misericordia Domini nostri Jesu Christi, cui cum Patre et Spiritu Sancto sit omnis honor et imperium. Amen.

26 Octobr. A° Dni. 1554.

Et adhuc, hoc 6 Augusti A°. Dni. 1557. [1555] persto eadem constantia, suffultus gratia et benignitate Domini mei, et Servatoris Jesu Christi, quo inspirante absolvi Psalterium versum metrice lingua vulgari; et scripsi defensionem conjugii Sacerdotum contra Thom. Martin.

3° Febr. A° Dni. 1552 [5?].

Hactenus coram Dei ita lætus, sorte mea contentus vixi, ut nec superioribus inviderim, nec inferiores despexerim: huc omnes conatus meos dirigens, ut Deo in pura conscientia servirem, utque nec major me despiceret, nec timeret minor.

14 Octobr. A° Dni. 1556.

Et adhuc lætus, sorte mea contentus, testimonio conscientiæ meæ in Domino confisus, et fretus verbo ejus, vivo; expectans redemptionem corporis mei per Christum Servatorem meum.

CONCIONES.

A°
1534. Coram Epo. Eliensi in sua visitatione, Balsamiæ.
1535. Coram Dna. Elizabeta, apud Hundeston.
1535. Coram Rege Henr. VIII. in aula, Dominica 3ª in 40ª, opla.
1539. Coram Edwardo Principe.
1540. Coram Dna. Elizabetha, apud Hatefeld.
1548. Coram Edwardo Rege in aula West. in 40ª, Dª 3ª, de Evangelio.
1551. Coram illustr. Rege Edwardo in quadragesima, scz. alternis diebus Mercurii, viz. 9. 23. 25. diebus Martii, collega meo M° Harlow Epo. Herfordiæ.
1559. Coram Dª Elizabeta regina, bis in 40ª.

484   APPENDIX.

A° ætatis meæ 43.
A° ætatis suæ 28.
Anno Domini.

An° Domini 1547. 24 Junii. Conjugatus sum cum Margareta filia Roberti Harlston de Matsall in Comitat. Norfolc. Gentleman. Quæ nata est A° Dni. 1519. lra. dominicali B., 23 Junii. Quo anno dies Corporis Christi fuit in vigilia S. Johannis Baptistæ.

1570. Hæc Margareta uxor mihi charissima et castissima, mecum vixit anuos plus minus 26. Et obiit Christianissime 17 Augusti, A° 1570. circa undecimam ante meridiem; *et sepulta est in sacello Duc. Norfolciæ apud Lamhith.*

[1548.] Ex qua suscepi filium Johannem anno Domini 1548, 5 Maii, litera dominicali G., mane hora sexta.

1566. Qui conjugatus est cum Joanna filia Episcopi Eliensis 28 Januarii.

[1550.] A° Domini 1550. 27 Augusti, litera dominicali E(?)sera hora undecima suscepi alterum filium, Matthæum, qui e vita decessit 8 Januarii eodem anno.

[1551.] Anno Dom. 1551. primo Septemb. inter horam secundam et tertiam post meridiem, litera dominicali D., suscepi tertium filium, Mattheum.

1569. Qui conjugatus est cum Francisca, filia Episcopi Cicestren. 29 Decemb.

[1556.] Anno Dom. 1556. 12 Septemb. inter 7 et 8 pomeridianam, suscepi quartum filium Joseph.: et decessit eodem anno.

[1559.] 17 Decemb. A° 1559 consecratus sum in Archiepiscopum Cantuar.

Heu, heu, Domine Deus, in quæ tempora servasti me. Jam veni in profundum aquarum et tempestas demersit me. O Domine, vim patior, responde pro me: et spiritu tuo principali confirma me: homo enim sum, et exigui temporis, et minor etc. Da mihi fidium tuarum etc.

Johannes Parker nat. 5 Maii, 1548 duxit Joannam Cox nat. 1° April. a° 1551 ex quæ genuit.
Margaretam, nat. Lamhethi 21 die Martii 1568.
Mathæum, primogenitum Cant. 19 Maii a 1570.
Janam, nat. Lamhethi 19° Martii a 1572.
Richardum, nat. Cantuariæ [?] 20° Maii a° 1577.
Jacobum, nat. Bekesborniæ, 30° Maii a° 1585 [?].
Johannes natus in Insula Elien. 4° Maii a° 1589.
Elizabeth et Johannes obierunt parvuli.

No. II.

DR MATTHEW PARKER TO SIR WILLIAM CECIL.

30th March [1559]. The King's Visitatorial power asserted, by Nathaniel Johnston, 4to, Lond. 1688. p. 215. From "Paper Office; Ecclesiastica, 1550 to 1559."

PLEASETH it your honourable[1] goodness. Upon the occasion of sending up to your honour for the matter which Mr Vice-chancellor writeth of, I thought it good to signify to you that the matter which ye have delegated to us is in hand, with as good expedition as we can make, by reason of the absence of some who were meet to be communed with, though some doubt is made, whether your authority of Chancellorship extendeth to College Statutes for any[thing?] beyond limitation contained in them. So may they doubt of your *delegatum*, [delegation?], though Bishop Gardiner would not be so restrained in his doings; whether upon warrant of the Queen's letters of commission, the copy whereof I sent to you[2], or by authority of his office, I leave that to your prudence to expound. Our statutes and charters prescribe here to officers, that they must in pleas proceed *summarie et de plano, sine strepitu judiciali*, that scholars may be sooner restored to their books. Yet here be wits, which, being thereto admitted, would entangle matters *extremis juris apicibus*, that controversies might be infinite and perpetual, never to have an end. But, according to our old ancient customs, we shall proceed to hearing, with cutting off all such superfluous and perplex solemnities of their cavillations, and so refer the matter to your understanding to be resolutely determined, as the last clause of your letter pretendeth to will us. And if I shall perceive any like incident to be signified to your honourable wisdom, I shall be bold in secret[3] to write it, lest[4] things borne by partialities might prevail under your authority not rightly instructed, and to avoid some stomach that else might be taken. Without doubt, sir, the university is wonderfully decayed, and if your visitation intended be too stoutly executed in some like sorts as hath been practised, that will I fear so much ruffle the state thereof that it will be hardly recovered in years, and yet authority must bridle wilful and stubborn natures, and high time it is here. I trust the prudence of the visitors, for good will toward you, will diligently note how ye received [?] the universities after others, for comparison of the

[1 honorables, Johnston. The original of this letter cannot now be found in the State Paper Office.]
[2 See p. 54, n. 3.]   [3 secietys, Johnston.]   [4 less, Johnston.]

sequel, well hoped for at your hands. Except that be looked to in time, the Queen's Majesty shall not have half sufficient ministers for her years, which I pray God may be many, to uphold Christ's faith in her realms. Youth here is of some inclination if they had but three or four good Heads resident to lean unto, to comfort them against some [?] four[1] talkers in their stoutness; but time must be expected, and God's furtherance craved. Sir, I pray you pardon my boldness, and not to be offended, though I write thus homely and in English letters. While peradventure I might busy my head to write *Latinius*, somewhat to avoid offending of your exact and exquisite gift in your Latin tongue, I might chance to write *obscurius*, not *significantius*, and so the longer to detain your perusing these small causes, to hinder your others much more weighty, which I beseech Almighty God to prosper.

Your unfeigned and bound bedesman,
M. P.

*From Corpus Christi College in Cambridge,
the 30th day of March.*

[1 fower, Johnston.]

INDEX.

A.

ABBEYS, application of their revenues, 215.
Abergavenny (Hen. lord), v. Neville.
Absolution of certain excommunicated foreigners, 247.
Achates, provisions, xii.
Acworth (Geo.), notice of him, 440 n.
Admonition controversy, the Admonition to the Parliament reprinted, 395; Cartwright answered by Dering, 434; Cartwright's Reply to an Answer made by Whitgift, 453 n.
Advertisements, notice of the book of, (or Articles, or Ordinances) devised by certain bishops, 1564, 233, 271.
Affliction, letter of consolation to lord Burghley on occasion of severe illness, 453.
Agletts, Fr. aiguilettes, figuratively, finishing touches, 12.
Aglionby (Edw.), lent Parker a MS., 388 n.
Ainsworth (Ralph), master of Peter-house, 38 n.
Aldborough, Suffolk, contest between Levers and Willoughby about the benefice, 404; the chancel quite down, &c., ib.
Aldrich (Tho.), master of Benet College, Cambridge, 358; a great maintainer of Cartwright, 427, 429; sent for by the ecclesiastical commissioners, 433; he and the fellows appeal to lord Burghley, as chancellor of the university, 436, 438; his insolence too great, 436; most of the heads against him, 439; resigns his prebend at Westminster, 439; doubts as to the mode of determining the controversy in the college, 440; he desires to resign rather than be deprived, 443.
Alexander (Mr), i.e. A. Citolini, q. v.
Allen (Tho.), skinner, 211.
Alley (Will.), bp of Exeter, his share in the Bishops' Bible, 335 n.
Alvey (Jo.), master of the Temple, applies to Parker about Corranus, 476.
Ambrose (St), says Helena worshipped the king, not the wood, for that is a gentile error and vanity of the wicked, 8; tells Theodosius that it neither becomes an emperor to deny liberty of speech, nor a priest not to say what he thinks, &c., 94.
Anabaptists, a great number taken in 1575, on Easter day, 479.
Andrews (——), brought in Saunders's book, 409.
Anglo-Saxon tongue, 253, 266, 271; type cast for Day, 468 n.
Anne Boleyn, second queen of Henry VIII., sends for Parker, 1, 2, 482; her liberality towards students, 2; Latin letter to Rich. Nix, bp of Norwich, 4; her charge to Parker about her daughter Elizabeth, 59, 391, 400; her favour to Parker, 70, 178; her marriage thought to be confirmed by a pope's bull, 414, 420.
Apparitions, an alleged one at Blackburn, 222.
Aquila (the bishop of), ambassador from Spain, desires a conference with Parker, 201.
Archbishops, many desired that the name might be abolished, 373.
Archdeacons, one not in orders, 142 n.
Archers, their outfit, 15.
Arden (Jo.), deprived by bp Sandys, 125.
Armour, how to be provided by the clergy, 345—348.
Arnobius, mentions the heathen objection that Christians had neither temples, images, nor altars, 86.
Articles, v. Advertisements.
  A book of articles was presented to Elizabeth by the returned Marian exiles, 290; articles were sent from some learned men in Germany soon afterwards, 118.
Articles (XXXIX.), a bill introduced respecting subscription to them, 291—294; ultimately passed, 293 n.; on the citation of Augustine on the 29th article, 381.
Arundel (Hen. earl of), v. Fitzalan.
Arundell (Mr), 448.
Ashen, Essex, viii. 482.

Asplyn (Will.), a printer of Cartwright's book, 449.
Asser (Jo.), bp of Sherborne, his 'Ælfredi Res Gestæ' published by abp Parker, 468.
Astrology, v. Nostradamus.
Practised by Bomelius, 364.
Athanasius (St), says the invention of images came not of good but of evil, 83.
Atkins (Anth.), fellow of Merton College, committed to the Tower, 75.
Atkinson (Ric.), vice-provost of King's College, Cambridge, 18.
Aubrey (Dr), an insatiable cormorant, 267; Dr Abre, perhaps another person, 285.
Audley (Tho., lord), lord-chancellor, articles sent to him against Parker, 7; learned and eloquent, 315.
Augustine (St), commends the opinion of Varro that religion might be more purely observed without images, 86; says they serve rather to crook an unhappy soul than to correct it, 87; shews why scripture so frequently reminds us that they have mouths and speak not, &c., 87; he disallowed appeals to Rome, 111; on the chastity of John and that of Peter, 159; he is properly cited in the twenty-ninth article of the church of England, 381.
Augustine (St), abp of Canterbury, 425; his authority denied by the British bishops, 111; his doctrine not received by them, 265, 266.
Aylmer (Jo.), bp of London, recommended for that see, 350; he declines to answer the book 'De Disciplina' (ascribed to Travers), 477.
Aylond (Mr), 38.

B.

Babington (Dr), of Oxford, 138.
Backere (Romanus de), of the strangers' church at Sandwich, 247.
Bacon (Sir Nich.), a commissioner for the suppression of Colleges, &c., 33 n.; his house in Noble Street, London, 49 n.; lord keeper, 155, 156, 179, 328 n., 357, 381; at variance with Parker, 309—316; libelled, 444; letters to Parker, 49, 53, 68, 69, 71, 76, 120; letters to him, 50, 52, 57, 171.
Bacon, Anne, wife of Sir Nich., (daughter of Sir A. Cook), translates Jewel's Apology, 219; letters to her, 219, 309.

Bagnal (Sir Rich.), desires a commission against the clergy, 413, 424.
Baker (Jo.), married Parker's mother, 18 n.
Baker (Jo.), son of the last, and Parker's treasurer, ib.
Bale (Jo.), bp of Ossory, possessed many ancient MSS., 140, 198, 287; his preferment at Canterbury, 197 n., 199, 202.
Bangor, the diocese out of order, 257.
Bannester (Tho.), skinner, 211.
Barber (Rich.), warden of All Souls' College, letters to him, 296, 297, 300, 320, 324; enjoined to deface superstitious plate, &c., 301 n.
Barker (Will.), servant to the duke of Norfolk, 391.
Barley (Rob.), of Barley, and Elizabeth (Hardwick) his wife, 301 n.
Barlings, Linc., the prior heads an insurrection, 8.
Barlow (Will.), bp of Chichester (previously of St Asaph, of St David's, and of Bath and Wells), signs letters to the queen, 101, 294; his share in the Bishops' Bible, 335 n.; his death, 331; marriage of his daughter Frances to Matthew, son of abp Parker, x. 484.
Barnes (Rich.), bp of Carlisle, afterwards of Durham, letter to him, 392.
Baron (Jo.), a Scottish minister, and Anne Goodacre, his wife, 205, 209.
Baskerville (Dr), or Baxterville, 171.
Bateman (Tho.), of the strangers' church at Sandwich, 247.
Beard (——), vicar of Greenwich, 197.
Beaumont (Rich.), master of Trinity College, Cambridge, and vice-chancellor, 226 n., 264; to preach at Paul's Cross, 275.
Becon (Tho.), proposed as a preacher at Paul's Cross, 275.
Beddell (——) of Pancras, 278.
Bedford (Earls of), v. Russell.
Bekesbourne, Kent, Parker desires to take down a part of his house at Ford, to enlarge his house at Bekesbourne, 419; repairs intended, 446, 448.
Benefices, v. Dispensations — Impropriations — Ministers.
Informations for non-residence, 312; Godfrey's book, 348.
Benis (Tho.), rector of St Clement's, Norwich, vi. 481.

INDEX. 489

Bennett (Dr), 196.
Bentham (Tho.), bp of Coventry and Lichfield, signs a letter to the queen, 294; his share in the Bishops' Bible, 335 n.
Berkeley (Gilb.), bp of Bath and Wells, 408.
Betts (Will.) of C. C. C. C., chaplain to Anne Boleyn, his death, 1, 2.
Bible, the only necessary treasure, 338; the Geneva Bible, Bodley has a special licence to print it, 261; the Bishops' Bible, Parker desires Cecil to revise an epistle, 290; completed, 334; lists of the revisers, 334—336 n.; instructions sent to them, 336 n.; Parker's letter sent with this Bible to the queen, 337; the Welsh Bible, 265.
Bickley (Tho.), bp of Chichester, chaplain to Parker, 261; sent to preach at Cripplegate, 278; recommended for a prebend, 290; proposed as bishop of Oxford, 360.
Bill (Will.), unable to have his fellowship at St John's for want of money, 3; master of St John's, 38 n.; an ecclesiastical commissioner, 133.
Billmen, their outfit, 15.
Bindon (Tho. visc.) v. Howard.
Binneman (Hen.), seeks a privilege for printing some school books, 352.
Bishops, v. Coadjutors—Suffragans.
Letter to the deprived bishops, 109; the election of bishops confirmed by the primate, 306; the council complains of their negligence, and of consequent disorder amongst the people, 355; regarded as persecutors of the puritans, 410.
Blackburn, Lanc., an apparition there, 222.
Blethin (Will.), bp of Llandaff, 476.
Blyth (——), M.D., 18, 37.
Bobbing, Kent, the lazar-house, 169.
Bodley (Jo.), specially licensed to print the Geneva Bible, 261.
Boleyn (Mr), prebendary of Canterbury, 319.
Bomelius (Eliseus), his astrology and imprisonment, 363, 364; desires to go to Russia, 364 n.
Bonham (Will.), to be discharged, 464.
Book of Common Prayer, revised on the accession of Elizabeth, ornaments retained, 65; translated into Latin for certain collegiate churches, 133; approved by the cardinal of Lorraine, 398.

Book of Discipline, 382.
Books, superstitious church books at All Souls' College, 297.
Booksellers, ordered not to sell books without permission, 410.
Boulogne, taken by king Henry, 15 n., 30 n.
Bourne (Gilb.), bp of Bath and Wells, prisoner in the Tower, 122; in the custody of bp Bullingham, 253.
Bowen (——), 266, 267.
Boxall (Jo.), dean of Peterborough, &c., quarrels with the service-book, 65; to be deprived if he refuse the oath, 104; his character, ib. n.; prisoner in the Tower, 122; removed thence on account of the plague, 192—195; lives with Parker, 194 n., 203, 215, 217, 218.
Boyes (Edw.), recommended as a justice, 204.
Boys (Jo.), steward of Parker's liberties, letter to him, 452.
Brackinbury (Edw.), recommended as a notary, 393 n.
Brady (Hugh), bp of Meath, 117 n.
Brand (Will.), of the strangers' church at Sandwich, 247.
Brandon (Kath.), duchess of Suffolk, the ecclesiastical commissioners send for one Brown, her chaplain, 390.
Braye (Rich.), fellow of All Souls', 300, 301 n.
Bridges (Agnes), pretending to be possessed, she is examined before abp Parker, and does penance at Paul's Cross, 465.
Bridges (Edm.), lord Chandos, writes to Parker, 213 n.
Brill (Steph.), fellow of All Souls', 300.
Brimstone, made from stuff gathered on the shore, 341.
Broadways, Dorset? the rectory, 136.
Bromley (G.), ecclesiastical commissioner, 383.
Bromley (Sir Tho.), lord chancellor: previously ecclesiastical commissioner, 370, 383.
Brook (Will.), lord Cobham, lord warden of the Cinque Ports, 202, 203, 379, n. 437; letter to him, 379; Frances (Newton), his wife 341 n.
Brookesby (Humph.), 297.
Brooks (——), applies for the prebend of Rycall in the church of York, 361.
Brown (Ant.), visc. Montague, 285.
Brown (Rob.), 'one Brown' (probably the

celebrated Robert), chaplain to the duchess of Suffolk, 390.

Browne (Geo.), abp of Dublin, pulls down an image, 96 n.

Broyle, Sussex, a park near Lewes, 178.

Bruerne (Rich.), his irregular election as provost of Eton, 150 n.; receiver of Christ Church, Oxon., 240.

Bucer (Martin), letters to Parker, 41, 42; his death, 42 n.; his excellent qualities, 44; made Parker and Haddon his executors, 46, 47; some account of his goods, 47, Wibrand Bucerin, his widow, Cheke intercedes with the king for her, 43, 44; she goes to Strasburgh, 47.

Buckland Newton, Dorset, register, 393 n.

Bulls. a bull in Spanish brought to Parker, 397; one confirming the marriage of Anne Boleyn, 414, 420.

Bullingham (Nich.), successively bp of Lincoln, Worcester, Gloucester, and Bristol; assists in the compilation of the book of advertisements, 233; has the custody of bp Bourne, 253; signs a letter to the queen, 294; to preach at Paul's Cross, 318; his share in the Bishops' Bible, 336 n.; his preaching not suited to the court, 378; ecclesiastical commissioner, 383.

Bunge (Mr), of Norwich, vii. 481.

Bungey (Jo.), of Canterbury, 442.

Burghley (Will., lord), v. Cecil.

Burlingham, St Andrew's, Norfolk, viii. 482.

Busby (———), a doctor of law, 18.

Butterworth (Edw.), of Rochdale, 232.

Byron (Sir Jo.), lessee of the living of Rochdale, 231; letter to Mr Byron, his son, 232.

C.

Caius (Jo.), master of Gonville Hall, (now Caius College), 248; rash in expelling fellows, 249; but worthy of respect as a founder, *ib.*; accused of atheism, 251; apparently referred to as Mr Keyes, 295; letter by him, 298; his book De Antiq. Cantab. Academiæ, 298 n.
— (Tho.), registrar of the Univ. of Oxon., his Assertio Antiq. Oxon. Academiæ, 298 n.

Calendar, a new calendar of lessons directed to be made, 133, 135.

Caley (Rob.), a printer, 295.

Calfhill (Jo.), preaches an injudicious sermon before the queen, 218.

Calvin (Jo.), Parker desires his attendance at a conference in France, 147.

Cambridge, old parliaments held there, 300 n.

University: v. Caius (Jo.),—Universities; account of Parker's election as vice-chancellor, 17, 18; corrodies for decayed cooks, 20; many things out of order, 28; prayers and processions, 1545, for the king's success in war, 30; commission from Henry VIII. to inquire into its possessions, 34 n.; royal visitation, 1549, 38; letter of Mary, on her accession, to Gardiner respecting its condition, 54 n.; letter to the university from Gardiner, the chancellor, 56 n.; letter of abp Parker and others to the university desiring the immediate election of a preacher, 71; comedies and tragedies performed there, 226 n.; licenses to preachers, 238; proper style of the university, 239; dissensions respecting vestments, 245; the study of Hebrew there, 348; Parker promises to do something for increase of the living of the Hebrew reader, 467; devilish works there, 353; not two men there, able or willing to read the lady Margaret's lecture, 374; complaints of some young men against the masters of colleges, 393; letter from the ecclesiastical commissioners to the vice-chancellor about Tho. Aldrich, 433;

Benet or Corpus Christi College (v. Aldrich, T.): letter from Henry VIII. to the fellows, recommending Parker as master, 16; Parker's benefactions, xiii.; the mastership worth 20 nobles a year, 51; disorders there, 343; revision of the statutes in king Edward's time, 439; college leases, 469.

Caius College (formerly Gonville Hall), quarrels there, 248, 252; plate given by Parker, xiii.

Christ's College, a tragedy called Pammachius played there, and proceedings thereon, 21—29; some there objected to the surplice, 226 n.

St Mary's Hall, hosp. D. Mariæ, vii. 481.

Queens' College, dispute about election there, 64, 65; Peacock resigns the headship to Dr May, 67.

St John's College, some there objected to the surplice, 226 *n.*; a proposal to annex the college of Manchester to it, 365.

Trinity Hall, plate given by Parker, xiii.

The Schools, the highway to them, 455.

Campion (Edmund), his History of Ireland, 407.

Candles, retained in Queen Elizabeth's private chapel, 97.

Canerner (Mr), 18.

Canons, to be kept not precisely, but as edification shall require, 389.

Canterbury, a royal park there, 178; scheme for making the river navigable, 322; arrangements for Queen Elizabeth's visit, 441—444; the visit described, 475, 476.

Cathedral, church plate, &c., sold by deans Wotton and Godwin, 303, 304; Elizabeth reserves prebends for her chaplains, 319; custom on receiving princes, 442; how queen Elizabeth was received there, 475.

Archbishoprick, exchange effected between the crown and the see, 102 *n.*; the contention for the stewardship of the liberties, 285, *n.*; removed by the attainder of the duke of Norfolk, 452; the steward to hold a court annually, citing all who hold of the palace of Canterbury by knight service, *ib.*; the archbishop by prescriptive custom visits throughout his province, 115; power of the archbishop to visit vacant dioceses, 476.

Archbishop's palace, burned in Cranmer's time, repaired by Parker, xiii.;

St Augustine's, a royal palace, 442; queen Elizabeth lodges there, 475.

Hospitals, &c., return of hospitals and schools within the diocese, 163, 165—170; lazar house of St Lawrence by Canterbury, 166; hospital of John Baptist without the walls, 167; hospital of poor priests, 167; Maynerd's spital, 167; Eastbridge hospital, 168; the grammar school, 169.

Caps, appointed by injunction, 240.

Carey (Hen.), lord Hunsdon, goes against the rebels in the north, 388 *n.*

Carter (Dr), refuses the oath of supremacy, 105.

Cartwright (Tho.), 395, 434, 453 *n.*

Cartwright (——), brother of Thomas, and a lunatic, 469, 470.

Cathedrals, no women to live within their precincts, 146, 151, 158; the statutes for the new cathedrals finished, 395.

Catherine Parr, sixth queen of Henry VIII., letter to Parker, 16; letter to the dean and fellows of Stoke, desiring a lease for Edw. Waldegrave, 19; letter to the university of Cambridge, 36 *n.*

Cavallerius or Le Chevalier, (Ant. Rod.), notice of him, 349 *n.*

Cave (Sir Ambrose), signature as privy councillor, 103, 106, 155, 298.

Cavendish or Canndysh, (Sir Will.), letter signed by him, 307; Elizabeth (Hardwick), his wife, 301 *n.*

Cecil (Sir Will.), afterwards lord Burghley, chancellor of Cambridge, 54; restrains the queen from forbidding the marriage of the clergy, 148; created baron Burghley, 381; sends Parker a book containing an attack on himself and the lord keeper, 444; signature as privy councillor, 46, 73, 74, 76, 77, 103, 106, 122, 155, 179, 328 *n.*, 330, 357, 381; his letters to Parker, 53, 63, 67, 69, 77, 78, 104, 108, 138, 148, 161, 163, 172 bis, 183, 187, 223, 235, 301, 305, 354, 444; Parker's letters to him, see the Table of Contents.

Cecilia, margravine of Baden, sister of the king of Sweden, xii.

Celsus, objected that the Christians had neither altars, images, nor temples, 86.

Ceremonies, disorders in rites and ceremonies, 224, 227; the prince has power by law to ordain ceremonies in certain cases, 375.

Chafin (——), married two sisters, 176.

Chamber (Edw.), beneficed near Abington, 96.

Chancels, the use of chancels upheld by Parker, 132, 185, 186, 376, 450.

Chandos (Edm. lord), *v.* Bridges.

Chapman (Edm.), prebendary of Norwich, 450.

Charing, Kent, a lease of it obtained by Sir Richard Sackville, 372.

Charlemagne, emperor, his book against the second council of Nice, 92, 141.

Chartres (Jean, Vidame of), v. Ferriers (J. de).
Cheke (Sir Jo.), letters to Parker, 2, 39, 43, 48; translates a book De re militari, ascribed to the emperor Leo III.; and dedicates it to Henry VIII., 90.
Chelius (Ulric.), 46 n.
Cheshire, divers gentlemen committed to ward for refusing to answer the bishop on oath, 329.
Chester, a benefice annexed to the bishoprick, 100; a seditious paper cast abroad there, 163 n.
Cheyne (Sir Tho.), a privy councillor, 46.
Cheyney (Rich.), bp of Gloucester, letter to Cecil, 138 n.; letter to him, 213; Parker complains of him, 332.
Chimere, an episcopal vestment, 475.
Chipley, Suffolk, a manor belonging to Stoke college, 19.
Christopher, margrave of Baden, xiii. n.
Christopherson (Jo.), afterwards bp of Chichester, 38.
Chrysostom (St Jo.), shews why a bishop may be the husband of one wife, 159; a passage from the Opus Imperfectum in Matthæum wrongly ascribed to him, against the love of relics, 8, 511.
Church of England, its order explained to a French ambassador, 216.
Church lands, an act passed empowering the crown to exchange them, 98 n.
Churches, much neglected, especially the chancels (v. chancels), 132.
Citolini (Ales.), an Italian protestant exile, 420 n., 421, 470.
Clare, Suffolk, 7, 8.
Clarke (——), fellow of Gonville hall, 248.
Clarke (Will.), of Cambridge, 433.
Clement VII. pope, mention of a bull (of this pope, or Paul III.?) confirming the marriage of queen Ann Boleyn, 414.
Clement (Tho.), a prebendary, 114.
Clergy, v. ministers.
Armour to be provided by them, 345—348; their impoverishment, and its effect, 374; commissions against them for discovery of concealed lands or goods, 413; terrible things to be contrived against them in parliament, 470.
Clerk (Barth.), engaged to refute Saunders, 411, 412; some account of his answer, 413, 414, 430; refuses to resign the deanery of the arches, 427—432.

Clerk (——), niece of abp Parker, xiii.
Cliffe, Kent, the benefice annexed to the see of Rochester, 100.
Clinton (Edw. lord), afterwards earl of Lincoln, signature as privy councillor, 74, 77, 106, 122, 155, 330, 357, 381; goes against the rebels in the north, 388 n.; created earl, 447 n.
Clyfford (Geo.), founded a lazar house at Bobbing, 169.
Coadjutors, their duty, 306.
Cobham (Will. lord), v. Brooke.
Colbyn (Tho.), of Beccles, letter signed by him, 307; Mr Colby, Parker's steward, apparently the same, 324.
Cole (Dr), 56; suspected of nonconformity, 264.
Cole (Mr), at court in his hat and short cloak, 237.
Cole (Rob.), of St Mary le Bow, a puritan, 278.
Cole (Tho.), archdeacon of Essex, 303 n.
Coligni (Odet de), cardinal de Châtillon, his lodging at Canterbury, 442.
Colleges, no women to live within their precincts, 146, 151, 158.
Colt (G.), of Clare, sends articles to lord chancellor Audley against Parker, 7.
Columna (Guido de), 295.
Commandments (X.), directed to be set up at the east end of the chancel, 133, 135.
Commendams, 208.
Commerouse, cumbrous, 249.
Commission (Ecclesiastical), suggestions for a new one, 369, 370; letter to the vice-chancellor of Cambridge about Tho. Aldrich, 433; letter from Parker and Sandys to a commissioner about the Puritans, 434; the commissioners commit some to prison, 447; the commission much abused, 450.
Commissions against the clergy for discovery of concealed lands or goods, 413.
Communion Tables, complaint of unseemly ones, with foul cloths, 133; enjoined to be placed within the quire, 375, 376.
Conspiracy, a supposed conspiracy against nigh friends of queen Elizabeth, 461.
Constance (bishop of), received by Parker, 214.
Constantine V., emperor of the East, called a council at Constantinople, 91; his bones burned by his daughter Irene, 92.

INDEX. 493

Constantine VI., emperor of the East, his mother Irene puts out his eyes, 92.
Convocation, slow in its pooceedings, 9.
Cook (Sir Anth.), an ecclesiastical commissioner, 370 n.; and visitor of colleges, 439; Anne his daughter married Sir N. Bacon, q.v.
Cooke (——), chaplain to the earl of Sussex, 458.
Cooper (Tho.), bp of Lincoln, afterwards of Winchester, notice of him, 316 n., 511; could not have the see of Oxford, 360; his Brief Exposition of such chapters of the Old Testament as usually are read in the Church...on Sundays, 462; he meets the queen at Canterbury, 475.
Corranus (Ant.), otherwise A. Bellerivus Corranus, or del Corro, reader at the Temple, letter by him, 339; his books, ib. n.; notice of him, 340 n.; thought to preach erroneous doctrine, 476.
Corringham, Linc., a prebend in the cathedral church, viii. 482.
Corrodies for decayed cooks, 20.
Cotton (Mr), son of a knight, married Sir Rog. Woodhouse's daughter, 401; very evil disposed, ib.; absconded, 402 n., 403, 415, 417.
Council (Privy), letters from the lords of the council, temp. Eliz., 103, 105, 117, 121, 179, 180, 182, 192, 195, 217, 327 n., 328, 355, 379, 384, 457 n.; letter to the council, 330.
Councils, Parker owns councils called by religious princes, 110; many ancient ones possessed by Jo. Tilius, 141; Carthage (252—256); Cyprian's sentences therein, 111; Carthage VI. (or Africa, 419?), where Augustine and 216 bishops forbade appeals to Rome, ib.; Constantinople (754), condemned image-worship, 91; Elvira (Eliberinum, c. 305), forbade pictures in churches, 93; Nice II. (787), condemned the decrees of the council of Constantinople, 91 n.; and established image-worship, 92; Charlemagne's book against it, ib.
Court of Exchequer, a writ therefrom, 163.
Court of Faculties, Parker desired its abolition, 363.
Court (Palace) of the abp of Canterbury, to be holden by the steward of his liberties, 45.

Court of Star Chamber, an order made for the expulsion of sundry of the perverse sort in religion from the inns of court, 384; referred to, 418, 427.
Courtenay (Will.), abp of Canterbury, attends a parliament at Cambridge, 300 n.
Coverdale (Miles), bp of Exeter, absent from the Lambeth conference about the vestments, 270 n.
Cowper (Rob.), Parker's tutor at C.C.C.C. vii. 481.
Cox (Rich.), bp of Ely, his election to that see, 101 n.; formerly dean of Ch. Ch. Oxon. 118; assists in the compilation of the Advertisements, 233; to preach at Paul's cross, 261; desires the enforcement of uniformity, 270; his part in the Bishops' Bible, 282, 336 n.; an ecclesiastical commissioner, 383; his opinion of Saunders, 410; libelled, 474; letters to Parker, 151, 281; signs letters to the queen, 101, 129, 294; and a letter to lord Burghley, 394; his daughter Joanna married to John, son of abp Parker. x. 484.
Craig (Jo.), minister of Edinburgh, letter from him and others to abps Parker and Young, 205.
Crane (Jo.), fellow of Ch. coll. Cambridge, 25, 26.
Cranmer (Tho.), abp of Canterbury, letters to Parker, 39, 40, 43; record of his disputation at Oxford, 160; some of his written books in private hands, 186, 187; further particulars respecting his MSS., 191.
Crinitus (Pet.), records a decree of Valens and Theodosius against representations of the cross (signum) of Christ, 90.
Crisp (Sir Hen.), of the Isle of Thanet, 204.
Croft (Sir James), signature as privy councillor, 381.
Cromwell (Tho. lord), afterwards earl of Essex, letter to Parker, 5; master of the rolls, 5 n.
Cross, v. Crucifix.
We should not worship the wood, and forget the mystery of the cross, 7; representations of the cross (signum) of Christ, forbidden by Valens and Theodosius, 90.
Crowley (Rob.), expelled divers clerks from St Giles's, Cripplegate, attending a funeral in surplices, 275, 276; a divine,

a poet, and a printer, *ib. n.*; his opinions declared to be anabaptistical, 276; imprisoned in his own house, 276, 278.

Crucifix, retained in queen Elizabeth's private chapel, 97, 105; removed, and brought back again, 379.

Culpepper (——), married the sister of Leonard Dacres, 366; a suspected person, 367.

Curteys (Rich.), bp of Chichester, made dean of Chichester, 290; recommended for the see, 331; meet to serve the court, 350; an ecclesiastical commissioner, 383.

Curwen (Hugh), or Coren, abp of Dublin, detects a pretended miracle, 95 *n.*, 96 *n.*; afterwards bishop of Oxford, 305; should have a coadjutor there, *ib.*

Cyprian (St), says Peter, on whom the Lord built his church, did not, when Paul disputed with him, challenge anything arrogantly, 110; shews that bishops are not subject to the judgment of each other, but only to Christ, 111.

D.

Dacres (Leon.), the rebel, son of William lord Dacre of Gillesland, 367; his sister married to one Culpepper, *ib.*

Damascenus (Jo.): records portions of an edict of Leo Isauricus against images, 90 *n.*

Danet (Gerard), his unlawful marriage, 353.

Danvers (Will.), an ecclesiastical commissioner, 301 *n.*

Dathenus (Pet.), letter to him, 471.

Davies (Rich.), bishop of St Asaph, and afterwards of St David's: his translation, 137 *n.*; his part in the Bishops' Bible, &c., 265, 267 *n.*, 280, 335 *n.*; letters to Parker, 137, 265, 279; signs a letter to the queen, 294; letter to him, 270.

Davies (Tho), bishop of St Asaph, 137 *n.*; seeks a licence to hold a living in commendam, 207; signs a letter to the queen, 294; his death, 446 *n.*

Day (Geo.), bishop of Chichester, 10.

Day (Jo.), the printer, his new Italian letter, 411; obtains a lease of a shop in St Paul's churchyard, *ib.*; Asplyn attempts to kill him and his wife, 449; Anglo-Saxon type cast for him, 468.

Day (Will.), bishop of Winchester, sometime provost of Eton, 162; meet for the see of London, 360; proposed as a commissioner, 370.

Deal castle, Kent, 203.

Dean (Mr), 258; Mr Dene, probably the same, 285.

Declaration, A Declaration in the name and defence of certain Ministers in London, 285 *n.*; A brief Examination, &c. in reply to it, *ib.*

Delamore (Humf.), parson of Kemisford, 213.

Denny (Sir Anth.) letter to the commissioners for the dissolution of colleges, 33 *n.*

Denny (——), vicar of North Elmham, 247.

Derby (Earls of), *v.* Stanley.

Dering (Edw.), a great learned man, 410; attempts to confute Saunders, 410; answers Cartwright, 434; the queen dislikes his reading, 476.

Dethick (——), fellow of Gonville hall, 248, 252, 298.

Dispensations, Parker refuses a dispensation to allow a child to hold a benefice, 136; a Roman dispensation to hold a prebend, whether still in force, 176; on the dispensing power of the prince, and of the archbishop, 351; a dispensation sought to make a child a prebendary, 362.

Dodds (Greg.), dean of Exeter: appointed to preach, 260, 275, 511.

Dorel (Mr), prebendary of Canterbury, 319.

Dorman (Tho.), his controversy with Nowel, 260.

Dover, Kent, state of the castle and town, 203, 204; the pier, 258, and haven, 259; a strange person examined there, 400; Parker sends a book about Dover to lord Burghley, 436, 439.

Downes (Fra.), of East Tuddenham, 402 *n.*

Downham (Will.), bishop of Chester, compounds for his visitation, 222; signs a letter to the queen, 294.

Doyly (Tho.), married a niece of Parker, xiii.

Drury (Will.), letter to him, 213; an ecclesiastical commissioner, 277, 345; Parker's officer, 363.

Dublin, a pretended miracle at Christ church, 95 *n.*

INDEX. 495

Dudley (Jo.), earl of Warwick, afterwards duke of Northumberland, 46.
Dudley (Ambrose), earl of Warwick, holds Newhaven, 179 n.; surrenders it, 183; letter by him, 319; goes against the rebels in the north, 388 n.
Dudley (Rob.), earl of Leicester, Parker intends to ask him for venison, 177; mentioned, 236, 237; he claims an advowson, 266; seeks a dispensation to make a child a prebendary, 362; slandered by a prisoner, 400; offended with Parker, 406, 408; supports the puritans, 428; still grieved, 439; expected to accompany the queen to Canterbury, 442; visited by the queen, 468; purposes to undo archbishop Parker, 572; letters by him, 190, 301; letters to him, 190, 405; signature as privy councillor, 328 n., 330, 357, 381.
Dugdale (Sir Will.), xi.
Duns (Jo.) Scotus, his opinion on the consecration of the eucharist, 251.
Dunstan (Ant.), alias Kitchen, q. v.
Durham cathedral, its statutes signed by Philip and Mary, and sealed with the great seal, 395.

E.

Eagles (Brazen), outcry against them in London, 450.
Earthquake, one in Yorkshire and the midland counties, 1574—5, 477.
Easter, the true meaning of Easter processions, 7.
Edward Fortunatus, son of Christopher, margrave of Baden, baptized by Parker, xii.
Eleutherius, bishop of Rome, his alleged mission to Lucius, 295.
Elizabeth, queen of England, her mother's charge to Parker, 59, 391, 400; she resides at Hunsdon and Hatfield, (1535, 40), ix. 483; on Lever's suggestion she declines the title of supreme head, 66; Parker's letter to her begging to be excused taking the archbishoprick, 69; letter to her from Parker and others against images in churches, 79—95; she consents to the casting out of images, 96 n; but retains a crucifix and lighted tapers in her private chapel, 97, 105; letter to her from Parker and other bishops elect against the inequitable exchange of the lands of bishopricks, 97; the queen's letter to the lord treasurer, &c., on this matter, 101; she dines at Lambeth, 120; letter to her from Parker, Grindal, and Cox, 129; advised to marry, 131; letter to the ecclesiastical commissioners respecting a new calendar of lessons, tables of the commandments, &c., 132; letter to Parker respecting the re-edifying of St Paul's, 142; order prohibiting the residence of women in colleges and cathedral precincts, 146; letter of bp Cox, complaining of this order, 151; letter of abp Parker severely condemning it, 158; she disapproves the marriage of the clergy, but is restrained by Cecil from forbidding it, 148; letter to Parker about the unauthorized election of a provost at Eton, 149; Parker horrified by her words concerning holy matrimony, 156; writ addressed to Parker commanding him to make a return of the hospitals and schools in his diocese, 163; grant to abp Parker to retain forty persons with his livery badge, 175; letter respecting prayer and fasting, 1563, 184; sends Parker a deer killed with her own hand, 190; letter to Parker on the reception of a French ambassador, 212; dines with Sackville, 219; intends to go towards Stamford, ib.; letter to Parker on the correction of many disorders in opinions, and especially in rites and ceremonies, 223; letter to her from the bishops praying that a bill for uniformity may be allowed to proceed, 292; she chides Parker, 311; letter to Parker requiring him to make inquiry respecting the numerous strangers in England, 321 (see 323); Parker's letter to her with the Bishops' Bible, 337; letter to Parker respecting a vacant prebend at Canterbury, 340; Parker's letter to her respecting certain lands in Kent claimed by the crown from the archbishop, 371; the cross, which had been removed from her chapel, is brought back again, 379; letter to Parker on the enforcement of uniformity in divine service, 386; slandered by a prisoner, 400; two letters to her from Parker, about Dr Clerk, dean of the arches, 428, 429; she visits Kent, 436, 437, 441; received by the archbishop at Folkestone and Canterbury, 475; cere-

monics at the cathedral, *ib.*; her opposition to prophesyings, 456, 457, 459; returns from the west, 466; comes to the earl of Leicester, 468; proposes to go to the north, 475.

Elizabeth, queen of Bohemia, 471 *n.*

Ellis (Dr), not a fit person for the see of Bangor, 257, 261; sometime sheriff of the county, 258.

Ellys (Tho.), founder of Ellys's hospital, Sandwich, 168.

Elmham (North), Norfolk, the vicarage, 247.

Elvan (St), sent from Rome to Lucius, 295.

• Ely cathedral, but one prebendary resident there, 151.

England, rudeness of the people in the north, 123; rebellion in that part, 388.

Epiphanius (St), destroys a picture of our Lord in a church at Anablatha, 88.

Erle (Jo.) prebendary of Winchester, in prison for nonconformity, 103.

Essex (Tho. earl of), *v.* Cromwell.

Eton college, letter by queen Elizabeth on the unauthorized election of a provost, (R. Bruerne), 149; letter from Parker to the provost and fellows, 162.

Eusebius Pamphilus, ascribes the invention of images to the heathen, 83.

Eutropius, says when the eyes of Constantine VI. were put out, the sun was darkened for 17 days, 92.

Execution of laws, the first and last part of good government, 246.

Exeter, letter to the chapter respecting divine service, 107.

Excommunication of certain members of the Strangers' Church at Sandwich, 247.

Eye (At), at a glance, 130.

F.

Fabyan (Edw.), sheriff of Oxon. and Berks., letters to him, 145.

Farrar (Rob.), bp of St David's; taken in hand by the council, 281.

Farrar (Sam.), son of the last, 267.

Fasting, on Fridays, 216; the Wednesday fish-day dispensed with at Oxford, Cambridge, and Winchester, 235.

Feckenham (Jo.), abbot of Westminster; prisoner in the Tower, 122.

Felton (Jo.), or Fenton, who published the bull for the dethronement of Elizabeth, 445 *n.*

Felton (Tho.), letter signed by him, 307.

Feria (The count de), ambassador from Spain, 66.

Ferriers (Jean de), vidame of Chartres; Parker's epistle to him, prefixed to Marlorat's Thesaurus, 455.

Feuguereius (Gul.), 455.

Fitzalan (Hen.), earl of Arundel; a privy councillor, 73, 76; mentioned, 266; lent Parker a MS., 388 *n.*

Fitzwilliam (Sir Will.), a privy councillor, 364.

Flacius (Matthias) Illyricus, letter to Parker, 139; letter to him, 286.

Flanders, embassy from churches of, 332.

Fletcher (Will.), skinner, 211.

Fogg (W.), 375

Folkestone, Kent, Parker meets the queen there, 475.

Fonts, outcry against them in London, 450.

Ford, Kent, Parker desires to take down a part of his house at Ford, to enlarge his house at Bekesbourne, 419, 424.

Foreigners, Parker enjoined to make inquiry respecting the numerous strangers in England, 321, 323.

Foster (R.), of All Souls' College, 297, 301 *n.*; his widow, 320, 324.

Fox (Jo.), letters to Parker, 160, 230; finishes Haddon's second reply to Osorius, 217 *n.*

France, war against France, 1544, 15; Parker desires the re-edifying of the church there, 147; the conference at Poissy, 147.

Franklin (Rob.), fellow of All Souls', 300.

Frederick III., elector Palatine, 471 *n.*; letter to him, 317.

Frederick IV., elector Palatine, 471 *n.*

Frederick V., elector Palatine, and afterwards king of Bohemia, married Elizabeth, daughter of James I., 471.

Free-will, errors thereon, 140.

Freke (Edm.), bp of Rochester, afterwards of Norwich, 318, 319; his opinion on prophesyings, 459 *n.*; meets the queen at Canterbury, 475; his translation, 477 *n.*

G.

Gardiner (Steph.), bp of Winchester, letter to Parker and Smith, 20; to Parker, 22,

INDEX. 497

27; as chancellor of Cambridge he determines the pronunciation of certain Greek letters, 28; signature as privy councillor, 30; letter to him from queen Mary, 54 n.; letter to the University of Cambridge, 56 n.
Gascoyne (——), 'Gasconus,' 65.
Gavell (Rob.), keeper of Nonsuch park, 387.
Geoffrey of Monmouth, a copy in MS., 265.
Germanical natures, 125.
Gerrard (Sir Gilb.), or Gerald, letters to him, 308, 325; an ecclesiastical commissioner, 370 n.
Gerrard (Mr), a justice, 375.
Gervase of Tilbury, Parker sends a transcript of a treatise by him to Lord Burghley, 424.
Geste (Edm.), bp of Rochester, afterwards of Salisbury, 123 n.; to preach at Paul's cross, 240; letter by him, 250; his share in the Bishops' Bible, 250.
Gibbes (Mr), defames the dean of Exeter, 261.
Gibbon (Edw.), xiv.
Giraldus Cambrensis, a copy in MS., 265.
Glover (Rob.), Somerset herald, xiii.
Glyn (Will.), afterwards bp of Bangor, 18, 38.
Gnostics, Irenæus mentions that they had an image of Christ, 86.
Godfrey (——), his book of benefices, 348.
Godwin (Tho.), bp of Bath and Wells, falsely charged, when dean of Canterbury, with the misappropriation of church plate and ornaments, 303; an ecclesiastical commissioner, 370 n.
Goldastus (M. H.), his 'Imperialia Decreta de cultu Imaginum,' 90 n.
Gonell (Mr), 38.
Gonour (Mons. de), French ambassador, 212; received by Parker, 214.
Goodman (Chr.), his book, 'How superior powers ought to be obeyed,' 61 n., 449; a puritan, 382.
Goodman (Gab.), dean of Wesminster, his share in the Bishops' Bible, 336 n.; not meet for the see of London, 360; an ecclesiastical commissioner, 370, 383, 390; mentioned, 407, 409, 411, 438, 447, 469; recommended for the bishoprick of Norwich, 473, 476, 477.

Goodrich (Tho.), bp of Ely, 30 n.; an upright chancellor, 315.
Goodrik (Hen.), a prebendary, 202.
Googe (Barnaby), notice of him, 198.
Gordon (Alex.), bp of Galloway, a commissioner for the release of Mary queen of Scots, 378.
Gosnold (Jo.), a commissioner for the suppression of colleges, &c., 33 n.
Gough (Jo.), or Gouff, a puritan, 382.
Government, mischievous books on government, 60, 61.
Gown, Parker is desired to bring a long one to court, 2.
Grafton (Rich.), letter by him, 295.
Gray (Jo.), scribe of the general assembly of the church of Scotland, 206, 207.
Greek, Gardiner's determination (as chancellor of Cambridge) respecting the pronunciation of certain Greek letters not attended to, 28; disputes respecting pronunciation at Oxford, 138 n.
Greenwall (Nich.), fellow of Ch. coll. Camb., 25, 26.
Gregory I., pope, allowed images, but forbade them to be worshipped, 89; his saying as to one universal bishop, 112.
Grigby (Justinian), and Jane his wife, 303.
Grindal (Edm.), bp of London, afterwards abp of York, and finally of Canterbury, minor proctor at Cambridge, 38; signs letters to the queen, 100, 129, 294; his election to the see of London, 100 n.; an ecclesiastical commissioner, 107, 298, 344 n., 345; assists in the compilation of the book of Advertisements, 233; to be urged to execute the laws and injunctions, 233, 235; supposed to favour the puritans, 236; deemed by Parker too tolerant, 284; his share in the Bishops' Bible, 335 n.; shews favour to strangers, 340; recommended for the see of York, 350; his election thereto, 359 n.; confirmed archbishop, 361 n.; letters by him, 165, 196, 115, 120, 127, 134, 143, 152, 160, 227, 201, 261, 267, 348, 394; letters to him, 242, 272, 308, 323, 345, 474.
Gwynne (Lewis), a prebendary, 114; and parson of Llanddewi Brefi, 266, 280.

H.

Haddon (Walter), an ecclesiastical commissioner, 72, 133, 370 n., 439; answers

32

Osorius's letter to Elizabeth, 216 n.; letters by him, 218, 262; letter to him, 264.
Hales (Sir Chr.), lessee of an hospital at Canterbury, 167.
Hales (Jo.), 5 n.
Halford, Warwick, the benefice, 138 n.
Hallowmas, the feast of All Saints, 473.
Hamber, hammer? 425.
Hamond (Mr), desired to make his child prebendary of York, 361, 362; an ecclesiastical commissioner, 447.
Harbledown, Kent, the hospital, 167.
Hardiman (Jo.), vicar of Lydd, his evil behaviour, 342.
Hardwick (Jo.), of Hardwick, and his daughter Elizabeth, 301 n.
Hargreves (Geo.), recommended to be vicar of Rochdale, 221.
Harleston (Rob.), Parker married to his daughter Margaret, x, 46 n., 484.
Harley (Jo.), bp of Hereford, mentioned as M. Harlow ep. Herfordiæ, x, 483.
Harrison (Lucas), warden of the printers, 449.
Hartgill (Jo. and Will.), murdered by Cha. lord Stourton, 442 n.
Harvee (——), prebendary of Sarum, a layman, 176.
Harvey (Hen.), a doctor of law, 18, 196.
Hastings (Hen.), earl of Huntingdon, befriends Sampson, 243, 245; letter to him, 245.
Hatcher (——), M.D., 18, 38.
Hatfield, Herts., Parker preaches there, 1540, before the princess Elizabeth, ix, 483.
Hatton (Sir Chr.), K.G., 400, 442.
Havre de Grace, or Newhaven, besieged, 179; surrendered, 183.
Hayward (Sir Rowland), 465.
Heath (Nich.), successively bp of Rochester and Worcester, and abp of York, 18; letter to him and other deprived bishops, 109; prisoner in the tower, 122.
Hebrew language, its study at Cambridge, 348, 467.
Helena, empress, worshipped not the cross but the king, 8.
Hell, controversy on Christ's descent thither, 305.
Heneage (Sir Tho.), 320.
Henry III., king of England, caused the chronicles to be searched concerning the superiority of the English crown over Scotland, 327.
Henry VII., king of England, reason of his reputation for wisdom, 461.
Henry VIII., king of England, warrant for a doe for Parker, 4; his diligence in reclaiming the people from superstition, 11; letter to the dean and prebendaries of Stoke, requiring them to send four able men to his army, about to invade France, 15; takes Boulogne, 15 n., 30 n.; letter to the fellows of Corpus Christi College, Cambridge, recommending Parker as master, 16; commission to Parker, Redman, and May to inquire into the possessions of the university of Cambridge, 34 n.; his marriage with Anne Boleyn confirmed by a papal bull, 414, 420.
Herbert (Will.), earl of Pembroke, signature as privy councillor, 46, 103, 156; recommends Dr Ellis for bishop of Bangor, 258; claims an advowson, 266.
Herd (Mr), preserves some writings of Cranmer, 187.
Hereford, proposed visitation of the cathedral, 165.
Heresy, said to be prevalent in England, 61, 474.
Herle (Tho.), chaplain to the queen, and warden of Manchester, suggested for bishop of Bangor, 259; desires to surrender the college, 365.
Heth (Jo.), married a niece of Parker, xiii.
Hewet (Tho.), proposed for the see of Bangor, 257, 261.
Hewick (Dr), 177.
Heydon (Chr.?), his son and heir, 417.
Heydon (Will.), made a great stir about the suppression of prophesyings, 459.
Hill (Mr), 223.
Holt (Sir Jo.), letter to him, 231.
Homilies, publication of the second book, 177 n.
Hooper (Jo.), bp of Gloucester, his opinions on vestments opposed by the council, 234, 280.
Hopton (Jo.), bp of Norwich, died in debt, 58.
Hopton (Rob.), 307 n.
Hopton (Will.), letter signed by him, 307.
Horne (Rob.), bp of Winchester, an ecclesiastical commissioner, 72, 383, 439; assists in compilation of book of advertise-

ments, 233; signs a letter to the queen, 294; appointed to preach, 318; his share in the Bishops' Bible, 335 n.

Hoveden (Rob.), warden of All Souls' College, 398.

Howard (Sir Geo.), letter to him, 197.

Howard (Lord Hen.), afterwards earl of Northampton, Parker begs for his liberty, 394.

Howard (Tho.), duke of Norfolk, part of a letter to Parker, 255 n.; letter from Parker to him, 255; mentioned, 310; signature as privy councillor, 328 n., 330; his treason, 391; beheaded, 394 n.; his attainder terminates a dispute about the stewardship of the archbishop's liberties, 452.

Howard (Lord Tho.), probably third visc. Howard of Bindon, letter to him, 136.

Howard (Will. lord), of Effingham, signature as privy councillor, 77, 103, 106, 117, 155, 328 n., 330, 357, 381.

Howel (Cha.), of Rochdale, 232.

Hubert (Conrad), 46 n.

Hughes (Will.), bp of St Asaph, 446 n.

Hugo, second abbot of St Augustine's, Canterbury, 166.

Humphrey (Lau.), a conference to be held with him, 233; remains immovable, 234; appointed to preach at Paul's cross, 239; his nonconformity, 240.

Hunsdon, Herts., Parker preaches there, 1535, before the princess Elizabeth, ix, 483.

Hunsdon (Hen. lord): v. Carey.

Huntingdon (Hen. earl of): v. Hastings.

Hutton (Hen.), farms the manor of Chipley, 20.

Hutton (Matt.), afterwards abp of York, a professor at Cambridge, 252; not meet for the see of London, 360.

Huyck (Tho.), signs a letter, 107.

Hythe, Kent, hospital of St Bartholomew, 169; hospital of St John, ib.

Hythe (Haymo de), or Hethe, bp of Rochester, founded St Bartholomew's hospital near Hythe, 169.

I.

Images, v. Cross, Crucifix, Pictures.
Letter from Parker and others to queen Elizabeth containing reasons from scripture, the fathers, and councils, against the use of images in churches, 79—95; they divided the church and the empire, 93; called laymen's books, 93.

Impropriations, 99.

Improve, to disprove, 130.

Incent (Jo.), Parker's registrar, 161, 214, 328 n.

Infymacion, confirmation, 268.

Innocent III., pope, his opinion on the consecration of the eucharist, 251.

Interim (The), 141.

Ireland, Parker fears the people of the north of England will become 'too much Irish and savage,' 123; the prince of this realm (England) reported to be by ancient right not lord, but king, of Ireland, 328; Campion's History, 407.

Irenæus, mentions that the Gnostics had an image of Christ, 86.

Irene, empress of the East, calls the second council of Nice, 92; burns her father's bones, and puts out the eyes of her son, ib.

Isle of Wight, 478.

J.

Jackson (Hen.), of Merton college, 301, 302.

Jerome (St), translates the epistle of Epiphanius to John, bp of Jerusalem, 88; shews that a bishop, a priest, may be the husband of one wife, 159, 160.

Jewel (Jo.), bp of Salisbury, his Apology, 148, 161; translated by lady Bacon, 219; the Defence of the Apology published, 319; his Answer to Harding placed in churches, 417; letter to Parker, 176.

Joan, pope, 'merry as pope Joan,' 222.

John, bp of Jerusalem, epistle of Epiphanius to him, 88.

Johnson (———), had four prebends, 450.

Johnston (Nath.), 'The King's Visitatorial Power asserted,' 485.

Jones (Hugh), bp of Llandaff, 257.

Jones (Nich.), at Cambridge, 339 n.

Joscelin (Jo.), or Josseline, wrote the volume 'De Antiquitate Britannicæ Ecclesiæ,' xiii.; Mr Joscleyn mentioned, 298; notice of his book, 425, 426.

Joscelin (Sir Tho.), or Josseline, brother of the last, xiii.

Josephus (Fl.), relates how Herod, Pilate, and Petronius sought to place images in the temple, and how the Jews opposed them, 82.

Judd (Sir And.), founds a school at Tonbridge, 210.
Judex (Matthias), letter to him, 286.
Jugg (Jo.), one of the queen's printers, 281; prints the Bishops' Bible, 337.
Julian, bp of Ostia, granted to the university of Cambridge power to license twelve preachers, 238.

K.

Kempe (Sir Tho.), 169.
Kent, v. Canterbury—Lambard (W.); defenceless condition of the coast, 202; state of the castles, 203; salt-works there, 238.
Kett (Will.), the story of his rebellion written by Alex. Nevile, xiii.
Keyes (——), Parker's messenger, 441.
Keyes (Mr), perhaps Dr Jo. Caius, 295.
Keyes (Tho.), sergeant porter to queen Elizabeth; letter to Parker respecting his marriage with lady Mary Grey, 366 n.
Kilburn (Sir Pet.), 417 n.
Kitchen (Anth.), alias Dunstan, bp of Llandaff, his death, 208 n.
Knight-service, the archbishop's tenants by knight-service, 388 n., 452.
Knollys (Sir Fra.), privy councillor, 73, 75, 76, 77, 103, 106, 298, 357, 457 n.; letter to Parker, 96.
Knollys (Hen.), 333.
Knox (Jo.), his 'First Blast against the Regiment of Women,' 61 n.; his turbulent reformation, 105; letter from him and others to abps Parker and Young, 205.

L.

Lacedemonians, no images allowed in their council-chamber, 85.
Lactantius, says there is no religion where there is an image, 86.
La Ferte (M. le baron de), hostage for the French king, 172.
La Haye (Mons. de), 170.
Lambard (Will.), Parker sends his Perambulation of Kent, not yet published, to Lord Burghley, 424, 441.
Lambeth, Surrey, queen Elizabeth dines at Lambeth palace, 120; conference in the chapel respecting the vestments, 268–270; the burial and monument of abp Parker, xi., the Norfolk chapel in Lambeth church, x., 369, 484; Lambeth bridge, i. e. landing place, 311.
Lances, abp Parker's 'poor lances' at York, 388.
Landbeach, Cambridgeshire, vii., viii., 481, 482.
Langrige (Peter), in prison for nonconformity, 103.
Latham (R.), fellow of Merton college, 308, 326.
Latimer (Hugh), bp of Worcester, letter to Parker, v.; record of his disputation at Oxford, 160; his saying respecting watchmen, 353.
Lawes (Tho.), prebendary of Canterbury, 442.
Lawrence (Mr), a preacher near Ipswich, removed by the archbishop's visitors, 307.
Lawyers, keep their old trade, 352.
Lee (Sir Hen.), K. G., favoured by Parker, 354, 359.
Leeds (Edw.), letters to him and others, 63, 64.
Leicester (Rob. earl of), v. Dudley.
Leigh (Rich.), his pious fraud at Christ church, Dublin, 95 n.
Lent, v. Fasting.
Lent licenses sought; for Sir Rog. North, 108; for the baron de la Ferte, 172; for the lord of Lethington, ib.; for Jo. Fox, 230; for Philip Sydney, 316.
Leo III., called Isauricus, emperor of the East, a treatise, 'De re militari' ascribed to him, 90; he abolished and burned images, ib.
Leonard (Jo.), and Leonard (Tho.), 198.
Lessons, v. Calendar.
Bp Cooper's 'Brief Exposition' of the first lessons for Sundays, 462.
Lethington (The lord of), v. Maitland.
Lever (Tho.), on his suggestion, queen Elizabeth declines the title of supreme head, 66; married of late, ib.; complains of the state of Sherborne hospital, 348; about to be examined, 382.
Levers (——), farms Aldborough benefice, 404.
Lewis (Dav.), mentioned as 'Dr Lewes,' 257; an ecclesiastical commissioner, 277, 370 n.
Lewisham, Kent, the advowson, 239.

Linacre (Tho.), his lecture at Merton college, Oxford, 326.
Lincoln, value of the deanery, 51; misconduct of a certain lady of Lincoln, 147.
Lincoln (Edw. earl of), v. Clinton.
Lincolnshire, rebellion there under the prior of Barlings, 8 n.
Linney (Rog.), vicar of Blackburn, 222.
Livery, Parker receives permission to retain forty persons with his livery badge or cognizance, 175.
Llandaff, vacancy of the see, 208.
Llanddewi-Brefi, Cardigan, the advowson, 266, 271, 280.
Lockwood (Hen.), 25, 26
Loftus (Adam), abp. of Armagh, 117 n.
London, v. Ministers—Plague.
 St Paul's, letter from queen Elizabeth about its re-edification after the fire of 1561, 142; letters by Parker on the same, 143, 152; the works at a stand for want of money, 178; inconvenience of a thanksgiving communion there, 201.
 Paul's Cross, Parker appointed to preach there, ix. n., 5, 39, 45; arrangements about preachers there, 239, 261, 275, 318; penance done there by two girls who pretended to be possessed, 465 n.
 St Giles's Cripplegate, disorder at a funeral there, 275, 276.
 Inns of Court, disordered about religion, 384, 385; (Temple, v. Corranus).
 Spital, sermons there, 263.
 Whittington College, 72 n.
 Skinner's Company, letter to Parker respecting a grammar school at Tunbridge, 210.
 Tower, prisoners there for ecclesiastical causes, 121, 122.
 Houses, Bergavenny house, 49, 52; Shelley house, afterwards Bacon house, 49 n.; Day's little shop in St Paul's church-yard, 411, 412.
Longbeach, a wood in Kent, 372.
Lorraine (Cha. card. de), his opinion of the Prayer Book, 398.
Louis VI., elector palatine, 471 n.
Love (W.), a priest at St Stephen's, Norwich, vi., 481.
Lovelace (Will.), serjeant, recommended to be steward of abp Parker's liberties, 405.

Lowther (——), exercises spiritual jurisdiction without ordination, 474.
Lucian, his declamation, 'Pro Tyrannicidia,' 445.
Lucius, king of Britain, the alleged embassy to him from Eleutherius, 295.
Lydd, Kent, letter from Parker to the bailiff and jurats on the evil behaviour of Dr Hardiman the vicar, 342.
Lylye (——), an artist skilful in supplying wanting portions of MSS., 254.

M.

Madew (Jo.), master of Clare hall, 38 n.
Maidstone, Kent, the grammar school, 170.
Maitland (Will.), lord of Lethington, sent from the queen of Scots, 172.
Malachias, an Irish bishop, v. O'Molana.
Malet (Fra.), dean of Lincoln, viii, 482.
Mallocke (Jo.), fellow of All Souls', 300.
Manchester, Herle desires to surrender the college, to be annexed to some college at Cambridge, 365.
Mann (Jo.), warden of Merton college, ambassador to Spain, 326.
Manred, man-rent, 99.
Manthorp (R.), a clerk of St Stephen's, Norwich, vi, 481.
Manuscripts, v. Bale (J.), Cranmer (T).
 Rare MSS. should be brought together into well-known places, 140; Bale's and other MSS., 140; those of Tilius, 141; MSS. at Rome, ib.; no old ones at St David's, 265; letter from the council respecting writings and records formerly kept in divers abbeys, but then in private hands, 327; a curious one of the Old Testament, or part thereof, in Latin and Anglo-Saxon, 253.
Manwood (Sir Rog.), lord chief baron, willing to endow a school at Sandwich, 187, 188, 192; letter to him when serjeant, 338; made a justice of the Common Pleas, 405 n.
Marley (Mr), called Cecil's old master, 260.
Marloratus (Aug.), his Thesaurus, 455.
Marriage, that of the clergy proposed to be winked at, not established by law, 66; disliked by Elizabeth, 148, 157; defended by bp Cox, 151; and by abp Parker, 157; pensionary concubinage continued in Wales, notwithstanding leave of mar-

riage, 257; marriage with a deceased wife's sister, Jewel would have had it declared lawful, 176; of a brother and sister german, 353.

Marshall (Rog.), keeper at Norwich, 387.

Martin (——), young Martin, 470.

Martin (Tho.), Parker wrote a defence of the marriage of priests in reply to him, ix, 483.

Martyr (Pet.), Parker desires his attendance at a conference in France, 147.

Marven (Mr), of Chichester diocese, 371.

Mason (Sir Jo.), signature as privy councillor, 155.

Mary, queen of England, letter to bp Gardiner, 55 n.

Mary, queen of Scots, her arrival in England, 325, referred to, 398, 446 n.

Matchett (Mr), parson of Thurgarton, Parker writes to him against prophesyings, 456, 457 n.

Mathewe (——), vicar of Howe, sent to the Marshalsea, 76.

Matthew Paris, extracts from his chronicle sent to Parker, 140; Parker borrows his chronicle of Cecil, 353; it is printed, 388 n.

Mattishall, Norfolk, x., 484; abp Parker's benefaction to the poor, xiii.

May (Will.), has an interview with Henry VIII., 34; letter to Parker, 38; president of Queens' college, Cambridge, 38 n., 67; an ecclesiastical commissioner, 107, 439; dean of St Paul's, nominated abp of York, but died unconsecrated, 123 n.

Maynard (Hen.), 469.

Medwin (St), sent from Rome to Lucius, 295.

Mere (Jo.), letter to Parker, 17; notice of him, 19 n.; mentioned, 38.

Mershe (Jo.), an ecclesiastical commissioner, 383.

Metcawffe, (Jo.), skinner, 211.

Mildmay (Sir Walter), a privy councillor, 357, 457 n.

Mills (Mr), of All Souls' college, 297 n.

Ministers, v. Clergy, Declaration, Preachers. Artificers and unlearned men admitted to the ministry, 120; some beneficed ones neither priests nor deacons, 128, 154, 308 (v. Lowther); laymen presented to benefices, 311; and made prebendaries, 312, an archdeacon not in orders, 142 n.; certain London ministers summoned to Lambeth, 233; some of them refuse conformity, 268, 269, 270, 272; churchwardens, &c. not to suffer unlicenced persons to minister, 383.

Miracle, a pretended one at Dublin, 95 n.

Monson (B.), an ecclesiastical commissioner, 390.

Montgomerie (The count), a French protestant exile, 420.

Moptyd (Lau.), master of C. C. C., viii, 482.

More (Sir Tho.), Parker alludes to a book of his on Fortune, 60; his eloquence and wit, 315.

Morris (Mr), slandered, 368.

Mownt (——), servant to Cecil, 258.

Mullyns (Mr), 377.

Muncer (Tho.), the anabaptist, 426.

Munster (Seb.), his character as a translator of Scripture, 257.

Music, not expelled from the church of England, 215.

N.

Neve (Will.), of Norwich, vi, 481.

Nevenson (Steph.), or Nevison, letter to him as commissary of Canterbury, 165; had certain MSS. of Cranmer, 191, 195; prebendary of Canterbury, 319.

Nevile (Alex.), Parker gave him £100 for writing the story of Kett's rebellion, xiii.

Neville (Hen.), lord Abergavenny, letter to him, 285; he claims the stewardship of the liberties of Canterbury, 285 n., an ecclesiastical commissioner, 370 n.

Neville (Hen.), earl of Westmoreland, a commissioner, 105.

Newton (Francis), dean of Winchester, made prebendary of Canterbury in the room of his brother, 341.

Newton (Theodore), prebendary of Canterbury, 340.

Nix (Rich.), bp of Norwich, Latin letter to him from queen Anne Boleyn, 4.

Nonsuch park, the earl of Arundel's, 387.

Norfolk (the duke of), v. Howard.

Norgate (Rob.), master of C. C. C., extract from a letter to abp Parker, 469; letter to him, ib.

North (Sir Rog.), afterwards second lord North, requires a Lent licence, 108.

INDEX.   503

North. (W.), this signature as a privy councillor means Will. marq. of Northampton, *v.* Parr.
Northampton (Hen. earl of), *v.* Howard.
Northampton (Will. marq. of), *v.* Parr.
Northfolk (Will.), deprived by bp Sandys, 125.
Northumberland (Jo. duke of), *v.* Dudley.
Norwich, Parker's birthplace, mention of some localities, vi., 481; foreigners there, 247 *n.*; a church assigned to them, 255; the Green yard, a place for preaching, 313; cathedral, a serving man made prebendary, 312; miserable state of the church; only six prebendaries, only one at home, some of them puritans, 450; diocese, visited by Parker, 473; dispute between the archbishop and the chapter about visitation, 476.
Nostradamus (Mich.), threatens the world with peculiar evils in 1559-60, 59 *n.*
Notaries, application of one to be a notary, 392.
Nowell (Alex.), dean of St Paul's, 145; approves rules for Tunbridge school, 211 *n.*; the queen is offended with a sermon by him, 235; letter by him, 251; will not preach before the queen unless she will favour him, 254; being occupied against Dorman, begs to be discharged from Lent preaching, 260.

O.

O'Molana (Malachias), bp of Ardagh, 421.
Onslow (Rich.), solicitor-general, 'Mr Onssley,' 302, 303 *n.*
Origen, reports that Celsus objected the lack of images against Christians, 86.
Osborne (Pet.), an ecclesiastical commissioner, 277, 302, 383; his office, 280.
Osorius (Hieron.), bp of Silvas, his letter to queen Elizabeth answered by Haddon, 216 *n.*
Ostia (Julian, bp of), *v.* Julian.
Oxford, disputation there, 1555, 160; the Bear, 138 *n.*; the common jail, 145; the see long vacant, 145 *n.*
   University (*v.* Caius (T.), Universities), it lives quietly with fewer privileges than Cambridge, 24.
   All Souls' College, letter from Parker to the warden, Dr Barber, requiring an inventory of superstitious plate and vestments retained by the college, 296; letter from Parker and others requiring the warden to deliver up certain superstitious books, 297; letter from Parker and other ecclesiastical commissioners to the warden citing several fellows before them, 300; order of the commissioners respecting the plate, &c., 301 *n.*; disposal of the plate and church-books, 304; letters from Parker to the warden to procure the renewal of a lease from the widow of an old tenant, 320, 324; the founder ordered that the fellows should all be priests, 396; but in 1572 only two of the forty were priests, *ib.*
Christ Church, commission respecting its statutes, 118.
St John's College, a dispute there, 436.
Merton College, an order made that only three priests should be within the college, 325; one physician there for reading Linacre's lecture, 326.

P.

Paget (Sir Will.,) afterwards lord Paget, signature as privy councillor, 30.
Pammachius, a tragedy, played at Cambridge, 21—29.
Papists, should be disarmed, 399.
Paris, massacre of St Bartholomew, 399—401.
Parker family, the archbishop's parents, vi., 481; his descendants, x., 484.
Parker (Sir Jo.), son of the archbishop, his birth, x., 484; Mere's legacy to him, 19 *n.*; his statement of his father's revenue and expenditure, xii.; note by him, 115 *n.*; marries Joanna, daughter of bp Cox, x., 484; his children, *ib.*
Parker, (Sir Jo.), the archbishop's grandson, note by him, 103 *n.*
Parker (Matt.), abp of Canterbury, his autobiographical memoranda, in English, vi.; the original Latin, 481; his birth, education, and ordination, vi., vii., 481; summoned to court by queen Anne Boleyn, vii., 1, 2, 482; dean of Stoke by Clare, vii., 4, 482; appointed to preach at Paul's cross, 5, 39, 45; chaplain to Henry VIII., vii., 6, 482; articles against him sent to lord chancellor Audley, 7; preferments, vii., viii., 482; being recommended by the king, he is

elected master of Corpus Christi College, Cambridge; viii., 16, 17, 482; chosen vice-chancellor, viii., 17, 482; his letter to the council of Queen Catherine Parr against the dissolution of Stoke college, 31; minute of an interview with Henry VIII., 34, his marriage, x., 46 n., 484, again chosen vice-chancellor, viii., 37, 38, 482, appointed to preach before king Edward VI, x., 40, 41, 43, 483; made dean of Lincoln, but shortly deprived, viii., 482, his retired life in queen Mary's time, viii., 199, 483; summoned to London on the accession of Elizabeth on the queen's service, 53; unwilling to accept the archbishoprick, 57, &c.; resolution that he should be archbishop, 68; again summoned to court, 68, 69; writes to the queen begging to be discharged from the office, 69; but refers himself to the queen's pleasure, 71; a second resolution that he should be archbishop, 71; the queen assents to his election, 76; he is consecrated, x., 484; Tonstal committed to his custody, 77, 78; exchange effected between the queen and the archbishop, 102 n.; refuses a dispensation to allow a child to hold a benefice, 136; the queen thought him too easy, his brethren thought him too sharp, 173, the queen grants him permission to retain forty persons with his livery badge, 175; he appoints days for prayer on account of war, pestilence, and famine, 182; his armoury, 216; perplexed through want of support in his endeavours to enforce uniformity, 262; his measures for that purpose, 270, 272–274, 278; his part in the Bishops' Bible, 335 n., 336 n.; refuses a dispensation to make a child a prebendary, 362; his lances at York, 388; forged letters in his name, 418; sends the *Antiquitates Brittanniæ Ecclesiæ* to lord Burghley, 425; meaning and object of that book, *ib*.; intends to keep it private during his life, 426; has various artists and workmen in his house, *ib*.; his seal, 452 n.; statement of his yearly expenses, 455; his son's statement of his revenue and expenditure, xii.; his illness, 464, 477; publishes Asser's *Ælfredi Res Gestæ*, 468, disliked by the precisians, 472; spends his time in copying books, devising ordinances for scholars, in genealogies, &c., 474; receives the queen at Folkestone and Canterbury, 475; visits in the diocese of Winchester, 478; cared neither for cap, tippet, surplice, nor wafer bread, but for the laws established, 478; his death and burial, xi.; dates of sermons preached by him on remarkable occasions, vii., ix., 481, 483.
— Margaret, his wife, daughter of Rob. Harleston, 46 n., 483, 484; Mere's legacy to her, 19; her death and burial, 369 n., 484.
— his children and descendants, 484.
Parker (Tho.), mayor of Norwich, the archbishop's brother, 19 n.
Parker (Will.), and Alice his wife, the archbishop's parents, vi., 481.
Parkhurst (Jo.), bishop of Norwich, said to wink at schismatics and anabaptists, 149; to be pressed to execute the laws, 234; his share in the Bishops' Bible, 248, 335 n.; his death, 446 n.; letter by him, 247; letters to him, 389, 401, 403, 415, 416, 417, 457, 459.
Parliament, *v.* Cambridge.
Abp Parker and lord Cobham ordered by the council to confer with the sheriff and principal persons in boroughs that fit persons might be chosen, 380.
Parr (Will.), marq. of Northampton, signature as privy councillor (sometimes 'W. North'), 73, 75, 76, 106, 122, 155, 328 n., 330, 357, 381.
Parry (Sir Tho.), privy councillor, 74, 75, 76, 77, 103, 106, 117, 122; letter from him and Cecil to Parker, 104.
Pate (Rich.), or Pates, bp of Worcester, prisoner in the Tower, 122; 'patesing,' a supposed allusion to his name, 124.
Paulet (Will.), earl of Wiltshire, afterwards marq. of Winchester, signature as privy councillor, 46, 155; letter to Parker, 119.
Peacock (Tho.), president of Queens' college, Cambridge, resigns, 67.
Peculiars, a return of them required, 181.
Pegson (Tho.), and his wife, 303.
Pembroke (Will. earl of), *v.* Herbert.
Penance, *v.* London, *Paul's cross.*
Dr Turner causes an adulterer to do penance in a priest's square cap, 241.
Peny (Mr.), suspected of nonconformity, 264.
Perne (And.), master of Peterhouse and

INDEX. 505

dean of Ely, to preach at Paul's cross, 261; his share in the Bishops' Bible, 335 n.
Peter (St), claimed no subjection, 110.
Petre (Sir Will.), signature as privy councillor, 75, 117, 155; letter to Parker, 118.
Philotus (Laur.), 60 n.
Pierpoint (Geo.), or Perpoynt, viii., 482.
Piers (Jo.), bp of Rochester, then of Salisbury, and ultimately abp of York, recommended for the see of Norwich, 476, 477.
Pierson (And.), prebendary of Canterbury, 197 n., 442, 444; his supposed share in the Bishops' Bible, 335 n. (bis).
Pighius (Alb.), says the writings of the apostles should not be above, but subject to, our faith, 110.
Pilgrimage of Grace, 8 n.
Pilkington (James), bp of Durham, at Cambridge, 38; made bishop, 123 n.; letter by him, 221; supposed to favour the puritans, 237; mentioned, 264; signs a letter to the queen, 294.
Pilkington (Leon.), made master of St John's college, Cambridge, 149 n.
Pinder (Rachel), does penance at Paul's cross for pretending to be possessed, 465 n.
Plague, pestilence in 1563, 182—184; Thirlby and Boxall removed from the tower, 192—195; feared at Canterbury, 1564, 208; in London and Lambeth, 1574, 466.
Plancher, cornice, 231.
Playter (Tho.), letter signed by him, 307.
Points, tags or pins, 472.
Poissy, France, the conference there, 147.
Pole (Reg. card.), his income as archbishop of Canterbury, xii.
Polycrates, his reply to the bishop of Rome, 111.
Pope (Rich.), a priest at Norwich, vi., 481.
Porie (Jo.), master of C. C. C. C., and vice-chancellor, letters to him and others, 63, 64; mentioned, 298; desires to resign his prebend at Westminster to Mr Aldrich, 358.
Possession, the case of Agnes Bridges, examined by Parker, 465; she and Rachel Pinder do penance at Paul's cross for their imposture, ib. n.; books published on the subject, 465, 466.
Postmasters' endorsements, 289.

Poynt (——), a doctor of law at Cambridge, 18.
Prayer (Occasional forms), letters respecting a form of prayer, 1563, 182—185; remarks on a form of thanksgiving set forth, 1563-4, 201; a form prepared for the preservation of Christian countries invaded by the Turks, 1566, 289; notice of a form set forth in 1572, 402.
Preachers, v. Cambridge, *University*— London, *Paul's cross.*
to be appointed in vacant dioceses, 119; their licences, 242, 383, 389; few in Suffolk, 307.
Prebendaries, serving-men made prebendaries, 176, 312; a dispensation sought for a child, 362.
Priour (Will.), of St Benedict's church, Norwich, vi., 481.
Prophesyings, the queen will have them suppressed, 456, 457; favoured by bp Parkhurst, 457, 459; also by bp Sandys, and some others of the Council, 457 n.; stir made by Will. Heydon, on measures being taken to suppress them, 459.
Prosper (St), his 'Sentences out of Augustine,' 381.
Psalms, turned into metre by Parker, ix., 483; a curious MS. (apparently a psalter), Latin and Anglo-Saxon, 253.
Puritans, v. Uniformity.
their works found in the Low Countries, 283; termed precisians, 377, 472, &c.; a question amongst them on obedience to the prince, 377; commonly regarded as persecuted, 410; their private press, ib.; danger to the state apprehended from them, 418, 419, 426; the queen offended with their dissolute writing, 426; their faction democratic, 437; under colour of reformation, they seek the ruin of learning and religion, and seek a popular state, 434; disliked fonts and brazen eagles, 450.

Q.

Queenborough castle, Kent, 203.
Questions, cast abroad at Chester, 163 n.

R.

Radclyff (Randall), recommended by queen Catherine Parr as bailiff of Stoke college, 16.

Randolph (Edw.), marshal of Newhaven, 180 *n.*
Rastell (Will.), 114.
Ratcliffe (Tho.), earl of Sussex, in Dublin, 95 *n.*; seeks the preferment of Mr Rush, 283; signature as privy councillor, 381; commands an army against the rebels in the north, 388 *n*; lord chamberlain, 442, 443; letters to him, 416, 458, 466, 467.
Ratclif (Cha.), of Rochdale, 232.
Reade (Mr), recommended to bp Parkhurst, 460.
Redman (Jo.), master of Trinity college, Cambridge, 34, 38.
Relics, citation [from the Opus Imperfectum in Matthæum, wrongly ascribed to Chrysostom,] against those who esteem the garments of Christ more than his body, 8, 511.
Relic Sunday, the third Sunday after Midsummer day, 7.
Rice (Will.), or Rise, sent to the tower, 155.
Riccall, Yorkshire, a prebend in the cathedral church, 361.
Ridley (Nich.), bp of Rochester, afterwards of London, candidate for the vice-chancellorship of Cambridge, 17; letter to Parker, 45; record of his disputation at Oxford, 160.
Robinson (Nich.), bp of Bangor, 261; signs a letter to the queen, 294; and a letter to lord Burghley, 394.
Rochdale, Lanc., the living, 221, 231 *n.*; the school, 231, 232.
Rochester, a benefice annexed to the bishoprick, 100.
Rochet, an episcopal vestment, 475.
Rogers (Ed., incorrectly printed G.), a privy councillor, 75, 76, 77, 103, 106, 117.
Rogers (Rich.), bp of Dover, an ecclesiastical commissioner, 370; attends queen Elizabeth at Canterbury, 475.
Rolfe (Mr), a gentleman of Kent, 258.
Rome, MSS. there, 141.
Romney (Old), Kent, the living, 339 *n.*
Rush (Mr), recommended to be teacher in the grammar school at Canterbury, 144; notice of him, *ib. n.*; recommended for preferment, 283.
Russell (Jo. lord), afterwards earl of Bedford, signature as privy councillor, 30, 46.

Russell (Fra.), second earl of Bedford, signature as privy councillor, 73, 357, 381; mentioned, 464.

S.

Sabbath, part of the precept ceremonial, 81.
Sackville (Sir Rich.), signature as privy councillor, (in some instances printed incorrectly 'Ed.' instead of 'Ryc.') 103, 117, 122; letter from, referred to, 171 *n.*; obtains a lease of Charing, 372.
Sackville (Tho.), afterwards lord Buckhurst, and at last earl of Dorset, the queen dines with him, 219.
Sadler (Sir Ralph), signature as privy councillor, 357; supposed to be a supporter of the Puritans, 428.
Saint David's, no old MSS. in the library there, 265.
Saint-Leger (Sir Ant.), K.G., and Agnes (Warham) his wife, 113 *n.*
Saint-Leger (Sir Warham), letter to him, 113; notice of him, *ib. n.*
Saint-Leger (Mr), prebendary of Canterbury, 319.
Saint-Loe (Sir Will.), and Elizabeth (Hardwick) his wife, 301 *n.*
Salford, Oxon? an estate belonging to All Souls' college, 320 *n.*
Salisbury, a serving man prebendary there, 176.
Salisbury (Jo.), bp of Sodor and Man, 265 *n.*
Salisbury (Will.), antiquary, 265 *n.*, 271.
Salt, made in Kent and Norfolk, 258.
Sampson (Tho.), a conference to be held with him, 233; he remains immoveable, 234; appointed to preach at Paul's cross, 239; his nonconformity, 240; letter to Parker, and his answer, 243, 244; the earl of Huntingdon applies to Cecil that he may be set at liberty, 243, 245; Parker's clemency to him, 244; about to be examined, 382.
Sancroft (Will.), abp of Canterbury, reburied the bones of abp Parker, and restored his monument, xi.
Sandwich, Kent, the town visited by Parker, 188; service at the church, 189; state of the refugees and their church, *ib.*; some members thereof excommunicated, 247; hospital of St Bartholomew, 168; Ellys's hospital, *ib.*; St John's

INDEX. 507

house, 169; Manwood's free school, 178, 188.
Sandwich (Sir Jo.), founder of an hospital, 168.
Sandys (Edwin), bp of Worcester, then of London, and at last abp of York, at Cambridge, 38; his share in the Bishops' Bible, 256; signs a letter to the queen, 294; translated from Worcester to London, 369 n.; dangerously ill, ib.; thought by Parker not sufficiently severe against the Puritans, 382; an ecclesiastical commissioner, 383, 390, 434; favours prophesyings, 457 n., 459 n.; letters to Parker, 65, 124, 256; letters signed by him and others, 390, 394, 434; letters to him, 384, 402, 451.
Sandys (Will.), F.S.A., xi. n.
Saunders (Mr), a parson, 18.
Saunders (Sir Edw.), lord chief baron, 164.
Saunders (Nich.), his book De visibili Monarchia Ecclesiæ, 409, 410; answered by Dering, 410; by Dr B. Clerk, 411—414, 430; by Acworth, 440 n.
Saxon, v. Anglo-Saxon.
Sayer (——), a deputy of London, 276.
Scambler (Edm.), bp of Peterborough, afterwards of Norwich, to preach at Paul's cross, 261; his share in the Bishops' Bible, 335 n.
Schisure, schism, 14.
Scory (Jo.), bp of Hereford (previously of Rochester and Chichester), signs a letter to the queen, 101, 294; forbidden to visit his diocese, 117 n.; often conferred with Sandys, 126; Parker and Grindal seek the queen's permission for him to visit the cathedral of Hereford, 165; not fit for the see of London, 359.
Scot (Cuthb.), bp of Chester, apparently referred to as Mr Scot, 25, 26, 28, 29; absconds without regard to his sureties, 218.
Scotland, supremacy of the crown of England, 328; letter sent by order of the general assembly to abps Parker and Young in the case of Jo. Baron's wife, 205; Parker's view of the request contained in the same letter, 209.
Seckforde (Tho.), or Sekford, letter to Parker, 142; an ecclesiastical commissioner, 370 n.
Sedgrave (Chr.), mayor of Dublin, 95 n.

Sedgwick (Dr), or Seggiswick, refuses the oath of supremacy, 105.
Serenus, bp of Marseilles, destroyed images, 89 and n.
Seymour (Edw.), duke of Somerset, lord protector, 40.
Seymour (Edw.), earl of Hertford, son of the protector, his stolen marriage with the lady Kath. Grey, 149.
Sherborne hospital, Durham, Lever complains of its state, 348.
Shorton (Rob.), dean of Stoke by Clare, his death, 4.
Shrewsbury (Geo. earl of), v. Talbot.
Simony prevalent in Norfolk, 311.
Sin (Original), Flacius Illyricus sends a disputation on original corruption and free will to Parker, 140.
Skinner (Ralph), dean of Durham, 124.
Skrimsham (R.), of All Souls' college, 301 n.
Skypp (Jo.), bp of Hereford, letters to Parker, 1, 2, 6, 9; sometime chaplain to Anne Boleyn, 3; dates of his election and death, 6 n.
Smith (Rich.), or Smyth, regius professor of divinity at Oxford, and master of Whittington college, 72—74.
Smith (Sir Tho.), fellow of Queens' college, Cambridge, when 19 years old, 64 n.; gives up the office of vice-chancellor of Cambridge, 17, 18; chancellor to Goodrich, bp of Ely, 30; mentioned, 36 n.; an ecclesiastical commissioner, 370 n; a privy councillor, 457 n.; letter to him and Parker from Gardiner, 20; letter from him to Porie, Parker and Leeds, 64.
Smith (Will.), M.A. Camb., recommended as a fellow of Eton, 162.
Smyth (Jo.), provost of Oriel college, 138 n.
Smythe (——), a layman, but prebendary of Norwich, 312, 313.
Somerset (Edw. duke of), v. Seymour.
Somersham house, 474.
Somner (Mr), 400.
Sonds (——), his vain prophecies, 60.
Southampton (Tho. earl of), v. Wriothesley.
Southcoots (Mr), a justice, 375.
Southworth (Sir Jo.), committed to prison, 329; refuses to submit, 330.
Sowode (Will.), master of C. C. C. C., 16.

Spencer (Dr), prebendary of Riccall in the church of York, 362.
Spensor (——), fellow of Gonville hall, 252.
Sporis, spurs, 13.
Spottiswoode (Jo.), superintendent of Lothian: letter from him and others to abps Parker and Young, 205.
Stafford (Mary lady), wife of Edw. lord Stafford, 1562—1603, daughter of Edw. Stanley, earl of Derby, 358.
Stafford (Edw. lord), who succeeded 1603, at C. C. C. Cambridge, 358.
Stallard (——), of Benet college, 344.
Standysh (Dr), candidate for the vice-chancellorship, 17.
Stanley (Edw.), third earl of Derby, Anne his daughter marries Cha. lord Stourton, 424 n.
Stanley (Hen.), fourth earl of Derby, 424 n.
Stanley (Tho.), bp of Sodor and Man, 222.
Starky (Tho.), skinner, 211.
Statutes, 21 Hen. VIII. c. 13, benefices, 136; 1 Eliz. c. 19, exchange of church lands, 98 n.; 5 Eliz. c. 1, supremacy, 174; 13 Eliz. c. 2, subscription, 293 n.
Steward (Mr), perhaps a name of office, 460.
Steward (Dr), 476.
Stifflers, sticklers, 252.
Still (Jo.), afterwards bp of Bath and Wells, recommended for a prebend at Westminster, 439; and for the deanery of Norwich, 449.
Stoke-by-Clare, Suffolk, the college, Parker made dean, vii., 4, 482; letter from Henry VIII. to the dean and prebendaries requiring them to send four able men to his army, about to invade France, 15; R. Radclyff recommended by queen Catherine Parr as bailiff, 16; letter from queen Catherine Parr to the dean and fellows, desiring a lease of the manor of Chipley for Edw. Waldegrave, 19; Parker opposes the dissolution of the college, but without success, 31—33, 482; pensions granted to the dean, &c., 40; the schoolmaster's stipend restored by Elizabeth, 188.
Stokes (Dr), Austin Friar, letter from Parker to him, 10; he preaches against Parker, and is imprisoned, 14 n.
Stonden (——), to be discharged, 464.
Stourton (Cha. lord), executed for murder, 422 n.; Anne (Stanley) his wife, 424 n.

Stourton (Jo. lord), notice of him, 422 n.; committed to the custody of Parker, 422 —424, 441; comes to chapel, and behaves orderly, 448.
Stowell (Jo.), accused of bigamy, 405, 406, 407, 408; imprisoned, 447 n.
Stowmarket, Suffolk, 417 n.
Subsidy, arrears of one granted in Mary's time, 196.
Suffolk, only one preacher in an extensive district there, 307.
Suffolk (Kath. duchess of), v. Brandon.
Suffragans, Parker had one [Rich. Rogers, bp. of Dover], 370, 475.
Sugill, to defame or slander, 11, 157.
Supper of the Lord, wafer bread enjoined by Elizabeth, 240, 277, 278; i.e. bread like singing cakes, but somewhat larger, 375; the rubric which speaks of 'usual' bread regarded by Parker as permissive, not as forbidding wafer bread, 376; form of sacramental bread appointed by Parker and Grindal, 378; directions respecting it, 458; loaf bread not to be permitted, 460.
Supremacy, v. Statutes.
That of the prince once affirmed by Gardiner, 23; Elizabeth, on Lever's suggestion, declines the title of supreme head, 66; the prince has power by law to ordain ceremonies in certain cases, 375.
Surplice, v. Vestments.
Not worn in the diocese of Norwich, 149; opposed by some at Cambridge, 226 n.; disorders at St Giles, Cripplegate, 275, 276; Parker's chaplains, for lack of a surplice and wafer bread, at certain places did but preach, 277.
Sussex (Tho. earl of), v. Ratcliffe.
Sydney (Sir Hen.), letter by him, 316; he lent Parker a MS., 388 n.
Sydney (Sir Phil.), his father seeks a Lent licence for him, 316; notice of him, ib. n.

T.

Talbot (Geo.), earl of Shrewsbury, marries the lady St Loe, 301 n.
Tamworth (Mr), 202.
Tanner (Mr), 18.
Taylor (Jo.), bp of Lincoln, viii., 482.
Taylor (Rowland), his widow married a minister named Wright, 221.

INDEX. 509

Temple at Jerusalem, no images allowed there, 81, 82.
Tempsis, the Thames, 250.
Tenterden, Kent, the grammar school, 170.
Tertullian, expounds St John's caution against idols, 83; in his time Christians abhorred images, 86; he burned incense in private, but not as idolaters did, 88; says whatever was first, is true; whatever afterwards, is spurious, 93.
Thanksgiving, v. Prayer.
Theodosius, emperor, v. Valens.
Thirasius, patriarch of Constantinople, 92.
Thirlby (Tho.), bp of Westminster, then of Norwich, lastly of Ely, 18; prisoner in the tower, 122; removed thence on account of the plague, 192—195; lives with Parker, 194 n., 203, 215, 217; his death, 369 n.; buried at Lambeth, 194 n.; letters to Parker, 41, 193; letter to him, 193.
Tilius (Jo.), bishop of Angoulesme, possessed many ancient councils, 141.
Tilney (Mr), seeks a dispensation, 351.
Tippets, some preached before the queen without the tippet, 264; the sarcenet tippet worn by act of parliament, 268.
Tonbridge, Kent, the grammar school founded by Sir And. Judd, 210.
Tonstal (Cuthb.), bp of London, afterwards of Durham, committed to Parker's custody, 77, 78, 106 n.; his executors, and funeral, 106.
Trappes (Mr), of London, 167.
Travers (Walter), supposed author of a treatise, *De Disciplina*, 477 n.
Tremellius (Imm.), letter to Parker, 332; notice of him, *ib. n.*
Tufton (Mr), 198.
Turbervile (James), bp of Exeter, prisoner in the tower, 122.
Turner (Will.), dean of Wells, makes one do penance in a priest's square cap, 241; his 'Hunting of the Wolf,' 455.

U.

Undertree (——), scheme to take him, 460, 462, 463; examined, 464; should be hanged, *ib.*
Uniformity, letter of Elizabeth requiring uniformity in rites and ceremonies, 223; letter of Parker on the same, 227; proceedings relative thereto, 233, 234, 236, 237; Parker perplexed through want of support in his endeavours to enforce it, 262; course to be adopted, 267; enforced by Parker, 270, 272—274, 278; another letter of the queen, 386; her care for it and proceedings to enforce it, 451.
Universities: v. Cambridge—Oxford—Colleges;
racket stirred up by Withers for the reformation of the university windows, 234; the Wednesday fish-day dispensed with in the universities, 235.

V,

Valens and Theodosius, emperors, their decree against representations of the cross (signum) of Christ, 90.
Vanderstad (Corn.), of the strangers' church at Sandwich, 247.
Varro, his opinion against images, 86.
Venison, Henry VIII.'s warrant for a doe for Parker, 4; begged by Parker, 177; the queen sends him a deer killed with her own hand, 190; order of Henry earl of Arundel for the supply of deer to him, 387.
Vestments, v. Cap—Chimere—Gown—Rochet—Surplice—Tippet:
dissensions at Cambridge, 226 n., 245; the nonconformity of Sampson and Humfrey, 240; Parker's proceedings in order to uniformity, 267.
Vigilius, an African bishop, his works published, 288 n.
Visitation, v. Canterbury—*archbishop*.
Parker forbids the bishops of his province to visit their dioceses, 115, 116; is offended with the visitation of Worcester by bp Sandys, 125, 126.

W.

Waldegrave (Sir Edw.), notice of him, 19 n.
Wales, pensionary concubinage continued there notwithstanding liberty of marriage granted, 257.
Waley (Jo.), 265.
Walker (—— and ——), two doctors of medicine, 18.
Walker (Mr), a preacher at Norwich, 312, 313; a puritan, 382.
Walloons, at Sandwich, 189.
Walmer Castle, Kent, 203.
Walsingham, Norfolk, salt-works near it, 250.

Walton (West), Norfolk, 18.
Ware (Sir James), his 'Hunting of the Romish Fox,' &c., 95 n.; he publishes Campion's History of Ireland, 407 n.
Ware (Rob.), 95 n., 109.
Warehorn, Kent, the benefice, 214.
Warner (Mr), 114.
Warner (Sir Edw.), lieutenant of the tower, 121; letter to him 122.
Warwick (Earls of): v. Dudley.
Watson (Tho.), bp of Lincoln, prisoner in the tower, 122.
Wattes (Tho.), an ecclesiastical commissioner, 344 n., 369.
Welles (Mr), 333.
Wendesley (Rich.), an ecclesiastical commissioner, 383, 390, 447.
Wendon (Nich.), archdeacon of Suffolk, 142; not in orders, ib. n.
Wendy (Tho.), 25, 26.
Westfaling (Herb.), bp of Hereford, previously proposed for bp of Oxford, 360.
Westminster, Canon Row,—the house of the abp of York, 291 n.; the Gatehouse, a prison, 465, 470,
Westmoreland (Hen. earl of): v. Neville.
Weston (Rob.), dean of the arches, 129 n., 428, 430.
Westwell, Kent, the manor, 373.
Weybridge, Surrey, the forest, 4.
Whalley, Lanc., 222.
Whalley (Will.), canon of Lincoln, viii, 482.
Whitgift (Jo.), bp of Worcester, afterwards abp of Canterbury, occupied about his book, 439; recommended for the see of Norwich, 476, 477.
Whitstable, Kent, brimstone made from stuff gathered on the shore there, 341.
Wiburn (Perceval), about to be examined, 382.
Wigan (Edw.), 25, 26.
Wigand (Jo.), letters to him, 286.
Wilbraham (Tho.), proposed as a commissioner, 370.
Williams (Mr), in the Marshalsea, 423.
Willoughby (Dr), of Aldborough, 404; spent £4 for painting a pulpit, ib. n.
Wilson (Tho.), an ecclesiastical commissioner, 383; Dr Wilson, probably the same, 420.
Wiltshere (Will. earl of): v. Paulet.
Winchester, the Wednesday fish-day dispensed with at the college, 235; the diocese visited by Parker, 478.

Winchester (Will. marq. of), v. Paulet.
Wingfield (Sir Rob.), letter by him and others, 306.
Winsloo (Mr), 461.
Witchcraft, case of an old woman at Stowmarket, 417 n.
Withers (Geo.), stirs up a racket for the reformation of the university windows, 234, 236; his license to preach informal, 238.
Women, books on government by them, 60; not to reside within colleges, &c. 146.
Wood (Mr), seeks to be placed in physic in All Souls' college, 396.
Workington, Cumberland, Mary queen of Scots lands there, 325 n.
Wotton, (Nich.), dean of Canterbury, a privy councillor, 74, 75; letter to him, 144; he had his dividend of church plate, 304.
Wotton (Tho.), or Wootton, 304; an ecclesiastical commissioner, 370 n.; visited by the queen in Kent, 441.
Wright (——), married Rowland Taylor's widow, 221.
Wright (Dr), archdeacon of Oxford, 138 n.
Wriothesley (Tho. lord), afterwards earl of Southampton, 30.
Wye, Kent, the almshouse, 169; the grammar school, 170.
Wykes (Hen.), printer, 319 n.

Y.

Yale (Tho.), letter to him as Parker's chancellor, 128; an ecclesiastical commissioner, 300, 301 n., 344 n., 345, 370, 383, 447; dean of the arches, 428.
Yate (Mr), placed in the custody of the earl of Sussex for nonconformity, 458.
York, letter to the dean and chapter on their provision of armour, 347.
Young (Jo.), afterwards bp of Rochester, chaplain to bp Grindal, 275; to preach at court, 378.
Young (Tho.), abp of York, translated from St David's, 115 n., 123 n., 134 n.; signs a letter to the queen, 294; his death, 115 n., 328 n.; his letters to Parker, 114, 291 n.; letter to him, 205.

Z.

Zephyrus (Fra.), says Christians in Tertullian's time abhorred images, 86.

ADDENDA AND CORRIGENDA.

Page 8, n. 2. The passage alluded to is a quotation from the Opus Imperfectum ascribed to St Chrysostom (Opera Lat. II. 920. edit. Par. 1570) See Calfhill's Answer to Martiall (Parker Society), pp. 95, 286.

— 15, last line, *for* "1554," *read* "1544."
— 119, n. 3, *for* "Sir H." *read* "Sir W."
— 144, reference to oiig. of Letter CIII. *for* 283 *read* 583.
— 260, n. 2. The Dean alluded to is said by Strype, (Parker, Book III. c. 5,) to have been Dr Carey, but that seems to be a mistake. Gregory Dodds was at that time Dean of Exeter. Dr Carey was not appointed until 12 Jan. 1570-1.
— 291, sixth line of n. 4, *for* "27 th" *read* "26 th."
— 316, n. 1, *for* "Gloucester" *read* "Winchester."